TRANSFORMATION OF A CONTINENT

TRANSFORMATION OF A CONTINENT

Europe in the Twentieth Century

EDITED BY

Gerhard L. Weinberg

UNIVERSITY OF NORTH CAROLINA
CHAPEL HILL, N.C.

BURGESS PUBLISHING COMPANY • MINNEAPOLIS, MINNESOTA

To Alex Fraser 1923-1974
A Man of Insight and Vigor

Copyright © 1975 by Burgess Publishing Company
Printed in the United States of America
Library of Congress Card Number 75-16797
ISBN 0-8087-2332-4

0   9   8   7   6   5   4   3   2   1

Contents

GERHARD L. WEINBERG

Introduction

AT THE BEGINNING of the twentieth century, Europe dominated the globe in a way no single continent had ever previously
controlled the earth as a whole. The direct ownership of colonies,
the indirect dominion of spheres of influence, and the effective
control of world trade by banks, navies, and shipping lines, reached
out of the narrow confines of the European continent to the
farthest portions of the earth. The ancient empires of south and
east Asia had come under the influence—if not direct management
—of Europeans at the same time as economic ties had replaced the
sundered political bonds which had once held much of the Western
Hemisphere. The African continent had been divided among the
European powers; and the arguments over the Sudan, South Africa, and Morocco that threatened the peace of the world near the
turn of the century revolved primarily around the question of
which European nation would exercise predominant influence in
different portions of the partitioned continent.

The preeminence of Europe was not limited to political, economic, and military aspects. The scientific and technological
changes within Europe that had contributed so greatly to the
extension of European power were beginning to be adopted
elsewhere. In some parts of the world, like Japan, this might take
the form of voluntary imitation and adaptation; in others, like

1

India, there was the direct exportation implicit in railroad building. Furthermore, at least some nonmaterial aspects of European
civilization were being exported. The great revival of European
missionary activity in the nineteenth century did not leave as great
a mark on the previously non-Christian populations of the globe as
many anticipated, but other European ideologies took hold in
ways that would transform both the non-European areas and their
relationship to the European powers. The Europeans exported
their concepts of state organizations with centralized bureaucra-
cies and formal legal systems to areas previously characterized by
tribal structures and customary law; their most fateful export,
however, was the very ideology that had played such a prominent
part in firing up the great burst of imperialism in the last decades
of the nineteenth century: the ideology of nationalism.

The weakening of the European powers by two world wars, the
appearance of new systems of government, the rising tide of
nationalism outside Europe, and the changing self-perceptions of
people inside as well as outside Europe, would completely alter the
world situation and Europe's place in it by the 1970s, but only the
faintest signs of such changes could be perceived in the years between 1900 and 1914. This period of rapid development and substantial change has only recently come to be seen as an era worth
examining on its own terms; Oron J. Hales's superb work, *The
Great Illusion 1900-1914* (New York: Harper & Row, 1971), in
the "Rise of Modern Europe" series is likely long to remain the
best introduction to the period and its opportunities. The war
which began in August of 1914 and continued for more than four
years would end those promises and set the framework out of
which the major characteristics of twentieth-century Europe
emerged.

This is not the place to recite the arguments over the causes of
what came to be known as the Great War, but one critical point
about the war plans of the belligerents needs to be mentioned
because its implications are so often overlooked. The military
plans of all the major European powers in the late nineteenth
century were consonant with a short war, leading either to victory
for one side or to a stalemate that would have occurred sufficiently close to the borders of the participants so that the powers
engaged might have considered a return to the prewar borders as
one possible way of ending the conflict. The new German plan
generally identified with General Alfred von Schlieffen differed
fundamentally from all the others because the alternatives it

presented were a victory or a stalemate deep inside France. It was the political and psychological obstacle of a stalemate whose geographical location gave one side the illusion of great advantage and the other a constant incentive to continuing exertions that would make it so difficult for the European powers to disengage themselves from the disaster of death and destruction into which they had fallen together.

The piece by Professor Coffman shows by a specific and very dramatic example how the exigencies of a long war from which the participants could or would not extricate themselves changed the United States from a peripheral observer of the European scene into a significant factor on the battlefields of the Marne. Unable to defeat France in the initial onrush of 1914, the Germans had been forced to go on the defensive in the West in 1915 while assisting their Austrian ally in the East. This pause in the West had given the British time to build up a large continental army whose offensive on the Somme in the summer of 1916 so shook the Germans that they could not take advantage of the staggering losses inflicted on the French army at Verdun earlier that year. Shifting now to the British as their main enemy, the Germans hoped to knock the island empire out of the war by the submarine blockade, which failed in its purpose but did bring American intervention into the war. It was this American role that, as Coffman illustrates, made it impossible for the Germans to draw victory in the West in 1918 from their victory in the East over Russia in 1917. The changed situation of Europe, where a non-European power furnished the troops to turn the tide at the Second Battle of the Marne, points to an exhausted continent no longer master of its own fate.

This shift was evident in other ways as well. The "Black Day of the German Army," the 8th of August 1918, which is referred to by Coffman, was the day on which an attack on the German Second Army practically collapsed a section of the German front. This attack was conducted by the British Fourth Army supported by a French corps. It was symbolic of the impact of war on the European empires that the British Fourth Army consisted of one English, one Australian, one Canadian, and one cavalry corps. If the use of over five hundred tanks and almost five hundred planes in the attack symbolized the new role of armor and airplanes on the field of battle, the reliance on soldiers from the British empire indicates the extent to which the demands of war forced the mobilization of manpower outside the home countries. This dependence of Europeans on non-Europeans was recognized when Australia and Canada, as well as other British dominions, signed the peace treaties and assumed roles in the new League of Nations and world affairs generally as independent powers for the first time.

If the empires of the victors were weakened by the exertions of battle, those of the defeated collapsed in disarray. The extra-European territories of the German and non-Turkish portions of the Ottoman Empires were partitioned among the victors, but their designation as "Mandates" under a tenuous League of Nations supervision showed that new perceptions of imperial relationships were coming to the fore, even if reality still lagged behind professions of purpose. Inside Europe, however, the national ideology that had been contained, if not suppressed, at the last great peace settlement—that of Vienna in 1814-15—broke forth in full strength. Out of the ruins of the Russian empire that had been defeated by the Central Powers and the wreckage of the German and Austrian empires subsequently defeated by the Western Powers, there arose a group of entirely new nations, while some of those that had secured their independence in earlier stages of the national revival in Southeast Europe in the nineteenth century benefitted by alignment with the victors. In the extraordinary situation of 1918-19, where *all* the great powers of Central and Eastern Europe had been defeated in war, and where no major power had a commanding military presence in the area, the smaller nationalities attempted to realize their hopes and ambitions. Encouraged by the belief of the victors that the suppression of national aspirations had contributed to the outbreak of war, the leaders of the new states did their best to take advantage of the unique situation.[1]

The account by Dr. Dagmar Horna-Perman of the drawing of Czechoslovakia's borders at the peace conference illustrates this process in all its complexity. It shows how the needs of war, the new perceptions of diplomacy, the seizure of initiative on the spot, and the eager reach of the newly freed combined with the situation of the moment to create a new map of Europe. The revival of Poland, the independence of Finland and the three

---

[1]It should not be overlooked that some of the nationality groups with elements hoping for independence failed to secure, or retain more than temporarily, the statehood they hoped for. The Ukrainians and the nationalities of the Caucasus area, as well as at least some elements among the Slovaks, Croatians, and Macedonians, belong in this category.

Baltic states of Estonia, Latvia, and Lithuania, the creation of Yugoslavia, and the enlargement of Rumania all resulted from processes not far different from those described by Dr. Horna-Perman; and all left behind new problems which differed in detail but not in essence from those of the new Czechoslovakia. The difficulties of internal consolidation, problems of national minorities, disputes over boundaries, pressures of economic adjustment and development, and the inherent factor of relative weakness in the face of Germany and Russia when either or both recovered their strength, would hang like menacing clouds over the prospects of all the countries of east-central Europe.

The victory of the Allies over the Central Powers was to mark not only the triumph of nationalism in Europe and its accelerated export to the rest of the world; it was also seen as a victory for democracy. The largest of the democracies, the United States, turned its back on Europe. Having first denounced the administration of President Woodrow Wilson as too soft on Germany, the opposition next denounced it as too hard on the Germans, too accommodating toward the allies, and too willing to allow the sovereignty of the United States to be subordinated to the League of Nations with its potential for future American involvement in Europe. This left the European allies to fend for themselves, something that they were theoretically quite willing but in practice unable to do. Some sense of the impact of war on one of the European democracies, that of England, can be seen in Professor Arthur Marwick's study of the British elite in the interwar years. The peculiar English combination of stability and change is revealed by an analysis of the ruling element that Professor Marwick believes less altered by the impact of disproportionately heavy casualties among sons of the upper classes than has often been asserted.

If democracy in one form or another managed to muddle through the years between the wars in Britain, France, and some of the smaller countries of western and northern Europe, the rest of the continent saw entirely new ideologies coming to dominance. The government of Russia had come into the hands of advocates of a system which called for the dictatorship of the proletariat even before the armistice of November, 1918. Almost exactly a year earlier, a determined group of revolutionaries had ended the attempted establishment of a pluralistic democratic government in place of the Czarist autocracy that had disintegrated under the impact of the war. The dictatorship of the proletariat was in fact simply the dictatorship of a series of dictators, operating through the mechanism of the Communist Party of the Soviet Union. The first of these, Nikolai Lenin, had been the leader of the 1917 revolution; his successor Joseph Stalin emerged in control as a result of struggles within the Party before and after Lenin's death in 1924. Professor John Armstrong, who has previously provided a reliable analysis of the Party as the dominant element in the Soviet system in his *The Politics of Totalitarianism* (New York: Random House, 1961), here offers a detailed study of the rise of Nikita Khrushchev as Stalin's successor in the critical period immediately following the death of the latter in 1953. Khrushchev himself was to be displaced in 1964 before his death, the first such transfer of power since the beginning of the Soviet system; but the very mechanics of the latest transfer, like the one examined here, showed the monopoly of power held by a small circle of Party leaders.

While the Soviet system had been installed in a defeated Russia in November, 1917, the victory of the Allies did not preserve the tottering political system of Italy. Alone among the major powers, Italy when entering the war in 1915 was a country strongly divided over the wisdom of participation. If the ordeal of war proved terrible enough for those peoples united at least at the beginning of hostilities, it proved in some ways even more traumatic for a country that had taken the plunge in the face of massive internal division. The calamitous defeat at Caporetto did shock the Italian public into a sense of desperate cohesion, but Italy's political and social system came apart under the stress of enormous sacrifices imposed on a country basically weaker than its power aspirations required. The fascist movement under Benito Mussolini's leadership which came to power in Italy in 1922 in a semilegal fashion would control the country for over two decades, strengthening its hold internally in the 1920s and attempting to assert imperial power outside the Italian peninsula in the 1930s. Starting out as a Marxist like Lenin, Mussolini developed an alternative variant of dictatorship based on an international division of states into classes instead of an internal division of each state into classes. The nature and development of this ideology are traced in Professor A. James Gregor's piece on "The Ideology of Fascism." Because there was a substantial number of years when it was widely asserted that fascism had no ideology, a view that occasionally still occurs in textbooks, there is an especially useful corrective in juxtaposing an essay on the Soviet system depending heavily on the analysis of career patterns of Party officials with one on Italian fascism that examines its theoretical bases and the application of that theory to issues ranging from women's suffrage to international relations. Not everyone will agree with Professor Gregor's implied suggestion that Mussolini is the unacknowledged prophet of the "Third World," but there is here surely a fruitful basis for examining the Ghana of Nkrumah, the Indonesia of Sukarno, and the Uganda of Amin.

World War II, which accelerated the collapse of the colonial empires sufficiently for these last-named countries to gain their independence, was primarily due to the aggression of Hitler's Germany. The shaky democracy established on the ruins of the German empire succeeded in maintaining the basic unity achieved by the Germans less than half a century earlier, but both this achievement itself and its import for future international relations were obscured from the eyes of contemporaries by the extraordinary depths to which the proud German empire seemed to have fallen. The new government of the Weimar republic reaped much of the blame for the defeat and peace settlement which were as much a part of its heritage as the political inexperience of its political parties and leaders who had been so carefully excluded from any share in the management of imperial institutions. Only as long as the opponents of the republic balanced each other out at the "left" and "right" extremities of the political spectrum could those supporting its institutions maintain themselves in authority. When the opponents on the "right" gained sufficient adherents among the population at large and the assistance of a small group of intriguers around the president, Adolf Hitler was appointed chancellor and soon consolidated his hold on the nation.

A shrewd organizer who combined grim determination with total lack of scruples, Hitler recognized the need for domestic change before foreign expansion. As he had previously promised the German public, dictatorship replaced democracy. Rearmament provided the basis for short-term economic recovery from the depression and the means for the contemplated conquest of vast living space once Germany had regained her strength. The semilegal way in which Hitler had come to power and the dependence on the existing officer corps imposed by Hitler's own aggressive intentions combined to make the National Socialist revolution in Germany a process over time rather than an event on a certain date. But as Hitler shifted focus from the domestic to the external portion of his program, as the state of German rearmament seemed to offer opportunities for conquest, but also alerted other powers to the new danger and thus frightened them into rearmament programs of their own which would at some point overtake Germany's, the German dictator took the reins more closely into his own hands. This stage in the National Socialist revolution served to bring together those inside the country who were opposed to the regime; it is this set of events that Professor Harold Deutsch illuminates in his study of "The Genesis of the Military Conspiracy Against Hitler." The problems and eventual failure of the opposition illustrate the difficulties faced by those who oppose a dictatorial regime from within. In the German case, this also meant that Hitler was able to launch his war; but instead of remaining within his intended bounds, namely a series of separate short wars, it soon spread into precisely the kind of all-encompassing total global conflict that the *Blitzkrieg* (lightning war) concept had been designed to avoid. In such a conflict, Germany was certain to lose, and the National Socialist system was only one of the things buried under the ruins. The energies harnessed to its purposes by a great modern totalitarian state can bring about cataclysmic changes; in the case of Germany they achieved the disruption of the continent's political and economic order, the murder of millions of Jews and other so-called undesirables, and the conversion of the whole range of human instincts and emotions into the two stark feelings of fear and hate.

The end of World War II saw a shattered and divided Europe. There was the physical destruction of war. There was the psychological shattering of defeat, experienced at one time or another during the war years by all the major European countries except England and the Soviet Union—and even these two powers had been severely shaken by military disasters. Furthermore, while World War I had ended with Germany acknowledging defeat before the victors had occupied the central portion of the continent, World War II ended with the armies of the allies in physical control of Europe. Most of the smaller countries of east-central Europe which had gained their independence when all the major powers of that area had been defeated in World War I now lost it when one of these—the Soviet Union as it turned out—emerged victorious in World War II. The unity of Germany, which had survived the first, did not survive the second conflict. The division between the Soviet and the Western zones of occupation came to be a permanent barrier, made evident by the creation along the border of the Soviet zone, which became the German Democratic Republic, of a death-strip designed to keep its inhabitants from fleeing to the Western zones which in turn became the German Federal Republic. This border was reinforced in 1961 by the Berlin Wall, designed to close the major escape route remaining for those in the east and symbolizing the stabilization of the new situation and boundaries in Central Europe.

The division so conspicuously marked by death-strip and wall in Germany affected the rest of the continent: eastwards the area was dominated by the Soviet Union, and most of the countries there were absorbed into Russia itself or remolded on the Soviet pattern; westwards a variety of institutions emerged or reemerged, assisted and defended by the United States and closely allied with her. A significant differentiation between the major countries on the two sides of what came to be called the iron curtain has frequently been overlooked. The Soviet Union retained control of the territories acquired by Russia in the imperialist scramble of the late nineteenth century, but the countries on the western side of the iron curtain relinquished their acquisitions, more or less willingly.

In the years after the war, not only Italy's colonial empire but the empires of France, Holland, and Belgium as well as the remaining parts of England's empire were transformed into independent countries. By far the largest of these in both area and population was India, but for an illustration of the process of decolonization in the postwar years this volume includes a piece on the first of the Black African states to emerge from colonial status. Professor Godfrey Uzoigwe's "From the Gold Coast to Ghana" records the transformation of one African colony into a distinctive and independent country; it also suggests an approach to the interaction between the colonial power and different segments of the colonial elite that can be fruitfully used in examining the process of decolonization in other territories.

If the reorientation of Europe towards the United States and the Soviet Union—one partly European itself, the other once a European colony—and the dissolution of the colonial empires mark a great shift in European as well as world affairs, one should not assume that this means the complete end of European leadership in world affairs. The trends of the 1970s suggest that new approaches to supranational institutions are being worked out in Western Europe, while national distinctiveness in new forms is reaserting itself in Eastern Europe. If Europe provided a model to the world at the beginning of the twentieth century, it may do so again in entirely different ways in the century's last decades.

●   ●   ●   ●   ●

The seven studies in this book deal with different significant aspects of the transformation of Europe in the twentieth century. They also illustrate the way in which the historian of the recent past works with diverse materials to prepare his account and develop his understanding of events. In some cases, the scholar can turn to extensive collections of unpublished archival materials; this is particularly true of the piece by Professor Horna-Perman. In other cases—such as the Coffman and Marwick articles—unpublished items primarily serve to supplement what is already in print. For certain topics—such as Gregor's analysis of fascist ideology—published materials are the appropriate basis of research; while in others—such as Uzoigwe's account of the origins of independent Ghana—it would be helpful to have access to the archives, but for the most recent period these are not open to researchers. Sometimes an essentially closed society like the Soviet Union imposes special difficulties on the scholar who must exercise his ingenuity to locate and identify—and when appropriate quantify—whatever scraps of evidence might be used; and Professor Armstrong, like Gregor a political scientist rather than historian, has been one of the more resourceful of those working under such handicaps. The piece on the military opposition to Hitler by Professor Deutsch points to an advantage in research restricted to the historian of recent events: he may be able to talk to participants and obtain their recollections as well as private papers. There are dangers to the use of what has come to be known as "oral history," but in the hands of a careful scholar, it can add both basic information and interpretive dimensions to the study of this century.

EDWARD M. COFFMAN

The Second Battle of the Marne

$\mathbf{A}$T 9:15 ON THE MORNING of July 21, 1918, exhausted but victorious American infantrymen took possession of the ruins of Berzy-le-Sec. This was the fourth day of heavy fighting for these survivors of the Second Brigade, First Division. They had driven back veteran German troops some nine kilometers to the edge of the plateau where Berzy-le-Sec perched with deep ravines on three sides. It took two attempts, but after five hours of bitter combat they seized this tiny village. From this position, Allied guns could fire on the Germans' main line of communication in the Marne salient. This meant that the Germans either must retake these heights or retreat. They chose the latter course.

Significantly, Berzy-le-Sec had not been the original objective of the Americans, but the French corps commander, Pierre Berdoulat, had taken it away from the lagging French 153rd Division and had given it to the Americans. (See Source 4.) Throughout the Soissons counteroffensive, the Americans of the First and Second Divisions led the way, even pushing ahead of the crack Moroccan troops. In those four terrible summer days, the Americans demonstrated that their intervention in what came to be known as World War I was crucial.

Within a week the Allies not only had stopped a massive German offensive but also had reacted quickly and very successfully in this

11

counterattack. American troops made significant contributions in both actions, but it was the prospect of American reinforcements that made the future seem so gloomy for the Germans. Thousands of Americans were arriving daily. (The average for the month of July was approximately 10,000 a day.) The Germans, who had more men on the Western Front than the Allies in the early part of 1918, simply could not match this great reinforcement. This was the beginning of the end or—in a phrase used at the time—"the turning of the tide." German troops would never take the offensive again in this war.

●   ●   ●   ●   ●

World War I had been in progress a few days short of four years when those Americans seized Berzy-le-Sec. Unrest in the Balkans led to the assassination of the heir to the Austro-Hungarian throne on June 28, 1914. A month later, the Austrians went to war against Serbia. Germany, France, Russia, and England also went to war within days. The major powers, with the exception of England, had large armies available to put in the field since they had instituted conscription and mobilization systems for such an emergency. Originally the generals and their planners had anticipated a short war—won by overwhelming offensives. They believed that masses of infantry if imbued with the proper spirit would dominate the battlefield and win quickly and decisively.

The French, who longed to revenge their humiliating defeat by the Prussians in 1870, were particularly outspoken in their emphasis on the offensive. Ferdinand Foch, a professor at the French War College before the war, was a leading advocate of this doctrine. The development of increased firepower—improved rifles and machine guns—only seemed to Foch to help the attacker.[1]

The Germans also emphasized the attack. A German General Staff officer, Hermann Foertsch, wrote in the 1930s of the attitude held prior to World War I: "The German Army was trained for attack. The strategic situation called for attack. Technology seemed to have distributed her favors evenly between friend and foe. Superiority, therefore, depended on which side showed the greater spirit or dash." Foertsch added: "But in this chain of reasoning the defensive had been overlooked."[2]

---

[1] Theodore Ropp, *War in the Modern World* (New York: Collier Books, revised paperback edition, 1962), p. 218. Chapters 7 and 8 are about the events prior to the war and the war itself. The footnotes contain an excellent annotated bibliography.

[2] Hermann Foertsch, *The Art of Modern Warfare* (New York: Veritas Press, 1940), p. 88.

The Germans came closest to success in those early weeks of war. They expected to fight a two-front war against the French and the Russians. By sending the bulk of their force in the West on a wide enveloping march through Belgium, they hoped to trap and defeat the French and then turn their effort against the Russians. The von Schlieffen Plan, named for its originator—a former Chief of the General Staff—did not work. In mid-September the French with the help of the small British Expeditionary Force stopped the Germans in the First Battle of the Marne.

By the end of 1914, the Germans, French, and British had settled into trenches and dug-outs along what became known as the Western Front from the mountains of eastern France to the seacoast of Belgium. The Germans were also engaged with the Austrians in fighting on the Eastern Front against the Russians. There the fighting was not as stabilized as it was in the West. Other theaters of war included the Balkans, the Middle East, and East Africa.

As the casualty lists mounted and the war stretched into months and then years, neither side was able to win a decisive victory on the Western Front. The Germans, in fact, concentrated their efforts in the East in 1915, remaining on the strategic defensive in the West. The problem which the generals could not solve was how to break through the defensive lines of the enemy. The standard solution was that a lengthy artillery barrage would weaken the enemy's resistance. Then waves of infantry would charge and make the initial crack in the line. Finally, cavalry would exploit the penetration by probing far in the rear of the trench system. Presumably the defenders would then at least have to withdraw. If the offensive force was powerful enough and could sustain itself long enough, it might crush the defenders and bring about such an overwhelming defeat that the enemy might sue for peace. Those who supervised these attempts underestimated the advantage artillery and machine guns gave to the defense in this situation, so these tactics simply did not work.

The front in the area where one of these offensives occurred was a barren and desolate place with the ground torn up and churned by the intensive shelling. The men who faced each other across the No Man's Land between the trenches harassed each other with snipers and occasional raids. In Flanders, the often waterlogged trenches added to the misery of the British and the Germans. On other sectors, if there had not been any heavy fighting in the particular vicinity, life would be better as the opponents might try to avoid stirring up trouble. Even in the quiet sectors, however, sanitation problems and the lice as well as the ever-present danger made for misery enough.

Robert Graves, the poet, who as a young officer in the Royal Welsh Fusiliers was left for dead in one of these battles, concisely summed up the experience of trench warfare some fifty years later. "The grossly mismanaged First World War, into which I plunged as soon as I left school, gave us infantry men so convenient a measuring-stick for discomfort, grief, pain, fear and horror, that nothing since has greatly daunted us. But it also brought new meanings of courage, patience, loyalty and greatness of spirit; incommunicable, we found, to later times."[3]

In 1916, the Germans launched an offensive which they hoped would cause the collapse of the French. Erich von Falkenhayn, the Chief of the General Staff, did not think a breakthrough was necessary. If he could send his troops against a place that the French must defend, he could force them to spend their army in its defense. This callous attrition plan presupposed that the German losses would be a great deal less than the French. For ten months the two armies fought in the vicinity of Verdun. The Germans did not capture the town but they did exact a toll of more than 377,000 French casualties and weakened the French Army so that it did not fully recover in the two years remaining in the war. But the Germans also lost heavily (their casualties numbered perhaps 337,000) and one might argue that their army was also never the same after this campaign.[4] Then, too, the Germans had to defend simultaneously against a British offensive near the Somme River from the first of July through mid-November. No one really knows what the exact casualty figures were for that battle, but one recent estimate is that both sides lost a combined total of a million men.[5] Despite the appalling losses, the belligerents remained deadlocked on the Western Front.

New weapons were not the answer. Poison gas, which the Germans introduced in April 1915, simply added to the horror of trench warfare. Air warfare developed rapidly with improved aircraft, new techniques and organizations; and the fighter pilots

[3]Frank Richards, *Old Soldiers Never Die* (New York: Berkley paperback edition, 1966). Robert Graves wrote the introduction to this interesting memoir of a veteran of his regiment. The quotation is from page 5.

[4]Alistair Horne, *The Price of Glory: Verdun, 1916* (New York: St. Martin's Press, 1962), pp. 36, 327.

[5]Brian Gardner, *The Big Push: A Portrait of the Battle of the Somme* (New York: Morrow, 1963), pp. 157-58. Accurate casualty figures are difficult to ascertain because of the attempts of the belligerents to hide the extent of their losses.

provided a cavalier aspect to a war which had become very drab. But the air weapon was not capable of winning the war—no matter the superiority one side might gain over the other—in World War I. In September 1916 tanks made their appearance on the battlefield. At that time the British threw away the initial advantage of surprise by using too few too soon. Later, they would use tanks more effectively. The Allies had a great superiority in this weapon, but, as in the case of the airplane, it could not be decisive in this war. Neither the aircraft nor the tank had reached that stage of technological development which would allow full exploitation of its capabilities.

There was one weapon which did come very close to being decisive—the submarine. The Germans found it difficult to use their U-boats in their most effective manner—namely, to sink merchant ships without warning—however, because of their desire to keep the Americans neutral. Such sinkings which did result in the loss of American lives aroused President Woodrow Wilson and caused him on occasion to issue threats against the German government. It was useless for the Germans to point out the awful effect of the British blockade on their civilians. Finally, in December 1916, the German High Command decided to risk American intervention by ordering unrestricted submarine warfare. This eventually did bring the United States into the war on April 6, 1917, but it also almost won the war for the Germans. When an American admiral, William S. Sims, arrived in London in April to discuss the naval war, the First Sea Lord, Admiral Sir John Jellicoe, bluntly informed him of the British losses of more than a million tons of shipping in February and March and concluded: "It is impossible for us to go on with the war if losses like this continue." The current secret estimate was that Britain could not hold out until the next winter. Adoption of the new technique of convoying merchant ships and the reinforcement of American destroyers prevented the defeat Jellicoe had feared.

When the United States went to war, there seemed to be little reason for the Germans to fear and the Allies to hope for much in the way of American troops in battle. Economic aid in the form of credits and material was another matter, but an army of just under 128,000 and some 13,419 Marines did not appear formidable when compared to the millions under arms in Europe.[6] German

---

[6]The Army strength is from Marvin A. Kreidberg and Merton G. Henry, *History of Military Mobilization in the United States Army, 1775-1945* (Washington, D.C.: Government Printing Office, 1955), p. 221. The Marine statistic is from Clyde H.

observers who had seen the American Army in maneuvers in 1911 had not been impressed. (See Source 1.) It seemed most unlikely that the United States could mobilize, equip, and train an army of sufficient strength quickly enough to play a significant role in the war. Even if Americans could field such a large force, they would have to get it across the Atlantic, and in the spring of 1917 it seemed realistic to assume that the U-boats could hamper the flow of men as well as supplies.

Although the Allies were pleased at the prospect of open American support, they had some idea of the sad state of American preparations and wondered how much help the Americans could give. The same month, April 1917, that Congress declared war, both the British and the French sent missions to Washington to consult with the American leaders. A former Prime Minister, the current Foreign Secretary, Arthur J. Balfour, headed the British mission while one of the most famed soldiers of the war, Marshal Joseph Joffre, was in the French party. These dignitaries explained the war situation, asked questions about what the United States government expected to do, and gave advice as to appropriate preparations. Manpower was a peripheral issue. The problems of building an army and transporting it to France seemed insoluble. It was more pragmatic to concentrate on supplies. Marshal Joffre, who had the pomp and glitter of a great reputation despite his relief from command and discrediting by political leaders, was not satisfied with that rationale. He bluntly stated, "We want men [and he emphasized], men, men."[7] He knew that the much vaunted French offensive had failed earlier that month, and he believed that even a small "show-the-flag" force of Americans would bolster French morale.

The others could see the logic in the old Marshal's plea. A few thousand American soldiers might serve as a psychological lift to the war-weary French and British. More than that, however, would take up ship space that might better be used for munitions—that is, assuming that the discussion was about an independent army complete with staffs and support troops. If the Americans were willing to send merely replacements to be used within the Allied armies, this would put the question into a different, and to the

---

Metcalf, *A History of the United States Marine Corps* (New York: Putnam, 1939), p. 450. The wartime Secretary of Navy, Josephus Daniels, in his book, *Our Navy at War* (New York: George H. Doran Co., 1922), p. 311, said that there were 69,056 officers and men in the Navy when the United States entered the war.

[7]Francis W. Halsey (ed.,), *Balfour, Viviani and Joffre* (New York: Funk & Wagnalls, 1917), p. 364.

Allies, more pleasing perspective. They could use replacements when and where they saw a need to replenish their ranks.

Amalgamation, as it was called at the time, certainly had major advantages. An independent army would necessitate large numbers of officers and men to command, staff, and support combat troops. These people would take up valuable ship space. It would also take time to develop the facilities for such a force. Rather than fitting into existing military systems, the Americans would have to build an entirely new system behind the battleline. Then it seemed to those who had been in the war since 1914 not only wasteful but also possibly disastrous for untried commanders and staffs to attempt to match wits with the experienced Germans. The logic seemed irrefutable.

Nationalism, however, shattered that kind of logic. President Wilson desired to play a key role in the making of peace. Although apparently he did not initially think much about this point, others did believe that the contribution of an independent national army would be obvious and presumably would give the President a high card at the conference table. If Americans fought under foreign leadership and perhaps even in foreign uniforms, their efforts would appear nebulous and much less impressive. There also was a suspicion that the difficulties implicit in forcing men of different nations to work closely together in a dangerous enterprise might outweigh other advantages. Language differences alone would create problems. Few Americans spoke French, and the English vernacular was confusing. A British officer's comment about heavy casualties—"things here are a bit fruity"[8]—would perplex the average American. Finally, the American professional soldiers were confident that they could do as well if not better than the Allies against the Germans, and they wanted the opportunity which only an independent army could afford.

Although this issue surfaced in the spring of 1917, it did not become a major controversy until the following winter. A series of disasters made American manpower seem much more necessary in December than in April. The first of these came in April. With much fanfare and boasting that his offensive would drive the Germans out of France, General Robert Nivelle, the French commander-in-chief, raised the hopes of his war-weary troops. When the attack failed, the morale of the French Army snapped and many units mutinied. A new commander, Philippe Pétain,

[8]As quoted in Edward M. Coffman, *The War to End All Wars: The American Military Experience in World War I* (New York: Oxford University Press, 1968), p. 286.

restored morale and discipline by a combination of better treatment of soldiers generally and executions of so-called ring-leaders.

During that spring, the British were successful in two offensives with limited objectives. Encouraged by this, the British com-mander, Sir Douglas Haig, decided to launch a more ambitious offensive in the summer. His objective was to force the Germans out of the Belgian ports they were using as submarine bases. There also was the possibility, since he had heard that the enemy forces were deteriorating, that the German Army might collapse. In the Third Battle of Ypres, which began on July 31 and lasted into November, the British made minimal gains in the Flanders mud at a loss of some 300,000 men.[9] Then, before the end of this battle which is sometimes known as Passchendaele, the Allies suffered a severe defeat in Italy. The Austrians and Germans broke through the Italian front in the battle of Caporetto and came close to eliminating Italy from the war.

The culminating disaster to the Allied cause was the Russian Revolution. It began in March 1917, but moderate successors to the czar kept Russia in the war until November. At that time, the Bolsheviks came to power and began to seek peace. If the Eastern Front ceased to exist, the French and British faced the grim prospect of having German forces superior in strength to their combined total on the Western Front. Up to this point, the Germans had been able to maintain a stalemate even though outnumbered. The Allies, understandably, feared the effect of a shift in the numerical balance.

In the face of these disasters, David Lloyd George, the British Prime Minister, led the way in forming a Supreme War Council of the Allies and the Americans in an effort to coordinate strategy. American manpower was a primary matter on the agenda. Pétain emphasized this point in a directive summing up his view of the strategic situation after the collapse of Russia:

The Entente will not recover superiority in fighting forces until the American army is capable of sending a certain number of large formations into the line; until then we must, under the threat of inevitable wastage of our forces, keep

---

[9]In his *President Wilson Fights His War: World War I and the American Intervention* (New York: Macmillan, 1968), p. 191, Harvey A. DeWeerd gives this figure which he derived from an article by Sir Basil Liddell Hart. Leon Wolff in his book *In Flanders Fields: The 1917 Campaign* (New York: Time, Inc., 1958), pp. 259-60, gives both higher and lower estimates and discusses the controversy over the casualty figures.

up a waiting attitude, with the definite idea of taking up again, as soon as we can, the offensive which alone can give us the final victory.[10]

The situation had also changed greatly for the Americans. In mid-June, Major General John J. Pershing and a small advance party arrived in France. During the last week of that month, four infantry regiments landed. Pershing, a handsome, tall cavalryman who had made his reputation in fighting in the Philippines and as leader of the 1916 Punitive Expedition into Mexico, was impressed by the seriousness of the situation following the French mutinies. He cabled to the War Department a recommendation to expand the American Expeditionary Force to three million men. At that time most of the American and Allied leaders anticipated a far smaller AEF. By the end of November, Pershing had erected the structure of an independent force, but there were only 126,000 men under his command.

Off and on, through the winter and spring of 1918 into June, the French Premier, the aged but fiery Georges Clemenceau, the British Prime Minister, and their military assistants discussed the manpower problem and how best to use the American reinforcements with Pershing. From the American commander's standpoint, the problem was shipping. The best way to blunt the dreaded German offensives which everyone thought were coming in 1918 would be to get as many Americans across the Atlantic as possible so that the AEF could take the field in great numbers and shift the balance against the Germans. To counter this argument, the British and the French emphasized the importance of time. It would take longer to get an independent force into effective action than it would to push a much larger number of combat replacements to the front. The difference in months might well be crucial.

President Wilson and various other American leaders—political and military—were willing to concede to the Allies—particularly after the German offensives began. But Wilson believed that the decision was a military one and that the final judgment should be that of his semi-autonomous commander. While Pershing did relent on occasion and permit American units—at times as small as

---

[10]The quotation is from Richard M. Griffiths, *Pétain: A Biography of Marshal Philippe Pétain of Vichy* (Garden City, N.Y.: Doubleday, 1972), p. 52. David F. Trask in *The United States in the Supreme War Council: American War Aims and Inter-Allied Strategy, 1917-1918* (Middletown, Conn.: Wesleyan University Press, 1961) discusses the amalgamation issue as well as other matters.

platoons—to serve temporarily in Allied ranks, he remained ada-
mant about the continued build-up of the AEF. He was
determined that Americans would make their battlefield contribution in their own army. Scattering American soldiers throughout the Allied armies, he believed, would be not only less
beneficial to Allied morale but also hurtful to American morale.
More importantly, he envisioned a fresh American Army breaking
the stalemate on the Western Front with open warfare tactics and
administering the "knock-out blow" to the Germans. Thus, to
him, amalgamation seemed to be an ineffectual dissipation of the
most critical resource—American manpower—the Allies had in
1918. Pershing won the argument and his side won the war
months before most people deemed it possible. The results
indicate that he was right; nevertheless, the concern of the Allies is
understandable. It was a gamble.

The Germans were optimistic during that winter. Erich Ludendorff, Quartermaster General and chief strategist, the man who
virtually ran the German war effort in that period, directed that
the troops devote their time that winter to training for the
offensive. They learned the attack techniques which the German
Army had already used successfully on the Eastern Front and at
Caporetto. The emphasis was on surprise—a heavy but brief artillery
barrage immediately preceding the assault. Then infantrymen,
organized in small assault teams, probed the front. When they
located weak points, they called for reserves and made small
breakthroughs. These would make the strong points untenable and
quickly lead to a collapse of the entire defensive line. The planners
also carefully studied Haig's dispatches during the British offensives of 1917; as Sir Basil Liddell Hart, the famed British military
historian, commented—"because they showed how not to do
it."[11]

The German efforts met with success. Since August 1914, the
belligerents had meshed in a stalemate on the Western Front, but
in the spring of 1918 the Germans seemed to be able to break the
line at will. Through the fog on the morning of March 21, they
swept over the British. After several days, they were halted after
making a forty mile breach and rolling back their enemies some
forty miles. Less than three weeks later, on April 9, they again
staggered the British with another breakthrough. In late May, they
turned their devastating attention to the French and smashed to

[11]Basil H. Liddell Hart, *The Real War: 1914-1918* (Boston: Little, Brown, paperback
edition [original copyright 1930]), p. 391.

the banks of the Marne—some fifty miles from Paris. At this time, French government officials made preparations to move their offices to Bordeaux.

The events of this terrible spring had two major results on the Allied High Command. Immediately, the Allies moved toward greater coordination through the Supreme War Council and named a French general, Ferdinand Foch, as Supreme Commander. Although limited in authority (the particular national army commanders could appeal his orders to their respective governments), Foch did plan strategy and was generally successful in persuading the commanders to follow his guidance. The second result was an increased awareness of the need for American manpower. The weary French and badly worn British pressed harder than ever before for American replacements who were their only hope of attaining superiority in manpower over the Germans. After the two German offensives, the British divisions, as Cyril Falls, the noted historian pointed out, "were often ghosts"[12] and the French were not much better off. While Pershing still fought the theory of breaking up American units to provide replacements in Allied ranks, he readily offered the units he had to the Allies. He visited Foch at his headquarters on March 28 and told the new generalissimo, "All that we have are yours."[13] Foch was touched and did make use of these American divisions then in France— mostly to relieve experienced French units from quiet sectors.

The German spring offensives were, in the final analysis, failures. Although they did crack the British and French fronts and were successful, tactically, they did not achieve the basic strategic goal of winning victories so decisively that the Allies would have to sue for peace. At the same time, the Germans rapidly used up their superiority in manpower. While they also inflicted heavy losses on the Allies, they did not have the prospect of hundreds of thousands of fresh troops coming to their aid.

In the month beginning on May 28, in two separate actions, the AEF, which then numbered some 650,000, gave Allied morale a sturdy lift by defeating German units. These were the first American attacks; heretofore, they had merely held quiet sectors of the front and conducted or countered trench raids.

At Cantigny, on May 28, the 28th Infantry Regiment of the

---

[12]Cyril Falls, *The Great War* (New York: Capricorn paperback edition, 1961), p. 339.

[13]John J. Pershing, *My Experiences in the World War,* 2 vols. (New York: Frederick A. Stokes Co., 1931), I: 365.

First Division staged the first assault. Reinforced by machine gun units and two rifle companies from other First Division regiments and supported by artillery, twelve French tanks, a few flamethrowers, and aircraft, this regiment quickly overran the small German garrison. General Pershing, who was present, was pleased. His troops had demonstrated that they could mount a successful regimental attack. He then went on his way, but the infantrymen stayed and battled desperately for several days against German counterattacks. The Germans did not retake Cantigny, but the First Division was forced to sacrifice a good many men holding this tiny village.

Another German offensive far overshadowed the Cantigny battle. The day before the American attack the Germans surprised the French and sent seventeen divisions through the French lines in the Chemin des Dames sector. They advanced twelve miles the first day. By the third day the Germans were again on the banks of the Marne River. Less than fifty miles away the French began to evacuate Paris and many feared that the war was lost. Pershing sent two divisions (the American divisions contained 28,500 officers and men, twice as much as their European counterparts) to the vicinity of Chateau-Thierry on the Marne to help stop the Germans.

In early June, the Marine Brigade of the Second Division made a counterattack west of Chateau-Thierry which became a much larger and longer battle than Cantigny and appropriately received much more attention. Aided by Army units, the Marines fought for twenty days to retake Belleau Wood, a small forest seized by the Germans as their offensive ground to a halt. Militarily, one could argue that there was no need for a battle at that particular place or that the Americans, if they had been more skillfully led, should have cleared the Germans out of that wood sooner. The importance of this fierce battle, however, was symbolic. At a time when Paris was threatened, Frenchmen learned that Americans had come between their beloved capital and the German hordes. Then, as the commander of one of the German divisions bested by the Americans in this fighting explained to his troops when they went into action—". . . it is not a question of the possession or nonpossession of this or that village or woods, insignificant in itself; it is a question whether the Anglo-American claim that the American Army is equal or even the superior of the German Army is to be made good."[14]   Field Marshal Paul von Hindenburg, the

[14]Ernst Otto quoted this June 8 order of General Böhm, commander of the 28th

foremost German commander, tactfully summed up the result: "With the appearance of the Americans on the battlefield the hopes which the French and English so long cherished were at length fulfilled." He added: "Thanks to the arrival of American reinforcements, time was working not for us but against us."[15] Time was running out for the Germans and the leaders obviously knew it.

As he contemplated the strategic situation, Ludendorff still believed that the key to victory was to defeat the British in Flanders. Yet, before he could stage another offensive against the British, he wanted to make the Marne salient, the bulge in the line created by the Chemin des Dames offensive in May, less vulnerable to enemy counterattacks. By attacking simultaneously east and west of Rheims he hoped to capture that city and the commanding terrain south of the Marne, thus flattening the salient. At the same time, Ludendorff hoped that the attack would draw reserves away from the Flanders front and thus help prepare the way for a successful attack on the British. Meantime, the military attempted to rejuvenate morale at home and in the army by referring to these summer offensives as the "Peace Offensives" with the obvious connotation that they would bring about the end of the war. In turn, the French feared that the Germans, if they attacked the Marne sector, might take Paris. Even before the battle began, people on both sides thus misunderstood the intention of the German planners.

In mid-June the Germans began their meticulous preparations for the offensives. They built up ammunition dumps, stockpiled supplies generally, increased the size of air fields, and even laid some railroad tracks to facilitate the movement of material. The son of the Kaiser, Crown Prince Wilhelm, was in command of the army group (47 divisions in three armies) designated for the attack. Many of these men had taken part in the Chemin des Dames offensive. Others were from recent drafts and, as the Crown Prince pointed out, "no longer of the best stamp."[16] Since success depended greatly on surprise, the Germans took particular precautions to conceal their activities. Nevertheless, a staff officer in

Division, in "The Battles for the Possession of Belleau Woods, June, 1918," United States Naval Institute *Proceedings,* vol. 54, no. 11 (November 1928), p. 951. The best account of Belleau Wood is Robert B. Asprey, *At Belleau Wood* (New York: Putnam, 1965).

[15] Paul von Hindenburg, *Out of My Life* (London: Cassell, 1920), pp. 366, 374.

[16] Crown Prince Wilhelm Hohenzollern, *My War Experiences* (New York: Robert McBride & Co., 1923), p. 330.

one of the assault divisions, Rudolf Binding, was doubtful about the surprise. He wrote in his diary on the night of July 14: "It looks as if the enemy suspected nothing, but that is hardly credible. The dust-clouds over the roads, which mark the path of the troops and transport even in the morning, would alone be sufficient to give us away."[17]

The French did know about the offensive. They began to suspect the possibility in late June. Aerial photographs and prisoners confirmed these suspicions and indicated the area to be attacked. Finally, on the night of July 14, a few hours before the Germans planned to attack, they captured 27 prisoners who revealed the exact time. (See Source 2.)

Because he knew the time and place of the offensive, Pétain planned a trap for the Germans. He knew their new offensive tactics and thought that a flexible defense in depth would defeat this heretofore successful ploy. His idea was to evacuate secretly the front except for suicide squads and concentrate his force in a main defensive line some distance in the rear. Thus the heavy barrage would fall on virtually empty trenches and the assault teams would quickly overrun the lightly held front. They would presume that a general breakthrough was at hand and so would call on reserves to go through the gap in the lines. As they advanced, however, they would be exposed to French artillery fire. By the time they reached the actual defense line, the tired assault troops, riddled with losses, would be no match for the defenders.

Pétain had three armies in this area. These included 32 French, two Italian, and five American divisions. Another American infantry regiment—the 369th which consisted of white officers and black enlisted men—was assigned to one of the French divisions. Not all of these troops would actually face the German attack. For example, only two American divisions, part of a third, and the black regiment were exposed to the brunt of the attack.[18]

When Pétain discussed his defensive plan with the three army commanders he ran into resistance. None wanted to give up ground without a fierce fight. In the end, the two who commanded the Fifth and Sixth Armies west of Rheims did not position their soldiers according to this plan. East of Rheims, in

[17]Rudolf G. Binding, *A Fatalist at War* (London: Allen & Unwin, 1929), p. 233.

[18]Preface and Order of Battle in *Military Operations of the American Expeditionary Forces: Champagne-Marne and Aisne-Marne*, vol. 5 in *United States Army in the World War: 1917-1919*, 17 vols. (Washington, D.C.: Government Printing Office, 1948), pp. 1-2. Hereinafter cited as *United States Army in the World War*, 5.

Map I

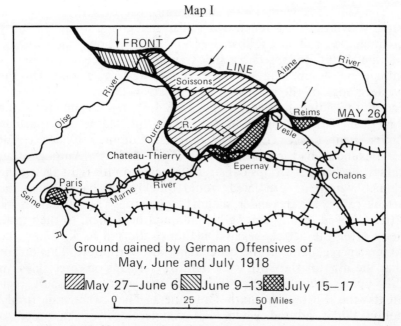

Ground gained by German Offensives of
May, June and July 1918
May 27—June 6 June 9–13 July 15—17
0   25   50 Miles

From American Battle Monuments Commission, *A Guide to the American Battle Fields in Europe* (Washington, D.C.: Government Printing Office, 1927), p. 25.

Champagne, Henri Gouraud, a charismatic leader with a red beard and one arm (he had lost the other in an earlier battle), reluctantly ordered his Fourth Army to comply with Pétain's plan.

In the early morning darkness on Monday, July 15, the Germans started their attack (see Map I). Already the French had surprised them by heavy shelling just before the German artillery commenced firing the barrage. In Champagne, the assault troops were pleased and perhaps a little puzzled to find so few of the enemy in the trenches. Then, the trap sprang shut. A newly promoted brigadier general in the American 42nd Division, Douglas MacArthur, described what happened in front of his unit. "As the enemy stormed our now abandoned trenches, our own barrage descended like an avalanche on his troops. The ease with which their infantry had crossed this line of alert, so thinly occupied by our suicide squads, had given them the illusion of a successful advance. But when they met the dikes of our real line, they were exhausted, unco-ordinated, and scattered, incapable of going further without being reorganized and reinforced."[19]

[19] Douglas MacArthur, *Reminiscences* (New York: McGraw-Hill, 1964), p. 58.

The Germans were more successful west of Rheims as they rapidly overran the French and Italian defenders. Since the army commanders had not followed Pétain's instructions, their section of the front collapsed as the Germans advanced five or six kilometers before the defenders could restore a line. On the western edge of the offensive, near Chateau-Thierry, the Germans found the going less easy. The 38th Infantry Regiment of the American Third Division held firm on the Marne for fourteen hours against six German regiments. Colonel Ulysses Grant McAlexander had carefully planned his defense. Among other things, he had his troops construct trenches on his right facing the French whom he predicted would quickly fall back. When the attack came, McAlexander, a short, solid, tough, bald man in his fifties, moved calmly among his men and held them to their task. Soon after the attack began the French did fall back. Later, the American regiment on the other flank also withdrew. This meant that the men of the 38th were fighting Germans on three sides. In this fight, they virtually destroyed two German assault regiments—the Fifth and Sixth Grenadiers. They were still firmly holding their ground when McAlexander received an order to withdraw. By that time the German attack in that vicinity was spent. Since then, the 38th has been officially known as the "Rock of the Marne" regiment.[20]

The offensive was a failure. Within 36 hours after it began, Ludendorff ordered it stopped. The trap set by Gouraud's troops forced this decision. They had not only stopped elements of two German armies but also exacted a heavy cost. On Wednesday, the 17th, Ludendorff decided to withdraw from the southern bank of the Marne on the night of the 20th. It was a crushing disappointment—analogous to that of the French upon the failure of the Nivelle offensive in 1917. As in that situation, it was made worse by the high hopes for an end-the-war blow which the propagandists had generated. Even the Kaiser had come to see the great victory only to hear the bad news from the Crown Prince.

Within a few days there was more to depress the Germans.

In mid-June, Foch had begun plotting a counterattack to drive the Germans out of the Marne salient. Although knowledge of the upcoming July 15 offensive caused him to modify his plans, he

[20]See Source 3 and Robert L. Bullard, *Fighting Generals* (Ann Arbor, Mich.: J. W. Edwards, 1944), pp. 133-81. This is an interesting biographical sketch of McAlexander by his former commander, Lt. General Bullard. It includes a detailed description of the battle.

refused to discard them. Now that the Americans were available in increasing number, he had enough men to go on the offensive. His revised plan was to attack the western face of the Marne salient with two French armies—the Tenth and the Sixth—which included four American divisions.

The key sector was near the western base of the salient in the vicinity of Soissons. If his troops could push the Germans back six or seven miles at that point, they would be in position to cut the German supply and communications lines into the salient and force a general withdrawal. He gave this assignment to the Tenth Army's XX Corps which consisted of the Moroccan Division and the First and Second American Divisions (see Map II).

Both of these divisions had experienced combat although many in their ranks were recent replacements. The First had been in France longer and had more time in the trenches. The Second, whose infantry was a unique combination of two Marine regiments and two Regular Army regiments, however, had just come out of the severe fighting at Belleau Wood and near Chateau-Thierry.

Map II

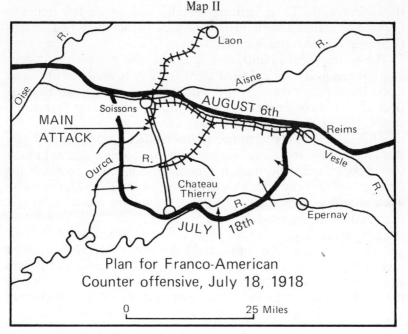

From American Battle Monuments Commission, *A Guide to the American Battle Fields in Europe* (Washington, D.C.: Government Printing Office, 1927), p. 27.

They were as good as any American unit and those who served in them could argue—with real justification—that they were the best.

The French set H Hour and D Day at 4:35 a.m. July 18. The Corps Commander, General Berdoulat, issued his attack order on July 16:

At H hour, supporting, counterbattery and prohibition [artillery] fires contemplated in the plans of engagement will start with the utmost violence and infantry will rush in groups made for speed, so as to get rapidly in touch with the enemy, to outflank him and to drive him back relentlessly.[21]

At this time the Americans were still moving toward their assault positions. The First Division, which had less problems with its transportation, arrived earlier and was able to get some rest. The Second had more difficulty in its journey. There was a good deal of confusion as French transportation officers moved elements of the division without telling unit commanders where their troops were going. Changes in command at the top level probably amplified this confusion. A new division commander took over on July 15, and both infantry brigades received new commanders on the seventeenth. These officers literally had only a few hours to become acquainted with their new jobs before they had to lead their men into the attack.

The Marines and infantrymen in the Second went without sleep and hot meals as they travelled night and day toward the Forest of Retz. During their second night without sleep, they completed the final lap of their journey on foot through the dense forest in a storm. Horses, mules, artillery, long columns of infantry, and the rain turned the roads to mires. Neither officers nor men had seen this area before and there was no time for reconnaissance. In fact, two regiments actually had to doubletime in order to reach the front in time for the attack. A lieutenant of the Fifth Marines who made that march recalled: "Just to keep moving was a harder test than battle ever imposed."[22]

They made it just in time. The artillery opened up at H Hour and the tired, hungry troops started the attack. The First Division was on the left in relatively open ground. The Moroccan Division which included the famous Foreign Legion was in the center and the Second was on the right with part of its line still in the forest. The First Division had to anticipate the most formidable terrain

[21] *United States Army in the World War, 5:292.*
[22] John W. Thomason, Jr., *Fix Bayonets!* (New York: Scribner's, 1926), p. 90.

obstacles in the form of four large, steep, wooded ravines. The Moroccans and the men in the Second Division had only one such ravine in their path.

The initial attack was a surprise and the Tenth and Sixth Armies rolled over the defenders. The Germans had left only a light defensive force in the Soissons sector and many of these men were ill with influenza. They were simply unable to cope with the fury of the attackers, strongly supported by French tanks and airplanes.

It was a clear, sunny, hot day as the First and Second American Divisions swept forward through the fields of waist-high wheat. Their enthusiasm and daring impressed the French who lagged behind them on their flanks. Even the Moroccan Division, which was considered one of the best in the army, was left behind by the spirited Americans. The French were also quick to point out that this headlong rush cost heavy casualties and brought about a breakdown in control, particularly in the Second Division, and a loss in liaison with adjacent units. Of course, the heavy toll of officers which left some companies without officers contributed to these problems.

On the second day, the trial of fighting through the ravines slowed down the First and exhaustion overtook the Second. The loss of many of their tanks and the inability of the artillery to provide as much support as on July 18 also hampered them. Yet, both divisions continued to advance against increased resistance. The Germans recognized the seriousness of their predicament and poured reinforcements into the sector. The commander of the Army Group, Crown Prince William, wrote later: "It was certainly the most critical situation in which I had found myself as Commander during the whole war."[23]

That night the Second Division was relieved. (See Source 5.) Many of these exhausted men had gone without food or water for twenty-four hours. The haste and confusion of the approach march combined with the rapid advance had been too much for the supply people. The Marines and infantrymen had gained six and a half miles and captured 2900 prisoners and 75 guns at a cost of 4000 casualties.

The First stayed for another three days. On Sunday, the 21st, it seized Berzy-le-Sec. The next day the tired infantrymen consolidated their position and waited for their relief which came that

[23]Hohenzollern, *My War Experiences*, p. 338.

night. They had lost 7317 casualties in their drive of almost seven miles and they had taken 3400 prisoners and 75 guns. (See Source 4.)

They had won a great victory and, in fact, had turned the tide of the war by giving the initiative to the Allies. There was rejoicing at the time and, on the part of some, a realization of the consequence of this battle. (See Source 7.) But even the optimistic Americans thought it would take months of hard fighting into the spring of 1919 before the Allies would be able to force the Germans out of the war.

Immediately, there would be much hard fighting before the French and the Americans could regain the Marne salient. The French Fifth Army joined in the attack on July 20 by moving against the eastern face of the salient. Two days later the Germans decided to evacuate. For twelve days, until they reached the Vesle River at the base of the salient, they gave up ground slowly and deliberately, exacting heavy casualties from the attackers. The Second Battle of the Marne came to an end in the first week of August. Altogether, eight American divisions had participated in this great battle.

At the time some Germans tried to de-emphasize the importance of the battle. They pointed out that troops had eventually held the attackers and had inflicted heavy casualties. The Crown Prince did not agree with this attempt at optimism. He wrote his father at the end of July and told him of the seriousness of the "ever-growing numerical superiority" of the Allies because of the Americans. He later spoke of the battle as the "turning point" and gave the reason: "From being the attackers we had been thrown on the defensive."[24] Because of their own heavy casualties, the Germans had to draw replacements from the armies poised for the planned attack against the British. This meant postponement and eventual cancellation of that offensive of which Ludendorff had expected so much.

Ludendorff, despite these setbacks, was one of those who tried to be optimistic. When he reviewed the events of the last two weeks in July, he emphasized the successful withdrawal and noted: "The shadow cast by the events of July 18 had passed." He considered August 8 the "black day of the German Army." For on that day the British attacked near Amiens and gained seven miles.

---

[24] Hohenzollern, *My War Experiences*. In order, these quotations appear on pp. 342, 341, and 339.

Then he realized the truth: "The balance of numbers had moved heavily against us; it was bound to become increasingly unfavorable as more American troops came in. . . . We had to resign ourselves now to the prospect of a continuation of the enemy's offensive."[25]

Before the attack at Soissons and the culmination of the Second Battle of the Marne, American staff officers created the organizational plan for a field army. At St. Mihiel, in mid-September, this Army scored a spectacular success. Later that month, it launched the Meuse-Argonne offensive. Throughout September and October, the Allies hammered the Germans. For the hard-pressed Germans, it was no longer a question of when they could regain the initiative, it was simply a matter of how long could their understrength, war-weary units stand the beating. In early November, another American field army went into battle and the First Army broke the German line in the Meuse-Argonne. There were two million Americans in France and more were coming. The Germans signed the Armistice on November 11.

The war was over. For more than four years, the belligerents had fought and lost enormous casualties. After the collapse of Russia, it seemed that the Germans, because of their increased strength and new tactics, would be able to force a decision on the Western Front. The arrival of the two million American soldiers more than offset this advantage. Although they participated in large numbers only in the last four months of the war, the actual role they played in those battles and the sheer weight of their numbers were crucial to the Allied victory. They were inexperienced and they faced veteran German troops, but their numbers and vigor were eventually too much for war-weary German units, depleted in strength and suffering from shortages of food and other supplies.

In the Second Battle of the Marne the Germans lost the initiative and never regained it. The Allies were able to seize the initiative and maintain it because of their American reinforcements. The AEF tipped the balance and made victory possible.

FOR FURTHER READING

Bullard, Robert L. *Fighting Generals,* Ann Arbor, Mich.: J.W. Edwards, 1944.
Coffman, Edward M. *The War to End All Wars: The American Military Experience in World War I.* New York: Oxford University Press, 1968.

[25] Erich Ludendorff, *Ludendorff's Own Story: August 1914-November 1918*, 2 vols. (New York: Harper Brothers, 1919), II: 321, 326, 330-31.

De Weerd, Harvey A. *President Wilson Fights His War: World War I and the American Intervention.* New York: Macmillan Co., 1969.

Falls, Cyril. *The Great War: 1914-1918.* New York: G. P. Putnam's Sons, Capricorn paperback edition, 1961.

Foch, Ferdinand. *The Memoirs of Marshal Foch.* Garden City, N.Y.: Doubleday, Doran & Co., 1931.

Harbord, James G. *The American Army in France: 1917-1919.* Boston: Little, Brown & Co., 1936.

Hindenburg, Paul von. *Out of My Life.* London: Cassell & Co., 1920.

Hohenzollern, Wilhelm. *My War Experiences.* New York: Robert McBride & Co., 1923.

Liddell Hart, Basil H. *The Real War: 1914-1918.* Boston: Little, Brown & Co., paperback edition, copyright 1930.

————. *Through the Fog of War.* New York: Random House, 1938.

Ludendorff, Erich. *Ludendorff's Own Story: August 1914-November 1918.* 2 vols. New York: Harper Brothers, 1919.

Paxson, Frederic L. *America at War: 1917-1918.* Boston: Houghton Mifflin Co., 1939.

Pershing, John J. *My Experiences in the World War.* 2 vols. New York: Frederick A. Stokes Co., 1931.

Stallings, Laurence. *The Doughboys: The Story of the AEF, 1917-1918.* New York: Harper & Row, 1963.

Vierick, George S., ed. *As They Saw Us: Foch, Ludendorff and Other Leaders Write Our War History.* Garden City, N.Y.: Doubleday, Doran & Co., 1929.

Wise, Jennings C. *The Turn of the Tide: American Operations at Cantigny, Chateau Thierry, and the Second Battle of the Marne.* New York: Henry Holt & Co., 1920.

SOURCES

1

German Attitude toward the Prewar American Army

The American Military Attaché in Berlin, Captain Samuel G. Shartle, forwarded this translation of a newspaper article to the American General Staff on June 5, 1911.

SOURCE: Document No. 6553-3, War College Division File, Record Group 165, National Archives.

EVENTS OF MILITARY INTEREST IN GERMANY
DURING THE MONTH OF MAY, 1911

From: Captain Samuel G. Shartle, C.A.C., American
Military Attaché, Berlin, Germany, June 5, 1911

The Schlesische Zeitung, May 28, 1911, publishes the following comments of a German officer who visited the camp at San Antonio:
The rapidity with which the marching orders were carried out by the troops on the Rio Grande, and the smooth execution of the concentration of General Carter's demonstration Corps, for the conditions of the Union, merit recognition. But between the frequent mobilization tests, which we make on our western border, where in earnest the troops would march out in a few hours, and the military practice trip in Texas a gap, very striking to German eyes, appears. Even if our Lorraine companies, which on mobilization march out at once, should be on an approximate peace strength, thanks to the absent and sick, they would present a very different service type from the skeleton formations which ten weeks ago united in the Carter Division and even today cannot be brought to the full prescribed strength.

In spite of the high pay and the prospect of a sort of campaign, recruiting of the maneuver troops has great difficulties. This circumstance is explained in part by the fact that even after the victorious war against Spain and the many successful expeditions to Cuba, China, Panama and the Philippines, where every place the American soldier brought himself honor, still officers in uniform are not allowed to go to a ball with their ladies in a public pleasure place at San Antonio. The non-commissioned officers and the privates are not allowed to go to any of the best theaters—so low stands the recruited defender of the fatherland in the eyes of a free people! It is not therefore surprising that in the last bunch of recruits there are many foreigners, especially new immigrants; so that, in the infantry at least, one might believe there is an American Foreign Legion. That there are many German countrymen in the olive green of Uncle Sam can hardly excite surprise in view of the French-African example.

The infantry is the worst reduced; in this the number of stragglers on even short and not strenuous practice marches, at present on account of the strong recruit detachments in the companies, was according to our conception simply enormous. Also the leadership of the higher officers, unaccustomed to the disposition of large masses of troops, has failed considerably in the various field exercises. On the other hand, the arrangements and sanitary measures in the tent camp are excellent; these are recognized as models,

among others by the German Military Attaché, Major Herwarth von Bittenfeld.

2

The French Fourth Army in the
Second Battle of the Marne

General Henri Gouraud, the Army Commander, gives his report
of the operations in mid-July.

SOURCE: *Military Operations of the American Expeditionary
Forces: Champagne-Marne and Aisne-Marne,* vol. 5 in *United
States Army in the World War: 1917-1919.* 17 vols. Washington,
D.C. Department of the Army, 1948, 150-153. Hereinafter cited
as *United States Army in the World War, 5.*

Operations Report   FRENCH FOURTH ARMY,
3d Section, General Staff   July 18, 1918.

[Extract]

I. SUCCINCT HISTORICAL ACCOUNT: The battle begun July 15 on the
CHAMPAGNE front formed part of the general offensive opened the same
day by the German armies with the purpose of pinching off the MONTAGNE-
de-REIMS by capturing a position on the MARNE in the CHALONS-CONDE
REGION ON ONE SIDE of REIMS and in the region of EPERNAY on the
other.

Swiftness of execution sought through surprise was the condition indispensable to success. Moreover, on the Champagne front, the enemy had taken
every precaution to preserve secrecy and not to attract the attention of the
French High Command: Almost no artillery and aviation activity—quiet of
the infantry which evacuated its front lines and showed its presence neither
by raids nor by extensive patrolling—very great care to avoid letting prisoners
fall into our hands—instruction of men in case they should be made prisoners.

However, beginning with the end of June, certain indications pointed to a

German offensive on the army front: The equipment of the front revealed by photographs, the construction of new railways, the increase in the size of aviation fields, and ammunition dumps, the statements of prisoners, activity back of the front, special information.

By July 1, the indications were such that an attack could not but be expected in a short time on the front east of the SUIPPE.

As early as July 2 the general commanding the army informed the corps and division commanders of the situation, reminded them once more of the position on which the army was to make its defensive stand, gave each one his mission and the troops at his disposal (Personal and Secret Instructions No. 6459/3 of July 2).

The army corps commanders received the order to make frequent and deep raids along the whole front. Everyone bearing in mind the imperative necessity of making prisoners, numerous and profitable raids were carried out with extraordinary vigor and zeal.

The interrogation of prisoners left no doubt about the preparations for attack.

The air service reported the increase in traffic behind the front, particularly in the stations (the number of cars has doubled and even tripled in some stations). Reconnaisance by night and day confirmed the information from photographs. Night patrols reported the increased activity in the bivouacs and billets and made it possible to follow the movement towards the point of attack of troops formerly in reserve in the region of SEDAN–MEZIERES–HIRSON, the establishing of numerous dumps of material and ammunition located well toward the front, the construction of numerous battery emplacements, and the repairing of roads up to the front line trenches.

July 6, the general commanding the army prescribed the dispositions to be made each evening in order to be ready to receive the attack and avoid any shifting of troops during the artillery preparation which we expected to see begin about midnight (Memorandum 6604/3). As soon as the alarm was given the night guard balloons were to ascend.

The 1st position, entirely under the fire of the trench mortars, was not to be held—the position of resistance was the intermediate position; its density of occupation was to be such that no enemy infiltration would be possible. This density was to be attained by taking troops beforehand from the 2d position. Units not employed were to occupy the 2d position. Observation detachments commanded by selected officers were designated to remain in our 1st parallel and signal the jump off of the enemy assault waves. Behind on the line of the reserves of the 1st position advanced detachments had the mission of delaying the assault waves and breaking up the attack by sacrificing themselves. Everyone understood the duty he would have to perform.

This disposition for combat was taken when the alert was ordered.

Meanwhile, as the information became more accurate, it appeared that the anticipated attack would extend more to the west than had been supposed at first and would include the front of the IV Army Corps and the right of the Fifth Army.

From July 13 the general commanding the army had reached a definite opinion as to the front on which the attack would be delivered, and was certain it would extend from the region of La-POMPELLE to MAISONS-de-CHAMPAGNE Farm. He expected the attack might be made at any time after July 14.

Dispositions for a full alert were taken beginning with the night of July 13/14, and were to be put into effect each night at 11 p.m.

Instructions were given to yperite [mustard gas] the dugouts of the 1st position the evening of July 14.

Finally, at 8 p.m., July 14, a raid by the IV Corps brought back 27 prisoners who made known that the attack would take place the 15th between 3 a.m. and 5 a.m. and that the preparation would begin about midnight.

At 11 p.m. the general commanding the army gave the order to fire the counter-preparation. This order was carried out beginning at 11:30 p.m., according to prearranged plan. Batteries that had been silent until that time, revealed themselves. German officers taken prisoner later declared their astonishment at the number of our batteries that had not been detected previously, and did not appear on their maps, which suddenly disclosed their existence at the moment of the attack, and the surprise they experienced in consequence.

This was the situation, our troops occupying their battle posts, the counter-preparation being fired along the whole front, when the German artillery preparation opened at 12:10 a.m., July 15.

During the period preceding the attack the French command sought by all the means at its disposal to discover the intentions of the enemy. The German command on the contrary showed a passiveness, certainly intentional, to maintain secrecy, made no attempt to discover the dispositions taken by its opponent for the defense of his positions nor to know what positions would be encountered.

II. BATTLE OF JULY 15: At 12:10 a.m. the enemy preparation broke loose, sudden and terrific violence, by cannon of all calibers (77, 150, 105 and 210). The trench mortars came into action about 2 a.m. and reached their maximum intensity towards 4 a.m.

A large proportion of gas shells was reported, but little mustard.

The bombardment affected the front of the IV and XXI Army Corps and of the 161st Infantry Division, continuing, but in decreasing intensity, east as far as the AISNE. The 1st position was the most violently shelled. The intermediate and 2d positions were subjected to less violent fire. Only these batteries that had been in action before the attack were clearly engaged. The majority of our silent batteries were not shelled.

Interdiction fire extended along lines of communication and billets as far as 20 km. to the rear.

At 4:15 a.m. the infantry came out of its trenches and leaped to the assault, preceded by a rolling barrage. The attack was reported by rockets set off by our observation groups.

On the front of the IV corps the enemy made only painful progress, delayed by the fire of the advanced elements, and in particular by machine guns placed in the pill boxes south of [the heights of] Le CASQUE and Le TETON.

At 6:30 a.m. the enemy was still engaged with elements of the front line battalions which had fallen back to the general line: VOIE-ROMAINE [Roman Road] –St-CYR Parallel–Ouvrage GOURAUD [fieldwords] –HAIE-CLAIRE–Bois-en-ESCALIER–Bois-du-CHIEN–Hill 181–former French 1st position in the eastern part of the corps zone.

At 7 a.m., the enemy who had just taken PRUNAY, was advancing toward the southeast. Dispositions were taken at once to check this advance.

Between 7 a.m. and 7:30 a.m. the enemy came up to the intermediate position. The most vigorous pressure was experienced, especially in the direction of PROSNES. To the north of this village, the enemy penetrated our intermediate position as far as the ROMAN ROAD, in spite of sharp hand-to-hand fighting. Everywhere local counterattacks threw back the few attackers who had penetrated within the position.

On the front of the XXI Army Corps after having crossed the line of observation, the attack infiltrated through the works of the reserve line of the 1st position occupied by the advanced elements which resisted with energy. Toward 8 a.m. they came up against the intermediate position. The attack of this position, supported by tanks, was particularly violent. At some points the enemy attempted as many as seven times to penetrate within our lines, without obtaining the least success. The village of PERTHES, taken and retaken, finally remained in our hands. It should be noted that at no point did the tanks reach our line, that many were destroyed either by our cannon or by the lines of land mines, placed according to the plan of defense, in the 1st position.

Opposite the VIII A. C. the action of the enemy was limited to the MAIN-de-MASSIGES.

An advance took form south of La BUTTE-du-MESNIL in a southwesterly direction.

At 5 a.m. the enemy infantry came up to the reserve line of the 1st position and advanced slowly toward the MARSON. Twice he attacked Le MESNIL Redoubt; each time he was repulsed and his attempts toward the village of MESNIL had no more success.

This first part of the battle, from the jump off to the attack on the intermediate position, developed exactly as the command had foreseen.

● ● ● ● ●

At midday the enemy appeared definitely blocked and from thence on his activities became limited to artillery concentrations and fire of interdiction.

The battle position fixed by the general commanding the army was intact.

● ● ● ● ●

GOURAUD
General Commanding the Army

3

The 38th Infantry Regiment
in the Second Battle of the Marne

Colonel Ulysses G. McAlexander reports on the battle of July 15
and 16 on the banks of the Marne.

SOURCE: *United States Army in the World War*, 5:81-82.

Operations Report   38th INFANTRY, A.E.F.,
                                                    Crezancy, Aisne, July 31, 1918.

[Extract]

5. The Action: The action began at midnight July 14/15, 1918, with a
bombardment of guns of various caliber, reported to consist of eighty-four
(84) batteries. The firing was rapid until 1:55 a.m., when it became moderate
and remained so all over the area occupied by this regiment, with one
exception, up to the moment of starting the rolling barrage along the railroad
line at about 3:45 a.m.

Immediately preceding the rolling barrage there was apparently a concentration of artillery fire on the railroad line. The Germans pushed forward
their preparations for crossing the MARNE under cover of smoke, tear and
sneezing gas near the river, and lethal gas farther south. The French batteries
of artillery in the subsector east of me are reported to have withdrawn at
about 1 a.m., July 15, 1918, and the French infantry withdrew at about 4
a.m., after probable severe loss. This withdrawal exposed my right flank to
hostile attack on a front of over four (4) kilometers. Attempts to cross the
MARNE at three (3) places in my subsector were made; one in front of Co. E
and another in front of Co. H were repulsed by rifle and Chauchat fire and
hand grenades. The third place was in front of Co. G, made by the 6th
Grenadiers. This was successful after the complete extermination of the
platoon of that company on the river bank. A second platoon of Co. G on the
north side of the railroad embankment was likewise exterminated after
desperate hand-to-hand fighting. The third platoon of this company advanced
over the railroad and engaged the enemy in similar manner and drove them
off, which permitted the fourth platoon to first counterattack, then to resist
a flank attack coming from the southwest of MEZY. The do-or-die spirit of

this battalion prevented any Germans from entering our lines except as prisoners, of whom there were over 400 from this one point. It was here that by aid of Co. H the 6th Grenadiers were destroyed.

On the right flank of the front line battalion, Company F occupied trenches specially constructed to meet any possible contingency of retirement by the troops of the sector adjoining me on the east. Here this company fought throughout the day of the 15th and repeatedly repulsed and counterattacked the 5th Grenadiers until they, too, were driven, defeated and all but destroyed back towards JAULGONNE. That regiment did not again appear in action.

The battalion was withdrawn by order of higher authority to the aqueduct line on the night of July 15, after having sustained an action on its front and both flanks for over 14 hours. As far as known, not an officer or man abandoned his duty during those trying hours. The annals of our army do not record a more heroic action.

Companies B and D, during the 15th/16th, protected the rear and right flank of the 2d Battalion in a series of attacks that made possible the holding of the valley behind them.

To the 3d Battalion fell as hard a lot as can be imposed upon soldiers, that of having to remain constantly exposed under fire with no opportunity to return it. My praise for these battalions must, in fairness, be equally divided.

It is of interest to note that at the time the shelling first started, practically every company, except those in the front line, had working details of from seventy-five to one hundred men under supervision of the engineers engaged in digging trenches. In a great many instances these details were over half a kilometer from their respective positions, especially in the support battalions. In spite of the heavy bombardment, the officers in charge kept perfect control of their men, held them under cover, separated and organized their own men, and reported them back to their companies and positions when the barrage lifted.

The action of July 16 consisted principally in repulsing repeated attacks by the enemy from the northeast and east along the ridge east of the SURMELIN and as far south as CONNIGIS. During the afternoon the pressure became so great that a change of front along the Surmelin was required under a severe fire. On the night of the 16th, superior authority ordered the occupation of the woods line.

6. Result: This regiment fought the German 10th and 36th Divisions to a standstill and captured prisoners from each of their six attack regiments.

●   ●   ●   ●   ●

U. G. McALEXANDER
Colonel, 38th Infantry
Commanding

4

The First Division
in the Soissons Counteroffensive

Colonel Campbell King, the division Chief of Staff, reports the
division's actions throughout the battle.

SOURCE: *United States Army in the World War,* 5:325-27.

Report on Operations   1st Division, A.E.F.
South of Soissons   Dammartin-en-Goele, Seine-et-Marne,
                                                        July 27, 1918

[Extract]

2. ATTACK:

   (a) July 17 orders were received from the XX Army Corps that the Tenth
Army would make an offensive to break the enemy's front between the
AISNE and the OURCQ, and to push in the direction of FERE-en-
TARDENOIS; that the XX Army Corps would participate with three
divisions in the first line and two in the second. The 1st Division was
designated as the left (north) front line division of the corps. The 1st Division
had on its right the Moroccan 1st Division; on its left the 153d D. I. of the
French I Army Corps. The attack was ordered for 4:45 a.m. July 18. It was
not to be preceded by artillery fire but the advance was to be covered by a
rolling barrage. Three objectives were assigned.***

   (b) In conformity with the above orders the 1st Division attacked as in
F. O. 27.*** In addition to the French artillery units as enumerated in F. O.
27, the division was supported by the following French units:

Groupment XI - Heavy Tanks
Escadrille Spad 42
Balloon 83

   All troops were in place in sufficient time to begin the attack at 4:35 a.m.
At 5:30 a.m. the first objective had been attained by all troops, with
comparatively few losses and there was little resistance encountered, mostly
on the right. At 7:15 a.m. the right of the attack had reached the second
objective. The left of the division was on the west side of the MISSY Ravine.

Shortly afterwards the second objective was reached by all troops. The 2d Brigade had heavy fighting in the MISSY Ravine.

After the halt at the second objective, the 2d Brigade was unable to continue the advance to the third objective on this day. The 1st Brigade advanced to the third objective and pushed patrols out in front of the objective. The failure of the 2d Brigade to advance was occasioned by very heavy enfilading machine-gun fire from machine-gun nests to the north and northeast. The 153d Inf. Div. on the left was unable to capture these nests, which lay in its zone, and the fire for the time being held up our attack.

At the end of the day the situation was: 2nd Brigade on second objective, in liaison with 153d Div.; 1st Brigade on third objective, in liaison with the Moroccan division, with left flank refused, to establish liaison with 2d Brigade. The casualties suffered during the advance to the second objective were very light. Quite heavy casualties were suffered thereafter by the 2d Brigade in attempting to advance and by the 1st Brigade, which had its flank exposed. The advance was a complete surprise to the enemy and he suffered heavily in casualties and prisoners. Approximately 2,000 prisoners were taken the first day, of which approximately 75 were officers. In the quarry 500 men, with battalion commander and several officers, were taken by a very small group of men. It is impossible to estimate the small material captured. Many machine guns were taken and operated against the enemy. Approximately 30 field guns (77's and 150's) were taken in the MISSY Ravine and neighboring positions. At 7:30 on the morning of this day the division P.C. was moved from MORTEFONTAINE to quarry 500 meters west of COEUVRES. Both brigades also established advance P.C.'s. The division reserves, other than the infantry battalions, were moved into the vicinity of the division P.C. One battalion, 18th Infantry, in division reserve, was moved to DOMMIERS, for entrucking, to support the II Cavalry Corps in case it was able to penetrate the enemy's lines.

(c) On the night of July 18/19 orders were received from the XX Army Corps that the Tenth Army would continue the attack at 4 a.m. July 19 and that the division would attack as part of the XX Army Corps in liaison with flanking divisions. The battalion of the 18th Infantry sent to DOMMIERS for entrucking was returned to the division as reserves. The objective given to the division was the front - BERZY-le-SEC (exclusive)–BUZANCY (exclusive)– to thus establish itself facing to the northeast to cover the left flank of the corps.

As soon as this objective was obtained the division was ordered to push out offensive reconnaissance parties until contact with the enemy was gained. The conditions for the execution of the attack were otherwise the same as for the first day.

(d) In conformity with these orders the division attacked at 4 a.m. Due to the lateness of the hour at which orders were received, it was impossible to notify some battalions until almost the hour of assault, but all battalions went forward at approximately 4 a.m. In liaison with the Moroccan division the 1st Brigade was able to sensibly advance and to occupy the line extending

from the head of the CHAZELLE Ravine and to its junction with the 2d
Brigade on the SOISSONS-PARIS Road. The 2d Brigade continued to suffer
heavily from machine-gun fire and was unable to advance beyond the
PARIS-SOISSONS Road at this time. Supporting tanks were able to advance
as far as the edge of the PLOISY Ravine. They suffered heavy casualties,
however, and from this time were unable to participate further in the attack.

At 5:30 p.m., in liaison with the 153d Div. on the left, the division again
attacked with the objective of advancing its left to the western edge of the
PLOISY Ravine and strengthening its front. This operation was successful,
although many casualties were suffered from machine-gun fire from strong
points to the north. Right of the division was marked by Fme du MONT-de-
COURMELLES—edge of PLOISY Ravine—CHAZELLE. The casualties suffered in this day's operation were very heavy — probably 3,000 for this day
and 4,500 for the two days. An additional thousand prisoners were taken and
about 35 officers. About 30 additional field guns were taken in the ravines
between PLOISY and CHAZELLE. Liaison was established for the night with
both flanking divisions.

(e) On July 20 orders were received from the XX Army Corps that on
account of the difficulties the 153 D. I. had encountered in its progress the
1st Division would be charged with the taking of BERZY-le-SEC, formerly in
the zone of the 153d Div. and that the zone of action of the 1st Division
would extend to the north of the village. In compliance with the above orders
the division attacked at 2 p.m. for the purpose of taking BERZY-le-SEC and
the heights to the north and strengthening the front of the division on the
general line BERZY-le-SEC—BUZANCY. For this purpose one battalion
divisional reserves were put under orders of Commanding General, 2d Brigade.
The divisional artillery, which had been moved into forward positions,
delivered a powerful preparation of two hours, and a rolling barrage from H
hour. The 2d Brigade suffered very heavily from machine-gun nest to north
which had not yet been taken and was unable at this time to take
BERZY-le-SEC. The 1st Brigade, in liaison with the Moroccan division,
crossed the railroad and advanced to the vicinity of Bois-GERARD, VIS-
IGNEUX and ANCONIN Farm, retiring its flank to connect with 2d Brigade.
The situation at nightfall was: 28th Infantry on plateau in front of
BERZY-le-SEC; 26th Infantry dug in along road between BERZY-le-SEC and
CHAZELLE; the 1st Brigade in liaison with the 2d Brigade and with the
Moroccan division at VISIGNEUX. Casualties continued heavy, approxi-
mately 1,000 for the day. Some prisoners and material were taken in PLOISY
Ravine and in the zone of the 1st Brigade.

(f) During night of July 20/21 orders were received from the XX Army
Corps that the corps would attack on the morning of July 21 at 4 h.; that on
this night the Moroccan division would be relieved by the 87th Inf. Div. and
the 153d Inf. Div. reenforced by one regiment of the 69th Inf. Div. The first
objective was given as BERZY-le-SEC (inclusive)—the heights north and east
of BUZANCY—BUZANCY (exclusive).***

(g) In conformity with these orders the division attacked at 4 a.m. July 21.

The situation was complicated by the necessity of maintaining liaison with the 87th Div. which attacked at 4 a.m. and with the 153d Div. which only attacked at 8 a.m. after three hours artillery preparation. To meet this situation the 1st Brigade was sent forward in liaison with the 87th Div., retiring its left to protect its flank, which was also covered by intense supporting artillery fire. This brigade, however, necessarily suffered severe casualties from flanking machine-gun fire in attaining its approximate objective on the heights north of BUZANCY. At 8:30 a.m., after the ground in front and flank had been subjected to heavy artillery fire, the 2d Brigade advanced under partial barrage and at 9:15 a.m. took BERZY-le-SEC. The rest of the day was spent in exploiting the success by the seizure of commanding heights and by pushing out patrols. The line at nightfall was the heights north of BERZY-le-SEC—the CHATEAU-THIERRY—SOISSONS Road south of the SUCRERIE—and the heights north of VISIGNEUX. Casualties continued heavy in the front line from machine-gun and increasing artillery fire and in the rear from machine-gun fire from the nest to the north and long range artillery fire from the north down the MISSY Ravine. Several hundred prisoners were captured, especially in region of BERZY-le-SEC which was held by one battalion. A battery of field guns and many machine guns were taken in BERZY-le-SEC and other guns captured. On this date the division was notified that the promised relief for the night of July 21/22 was impossible, as the relieving division could not be gotten into place.

(h) On July 22 the 26th Infantry occupied the SUCRERIE so as to straighten out the line at the front of the division on its given objective, in liaison with the 153d Div. on its left and with the 87th Div. on its right, north and west of BUZANCY which that division had been unable to take. Casualties were lighter. Few prisoners were captured. On this day a preliminary reconnaissance was made by the relieving division—15th Scottish Division. On the day of July 22 orders were received for the relief of the division by the 15th Scottish Division, beginning the night of July 22/23 with the relief of all infantry and one-third of the artillery, and ending July 23/24 with the relief of the remainder of the artillery. These orders also covered withdrawal of the division to reserve positions in the NANTEUIL area, afterward changed to the DAMMARTIN area. Due to the difficulties of ammunition supply for the relieving division and the fact that it was to attack on the morning of July 23, the Commanding General of the 1st Division considered it imprudent to withdraw any of his own artillery. On his own initiative, therefore, the artillery of the 1st Division was retained in the sector one extra day.

(i) In accordance with the above orders all elements of the division except the field artillery brigade, the ammunition trains, and the sanitary units were relieved and withdrawn from the sector on the night of July 22/23. Casualties were light.*** The Commanding General, 1st Division relinquished command of the sector midnight of July 22/23, and opened P.C. at DAMMARTIN the next morning.

(j) The elements left in the sector continued to function for the 15th

Scottish Division, the field artillery brigade supporting its attack on the morning of July 23. The artillery was relieved and withdrawn nights of July 23/24 and 24/25. It assembled on July 25 at rear echelons in vicinity of MORTEFONTAINE. ***

● ● ● ● ●

By command of Major General Summerall:

CAMPBELL KING,
Chief of Staff.

5

The Second Division on July 19

Major General James G. Harbord, the division commander, reports the events of the day and requests that his troops be withdrawn.

SOURCE: *United States Army in the World War,* 5:336, 338.

2d Division, A.E.F.
July 19, 1918

FROM: Commanding General
TO: Commanding General, XX Army Corps

1. The order of the XX Army Corps to the 2d Division to attack at 4 a.m. this date was received at 2 a.m. It was impossible to comply with the order to attack at 4 a.m. due to the delay in receiving the order.

2. With the exception of the 6th Marines, kept out of the fight as corps reserve yesterday, and the 2d Regiment of Engineers, which are armed with rifles, every infantry unit of the division was exhausted in the fight yesterday. It was necessary therefore to make the attack this morning with one regiment, the 6th Marines, supported by a battalion of the engineer regiment, a force regarded by me as inadequate to the task, but no other was available.

The attack has progressed favorably until the line has come to a north and south line approximately through TIGNY. It is held up on the right from the direction of PARCY-TIGNY, a place previously reported to us as being in French possession. On the left it is being held up and our left flank threatened, due to the fact that the Moroccan 1st Division has not apparently advanced as far as CHARANTIGNY.

3. I do not anticipate any great danger to my right flank, having a brigade of the 6th Dragoons constituting the liaison between my right and the left of the French 38th Division. The effect, however, of this cavalry is principally a moral one as I have been informed by their general and by the brigade commander himself that he preferred not to be used in actual fighting unless a gap occurred in the line. On the left I have sent a fraction of a battalion which was at VIERZY and which suffered the least of any battalions employed in the fight yesterday. This battalion has been sent to occupy the former French trenches along the front southwest and south of CHARAN-TIGNY.

4. The tank commander, who employed this morning 28 tanks, just now reported that 11 of his tanks have been put out by German artillery fire.

5. I do not anticipate that my division will not be able to hold what it has already gained but I desire to insist most strongly that they should not be called upon for further offensive effort. Due to the congestion of the roads through the Foret de RETZ, the regulation of which was not under our control, and the circumstances of our arrival from the Sixth Army without information as to destination or manner of employment after arrival, the troops in the fighting line of the division have many of them been without water or food for over twenty-four hours. This statement applies to practically the whole division, including the animals of the 2nd Field Artillery Brigade.

6. It is earnestly recommended that this condition which exists as a result of no fault of anyone connected with this division, be recognized and the further prosecution of the offensive in our front be done by divisions in the second line, passing them through our present position.

J. G. Harbord,
Major General, N.A.

6

A German Staff Officer Comments
on the Battle

An unidentified staff officer who kept the War Diary at the
headquarters of the Crown Prince's Army Group emphasized the
weakness of the defense, the impact of the tanks, and the great
success of the attack.

SOURCE: *United States Army in the World War,* 5:678-79.

War Diary
[Editorial translation]

GROUP OF ARMIES GERMAN CROWN PRINCE
July 18, 1918.

[Extract]

JOUAIGNES: On July 18 the enemy launched his double offensive, which
had been systematically prepared and was executed with the aid of a
tremendous amount of war material.*** The main attack, launched on a wide
front between the AISNE and CLIGNON Creek, almost completely shattered
the divisions of the Ninth Army which had been worn out by the incessant
local attacks [July 13] which had preceded.

In a certain sense the enemy had succeeded in effecting a strategic surprise,
although the concentration of his assault army in the VILLERS-COTTERETS
Wood had not gone unnoticed. Nevertheless, its numerical strength seems
not to have been recognized to its full extent. Furthermore, it was expected
that a successful advance of our own offensive against REIMS would compel
French G. H. Q. to take the forces placed in readiness for the attack against
the west front of the Seventh Army and the south part of the Ninth Army,
and throw them hurriedly into the salient: EPERNAY—REIMS—CHALONS-
sur-MARNE, in order to prevent a collapse there. Both lines of reasoning had
for their first premise that our own offensive would overrun a surprised and
weak enemy in an irresistible drive, in other words, that a catastrophe would
rapidly begin to develop in the REIMS Salient, into the whirlpool of which
the still available enemy strategic reserves would be drawn. This first premise
was based on a second: That the total number of full strength divisions at the

disposal of the enemy opposing Army Group German Crown Prince was so limited as not to permit of a concentration of strong forces in the VILLERS-COTTERETS Wood and a sufficiently strong occupation of the REIMS front at one and the same time. The remainder of the enemy's strategic reserves were assumed to be tied up by the threat against AMIENS.

Both premises were in error. The enemy early had gained exact knowledge of the preparations for the attack against REIMS and CHALONS and thus was able to prepare himself for the defense. In the main, he used the defensive system developed by us, consisting of a deep outpost area located in front of a rear zone in which the resistance of the artillery and infantry was concentrated. The enemy, using this, our method, achieved a complete strategic defensive victory.

Furthermore, the total number of strategic reserves available for his use against Army Group German Crown Prince was considerably higher than had been estimated by us. Not only could he finish a sufficient number of units for his defensive front, but he was able to place full strength divisions in readiness for his main offensive drive .***

Finally, the development by our enemies of the tank as an offensive weapon had not been fully realized or/and evaluated by us.

The November battle of 1917 at CAMBRAI might have given us a hint as to the success a surprise mass employment of tanks could achieve in an attack. That our enemies were able to learn this lesson and they have improved their tank weapons technically as well as increased their numbers, we realize today. We, for our own part, paid little attention to this weapon, no more than we did to its use by the enemy.

For that matter, it had made its appearance but seldom during our offensives of March and May 1918, since in the main it is an offensive weapon and therefore our enemies who at that time had been forced altogether on the defensive, could find no proper use for it. Thus, our underestimate of this weapon seemed justified. The experiences of July 18, 1918, for the first time, taught us differently. The tanks, employed in numbers never known before and much better developed technically, rolled ahead of the infantry in long, connected lines. Our defense was not adapted to this mass employment on a wide front and was effective only in spots, and the infantrymen opposing these fire-spitting, rapidly moving machines felt themselves deserted and lost their nerve. Later this evil was remedied. The mobile artillery of the rear divisions quickly adapted itself to this peculiar method of combat and firing from open positions destroyed a large number of the tanks. Robbed of its protection, the enemy infantry at once lost the impetus of its attack and because of the tactics used (which called for columns crowded closely together, which the enemy had dared to adopt because of his faith in his tanks) suffered heavy casualties.

Nevertheless, this controlled defense by our rear echelons was not put into effect until comparatively late. Even if the enemy attack, as mentioned above was not really a strategic surprise, but in a sense had merely made the improbable possible, his tactical surprise was complete. The enemy had further developed the surprise element which he had made use of at CAMBRAI in November 1917. In the wooded terrain the concentration found extraordinarily favorable conditions for a screen. An artillery preparation of long duration was dispensed with and the hostile infantry started forward following a brief and vigorous bombardment. What his infantry lacked in combat value which such a procedure demands, he made up for by the employment of his tank squadrons.

Thus on the first day the enemy was able to gain a great success, as figured in ground gained and men and matériel captured, but did not know how to exploit it to the limit on the same day. As the defense which had been formed quickly in rear became effective and as the counteraction against his tanks constantly grew in effectiveness, his advance already began to waver on the next day and he was unable to gain the objective doubtlessly planned: the cutting off of the German forces between the AISNE and MARNE, which would still have been possible on the 18th. Still, the restablishment [*sic*] of our front between the AISNE and MARNE and its temporarily needed reinforcement, required so many of our forces that Army Group German Crown Prince had to dispense with the idea of continuing its own offensive within a forseeable [*sic*] time. Indirectly, but nevertheless surely, this means a great strategic success for Marshal Foch's counteroffensive, and looking at it from this viewpoint July 18 is a turning point in the history of the World War.

7

An American Liaison Officer Reports French Reaction

Major Paul Clark, whose assignment was to observe the Operations Bureau at French Army Headquarters and to report what he heard and saw daily, was no doubt pleased at the French staff officers' appreciation for the American contribution to success at Soissons. In paragraphs 2 and 3, he refers to interrogation of prisoners about the July 15 attack.

SOURCE: Pershing-Clark Correspondence, John J. Pershing Papers, Record Group 200, National Archives.

French G. Q. G. 4:30 p.m. July 18, 1918

From: Major Paul H. Clark, QMC
To: C. in C. [Pershing]
Subj: Military situation

●　　●　　●　　●　　●

2. Captured prisoners confirm the very ambitious designs of the Boche [on July 15]; for example to reach Epernay, Chalons (2d day) etc.

3. The Boche prisoners gave as reasons for their check:

1. Lack of sufficient artillery to support the attack, explaining that there is not enough artillery in the German army to make all the attacks; 1/3 of their artillery was given to Von Eimen [sic] (attack on French IV army), 1/3 to Mudra, and 1/3 to OBEN, for use, probably in an attack on British. Also it is explained by prisoners that a part of the arty. used in the attack on Fr. IV army was to be withdrawn on the 15th, even, to be sent to the attack on British.

2. Insufficient effectives, many companies not having more than 50 men. Many are sick with Grippe [influenza].

3. Much discouragement on account of lowered effectives and the arrival of the Americans.

Hope: All their hope is now based upon a military alliance with Russia; they think they can influence the Russians to join them and fight the allies.

4. Our air service yesterday did well: they downed 9 avions, 8 balloons. To a large extent the improved work of our air service is due to the establishment in likely places of hangars, air domes, etc., so that our squadrons could upon arrival go at once to work, there being no time lost in getting installed in a new place. It is important to multiply aviation installations.

5. In Albania matters are progressing well. The Italians, French and troops of Essad Pasha have already advanced more than 20 km. They are approaching a region where the population is very favorable to Essad Pasha and against the Austrians. It is believed that our forces will move fast in that region.

6. IV army 10 a.m. today. "In the night, the actions begun yesterday afternoon in region of Massiges to occupy the line of Reduits of the 1st position have continued. They have enabled us to completely regain that line make 38 prisoners and 8 M.G. 13 other prisoners have been captured during the night region of MARSON.

On all the front until sun up our artillery executed fire of the habitual harassing variety.

Beginning at 4 a.m. general preparation on front of entire army. West of the Suippe it was forestalled by a hostile preparation on PROSNES followed at 4:30 by an attack by units of the Guards supported by flame. The enemy succeeded in entering the first parallel from which he was immediately ejected.

East of Suippe our infantry our infantry [sic] has succeeded in progressing, gaining a number of positions essential for the security of the line of resistance. The operations continue. 77 prisoners, 10 M.G."

7. V army 10 a.m. Night relatively calm—Italian front has been completely reestablished, since 22 o'clock.

8. IX army 10 a.m. Nothing to report save destruction of a section who made effort to cross Marne near Fossoy.

9. VI army, telephone connection interrupted.

11. The 3d Bureau is simply delighted over the success of the counterattack of today. At lunch, and even in the office, the bable [sic] of voices was very great. Every one's face was covered with smiles. One would impersonate Ludendorf[f] at the phone receiving the news of the counter attack and in mingled French and German give his conversation, two others would impersonate a meeting between the Kronprinz and Ludendorf[f] and convulse the audience with their gesticulations and conversation, another would pretend to mimic the Kaiser and so on. And between laughs they would read the latest message, mark it on the map, shake my hand and utter eulogies about the Americans. Such words as Superbe, Magnifique, Epatant were used many times in talking about the 1st and 2d and 4th Divisions U.S.

Several have said "Without the Americans this would never have been possible. We owe it all to you and your influence.["]

12. After lunch, sitting in the garden Gen. Dufieux said that: This is the greatest day since the Marne. We are now attacking the boche [sic] from Soissons to east flank of IV army—150 km.—and the initiative must never leave us, we must keep it up day in and day out, we must give the Boche no rest till he falls on his knees and begs for mercy. (I thought of your recent conversation with Gen. Rageneau on the subject of the German "Peace Offensive." It seemed to me Gen. Dufieux was not quite up to the vigor of your ideas, P.H.C.) Turning to General Clive he said that: the British must attack. If the Boche don't attack you today or tomorrow you must attack all along your line, not in one place, but all over.

Gen. Clive replied: that is what I told the Field Marshall [Haig] yesterday. Several broke in, "tell him again today."

Clive—Yes I will. We must attack, that is sure.

6:30 p.m.

13. I walked back to his office with Gen. Clive. I asked many questions. He said that: Yes it is a great day. The biggest for us since the Marne. The events of [the] last few days will have great effect in Germany. It is quite conceivable that they will find it opportune to make proposals that will lead to a discussion and this fall may see peace. The Boche has been seriously surprised. No, I have not seen Gen. Maurice's article* of which you speak. It

*Editor's Note: Sir Frederick Maurice, the former Director of Military Operations, had started a controversy in May by accusing in print the Prime Minister and another member of the Government of making misstatements as to the military situation and the strength of the British Army. This led to a parliamentary debate and a vote of confidence in the Prime Minister. Apparently this reference is to a later article published by Maurice. Lord Beaverbrook, *Men and Power: 1917-1918* (New York, 1956), Chapter VIII.

probably appeared in the Chronicle and was written, I imagine, in answer to the French contention that the British are not doing their fair share; that as prove [sic] of that assertion. France maintains 103 divisions with 39,000,000 people and Britain only 61 divisions with 49,000,000 population. They forget that England is the work house, the manufactory, and that in order to maintain the output you must have workmen. And then again the 103 French divisions are not divisions as you know, they are really equivalent to about 65 real divisions and yet they keep up the pretense of 103. When we wanted to reduce our divisions to a number we felt we could really maintain, Gen. Foch loudly protested and to satisfy him we acquiesced and filled up the nine divs. we were going to break up but we filled them with "B" men and just *entre nous.* They are no good.

14. I saw Gen. de Barescut. He received me very cordially, expressed his satisfaction on the day's events, congratulated me on the work of the 1st, 2, and 4th divisions U.S. for their part. Yes, said he, we attacked. We had mighty little to do it with, but it worked well. I am sorry the line is so thin for the Boche will counter soon and we have not much to throw in. We have on the ground or en route to put in to stiffen our line the 15 and 28 British, the 12, 25 and 62 French. The results have been about what I hoped for. I will not be surprised to hear that we have 8,000 to 10,000 prisoners. There is much confusion on the Boche side. Tomorrow we will undertake two small operations south of the Marne and then the following day we will put on an offensive north of the Marne with the 51 and 62 British and our 9th, not yet used. Thus while the Boche is trying to make his counter against our attack of today we will fall on his back again. It is because we need strength that I asked today that your 37 div. be sent to take its place behind our 77 to there complete its training because, you see, your 29th, behind the 32 U.S. is all the reserve we have in the east. I don't know just where we will send your 32d—somewhere near Chateau Thierry probably, for there is where Gen. Pershing wants it. Your 28th will not take part in the attack tomorrow for I understand they are tired. The Italians did not do very well. Their 8th div. did not do at all well; their 3d did much better. Yes the British will soon be attacked. My guess is the 24th, region of Ypres. No I do not think the British will attack, they are not ready to. They have sent two divisions to rear of our first Army.

15. According to reports received up to 6:30 p.m. they had advanced about 10 km. on front of 20, 5 km. on front of 20 and about 3 km. on front of 10.

Paul H. Clark
Major   7:30

8

French Officers' Attitude
toward American Aid

Clark, by this time a lieutenant colonel, tells of the conversations
he had with the officers in the Operations Bureau of the French
Headquarters on the day the war ended.

SOURCE: Pershing-Clark Correspondence, John J. Pershing
Papers, Record Group 200, National Archives.

French G.Q.G. 2 p.m., Nov. 11, 1918

From: Lt. Col. Paul H. Clark, QMC
To: Commander in Chief
Subj: Military situation

1. Lunch at the 3d Bureau today was impressive in that the officers felt
very deeply the termination of hostilities. They were very calm during the
meal, there was less conversation than usual. It was not until they were
drinking their coffee in an adjoining room, after the lunch, that they began to
be demonstrative. Then conversation glowed at white heat. All seemed to be
talking at the same time. It was a babel of voices.

2. The great idea seems to be—France victorious. France saved from an
ignominious fate.

3. Major Laure: Our G.Q.G. should be at METZ and I want to see *Marshal*
Pétain installed in the quarters of the late Emperor William. That sentiment
met with immediate acceptance by everyone. It was estimated that his
headquarters should be at Metz in about one week.

4. Col. Paillé: Pétain is too modest a man. He must overcome that retiring
nature now and show himself for the glory of France and the French army.

5. Col. Allehaut: When the French headquarters were at Chantilly we
always had a specially meritorious regiment detailed as guard of honor at
headquarters. I would like to see that custom resumed.

6. Col. Alexandre: What about marching the French army through the
Arch of Triumph at Paris?—(This idea was much discussed.) Col. Node
Langlois: I think the idea must be adopted, the General in Chief and his staff,
and a selection of about 100,000 men must march through the arch. You
may select a company from each regiment. No, broke in Col. Paillé, Chief of
Training section, the company is too small a unit, better select battalions or

better yet, one regiment per division. And then in Alsace we must have a review of the entire French army.

7. I saw General Duval last night. He came rapidly to greet me. He shook my hand with both of his and said with feeling—You are the first to offer congratulations and I thank you on this the greatest day of my life. We have longed for this day since 1870. I had a letter from my wife today and woman like she [is she] referred to our son, who was slain in battle, and she deplored that he is not here to rejoice with us at this glad day; but you know Clark there is superbe [sic] consolation for me in the great fact that he, my son, and the great multitude, did not die in vain.

And right here, now, before we begin to talk, let me say from my heart that we French we will feel an eteral [sic] gratitude to America, for without your aid, we would today be Boche provinces instead of a free people. You came not one hour too soon. We were nearly finished.

Our conception of America has undergone a profound change. Our people do not travel. We did not know America. Our popular conception of the American was that he was only a man of affairs; a giant, a superman, almost, in affairs. Our picture of the American was the portly pork packer of Chicago or the Coal Baron—both devoid of heart but wizards in affairs. We have been rudely awakened to learn better.

We fondly thought at first, when you entered the war, that you would as by magic, we didn't know just how, produce airplanes and cannon and munitions etc. in quantities almost limitless—that you would do in a month what it took us a year to do. In that we have had to amend our conception of you. But in your qualities of heart we are amazed. We have seen you ready to make any kind of sacrifice, ready to meet any demand of circumstances. We have seen an altruism unhead [sic] of. An idealism never before known in Europe. A renunciation of material benefits and an adhesion to principle that is unspeakably impressive. Take the all important attack of July 18. Without the presence in that attack of your troops the attack would have been an utter impossibility—it would never have taken place. Your presence was absolutely essential.

Your losses have been very serious and we will not forget the blood you Americans have spilt here so unselfishly. Your living here with us at G.Q.G. has done a great deal to assist us in understanding the American and his point of view.

We feel of course a great appreciation of the English, for when you have fought for four years alongside of a fellow you are bound to have formed a very great affection for him. Of course our feeling of admiration for the British is tempered by the realization that they are in this war from very different motives from you Americans. The English came in to this war for selfish reasons. They said it was to free Belgium but we know better. And then again we have often fought against the British. But I must say in all candor and gratitude that on the field of battle the British have been splendid.

The turn of affairs in Germany is beyond belief. No doubt a very great factor in the fall of Germany is their interal [*sic*] condition. But let me tell you that in one week more and we would be unable to find the German army. One of our armies has advanced 60 kilometers in 4 days. We have 64 divisions in rear, that is including the American divisions which are in rear. Our attack east of Nancy was to take place on the 14th on a front on which the Germans have only five divisions. We would have gone through very easily and it would have crashed what then remained of the German army. (End of Duval)

8. At lunch today Col. Alexandre said, Clark you don't know the Boche like we know him. Look at the dishonor. You can pardon the Kaiser's flight perhaps, but it is despicable in Hindenbourg [*sic*] to flee. He should stay and share the lot of his troops.

9. Discussing how the Boche plenipotentiaries should be treated by Marshall Foch, Col. Paillé said: We should give the S.O.Bs good food, our treatment of them should be correct in every particular. That sentiment was approved by everyone present.

10. Speaking of the advance of the allied armies Gen. Duval said "We are to wait four days and then advance. I suppose we will advance in our present battle order. I look tó see the French Hdqs. at METZ."

11. Herewith copy of a phone message of interest:

> Mission Américaine au G.Q.G.
> à Assistant Chief of Staff, G-3,
> Etat-Major Américain,
> Chaumont.

I am just in receipt of the following message from French G.Q.G. quoting the following wireless message just received here Quote To the High Command of the Allies from the High German Command period On the front STENAY dash BEAUMONT and on the Meuse the Americans continue to attack in spite of the conclusion of the Armistice period Please order the cessation of hostilities period Signed the German High Command Unquote.

Paul H. Clark

9

The Germans on the
American Role in the War

After the war, intelligence officers interrogated many Germans on the subject of their attitude toward the American soldiers. The Intelligence Section of Pershing's Headquarters compiled excerpts from these interviews into a lengthy typescript document in 1919. The excerpts printed below appear as they are quoted in that document. Keep in mind that these Germans may have been trying to please their interrogators.

SOURCE: "Candid Comment on the American Soldiers of 1917-1918 and related topics by the Germans: Soldiers, Priests, Women, Village Notables, Politicians and Statesmen" prepared by the Intelligence Section, GHQ, AEF, Chaumont, 1919. Folder # 777, AEF, GHQ, G-3 Reports, Records of the AEF, 1917-23, Record Group 120, National Archives.

CANDID COMMENT ON THE AMERICAN
SOLDIER OF 1917-1918

Interrogation of Antone Fuhrmann,
   of MAYSCHOSS.

Fuhrmann is 25 years old and served in the 128th artillery against the French at CHATEAU THIERRY, RHEIMS and ARRAS and the Americans and British at CAMBRIA [sic]. He states that his unit was kept utterly in the dark as to the number of Americans in France; in fact they knew nothing of their presence until the CAMBRAI action. He says there were only handful of Americans there but they fought like wildmen. Knowing what he does now of their numbers and fighting ability he thinks the Germans would have laid down their arms long ago if they had as much information about Americans then. The Germans were herded about like sheep and kept in absolute ignorance of the real political and military situation. They were watched very closely and all incoming mail was subject to censorship, especially toward the last when they were losing.

(42nd Div. Sum. of Int. no. 213,
January 9th, 1919)

Interrogation of Ludwig Weller,
  a discharged soldier.

Morale took a severe slump after the defeat in July, and from that time on it was common talk among the soldiers that they had been deceived by their leaders in regard to the Americans. The troops, Weller says, soon recognized that the American soldier was a brave and worthy opponent, that he advanced rapidly with little regard for cover and was daring in his night patrolling. The German troops had been told that the Americans would be poor soldiers and the actual experience was discouraging.

(3rd Army Corps. Sum. of Int. no. 29,
December 14, 1918)

● ● ● ● ●

Statement of Ernest Enelt of Gladbach:

Ernest Enelt of Gladbach served two and one half years in the First Pioneer Regiment. He had been on many fronts, but at Chateau Thierry had his first encounter with the Americans. After the first battle with this new foe, his regiment was ready to give up, and their officers were forced to drive them against the oncoming Americans. He claims that if the soldiers had had their way war would have been over after the start of the 2d Battle of the Marne.

(32nd Div. Summary of Intelligence no. 48,
January 5, 1919)

● ● ● ● ●

Interrogation of Matt Speinmann, of Holzweiler:

He is 33 years of age and is one of the few volunteer troops to enlist from this section. He was assigned to the 116th Artillery (77s) and after two month's training near Bonn was sent to the front in Flanders. During 1916-17 they were shunted from one front to another and in July and August, 1918, were against the Americans in the Chateau-Thierry drive and again in the Argonne in September and October. He says that the fighting of the American troops was terrible and as they had been given to understand by their officers that the Americans were green and untrained, the surprise caused many of the Germans to surrender where they were. With the first news of Americans in the line the German morale dropped and the general feeling among the troops was that they were defeated. From then on discipline failed to hold the troops and toward the end they paid little or no attention to their officers and were hardly more than a mob. He says that papers dropped on their lines by American planes caused great uneasiness among the troops and resulted in many desertions and surrenders.

(42nd Div. Summary of Intelligence no. 286,
March 23, 1919)

Interrogation of Peter Fuchs, Westum:

Fuchs is 32 years old and enlisted in the State Pioneers of Coblenz on February 20, 1915. After a period of training at Coblenz his regiment was sent to the western front where they immediately went to work putting up barbed wire and building dugouts. He took part in the July offensive on the Champagne front and was wounded in the head and foot. The morale of the people in the hospital was low and especially so when they heard that Americans were on that front in force and had a lot to do with the failure of their offensive. He thought that the war would be won by that offensive but realized after the failure that Germany had lost. The soldiers soon learned that the submarines had also failed because again Americans were met in Chateau Thierry with disastrous results to the Germans. This news got back to the hospital by wounded men. Some of the tales were greatly exaggerated because the Americans fought differently from what they were accustomed to. Some said that the Americans would not stop in the face of any kind of fire and their artillery was wonderful. All these stories helped still further to depress the low morale.

(42nd Div. Summary of Intelligence no. 287,
March 24, 1919)

Interrogation of Joseph Muller, Ringen:

Muller is 27 years of age and was called in May, 1915. He was assigned to the 47th Infantry Regt. and saw service in practically every important engagement during the war. He was wounded twice but was returned to the front after recovering each time. He says that during 1914-1915 everyone was confident Germany would be victorious in a short time; food and clothing were good and plentiful and the morale high. After serious defeats in 1915 and the shortage in food and material became apparent the morale dropped and desertions began. When the news finally got out that the Americans were in the front lines in great force the German soldiers knew that they were beaten and a great many surrendered to escape the chance of being killed in the trenches. He fought against Americans for the first time on the Marne in July and August and says that in open warfare there are no better troops. He thinks the system of the American army and the comradeship of the men is far better in the making of good soldiers than the strict discipline and machine-like actions of the German system.

(42nd Div. Summary of Intelligence no. 279,
March 16, 1919)

Interrogation of Matthew Guttis, Unkelbach:

Guttis was called into active service March 24, 1916. He saw very little service at the front until the summer of 1918 when he was sent with other replacements to Chateau Thierry where his regiment, the 294th was held in reserve at the beginning of the great offensive and was finally sent into the front line when they were forced to fight to the finish. He says the Americans were so strong that it was a futile effort so they finally broke and ran for their lives. He claims that at that time the Germans thought the Americans were either crazy or bullet proof.

(42d Div. Summary of Intelligence, no. 274, March 10, 1919)

•   •   •   •   •

Interrogation of Wilhelm Eschuriler, Vetterlhoven:

Eschuriler is 55 years of age so was not in service during the war. He is a cafe owner in Vetterlhoven. He says that the people at home and the soldiers were kept in ignorance for a long time of the fact that America had entered the war. After the news of our entrance into the war could not longer be kept from the people they were told that the U-boats were sinking our transports as fast as they left America and that there could never be more than one or two divisions of American troops in the line. He thinks that when the fact that the Americans were here in large numbers and had shown their fighting qualities it did more to break the German morale and hasten the end than any other one event during the entire war. The news of the terrible fighting of our troops was spread rapidly throughout Germany by returned wounded and A.W.O.L. soldiers. He thinks that America had no just cause for entering the war and he is sure that without our aid the Allies would have been defeated.

(42nd Div. Summary of Intelligence no. 276, March 13, 1969)

•   •   •   •   •

Interrogation of Fred Eiker,
    M.G. Co. 43d Inf. Regt.:

He said Bois de Belleau was well known in Germany. He also said they had never before met such a sudden shock and deadly machine gun and rifle fire, and that most of their losses were from the above mentioned arms. They came to Chateau-Thierry with a company strength of one hundred and fifty men and had lost only two per cent until they met the Americans the first day of June, and when relieved the 10th of June by the 108th Regiment had only thirty men left in his company. They were out of the line for three weeks then replaced being sent to the Champagne front, where again he met the Americans July 15, and here the American Artillery so badly wrecked his Regiment that what was left were given work behind the lines. He has three other brothers in the German Army and two in the English Army. He frankly admitted that Chateau-Thierry and Soissons were the turning points of the War and also said that if the Americans had not come to the aid of the French in June and July that they would have been in Paris by the last of July. He thought the American morale the best of any he had ever seen.

(2nd Div. Summary of Intelligence no. 181, January 15, 1919)

DAGMAR HORNA-PERMAN

The Making of a New State: Czechoslovakia and the Peace Conference, 1919

THE END OF WORLD WAR I presented the Allied and Associated Powers with a problem that had haunted Central and Eastern Europe since the revolutions of 1848: how to draw boundaries based on ethnic lines, and form viable national states in an area in which for many centuries political, geographic, and economic factors produced a crazy quilt of various nationalities within the structure of the traditional dynastic states. In 1848 German liberals had discovered that other nations' claims for self-determination clashed with their unification aims, and opted for aggressive German nationalism instead of seeking an accommodation with those claims within the framework of a liberal constitutional reform. Within months the revolution travelled the path from national egalitarianism to chauvinistic nationalism.

In Austria the revolution of 1848 also foundered when it met this problem. First setting out to resolve it in liberal terms that

This essay is based to a large extent on Dagmar Horna Perman, *The Shaping of the Czechoslovak States* (Leiden: E.J. Brill, 1963). The reader is referred to citations of sources and bibliography in that work.

would grant national equality, the revolution quickly abandoned this course in favor of one that would give free rein to the national rights of the German population only. The subsequent reorganization of Austria-Hungary in 1867, and the unification of Germany in 1871 confirmed the national rights of the Germans and the Hungarians in Central and Eastern Europe, but left the Polish, Czech, Slovak, Rumanian, Croatian, Slovene, and Serbian minorities struggling for recognition of their national claims. Their clamor for equality became a source of increasing concern to Austria-Hungary and her ally, Germany. The desire to maintain German-Hungarian dominance over the Austrian Slavs in 1914 spurred the Austrian leaders to launch what they hoped would be a quick local war against Serbia; instead they precipitated the worldwide holocaust of World War I.

Although the immediate cause of the war was national unrest in Austria-Hungary and in Eastern Europe, a reorganization of the Empire was not a war aim of the Western Powers. During the first three years of the war the Allies were preoccupied primarily with the German threat to Europe and showed no intentions to alter radically the structure of the "ramshackle Empire," as it was generally called, in the event of victory. France, Britain, and Italy sought to separate Austria from Germany and induce her to conclude a separate peace. As the war dragged on, limited autonomy for Austria-Hungary's nationalities was included in Allied statements of war aims, but it was a negotiable point, and the Allies were not committed to the destruction of the Monarchy. These were also the aims of the United States both before and after they entered the war. (Sources 1, 2.)

After the collapse of the Russian front and the defeat of Italian armies in 1917, the Allies faced the danger of a concentrated German onslaught on the Western front. They had to search for new weapons to use against their enemies. Recognizing the possibilities of psychological warfare which the Germans had employed in Russia, France and Great Britain threw their support to the national minorities in Austria-Hungary in order to weaken Germany's ally. The new policy was aimed at stirring up of nationalist discontent, but it stopped short of seeking the dismemberment of the Empire.

In the United States, Secretary of State Robert Lansing pointed out to President Woodrow Wilson that the German government had been "eminently successful in the disorganization of Russia" by appealing to the national jealousies and aspirations of the peoples of Czarist Russia, and advised the President to employ "the same methods."[1] Even Wilson eventually overcame his initial dislike "of setting the Austrian people against their own Government by plots and intrigues."[2] In May 1918 he joined the European Allies in an expression of "earnest sympathy" for the "national aspirations for liberty of the Czecho-Slovak and Yugo-Slav nations."[3] (Sources 3, 4.)

To stimulate the discontent of minority nationalities in Austria-Hungary, the Allies had to become increasingly specific in their promises for the future of these nations. The latter's representatives in exile besieged the Allies for assurances that after an Allied victory, Central Europe would be reorganized so as to safeguard their interests. After the fall of the Czarist regime, the Allies' concern for Russia's interest in the area no longer stood in the way of restoration of an independent Polish state as one of the conditions of a durable and just peace. Restoration of Poland would separate from Austria only a peripheral territory, and thus not endanger the existence of the Empire itself. But claims of other nationalities and especially the quest of the Czechs, Slovaks, and Southern Slavs in effect required a total dismemberment of the old Empire. The Allies hesitated to commit themselves to the destruction of the state which, as counterweight to Germany and Russia, held the balance of power in Central Europe.[4]

The Czechs pressed their claims skillfully and vigorously. They had little trust in reforming Austria-Hungary and had never forgotten the lessons of 1848. Then, the Czechs feared the Pan-German trend of German development and hoped that a federative Austro-Hungarian state would protect them against the expansionism of their northern neighbor. In the nineteenth century Czech leaders had proposed several plans for reorganization of the Empire to give equal opportunity to all nationalities. But the continuous frustration of Czech national desires in the decades following 1848, culminating in the *Ausgleich,* the constitutional

---

[1] Lansing to Wilson, May 10, 1918, United States, Department of State, *Foreign Relations of the United States, 1914-1920* (hereafter cited as *FRUS*), *The Lansing Papers*, (Washington, D.C.: Government Printing Office, 1939-40), II, p. 128.

[2] Notes of a conversation between Sir William Wiseman and President Wilson, *circa* May 1918; Arthur Willert, *The Road to Safety, A Study in Anglo-American Relations* (London: Derck Verschoyle, 1952), p. 158.

[3] Lansing to T.N. Page, May 29, 1918, *FRUS*, 1918, Supplement I, *World War* (Washington, D.C.: Government Printing Office, 1933) I, p. 809.

[4] Eduard Beneš, *Světová válka a naše Revoluce* (Prague: Orbis, 1927-28), I, *passim* and Tomáš G. Masaryk, *The Making of a State* (New York: F.A. Stokes, 1927), *passim.*

compromise of 1867, had taught the Czechs a bitter lesson. In the following decades they clung defensively to the tattered remnants of the historic rights of the old Bohemian Kingdom.

The quest for freedom of national development remained the central issue of Czech political life at the turn of the twentieth century. When the war broke out, Professor Tomáš Garrigue Masaryk, a Czech political leader, formulated a new plan for the future of the Czech nation. He foresaw that the war would be a long one and that Allied victory could be won only by complete defeat of Germany and Austria-Hungary. He anticipated the disintegration of the Empires under the pressure of a prolonged military struggle and perceived that the simultaneous defeat by the Entente of the two major Central European powers would present a unique historical opportunity for the Czech people to reestablish a state of their own.

As envisaged by Masaryk, the new state was to unite the historic provinces of the medieval kingdom of Bohemia and Moravia with Slovakia, a part of the territory of Hungary inhabited by the Slovaks, who were of close national affinity to the Czechs. Masaryk was keenly aware of the fact that a small state, wedged between Germany and Russia, would be in grave danger if it stood alone. As Palacky, the Czech leader of 1848, had tried to do, Masaryk sought security of the projected state in a close alliance with other small Slav states in Central and Eastern Europe. They were to create a block of mutually supporting states, stretching from Poland on the Baltic Sea to Yugoslavia on the Adriatic.[5]

In the 1918 German offensive, France faced once more the imminent danger of defeat on the Western front, and her leaders desperately sought new resources to throw into the precarious balance. At this crucial moment the Czechs and Slovaks offered a valuable service to the Allied cause. Masaryk, the Czech leader-in-exile, had organized the Czechs and Slovaks in the Allied prisoner-of-war camps into an autonomous Czechoslovak army fighting with the Allies against the Central Powers. By early 1918 France was convinced of the effectiveness of this army, not only because of its military valor but also because of its effect on other Austrian troops. When facing their compatriots in Allied lines, Austrian soldiers of Slav origin refused to fight and often deserted to the West. Although Italy was suspicious of any Slav movement and at

---

[5] R.W. Seton-Watson, *Masaryk in England* (Cambridge: Cambridge University Press, 1943), pp. 59-64, 116-34.

first had opposed the organization of these units, by 1918 even she sought to use them on her front. (Sources 5, 6, 7.) Masaryk had also organized a sizeable Czech army where the Allies had no troops at all—in Russia. Defying the terms of the Treaty of Brest-Litovsk, the Czechoslovak troops refused to surrender and tried to make their way across Siberia to the port of Vladivostok. From there they hoped to be sent by the Allies to the Western front to fight against Germany and Austria-Hungary. They had seized several major points on the Volga and held important sections of the Trans-Siberian Railway. In the generally chaotic situation in revolutionary Russia, the well-disciplined Czech troops, at the time the only effective military force in the whole country, had become suddenly a force to be reckoned with.

After the great German offensive brought the enemy once more to the gates of Paris at the end of May, Great Britain and France sought desperately to prevent further German military concentration of forces on the Western front. Their schemes for reopening of the Eastern front by Allied military intervention in Russia look in retrospect somewhat frantic and fantastic, but at the time they seemed completely warranted. The plan for a joint Allied military venture in Russia, proposed by Marshall Foch, called for Allied penetration of Russia from the East. Allied troops were to land in Vladivostok and move westward along the Trans-Siberian Railway. Under these circumstances, the Czech troops and their control of the railway assumed great importance.[6] (Source 8.)

In June 1918, France and Britain invited Japan to join in an Allied military enterprise in Siberia; at the same time France opened negotiations with Czech leaders-in-exile about the disposition of the troops in Siberia. France was increasingly anxious to undertake a joint military venture in Russia with Japanese and American participation and counted on Czechoslovak cooperation. But she also wanted to transport part of the Czechoslovak troops to the Western front, hoping that their presence there would stir further unrest in Austria and would cause Germany trouble on the southern flank. In return the Czechs pressed for a clear definition of Allied intentions for their future. As a result, France decided to make a definite commitment to the Czechs. The Ministry of

[6] John Albert White, *The Siberian Intervention* (Princeton, N.J.: Princeton University Press, 1950), pp. 211-55; for a different interpretation of American policy, see William A. Williams, *American-Russian Relations, 1781-1947* (New York: Rinehart, 1952), pp. 131-75.

Foreign Affairs on June 30, 1918, recognized as "equitable and necessary" the claims of the Czechoslovak nation to independence and pledged to secure "Czechoslovak aspirations to independence within the historical boundaries of her provinces finally liberated from the oppressive yoke of Austria and Hungary."[7] France—the nation most immediately threatened by the German advance in the West—acted without waiting for the other Allies to declare themselves.

Great Britain was disinclined to replace Austria by a number of small states, fearing that they would be "disjointed" and would "Balkanize" Europe.[8] The Foreign Office hoped that a non-German confederation of Central European and Danubian states would be formed, but made no clear plans for it. The British wanted to keep their options open, and they sought to avoid dealing with individual groups and with their political and territorial aspirations. But British plans for intervention in Russia and the need to secure a bridgehead in Vladivostok led the Foreign Office to negotiate about the future deployment of the Czechoslovak troops, and the form of recognition to be granted to their political leaders. A compromise solution was found; the exiles were acknowledged to be "trustees of the future Czechoslovak government" but no clear definition of the state they were to govern was attempted.[9] These semantic reservations did not hide the central fact that Great Britain, no less than France, had pledged herself to the dissolution of the Hapsburg Empire.

The President of the United States also hoped to keep issues fluid until a peace conference would convene after a decisive victory over the Central Powers. His Secretary of State urged him to declare "without reservation for an independent Poland, an independent Bohemia and an independent Southern Slav state,"[10] but he refused to do any more than to declare his sympathy for the national minorities of Austria-Hungary. It was not his dedication to national self-determination, but his policy towards Russia that changed his attitude. Wilson was opposed to the Allied plan for intervention in Russia, but was slowly giving way under the

---

[7]Pichon to Beneš, June 30, 1918, Czechoslovak Republic, Ministerstvo zahraničnich veci, *Archiv Dokumentů československých* (Prague: Orbis, 1927-28 [hereafter cited as *Archiv*]), I (no pagination).

[8]Wickham Steed, *The Fifth Arm* (London: Constable, 1940), p. 16.

[9]Beneš to Masaryk, August 11, 1918, *Archiv*, II.

[10]Lansing to Wilson, June 25, 1918, *Woodrow Wilson Papers* (Manuscript Division, Library of Congress).

constant pressure from the Allies, the émigrés, and domestic groups. In May, Masaryk arrived in the United States. His Czech followers had previously made themselves useful to the American wartime intelligence service, and he had the confidence of official Washington. Within a few weeks after his arrival in the capital new developments in Siberia made him the focus of intense interest. The Czechoslovak Legions, in open defiance of the Bolsheviks, held the Trans-Siberian railway; on June 29 they also seized the city of Vladivostok, becoming masters of this important port. This event brought the relationship of the military position of the Czechs in Siberia to the problems of Allied intervention under close scrutiny of senior State Department officials, and soon also to the attention of the President.

Wilson had never met Masaryk, but he had heard of him from a trusted personal friend and all he had heard inclined him favorably. He requested and received Masaryk's views on Russia because he was aware that Masaryk was both a scholar and a firsthand observer of the Russian developments. Wilson considered the military schemes of France and England absurd, but he thought about the possibility of sending a commission, modeled after that for relief of Belgium, to dispense economic aid to Russia. He grappled with the problem of how it could function in a territory held by the Bolsheviks. The position of the Czech forces in Siberia seemed to offer a way out of these difficulties, and even offered the possibility of penetration of Russia without the use of large military resources. On July 6, the President proposed a plan to send a small American and Japanese force to Vladivostok to help the Czechs to hold the railway in preparation for an American economic mission.[11] Masaryk did not want the Czech troops to be a springboard of an Allied military intervention in Russia. He did not believe that such an intervention could be successful. But he hoped that an Allied landing in Vladivostok would facilitate the withdrawal of the troops and their transfer to the Western front where, he felt, they could be used most effectively. He realized also that Wilson's decision to intervene in Russia and his public statement that the American troops were sent there to save the Czechoslovak Legions rendered a United States recognition of the Czechoslovak cause inevitable. He pressed for formal recognition, but the President still wanted to maintain his general policy of

[11] George F. Kennan, *The Decision to Intervene* (New York: Atheneum, 1967), pp. 381-404.

keeping the United States "free for the peace treaty."[12] In order
to reflect this attitude and to prevent other nations of the Habsburg Empire from demanding an endorsement of their claims to
independence, the State Department based its acknowledgment of
the Czechoslovaks on their co-belligerency with the Allied and
Associated Powers. No definition of what they were fighting for
was given. (Sources 9, 10, 11, 12.)

Two months later, in October 1918, militarily defeated, economically broken and politically divided, Austria-Hungary was
ready to capitulate. The Austrian government hoped to avoid a
complete dismemberment by addressing a request for armistice not
to the European Allies but to the United States. President Wilson's
Fourteen Points had stipulated as one of the war aims of the
United States a reform of the Austro-Hungarian Empire and
autonomy for its nationalities. The last hope of the Empire was
that Wilson would make these conditions the basis of peace
negotiations. In fact, Wilson confided to his adviser, Colonel
House, that he had "no idea of what should be done with Austria,
or how the Empire should be broken up, if indeed it was to be
broken up at all."[13]   But Wilson was keenly aware of the
commitments he had made to the Poles and Czechoslovaks, and
subsequently to the Yugoslavs in exile. He therefore informed the
Austrian government that the United States had recognized the
Czechoslovaks as a *de facto* belligerent government and that
"autonomy" could no longer be accepted as a basis of peace. He
insisted further that the nationalities themselves "be judges of
what action on the part of the Austro-Hungarian government will
satisfy their aspirations and their conception of their rights and
destiny as members of the family of nations."[14]   (Sources 13, 14.)

Wilson's note brought the end of the Austro-Hungarian Empire.
As it became clear that both the military power and diplomatic
influence of the government were broken, the component nationalities of the Empire quickly seized the reins of government and
became in fact independent. The only important question that
remained was not whether Austria-Hungary should be maintained
but how she should be divided. None of the Western statesmen

[12] August 30, 1918, Lansing's Desk Diary, *Robert Lansing Papers* (Manuscript
Division, Library of Congress).

[13] September 24, 1918, House Diary, *E.M. House Papers* (Charles Seymour Collection, Yale University Library).

[14] Lansing to Ekengren, October 19, 1918, *FRUS*, 1918, Supplement I, *World War*, I,
p. 368.

had a clear answer. The Germans in Austria wished to be incorporated into the German Reich. This, the French feared, would enable Germany to emerge from the war significantly strengthened in her position in Central Europe. Great Britian feared "Balkanization" of Europe. Nobody seemed to be clear about what precisely they had promised to the Czechoslovaks; each of the Powers had granted recognition on a different basis. And none, including the United States, had agreed on a general policy toward Austria-Hungary.[15]

Nor was there any understanding between the United States and the European Allies about what constituted suitable terms of armistice for the lands of the Dual Monarchy. The need to press the war effort against Germany finally dictated the provisions of the armistice. It was then assumed that the war would continue into 1919, and the Allies planned to launch a southern offensive through Austria. They therefore sought above all control over railways and communications to secure passage of Allied troops. In all other respects, the Empire was left intact. (Source 15.) As it turned out, the emphasis on military expediency in drawing up the terms was misplaced. German military collapse followed shortly after that of Austria-Hungary, on November 11, 1918, and the planned offensive turned out to be unnecessary. No Allied troops penetrated into Austro-Hungarian territory or seized any strategic railways or ports. The army of the Empire melted away and left a power-vacuum into which moved the embryonic governments of the various nationalities so long under Habsburg domination. They pushed for quick consolidation of their power and a takeover of administration of areas which they claimed by historical or ethnic reasons. Without guidelines on how the lands of the defunct Empire were to be administered or divided, each of them endeavored to occupy as quickly as possible the territories of their future states. Within days after the end of the war the Allies lost any opportunity to impose an overall political or administrative plan on the area.

Allied statesmen expected that the problems posed by the dissolution of Austria-Hungary would be solved at the Peace Conference. But when the Conference met in Paris two months later, in January 1919, the most important decisions had already been taken: several small states had replaced the Empire, and new

[15]Victor S. Mamatey, *The United States and East-Central Europe, 1914-1918* (Princeton, N.J.: Princeton University Press, 1957), pp. 233-245, *passim.*

political authorities had been established. Without waiting for guidance of the Allies, the small nations avidly sought to consolidate their territories. Thus the Allies could no longer regulate the relationships among these successor states and had no choice but to allocate boundaries to them in the articles of peace. Soon temporary demarcation lines hardened into permanent ones; military and political *faits accomplis* changed the map of Central and Eastern Europe.

In Prague, leaders of Czech political parties formed the nucleus of a national administration which joined with the leaders-in-exile to form a Czechoslovak government. When it realized that the transfer of power and lands would not be carried out under the auspices of the Allied armies, this Czechoslovak government quickly embarked upon a policy of territorial and diplomatic *faits accomplis*. An army was organized and nominally placed under Allied command as *de facto* co-belligerent of the Allied and Associated Powers. The Germans of Austria and the Magyars of Hungary likewise formed their national governments. In the absence of Allied forces, the only practical limit to the efforts of these governments to consolidate their positions in the disputed territories was their temporary political and military impotence. The Czech leaders were particularly anxious about the German districts of Bohemia and Moravia, for they feared that some would attach themselves to Austria, which in turn loudly declared her wish to become a part of the Great German Republic, and that others would seek a direct bond with their northern neighbor. The Czechoslovak government considered these territories vital for the creation of a geographically and economically viable state, an opinion held by all leading Czech thinkers since the Revolution of 1848. The Czechs therefore sought to prevent a Pan-Germanic consolidation of these territories and to bring them under Czech military and civilian administration without "open struggles and bloody riots"[16] which might expose the meagerness of the Czechoslovak military resources.

For several weeks the penetration of the German-inhabited boundary areas of Bohemia and Moravia proceeded apace; the Allies treated this move with tacit tolerance. The new Czechoslovak Minister of Foreign Affairs, Eduard Beneš, however, sought to clarify the diplomatic position of the new state for the Peace

---

[16]Beneš to Kramář, November 5, 1918, Eduard Beneš, *Světová válka a naše Revoluce,* III, p. 505.

Conference and therefore bent every effort to receive an official Allied sanction for the occupation of these territories. He pointed out to the Allies that once it was consolidated, the new state, would provide a bulwark of order, democracy, and political stability against both the spread of Russian Bolshevism into Central Europe and the unification of that area under German hegemony. France, especially sensitive to either of these dangers, authorized Czech occupation of the territory of the historic provinces in December. Less enthusiastically, Great Britain followed suit. The United States clung for a while longer to its attitude of no commitments but finally also gave way for fear of Bolshevism.

Vienna, in the grips of an extreme fuel shortage, was, in the opinion of the Allied observers, on the brink of a Bolshevik upheaval. When the Czechoslovak government was asked by the United States Relief Mission to ship fuel to Vienna, it pointed out that the border areas in which the coal mines were located were not under Czech military control. (Sources 16, 17.) In return for a promise of coal shipments to Vienna, the Czechs received the oral, unofficial consent of the United States representatives in Paris to a full occupation of the German-inhabited boundary areas of the historic provinces of Bohemia, Moravia, and Silesia. As a result, three weeks before the Peace Conference began, the German minorities of Bohemia and Moravia were incorporated into Czechoslovakia with full consent of the Allies. The leaders of the Austrian Germans continued to send notes and protests to the Western Powers but to no avail. (Sources 18-21.)

The annexation of Slovakia, a no less vital issue for the Czechoslovak state, proved more difficult to achieve. The Magyars maintained a tight hold on the land and repulsed the Czech forces. A newly established liberal government of Hungary proclaimed itself eager to grant rights to minorities in its territory, and tried to establish the credentials of its sudden dedication to self-determination with President Wilson. The Slovak population was much less nationally aware than the Czechs; and it was not at all clear whether, if the Hungarian administration were to force a quick plebiscite, the population would declare unequivocally for Czechoslovakia. Hungary was under the jurisdiction of the French command on the Eastern Front, and Marshall Foch was the ultimate arbiter of military demarcation lines there. Beneš worked closely with the French, who, after some initial muddling, finally asked the Hungarians to withdraw their forces from Slovakia, an area roughly delineated by the pre-1914 boundary in the North and a demarcation line which followed closely Masaryk's 1915 sketches of the southern Slovak boundary.[12] (Source 18.)

After the Armistice, President Wilson pursued a policy of noninterference in Central and Eastern European affairs until the emergence of governments which could enter into binding agreements. (Source 14.) This policy proved totally inadequate. The area was gripped by economic disaster and political and military chaos. "All the races of Central Europe and Balkans in fact are actually fighting or about to fight with one another. Just as the Russian, Austrian and German Empires have split into national groups, so the Great War seems to have split up into a lot of little wars," Lansing lamented.[18] When the Conference convened, the Allies feared that hunger and political chaos would lead to Revolution and Bolshevism, and they repeatedly warned the "emerging" nations that "if they expect justice, they must refrain from force and place their claims in unclouded good faith in the hands of the Peace Conference."[19] (Source 24.)

By January 18, 1919, when the Peace Conference convened in Paris, Czechoslovakia was in full possession of the territories claimed for the new state, with only one exception: Teschen. Occupation of this coal mining and industrial area in Silesia, wedged between Poland and Northern Bohemia, turned out to be a most troublesome and politically pernicious issue in Eastern Europe. In Teschen, Czech military advances were made under the auspices of an "Inter-Allied Mission" which had no official sanction from Paris and consisted of a few low echelon Allied officers. The Poles refused to respect this veneer of legality and put up armed resistance. Unlike the defeated Austrians and Hungarians, Poland claimed as much Allied support and sympathy as the Czechs did, and made equal demands for self-determination. The outbreak of hostilities in Silesia forcefully drew the attention of the Allies to the whole spectrum of Central European problems during the first sessions of the Conference.

The unauthorized use of Allied officers put Czechoslovakia in an unfavorable posture before the Allies, but their extreme

[17]Ferdinand Peroutka, *Budování státu* (Prague: F. Borovy, 1935-36), I, Rok 1918, *passim*.

[18]January 22, 1919, Confidential Memoranda, *Robert Lansing Papers* (Manuscript Division, Library of Congress).

[19]*FRUS*, 1919, Paris Peace Conference (Washington, D.C.: Government Printing Office, 1942-47), III, p. 715.

displeasure at this incident stemmed from deeper causes. The situation in Poland was serious. (Source 23.) The country was torn by internal strife, had no reliable army, and was economically bankrupt. Yet, she fought Germany on her Western frontier and Russia in the East, while Teschen added a military conflict with Czechoslovakia in the South. France was concerned lest Poland be overcome by her enemies before she could consolidate her position as Germany's counterweight in Eastern Europe. On one hand, the Allies feared a Russian victory over Polish forces and the penetration of Bolshevism to Central Europe. On the other hand, the Allies had strong misgivings about Poland's militant national policy. France had previously supported the Czech claims to Teschen and could not completely disclaim her former commitments; the Polish claims found sympathy and support among influential members of the American Delegation to Negotiate Peace. The Allies were split and, instead of resolving the complicated dispute, put it on the back burner; a Commission, endowed with neither expertise, authority, nor power, was dispatched to study and settle the situation in Teschen and to pacify the Poles.

Czechoslovakia at first refused to relinquish the territory she had seized in that area, but the United States used the one means of compulsion not available to the other Allies—food. After the Armistice, Wilson had set up a food administration to distribute vast amounts of American agricultural products to hungry nations in Europe. Herbert Hoover headed this American food relief agency and used it as a powerful instrument by which the Administration sought to contain Bolshevism and maintain American influence over victorious allies and defeated enemies alike. Wilson made it clear that food and economic support would be given only to those governments who "preserve their self control and the orderly processes of their governments" and do not seek the "treasures of liberty . . . by the light of the torch."[20] Czechoslovaks were starving, and the state badly needed American loans; the threat could not be ignored. The seized territories were ceded, but the claims of both states remained unresolved.

The Teschen clash was one of the very first issues considered by the Council of the Peace Conference. (Source 25.) It was a clear warning that social revolution was not the only threat to peace in Central Europe and that nationalism could become equally explo-

[20]Ray Stannard Baker and William E. Dodd, eds., *The Public Papers of Woodrow Wilson* (New York: Harper, 1925-27), II, pp. 294-302.

sive and violent. The indecisive, procrastinating manner in which the Conference treated the conflicting Polish and Czech claims to Teschen in time turned that issue into one of such national bitterness and political magnitude for the two countries that settlement proved to be beyond the ingenuity and power of the Allies. The break between Czechoslovakia and Poland was never healed, and had a disastrous effect on their relationship even when they faced danger from Hitler's Germany in 1938 and 1939.

In February, the Allied statesmen finally began to deal with the new nations of the former Austro-Hungarian Empire. The Council of Ten, the political summit of the Peace Conference, soon found itself overwhelmed by the intricacies of rival territorial and political claims and adopted the procedure, originally suggested by France, of referring them to technical commissions. (Source 25.) These were created *ad hoc,* as the new nations pressed their claims before the Council. Each of these commissions dealt with a separate fragment of the old Empire,.in some instances duplicating the work of others. The leaders of the conference gave the commissions no overall political blueprint, no outlines of a plan jointly agreed upon. Reorganization of Central and Eastern Europe became a maze of local questions. In fact, the Big Four of the Conference—Wilson, Lloyd George, Clemenceau, and Orlando—never discussed the reshaping of the former Austrian Empire as a 'complex of interdependent problems. When the piecemeal recommendations of the Commissions came back for their consideration, the pressures for a quick peace were such that they accepted routinely decisions reached by their experts, often without even reviewing their substance. The technical commissions were, in fact, the level on which political decisions were made; the experts had to make them to resolve technical problems. In nearly all instances their recommendations were accepted as final and were later formally ratified by the political echelons of the Conference.[21]

Czechoslovak claims were referred to the Commission on Czechoslovak Affairs. The Big Four agreed on only one thing: that a Czechoslovak state was to become part of Europe. The details were left to the Commission. The discussions in that body revealed the basic policies of the four powers in Central and Eastern Europe. France was determined to weaken Germany and increase

---

[21]Harold G. Nicolson, *Peacemaking 1919.* Being Reminiscenses of the Paris Peace Conference (Boston: Houghton, 1933), *passim*; Frank Swain Marston, *The Peace Conference of 1919* (New York: Oxford University Press, 1944) pp. 54-68, 115.

her own security. Although the French delegates officially adhered to President Wilson's principle of collective security, in all practical instances they sought to strengthen France's position in postwar Europe. The Franco-Russian alliance seemed irretrievably disrupted by the Bolshevik Revolution, and France sought to replace it by a close alliance with the small states in Eastern Europe which were to serve as a barrier to German expansion to the East and the South and Russian Bolshevism to the West. Czechoslovakia was vitally important because she was the central link in this double-purposed *cordon sanitaire.* The guiding principle of the French representatives on the Commission, therefore, was to secure as much territory and as strong strategic frontiers for Czechoslovakia as possible, and to prevent the annexation of Austrians of Bohemia to Germany. Within a few minutes after the Commission met for the first time, the French delegation was able to secure the acceptance of the pre-1914 Bohemian-German historic boundary as a point of departure for all discussions. This quick confirmation of the old boundaries, which left a sizeable German population in Czechoslovakia, was consistently supported by France. The French delegates remained unmoved by the arguments of their American colleagues that minor border areas should be given to Germany in order to diminish the German population of Czechoslovakia, or by the efforts of Czech representatives to smooth the jagged line of the boundary by exchange of territory with Germany. The French feared that once the historic boundary was modified, a precedent would be established for further cessions of territory to Germany. Above all, they did not want to set a precedent of application of self-determination which might lead to annexation of Austrian Germans to Germany. The French delegates also drew the boundaries of Slovakia in accord with their preference for strategic lines for their ally. In the North, the natural and strategically satisfactory old boundary of Hungary in the Carpathian Mountains was quickly approved. In the South there was no historical line to follow, and the terrain, sloping down to the Hungarian plains, offered few strategic landmarks. The line proposed by the Czechoslovaks disregarded ethnographic factors and followed the only distinguishable geographical line— the Danube and the small mountain ranges north of Budapest. Although the French were compelled by a determined resistance of the other delegates to abandon this line as including far too many Magyars, they tried systematically to save as many railroad connections as possible, maintaining that these were necessary in order to safeguard the communications and economic life of the new state.[22]

The clarity of their political guidelines was a great advantage for the French delegates on the Commission. In this respect their American colleagues, their chief antagonists on the Commission, worked under a heavy handicap. They sought a "just" settlement in the spirit of President Wilson's Fourteen Points, and ways to transpose the abstract idea of national self-determination onto the complexity of the geographic and demographic conditions in Central Europe; they encountered difficulties and received virtually no guidance from their political superiors. Neither the Secretary of State nor the members of the Delegation to Negotiate Peace had a clear idea about how to apply this general doctrine, how it could be adhered to in Central and Eastern Europe, and whether it was pertinent for small units of population without causing a revival of the most extreme forms of nineteenth century particularism in that area. "Phrases such as 'justice,' 'viability,' 'self-determination' were freely bandied about without clear definition of their meaning," one of those experts wrote in retrospect.[23] Furthermore, they were uncertain about what role the proposed League of Nations was to play in European affairs as a guarantor of peace and mediator of boundary disputes. The League had not yet been agreed upon by the Big Four, and thus the American experts' arguments that trust should be placed in the stabilizing influence of that international body were ineffectual. Rigid application of the principle of self-determination was compromised in favor of rounding out Czechoslovakia's boundaries so as to ensure a maximum of strategic defensibility, economic unity, and railway communications for the state. (Sources 26, 28.)

The position of the American members of the Commission was further weakened by lack of experience in negotiations; most of them were men of academic backgrounds, not of diplomatic experience. Perhaps that was the reason why they were more concerned than their diplomatic colleagues on the Commission about the internal political structure of the state they were helping to put on the map of Europe. They discussed repeatedly the danger to the new state from large irredentist minorities and, in

---

[22]France, Ministère des Affaires Étrangères, *Récueil des Actes de la Conférence,* (Paris, Imprimerie Nationale, 1922-34) Partie IV D (I), Procès Verbaux et Rapports de la Commission des Affaires Tchécoslovaques (hereafter cited as *Récueil*).

[23]Charles Seymour, "Versailles in Perspective," *The Virginia Quarterly Review* XIX, (1943), 487.

one or two instances, they succeeded in reducing their numbers somewhat. But on the whole they had little impact; their moderate suggestions to cut out some purely German territories on the Bohemian-Bavarian boundary and to draw a line closer to ethnographic realities in southern Slovakia were defeated.

The other European delegates supported the French in the Commission. The Italians seconded the French proposals for a policy that would give Czechoslovakia strategic boundaries and weaken Germany and Austria. Only in the case of Hungary did Italy diverge from that policy. There she sought to strengthen Hungary as a counterweight against a Yugoslav-Czechoslovak alliance and against any efforts to establish a connecting territorial corridor to Trieste, as a Slav outlet on the Adriatic. British delegates generally supported their French allies. They sought, on the whole, the same aims. In dealing with Bohemia they had no desire to cede extensive territory to Germany under the application of the rule of national self-determination; in the case of the boundaries of Slovakia, they stressed the importance of communication lines and were willing to grant railways and rail junctions to the new state, whether it enlarged the size of the Magyar minority or not. On the whole, they sought a "territorial settlement as closely in accordance with the principle of nationality as economic necessity would permit."[24]

After several months of meetings and discussions, the Commission was able only to ratify an already existing situation. The framework for the work of the Commission had been firmly set by previous Allied recognition and the *de facto* establishment of the Czechoslovak state prior to the Conference. Occupation of the historic provinces within their old boundaries before the Peace Conference had convened settled the basic territorial questions. Such modifications as occurred in the Commission were mere details, and in those instances France usually exerted her influence. Only once had the American delegates refused to give in—they insisted that a western salient of the historic Bohemian province inhabited largely by Germans be ceded to Germany. This minor rectification was all that remained of their efforts on behalf of national self-determination. When the Commission's report was presented to the Big Four, the American experts insisted on a minority opinion on this point.[25]

[24]Harold G. Nicolson, *Peacemaking 1919*, p. 111.
[25]*Récueil*, loc. cit.

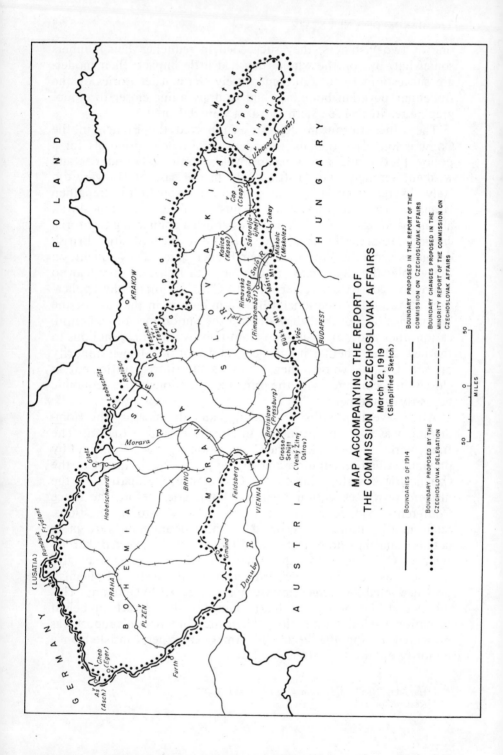

MAP ACCOMPANYING THE REPORT OF
THE COMMISSION ON CZECHOSLOVAK AFFAIRS
March 12, 1919
(Simplified Sketch)

BOUNDARIES OF 1914

BOUNDARY PROPOSED BY THE
CZECHOSLOVAK DELEGATION

BOUNDARY PROPOSED IN THE REPORT OF THE
COMMISSION ON CZECHOSLOVAK AFFAIRS

BOUNDARY CHANGES PROPOSED IN THE
MINORITY REPORT OF THE COMMISSION ON
CZECHOSLOVAK AFFAIRS

MILES

As pressure for conclusion of a treaty mounted, the Conference started to assemble from various Commissions the bits and pieces of the peace terms. Problems which had bedeviled the territorial commissions finally received the attention of the Big Four. Disagreements over issues such as the Rhineland, the Saar, and reparations soon brought on a crisis among them which lasted for three weeks. Lloyd George, surveying the transfers of territory to be made from the former German Empire, was deeply troubled by the prospect that many millions of Germans would be placed under foreign domination and recommended that German boundaries vis-à-vis smaller states be drawn along ethnic lines. Clemenceau took issue with Lloyd George, stating that Poland and Bohemia "have been able to resist Bolshevism up to now," because of a "strong sense of nationality." To deprive them of territories which historically, economically, strategically, and militarily they had to have to become viable states, he urged, would do such a violence to their national will that

... Bolshevism would find the two peoples an easy prey, and the only barrier which ... exists between Russian Bolshevism and the German Bolshevism will be shattered. The result will be either a Confederation of Eastern and Central Europe under the domination of a Bolshevist Germany, or the enslavement of the same countries by a reactionary Germany, thanks to general anarchy. In both cases the Allies will have lost the war. On the contrary, the policy of the French Government is resolutely to aid these young peoples with the support of the liberal elements in Europe and not to seek at their expense ineffectual attenuations of the colonial, moral and commercial disaster inflicted upon Germany by the Peace. If one is obliged, in giving to these young peoples frontiers without which they can not live, to transfer to their sovereignty the sons of the very Germans who had enslaved them, it is to be regretted and it must be done with moderation, but it cannot be avoided.[26]

President Wilson planned a European order based on a general limitation of armaments and the settlement of boundary disputes by the League of Nations. He opposed French demands for the Rhineland and the Saar, and considered Polish territorial claims exaggerated, but he formulated no opinion about the Czechoslovak boundaries. In the absence of clear leadership from the President, members of the American Delegation had to make their own interpretations of his policy in this matter. Secretary Lansing

[26] Clemenceau to Wilson, Observations générales sur la note de M. Lloyd George en date du 26 Mars. March 28, 1919, *Woodrow Wilson Papers.*

viewed with suspicion French insistence on strategic boundaries and was convinced that the mutual guarantees of boundaries included in the draft of the Covenant of the League of Nations would make strategic boundaries unnecessary. If the French attitude were to prevail, he feared "the guarantee, which is the heart of the Covenant, the storm center of the controversy, might as well be laid on the shelf... "[27] He supported the demand of the Commission's American members for minor frontier rectifications in Western Bohemia in favor of Germany. The French Minister of Foreign Affairs determinedly opposed Lansing's suggestion that a plebiscite be held in a small salient of Bohemian territory. France, he stated emphatically, was not in a position to neglect considerations of national defense for herself or her allies. This clash deepened the disagreement between the United States Delegation and France, and added to the discord of the Allies. (Source 29.)

Developments in Eastern Europe, meanwhile, caused the Allies to fear a complete Bolshevik take-over. On March 21, Hungary's government fell into the hands of a declared Bolshevik, Béla Kun. In Vienna, Allied observers were predicting a Bolshevik revolution. While these pressures mounted, the negotiations in Paris reached a complete deadlock. On April 3, President Wilson suffered an illness, then diagnosed as influenza, but probably a minor stroke. During his absence Colonel House, the President's *alter ego* and adviser, took his place in the deliberations of the Big Four. The Colonel was determined somehow to bridge over the disagreements between the Allies; when the German-Bohemian boundary was discussed he thought he had found an issue on which agreement could be reached. He quickly decided with Clemenceau to maintain "the old historic boundary," which seemed "much simpler and less full of possibilities for trouble."[28] Together they had little difficulty in persuading Lloyd George to accept this conclusion, for the British statesman seemed "to know but little about it."[29] Colonel House was well pleased and considered the situation "rather improved."[30] But it was French policy that won the day; the United States and the British delegations abandoned their reservations about inclusion of the German minority in the Czechoslovak state, and thus this blow to the principle of

[27]March 20, 1919, Confidential Memoranda, *Robert Lansing Papers.*
[28]April 4, 1919, House Diary, *E.M. House Papers.*
[29]*Ibid.*
[30]*Ibid.*

self-determination was struck by President Wilson's closest friend. (Source 30.)

The old frontier, as it had existed on August 3, 1914, between Austria-Hungary and the German Empire, was incorporated in the Treaty of Versailles. It was not challenged by the German delegation, which deliberately steered away from any claims to Bohemian territory. Count Ulrich von Brockdorff-Rantzau, head of the delegation, rejected requests by the Austrian government that he seek incorporation of Bohemian Germans into Germany. He bluntly stated that such a step would not be in Germany's interest. Rantzau knew that a conflict with Czechoslovakia could endanger Germany's southern boundary. After receiving the terms of the peace treaty, the German government seriously considered rejecting the peace terms and facing a renewal of hostilities on the Western front. Rantzau was advised by General von Seeckt, the War Ministry's representative on the delegation, that were Germany attacked by the Allies in the West, a joint Czech-Polish attack could not be resisted. Under such conditions the German government did not consider it wise to stimulate the hostility of its southern neighbor, although it hoped to achieve an Anschluss of Austria. The question of the so-called Sudetenland is conspicuous by its absence from the documents of the German government and of its delegation to Versailles. Although Hitler subsequently styled Germany as their protector, the disinterest of the German government in the German minorities in Czechoslovakia during the peace negotiations is a matter of historical record.[31]

In concluding the treaty with Germany, the Big Four had approved only a part of the Czech boundaries, leaving for later determination the frontiers with Austria, Hungary, Poland, and Rumania. Preoccupied with their disagreements over the settlement with Germany, the Big Four devoted no attention to the reorganization of the territories of the former Empire although conditions there deteriorated to a point where they were no longer amenable to diplomatic intervention unsupported by military means. In Hungary a Bolshevik government seized power after a request of the Allied Command that Hungary evacuate a large section of Transylvania. Its leader, Béla Kun, defied the Allied order. The Big Four were unwilling to undertake military interven-

---

[31] Alma Maria Luckau, *The German Delegation at the Paris Peace Conference* (New York: Columbia University Press, 1941), pp. 197-98.

tion in Eastern Europe, but were worried by Hungary's open defiance of Allied orders and the danger of the further spread of Bolshevism. (Sources 31, 32, 33.)

Once more a mission was dispatched to the trouble spot. The Big Four selected Lt. General Jan C. Smuts, soldier-diplomat and ex-Prime Minister of the Union of South Africa, to handle the situation in Budapest. Smuts went, but he did not get Béla Kun to accept the new demarcation line in Transylvania, nor was he able to arrange a *modus vivendi* with Communist Hungary; the results of his mission were negligible. But on the basis of his trip through the territories of the former Empire, Smuts became convinced that the problems of that area had been neglected too long. He therefore proposed a conference to deal with all the problems of the successor states of the old Empire. (Source 34.) But when he returned to Paris, the Big Four were in the midst of another crisis, due to the opposition of the United States to territorial annexations by Italy. The Italian delegation had left the Conference; during its absence, no settlement of the territories of the former Austro-Hungarian Empire could be reached since Italy was the most powerful neighbor of several of the new states. Smuts's proposal, therefore, was never considered. Once more, the problem of the new states was shelved and the Allies waited for the dust to settle in Eastern Europe.[32]

But fear that the Austrian government might also turn to Bolshevism forced the Conference into action a month later. Even before they had settled the peace terms for Austria, the Big Four decided to invite the Austrian delegation to Paris. The same procedure was followed as in preparation of the treaty of Germany. Fragments of Austria's boundaries were assembled from the reports of various Commissions and approved, mostly without a review, by the political echelons of the conference. The Commission on Czechoslovak Affairs recommended that the boundary of Czechoslovakia follow the old administrative line between Bohemia and Upper and Lower Austria, with some rectification in favor of the new state. This line was endorsed by the Big Four and the fate of the German minority was definitely decided: the Germans of Bohemia were to remain in Czechoslovakia.

The treaty was presented to the Austrian delegation on June 2, 1919; the following three months were devoted to consideration

[32] Stephen Bonsal, *Unfinished Business* (New York: Doubleday, 1944), pp. 85, 141; Harold G. Nicolson, *Peacemaking 1919*, p. 307; René Albrecht-Carrié, *Italy at the Paris Peace Conference* (New York: Columbia University Press, 1938), pp. 131-52.

of Austrian objections to it. The Austrians sought radical changes in the boundary and tried to reopen the decisions taken in the Treaty of Versailles about the German minorities remaining in the Czechoslovak Republic. The delegation requested that a plebiscite be held in every community in the provinces, no matter how small, which had German inhabitants. The plebiscite was to be held "under neutral control, in absence of Czech troops" and the population was to be free to decide "to what state" it wanted to belong.[33] The German areas in Northern Bohemia and Moravia and in Western Bohemia could practically incorporate only into Germany. Such incorporation would have necessitated changes of the terms of the treaty for Germany. The Allies considered the whole matter a *res iudicata*, and had no intentions of holding a plebiscite in the areas stipulated by the Austrian delegation. France feared above all Pan-German unification in Central Europe. But there were also practical obstacles to such an undertaking. The Allies would have had to take over the administration of half of Czechoslovakia and to establish numerous commissions to supervise the plebiscite. This could not have been accomplished without the commitment of many troops. The Allies were utterly unwilling to use their dwindling military resources for such an undertaking. They were ready, if necessary, to make a major military effort to force Germany to sign the peace treaty, but not ready to get their armies bogged down in supervising plebiscites to guarantee the right of self-determination to German Austrians.[34]

Some members of the United States delegation attempted to respond to Austrian objections by proposing radical changes of the boundary lines. They were stopped by President Wilson himself, who, for the first time, defined the limitations of the self-determination principle. In regard to the Austro-Bohemian boundary, he stated, when an ethnographic line dissects a geographic and economic unit, it "cannot be drawn without the greatest injustice and injury."[35] The boundary was modified only in minor detail.

---

[33] Austria, Ministry of Foreign Affairs, *Bericht über die Tätigkeit der deutsch-österreichischen Friedensdelegation in St. Germain-en-Laye* (Vienna: Deutsch-österreichische Staatsdruckerei, 1919), Annex A to Mémoire des Représentants des pays allemands des Sudètes en réponse aux conditions de paix des Puissances Alliées et Associées, p. 102.

[34] See, for example, Notes of a Meeting of Council of Four, June 16, 1919, *FRUS 1919*, Paris Peace Conference (Washington, D.C.: Government Printing Office, 1942-47), VI, pp. 501-09; also, Notes from Marshal Foch, June 17, 1919, *ibid.*, pp. 525-26.

[35] Wilson to Lansing, July 2, 1919, *Wilson Papers*.

Settlement of the boundary with Austria left two portions of the Czechoslovak boundaries, the frontiers with Poland and Hungary, still to be determined. The Czechoslovak-Polish armed conflict over the region of Teschen and the violent Hungarian opposition to Czech occupation of Slovakia rendered these problems increasingly complicated. A provisional demarcation line between Slovakia and Hungary, it will be remembered, had been established as early as November 1918, by a decision of Marshall Foch. French military authorities later changed the line in order to secure some railroad junctions to facilitate Czech occupation of Slovakia. After the Bolshevik revolution in Hungary, the Czechs requested Foch's permission to occupy additional railroad connections to Rumania, with whom they hoped to establish territorial links and a united front. When this additional change of demarcation line was effected, without prior notification to the Hungarians, the Béla Kun government, till then occupied in stopping the Rumanian advances in Transylvania, attacked the Czechs. Hungarian forces invaded Slovakia. The Big Four hastily approved the terms of the treaty for Hungary, incorporated the boundary lines as drawn by the Commissions into it, and communicated them to Hungary.[36]

How to force Hungary to accept the treaty and to abide by the decisions of the Conference became a problem that plagued the Allies for months to come. They no longer had any means of compulsion at their disposal. The time was most inopportune: Germany had not yet signed the treaty and what military resources the Allies still could muster were reserved for action against Germany should she refuse to accept the treaty. The unrest in Vienna caused by the publication of the peace terms for Austria led to increased fears of an outbreak of Bolshevism there. The only forces available for possible action in Eastern Europe were those of Rumania and the French troops in the Eastern Theater. President Wilson, distrustful of the political aims of both countries, tried to block the use of these troops. As a result, no action was taken and the situation was once more allowed to drift. Béla Kun was neither overthrown nor granted recognition by the Allies. Finally a successful Czechoslovak offensive forced him to negotiate and retreat behind the demarcation line stipulated by the Conference. During the first days of July Hungarian forces

---

[36]Notes of Meetings of Council of Four, June 5, 9, 10, *FRUS, 1919*, Paris Peace Conference, VI, pp. 189, 254-61, 281-88.

withdrew from Slovakia, but no Hungarian delegation came to Paris to accept the treaty.

Allied military potential had decreased considerably, and even France finally stopped proposing military intervention in Eastern Europe. Orders of the Conference were openly defied not only by Hungary but also by Rumania. Béla Kun's regime finally fell not by Allied action but rather because of defeats inflicted on his forces by the Rumanian armies, who disregarded Allied orders to stop their advance on Budapest. Only after their occupation of the Hungarian capital in February of 1920 did a Hungarian delegation come to Paris to receive the peace conditions. The Hungarians immediately sought major modification of the boundary line in Slovakia. They were supported by Italy but met opposition from France and Great Britain, who were not willing to grant territories to Hungary after her defiance of the Conference. But, although only minor changes were made in the original line, the Allies also held out hope for later far-reaching changes.

The reason for this change in Allied posture was that the whole international situation was radically changing. The peace treaties had run into opposition in the Senate of the United States, and Great Britain and France were more than ever aware that the United States would play a very minor role in the maintenance of peace in Europe. They were, therefore, eager to strengthen the old system of balance of power. France, deprived of the international guaranties of her security, sought new allies. For a brief interlude, Hungary seemed a likely prospect; a hope of future redrawing of the northern Hungarian boundaries was held out as bait. The covering letter under which the final peace terms were presented to the Hungarian delegation mentioned the possibility of further technical rectifications but failed to define their scope clearly. France encouraged the Hungarian government to interpret the letter as a definite promise of far-reaching rectifications. The covering letter soon became the basis of an irredentist movement which sought wholesale redrawing of the Hungarian frontier. These hopes and the propaganda they generated bore fruit in 1938, when Hungary claimed and received large sections of Slovak territory.[37]

The Polish-Czechoslovak contest for Teschen also led to lasting

---

[37]Francis Déak, *Hungary at the Paris Peace Conference:* The diplomatic history of the Treaty of Trianon (New York: Columbia University Press, 1942), pp. 282-83.

hostility and disastrous consequences in 1938. Throughout 1919, three Commissions dealt with the Teschen dispute; under pressure from the United States the Big Four finally decided to hold a plebiscite in the disputed area, and dispatched an inter-Allied Commission to supervise it. But the Commission was not supported by troops, and met systematic obstruction; the dispute reached an impasse once more in early 1920. Teschen had become a national *cause célèbre* in both countries. National fervor threatened to undermine the Czechoslovak government when, in order to defuse public excitement after the Conference had failed to settle the issue, it proposed to submit it to arbitration by King Albert of Belgium.[38] Poland rejected this offer because she was engaged in war against Russia, and hoped to obtain a favorable settlement after a brilliant victory on the Russian front. After these hopes were dashed by military defeat, the Inter-Allied Conference of Ambassadors at Spa, while considering other parts of the Polish boundaries, persuaded the Polish government to agree to a settlement of the dispute as a condition for further military help from the Allies. Previously, the United States delegation had been the strongest supporter of Poland's position in Teschen, but at Spa the United States no longer participated in the negotiations, because the peace treaties had been defeated in the Congress. The Conference reached a compromise solution: to divide the contested territories between Poland and Czechoslovakia.[39] The settlement was bitterly resented by Poland and met with a storm of popular indignation in Prague. The break between the two states never healed; instead of becoming Czechoslovakia's ally, Poland concluded an alliance of interest with Hungary.

In retrospect, the haphazardness of the manner in which the new state was created is truly remarkable. During the war the Allies hoped to maintain Austria-Hungary; when she crumbled precipitously they were left without a plan to guide them in reorganization of the area. After Russia collapsed, France, fearful of Germany, saw Czechoslovakia as a natural ally in the East. The French government used Czech armies and promised in return to secure independence and territories for the new state. The British Foreign Office vaguely entertained during the closing stages of the

---

[38] Minutes of Meeting of the Conference of Ambassadors, June 23, 1920 Conference of Ambassadors Bulletins Series No. 53 (Hoover Library, Stanford University).

[39] Décision de la Conférence des Ambassadeurs, 28 Juillet 1920, *Récueil*, IV C (3) F, 275 ff.

war a plan to replace the structure of the old Empire by some other form of confederation or collaboration among the many nationalities in Eastern Europe but failed to implement this policy. The United States declared the principle of self-determination, but supported the Czechs for reasons of American policy toward Russia.

The Peace Conference had no overall policy toward the successors of Austria-Hungary, and there are few traces of any coherent position towards Czechoslovakia in the documents of the Conference. Occasional brave beginnings of a plan or a purposeful action were immediately crossed and deflected by conflicting interests of the Big Powers and ultimately lost altogether. That Masaryk's plan of a close alliance and community of interests between Czechoslovakia, Poland, and Yugoslavia was not going to work became obvious as soon as the Conference met. But the Allied statesmen let matters drift. Their deliberations about Czechoslovakia and Eastern Europe dealt with details of territorial delimitation, leaving major questions of balance of power, regional economic development, and adjustment of national claims in that area unsolved. The Big Four avoided discussion of the problems of the area of former Austria-Hungary for fear of discovering some unbridgeable disagreements and because of the pressure of other matters. The specter of Bolshevik revolution, lack of political support at home, dwindling military resources, all drove the Allied statesmen to expediency and compromises in determining the shape of the new states piecemeal, without consideration of their political and economic balance. The manner in which Czechoslovakia was created by the Conference bore evil omens for the future of that state. (Source 35.)

The Czechoslovaks owed much of their initial success to the United States. In the decisive moment in 1918 President Wilson supported them and made final the dismemberment of the ramshackle Empire. But the United States had no vital interest in their own creation. The American Delegation to Negotiate Peace had no great influence on the formation of the new state, and showed no desire to exercise such influence. Decisions were left in the hands of technical experts who had no guidelines to help them and who were left in darkness about the ultimate aims of United States policy. President Wilson did not concern himself with the fate of Czechoslovakia and gave his subordinates no guidance. Some of the technical experts sometimes showed sound judgment and understanding of the political and economic problems the new state was to face; others followed their personal inclinations and prejudices. The entire delegation vacillated between rigid adherence to the principle of self-determination and compromises with the French search for strategic security for her Eastern ally.

France lacked the military resources to carry out a decisive policy in Eastern Europe alone and was unable to secure support of the other Allies for intervention. She had missed the opportunity to nip in the bud the pernicious Polish-Czechoslovak dispute, and later could not prevent it from undermining the foundations of a Czechoslovak-Polish-French collaboration designed to hold the balance against Germany in the East. Nor could France hinder Italy's efforts to weaken a Czechoslovak-Yugoslav link. Italy sought to weaken Germany by denying her acquisition of German-inhabited territories in old Austria, and therefore supported the 1914 boundaries of Bohemia. But above all she sought to contain Czech and Yugoslav penetration to the Mediterranean. She therefore supported Czechoslovakia's potential opponents, Poland and Hungary. The three Slav states failed to form a barrier against Germany's expansion to the East and to the South.

In trying to strengthen France's role on the Continent, the British delegation tended to subscribe to the demands France was making on behalf of her future Czechoslovak ally. But Britain was also trying to hold the balance between France and the United States. Thus, on occasion, she sought to restrain France by supporting the American delegation, particularly in matters of national self-determination. Her conviction that new states like Czechoslovakia must be strong enough to survive after Germany's recovery from defeat was tempered by a fear of an all-powerful France and a helpless Germany.

In retrospect it is easy to see the weaknesses that were built into the structure of the new Czechoslovak state. When Masaryk set out to work for Czechoslovak independence he sought a new solution to the old problem of survival of the small Czech and Slovak nations wedged between two powerful neighbors—Germany and Russia. Above all, he sought to avoid the creation of an independent but isolated state. It was the tragic irony of his life that while the major part of his territorial blueprint for the new state was realized, the basic promise of his Central European order was never achieved. At the close of the Conference the Czechoslovaks were facing on the northern, western, and southern frontiers the danger of German hostility heightened by the existence of a large German minority in the strategic border regions.

Slovakia was perilously wedged between Poland and Hungary, tacit allies in coveting Slovak territories. In the north stood Poland, embittered by the loss of Teschen territory. Yugoslavia, a friend in the South, was separated from Czechoslovakia by the whole width of irredentist Hungary. There were no friends within reach. Czechoslovakia was born an isolated state and remained so. Whatever the dangers to confront her, she was to face them alone.

There were indications even before the Conference was over that the Allies themselves were not convinced that the boundaries of Czechoslovakia would last. Western influence was waning. The United States retired across the sea into splendid isolation and Great Britain assumed a posture of insular aloof disinterest towards Czechoslovakia. And even France briefly abandoned her new ally for a fitful speculation with the terms of the treaties to lure Hungary into her camp. The result of this flirtation was a lasting weakening of international acceptance of the lines drawn in Paris as final and equitable. The seeds of the movements towards appeasement were sown before the Allies left Paris. In Munich, not quite twenty years later, Great Britain and France set out ostensibly to correct deviations from the principle of self-determination, the application of which they had so skillfully opposed in 1919. They redrew Czechoslovakia's boundaries and destroyed the state they had created. The precarious balance of Europe collapsed a year later, and war once more engulfed the world.

FOR FURTHER READING

Bonsal, Stephen. *Suitors and Suppliants: The Little Nations at Versailles.* New York: Prentice-Hall, 1946.

Mamatey, Victor S. *The United States and East-Central Europe, 1914-1918.* Princeton: Princeton University Press, 1957.

Masaryk, Tomáš Garrigue. *The Making of a State; Memoirs and Observations.* An English version arranged and prepared with an introduction by Henry Wickham Steed. New York: F.A. Stokes, 1927.

Mayer, Arno J. *Politics and Diplomacy of Peacemaking: Containment and Counterrevolution at Versailles, 1918-1919.* New York: Alfred A. Knopf, 1968.

Nicolson, Harold G. *Peacemaking 1919. Being Reminiscenses of the Paris Peace Conference.* Boston: Houghton, 1933.

Perman, Dagmar Horna. *The Shaping of the Czechoslovak State: Diplomatic History of the Boundaries of Czechoslovakia, 1914-1920.* Leiden: E.J. Brill, 1962.

Seton-Watson, Robert William. *A History of the Czechs and Slovaks.* London: Hutchinson, 1943.

Seymour, Charles. *Geography, Justice and Politics at the Paris Conference of 1919*. Bowman Memorial Lectures, series 1. New York: American Geographic Society, 1951.

SOURCES

I. Statement of United States War Aims and Preparations for Peace Conference

1

The Inquiry — Memorandum Submitted December 22, 1917

SOURCE: United States, Department of State, *Foreign Relations of the United States* (hereinafter cited as *FRUS*), 1919, Paris Peace Conference (Washington, D.C.: Government Printing Office, 1942), I, 41-53.

THE PRESENT SITUATION: THE WAR AIMS AND PEACE TERMS IT SUGGESTS

OUR OBJECTIVES

The Allied military situation and Berlin-Bagdad.

The Allies have had various opportunities to destroy Middle Europe by arms, to wit: the Russian invasion of Galicia, the protection of Serbia, the intervention of Rumania, the offensive of Italy, the expedition at Gallipoli, the expedition to Saloniki, the Mesopotamian campaign, and the Palestinian campaign. The use made of these opportunities has produced roughly the following results: The Russian army has ceased to be an offensive force, and Germany occupies a large part of that territory of the Russian Empire which is inhabited by more or less non-Russian peoples; Rumania is occupied to the mouth of the Danube; Serbia and Montenegro are occupied; the Austrian and German are deep into Italian territory. As the Russian, Rumanian, Serbian, and Italian armies cannot be expected to resume a dangerous offensive, the invasion of Austria-Hungary has ceased to be a possibility. . . .

The problem of Berlin-Bagdad.

The problem is therefore reduced to this: How effectively is it possible for Germany to organize the territory now under her political and military influence so as to be in a position at a later date to complete the scheme and to use the resources and the manpower of Middle Europe in the interests of her own foreign policy? She faces here four critical political problems: 1) The Poles; 2) the Czechs; 3) the South Slavs; and 4) Bulgaria. The problem may be stated as follows: If these peoples become either the willing accomplices or the helpless servants of Germany and her political purposes, Berlin will have established a power in Central Europe which will be the master of the continent. The interest of the United States in preventing this must be carefully distinguished before our objectives can become clear. It can be no part of our policy to prevent a free interplay of economic and cultural forces in Central Europe. We should have no interest in thwarting a tendency toward unification. Our interest is in the disestablishment of a system by which adventurous and imperialistic groups in Berlin and Vienna and Budapest could use the resources of this area in the interest of a fiercely selfish foreign policy directed against their neighbors and the rest of the world. In our opposition to Middle Europe, therefore, we should distinguish between the drawing together of an area which has a certain economic unity, and the uses of that unity and the methods by which it is controlled. We are interested primarily in the nature of the control.

The chief binding interests in Middle Europe.

The present control rests upon an alliance of interest between the ruling powers at Vienna, Budapest, Sofia, Constantinople, and Berlin. There are certain common interests which bind these ruling groups together. The chief ones are: 1) the common interests of Berlin, Vienna, and Budapest in the subjection of the Poles, the Czechs, and the Croats; 2) from the point of view of Berlin the present arrangement assures a control of the external affairs and of the military and economic resources of Austria-Hungary; 3) from the point of view of Vienna and Budapest it assures the German-Magyar ascendency; 4) the interest that binds Sofia to the alliance lay chiefly in the ability of Germany to exploit the wrong done Bulgaria in the treaty of Bucharest; 5) the interest of Constantinople is no doubt in part bought, in part coerced, but it is also in a measure due to the fact that in the German alliance alone lies the possibility of even a nominal integrity for the Turkish Empire; 6) at the conclusion of the war, the greatest tie which will bind Austria-Hungary, Bulgaria, and Turkey to Germany will be the debts of these countries to Germany.

The disestablishment of a Prussian Middle Europe.

It follows that the objectives to be aimed at in order to render Middle Europe safe are the following:

1. Increased democratization of Germany, which means, no doubt, legal changes like the reform of the Prussian franchise, increased ministerial responsibility, control of the army and navy, of the war power and foreign policy, by representatives responsible to the German people. But it means something more. It means the appointment to office of men who represent the interests of south and west Germany and the large cities of Prussia—men who today vote Progressive, Centrist, or Social Democrat tickets—in brief, the men who stood behind the Bloc which forced through the Reichstag resolution of July.

2. In addition to increased democratization of Germany, we have to aim at an independent foreign policy in Austria-Hungary.

3. We must aim at preventing the military union of Austria-Hungary and Germany.

These being our objectives, what are our present assets and liabilities?

ASSETS

I. Our economic weapon.

The commercial control of the outer world and the possibility of the German exclusion both from the sources of raw materials and the richer markets and from the routes of communication, lie in our hands. . . .

II. Our assets in Austria-Hungary.

In Austria-Hungary we have a number of assets which may seem contradictory at first, but which can all be employed at the same time. There is the nationalistic discontent of the Czechs and probably of the South Slavs. The increase of nationalistic discontent among the Czechs and the possibility of some kind of Poland will tend to break the political coalition which has existed between the Austrian Poles and the German Austrians. On the part of the Emperor and of the present ruling powers in Austria-Hungary there is a great desire to emerge from the war with the patrimony of Francis Joseph unimpaired. This desire has taken two interesting forms: 1) it has resulted in the adoption of a policy of no annexations, which is obvious enough; and 2) in the adoption, evidently with much sincerity, of a desire for disarmament and a league of nations. The motive here is evidently a realization that financially Austria cannot maintain armaments at the present scale after the war, and a realization that in a league of nations she would find a guarantee of the *status quo.* It follows that the more turbulent the subject nationalities become and the less the present Magyar-Austrian ascendency sees itself threatened with absolute extinction, the more fervent will become the desire in Austria-Hungary to make itself a fit partner in a league of nations. Our policy must therefore consist first in a stirring up of nationalist discontent, and then in refusing to accept the extreme logic of this discontent, which would be the dismemberment of Austria-Hungary. By threatening the present German-Magyar combination with nationalist uprisings on the one side, and by showing it a mode of safety on the other, its resistance would be reduced to a minimum, and the motive to an independence from Berlin in foreign affairs would be enormously accelerated. Austria-Hungary is in the position where she must be good in order to survive.

It should be noted that the danger of economic exclusion after the war affects Austria-Hungary as well as Germany very seriously and no amount of ultimate trade in transit to Turkey will be able to solve for her the immediate problem of finding work for her demobilized army, of replenishing her exhausted supplies, and of finding enough wealth to meet her financial burdens. . . .

A PROGRAM FOR A DIPLOMATIC OFFENSIVE

Austria-Hungary.

Towards Austria-Hungary the approach should consist of references to the subjection of the various nationalities, in order to keep that agitation alive, but coupled with it should go repeated assurances that no dismemberment of the Empire is intended, together with allusions to the humiliating vassalage of the proudest court in Europe. It will probably be well to inject into the discussion a mention of the fact that Austria-Hungary is bound to Germany by huge debts expended in the interest of German ambition. In regard to Austria-Hungary it will probably not be wise to suggest frankly the cancellation of these debts, as in the case of Turkey. Reference to their existence and to the bondage which they imply will, however, produce a useful ferment. The desire of Austria-Hungary to discuss the question of disarmament should not be ignored. The discussion should specifically be accepted and the danger of disarmament in the face of an autocratic Germany explained again. . . .

Germany.

As against Germany the lines of the offensive . . . should be more explicit assertion that the penalty of a failure to democratize Germany more adequately must mean exclusion from freedom of intercourse after the war, that the reward for democratization is a partnership of all nations in meeting the problems that will follow the peace. . . .

A SUGGESTED STATEMENT OF PEACE TERMS

What follows is suggested as a statement of peace terms in case a general statement of terms at this time is desired. The different items are phrased, both with a view to what they include and exclude, in their relationship to the present military and diplomatic situation. The purpose is to make them serve both as the bases of an ultimate just peace and as a program of war aims which would cause the maximum disunity in the enemy and the maximum unity among our associates. . . .

Austria-Hungary.

We see promise in the discussions now going on between the Austro-Hungarian Governments and the peoples of the monarchy, but the vassalage of Austria-Hungary to the masters of Germany, riveted upon them by debts for money expended in the interests of German ambition, must be done away with in order that Austria-Hungary may be free to take her rightful place among the nations.

The object of this is to encourage the present movement towards federalism in Austria, a movement which, if it is successful, will break the German-Magyar ascendency. By injecting the idea of a possible cancellation of the war debts, it is hoped to encourage all the separatist tendencies as between Austria-Hungary and Germany, as well as the social revolutionary sentiment which poverty has stimulated. . . .

2

President Wilson's Address to Congress, January 8, 1918

SOURCE: *FRUS*, 1918, Supplement I, The World War (Washington, D.C.: Government Printing Office, 1933), I, 12-17.

Gentlement of the Congress:
Once more, as repeatedly before, the spokesmen of the Central Empires have indicated their desire to discuss the objects of the war and the possible bases of a general peace. . . .

It will be our wish and purpose that the processes of peace, when they are begun, shall be absolutely open and that they shall involve and permit henceforth no secret understandings of any kind. The day of conquest and aggrandizement is gone by; so is also the day of secret covenants entered into in the interest of particular governments and likely at some unlooked-for moment to upset the peace of the world. . . . What we demand in this war, therefore, is nothing peculiar to ourselves. It is that the world be made fit and safe to live; and particularly that it be made safe for every peace-loving nation which, like our own, wishes to live its own life, determine its own institutions, be assured of justice and fair dealing by the other peoples of the world as against force and selfish aggression. All the peoples of the world are in effect partners in this interest, and for our own part we see very clearly that unless justice be done to others it will not be done to us. The program of the world's peace, therefore, is our program; and that program, the only possible program as we see it, is this:

I. Open covenants of peace, openly arrived at, after which there shall be no private international understandings of any kind but diplomacy shall proceed always frankly and in the public view. . . .

IV. Adequate guarantees given and taken that national armaments will be reduced to the lowest point consistent with domestic safety. . . .

VI. The evacuation of all Russian territory and such a settlement of all questions affecting Russia as will secure the best and freest co-operation of the other nations of the world in obtaining for her an unhampered and unembarrassed opportunity for the independent determination of her own political development and national policy and assure her of a sincere welcome into the society of free nations under institutions of her own choosing; and, more than a welcome, assistance also of every kind that she may need and may herself desire. The treatment accorded Russia by her sister nations in the months to come will be the acid test of their good will, of their comprehension of her needs as distinguished from their own interests, and of their intelligent and unselfish sympathy. . . .

IX. A readjustment of the frontiers of Italy should be effected along clearly recognizable lines of nationality.

X. The peoples of Austria-Hungary, whose place among the nations we wish to see safeguarded and assured, should be accorded the freest opportunity of autonomous development. . . .

XI. Rumania, Serbia and Montenegro should be evacuated; occupied territories restored; Serbia accorded free and secure access to the sea. . . .

XIII. An independent Polish state should be erected which should include the territories inhabited by indisputably Polish populations, which should be assured a free and secure access to the sea, and whose political and economic independence and territorial integrity should be guaranteed by international covenant.

XIV. A general association of nations must be formed under specific covenants for the purpose of affording mutual guarantees of political independence and territorial integrity to great and small states alike. . . .

For such arrangements and covenants we are willing to fight and to continue to fight until they are achieved; but only because we wish the right to prevail and desire a just and stable peace such as can be secured only by removing the chief provocations to war, which this program does remove.

We have no jealousy of German greatness, and there is nothing in this program that impairs it. We grudge her no achievement or distinction of learning or of pacific enterprise such as have made her record very bright and very enviable. We do not wish to injure her or to block in any way her legitimate influence or power. We do not wish to fight her either with arms or with hostile arrangements of trade if she is willing to associate herself with us and the other peace loving nations of the world in covenants of justice and law and fair dealing. We wish her only to accept a place of equality among the peoples of the world—the new world in which we now live,—instead of a place of mastery. . . .

An evident principle runs through the whole program I have outlined. It is the principle of justice to all peoples and nationalities, and their right to live on equal terms of liberty and safety with one another, whether they be strong or weak. Unless this principle be made its foundation, no part of the structure of international justice can stand. The people of the United States could act upon no other principle; and to the vindication of this principle they are ready to devote their lives, their honor, and everything that they possess. The moral climax of this, the culminating and final war for human liberty, has come, and they are ready to put their own strength, their own highest purpose, their own integrity and devotion to the test.

II. Decision of the United States to Support the Oppressed Nations of Austria-Hungary

3

The Secretary of State to President Wilson, Washington, May 10, 1918

SOURCE: *FRUS,* 1914-1920, The Lansing Papers (Washington, D.C.: Government Printing Office, 1940), II, 126-28.

Washington, *May 10, 1918*

My Dear Mr. President: I feel that the time has arrived when it is wise to assume a definite policy in relation to the various nations which make up the Austro-Hungarian Empire.

The ill-considered disclosure of the "Sixtus letter" by M. Clemenceau has compelled the Emperor and Government of Austria-Hungary to take a position in regard to Germany which makes further peace approaches to them well-nigh impossible, while their attitude toward Italy will be, as a result, generous in order to influence the latter country to withdraw from the war, and so release Austrian troops for the front in Flanders.

Like all these questions arising at the present time I think that they should be considered always from the standpoint of winning the war. I do not believe that we should hesitate in changing a policy in the event that a change will contribute to our success provided it is not dishonorable or immoral.

In the present case it seems to me that the pertinent questions are the following:

1. Is there anything to be gained by giving support to the conception of an Austria-Hungary with substantially the same boundaries as those now existing?

2. Is there any peculiar advantage in encouraging the independence of the several nationalities such as the Czech, the Jugo-Slav, the Rumanian, &c, and if so, ought we not to sanction the national movements of these various elements?

3. Should we or should we not openly proclaim that the various

nationalities subject to the Emperor of Austria and King of Hungary ought to have the privilege of self-determination as to their political affiliations?

4. In brief, should we or should we not favor the disintegration of the Austro-Hungarian Empire into its component parts and a union of these parts, or certain of them, based upon self-determination?

It seems to me that the time has come when these questions should be answered.

If we are to check the effect of the possible bribe of territory which will doubtless be offered to Italy, is not the most efficacious way to offset this inducement to declare that the aspirations of the subject nations of Austria-Hungary should be determined by the people of those nations and not by the power which has compelled their submission? Italy in such circumstances will undoubtedly consider the possibility of obtaining far greater concessions than Austria-Hungary can offer. She will therefore remain true to the common cause. Furthermore the revolutionary spirit of the nationalities concerned would be given a new hope. Unquestionably a revolution or its possibility in the Empire would be advantageous. Ought we or ought we not to encourage the movement by giving recognition to the nationalities which seek independence?

I have no doubt that you have been, as I have, importuned by representatives of these nationalities to give support to their efforts to arouse their fellow-countrymen to opposition to the present Austrian Government. This importunity is increasing. What should be said to these people? Some answer must be made. Should we aid or discourage them?

I do not think in considering this subject we should ignore the fact that the German Government has been eminently successful in the disorganization of Russia by appealing to the national jealousies and aspirations of the several peoples under the Czar's sovereignty. Whether we like the method or not, the resulting impotency of Russia presents a strong argument in favor of employing as far as possible the same methods in relation to Austria's alien provinces. I do not think that it would be wise to ignore the lesson to be learned from Germany's policy toward the Russian people.

I would be gratified, Mr. President, to have your judgment as to whether we should continue to favor the integrity of Austria or should declare that we will give support to the self-determination of the nationalities concerned. I think that the time has come to decide definitely what policy we should pursue.

Faithfully yours,

Robert Lansing

4

The Secretary of State to the Ambassador in Italy (Page), Washington, May 29, 1918

SOURCE: *FRUS*, 1918, Supplement I, The World War (Washington, D.C.: Government Printing Office, 1933), I, 808-9.

[Telegram] Washington, *May 29, 1918, 1 p.m.*
The Secretary of State has made public the following announcement:
The Secretary of State desires to announce that the proceedings of the Congress of Oppressed Races of Austria-Hungary, which was held in Rome in April, have been followed with great interest by the Government of the United States, and that the nationalistic aspirations of the Czecho-Slovaks and Jugo-Slavs for freedom have the earnest sympathy of this Government.

Explain confidentially and orally to the Italian Minister for Foreign Affairs that it was believed that this announcement would result in benefit both to the Czecho-Slovaks and Jugo-Slavs, to the cause of the Entente in general and to that of Italy in particular, since it was thought such an announcement would give great encouragement to the Czecho-Slovaks and Jugo-Slavs in the United States on their support of the United States in this war, would encourage and greatly increase enlistments in this country for the Czecho-Slav Legion now acting in Italy with Italian Army, and would encourage the Czecho-Slovaks and Jugo-Slavs in Austria in their efforts to hamper the Austrian military operations against Italy.

Lansing

III. Recognition of the Czechoslovak Aspirations to National Independence by the Allies

5

The British Embassy to the Department of State, Washington, June 7, 1918

SOURCE: *FRUS*, 1918, Supplement I, The World War (Washington, D.C.: Government Printing Office, 1933), I, 810-11.

Memorandum

His Majesty's Ambassador has received a telegram from Mr. Balfour, stating that in view of the fact that the Czecho-Slovaks on the Italian and western fronts have been so active in co-operating with the Allies, and also of the fact that there are approximately 50,000 men of this nationality in Russia, composed partly of prisoners and deserters, whom it is hoped to organize so as to use them against the enemy either in France or Russia, he has informed the representative of the Czecho-Slovak National Council that His Majesty's Government are prepared to recognize the Council in the same manner as it has been recognized by the French and Italian Governments. He is giving them an assurance of recognition of their Army as an organized unit labouring in the cause of the Allies, adding that His Majesty's Government will be ready to attach a British liaison officer to that Army as soon as such a step appears advisable. His Majesty's Government have also given an assurance that they will grant the Council the same political rights as regards the civil force of the Czecho-Slovaks as have already been accorded to the Polish National Committee.

Washington, *June 7, 1918.*
  [Received June 8.]

6

The French Ambassador (Jusserand) to the Secretary of State, Washington, June 20, 1918

SOURCE: *FRUS*, 1918, Supplement I, The World War (Washington, D.C.: Government Printing Office, 1933), I, 816-17.

[Translation] Washington, *June 29, 1918.*
[Received June 30.]

Mr. Secretary of State: I am informed by my Government that the President of the Republic will to-morrow deliver its flag to the Czech Army of France and on that occasion will make a solemn declaration affirming the wishes of our country for the independence of that nation.

This manifestation will take place at a moment which, owing to the agitation for freedom now going on in the Czech countries, appears to be particularly propitious. My Government believes that its effect will be greatly enhanced if similar sentiments among the Allies were manifested on that occasion, and would be glad if telegrams could be exchanged to that effect between the Ministers of Foreign Affairs of the countries united in the defense of the principles of liberty.

Referring to the oral statement by which I had given an intimation of the proposition to Your Excellency's Department, I have the honor to append hereto in compliance with my instructions the text of the telegram sent to you by His Excellency Mr. Pichon, and I should be very thankful to you if you should see fit to answer it so that your telegram could be published in the French newspapers on Tuesday. The fact that President Wilson's and Your Excellency's declarations again repeated yesterday entirely agree with our own inclinations affords me the hope that you will kindly accede to the proposition I have the honor to lay before you, and inform Mr. Pichon that the Government of the United States shares our views and is disposed to uphold them in accord with us.

Be pleased to accept [etc.]

Jusserand

7

The Secretary of State to Certain Diplomatic and Consular Officers, Washington, June 28, 1918

SOURCE: *FRUS*, 1918, Supplement I, The World War (Washington, D.C.: Government Printing Office, 1933), I, 817.

[Circular telegram] Washington, *June 28, 1918.*

Since the issuance by this Government on May 29 of the statement regarding the nationalistic aspirations for freedom of the Czecho-Slovaks and Jugo-Slavs, German and Austrian officials and sympathizers have sought to misinterpret and distort its manifest interpretation. In order that there may be no misunderstanding concerning the meaning of the statement, the Secretary of State has today further announced the position of the United States Government to be that all branches of the Slav race should be completely freed from German and Austrian rule.

Lansing

IV. Recognition of the Czechoslovak National Council as a Co-Belligerent Government by the United States

8

Consul in Vladivostok (Caldwell) to Secretary of State Vladivostok June 25 1918

SOURCE: *Woodrow Wilson Papers*, Manuscript Division, Library of Congress.

[Telegram] Vladivostok, *June 25, 1918, 7 p.m.*
(Received June 26, 2:49 p.m.)

Allied consuls here just met with the two principal members Czech national council, who state that even if willing, Soviets are powerless to prevent armed prisoners from interfering with movement Czech troops east, that Trotsky has ordered all Czech troops disarmed arrested and imprisoned and that the 15,000 Czech troops now here must return west to assist their fellows. To do this they require arms and munitions, and these they request from Allies, together with a supporting armed Allied force.

Allied consuls all agreed to recommend to their respective governments that favorable action be taken immediately on requests of Czechs, both as to supplying arms and supplies, and also the sending of an Allied force into Siberia for the double purpose of assisting a splendid body of Allied troops in their just fight against armed war prisoners, and of checking German activity in Siberia.

The strength of Soviets is decreasing, that of armed war prisoners is increasing constantly. Only a few days ago, the most important official of Soviet in Eastern Siberia stated in the presence of Consul McGowan, in answer to question put by private American, that Soviets will never ask foreign intervention. I believe intervention is necessary, and there is evidently no use in waiting for it to be requested by Soviets. If intervention is to be undertaken, favorable situation created by holding of large section of railway by Czechs should be taken advantage of.

Czechs (*) that action must be begun here within three weeks. They estimate that they require 13,000 rifles, three mounted batteries, 100 machine guns and 1,000,000 cartridges, and should be supported by from 50 to 100,000 Allied troops, to establish permanent front against Germany.

Caldwell

(*) omission.

9

The Acting Secretary of State to the Ambassador in Japan (Morris), Washington, August 3, 1918

SOURCE: *FRUS,* 1918, Russia (Washington, D.C.: Government Printing Office, 1932). II, 328-39.

[Telegram] Washington, *August 3, 1918, 4 p.m.*
Copy of following statement has been handed to Japanese Ambassador and given to the press:

In the judgment of the Government of the United States, a judgment arrived at after repeated and very searching considerations of the whole situation, military intervention in Russia would be more likely to add to the present sad confusion there than to cure it, and would injure Russia rather than help her out of her distresses.

Such military intervention as has been most frequently proposed, even supposing it to be efficacious in its immediate object of delivering an attack upon Germany from the east, would in its judgment be more likely to turn out to be merely a method of making use of Russia than to be a method of serving her. Her people, if they profited by it at all, could not profit by it in time to deliver them from their present desperate difficulties, and their

---

[1] The same, *mutatis mutandis,* on the same date, to the diplomatic representatives in Great Britain (for repetition to the Ambassador in Russia), France, Italy, and China (for repetition to the Consul at Harbin).

substance would meantime be used to maintain foreign armies, not to reconstitute their own or to feed their own men, women, and children. We are bending all our energies now to the purpose, the resolute and confident purpose, of winning on the western front, and it would in the judgment of the Government of the United States be most unwise to divide or dissipate our forces.

As the Government of the United States sees the present circumstances, therefore, military action is admissible in Russia now only to render such protection and help as is possible to the Czecho-Slovaks against the armed Austrian and German prisoners who are attacking them and to steady any efforts at self-government or self-defense in which the Russians themselves may be willing to accept assistance. Whether from Vladivostok or from Murmansk and Archangel, the only present object for which American troops will be employed will be to guard military stores which may subsequently be needed by Russian forces and to render such aid as may be acceptable to the Russians in the organization of their own self-defense.

With such objects in view the Government of the United States is now cooperating with the Governments of France and Great Britain in the neighborhood of Murmansk and Archangel. The United States and Japan are the only powers which are just now in a position to act in Siberia in sufficient force to accomplish even such modest objects as those that have been outlined. The Government of the United States has, therefore, proposed to the Government of Japan that each of the two governments send a force of a few thousand men to Vladivostok, with the purpose of cooperating as a single force in the occupation of Vladivostok and in safeguarding, so far as it may, the country to the rear of the westward-moving Czecho-Slovaks; and the Japanese Government has consented.

In taking this action the Government of the United States wishes to announce to the people of Russia in the most public and solemn manner that it contemplates no interference with the political sovereignty of Russia, no intervention in her internal affairs—not even in the local affairs of the limited areas which her military force may be obliged to occupy—and no impairment of her territorial integrity, either now or hereafter, but that what we are about to do has as its single and only object the rendering of such aid as shall be acceptable to the Russian people themselves in their endeavors to regain control of their own affairs, their own territory, and their own destiny. The Japanese Government, it is understood, will issue a similar assurance.

These plans and purposes of the Government of the United States have been communicated to the Governments of Great Britain, France, and Italy, and those Governments have advised the Department of State that they assent to them in principle. No conclusion that the Government of the United States has arrived at in this important matter is intended, however, as an effort to restrict the actions or interfere with the independent judgment of the Governments with which we are now associated in the war.

It is also the hope and purpose of the Government of the United States to take advantage of the earliest opportunity to send to Siberia a commission of merchants, agricultural experts, labor advisers, Red Cross representatives, and agents of the Young Men's Christian Association accustomed to organizing the best methods of spreading useful information and rendering educational help of a modest kind in order in some systematic way to relieve the immediate economic necessities of the people there in every way for which an opportunity may open. The execution of this plan will follow and will not be permitted to embarrass the military assistance rendered to the Czecho-Slovaks.

It is the hope and expectation of the Government of the United States that the Governments with which it is associated will, wherever necessary or possible, lend their active aid in the execution of these military and economic plans.

Polk

10

The Secretary of State to President Wilson, Washington, August 10, 1918

SOURCE: *FRUS,* 1914-1920, The Lansing Papers (Washington, D.C.: Government Printing Office, 1940), II, 139-41.

Washington, *August 19, 1918*
My Dear Mr. President: The Governments of France, Italy and Great Britain, as you have seen by the reports, have given recognition to the Czechs as a sovereign nation or at least to the Czech National Council, in terms which are assumed to be a full recognition. Doubtless this was induced by our public expression of sympathy with the national aspirations of the oppressed races.

In view of this action by the Allied Governments I think that we ought to consider whether it is expedient to make a further declaration giving more complete definition to our attitude in order to encourage the Czecho-Slovaks in their struggle against the Central Powers.

Although I feel strongly that Austria-Hungary as an Empire should disappear since it is the keystone of Mittel-Europa, I do not think that it would be wise to give full recognition to the Czecho-Slovaks as a sovereign nation. Without discussing the legal objections a serious embarrassment would be the effect on the Jugo-Slavs, who would undoubtedly clamor for similar recognition and feel offended if it was not granted. In any event I think the declaration would have to contain a reservation as to territorial limits, which would materially weaken it.

Two other courses seem open in case it is deemed to be advisable to make any declaration at this time:

First. We might recognize the belligerency of the Czecho-Slovak revolutionists in view of their military organization operating in Siberia and Eastern Russia against Austrian loyalists and their German allies. I think that it would be proper in such case to recognize the Czecho-Slovak Council with Masaryk at its head as a *de facto* Revolutionary Government and give to it such aid as seems expedient. Basing this action on the state of belligerency the Jugo-Slavs would have no similar ground to claim recognition. As you know the jealousy of Italy and the desire of Serbia to absorb the Jugo-Slavs rather than to become federated with them makes it necessary to be cautious in deciding on a policy.

Second. It may be wise, in order to avoid any future charge of deception or secretiveness, to adopt a more general policy by issuing a frank declaration that the utter subservience of Austria-Hungary to Germany, whether the result of coercion, fear or inclination, forfeits whatever right the Dual Monarchy had to be treated as an independent state; that the nationalities aspiring to be free from Austro-Hungarian rule are still more entitled to be saved from German domination; that such nationalities should receive not only the sympathy but the material aid of all nations who realize the evil ambitions of Germany's rulers; and that this Government is prepared to advance the cause of national freedom by assuming relations with any council or body of men truly representative of revolutionists against the Austro-Hungarian Government, who seek national independence by force of arms.

Such a declaration would avoid the question of defined territory and of naming any particular nationality, though the latter would later have to be done when a military organization was in actual operation.

If this course should be adopted, it would give Austria-Hungary notice that at the peace table we would oppose the continuance of the Empire in its present form and within its present boundaries. To that extent it would limit our freedom of action; but, if you have definitely decided that that should be the policy, its declaration can do little harm since Austria-Hungary is and will continue to be a tool of Germany.

It would cause a profound impression and would deeply affect the nationalities involved; it would put heart into the patriots now attempting to organize revolutions in the Empire; and it would be a notification to the world that this Government intends to support and give substantial aid to all little nations which have been held in subjection against their will by the exercise of superior force.

I submit the foregoing as a proper subject for discussion at this time.

Faithfully yours,

Robert Lansing

11

Confidential Memorandum of
Secretary Lansing, "Recognition of
the Czecho-Slovaks as a National Entity,"
August 23, 1918

SOURCE: Confidential Memoranda of Secretary Lansing, *Robert Lansing Papers,* Manuscript Division, Library of Congress.

August 23, 1918

There is being exerted in the press and by many sympathizers strong pressure to recognize the Czecho-Slovaks as an independent nationality adopting the course taken by Great Britain, France and Italy.

This sympathy mingled with the admiration is the natural consequence of the heroic and romantic withdrawal of Czecho-Slovak troops from the Ukrainian front and their remarkable migration across Siberia. No tale of military achievement in this war is more astounding. The fine spirit and discipline of these men and their firm determination to cross to France and fight against the Central Powers have aroused general enthusiasm. To help them and their fellow-countrymen who are scattered in groups from the Volga to Irkutsk is the unanimous sentiment of everyone who is susceptible to tales of valor. This emotional state of public opinion must be reckoned with. It is intense in this country and becomes more insistent for action and more impatient of delay as the details of the adventure are known.

With that feeling I am deeply impressed and would consider myself lacking in true sentiment if I was not stirred by the courage and temper of men who have overcome such great obstacles and faced unflinchingly so many dangers inspired by devotion to their national aspirations and by their intense hatred of Austrian mastery. It is, therefore, no easy matter to view the subject coldly and weigh fairly the reasons for and against recognition of the Czecho-Slovaks as a nation.

There is no doubt that the full recognition of these people as an independent state entitled to the possession of the territories included within Bohemia, Slovakia and Moravia is the course which would be the most politic and meet most fully the popular demand. It would undoubtedly give new courage to the Czechs and Slovaks in Russia, Siberia and everywhere else, and would bind them still more closely to the common cause. It would be in harmony with the declarations of the Allied Governments and receive the unanimous approval of the American people. This is the easy way—the natural way.

In spite of these apparent advantages I feel, nevertheless, that it is necessary to go very slowly before we take a step which commits this Government to the recognition of an independent state based upon the principle that a people who have been oppressed and their native land held in subjection by superior physical force are entitled to be free and to possess the land.

Immediately upon so broad a declaration by this Government the Central Powers would raise the question—at least I would if I had the conduct of their affairs—why, since we are so solicitous about oppressed nations, do we not take a definite stand for the independence of Ireland, Egypt, India and South Africa. It would be hard to deny that the question was justified, and even harder to explain the distinction between the suzerainty of an autocratic and of a democratic government. I hardly think that this explanation would be generally acceptable, and if it were not the consequences might be serious, particularly among the advocates of Irish independence in this country since it would invite the charge of inconsistency and prejudice. From the viewpoint of domestic politics it would be a very unwise policy.

In addition to this immediate result we would be, I think, embarrassed in no small degree at the peace table by having admitted beforehand the claims of the subject races of the Central Powers and of Turkey and by having ignored the claims of the Irish and others under the sovereignty of the Entente Powers.

I feel that we must so far as we can avoid committing ourselves to a policy or a principle which cannot be uniformly applied when a readjustment of nationalities takes place as it undoubtedly will. . . .

12

President Wilson to the Secretary of State, Washington, September 2, 1918

SOURCE: *FRUS,* 1914-1920, The Lansing Papers (Washington, D.C.: Government Printing Office, 1940), II, 144-45.

Washington, *2 September, 1918.*

My Dear Mr. Secretary: I respectfully suggest the following as a partial modification of your wording of the declaration which we must make with regard to belligerency of the Czecho-Slovaks:

The Czecho-Slovak peoples having taken up arms against the German and Austro-Hungarian Empires and having placed organized armies in the field which are waging war against those Empires under officers of their own nationality and in accordance with the rules and practices of civilized nations; and

The Czecho-Slovaks having, in prosecution of their independent purposes in the present war, confided supreme political authority to the Czecho-Slovak National Council,

The Government of the United States recognizes that a state of belligerency exists between the Czecho-Slovaks thus organized and the German and Austro-Hungarian Empires.

It also recognizes the Czecho-Slovak National Council as a *de facto* belligerent government clothed with proper authority to direct the military and political affairs of the Czecho-Slovaks.

The Government of the United States further declares that it is prepared to enter formally into relations with the *de facto* government thus recognized for the purpose of prosecuting the war against the common enemy, the Empires of Germany and Austro-Hungary.

It seems to me that you have successfully stated both the actual facts and the new legal relationship which we assume.

Faithfully Yours,

W.W.

V. Breakup of Austria-Hungary

13

The Secretary of State to the Swedish Minister (Ekengren), Washington, October 19, 1918

SOURCE: *FRUS*, 1918, Supplement I, The World War (Washington, D.C.: Government Printing Office, 1933), I, 368.

No. 466   Washington, *October 19, 1918.*

Sir: I have the honor to acknowledge the receipt of your note of the 7th instant in which you transmit a communication of the Imperial and Royal Government of Austria-Hungary to the President. I am now instructed by the President to request you to be good enough, through your Government, to convey to the Imperial and Royal Government the following reply:

The President deems it his duty to say to the Austro-Hungarian Government that he cannot entertain the present suggestions of that Government because of certain events of utmost importance which occurring since the delivery of his address of the 8th of January last, have necessarily altered the attitude and responsibility of the Government of the United States. Among the fourteen terms of peace which the President formulated at that time occurred the following:

X. The peoples of Austria-Hungary, whose place among the nations we wish to see safeguarded and assured, should be accorded the freest opportunity of autonomous development.

Since that sentence was written and uttered to the Congress of the United States the Government of the United States has recognized that a state of belligerency exists between the Czecho-Slovak and the German and Austro-Hungarian Empires and that the Czecho-Slovak National Council is a *de facto* belligerent Goverment clothed with proper authority to direct the military and political affairs of the Czecho-Slovaks. It has also recognized in the fullest manner the justice of the nationalistic aspirations of the Jugo-Slavs for freedom.

The President is, therefore, no longer at liberty to accept the mere "autonomy" of these peoples as a basis of peace, but is obliged to insist that they, and not he, shall be the judges of what action on the part of the Austro-Hungarian Government will satisfy their aspirations and their conception of their rights and destiny as members of the family of nations.

Accept [etc.]   Robert Lansing

14

President Wilson to Colonel House, Washington, November 1, 1918

SOURCE: *Woodrow Wilson Papers*, Manuscript Division, Library of Congress.

[Telegram]

Washington, November 1, 1918

Referring to your number twenty-seven strongly advise the most liberal possible concurrence in transfer of actual armed force to Czecho-Slovak and Jugo-Slav local authorities as the best proof of our utter good faith towards them, but more caution with regard to Hungary. Local control of course infinitely better than foreign on every account. On principle and for the sake of the incalculable difficulties of the future keep hands off the pieces of Austria-Hungary and reduce outside intervention to minimum.

This is the time to win the confidence of the populations there and the peace of Europe pivots there.

VI. Armistice with Austria-Hungary

15

The Special Representative (House) to the Secretary of State, Paris, November 1, 1918

SOURCE: *FRUS*, 1918, Supplement I, The World War (Washington, D.C. Government Printing Office, 1933), I, 433-34.

[Telegram] Paris, *November 1, 1918, 2 a.m.*
[Received 5 a.m.]

24. Following is the final proposal of the Austrian armistice:[1]

I. MILITARY CLAUSES

1. The immediate cessation of hostilities by land, sea and air.

2. Total demobilization of the Austro-Hungarian Army and immediate withdrawal of all Austro-Hungarian forces operating on the front from the North Sea to Switzerland.

Within Austro-Hungarian territory, limited as in clause 3 below, there shall only be maintained as an organized military force a [maximum of 20 divisions], reduced to pre-war [peace] effectives.

Half the divisional, corps and army artillery and equipment shall be collected at points to be indicated by the Allies and United States of America for delivery to them beginning with all such material as exists in the territories to be evacuated by the Austro-Hungarian forces.

3. Evacuation of all territories invaded by Austria-Hungary since the beginning of war. Withdrawal within such periods as shall be determined by the commander in chief of the Allied forces on each front of the Austro-Hungarian armies behind a line fixed as follows; . . .

All territory thus evacuated [will be occupied by the troops] of the Allies and of the United States of America.

---

[1] Telegraphic text brought into accord with that appended to the minutes of the Supreme War Council, Oct. 31, 1918.

All military and railway equipment of all kinds, including coal, belonging to or within those territories, to be left *in situ* and surrendered to the Allies according to special orders given by the commanders in chief of the forces of the Associated Powers on the different fronts. No new destruction, pillage or requisition to be done by enemy troops in the territories to be evacuated by them and occupied by the forces of the Associated Powers.

4. The Allies shall have the right of free movement over all road and rail and waterways in Austro-Hungarian territory and of the use of the necessary Austrian and Hungarian means of transportation.

The armies of the Associated Powers shall occupy such strategic points in Austria-Hungary at such times as they may deem necessary to enable them to conduct military operations or to maintain order.

They shall have the right of requisition on payment for the troops of the Associated Powers wherever they may be.

5. Complete evacuation of all German troops within 15 days, not only from the Italian and Balkan fronts, but from all Austro-Hungarian territory.

Internment of all German troops which have not left Austria-Hungary within that date.

6. The administration of the evacuated territories of Austria-Hungary will be entrusted to the local authorities under the control of the Allied and Associated armies of occupation.

7. The immediate repatriation without reciprocity of all Allied prisoners of war and interned subjects and of civil populations evacuated from their homes on conditions to be laid down by the commanders in chief of the forces of the Associated Powers on the various fronts.

8. Sick and wounded who can not be removed from evacuated territory will be cared for by Austro-Hungarian personnel who will be left on the spot with the medical material required.

II. NAVAL CONDITIONS

1. Immediate cessation of all hostilities at sea, and definite information to be given as to the location and movements of all Austro-Hungarian ships. . . .

16

The United States Director General of Relief (Hoover) to President of the Czechoslovak Republic (Masaryk), Paris, December 13, 1918

SOURCE: *Herbert Hoover Papers,* Paris Peace Conference Files, Hoover Library, Stanford University.

Paris, *13th December 1918.*

Dear Mr. President:

Since my conversation with you this afternoon I have had further opportunity of discussing with my colleagues the coal situation in Vienna, and they inform me that the coal sources of Vienna were Moravia, which is under the political jurisdiction of the Czecho-Slovak Government, and Silesia.

We, of course, have no information as to the situation in either place, except the inquiries made by our own agents. They are under the impression, however, that the Bohemian Government could possibly intervene to secure the transport of coal from Moravia and that the Viennese could arrange for the production of coal in Prussian Silesia, but that at present there is an embargo against the transit of coal from Silesia through Bohemia.

I think our common object is to prevent the rise of disorder and anarchy in such important centers as Vienna, and it is for these reasons that the Allied Governments are making strenuous efforts to organize food supplies to this city and other points. It will be hopeless, however, for us to protect this population even with food if they are short of coal. I can only repeat the thought of Colonel House, that no service could be so gratefully received by our Government as for you to intervene to cooperate in securing the purely humane issues in the city of Vienna, through the furnishing of coal and potatoes from Bohemia, while we intervene to furnish bread stuffs via Trieste. It seems to me the matter practically rests in the hands of the Czecho-Slovak Government to break through the difficulties in some manner to solve the coal situation as there is no hope of solution from any other quarter.

I cannot too strongly represent that the urgency of the matter as to the actual need of the city is not based on any Austrian assertion but on the investigation of our own agents who represent to me that the situation is one of hours and not of days.

Yours faithfully,

HCH:k

Herbert Hoover

President Mazaryck *[sic]*
Hotel Meurice.

17

President of the Czechoslovak Republic (Masaryk) to the United States Director General of Relief (Hoover), Paris, December 14, 1918

SOURCE: *Herbert Hoover Papers,* Paris Peace Conference Files, Hoover Library, Stanford University.

Paris, *December 14, 1918*

Dear Mr. Hoover:

Right after our conversation I sent orders home to send to Vienna all coal available: I myself hope to be in Prague next Thursday, and shall take care of the matter personally.

The situation in Vienna seems grave—but I am not quite sure of the good will of the Vienna Government and of some of the political leaders. Our Government has positive evidence of the fact that Vienna is sending arms to the German population in Bohemia through Bavaria and to the German population in Silesia through Prussia; and just the coal-mining districts of Silesia and Moravia have been occupied by the German bands, and, I am sorry to say, by the Poles. By reason of this fact it is not only Vienna, but also our cities, especially our capital, Prague, which suffer of serious coal-shortage. Another factor in the situation is the very great shortage of rolling stock, locomotives and freight cars, many thousands of which were taken by the Italians in the last Austrian debacle. The Prussians, allowing the transit of arms, could by the same rounte [*sic*] send coals to Vienna, which, before the war was chiefly supplied by coal from the Katowits mining district in Prussian Silesia, now held by the Poles.

At any rate you must take into account the evident endeavor of the Austrian Germans (I mean the known Pan-German leaders) to discredit us. There is a whole system of propaganda and agitation to this end. I see from the reports of American and Allied correspondents that the latter do not know the true situation, and even publish distorted facts the German propagandists tell them. It is significant that although several correspondents have already reported from Vienna, none of them even thought of going to

Bohemia and reporting on the situation there. I want to say that I am not quite sure whether your agents are not served by German propagandists.

Believe me, Dear Mr. Hoover,

Yours sincerely,

T.G. Masaryk

Mr. Herbert Hoover,
Paris

VII. Between War and Peace: Creation of the Czechoslovak State

18

The Chargé in Denmark (Grant-Smith) to the Secretary of State, Copenhagen, December 2, 1918

SOURCE: *FRUS,* 1919, Paris Peace Conference (Washington, D.C.: Government Printing Office, 1942), II, 376.

[Telegram] Copenhagen, *December 2, 1918–3 p.m.*
[Received December 2–11:32 a.m.
Department's 1221, November 8 *[18]* , 7 p.m.

Query 3. According to German and Danish press reports, the government in Prague has had some success in establishing authority by force of arms over the Czecho-Slovak districts of Hungary, but it is impossible to determine to what extent this has taken place. On the 20th ultimo a note was sent to the Karolyi Government, stating that the terms of the Armistice were not binding for the Czecho-Slovak Government, and that according to the acknowledgment of the Entente the districts in Hungary inhabited by Czecho-Slovaks no longer belonged to the Hungarian State. Simultaneously, a partial mobilization in Bohemia was ordered and it was announced in Prague that

Marshal Foch was despatching French and Czecho-Slovak troops to the aid of
the Home Government against Hungary. In the German districts of Bohemia
some armed resistance to the efforts of the Prague Government to secure
control has also been reported. . .

                                                              Grant-Smith

19

The Swedish Legation to the Department
of State, Washington, December 13, 1918

SOURCE: *FRUS*, 1919, Paris Peace Conference (Washington,
D.C.: Government Printing Office, 1942), II, 377.

MEMORANDUM

On the 12th inst., the Legation received a cablegram from the Royal
Swedish Foreign Office requesting the Legation to transmit to President
Wilson the following communication from the Austro-German Government:

It appears from a communication from the Czecho-Slovak Government
that the Allied Powers intend to incorporate with the Czecho-Slovak State
those large, coherent territories of Bohemia and Moravia, which are populated
by more than three million Germans. This measure, it is said, will be taken
without awaiting the results of the peace conference. Notwithstanding that
the Austro-German Government supposes that this is due to incorrect
information from the Czecho-Slovak Government, it feels obliged to call this
fact to everybody's attention and to insist upon that tendencies of this kind
are not practically carried out. There can be no doubt as to the German
character of the territories in question. Their population has on several
occasions manifested their ardent desire to maintain their liberty and their
independence of the Czecho-Slovak state. This desire of the people has been
expressed especially by the unanimous vote of its representatives, elected on
basis of equal suffrage. If, however, the Allied Powers have any doubts in this
regard, the Austro-German Government proposes to make clear without delay
the situation by a plebiscite superintended and guided by neutral authorities

and to give every guarantee besides, as to the liberty of vote. In such a case, the Austro-German Government asks the Allied Powers not to decide upon the fate of the people in question except upon basis of the results of this plebiscite. This way of procedure seems to be the only one in conformity with the principles recently proclaimed by the Entente itself and expressed in President Wilson's message of the 8th of January, 1918, in articles 2 and 4 of his speech of the 12th [*11th*] of February, 1918, and in his speech of the 4th of July, 1918, that is to say, in conformity with the principles of justice, of the world's peace and the nations' rights of self-determination.

Washington, *December 13, 1918*

20

The Czechoslovak Minister of Foreign Affairs (Beneš) to the Secretary of State, Paris, December 20, 1918

SOURCE: *FRUS*, 1919, Paris Peace Conference (Washington, D.C.: Government Printing Office, 1942), II, 378-82.

Paris, *December 20, 1918.*

Excellency: The Government of MM. Bauer-Renner in Vienna has recently sent a note to the Entente Powers and to the United States in which it requests the Allies not to reach a definite conclusion concerning the status of the Germans of Bohemia until a plebiscite has been held. It further demands that this German population be not included within the confines of the Czecho-Slovak Republic.

It is with reference to these matters that I take the liberty of calling your attention to the following important facts:

1. When impartially examined, the problem presented by the presence of the Germans in Bohemia, appears in quite a different light from that in which M. Bauer presents it. Herewith, I take the liberty of sending you a detailed communication on this subject.

2. The German population of Bohemia, mixed as it is with a very large percentage of Czechs, is quietly accepting its incorporation with the Czecho-

Slovak State. It is only the Government in Vienna that during the last four weeks has sought to avail itself of every possible means to agitate Bohemia with the purpose of embarrassing our Government and discrediting us in the eyes of the Entente.

With this purpose in view the Vienna Government threatens the Entente with an outbreak of Bolshevist revolution in Vienna and attributes the responsibility for the same to the Czechs because they refuse to supply Vienna with food and coal, but at the very same time it should be noted that the Vienna Government continues to send arms across Bavaria and Saxony to equip the German bands in the north of Bohemia and in Silesia, lawless bands composed of the very people who have prevented the mining of coal and its transportation not only to Vienna but even to the Czechs and German districts of Bohemia.

At one and the same time, the Vienna Government carries on a treacherous campaign in the neutral countries by deluging the newspapers with accounts of violent acts reported to have been committed by the Czechs to the detriment of the Germans in the regions of mixed populations, acts, which as a matter of fact, have never taken place.

3. M. Bauer, Minister of Foreign Affairs in Vienna, is a minority Socialist who participated in the Bolshevist revolution in Petrograd in the year 1917. He undoubtedly favors by every means the extremist movement in other countries. The Czecho-Slovak Republic is making headway, order is restored and a normal economic life is developing. In this respect it stands alone in Central Europe, but at present our Republic is seriously menaced by this Bolshevist movement acting from without. Every day bands of Bolshevists are going from Germany across the frontiers of northern Bohemia for the purpose of carrying on their propaganda among us. This is only possible because the German population of northern Bohemia, incited so to do by the Vienna Government, opposes the establishment of law and order by our authorities on the actual frontiers of Bohemia. In this way, it may be said, as a result of this activity, the Czecho-Slovak Republic has no frontiers against Germany and consequently is always exposed to the dangers arising from this movement and from the constant sending of arms to our enemies from Vienna.

This situation cannot be permitted to continue indefinitely although the note of M. Bauer has for its particular object such a continuance and for as long a time as possible. Certainly such a continuance would tend to the complete disorganization of the recently formed Czecho-Slovak State.

4. The Czecho-Slovak Republic is being organized economically and financially as allied territory and this is one of the most difficult tasks that the situation presents, and, of course, the liquidation of Austria in this connection presents a formidable problem. However, we are endeavoring to leave nothing undone that will aid towards establishing a normal state of affairs and preparing ourselves for the Peace Conference.

However, the Government of German Austria leaves nothing untried that might tend to make our tasks more difficult. It simply floods our country with its depreciated paper money which spells disaster for us. It is constantly urging the German population of Bohemia to export into Germany its manufactured articles, its food supply and raw materials. All this goes on in spite of the fact that ours is an allied country, Germany an enemy country and that the orders for the blockade still remain in force.

It was only possible to bring about the conditions by which we are confronted because the Czecho-Slovak Republic wishing to proceed tactfully and moderately, and believing that its views on this subject were shared by the Allies, tried to bring order and a settled state of affairs into the mixed regions of northern Bohemia without violence and in harmony and coopera-tion with its inhabitants.

The Vienna Government by its disloyal action has prevented the realization of our plan and by its note which we are now reviewing asks for a continuance of this impossible state of affairs.

The Government of the Czecho-Slovak Republic confronted by this situation is of the opinion that the following stringent and categorical measures must be taken.

1. That the Government of Prague, which is the only Government in Central Europe recognized as an allied government, be permitted to establish order within its territory.

2. That the frontiers of the territory to which it is entitled must be settled in agreement with the Allies and the United States and that it must be empowered to exercise its authority so that a continuance of the deplorable conditions indicated above may be avoided.

3. These measures, of course, may be of a provisional nature because it is only within the province of the Peace Conference to lay down definite decisions on this subject. But, in the meantime, in order that an endurable state of affairs may be established, it is absolutely necessary to take some such steps as I shall indicate in the following paragraph:

It might be well for the Allies to make a declaration in the following sense: The Czecho-Slovak State shall organize and govern the peoples living within the historical boundaries of Bohemia and Moravia, of Austrian Silesia and Slovakia (bounded by the Carpathians, March, Danube, Ipola [Eipel] as far as the city of R. Szombath, from there following a straight line towards the east, to the River Bodrog and the Ung down to the Carpathians). This temporary decision shall be later examined by the Peace Conference which will give to the problem its definite solution. But, for the present the German inhabitants and adjacent Governments would have to submit to the arrangement that is outlined above.

I appeal to your Government, Excellency, in requesting you to make an examination of this difficult question. During the war our Nation has pursued a loyal, open and sincere policy in all its relations with the Allied Govern-ments. We have made sacrifices and have not failed to show our devotion to the ideals which we have in common. Even today, when the fighting in the west is at an end, our people continue to shed their blood in the defense of our common interest on the far away Siberian plains. This is done very willingly, but at the same time our Nation cannot remain indefinitely at the mercy of those enemies of the olden days which we also have in common.

The prestige of the Allies and the United States cannot be disputed by our enemies and it is certain that all would accept without protest such a decision as is indicated above.

I take the liberty, Excellency, of placing before you this memorandum in the hope that it may be helpful in making clear the purpose of the note that has reached you from the Vienna Government and with the request that you may be good enough to examine this communication although it is of a somewhat cursory character, and in conclusion I beg to present to you, Excellency, the assurance of my deepest consideration.

                                                                    Dr. Eduard Beneš

[Enclosure]

Copy of the Reply of the French Government to the Government of German-Austria, Communicated Through the Swiss Legation

The Swiss Legation has been good enough to communicate to the Ministry of Foreign Affairs under the dates of December 13th and 16th two communications from the Government of German Austria.

The first of these notes is in the form of a protest against the alleged intention of the powers of the Entente to place in subjection to the Czecho-Slovak state the Germans of Bohemia and of Moravia. In this note it is affirmed that the Germans in question are desirous of separating themselves from the Czecho-Slovak state and a plebiscite is proposed at an early date for the purpose of clearing up the situation.

In the second note it is proposed to submit to arbitration all questions relating to the frontiers between German Austria and both the Czecho-Slovak and the Jugo-Slav states.

These requests cannot be favorably received; the boundary questions which are here presented cannot as a matter of fact be settled except by the Peace Congresse and they must be carefully examined with this purpose in view at an early date by the Allied Governments.

In the meantime as far as the Czecho-Slovak State is concerned the French Government holds that it should in conformity with the recognition which has been extended to it by the Allied Governments, have for its boundaries, at least until the decision of the Peace Conference is reached, the boundaries of the historic provinces of Bohemia, Moravia, and of Austrian Silesia.

In regard to Slovakia the boundary line should be drawn in the following manner: along the Danube from the present western boundary of Hungary to the river Eipel, along the stream of the Eipel to the town of Rima Szombat, then in a straight line proceeding from west to east to the river Ung, then following the course of the Ung to the frontier of Galicia.

This boundary line is identical with the one behind which General Franchet d'Esperey has invited the Hungarian Government to withdraw its troops. This request has been complied with and is already an accomplished fact.

Paris, *on 19th of December 1918.*

Pichon

21

The British Secretary of State for Foreign Affairs (Balfour) to the American Chargé (Laughlin), London, November 13, 1918

SOURCE: *FRUS,* 1919, Paris Peace Conference (Washington, D.C.: Government Printing Office, 1942), II, 383-84.

London, *November 13, 1918*

Sir: With reference to Mr. Page's Note, No. 1272, of the 30th of September last, relative to the future boundaries of the Czecho-Slovak State, I am directed by Mr. Secretary Balfour to transmit to you, herewith, a memorandum as to the difficulties with which this question is connected, and to assure you that His Majesty's Government would be glad to receive any views which the Government of the United States may entertain on the subject.

I have [etc.]   For the Secretary of State,
                                                                     R. Graham

[Memorandum]

Suggestions for Reply to the American Ambassador Concerning Boundaries of the Czecho-Slovak Nations

1. The Czechs and Slovaks having repeatedly declared their desire to form one single State, H.M.G. treats their territories as those of one single State.

2. The enclosed map, which may be taken as reliable, shows the ethnic

distribution of the Czecho-Slovaks. It will be noted that they inhabit the Austrian provinces of Bohemia and Moravia and part of Austrian Silesia, and the north-western and northern districts of Hungary.

3. The northern and north-western frontier districts of Bohemia are predominantly German in population. With regard to them we shall be confronted by a very difficult problem—to what extent the new Czecho-Slovak State should inherit the historic frontiers of Bohemia, which are also its natural geographical frontiers, and to what extent the ethnic divisions could be made the basis. In some districts, e.g. round Eger and Reichenberg, the frontier might perhaps be rectified to some extent without unduly impairing Bohemia's strategic defences or economic resources; in other districts these interests are of such paramount importance as to override all other considerations.

4. The matter has not hitherto been the subject of official considerations. We are of course collecting materials bearing on this and similar problems, and it would be of great advantage if those who do the work for H.M.G. were given opportunities for exchanging views with those who do similar work for the American government.

4/10/18

                                                                          L.B.N.

VIII. Between War and Peace:
Chaos in Central and Eastern Europe

22

From the Diary of General Tasker H. Bliss,
Friday, January 17, 1919

SOURCE: Diary of General Tasker H. Bliss, Member of the American Commission to Negotiate Peace, *T.H. Bliss Papers,* Manuscript Division, Library of Congress.

Friday, January 17, 1919

. . . In the afternoon, at 5 o'clock, Dr. [Alonzo] Taylor came into my rooms and gave me a general picture of what he had observed in Austria-Hungary during the last month on his visit there. He reports conditions in those countries to be literally horrible. Each of the dissolved parts of the former Austro-Hungarian Empire has now set up its own government and amuses itself by putting embargoes on all of its neighbors. German Austria has most of the storehouses of the former military supplies of clothing, etc., and that government has taken possession as though they belonged exclusively to it. The result of the embargo is very disastrous on the food supply. Dr. Taylor says that one community may be almost starving while another has plenty of food but the embargoes and seizures of railway transportation by the different governments prevent the food from being distributed. He says that he did not see a single potato on the market or on the table in Vienna although millions of bushels of them were to be obtained in Hungary. Each state seizes the former imperial government railway rolling stock, in order to build up its own railway equipment. Bohemia cuts off the supply of coal for Vienna; the Yugo-Slavs refused transport of flour to Vienna until they could get salt. He says that there is absolute and universal social disorganization. He says that some form of Allied commission government together with military occupation is necessary to save the situation. He thinks that the military force could be very small as he believes that it could effectually operate by moral force. . . .

23

Prime Minister of the Polish Republic (Paderewski) to Colonel House, February 4, 1919

SOURCE: *Woodrow Wilson Papers,* Manuscript Division, Library of Congress.

WARSAW
Feb. 4, 1919.

Colonel House Hotel Crillon Paris

Surrounded by enemy from all sides Danzig being in German hands Poland cannot communicate with civilized world. To our Commission and delegates about thirty people carrying important documents and material for Peace Conference unable to leave Warsaw. The Polish Government respectfully asks Peace Conference to deliver safe conducts for this Commission. Invasion of Polish South Galicia territory continues. Several important positions and villages have been occupied by their troops. Their patrols have been already seen in our oil districts. Six hundred prominent citizens all leaders of Silesian peoples arrested and deported. College students mere children hanged. Tcheque minister Foreign Affairs Shehla [Švehla] affirmed in Parliament that occupation of Silesia took place with approval of Polish Government and with consent of entente powers and United States. The first assertion is untrue. The Government as Government considers the second equally false but public opinion greatly alarmed and concerned. People cannot conceive why at this moment of ever growing Eastern danger no assistance is being given and General Hallers Army is detained in France while the Tcheques are allowed to make war on us because we possess what they would like to have. Kindly forgive my troubling you again and help before it is too late.

J. Paderewski

24

Secretary's Notes of a
Conversation Held in M. Pichon's Room
at the Quai d'Orsay, Paris, on Friday,
January 24, 1919, at 12:15 O'clock p.m.

SOURCE: *FRUS*, 1919, Paris Peace Conference (Washington, D.C.: Government Printing Office, 1943), III, 715.

Present

America United States of	British Empire	France
President Wilson	The Rt. Hon. D. Lloyd	M. Clemenceau
Mr. R. Lansing	George, M.P.	M. Pichon
Mr. A.H. Frazier	The Rt. Hon. A.J.	M. Dutasta
Mr. L. Harrison	Balfour, M.P.	M. Berthelot
Col. U.S. Grant	Lt. Col. Sir M.P.A.	Capt. Portier
	Hankey, K.C.B.	
	Major A.M. Caccia,	
	M.V.O.	
	Mr. H. Norman	

Italy	Japan
M. Orlando	Baron Makino
Baron Sonnino	H.E.M. Matsui
Count Aldrovandi	M. Saburi
Major Jones	

Interpreter: Professor P. J. Mantoux

1. President Wilson read the following communication, which he suggested should be published and transmitted by wireless telegraphy to all parts of the world:—

Warning To
Be Issued To
Belligerents

"The Governments now associated in conference to effect a lasting peace among the nations are deeply disturbed by the news which comes to them of the many instances in which armed force is being made use of, in many parts of Europe and the East, to gain possession of territory, the rightful claim to which the Peace Conference is to be asked to determine. They deem it their duty to utter a solemn warning that possession gained by force will seriously prejudice the claims of those who use such means. It will create the presumption that those who employ force doubt the justice and validity of their claim and purpose to substitute possession for proof of right and set up sovereignty by coercion rather than by racial or national preferences and natural historical association. They thus put a cloud upon every evidence of title they may afterwards allege and indicate their distrust of the Conference itself. Nothing but the most unfortunate results can ensue. If they expect justice, they must refrain from force and place their claims in unclouded good faith in the hands of the Conference of Peace."

(This was agreed to.)
The meeting adjourned until 3 o'clock in the afternoon.

24 January 1919.

IX. Paris Peace Conference and the Problems of Central and Eastern Europe

25

Secretary's Notes of a Conversation Held in M. Pichon's Room at the Quai d'Orsay, Paris, on Thursday, January 30, 1919 at 15 Hours 30 [The Council of Ten]

SOURCE: *FRUS,* 1919, Paris Peace Conference (Washington, D.C.: Government Printing Office, 1943), III, 797-815.

Present

America,
United States of

President Wilson.
Mr. R. Lansing.
Mr. A.H. Frazier.
Mr. L. Harrison.
Col. R.H. Williams.
Mr. G.L. Beer.
Prof. E.T. Williams.
Mr. D.H. Miller

British Empire

The Rt. Hon. D. Lloyd George, M.P.
The Rt. Hon. A.J. Balfour, M.P.
The Rt. Hon. Sir R.L. Borden
The Rt. Hon. Sir W.M. Hughes
Gen. The Rt. Hon. L. Botha.
The Rt. Hon. W.F. Massey.
Mr. C.J.B. Hurst.
Lt. Col. Sir M.P.A. Hankey.
Major A.M. Caccia.
Mr. H. Norman.

France

M. Clemenceau.
M. Pichon.
M. Simon.
M. Dutasta.
M. Berthelot.
Captain Portier.

Italy

M. Orlando.
Baron Sonnino.
M. Salvago-Raggi.
Count Aldrovandi.
Major Jones.

Japan

Baron Makino.
Viscount Chinda.
H.E.M. Matsui.
M. Saburi.
M. Kimura.

Interpreter: Professor P. J. Mantoux.

. . . M. Clemenceau said that the Roumanians wished to be present the next day.

Mr. Lloyd George said that raised the question of the agenda and he thought it was very important that some sort of agenda should be formulated. He was not complaining. But he did not know that the Belgians were coming there that afternoon and they were putting up a claim which very specially affected the British and he found himself without experts on this question and without maps, etc.

In regard to Roumania, Mr. Lloyd George enquired if that meant that they were beginning the following day with the discussion of the territorial questions in Europe. He thought the discussion on Czecho-Slovakia and Poland the other day was absolutely wrong. He would not use the term "a waste of time" because that was a very provocative one, and he could already see the glare in the President's eye! At the same time he thought it was not quite the best method of dealing with the business. If they were going to begin to hear them in part, let them each make their statements before the matter had been broached at that Conference. Unless they began business with Roumania and considered her claims the next day, he did not think the Roumanian representatives ought to be present. If they came without intending to do business, it would be a waste of time.

M. Sonnino thought that the question of the Czechs and the Poles could not be considered as a waste of time. They knew that the Poles and Czechs were fighting and they wanted to stop that, consequently they had decided to send a Mission to Warsaw. It was their duty to hear the Czechs and the Poles with the least possible delay, instead of sending a Mission which would take a fortnight. If the Poles put out all their aspirations, that was another question.

Mr. Balfour said that was their fault.

M. Sonnino thought that the talk with the Czechs and the Poles was very useful and if, as a consequence of that conversation, they could decide how to put a stop to the fighting, they would have gained and not lost time.

M. Clemenceau said that those present did not always share the same views. President Wilson had proposed that they should begin to deal with territorial questions. They began with the Pacific, then passed to Africa. Now they had come to Europe, beginning with Poland, because there was a pressing necessity and fighting was taking place there. If it were decided not to hear the Roumanian case the following day, well, let it be so; but they must have courage to begin with those questions one day or other. If Mr. Lloyd George wished to have another agenda, of course he (M. Clemenceau) was ready to accept his suggestion, but he only wished that suggestions should be other than negative ones. If it was suggested that they should leave out the Colonial question, that they should not deal further with Poland, that they should not hear the Roumanian case, then that would lead them to a *cul de sac.* President Wilson had given very important reasons why the discussion of the Colonial questions should be postponed for the moment. They had reached an agreement on the proposal made by Mr. Lloyd George that morning, and President Wilson had said he wished to stop at that stage for the present. Now, if they did not courageously deal with the European questions, what else was there for them to do? M. Clemenceau said that he expected to receive a report from the Committee on the Czecho-Polish dispute the following day, and it would be ready for issue the same afternoon.

Mr. Lloyd George said that he was afraid he had not made himself very clear but did not object to Roumania being taken. What he said was that if they took Roumania they must examine the territorial question. That was what he meant. If Roumania was to be taken as a serious examination of the problem, he had not a word to say. If the Roumanian and Serbian delegates had come there for the conference to hear what they had to say, then he had not the slightest objection to Roumania being taken the following day, so long as it was with a view to serious discussion.

President Wilson said that he had a suggestion to make, which at least looked practical. Discussions such as they had heard on the previous day he admitted were most instructive. His only objection was that they did not bear upon a single point that was in doubt in their minds. Now he wanted to hear the full Roumanian case and it was probable that an opportunity could not be found the next day. His suggestion was that the British students of the subject, and the Americans, French, Italians, and Japanese if they had a body of students conversant with those things, should take up any one of those questions and find how near they were in agreement upon it, and then submit to the conference for discussion their conclusions as to what, for example, the territory of Roumania should be. Then they should submit their conclusions to the Roumanians for their opinion. By this means they would eliminate from the discussion everything in which they were in agreement.

Continuing, President Wilson said that he had on his desk the recommendations of the American students on all those questions, in a digested form, so that he would not be laying them before the conference as American proposals, but as a basis of discussion.

Mr. Balfour said that the only observation he had to make was that he was quite sure that the President was right in thinking that a discussion among the experts who had studied those questions would be most valuable, and that it would tend to eliminate a great many agreed points, and therefore enable them to concentrate their attention on points upon which agreement had not been reached. He was not sure that it would not be wise to allow those people to have their day to explain their case. He thought they would be much happier, although he admitted it took up a great deal of time. He thought it would make a great difference to them if they came there and said that they would put their whole case before the conference.

The second part of his suggestion was that they should have representative experts there.

Mr. Balfour, continuing, said that with regard to the suggestion for allowing each of these groups to have it out before the conference with their experts, he thought that the discussions would be more fruitful, and they would know exactly what these people were thinking in their own minds. The Americans had done most of their work in America. The British had done

their work in England and France. They had had books but more than that
they had seen the representatives of these countries. If they could come face
to face with the actual living feelings of the people concerned, he thought it
would be beneficial. That is why he suggested they should have the
Roumanians there the following day.

M. Clemenceau said that he agreed.

Mr. Lloyd George added that Serbia must also be present . . .

26

Confidential Memorandum of Secretary Lansing, "Discouraging Outlook for Peace," December 29, 1918

SOURCE: Confidential Memoranda of Secretary Lansing, *Robert Lansing Papers*, Manuscript Division, Library of Congress.

December 29, 1918.

It is evident to me that the President is determined to incorporate in the
peace treaty an elaborate scheme for the League of Nations which will excite
all sorts of opposition at home and abroad and invite much discussion.

The articles relating to the League ought to be few and brief. They will not
be. They will be many and long. If we wait till they are accepted, it will be
four or five months before peace is signed, and I fear to say how much longer
it will take to have it ratified.

I am really distressed over the prospect because Germany and Austria may
be in social chaos by the time the peace treaty is ready to sign, and there will
be no governments to make peace with.

It is perhaps foolish to prophesy, but I will take the chance. In two
months we will still be haggling over the League of Nations, and an
exasperated world will be cursing us for not having made peace.

27

Confidential Memorandum of Secretary Lansing, "Review of the Present Condition of the Peace Conference," January 22, 1919

SOURCE: Confidential Memoranda of Secretary Lansing, *Robert Lansing Papers,* Manuscript Division, Library of Congress.

January 22, 1919.

The "Supreme Council of Ten," which is running the Conference on Preliminaries of Peace has been in operation for ten days. It has the same membership as the Supreme War Council, namely: MM Clemenceau and Pichon for France, Messrs. Lloyd George and Balfour for Great Britain, Signor Orlando and Barone Sonnino for Italy, Baron Makino and Baron Matsui for Japan, and the President and I for the United States. Clemenceau is the presiding officer and M. Dutasta is the secretary, so the conduct of affairs is entirely in French hands.

This Council determines everything which pertains to the Conference. It arbitrarily takes control, decides what the Conference may or may not consider and what action is to be taken. A more autocratic oligarchy never existed... Possibly it is the only practical way to reach results. However "the equality of nations" the independent voice of small nations and all those ideals, which have been cherished and exalted during the past ten or fifteen years as a basis for international relations, have been scrapped. It seems to me that the Congress of Vienna is reincarnated in the Council of the Quai d'Orsay. It is a fact, which there is no use blinking, that might is more firmly seated in the saddle than it has been for many a year. One constantly hears of the "Five Great Powers" and what they intend to do. Now the "Great Powers" are those which possess the military strength backed by sufficient resources to impose their will on the rest of the world. If they are just and generous, it will be well. If they are not, the little fellows will simply have to grin and bear it. Of course there is one great difference between the Congress of Vienna and the Council of Ten, the former was inspired by the monarchical spirit, the latter by the democratic. This may save the Council from the justified criticism which posterity has made on the Congress of a century ago.

I know that the United States means to be just and generous and is entirely unselfish in its policies, but I cannot say the same of the other four great powers.

Great Britain has, I believe, good intentions and does not mean to be unjust. Unfortunately the British Government under apparent necessity made some bad treaty agreements during the war and then under the stress of the political campaign in December they made a lot of very rash promises about indemnities and punishments. . . .

France's policy seems to be a very selfish one and, therefore, a dangerous one. The Government has made all sorts of promises to the people. . . During the war France has borrowed enormous sums to meet the expenses of the Government. They seemed afraid to tax the people. The debt is immense. . . They want to keep up this uncertain state between peace and war until they get possession of territory and property by means of new armistice terms so that they can go before the people and tell them that, though they were unable to get funds they have succeeded in securing all these valuable assets for France. . . .

Italy is in some ways worse than France. She entered the war to gain territory. . . The Pact of London acknowledged her territorial claims, and she is holding the Allies strictly to its terms. The Italian Government is, however, very nervous over the attitude of the United States. . .

Japan is, as usual, grabbing for everything in sight. . . Great Britain bought Japanese aid in the war by promising to support her claims to the German islands north of the equator. . .

This is the way things line up in the Council of Ten. It is full of trouble and with no end of possible quarrels. The United States is apparently to be charged with the duty of saving everybody from all sorts of undesirable promises and agreements. We will gain few friends and make some enemies if we do this. Yet we must be just.

Meanwhile Poles, Czecho-Slovaks, Ukrainians, Jugo-Slavs, Montenegrins, Serbs, Albanians, all the races of Central Europe and the Balkans in fact, are actually fighting or about to fight with one another. Just as the Russian, Austrian and German Empires have split up into national groups, so the great war seems to have split up into a lot of little wars. Heaven knows how this all will end.

There seems to me only one possible solution, and that is peace at the earliest moment. The President and Colonel House push everything aside in order to advance their pet project of a League of Nations. Personally I feel that the immediate peril demands our first attention. We ought to make peace without delay, if we do not we may have no German Government with which to make peace. In fact so great is the necessity that I shall pay little attention to the League, which can wait while peace cannot. . .

The crying need of the world today is Peace. If the acceptance of an elaborate scheme for a League of Nations interferes, I would throw the scheme overboard. . .

As it is we must go stumbling along in the present unsatisfactory way, delaying and delaying while the flames of Bolshevism eat their way into Central Europe and threaten the destruction of social order. I feel a deep and growing concern over the situation.

X. Problems of Implementation of the Policy of Self-Determination of Nations

28

Confidential Memorandum of Secretary Lansing, "Certain Phrases of the President Contain the Seeds of Trouble," December 20, 1918

SOURCE: Confidential Memoranda of Secretary Lansing, *Robert Lansing Papers,* Manuscript Division, Library of Congress.

December 20, 1918.

There are certain phrases in the President's "Fourteen Points" which I am sure will cause trouble in the future because their meaning and application have not been thought out. The principal ones, as I see them today, are those which declare that open covenants between nations should be "openly arrived at," that in imposing government over people they should have the right of "self-determination", and there should be "freedom of the seas." These three phrases sound well and will obtain popular applause but each one contains the seeds of discord.

Of course everyone, who has had any experience, knows that negotiations cannot be conducted like a town meeting. It is silly to declare a doctrine like that, because it never will work and I am sure that the President will not attempt to follow it himself, and he will be criticized and ridiculed for not doing so.

When the President talks of "self-determination," what unit has he in mind? Does he mean a race, a territorial area or a community? Without a definite unit which is practical, application of this principle is dangerous to peace and stability.

As for the "freedom of the seas," which sounds so attractive, I do not know what it means and I do not believe that the President does, because whenever I have asked him to define it he has always avoided an answer.

These phrases will certainly come home to roost and cause much vexation.

The President is a phrase-maker par excellence. He admires trite sayings and revels in formulating them. But when he comes to their practical application he is so vague that their worth may well be doubted. He apparently never thought out in advance where they would lead or how they would be interpreted by others. In fact he does not seem to care so that his words sound well. The gift of clever phrasing may be a curse unless the phrases are put to the test of sound, practical application before being uttered.

29

Secretary's Notes of a Meeting in M. Pichon's Room at the Quai d'Orsay, Paris, on Tuesday, April 1, 1919, at 3 p.m. [The Council of Foreign Ministers]

SOURCE: *FRUS*, 1919, Paris Peace Conference (Washington, D.C.: Government Printing Office, 1943), IV, 536-47.

Present America, United States of	Also Present America, United States of
Hon. R. Lansing	Mr. Shotwell
	Mr. Dulles
Secretary	Mr. Robinson
Mr. L. Harrison	Mr. Seymour
British Empire	British Empire
The Rt. Hon. A.J. Balfour	Item 2
Secretaries	
Mr. H. Norman	Rt. Hon. G.N. Barnes
Hon. T.A. Spring-Rice	Sir M. Delevingne

<table>
<tr><td>

France

M. Pichon
M. Tardieu

Secretaries

M. Berthelot
M. Arnavon
M. de Bearn

</td><td>

Item 3

Sir Eyre Crowe
Mr. C.J.B. Hurst
Lt. Comdr. J.G. Latham

France

M. Cambon
M. Hermitte
M. Laroche

</td></tr>
</table>

Italy	
H.E. Baron Sonnino	Japan
Secretary-General	M. Oka
Count Aldrovandi	
Secretary	
M. Bertele	

Japan

H.E., Baron Makino

Secretary-General
M. Otchiai

Secretary
M. Kawai

... Mr. Lansing suggested that only that part of the report dealing with the frontier between Czecho-Slovakia and Germany should be considered, as it

Report of the
Czecho-Slovak
Commission

was desired to collect all the elements of a preliminary treaty with Germany. The boundaries between Czecho-Slovakia and other countries might be considered at a later

stage.

M. Sonnino agreed to this procedure.

Mr. Cambon said that the task of the Commission had been one of considerable intricacy. It has attempted to do justice to ethnic claims but economic and strategic considerations had also to be given weight as a purely racial frontier would have left Czecho-Slovakia defenceless and economically crippled. He did not propose to explain the frontier in minute detail, as many points had been left to the decision of the Frontier Commission which would ultimately be sent to mark the boundaries. The Eastern point of contact with Germany began at Neustadt.

Mr. Balfour observed that it could not be laid down as certain that this would be the point of contact between Czecho-Slovakia and Germany until the frontier between Poland and Germany had been fixed.

M. Cambon said that the Commission had framed certain proposals regarding Teschen and Ratibor, but had found that its recommendations did not accord with those made by the Polish Commission at Warsaw. These areas were therefore reserved, pending a joint session of representatives of the Committee on Polish Affairs and of the Committee on Czecho-Slovak questions, which, it was hoped, would be able to harmonise the views of both. In any case it was probable that the point of contact of Germany would be in the region of Neustadt. The boundary from this place westward followed as a rule the old administrative boundary along the mountains. Some alteration of this line, however, was recommended near Glatz. The red line on the map indicated the claims of the Czecho-Slovaks. The Commission had not thought it right to grant them, but by diminishing the salient made by the German territory surrounding Glatz, had improved the strategic position of the new State in this quarter.

Mr. Balfour enquired whether this modification transferred a German population to Bohemia.

M. Cambon replied that the population transferred was not numerous.

Mr. Lansing asked whether the reservations made by the American delegates applied to this area or not.

M. Cambon said that they did not apply to this area.

Mr. Lansing thought that the reservations had a general character and a general application. The American Delegates objected to the whole method of drawing frontier lines on strategic principles.

M. Cambon said that it was not strategic interests but considerations of national defence that guided the Commission.

Mr. Lansing enquired whether there was any difference.

M. Cambon replied that he had himself heard President Wilson declare that the new States should be set up under conditions which would enable them to survive. The Commission had been entrusted with the task of setting up a new State in Central Europe. This State had perforce an odd shape, its territory was so narrow as to run the risk of being over-run at the very outset of hostilities. It was for this reason that the Commission had thought it advisable to reduce the glacis surrounding Glatz.

Mr. Lansing said he did not wish to debate the question of Glatz. He wished, however, to point out that the fixing of frontier lines with a view to their military strength and in contemplation of war was directly contrary to the whole spirit of the League of Nations, of international disarmament, and of the policy of the United States as set forth in the declarations of President Wilson.

M. Cambon, in reply, said that the report would reveal that the American delegates had not made any general reservations. They had only made two reservations on special points, to which he would refer later. It was not his province to discuss general policy, but he thought he might be allowed to say that the ethnological principle was not the only one the Commission was to apply. If a nation was to be composed strictly according to the national sentiments of each village, the result would be a country as discontinuous as the spots on a panther's skin. Such, he presumed, was not the result the Conference desired the Commission to recommend. The Commission had received deputations from many localities requesting the constitution of numberless small republics on the pattern of San Marino and Andorra. He assumed that the Conference did not wish this tendency encouraged, especially in Central Europe, where national security was not well established.

M. Cambon, continuing, said that there was not much to say about the line traced to the West of the Glatz salient until it reached the neighbourhood of Reichenberg. At this point the Commission had ceded a salient of territory surrounding Friedland to Germany, though it had previously been Austrian territory. This was done as a compensation for the ground lost by Germany near Glatz. Germany, moreover, gained the advantage of holding the railway from Zittau to the North, and therefore gained more than she lost. Further West, near Romburg, the Bohemian frontier made a bulge into Germany. The majority of the Commission, namely, the British, French and Italian delegates, had been in favour of maintaining the old administrative line. The American delegate, however, had made a reservation on this point.

Mr. Balfour asked M. Cambon to explain for what reasons the Commission had decided to leave the salient within Bohemia.

M. Cambon said that there were historical reasons for doing so.

Mr. Lansing observed that in this salient there were 90,000 Germans and no Czechs.

M. Cambon replied that the Commission had come to the conclusion that nature had so clearly marked the outlines of the country that it was undesirable to alter them without very cogent reasons. Further, it had thought it inadvisable to make a gratuitous offer to Germany of additional population, and thereby to create a precedent for the attribution of other Austro-Germans to the main federation.

Mr. Lansing remarked that the Commission had, nevertheless, done this in respect of Friedland. He further pointed out that the line recommended by the American Delegation was a better geographical line than that proposed by the majority of the Commission.

M. Cambon said that the majority had thought it reasonable to follow the old administrative border, which roughly followed the crests of the hills and had seen no sufficient reasons for disturbing the habits of the people formed by long connection with the administrative unit of Bohemia.

Mr. Lansing asked whether the Commission would approve of a plebiscite in this area.

M. Laroche said that this question had been raised in the Commission, which, after consideration, had decided that a plebiscite could not be proposed in an isolated salient without extending it to the remainder of the German Bohemians. If this were done, the Czecho-Slovak State would be reduced to very slender proportions.

Mr. Lansing observed that this was not a good reason to justify an injustice.

M. Laroche denied that an injustice was being done. The inhabitants of these regions were accustomed to live in close connection with the rest of Bohemia, and did not desire separation. Moreover, the German colonisation was of recent date. The result of the policy suggested by Mr. Lansing might be that the whole of Bohemia would elect to join Germany in order not to be separated from the German-Bohemians.

M. Cambon said that there was little to remark about the boundaries further West up to Asch. This place the Czecho-Slovak Government had agreed to give up. The Commission took note of this, but the American Delegation desired to cut off a considerable salient in addition. The British, French and Italian delegates had not concurred, and had thought it better to leave the people in this area in their old entourage.

Mr. Lansing observed that in the two salients discussed the line drawn by the American Delegation cut four railroads whereas that adopted by the other delegations cut ten. In the last salient mentioned there were 175,000 Germans and 3,000 Czechs. As far as he was able to judge, there was no valid reason against assigning this salient to Germany. Bohemia would lose nothing essential. There were in it some lignite mines, producing 7 per cent of the lignite in Bohemia, but as Bohemia exported lignite it was clear that it could get on without these mines.

M. Cambon said that it was for the defence of Bohemia that the Commission had decided to keep the railway lines alluded to by Mr. Lansing within Czecho-Slovakia.

Mr. Lansing said that he made reservations on this point.

M. Pichon said that on behalf of France, he also had reservations to make. He could not allow Germany to be fortified by populations taken from what had been Austrian Dominions, taken, moreover, from Bohemia, which, he trusted, would remain an Ally of France, and handed over to Germany, which, as far as he was concerned, still remained a country to be feared. If America refused to take into account considerations of national defence, France was not in a position to neglect them.

Mr. Lansing asked whether M. Pichon had noted that in yielding Friedland to Germany the Commission had reinforced Germany by 60,000 inhabitants.

M. Pichon said that he was not prepared to generalise this practice.

M. Cambon observed that this was done in compensation for the readjustment of the frontier near Glatz. He further pointed out that the railways at Eger were all directed towards Czecho-Slovakia. They were lines of penetration and any power commanding the junction would have control of the lines.

The boundary further South called for no special remark.

(Further Discussion on the Commission's Report was deferred until a solution of the differences between that Committee and the Committee on Polish Affairs had been adjusted.)

(The Meeting then adjourned.)

Paris, *2nd April, 1919.*

30

Notes of a Conversation of Colonel House, Mr. Lloyd George, M. Clemenceau and M. Orlando, Held on April 4, 1919, at 4 p.m.

SOURCE: *Woodrow Wilson Papers,* Manuscript Division, Library of Congress.

April 4, 1919

M. Clemenceau. I looked at the report of the Commission on Czechoslovak Affairs on the boundary between Behoemia and Germany. The solution is very complicated and makes all sorts of changes, some of which entail cession of territory to Germans: this seems to me very unnecessary. It is simpler to maintain the boundary such as it was before the war and to leave to Bohemia and Germany the problem of making exchanges of territories if they wish to do so.

As far as the question of the Germans of Bohemia is concerned, it has nothing to do with the preliminaries of peace between us and Germany.

Mr. Lloyd George. That question is in fact pertinent to the problem of division of the old Austrian empire. I agree with you about preserving the old boundary between Bohemia and Germany. As for the question of Teschen, that also is part of the Austrian problem.

Colonel House. This solution seems to me to be the best. We could establish a commission on Teschen which would report to the League of Nations.

M. Clemenceau. The problem of Ratibor and Upper Silesia, which are of interest to both Poland and Behemia, could be dealt with together with the Polish questions.

We decide therefore—reserving the opinion of President Wilson—to maintain purely and simply the old frontier between Bohemia and Germany. . .

XI. The Specter of a Bolshevik Takeover in Central and Eastern Europe

31

Confidential Memorandum of Secretary Lansing, "Effect of Secret Diplomacy on the Public Mind," April 4, 1919

SOURCE: Confidential Memoranda of Secretary Lansing, *Robert Lansing Papers,* Manuscript Division, Library of Congress.

April 4, 1919.

Gloom is everywhere. Paris is steeped in it. Distrust and depression have succeeded the high hopes with which the Council of Four was greeted.

There is nothing to indicate that we are nearer peace than we were ten days ago.

Meanwhile Central Europe is aflame with anarchy; the people see no hope; the Red Armies of Russia are marching westward. Hungary is in the clutches of revolutionists; Berlin, Vienna and Munich are turning toward the Bolsheviks.

A gentleman once fiddled while Rome burned. It is time to stop fiddling while the world is on fire, while violence and bestiality consume society.

Everybody is clamoring for peace, for an immediate peace. . .

32

Professor A. C. Coolidge to the Commission to Negotiate Peace Transmitting a Report from Captain Nicholas Roosevelt, Vienna, April 2, 1919

SOURCE: *FRUS,* 1919, The Paris Peace Conference (Washington, D.C.: Government Printing Office, 1947), XII, 282.

[Enclosure] Vienna, *April 2, 1919.*

Subject: Interview with Chancellor Renner.

1. In an interview which I had with the Chancellor Dr. Renner on April 1st, he stated that the situation was well in hand, and complete quiet was to be expected unless some unexpected incident should turn up. . .

2. In speaking of Karolyi's abdication he expressed the opinion that the revolution in Hungary had come as a surprise and despite Karolyi's efforts to withstand it. It had in no way been premeditated. But he added that as regards German Austria, it had already been decided that if the country was dismembered—especially referring to German Bohemia and German Tyrol—the German Austrian Government would resign, just as had done the Hungarian Government, and would turn the Government over to whoever would take it. He added that this would mean inevitably Bolshevism.

Nicholas Roosevelt

33

Professor A. C. Coolidge to the Commission to Negotiate Peace, Vienna, April 7, 1919

SOURCE: *FRUS,* 1919, The Paris Peace Conference (Washington, D.C.: Government Printing Office, 1947), XII, 287-88.

Vienna, *April 7, 1919.*
[Received April 10.]

Sirs: I have the honor to report that my impressions since my return to Vienna of the situation here are depressing. It is not so much that anything has got seriously worse but there are almost no signs of improvement anywhere, and several of increasing disintegration.

To begin with, there is a shortage of almost everything. The recent arrivals of food trains have not been sufficient to make conditions in the city appreciably better—people are on their fourth meatless week—but merely to prevent them from becoming more critical.

The same is true of coal, so urgently needed for the revival of industry.

Prices are soaring ever higher.

The number of unemployed is great, and those that are employed are constantly demanding an increase of wages, which the employers find it increasingly difficult to pay.

The economic and financial situation is disastrous, and the prospect of immediate improvement is slight. The dissolution of the former Austro-Hungarian Empire into a number of separate territories has naturally dealt a particularly heavy blow to the capital, which was the center of finance and control for the whole. This blow is rendered far worse by the almost complete closing of so many frontiers, which makes normal relations impossible. The last stroke has been the Hungarian revolution which, among other things, threatens the great Austrian interests in Hungary.

The condition of the currency looks desperate. The Krone has been going steadily down and one sees no end to the process. The restamping of money in Czecho-Slovakia could not but harm the Austrian currency, and now the Hungarian revolution, which is likely to mean an unlimited issue of fresh notes similar to the old ones, threatens further disaster to finances here. Under these circumstances, the rate of exchange makes the importation of anything except the most immediate necessaries impossible, and the lifting of the blockade is regarded as a platonic measure.

The political situation is no more cheerful than the economic. The government, though honestly struggling with the difficulties that beset it, is weak and not too well united. It has to lead or follow its supporters but cannot control them. It is helpless against the excesses of its own unreliable military force, the Volkswehr, for it has nothing else to fall back on in case of disorder. One cannot well see what could prevent it from falling tomorrow if the Volkswehr, supported by a section of the laboring class, should order it out. Already the illegal and arbitrary measures of the Volkswehr are beginning to terrorize the property-holding classes, who are also looking forward to a process of taxation and socialization which may amount to wholesale confiscation in the end.

A further sign of the weakness of the government and of the general disintegration, is the increasing independence of the provinces, which show a disposition to pay little attention to orders from Vienna. At the present moment not only are the peasants keeping their food supplies in a great measure for themselves, but there is a movement on foot to shut out all strangers this summer; that is to say, that people in this city are to be left to their plight here and not allowed to go into the country where conditions are better. The government has declared such resolutions on the part of the provinces to be illegal, but whether it will be strong enough to prevail in the end is uncertain. Its own small authority may soon have a rival in the system of Councils of Workmen who are to be called into existence by election next week.

Finally, there is an undoubted growth of Bolshevism. Its progress has been slow indeed—rather surprisingly so—and I do not believe it is yet either very deeprooted or widespread. But for months conditions have been such as to promote its increase, and now the example of Hungary has undoubtedly given a stimulus to those who favor a similar movement here. Relations between Austria and Hungary are still close, and what happens in Budapest inevitably affects Vienna, and vice versa. Some 800 or 900 of the Volkswehr have joined the Hungarians and this will react here; and from Hungary several prominent agitators are said already to have come to Vienna to begin work. If Bavaria goes Bolshevist, the situation will be blacker still.

When we add to all the above causes the strain of 4½ years of war, the depression of defeat, the long lack of sufficient food, the uncertainty as to the political future of many German-speaking regions, and finally the strain produced by months of waiting for the final conclusion of peace, we can see why pessimism here is so widespread.

On the other side of the ledger we can find little to note except the extraordinarily quiet, docile, and orderly, not to say apathetic, character of the population. Their patience and resignation have been admirable, and one can only hope that it will continue to be so. . . .

Archibald Cary Coolidge

XII. The Smuts Mission to Central and Eastern Europe: An Abortive Attempt at a Comprehensive Settlement

34

The Mission to Austria-Hungary (Report by General Smuts)

SOURCE: *Woodrow Wilson Papers,* Manuscript Division, Library of Congress.

April 9, 1919

The mandate which I had from the Great Powers was principally concerned with the working of the two Austro-Hungarian armistices of the 3rd and 13th November, 1918, and the regulation of a neutral zone between the Hungarian and Roumanian forces. It was, however, impossible to enquire into those subjects without hearing and seeing much about other matters more or less closely connected with them. The advance of Bolshevism into the territories of former Austria-Hungary, the position and attitude of the new Governments, and the urgent economic questions arising out of the carving up of the old Empire and the drawing of new economic and political frontiers,—all those and similar matters were continually pressed. on my attention. As I was asked to report generally I shall, therefore, in this report deal as briefly as possible with all the matters which are of special interest to the Great Powers or which call for urgent action. . . .

II. AN ECONOMIC AND TERRITORIAL CONFERENCE.

The Hungarian Government were at great pains to explain to me that, as a Soviet Government, they were not so much interested in territorial questions. Hungary had had an imperialist policy in the past which was one of the causes of its present downfall, and the national sentiment among the people was still strong. The present Government, however, occupied a somewhat different standpoint, and would prove more accommodating on the question of territorial boundaries than a Government inclining more to the Right could be expected to be. They were, however, profoundly interested in the economic questions which were arising from the great territorial re-adjustments. As it was now proposed to cut up Hungary, the country would cease to be an economic entity and would, indeed, become economically impossible, unless its position was safeguarded by economic arrangement with the neighbouring States. They were completely cut off from the territories occupied by the Czecho-Slovak, Jugo-Slav, and Roumanian forces, and both from a food and an industrial point of view the position was becoming impossible.

They, therefore, pressed very strongly that the settlement of political frontiers should be accompanied by a simultaneous arrangement of urgent economic questions, and they pointed out that an economic settlement would help to render the territorial settlement palatable. This view was so obviously reasonable and sound that I was not surprised to find the members of the German-Austrian Government who saw me also strongly pressing for it. I, therefore, decided to go to Prague in order to ascertain the views of President Masaryk. He agreed that a settlement of urgent economic questions would be most necessary, and that a conference of the neighbouring States, comprising the former territories of Austria-Hungary, should be called immediately for the purpose. President Masaryk considered it, however, essential that this Conference should meet under the aegis and presidency of the Great Powers.

In view of this general agreement, the necessity for such a Conference needs no further argument from me. It is, indeed, not only Hungary's position which will become economically impossible under the new territorial arrangements. German-Austria is in as difficult a plight, and unless she can obtain suitable economic arrangements with her neighbours, she must inevitably be driven into the arms of Germany. Besides, the drawing of new lines across the old Austria-Hungary and the prevention of intercourse and communication in which the various States are freely indulging, destroy all chance of the resumption of normal industrial and commercial life, strangle the economic life of these large areas, and by rendering impossible all production and industry, are making it a sure breeding place for Bolshevism and anarchy. As it is both the duty and interest of the Great Powers without any further delay to put an end to this intolerable situation, it is incumbent upon them to call the economic Conference for which these States are clamouring.

By assuming their proper role of guidance and help in this grave emergency the Great Powers will not only contribute to the salvation of the suffering peoples of this part of Europe, but they will establish their moral authority and enhance the prestige of the League of Nations, which will in its early stages, be mostly an expression of the joint action of the Great Powers.

The question is what form this Conference should take. As I have said, the Hungarian Government were most anxious that economic arrangements should be settled and announced *pari passu* with territorial frontiers, and they therefore asked that the neighbouring States should be called together under the presidency of a representative of the Great Powers to discuss both boundary and economic questions. They suggested Vienna or Prague as the place of meeting.

The Great Powers will have to decide whether and where such a Conference should be held. To my mind, the balance of convenience is in favour of Paris as the meeting place. In the first place, the Hungarian and Austrian representatives will, in any case, have to be invited there for the signature of the Peace Treaty. In the second place, the Prime Ministers of Czecho-Slovakia and Roumania, as well as the representatives of Yugo-Slavia are delegates to the Peace Conference, and it would in many respects be inadvisable to call them away from their duties at Paris in order to attend a Conference at, say, Vienna. In the third place, this meeting should be held not only under the presidency of a representative of the Great Powers, but also under their influence and general control, and for that purpose Paris is obviously the only suitable place.

If the Conference idea is accepted I would suggest that business be expedited by the parties being called together not in a general debating conference but in pairs (Roumania and Hungary, Hungary and Czecho-Slovakia, German-Austria and Czecho-Slovakia, etc. etc.) with the representative of the Great Powers as chairman and umpire, and that all questions be rapidly disposed of. The countries represented would state their respective territorial cases, and in the absence of agreement between them, the chairman or the Great Powers on references from him could finally decide on all points of difference. The economic questions could, at the same time, be agreed upon between the parties and could probably be announced simultaneously with the signature of the Peace Treaty. The economic questions to be dealt with should be those of most urgent necessity, such as freedom of inter-communication and exchange of necessary raw materials and urgent currency questions.

III. A MANDATORY OF THE GREAT POWERS FOR AUSTRIA-HUNGARY.

I have said enough to show that a sufficient community of interests will remain among the new States arising from the old Austro-Hungarian Empire to call for a common handling of them by the Great Powers. The new Governments are mostly weak, and some of them are sadly deficient in administrative experience. The peoples are actuated by old historic feelings of hostility towards each other. Without helping hand and the wise guidance of the Great Powers, I am doubtful whether any of them would achieve success in the immediate future, and their failure will involve grave dangers to the peace of Europe. I, therefore, consider it advisable that for the present, and for some time to come, the Great Powers should, in addition to their individual representatives with the several states, have a common representative of high standing, under whom all the Missions of the Great Powers should work, and who would be responsible for advising the Great Powers, and later on the Executive Council of the League of Nations, on all important questions involving the common interests of the new States. Such an official would not only represent the Great Powers, but also be the symbol of the surviving unity and the common interests which would continue to bind together the new States. His experience and authority would be necessary to help them to solve the very difficult questions of common concern which otherwise might well prove beyond their powers. He would inaugurate a policy of Conferences between them to discuss common interests which while teaching them new habits of co-operation, would help to allay the old historic bitternesses which still survive.

In that way German Austria might be kept away from union with Germany, and Czecho-Slovakia might thus be secured from the danger of being outflanked by such a union. Co-operation among the new States under the beneficent unifying guidance of the Great Powers would raise a happier temper among the peoples, and in this new atmosphere the load of despair, which is now one of the most fruitful sources of Bolshevism, would be lifted from the minds of the peoples. Nothing has impressed me more in all my enquiries on this Mission than the urgent need of common action by the Powers in all these countries and of their joint representation through a mandatory of wide experience and authority. . .

J.C. Smuts

XIII. An Epilogue and a Prediction

35

Confidential Memorandum of Secretary Lansing, "The New Map of the World," June 21, 1919

SOURCE: Confidential Memoranda of Secretary Lansing, *Robert Lansing Papers*, Manuscript Division, Library of Congress.

June 21, 1919.

The making of treaties has now reached a stage where the new map of Eastern Europe and Western Asia is practically settled except as to certain minor details which, however troublesome they may be, will not materially change national boundaries.

Whatever impression these new political frontiers make upon others and whatever satisfaction they may derive from the work which has been done, my own impression is that we have "Balkanized" the territories extending from the Baltic to the Aegean and from the Aegean to the Euphrates and the Caspian Sea.

It seems to me that, instead of reducing the area of political instability, where the jealousies and hatreds of the various nationalities are as inflamable as tow and liable to take fire on the slightest pretext, the area has been enlarged many times. Probably this was, in a measure at least, unavoidable in view of two things which were bound to happen, namely, the dissolution of the Austro-Hungarian Empire and the cutting up of the Turkish Empire and its consequent disappearance as a great power.

While these events were certain to take place, the consequences are that we have left a mass of small, covetous and quarrelsome nations. Along the boundaries of these little independent states there are sections inhabited by peoples whose blood is alien to their allegiance and who really desire union with a neighboring state which covets the territory occupied by them. Here is a ceaseless cause of trouble and unrest. For a time open rupture may be avoided, but it will certainly come in the near future because each country with alien population within its borders will seek to impose its nationality upon these aliens through the means of education, social usage, political practices and religious teaching.

An honest effort has been made to fix boundaries along ethnic, economic and strategic lines. This disposition of the United States and in a measure of Great Britain has been to give the ethnic and economic bases the first consideration while France and Italy have given preference to the strategic frontiers. Furthermore both Great Britain and France in order to induce certain nations to aid them against the Central Powers agreed to territorial compensations in the event of being victorious. The results have been that there have been introduced into the negotiations compromises which by including both elements are dangerously inconsistent.

No one, who has given thought to these questions, can view them without apprehension as to the future. The Balkan Situation was in the past a constant menace to the peace of Europe. Peace was always in precarious equilibrium. The reason that those little peoples did not fly at one another's throats was that they were checked by the Empires of Russia, Austria-Hungary and Turkey. Today those three Empires exert no restraining influence on the Balkans. New political and social forces are at work; new and greater ambitions inspire their policies. That, which was to them impossible, has become possible, and their avarice seems almost unlimited.

While these nationalistic impulses to become great and powerful absorb the energies and pervert the thoughts of the Balkan States, the same impulses affect the newly-created nations freed from the imperial yoke of the defeated Empires. All those evils of nationalism, which cursed the world during the 18th and 19th centuries, are again dominant over these peoples impelling them to prey upon one another.

The boundaries, which have been marked on the new map are certainly in many cases artificial. They will continue only so long as the dissatisfied grumbling nations feel themselves too weak to change them and only so long as they fear the Great Powers will exercise force to maintain them. It is weakness and fear rather than contentment and good will which will preserve peace between these fiery tempered peoples. When one of these nations is confident of its strength and believes it can take and hold contiguous territory, we may expect a new conflagration in Europe.

ARTHUR MARWICK

The British Elite in the Inter-War Years

C AREFUL HISTORIANS, and social scientists, usually prefer to
speak of "elites" rather than "the elite", even if, in the end, their
concern is to pin down the real holders of political power, the
"political" or "power" elite. Certainly, Britain, as distinct from
other twentieth-century industrialized countries, has the reputation of inclining towards one consolidated elite, or, at least, an
overlapping series of closely related elites. If the historian can
agree with the social scientist in defining elites as those minorities
which are set apart from the rest of society by their pre-eminence
in authority, achievement and reward (or any one or two of
these),[1] he would certainly wish to insist that the nature of
particular elites springs out of the special historical circumstances
of any given society. British elites in the inter-war years were
defined by the shape taken by the development in that country of
industrialisation and modern technology together with other
historical forces; the whole structure as it had established itself by
1914, had been given a mighty shake-up in the holocaust of the
First World War.

My central concern in this paper will be with the political, or

---

[1] Suzanne Keller, "Elites," in *International Encyclopaedia of the Social Sciences*, vol.
V (New York: Macmillan and Free Press, 1968), p. 26.

power elite, and, after a brief historical and social survey, I shall start by looking (1) at the country's political leadership— Conservative, Liberal and Labour—in the inter-war period, then (2) at the country's top administrators. Moving away from the power elite as such (though it will be necessary to identify areas of overlap), I shall look more briefly at (3) economic and industrial leaders, (4) labour leaders, (5) the dominant figures in the newspaper and communications world, and other social and cultural leaders, (6) local leaders; and finally, appropriately enough, since the period begins and ends with a major war, (7) the military leadership. The questions to which I shall address myself are: what was the social composition and recruitment pattern of these different elite groups?; how far, as British society moved into the era of mass democracy, was composition and recruitment changing?; what was the relative power of the different elite groups?; and, finally, recalling that this period is often regarded as one in which Britain adjusted badly to a changed world situation, how competent were these elite groups? The sources for the first two questions are essentially statistical. Yet the relevant statistical tables have, in the end, to be compiled largely from biographical material; thus this essay depends quite heavily on that strange, but indispensable source, *the Dictionary of National Biography.*

The judiciary does not have the autonomous significance that it has, say, in the United States, and I have not thought it worthwhile to make more than passing reference to this elite group. Politics, in fact, in keeping with the nineteenth-century adaptation of a venerable parliamentary tradition, were central in British inter-war society, and form the glue which kept the power elite together. Thus while in, say, Weimar Germany able men often tended to shun politics, in Britain it was still in politics (rather than, for example, in industry or in academia) that a name could most readily be made. This tradition, along with that of gross inequality of political opportunity, was underpinned at the two ancient English Universities, Oxford and Cambridge, where the Union Societies were consciously modelled on parliament, and where aspiring politicians got their training in debate. Another important point to be stressed about British society (particularly in comparison with the United States) is its tightly knit and homogeneous character, making conditions, particularly after the completion of the railway network and the establishment of the modern newspaper industry, favourable for the establishment of closely overlapping elite groups, and putting local leadership at a considerable disadvantage when compared with national leadership. At the same time, it has to be remembered that the United Kingdom contains Wales, Scotland, and Northern Ireland (after 1921) as well as England. We shall note on several occasions that a "Celtic" background could often enable a man to compensate for humble social origins in a fashion which was not usually open to an Englishman. A very brief preliminary word needs, too, to be said about the peerage and honours system. The old territorial aristocracy was still very much alive, but titles could also be given to men who had cut some sort of figure in politics, industry or elsewhere, and this obviously implied a form of recognition, though old titles would continue to carry more prestige than new titles. Holders of English peerages, together with a selection of Scottish peers, sat in the House of Lords. Sons of English peers, together with the other Scottish peers, and all Irish peers, *could* sit in the House of Commons, if elected. The two lowest rungs on the hereditary honours ladder, baronetcies and knighthoods, entitled holders to the sobriquet "Sir", but were not peerages, and did not carry a seat in the House of Lords.

It would not be correct to think of the First World War as having had a totally revolutionary effect on the British class structure; Britain remained an extremely class-conscious society, yet, undoubtedly, the war had brought significant modifications to the pattern of class relationships existing in the Edwardian period. The politically and socially dominant group in the Edwardian period had been essentially an amalgam of the older landed aristocracy and the outstandingly successful leaders of finance and industry, with the standards still being set by the landed element. The war had both material and psychological effects. High wartime taxation had quite a serious effect on the landed class, as did death duties, which sometimes hit one family several times over in the space of a few years, as fathers died, and sons and heirs were killed in the battlefield. The psychological effect of the war can be best seen in the various utterances of politicians and publicists during the war to the effect that in one way or another the war was a gigantic upheaval and had turned society "topsy-turvy".[2] This was not necessarily a lasting emotion; yet, taken with the equally strong wartime sentiment that the whole nation was united together in common citizenship in waging war against the

[2] See Arthur Marwick, *The Deluge: British Society and the First World War* (London: Bodley Head, 1965, 1967 edition [London Penguin]), p. 144.

Germans, it should not be neglected either as a factor in modifying accepted attitudes about the relative positions of various social groups.

Much attention was given immediately after the war to the changing fortunes of the old landed aristocracy, evidence in itself of the continuing social hold of this particular group. The balance of statistical and descriptive evidence certainly strongly indicates that at the end of the war there was a considerable decline in the proportion of wealth and income held by owners of land, and an acceleration in the breaking up of the great landed estates. C. F. G. Masterman was a rather unsuccessful liberal politician, but an extremely shrewd social commentator. (See Source 6.) His remarks about the vanishing of the feudal system in the blood and fire of 1914-1918 in his contemporary study, *England After the War* (1922) deserve careful study: he is very shrewd in his description of the way in which the pre-war aristocracy absorbed commercial and industrial wealth; he is right in his prediction that there could be no going back to pre-war conditions; but he obviously exaggerates the abruptness and the extent of the change, and underestimates the considerable resilience of the old ruling class. Yet, in dealing with a topic such as elites, though, in the end, it is important to get at the actual realities of the power structure, it is also important to take into account what people perceived these realities to be; if enough people believe that the position of the landed aristocracy has been diminished, then the actual power of that aristocracy will be sensibly diminished, even if not to the extent of popular belief. Thus there is much significance in the stock remark bandied around at the end of the war, "England is changing hands".

By March 1919 about half a million acres were on the market, and by the end of the year over a million acres had been sold. In 1920 sales were still greater, with the Duke of Rutland setting the pace by selling off about half of the Belvoir estate, 28,000 acres in all, for £1½ million. Undoubtedly high taxation, initiated in the years before 1914, but greatly extended during and at the end of the war, was an important cause of these sales. In other cases sales simply represented the continuation of a policy developed from the beginning of the century whereby a landowner aimed to consolidate his income by selling off outlying holdings; in such cases financial impoverishment was not necessarily involved. Finally, there was the fact that, because of wartime exploitation of agriculture, land values had greatly risen, while rents had not; by selling, the landowner could put the increased value straight into his pocket.

Professor F. M. L. Thompson has therefore concluded that economically the position of the great landowners was by no means as serious as suggested by Masterman and others; they

emerged into the inter-war period still in residence in their country-seats with their territorial empires considerably reduced, but with their incomes—once debts had been cleared and reinvestments made—probably much healthier than they had been for very many years.[3]

What was seriously dented was the feudal social dominance of the countryside formerly exercised by the great landowners, since their own tenants had now seized the opportunity presented by the land sales to set themselves up as owner farmers. The sale of urban land, opening the door to the small domestic landlord, and to a new type of property developer, took place at the same time as the sale of landed estates. Town houses, now that the up-keep of large establishments was so difficult, were sold too, symbolising the movement of aristocratic high society away from the centre of the London political stage.

Apart altogether from the question of land sales, much was written in the years after 1918 on "the lost generation", particularly with reference to the fact that, whereas over the population as a whole roughly one in ten of the generation aged between 20 and 45 was killed, losses were considerably higher among the elite groups who supplied the junior officers. For example, out of Oxford University's total roll of service of 14,561, 2,680 were killed; this figure of more than one in six can be taken as representative. To avoid getting one's generations hopelessly mixed, it is worth recalling that the survivors of the lost generation were men like Clement Attlee and Harold Macmillan, who only reached political eminence in the forties and fifties, when they were not noticeably deficient in colleagues of high calibre. However, the inescapable fact remains that the old leadership was hit particularly hard by the war. Undoubtedly, younger, middle range leaders, who might have served to mediate between the old men at the top and a still more disillusioned younger generation, were noticeably lacking. This lack assisted another trend which was

[3]Francis M. L. Thompson, *English Landed Society in the Nineteenth Century* (London: Routledge, 1963), p. 337.

taking place anyway: the upward flow of a new class of business leadership.

The new flow of political power within the topmost class was given its first big impetus by the events of December 1916, when Lloyd George ousted Asquith in order to form his own coalition government, and was ratified in the 1918 general election. For some months before the crisis of December 1916 many news-papers had been calling for "a businessman's government", so that the social climate, as with other changes associated with Lloyd George, was favourable to his innovations in governmental per-sonnel. There was nothing new about the businessman in politics: indeed, as I have already suggested, politics from Victorian times to 1914 was very much the politics of a class welded out of the old aristocracy and the newer aristocracy of commercial and industrial wealth; but to reach high office the businessman had to climb a political ladder. If the first distinctive characteristic of Lloyd George's ministerial businessmen was their numerical strength, the second was that in a large number of cases they had served little or no political apprenticeship at all. In this category were Sir Albert Stanley, manager of the London Underground and General Omnibuses Combine, Joseph Maclay, a Glasgow ship-owner who refused to take a seat in either house of Parliament, Lord Rhondda, a coal owner, Lord Devonport, an ennobled shopkeeper, Sir Alfred Mond, a chemicals manufacturer, Sir Frederick Cawley, and Albert Illingworth. Two further con-siderations enhance the long term significance of this new recruitment to government office: first, it coincided with a great extension in the powers and functions of government, and secondly, it was bolstered and consolidated by the great patriotic prestige which businessmen had acquired in this war of machines and industrial systems.

The traditional dominance of conservative representation in parliament by landowners or by businessmen of national eminence can be seen in some of the election figures for January 1910: of new members returned then, those in county (i.e., rural) constit-uencies were mainly (65 per cent) local men, while those sitting for boroughs were mainly (64 per cent) non-local. The changes reflected in the general election of 1918 are striking. Among the new Conservative M.P.s returned in this election it was in the borough constituencies that local men predominated (82 per cent), while the counties now had a majority of outsiders (54 per cent). What these statistics represent is a great swelling in the number of local businessmen on the benches of the powerful Conservative Party; most of them had little or no experience of national politics.[4]

The other significant new development which we shall have to take account of in our study of the inter-war years is the growth in prestige and influence of organised labour. The political Labour movement since the end of the nineteenth century was the obvious vehicle for the ambitious member of the working classes. The first Labour man to reach cabinet office was Arthur Henderson who was brought in by Asquith in May 1915 in recognition of the essential contribution which Labour was making to the war effort; Henderson had done sterling work as general secretary of the Labour Party. In Lloyd George's coalition, Henderson was joined by three other Labour men, Clynes, Barnes and Roberts. As the war weakened Liberalism, so it increased the potential opportunities for the Labour Party: ineffectually led, and dominated by ageing trade unionists, the Labour Party did not play a very significant role in parliament immediately after the war, but in reality it was already establishing its place as the only viable alternative to the Conservatives.

At the beginning of the inter-war period, then, the upper class was still, as in Edwardian times, a composite class, but the balance had moved definitely from the landed to the business interest. It was this class, or the younger members of it, which, drawing upon the hectic hedonism of the war, created the gay high life associated with the 1920s. It was this class which occupied the literary attentions of Aldous Huxley (see Source 9), and of John Galsworthy, the chronicler of the fortunes of a Victorian business family. Galsworthy, making a not very funny joke at the expense of social investigators who talked of the 10 per cent below the poverty line, said that he was concerned only with the 10 per cent above the property line. Inequality in the division of income and wealth was still very marked, but not quite as marked as before the war: in 1910 1.1 per cent of the population took 30 per cent of the income; in 1929 1.5 per cent took 23 per cent of the income, and two thirds of the wealth was owned by 2.5 per cent of the population. Bowley and Stamp, in their analysis of the national income as it was in 1924, pointed out that, while in 1911 individuals with incomes above £5,000 drew 8 per cent of the aggregate national income, in 1924 those earning £9,500 (the

[4] John M. McEwen, "The Coupon Election of 1918 and the Unionist Members of Parliament," in *Journal of Modern History,* 34 (1962):295, 300. Cf. Source 1.

equivalent, given the rise in prices between 1914 and 1924) drew only 5.5 per cent. They then proceeded to a very cautious summing-up:

When the full effects of taxation are taken into account the real income available for saving or expenditure in the hands of the rich is definitely less than before the war. The sum devoted to luxurious expenditure is (allowing for the rise in prices) definitely less than in 1911, but it is still sufficient to bulk large in the eyes of the public, since it is concentrated in small areas, enlarged by the spending of visitors from overseas and advertised by the newspapers.[5]

When we move into the middle classes, the outstanding and incontrovertible statistical fact is the increase over the war period in the salaried class from under 1.7 millions in 1911 to over 2.7 millions in 1921, a rise from 12 per cent to 22 per cent of the occupied population. The figures themselves are inflated because of the inclusion in this category of low paid shop assistants, clerks, etc., and the expansion is exaggerated because the classification used in 1921 was slightly different. Nonetheless the growth is striking. Itself a social phenomenon of outstanding importance, it reflects the expansion of four important groupings in the community: professions, for whom rising material and welfare standards brought a new demand; the civil servants and clerical administrators, needed by the growing bureaucracy; the managerial class required for the running of large-scale modern industry; and those women who held on to the opportunities open to them during the war. The other important feature of note is the decline in servant keeping among middle class households. The total decrease in the number of servants in the country over the war period, about a third, is less than is sometimes suggested; despite what observers during the war thought, many women, in conditions of post-war depression, were forced back into this occupation. Still, the decrease that did take place came largely out of the households of the middle class. In the commuter areas of London the number of resident servants per hundred families declined from 24.1 to 12.4, whereas in the West End it only edged down from 57.3 to 41.3. In the whole of Liverpool the decline was from 13.5 to 8.3; in suburban Wallesey from 22.4 to 14.5.[6]

[5] Sir A. L. Bowley and J. C. Stamp, *The National Income 1924* (Oxford: Clarendon Press, 1927), pp. 57-59.
[6] Marwick, *The Deluge*, p. 327.

Against these forces of change, we must pose one of the most unchanging and central institutions relevant to the nature of British elites: the educational system. At the core of the problem lay the so called "Public Schools", in reality, as is well known, expensive, fee-paying, privately controlled, boarding schools. However, within the broad term public schools lay a range of subtle, and not so subtle, distinctions. First in social prestige were certain old established schools which had already achieved such eminence in the mid nineteenth century that they were the subject of a special inquiry by the Clarendon Commission in the 1860s, and were thus sometimes called the "Clarendon Schools". These are Eton, Winchester, Westminister, Charterhouse, St. Pauls, Merchant Taylors, Harrow, Rugby and Shrewsbury. Almost rivalling the Clarendon Schools in prestige were a further short list of well established schools: Cheltenham, Clifton, Fettes, Haileybury, Loretto, Malvern, Marlborough, Oundle, Radley, Repton, Rossall, Sedbergh, Sherborne and Uppingham. In his analysis of the higher civil service in Britain, Professor R.K. Kelsall has for some purposes taken the Clarendon schools as a separate category, for other purposes he has taken all of the schools together as a first category of the most expensive and most prestigious schools. Many other schools claimed the title Public School, most of them set up during the nineteenth century in imitation of the great reforms carried through by Thomas Arnold at Rugby.

If we move on now to look at the country's political leadership as it actually developed in the inter-war years, we find right at the centre the Conservative Party. Effectively this was the governing party throughout the period, save for two short intervals, one of nine months in 1924, the other of eighteen months in 1929-31, when the Labour Party was uneasily in office. Conservative dominance of the British political scene is first of all attributable to the strongly Conservative nature of a large section of the British public, working-class as well as middle and upper-class. In 1922 the Conservatives secured 28.2 per cent of all votes cast, in 1923, 38.1 per cent; in 1924, 48.3 per cent; and in 1929, 38.2 per cent. In 1918, the Conservatives were the overwhelmingly dominant component of the coalition government then formed with Lloyd George's segment of the Liberal Party; and their dominance was still greater in the "National" governments elected in 1931 and 1935, and in the House of Commons upon which these governments depended. The Conservative position, certainly, was strengthened by the division in the anti-Conservative forces between the declining Liberal Party, and the emerging Labour Party; but it was far from clear that Liberal voters, given no Liberal candidate, would necessarily vote Labour. Able at all times to present themselves as the party of patriotism and the party of stability, the Conservatives always benefited from any national crisis; indeed the "khaki" election of 1918 (fought at the high-tide of patriotic hysteria) had given them a gigantic electoral head start. Such events as the "red letter" scare of 1924 (the scare was that a vote for Labour would be a vote for Bolshevism), the general strike of 1926, and the Abdication Crisis of 1936, all probably enhanced the electoral position of the Conservatives.

Throughout the period, young men with the right educational background, however critical they might be of the Party leadership, still went into the Conservative Party, the Party with the tradition of ruling, and the Party which seemed most likely to go on ruling (some of the best younger men, of course, were dead; and some of the survivors of the "lost generation" showed a thorough disenchantment with politics). In the constituencies the local Party organisations had a great deal of independence, which, since the Party was seldom afflicted by great ideological disputes, was not a source of any great trouble to the central organisation. But in the last analysis, in any case, the Conservative Party was essentially based on the hierarchical instinct inculcated at the great public schools. There was no formal machinery for electing the Party leadership, but once a leader had "emerged" then, as has been said, loyalty to that leader was the Conservatives' "secret weapon". At the level of national policy the important figures were the leader of the Party himself, the men he chose for important public offices (many of these, of course, were to some extent self-selecting), a handful of backbenchers, almost always from particularly rich and influential families, and, from time to time, behind the scenes figures within the Conservative Party organisation such for instance as J. C. C. Davidson. Son of a Scottish surgeon, Davidson epitomised discreet management, but ultimately he was at Baldwin's disposal, rather than the other way about. It was natural that business and commercial elements, however much they might dislike individual items of Conservative policy, should regard the Party as the best available defence of their special interests: the Party, therefore, was well-off financially. Constituency Parties were run by local people of wealth and influence, and it was an accepted convention that a candidate should pay his own campaign expenses. The major organs of the daily Press, with the exception of the *Daily News*, the *Daily Chronicle,* the *Manchester Guardian* (all Liberal) and the limping *Daily Herald* (Labour), were all Tory in outlook, though Rothermere (*Daily Mail*) and Beaverbrook (*Daily Express*) were personally bitterly hostile to the Conservative leader Stanley Baldwin.

As the Liberal Party was pushed further and further from the real possibility of political power, the Conservative Party assumed the form of being practically the sole vehicle for upper-class political aspirations. Of the Conservative M.P.s in the inter-war period, over 27 per cent had been educated at Eton, around 10 per cent at Harrow, and around 41 per cent at the various other public schools.[7] As it happened, the leader of the Conservative Party, from immediate pre-war days right through into the first post-war years, was not very typical of the top Conservative parliamentary leadership. Andrew Bonar Law had been born in Canada of Scottish stock, and made his fortune as an iron merchant in Glasgow in Scotland. He did not have the deep atavistic loyalty to Tory tradition which characterised most public school educated Conservative leaders, and it was probably partly for this reason that he was so ready to work closely with Lloyd George. But other important Conservatives increasingly chafed over a situation in which, though in a substantial majority in the House of Commons, they had to serve under a coalition led by Lloyd George. At a famous meeting held in the Carlton Club on 19th October 1922, Conservative discontent was organised and expressed by Stanley Baldwin. Baldwin's father had been the head of an old fashioned family iron foundry. Stanley Baldwin (see Source 4) went through the proper upper-class educational progression from preparatory school, to Harrow, to Trinity College Cambridge, where he revealed that he was not particularly blessed with brains by taking a third class degree in history. At the Carlton Club meeting the Conservatives voted to withdraw from the coalition, and in the general election which followed they received a secure majority (367 seats to 142 for Labour and a combined total of 117 for Asquith's and Lloyd George's Liberals). When Bonar Law was forced by ill health to retire from the Prime Ministership in May 1923, Baldwin was invited by King George V to become Prime Minister. Undoubtedly this was the most sensible available choice, but in that it meant the passing over of the most glorious figure in

[7]William L. Guttsman, *The British Political Elite* (London: McGibbon & Kee, 1963), p. 105.

the Conservative Party, the former Viceroy of India, the Marquis Curzon, it effectively established the principle that no peer could in future hope to hold the Prime Ministership, and further symbolised the decline of aristocratic influence within the ruling class.

Well within a year there followed the brief interlude in which Labour had office, though scarcely power. Baldwin had held a sudden election in the hope of securing support from the electorate for a switch away from free trade to full-scale protectionism, a tactic which, anyway, had the merit of reunifying the entire Conservative Party. After nine months of uneasy Labour government, the Conservatives did in fact return triumphantly to power.

It is worth pausing for a moment on the composition of the Conservative cabinet which governed the country from November 1924 to June 1929. Two influential posts, which carried no specific responsiblities, Lord President and Lord Privy Seal, were filled respectively by the Marquis Curzon, and by Lord Salisbury, head of the most eminent of all Conservative landed families. The Chancellor of the Exchequer was the former Conservative, turned Liberal, now returned to the Conservative fold, Winston Churchill, scion of the very aristocratic Marlborough family. Churchill's relatively easy switch in 1904 from Conservative to Liberal represents well the manner in which in these days Conservatives and Liberals were essentially grown from the same ruling class; his final departure from the Liberals back to the Conservatives symbolises the way in which the Conservatives were now the sole ruling-class Party. The Lord Chancellor, Viscount Cave, was a former barrister who had become a Lord of Appeal in 1918. At the Home Office was one of Conservatism's great gifts to the cartoonists, Sir William Joynson-Hicks (known as Jix), son of a city of London merchant, educated at Merchant Taylors, a wealthy solicitor and fervent Evangelical, prepared to go to ridiculous lengths in his hostility both to any signs of moral permissiveness and to the British Communist Party (a harmless body whose leadership, if anything, was even more incompetent than the national political leadership we are studying in this paper). The return of Austen Chamberlain (who had wished to stand by Lloyd George in 1922) as foreign secretary, was a great triumph for Baldwin: Chamberlain, of course, was the son, by his first wife, of the great late nineteenth-century statesman Joseph Chamberlain. At the Colonial Office was a great disciple of Joseph

Chamberlain, Leopold Amery, whose education (naturally) had been at Harrow and Oxford. The Secretary for War, Sir Laming Worthington Evans, was the son of a London solicitor; the Secretary for India, Lord Birkenhead, was the former F. E. Smith, a brilliant grammar school and Oxford University product; and the Secretary for Air, Sir Samuel Hoare, was the descendant of a venerable Norfolk banking family, his father having been a Conservative M.P. and baronet, and was educated at Harrow and Oxford. The Secretary of State for Scotland was a leading figure in the Scottish Conservative Party, Sir John Gilmour, son of a Scottish landowner and baronet. The President of the Board of Trade, Sir Phillip Cunliffe-Lister, went through even more changes of name than was customary in this class of Conservative politician: he started off life as Lloyd Greame, and later became Viscount Swinton. Another old landed family was represented at the Board of Education in the person of Lord Eustace Percy; while another ornament of the family of which Lord Salisbury was the head, Lord Cecil, was Chancellor of the Duchy of Lancaster. The head of a great nineteenth century family, Lord Peel, was First Commissioner of Works. At the Admiralty there was a country landowner, W. C. Bridgeman. Joseph Chamberlain's son by his second wife, Neville Chamberlain, was at the Ministry of Health. Sir Arthur Steel-Maitland, the Minister of Labour, had been educated at Rugby and Balliol College Oxford. The Minister for Agriculture, E. F. L. Wood (later Lord Irwin and, finally, Lord Halifax) came from an aristocratic nineteenth-century family and had been educated at Eton and Oxford. The Attorney-General Sir Douglas Hogg, also from a business background, had some claim to fame in that he had never actually been to University.

This cabinet well represents the balance of business and landed interests in the Conservative Party—with the preponderance being slightly with the former. Baldwin himself endeavoured to hold the ring against the older aristocratic figures (and above all against Winston Churchill) who were in favour of strongly right-wing, anti-trade union policies. Churchill, as Chancellor of the Exchequer, readily accepted the advice of the Treasury Civil Servants in returning the country to the Gold Standard with the pound at an unrealistic high parity. In the main, the government, in its domestic policies, followed a moderately collectivist line; and Neville Chamberlain's Local Government Act of 1929 was a considerable administrative achievement.

The general election of 1929 brought another minority Labour government to office. For eighteen months the Conservatives could sit back and watch Labour fail to control an increasingly desperate economic situation. But the reward was the 1931 general election in which the Conservative Party swept back into effective power, though the government was called a "National" one, and was led by the former Labour Prime Minister Ramsay MacDonald, together with one or two of his closest associates.

Neville Chamberlain proved to be the toughest character in the government of the thirties. In 1937 he replaced Stanley Baldwin as Prime Minister, and so was head of the government which concluded the Munich settlement in 1938 and somewhat reluctantly entered the Second World War in September 1939. In composition the governments of the thirties much resembled those of the twenties, not least because they were old governments set in old parliaments. In Edwardian times there had nearly always been one or two distinguished youthful figures both in parliament and in government—Winston Churchill, or F. E. Smith, for instance. Only one young man came to the political forefront in the thirties, Anthony Eden, who was made Minister responsible for League of Nations Affairs in 1935, and who, in 1936, succeeded Samuel Hoare as Foreign Secretary, before finally resigning in disgust with Chamberlain in February 1938. Younger men who in former times would have formed the basis of the middle political leadership, being survivors of the "lost generation", tended to remain detached from the official Conservative leadership. In the later twenties a number of them, including Robert Boothby, Harold Macmillan, J. de V. Loder and Oliver Stanley, had formed a group nicknamed the YMCA which criticised official Conservativism for its attempt to return to economic orthodoxy. In the thirties this group formed one of the centres of the inter- and non-party groups which well expressed the dissatisfaction with official party leadership at the time.[8]

One key to the actions and policies of David Lloyd George, Liberal Prime Minister of the coalition government from 1918-1922, is that he always felt himself to be an "outsider". He was never absorbed into the Conservative majority, which, of course, was one of the reasons for the revolt against his leadership successfully led by Stanley Baldwin in 1922. Had the Liberals still been a powerful Party, making a strong appeal to sections of the

[8] Arthur Marwick, "Middle Opinion in the Thirties: Planning, Progress, and Political 'Agreement'," in *English Historical Review*, 79 (1964): 285-98.

upper classes, Lloyd George could have continued to operate as in pre-war days as a rather exceptional figure bolstered by a Party which still found some acceptability among the British social and economic elite. But in fact the Liberal Party was in steady decline. The most reliable way of assessing this decline is to look not at the percentage of total votes cast, which is affected by the number of candidates put forward, but at the average percentage vote per candidate. In 1922 this was 38.4, in 1923 37.8, in 1924 30.9, and in 1929 27.7. (Over the same period the comparable Conservative percentage fluctuated between 39.4 and 51.9, and the Labour percentage between 38.2 and 41.0).[9] Since we are concerned not just with the composition and political affiliation of elite groups, but with their performance, it is important to note that some of the ablest elite figures of the period maintained their association with the Liberal Party. The trouble from the point of view of the country as a whole was that, however relevant and constructive the policies put forward by the Liberals, the Party itself was no longer in a position to implement them. The greatest economist of the twentieth century, J. M. Keynes, was a lifelong Liberal. In 1921 Ramsay Muir, Phillip Guedalla (both historians), William Beveridge (pioneer of Edwardian social reform, who in the twenties became director of the London School of Economics), Ted Scott (son of the distinguished editor of the *Manchester Guardian*), Walter Layton (Civil Servant and University teacher), and E. D. Simon (businessman and Lord Mayor of Manchester) launched the Liberal summer schools as a means towards scientific analysis of public policy. Keynes himself kept up the high level of polemic he had begun with the *Economic Consequences of the Peace*, denouncing the return to the gold standard in his *Economic Consequences of Mr. Churchill*. The grand culmination was the Liberal "Yellow Book" of 1928, *Britain's Industrial Future*, which a year later became the basis of the Liberal election manifesto, *We Can Conquer Unemployment.* The three major proposals of the Yellow Book were: a full scale attack on unemployment through massive schemes of public works; the establishment of an Economic General Staff (a phrase coined by Beveridge) to engage in continuous study of current economic problems, coordinate statistical information, call the attention of the government to coming economic difficulties and suggest

[9] David Butler, *The Electoral System in Britain 1918-1951* (Oxford: Clarendon Press, 1953), p. 177.

remedies; the replacement of a theoretical attachment to unadulterated individualism by an acceptance of a mixed economy in which public concerns would play an increasing part. Unhappily many active Liberals, particularly those who held seats in the House of Commons, found the Keynesian remedies too sharp an affront to the principles on which they had been reared. During the unhappy Labour government of 1929-1931 it was in fact the parliamentary Liberal Party which took the initiative in calling for economies in government expenditure. In the thirties the progressive Liberals gravitated towards the inter- and non-party groups mentioned above.

These Liberals were elite figures who did not have power. At the beginning of our period few Labour Party leaders were elite figures, and they were only operating on the very margins of political power. The new constitution of 1918 established the Labour Party as a mass national Party with individual membership (previously the Labour Party had been a federation of Trade Unions and individual Parties and societies, such as the Independent Labour Party and the Fabian Society). But in the 1918 election all of Labour's pre-war leaders were defeated, and until 1922 the Party cut a poor figure in Parliament as a merely trade union Party under the not very inspiring leadership of William Adamson, a Fifeshire miner. In the 1922 election the pre-war Labour leaders—in particular, Ramsay MacDonald, Arthur Henderson, and Phillip Snowden—returned to Parliament, and in 1923 the first Labour government took office with Ramsay MacDonald as Prime Minister, Phillip Snowden as Chancellor of the Exchequer, and Arthur Henderson as Home Secretary.

As with every historical figure, the rise of Ramsay MacDonald (see Source 4) was a unique phenomenon, yet it is very illuminating of certain aspects of the British elite. As the illegitimate son of a Scottish servant girl and a ploughman, Ramsay MacDonald would seem to have had immense natural disadvantages. Yet his Scottish environment did provide him with educational opportunities which probably would not have been open to a similar figure in most parts of England. His rise was made through journalistic and political activity, not in any way through the trade union movement. He might well have become a successful Liberal leader (indeed many of his political attitudes were essentially Liberal) but, of course, the growing Labour Party provided an admirable vehicle for him. A. J. P. Taylor has described Ramsay

MacDonald as the best leader the Labour Party has yet had;[10] and it is certainly important not to underestimate his intellectual qualities and his magnetism as a leader. His decision that his first minority government must above all establish its respectability in the eyes of the electorate and the influential newspapers was not a foolish one. "It's a lum hat government like all the rest" was the well-known judgement of one working man on MacDonald's first government.

Certainly respectability was well represented by former Liberal statesman, Viscount Haldane, who became Lord Chancellor, and by two non-party figures who if anything had Conservative leanings, Lord Parmoor who became Lord President, and Viscount Chelmsford who became First Lord of the Admiralty. Recent years had seen a number of important upper and middle-class converts to socialism and they too were well represented in MacDonald's government: Josiah Wedgewood, of the old established pottery family, became Chancellor of the Duchy of Lancaster; C. P. Trevelyan, of the famous Trevelyan family, became President of the Board of Education; and the Secretary for Air, a professional soldier, son of a general, who had joined the Labour Party at the end of war, and who was raised to the peerage as Lord Thomson.

Most of the remainder of the government was made up of respectable trade union figures. The only two left wing figures— both of working class origins, though through political and other activities they had really long since been far removed from real manual labour—were John Wheatley as Minister of Health, and F. W. Jowett as First Commissioner of Works. Neither this government nor MacDonald's second Labour government, which was remarkably similar in composition, had much effect on the course of British politics, and certainly could not be regarded as having brought any change in the composition of the political elite. What is of significance, is the way in which MacDonald was able to form his National Government in 1931 with Conservative support, and the way in which he gradually merged into the Conservative political elite. In the early stages MacDonald almost certainly hoped that it would be possible for him to rejoin the Labour Party. The fact that this did not happen was not so much due to

[10] Alan J. P. Taylor, *English History 1914-1945* (Oxford: Clarendon Press, 1965), p. 220.

his conscious decision, or even that of his former Labour colleagues, as to the very nature of the political elite itself. Ramsay
MacDonald was a gifted politician, and he proved extremely useful
to the Conservative elite: in a very real way, therefore, this elite,
in the traditional way so well described by Masterman, "absorbed"
MacDonald.

In general the higher civil service was even more restrictive in its
recruitment than the party political elite. Entry was either direct
by "open competition" or, less usually, by promotion from below.
As the 1931 Royal Commission on the Civil Service freely
admitted, considerable weight in the open competition was placed
on the "interview test", although it airily dismissed the argument,
in fact a very compelling one, that this interview "offered scope
for the display of class prejudice". (See Source 11.) In any case
the broad picture is pretty clear. In 1929 over a quarter of those
who entered the Higher Civil Service by open competition came
from the Clarendon schools; by 1939 this figure had dropped to
about a fifth, with a third of all successful candidates coming from
some type of Public School. Professor Kelsall further points out
that

amongst the most senior members of the 1939 and 1929 groups (the
Secretaries and Deputy Secretaries) the proportion of Clarendon school men
in the open competition entrants was as high as a third; and the percentage of
such men amongst other types of entrant of this rank was similar.[11]

It is in keeping with the traditions of the British Civil Service
that the names of individual civil servants are not usually widely
known either to contemporaries or to historians. However it is
worth giving attention to one or two "top" figures. As part of the
(modest) reorganization of the Civil Service which took place at
the end of the First World War, it was decided that the formal
position of permanent head of the Civil Service should rest with
the permanent secretary of the Treasury. This from October 1919
was a brilliant career civil servant, of impeccable social origins, Sir
Warren Fisher. Undoubtedly Fisher played an important part in
maintaining the general upper-class tone of the British Civil Service
and in insisting on the backward-looking economic orthodoxy
which characterised the Treasury in particular and British policy in

[11] Robert K. Kelsall, *Higher Civil Servants in Britain* (London: Routledge, 1955), pp.
15-18.

general. At the same time he was a convinced believer, in the 1930s, in a high level of rearmament in face of the German threat. Here he did not get his own way, and it is revealing of the relative strengths of a determined Conservative Prime Minister and a top Civil Servant, that Neville Chamberlain, in carrying through his Appeasement policies, was able to operate through the slightly less eminent, but more congenial figure of Sir Horace Wilson, technically Chief Industrial Adviser to the government. Likewise the permanent undersecretary at the Foreign Office, Sir Robert Vansittart, a strong anti-German, was virtually ignored by Chamberlain.

Perhaps the most important administrative change arising out of the First World War was the creation of a permanent cabinet secretariat. The first secretary was Sir Maurice Hankey, undoubtedly an important figure behind the British war effort. His successor, in 1922, was a further example of how an apparent outsider, aided by a Celtic background, could, like Ramsay MacDonald, get to the centre of the British power elite. Thomas Jones was born in an industrial village on the Welsh borders, son of an employee in the company store of the Rhymney Iron Company. After attending local schools, he became a time-keeper with the Iron Company. But in an environment favourable to learning and to nonconformist religion, young Jones, via being scripture gold medallist and a promising lay preacher, in 1890 entered the University College of Wales at Aberystwyth. In 1895 he moved on to the rather more prestigious Scottish University of Glasgow, where he took first class honours in economics. In 1909 he became Professor of Economics at Queen's University Belfast (in Ireland). His upward movement within the Civil Service came when he joined the newly established National Health Insurance Commission for Wales, set up by Lloyd George's 1911 Act, as its first secretary. Tom Jones had joined the Independent Labour Party in 1895, and though his later offices were incompatible with any political activity, he was certainly an important force behind the moderation and the collectivist social policies sometimes practised by the Baldwin and Chamberlain governments. Ironically, he was strongly disliked by Ramsay MacDonald.

A third leading administrator who deserves discussion both in his own right (he dominated Britain's domestic effort in the Second World War, when Churchill nicknamed him the "automatic pilot") and because he illustrates two important themes we have already touched on, and one other we have not yet mentioned (service in the Empire), is John Anderson (Sir John from 1919). Anderson's father owned a newspaper and fancy goods shop in Edinburgh, and sent his son to the most prestigious of the Scottish fee-paying day schools, George Watson's. After Edinburgh University, Anderson joined the National Health Insurance Commission—benefiting, like Tom Jones, from the civil service expansion resulting from the social reforms of the Edwardian period. He was secretary to the wartime Ministry of Shipping, and second secretary to the Ministry of Health set up at the end of the war. In 1922 he became permanent secretary at the Home Office, and while there was the man most responsible for preparing the government plans to defeat the General Strike. He was also responsible for initiating Britain's air raid precaution plans. In 1932 Anderson was appointed Governor of Bengal, showing that the Empire was still an outlet for an aspiring member of the power elite. In 1938 Anderson took the unusual step for an administrator of entering parliament as an Independent.

However, concentration on one or two important individuals must not conceal the fact that, even if it was slowly changing, the British higher Civil Service was essentially recruited from the upper classes in British society, properly filtered through the best schools and the ancient English universities. The conservative and unimaginative attitudes put forward by the permanent civil service were reflected in the unfortunate deflationary policies pursued by governments, and are well seen in the Treasury White Paper of 1929 which, in reply to the Liberal Yellow Book, maintained that no amount of expenditure on public works could have any possible effect on the level of unemployment. (See Source 10.) When the Conservatives were in office, economic policy was determined by men of identical social background and outlook, divided between politics, the Civil Service, and the Bank of England, whose governor, Montagu Norman, was a man whose influence rivalled, or even surpassed that of Warren Fisher. When Labour were in office they nearly always had, in the end, given the intrinsic weakness of their parliamentary position and their own lack of self-confidence, to yield to the views of the Civil Service and Bank of England. (See Source 12.)

British business leaders in the inter-war period have been much criticised for their alleged inflexibility and for depending too much on the achievements of their predecessors. Certainly it was true that just as the Conservative political elite inclined further towards the business class, so that class tended itself to become an entrenched elite resistant to recruitment from below. In criticising the Lancashire cotton owners for failing to adapt to the new post-war conditions, J. M. Keynes also suggested that British business-men were too dependent on the fortunes made by their fathers and grandfathers. (See Source 8.) Again any such picture, while containing a good deal of truth, would be too crude.

Self-made businessmen were certainly far from unknown. Per-haps the most famous was the former bicycle mechanic W. R. Morris, founder of the Morris motor company, who became Baron Nuffield in 1934 and Viscount Nuffield in 1938. Nuffield was one of those business figures who stuck closely to business, playing no part in politics or administration. An earlier, largely self made figure was William Lever, the first Lord Leverhulme, builder of the mighty Unilever combine. If one is tempted to accuse British industry in the twenties of being guilty of nepotism, it is worth noting that although Leverhulme wanted his own son to succeed him as chairman of the company, he was in fact succeeded by the brilliant accountant (from the correct upper-class background, of course) Sir D'Arcy Cooper, a prototype of the rising managerial element in British industry. Other prominent businessmen did play an active part in fostering employers' associations which, in turn, through rationalisation and retrenchment often intensified depres-sion and unemployment: Sir William James Larke, for example, first director of the British Iron and Steel Federation, founded in 1934, had considerable influence in government circles in the thirties.

We have already noted a number of important political business-men in Conservative cabinets. I should also mention Sir Alfred Mond (Lord Melchett) who, symptomatic of a process mentioned earlier in this paper, left the Liberals for the Conservatives, in 1926. (See Source 7.) Mond was the principal architect of the giant chemicals combine, I.C.I.; he was also an advocate of peaceful consultation between labour and management. A few businessmen took on another role which can be influential in British govern-ment (though it isn't inevitably so), that of adviser, sitting on important commissions, and so on. A man of rather obscure origins, who became a leading figure in the steel industry was Sir Arthur Balfour (no relation at all of the aristocratic Conservative family), who as chairman of the influential Royal Commission on Trade and Industry of 1922, was very much on the side of economic orthodoxy. (See Source 5.)

There can be no ignoring the reality of industrial depression and unemployment in the inter-war years, and the social evils that often resulted from policies of amalgamation and rationalisation. Nonetheless recent economic historians are inclined to rate the achievements of British business leaders much more highly than used to be the case:

On the basis of the statistical evidence now available there would appear to be strong grounds for suggesting that there was a sharp break with past growth trends in the 1920s. The acceleration was most noticeable in industrial production and productivity, and to a lesser extent in national product, but most other indices of economic growth (e.g. real incomes and wages) show a distinct shift upwards in comparison with earlier periods. Furthermore, the growth rates of the 1920s compare favourably with those achieved after 1930. In fact, there is every indication that this decade saw a return to the high growth rates which characterised the middle decades of the nineteenth century. In this respect, therefore, the 1920s can be seen as the beginning of a new period of relatively high growth rather than a period of economic decline.[12]

The role of labour leaders began to change towards the end of our period. At the beginning of it they were prepared to contemplate direct confrontation with the government in order to maintain gains made during the war. The General Strike of 1926 was the ultimate expression of this policy. Labour leaders, too, believed that they could directly influence policy when the Labour party was in office: such ideas were severely disillusioned when the Labour government collapsed in 1931. Thereafter ideas of cooperation began to gain ground, and such men as Walter Citrine, general secretary of the Trades Union Congress, could expect to sit on government commissions, and even receive, as Citrine did in 1935, knighthoods. Citrine, in a way, was typical of the efficient labour bureaucrat, the counterpart of the managerial types coming to the fore on the employers' side. But the outstanding trade union leader throughout the entire period was the former elementary schoolboy, dockers' leader, and creator and general secretary of the Transport and General Workers Union, Ernest Bevin. It took the war crisis of 1940 to bring him directly into government.

The two big newspaper magnates of the period were Lord Rothermere and Lord Beaverbrook, who also had important

[12] Derek H. Aldcroft and Harry W. Richardson, *The British Economy 1870-1939* (London: Weidenfeld, 1969), p. 226.

interests in the British newsreel companies. Their newspapers played an important part in preserving the politically conservative character of large sections of the British public, but their attempts to intervene directly in politics were not successful. If we are looking for political influence we must turn to the limited circulation "quality press", in particular *The Observer* (weekly) and *The Times*, both in the thirties controlled by the Astor family (the first Lord Astor was an extremely wealthy American who became a naturalized British subject in 1899). The correspondence columns of *The Times* provided a valuable platform for influential figures on the fringes of politics, and in the thirties Geoffrey Dawson, editor of *The Times*, was an important influence behind the widespread acceptance in the political and social elite of the policies of appeasement. However, in my own view, if Chamberlain had been opposed to appeasement, I doubt if Dawson would have appeared to be anything like as influential. I would make a similar comment in regard to the group of top people who met at the Astor country residence, the so-called "Cliveden Set", who are sometimes said to have had a sinister influence over the British government's appeasement policies. University professors and administrators were not generally influential outside their own narrow sphere, nor were literary, artistic, or scientific figures (not even the popular novelist who had become very much part of the establishment, John Galsworthy). Individual members of All Souls College, Oxford (an exclusively graduate college) were sometimes influential in an advisory or completely unofficial behind-the-scenes role, but it would be quite wrong to think of the college as having a unified policy on anything (for example—again!—appeasement).[13] Sir William Beveridge, Director of the London School of Economics, was a rather exceptional university administrator, whose rise had been through the new Civil Service departments created to deal with Edwardian social reforms, and the war-time Civil Service: he was much in demand as a chairman of committees and commissions. The inter-war period was the period of the birth of broadcasting: it was partly in keeping with the ethos of British society, but partly also due to the remarkable influence of the Scottish Calvinistic Director-General of the British Broadcasting Corporation, Sir John Reith, that radio in Britain was a force, not of commercialisation, but on behalf of high cultural standards and decent respectability.

[13] See Alfred L. Rowse, *All Souls and Appeasement* (London: Macmillan, 1961).

Despite my remarks about the homogeneity of British society it was still true in the inter-war period that the actual reality of life for the British people could depend very much on the nature of local leadership. In general, in the county areas, the picture was one of the rule of local landed figures giving way to that of salaried officials,[14] yet in some districts feudal attitudes (and even conditions) remained remarkably persistent. In large towns and in the London boroughs the Labour Party had greater success in local elections than it had nationally, and so was often able to foster local social services in a way in which Conservative-dominated councils did not.

However the Second World War was to reveal starkly that local government in Labour as well as Conservative areas was often incompetent and too tolerant of vested interests. While in its upper levels the judiciary very much reflected, or rather exaggerated, the attitudes and prejudices of upper-class society, the bottom level, the one most affecting ordinary citizens, the magistracy was very much dominated by small-scale local businessmen and property owners.

Finally back to major issues of war and peace, as we turn to the British military elite. Since the major reforms of the nineteenth century the military elite had ceased to be, for all practical purposes, synonymous with the political elite—it was tending to develop into a caste of its own, more determined than any other section of society to maintain nineteenth century principles.

In the 1920s, during the swift regression of the army from a national saviour to a backwater, it was seen how relatively superficial had been the impact of the pre-war reforms and of the war itself on "the Duke of Cambridge's army"—on the mental climate that derived from the intensely regimental outlook of the British soldier. The old, never really extinguished, conception of soldiering re-asserted itself—a gentleman's occupation that married well with social and sporting life in the countryside—smartness on parade and stiff regimental etiquette and custom. Victory itself also led by the late 1920s to a bristling complacency about existing doctrine and systems. Owing to the small size of the army, there was a bottleneck in promotion, and senior veterans of the Great War succeeded one another at the top of the army, ever older as the years passed. By the middle of the 1930s the average age of the higher commanders was seven years older than in 1914.[15]

[14]See J. M. Lee, *Social Leaders and Public Persons* (Oxford: Oxford University Press, 1963).

[15]Corelli Barnett, *Britain and Her Army* (London: Allen Lane, 1970), p. 411.

The two men who argued vociferously for new strategic and tactical doctrines, and, above all, for mechanization of the army, were both forced out: B. H. Liddell Hart (with the rank of captain) in 1924; J. F. C. Fuller (with the rank of major-general) in 1933. In fact the Secretary for War after 1937, Leslie Hore-Belisha was, with the help of Liddell Hart, subsequently military correspondent for *The Times*, able to carry through reforms which did ensure that Britain entered the Second World War with the only army in the world that had completely substituted motor for horse transport.

Since she also had a reasonable air force, and the inestimable boon of radar, the stewardship of those who had guided her fortunes since the previous war cannot by any means be accounted a total failure. Hore-Belisha was shortly forced out of office by the military leaders, but (revealingly) this was probably as much because he was a Jew, and therefore socially unacceptable, as because of his reforms. That Britain was involved in war at all was certainly in part due to the muddled policies pursued by her political elite. Events, perhaps, were too big for the men who sought to control them. But we have seen that in their composition and recruitment British elites were by no means as inflexible as is sometimes maintained—though, of course, to really succeed throughout most of the period it was necessary to adopt the style and manners of the traditional leadership. Towards the end of our period, though, we can clearly see the managerial type emerging: Chamberlain, indeed, was strongest as an administrator, and Clement Attlee, the new leader of the Labour Party, was to reveal a positive genius for chairmanship. Attlee was upper-middle class, public-school, and Oxford-educated. The Labour Party, too, was, in many respects, becoming respectable.

One final, topical point. Despite gaining the vote in 1918 and having a number of other disabilities removed in the following years women were almost totally excluded from the main elite groups. Margaret Bondfield, Minister of Labour in MacDonald's second Labour government, was the only woman cabinet minister throughout the entire inter-war period. Effectively women who got married were excluded from a career in the Civil Service, and in fact no woman achieved a top Civil Service post. It is not the whole truth, but there is indeed much to be said for the view that Britain's history between 1918 and 1939, under an elite that too often looked backwards rather than forwards, was one of wasted resources and missed opportunities.

FOR FURTHER READING

Andrews, P. W. S., and Brunner, E. *Life of Lord Nuffield*. Oxford: Blackwell, 1955.

Astor, Michael. *Tribal Feeling*. London: John Murray, 1963.

Barker, Theodore C., Campbell, Roy, and Mathias, Peter. *Business History*. London: Historical Association, 1960.

Barnett, Correlli. *Britain and Her Army*. London: Allen Lane, 1970.

Beer, Samuel H. *Modern British Politics*. London: Faber, 1965.

Bishop, Thomas J. H. and Wilkinson, R. *Winchester and the Public School Elite*. London: Faber, 1967.

Blake, Robert. *The Conservative Party from Peel to Churchill*. London: Eyre and Spottiswoode, 1970.

Bolitho, Hector. *Alfred Mond*. London: Martin Secker, 1933.

Boyle, Andrew. *Montagu Norman*. London: Cassell, 1967.

Carr-Saunders, Sir Arthur M., and Carradog Jones, D. *A Survey of the Social Structure of England and Wales*. Oxford: Clarendon Press, 1937.

Cole, George D. H. *Studies in Class Structure*. London: Routledge & Kegan Paul, 1968.

Galsworthy, John. *A Modern Comedy*. London: Harrap, 1929.

Guttsman, William L. *The British Political Elite*. London: McGibbon & Kee, 1963.

Huxley, Aldous. *Point Counter Point*. London: Chatto & Windus, 1928.

James, Robert Rhodes, ed. *Memoirs of a Conservative: J. C. Davidson's Memoirs and Papers, 1910-1937*. London: Weidenfeld & Nicolson, 1969.

Jones, Thomas. *Whitehall Diary*, 3 vols., ed. Robert K. Middlemass. Oxford: Oxford University Press, 1969.

Kelsall, Robert K. *Higher Civil Servants in Britain*. London: Routledge, 1955.

Lee, J. M. *Social Leaders and Public Persons*. Oxford: Oxford University Press, 1963.

McEwen, John M. "The Coupon Election of 1918 and the Unionist Members of Parliament." *Journal of Modern History*, vol. 34, 1962, pp. 294-306.

Marwick, Arthur. *Britain in the Century of Total War: War, Peace and Social Change, 1900-1967*. London: The·Bodley Head, 1967.

Marwick, Arthur. *The Deluge: British Society and the First World War*. London: The Bodley Head, 1965.

Middlemass, Robert K. and Barnes, John. *Baldwin: A Biography*. London: Weidenfeld & Nicolson, 1969.

Mowat, Charles L. *Britain Between the Wars*. London: Methuen, 1955.

Ross, James F. S. *Parliamentary Representation*. London: Eyre and Spottiswoode, 1943.

Stanworth, Philip, and Giddens, Anthony. *Elites and Power in British Society*. Cambridge: Cambridge University Press, 1974.

Taylor, Alan J. P. *English History 1914-1945*. Oxford: Clarendon Press, 1965. 1965.

Watt, Donald C. *Personalities and Policies*. London: Longman, 1965.

Waugh, Evelyn. *A Handful of Dust*. London: Chapman & Hall, 1934.

Wilson, Charles. *The History of Unilever*, vol. 1. London: Cassell, 1954.

Wrench, John Evelyn. *Geoffrey Dawson and Our Times*. London: Hutchinson, 1955.

SOURCES

1

The Effects of the War
on the Conservative Party

It can be shown statistically that among new Conservative (called
Unionists at this time) members elected in the 1918 General
Election there was a strong swing away from landed towards
business interests.

SOURCE: John M. McEwen, "The Coupon Election of 1918 and
Unionist Members of Parliament," *Journal of Modern History*
34(1962):302. Reprinted by permission of the University of
Chicago Press.

UNIONIST M.P.s 1919

	Old Members	New Members	Total	Per Cent
Land	45	12	57	15
Services	34	24	58	15
Professions	67	51	118	31
Business	68	81	149	39
Total	214	168	382	100

2

Public Schools and the Political Elite

British cabinets were largely recruited from that social class which
had its education at the so-called public schools (private preparatory schools), though the pattern was changing slightly over the
inter-war period.

SOURCE: Reprinted by permission of Faber and Faber Ltd. from
Winchester and the Public School Elite by Thomas J. H. Bishop
and R. Wilkinson, 1967, p. 37.

SCHOOLS ATTENDED BY CABINET MINISTERS OF ALL PARTIES
1886-1916 AND 1917-1936

Category of School	SOCIAL ORIGIN						Total	
	Aristo-cratic		Middle Class		Working Class			
	1886-1916	1917-1936	1886-1916	1917-1936	1886-1916	1917-1936	1886-1916	1917-1936
9 Clarendon Schools (7 represented by Cabinet Ministers)								
Eton	30	15	5	0	0	0	35	15
Harrow	10	4	3	6	0	0	13	10
Winchester	2	1	0	3	0	0	2	4
Rugby	1	0	5	5	0	0	6	5
Charterhouse	0	0	0	1	0	0	0	1
Shrewsbury	0	0	1	0	0	0	1	0
Westminster	0	0	0	0	0	0	0	0
M. Taylors'	0	0	0	1	0	0	0	1
St. Paul's	0	0	0	0	0	0	0	0
17 other 'most ex-pensive' Public Schools (4 rep. by Cabinet Ministers)								
Cheltenham	0	0	2	3	0	0	2	3

Category of School	SOCIAL ORIGIN						Total	
	Aristo-cratic		Middle Class		Working Class		Total	
	1886-1916	1917-1936	1886-1916	1917-1936	1886-1916	1917-1936	1886-1916	1917 1936
Marlborough	0	0	0	1	0	0	0	1
Mill Hill	0	0	1	0	0	0	1	0
Repton	0	0	0	1	0	0	0	1
Other Public Schools H.M.C. approx. 170 (8 represented)	2	1	7	5	0	0	9	6
Private Secondary	4	1	6	1	0	0	10	2
Grammar	0	0	10	23	0	4	10	27
Other U.K. Secondary	0	1	6	5	0	3	6	9
Elementary only	0	0	1	0	2	15	3	15
Aboard or no Information	0	2	3	5	0	0	3	7
TOTAL	49	25	50	60	2	22	101	07

3

Recruitment to the Civil Service

The higher Civil Service covers the ranks of Secretary, Deputy Secretary, Under Secretary, Permanent Assistant Secretary, and Assistant Secretary. Recruitment was largely by open competition, which greatly favoured those with public school and Oxbridge backgrounds.

SOURCE: Robert K. Kelsall, *Higher Civil Servants in Britain* (London: Routledge & Kegan Paul Ltd; New Jersey, Humanities Press, Inc., 1955), p. 16. Reprinted by permission.

ROUTES OF ORIGINAL ENTRY TO THE ADMINISTRATIVE CLASS
OF THOSE HOLDING CERTAIN RANKS IN 1929, 1939 AND 1950

Date and Rank	By Administrative Class open competition (including post-1918 reconstruction competitions)		By other forms of direct entry from outside				By Transfer from other Branches and Services Foreign, Diplomatic, Colonial, Irish, Indian C.S., etc.		Professional, Scientific, and Technical		By Promotion from the Ranks		All Routes (the number of women included in each total is shown in brackets)
			1939 and before		Since 1939 (Wartime entrants)								
	No.	%	No.	%	No.	%	No.	%	No.	%	No.	%	No.
1929:													
S. and D.S.	26	60.5	7	16.3	—	—	2	4.6	4	9.3	4	9.3	43 (0)
U.S. and P.A.S.	45	57.7	14	18.0	—	—	3	3.8	5	6.4	11	14.1	78 (2)
A.S.	96	54.8	22	12.6	—	—	4	2.3	18	10.3	35	20.0	175 (1)
All of the rank of A.S. and above	167	56.4	43	14.5	—	—	9	3.1	27	9.1	50	16.9	296 (3)
1939:													
S. and D.S.	35	64.8	11	20.4	—	—	—	—	3	5.6	5	9.2	54 (0)
U.S. and P.A.S.	78	62.4	12	9.6	—	—	3	2.4	8	6.4	24	19.2	125 (1)
A.S.	161	54.8	32	10.9	—	—	4	1.4	29	9.8	68	23.1	294 (2)
All of the rank of A.S. and above	274	57.9	55	11.6	—	—	7	1.5	40	8.5	97	20.5	473 (3)
1950:													
S. and D.S.	71	74.0	6	6.2	2	2.1	—	—	3	3.1	14	14.6	96 (1)
U.S. and P.S.A.	139	58.9	7	3.0	15	6.4	2	0.8	9	3.8	64	27.1	236 (5)
A.S.	246	34.5	14	2.0	101	14.2	11	1.5	44	6.2	297	41.6	713 (23)
All of the rank of A.S. and above	456	43.6	27	2.6	118	11.3	13	1.2	56	5.4	375	35.9	1045 (29)

4

Two Political Leaders

Stanley Baldwin was Conservative leader for the major part of the inter-war period. Ramsay MacDonald was Prime Minister of the first ever Labour government, though he then became Prime Minister of what was essentially a Conservative 'National' government.

SOURCE: *Dictionary of National Biography 1941-50* (Oxford: Oxford University Press, 1959), p. 43 (Thomas Jones on Stanley Baldwin) and *Dictionary of National Biography 1931-40* (Oxford: Oxford University Press, 1949), pp. 562-564 (Elton on Ramsay MacDonald). By permission of The Clarendon Press, Oxford.

BALDWIN, STANLEY, first EARL BALDWIN OF BEWDLEY (1867-1947), statesman and three times prime minister, was born at Lower Park, Bewdley, 3 August 1867, the only son of Alfred and Louisa Baldwin. His father's folk had been for centuries Shropshire yeomen who had settled as ironmasters within the Worcestershire border. Alfred Baldwin was the head of an old-fashioned business of patriarchal type, a model employer. Among his ancestors were country parsons and Quaker missionaries to the American colonies. Louisa, Stanley Baldwin's mother, was one of the remarkable children of the Rev. George Browne Macdonald, a Wesleyan minister of Highland stock who settled in Northern Ireland after the 'forty-five' and came under the influence of John Wesley. Macdonald married Hannah Jones, of Manchester, but Welsh from the vale of Clwyd. They had two sons and five daughters who survived infancy. Louisa's eldest sister Alice was the mother of Rudyard Kipling; Georgiana was the wife of Sir Edward Burne Jones; Agnes of Sir Edward Poynter [q.v.]

Stanley, an only child, was left much to himself and found his sustenance in the novels of Scott, the *Morte d'Arthur,* the *Pilgrim's Progress,* and the Lamb's *Tales from Shakespeare.* He was sent to Hawtrey's preparatory school, then in 1881 to Harrow, and in 1885 to Trinity College, Cambridge, where he was placed in the third class in the historical tripos in 1888. He entered the family business and (apart from a visit to the United States, significantly at a time when McKinley was running on the protectionist "ticket") for four years, until his marriage, he lived at home at Wilden where his father had built a church, a school, and a vicarage. He learnt to know every man in the works, became a parish and county councillor, a magistrate, and a member of the Oddfellows' and the Foresters' friendly societies. A farm was attached to the works and he learned about pigs and cows. His experience in industry was of a phase which was passing swiftly. "It was the last survivor of that type of works, and ultimately became swallowed up in one of those great combinations." In 1892 he married Lucy, the eldest daughter of Edward Lucas Jenks Ridsdale, of Rottingdean, a former assay master of the Mint. Three sons (the first stillborn) and four daughters were born to them.

•   •   •   •   •

MacDONALD, JAMES RAMSAY (1866-1937), labour leader and states-man, was born in a two-roomed 'but and ben' at Lossiemouth, Morayshire, a grey, lowland village of fishermen and farmworkers in the parish of Drainie, within a few hours' walk of the Highlands, 12 October 1866. Isabella Ramsay, his grandmother, a woman of exceptional courage and character, had successfully reared her four young children after being left penniless by an absconding husband. Of these, the youngest, Ann, said to have been the most intelligent of the family, when working at a farm in the parish of Alves, near Elgin, became with child by the head ploughman, John MacDonald, a Highlander from the Black Isle of Ross. She did not marry, and her son was born in her mother's cottage. The peculiar circumstances of MacDonald's childhood may well have accounted for the unusual later combination of mental toughness, physical courage, and extreme sensitiveness in his charac-ter.

At Drainie school, where the fees were eightpence a month, the boy studied Euclid and the ancient tongues, and devoured such books as were available in his grandmother's cottage or were lent him by a consumptive watchmaker, who introduced him to the works of Dickens. Before he was fifteen he was head of the school. For a short while, after leaving, he worked on a farm, but when he was about sixteen the 'dominie' of Drainie invited him to become a pupil teacher, at seven pounds ten shillings a year. With the free run of the 'dominie's' shelves he made the acquaintance of Shakespeare, of Carlyle's tory socialism, Ruskin's socialist aesthetics, and Henry George's then extremely influential *Progress and Poverty*. Although he was funda-mentally of a religious turn of mind, with an unfailing reverence for what he called 'the grand, crowned authority of life', an obstinate streak of ra-tionalism combined with that instinct of the insurgent, which sprang perhaps from his fatherless childhood, to prevent any of the rival Scottish orthodoxies from gaining his allegiance.

In 1885, at the age of eighteen, MacDonald obtained employment in Bristol from a clergyman who was inaugurating a boys' and young men's guild there. Chance thus brought him to what was at that time almost the only English city in which there was some nucleus of socialist activity. This was a branch of the Social Democratic Federation, founded in 1881 as the

Democratic Federation by H. M. Hyndman [q.v.], which professed those Marxian doctrines which MacDonald was to spend so much of his later life in combating. He joined the branch, and took his share in its members' persistent but unsuccessful efforts at outdoor evangelism. Meanwhile he became an enthusiastic geologist, and spent on books money which should have gone on food and clothes. Before the end of the year, however, he had returned to Lossiemouth with the few pounds which he had contrived to save, and the resolve that, when he next left home, he would return successful, or not return at all.

A few months later MacDonald went south again, this time to London. The post which he had hoped to obtain was filled a day before his arrival, and for a while he nearly starved, tramping the city in search of work and living mainly on oatmeal sent from home—for which he scrupulously paid—and hot water. He is said to have found employment on the very day on which his last shilling was spent—the addressing of envelopes, at ten shillings a week, for the newly formed Cyclists' Touring Club. A little later, as an invoice clerk in a warehouse at fifteen shillings, he 'lived like a fighting-cock', helped his mother, paid fees at the Birkbeck Institute and other places of education, and saved money into the bargain. In later life he seldom spoke of these early struggles, but they certainly coloured his political creed and reinforced the belief, which he sometimes afterwards expressed, in the power of extreme poverty to breed 'the aristocratic virtues'. Before long, however, thanks to underfeeding and overwork—he was spending every spare moment on reading science—his health broke down completely and he was compelled to return home.

By 1888 MacDonald was back in London, and, after another period of unemployment, was fortunate enough to be chosen as private secretary to Thomas Lough, Gladstonian parliamentary candidate for West Islington, with whom he remained until 1891. Thus for the first time he came into contact with the politically minded middle class. He was still speaking at open-air meetings for the Social Democratic Federation, and in 1887 he was present in Trafalgar Square on the celebrated 'Bloody Sunday' (13 November). But, what was far more significant, in 1886 he joined the Fabian Society. Conscious that by now 'almost all organisations contain elements making for Socialism' this body had set its face, almost from the first, against 'revolutionary heroics', and concentrated upon conciliating and harnessing, instead of antagonizing, the latent forces of the age as did the social democrats. MacDonald found its middle class and eminently practical environment a novel and congenial atmosphere. In particular the Fabians had wisely resolved to eschew all the distracting shibboleths of those vague idealists, so prominent in the 'eighties and 'nineties, who were ready to embrace any cult, from vegetarianism to bimetallism, provided that it was labelled 'progressive'. MacDonald was never a crank.

Nevertheless, the Fabians were scarcely more qualified than the Social Democratic Federation to convert the man in the street, and it was not until 1893, with the foundation of the independent labour party, that there appeared a body capable both of fusing the working class, skilled and unskilled, into political unity, and of popularizing socialist doctrines. It stood both for independent labour representation as against alliance with one or other of the traditional parties, and for socialism. Of both aims, MacDonald wholly approved and in 1894 he applied for membership in a personal letter to Keir Hardie. At the general election of 1895 he stood as independent labour party candidate for Southampton, polling only 886 votes. At this time he was earning a slender income by journalism, and it is remarkable evidence of the resolute process of self-education upon which he had embarked that he should have been invited to contribute a considerable number of articles to this Dictionary.

In the following year MacDonald married Margaret Ethel, daughter of John Hall Gladstone, F.R.S., of Pembridge Square, London, and a great-niece of Lord Kelvin [q.v.]. Her father was both a distinguished scientist and an active social and religious worker—he was one of the founders of the Young Men's Christian Association—and Margaret Gladstone had been attracted to socialism through her own social work in Hoxton and elsewhere. The marriage opened a new life for MacDonald. Not only did it mean financial independence, but the influence of his wife began insensibly to colour his own views. 'She saw spirit in everything', he wrote of her after her death; and thenceforth the faint streak of rationalism seems to fade out of him, and he was carried yet farther from the bleak materialism of Marx. Margaret MacDonald also possessed a genius for friendship which MacDonald himself had always lacked, and she made their new home at 3 Lincoln's Inn Fields the centre of a wide circle of friends. Here their six children were born, and despite the unceasing public activities of both parents their family life was exceptionally happy and united. The next few years were filled with expanding activities. There was foreign travel, which marriage had made possible, and for which MacDonald retained a passion to the end of his life. There were the regular gatherings in his home of labour and socialist protagonists, and friends and well-wishers from overseas. Moreover, in 1900 MacDonald had become secretary of the labour representation committee, the germ of the labour party: he held the post until 1912, and was treasurer from 1912 to 1924. Since 1896 he had been a member of the national administrative council of the independent labour party (where he was regarded as markedly cautious), and from 1894 to 1900 he served on the executive committee of the Fabian Society (which considered him a dangerous intransigent). From 1901 to 1904 he represented Central Finsbury on the London County Council. The acquisition through his marriage of an upper-middle-class social background undoubtedly accelerated MacDonald's rise to prominence in the labour movement. It was, for example, a strong recommendation for his secretaryship of the labour representation committee that he was not dependent upon the trade unions for an income.

With Hardie, MacDonald drafted the resolution by which in 1899 the Trades Union Congress convened a special congress to devise plans for returning more labour members to the next parliament. He was largely responsible for next year's decision representing a compromise between the traditional liberal-labourism of the Trades Union Congress and the class-war socialism of the Social Democratic Federation—to set up the labour representation committee, which in 1906 became the labour party. He had taken an active part in the resistance to the South African war, and his *What I Saw in South Africa* (1903) was based upon a journey undertaken with his wife on the morrow of the peace. More significant was *Socialism and Society* (1905), the whole argument of which is characteristically based upon the analogy between politics and biology. Not unnaturally this book rejects, as antiquated, Marxism and the doctrine of the class war, 'on the threshold of scientific sociology but hardly across it'. At the general election of 1906 he was returned for Leicester, which he had unsuccessfully contested in 1900. All but five of the twenty-nine successful labour representation committee candidates, and MacDonald among them, owed their success to an electoral arrangement made with the liberals, a fact which goes far to explain labour political strategy during the next few years. The new party was bound to support the liberals because the liberals were now about to establish the new system of social insurance, which was sound collectivist doctrine, but it was also bound to support them because it owed most of its own seats to liberal complaisance.

From the first MacDonald attended regularly, and spoke frequently, in the House of Commons, and at once established his reptuation; 'a born parliamentarian' was Lord Balfour's subsequent verdict. In public as in private life there was an impenetrable hinterland in MacDonald; it would often be his strength, and sometimes his weakness, that in a sense he was always a man of mystery.

5

A Top Industrial Leader

Balfour was essentially a self-made figure, who became very influential in the councils of government in the inter-war period. His advice was always very much in favour of economic orthodoxy.

SOURCE: *Dictionary of National Biography 1951-60* (Oxford: Oxford University Press, 1971), pp. 56-57 (Mary Walton on Arthur Balfour). By permission of The Clarendon Press, Oxford.

BALFOUR, ARTHUR, first BARON RIVERDALE (1873-1957), industrialist, was, by his own account, born in London 9 January 1873, the elder of the two sons of Herbert Balfour. The birth was not registered. He finished his education in 1887-9 at Ashville College, Harrogate, and was afterwards employed in the office of Seebohm and Dieckstahl, of Sheffield, a firm which sold crucible steel all over Europe. Balfour went to the United States for a few years to enlarge his experience, and did well; he thus began early the interest in overseas trade for which he and his firm became famous. He returned to Sheffield in 1897, and in 1899, when the firm became a limited company, he was appointed managing director, taking over also the work of local vice-consul for Denmark. In the same year Balfour married Frances Josephine (died 1960), a daughter of Charles Henry Bingham, a partner in the silver and electroplating firm of Walker and Hall. He chose a world tour for his honeymoon, opening new branches for his firm.

The company was then a considerable producer of rifles, interested in obtaining overseas markets for rifle parts steels; but at this time it was one of the first two in Sheffield to develop high speed steel, and in 1901 Balfour negotiated with American researchers to launch this product. The company prospered, establishing a research laboratory in 1905 and selling in the United States considerable quantities of tool steels. The engineers' tool department established in 1910 became the most considerable of the company's activities. The name of the firm was changed in 1915 to Arthur Balfour & Co., Ltd.

From 1911 when he was the master cutler, honours and interests came to Balfour yearly. He chaired a committee to deal with the new national insurance in Sheffield in 1912; he was a member of the royal commission on railways in 1913, and in 1914 became a member of the advisory committee on war munitions and of the industry advisory committee to the Treasury, on which he served until 1918. In 1915 he was made consul for Belgium, and undertook much work for the 9,000 Belgians who were given asylum in his district. He was a member of the manpower committee, the Advisory Council for Scientific and Industrial Research (of which he was chairman in 1937-46), the engineering industries committee, and the committee on commercial and industrial policy after the war under Lord Balfour of Burleigh [q.v.]. On a visit to Italy he had a long talk on the prospect of her entry into the war with the prime minister, Salandra, who thought his country unable to stand a long war. Only Great Britain, he remarked, could go to war for a right and just cause and stay in the war to the end.

During the period of reconstruction Balfour served on the coal industry commission (1919) and the therm charges committee (1922-3), and on the advisory councils of the Post Office, the Board of Trade, and the Department of Overseas Trade, as well as on the safeguarding of industries permanent panel. He was British delegate to the international conference on customs and other formalities in 1923. In the same year he was appointed K.B.D. and was a member of the government committee appointed to draw up the agenda for the Imperial Conference.

He was chairman, appointed in 1924, of the industry and trade commission which produced its important reports in six volumes up to 1929. He was a British delegate in preparing for and at the League of Nations economic conference of 1927. And in October 1930, as a member of the Economic Advisory Council, he wrote to the prime minister prophesying the severity of the approaching 'slump' in terms which shook both the Cabinet and the King, who considered him 'of almost unique experience'. An address which he gave to a meeting of business men in Sheffield in 1932 outlined his recipe for recovery; he was a shrewd if orthodox economist, with staunch faith in retrenchment and a wholesome hatred of inflation. In this, as in many spheres, his personal opinions were those which so often go with the political temperament of the Conservative.

He continued to serve, often as chairman, on innumerable committees and advisory bodies right up to the threshold of war. His last direct service to the Government was to lead the commission which went to Canada in 1939 to negotiate the scheme for training Royal Air Force pilots there, a difficult assignment successfully carried out. In 1942 he was promoted G.B.E. He had been created a baronet in 1929, and raised to the peerage as Baron Riverdale, of Sheffield, in 1935. He took the title from his home, Riverdale Grange, on the wooded slopes of western Sheffield. In 1921 he had headed a deputation to the United States on behalf of Sheffield firms to put their case to the Senate finance committee against certain sections of the Fordney tariff, and was instrumental in obtaining some modifications. In the midst of all the travel and work of national importance during the thirty years when he was a favourite of successive Governments, this energetic man was chairman and managing director of Arthur Balfour & Co., Ltd., of C. Meadows & Co., Sheffield, and of High Speed Alloys, Ltd., of Widnes, and a director of six other companies, besides serving on several Sheffield trade bodies, as a justice of the peace, and, for a short time, on the city council. In the words of another Sheffield business man: 'He was a great Sheffielder, and was always pushing Sheffield.' The university of Sheffield conferred on him the honorary degree of LL.D. in 1934.

Riverdale was continuously successful in promoting overseas trade both in his own business and as a national policy; he was a colleague of every economic expert of his day; but the reason why he achieved a general reputation as a necessary source of advice is not for brief description. He had a firm grasp of fact and a direct and courageous line of thought and conduct. He was always interested in the matter in hand and not in its effect on himself. He never consciously sought honours, and only incidentally sought wealth. He has been described as 'a big man, without conceit, willing to listen to humbler men' and 'a man of outstanding mental ability'. This ability was not of the intellectual order; it was a matter of practical grasp and judgement. He never put things off; he never took the easy things first. Added to boundless health and energy, these gifts enabled him to get through far more than a lifetime's work and to take more right decisions than would seem possible at such a speed of working.

Personally he was a jovial man, who loved fun, lived simply, and was easy and affectionate with his family. He died in Sheffield 7 July 1957, and was cremated.

6

The State of the Landed Aristocracy, 1922

Though unsuccessful as a Liberal politician, C. F. G. Masterman was a shrewd, if rather impressionistic social commentator. If his account is slightly exaggerated, it remains true that the position of the landed aristocracy was very seriously affected by the First World War.

SOURCE: C. F. G. Masterman, *England After the War* (London: Hodder, 1922), pp. 32-36. Reprinted by permission of the Estate of C. F. G. Masterman.

ENGLAND AFTER THE WAR

There is taking place the greatest change which has ever occurred in the history of the land of England since the days of the Norman Conquest: with the possible exception of the gigantic robberies of the Reformation. It is being effected, not by direct confiscation, but by enormous taxation, which is destroying the whole Feudal system as it extended practically but little changed from 1066 to 1914. Until now the land-owning class has always been able to absorb the intruders which came in with great wealth to obtain the prestige and amenities which belonged to ownership of great estates. Thus, in the eighteenth century, England saw the "nabobs," who had plundered India, purchase or build great country houses, with acres which gave them possession of the tenants, the labourers, and of many seats in Parliament. Later came the wealth of the Sugar Islands. And then the big manufacturers and traders commenced to see how they could obtain enjoyment, bought titles, and renovated bankrupt estates, and passed from allegiance to Nonconformity into the broad bosom of the Church of England. A courageous attempt to shore up the old system was made by the American marriages, in which the daughters of transatlantic millionaires were married to the heirs or owners of historic titles; and the marriage *dots* provided for the maintenance of unproductive estates. Then came the sudden influx of the South African gold mines, which threw the balance on the other side. And you would find in the remote countryside, in historic houses containing chapels with the tombs of Crusaders, men "with names like Rhenish wines" entertaining queer companies of appropriate friends.

Yet this tough old English landed system swallowed them all up, and compelled them to conform to its demands. In the second generation even the very names had been modified to those familiar in British rural life. The politics became Feudal, the religion State and Anglican, the attitude towards the tenants one of careless generosity, the attitude of the tenants one of respectful flattery, the attitude of the landless labourers one of acquiescence in an existence of semi-starvation in life sustained below the limits of decent existence, qualified by the flight of all the young men and women to the towns. In return for all the money spent on improvements and sport and noneconomic rents (for practically all the estates in Southern England were supported by incomes derived from outside), all that villages and farmers were asked to do was to vote for the nominee of their owners at infrequent elections, local or national; and most of them were very content to make the exchange, counting an infrequent vote as but of little importance in comparison with social comfort and liberal repairs, and the remission of rent in hard times. The system might have continued until the last aged labourer had been borne to his rest, and no one was left to till and dig and harvest the produce. But, with the most patriotic support to the Government in the great challenge of 1914, the Feudal system vanished in blood and fire, and the landed classes were consumed.

For it is impossible to imagine, in the vast changes now taking place, that much which is left of the old landed system will be able to assimilate the new owners. I have been unable, from Government or private returns, to obtain exact figures of this amazing transformation. But I note that in one year one firm of auctioneers declare that they have disposed of the area of an English county. I note that sales are being announced every day in the newspapers, of an average of perhaps half a dozen of greater or lesser historic country houses, and of estates running into many thousands of acres.[1] And wherever I have visited, up and down Southern England, I have come upon visible evidence of this transformation. The smaller squires went first, almost unnoticed, and with only occasional bitter complaint at passing from the homes of their ancestors to the suburbs or dingy flats of London or the villas of the salubrious watering-places. Then came the outraged cry of the owners of large historic estates, proclaiming that with the burden of income-tax and super-tax, and the fall in the value of securities, and the rise in the price of all estate necessities, they also would be compelled to relinquish the gigantic castles and houses which had been the pride of the countryside for hundreds of

---

[1] In one single page of the *Times* (I quote from the *Nation*) I find the following pieces of England offered for sale: Ingmire Hall, on a Northern Yorkshire border, castellated manor house, early sixteenth century, 5000 acres; Slains Castle and Longhaven in Aberdeenshire, 7700 acres; Hawkstone in Shropshire, 1285 acres; Glenfinart in Argyllshire, 7356 acres; Hamilton, 30,744 acres; Llanarmon Towers, twenty-three farms; Claremont in Surrey, which Clive built, 502 acres; Holmes Lacy in Herefordshire, 343 acres; Crawfurdton, Dumfriesshire, 3940 acres; Sudbourne Hall in Suffolk, 7650 acres; Oxford Castle in Suffolk, a large part of the village of Oxford and twenty farms; Colworth in Bedfordshire, 2300 acres; North Berwick estate in East Lothian, with ruins of Tantallon Castle, 2500 acres; Cassiobury Park, 370 acres, in Essex.

years. Their property perished in battle, no less than their children. They are not yet conscious of what has happened. They believe, many of them, that by borrowings and economies for a few years, better times will come with a return to something like "normal" conditions. But there are no "normal" conditions possible for them, for at least their generation, if not for ever. Their method of life has vanished as completely as that of the French Nobility after the march of the Revolution. Some new families may be founded by some rich men. But the greater number of these houses will become as the Châteaux and Castles of the Loire or the Indre; Chambord, a monstrous dead skeleton all cold and empty where once feasted and revelled beautiful women and gallent men; Blois, where Guise was murdered; Chenonceaux, built over a river; Langeis, an unchanged mediaeval fortress, a visiting place for tourists; Amboise, where once they drowned the Huguenots, now the home of a few old pensioners, supported by the charity of the Duc d'Orléans. Already the discussion has ceased to be academic. What use can the places be put to if no one can live in them: schools, centres for aerodromes, or convalescent homes for ex-soldiers or tuberculous children? Some of the smaller and less unwieldy are already turning into a kind of boarding-house, holding several families. One can even conceive of the adoption of methods which have frequently been put into force in other countries, and these gigantic castles being used as quarrying ground for constructing cottage homes for the poor. Half Rome and many of the great cities of Italy have been built literally from the stones of the buildings which were the glories of the Roman Empire. Such a fate—noble or ignoble—may await in these coming generations the historic houses of Britain.

There may be those who can rise to some sense of satisfaction, even at a transformation which has ejected them from the homes of their ancestors. After all, they have given property while others have given lives for the saving of England in a dark hour. They may feel pride in the thought that such houses may be used for beneficent purposes by the community long after they are dead, and neither destroyed nor put to some mean purpose. This is what they have "given" in the "Great War"—given, while other men have received increased wealth and emoluments by sharp contracts for munitions with a Government Department lax in cutting prices so long as the goods could be delivered speedily. The old generation passes with its children: the best of these children dead, the very type of its method of life, maintained for so long, vanished for ever.

Heine before his death confronted the future with dark forebodings, thinking it belonged to the Communists. "I can think only with fear and horror," he confessed, "of the time when these dark iconoclasts will have gained power. . . . They will tear from the soil of the social order the lilies that toil not nor spin, and are as wondrously arrayed as King Solomon in all his glory. . . . And my *Book of Songs* will be used by the grocer to make the little paper bags with which he will wrap up coffee or snuff for the old women of the future." At first he is filled with fury at the thought. Then reason prevails. "I cry aloud: 'It has been judged and condemned for long, the old social order, let it meet its due! Let it be destroyed, the old world, where cynicism flourished and man was exploited by man! Let them be utterly destroyed, the whited sepulchres where lies and injustice dwelt. And blessed be the grocer who one day will make paper bags of my poems, and will wrap up in them coffee and snuff for the poor, honest, old men who in our unjust world of to-day have perhaps to do without these pleasures.—*Fiat Justitia, pereat mundus.*' "

7

A Leading Liberal Businessman Joins the Conservatives, 1926

Sir Alfred Mond, an architect of I.C.I., was one of the most influential businessmen of his day. It was characteristic of the waning influence of the Liberal Party over the social and economic elite, that he should forsake it for the Conservatives.

SOURCE: Hector Bolitho, *Alfred Mond* (London: Martin Secker, 1933), pp. 271-273. Reprinted by permission of Martin Secker & Warburg, Ltd.

LETTER FROM SIR ALFRED MOND TO LORD OXFORD AND ASQUITH, 23RD JANUARY 1926

My dear Lord Oxford and Asquith,

The position of the Liberal Party has been steadily drifting from bad to worse. The unity which we have striven for, and which I did my best to promote, has in fact never been achieved and all efforts to revivify and reorganise the Liberal forces have been rendered hopeless by the introduction by Mr. Lloyd George of a Land Policy which has produced a new, profound cleavage and embarrassment in the Liberal ranks. I had hoped that when the compromise with the Liberal and Radical Candidates' Association had been reached, we had at any rate attained some measure of agreement, even if I felt that I must insist upon altering the proposals in the direction of the extension of freehold ownership. The resolution which the National Liberal Federation Executive is submitting to the Land Convention is so framed that it revives the original policy of the nationalisation of agricultural land as first advocated in the Land Report. To this policy in any shape or form I am absolutely and unalterably opposed, and the fact that it is being put forward by the chief Liberal organisation, apparently with your consent, proves to me how divergent my views are on this fundamental question of principle from those of a large and influential section of the party. It has become absolutely clear to me that this is a fundamental issue of principle and not of detail, which no attempted compromise can overcome or disguise. I have, however, no desire to be a source of fresh difficulties or divisions in the Party or to be engaged in controversy within its ranks. I have therefore, after the most careful consideration, decided that the only course for me to take is to sever my lifelong connection with the Liberal Party and, if I am to be able to render any further political service to the country, join the party with whom I feel I can most usefully co-operate, the Conservative Party. That such a step is a big break and wrench for me I need hardly assure you. I have passed all my life in the Liberal ranks, most of it under your leadership. I have done my best through its medium to render such services as I could to my country, and I had hoped it might be possible still to find a useful field of activity and influence in its ranks. But I find this impossible under the circumstances created and I prefer to be an open opponent than an internal dissentient. I shall, of course, after writing this letter, no longer consider myself a member of the Liberal Party, and shall take, in due course, the necessary steps resulting from my decision.

May I say that I cannot close this letter without expressing my thanks to you for all the personal kindness and help to me in all the many years of our political association.

Yours sincerely,
Alfred Mond

8

The Weaknesses of Lancashire's
Business Leaders, 1926

John Maynard Keynes was severely critical of many aspects of the
country's economic leadership. The criticisms made in this article
were strenuously denied by the Lancashire business leaders, and
by the local press.

SOURCE: *The Nation*, 13th November 1926, vol. XL, no. 6, p.
210. Reprinted by permission.

THE POSITION OF THE LANCASHIRE COTTON TRADE

Lancashire's first need is to face these figures. If they are substantially
correct, the termination of the short-time policy is urgently called for, and
the substitution for it of a "rationalizing" process designed to cut down
overhead costs by the amalgamation, grouping or elimination of mills. The
failure so far to eliminate weak mills is largely attributable to the banks, who
have been too ready to protect old loans by new ones. There are said to be
two hundred Lancashire mills on an unsound financial basis. It may be that
only the bankers of Lancashire are in a position to take the first step to break
down the ill-organized individualism which was well enough for an ever-
expanding industry, but spells universal loss when some curtailment is
necessary.

As it happens, Lancashire has just had a great stroke of luck, which may
make a revision of policy much easier than it would otherwise have been.
Owing to a cotton crop in the United States which has broken all records, raw
cotton has suffered a catastrophic fall of price. It costs today about
two-thirds of what it cost a year ago, although the price then was already
moderate on post-war standards. It will be paradoxical if this fall of price
does not stimulate consumption considerably. The cotton trade of the world
is justified in expecting an increased turn-over during the next year or two.
Now since the unoccupied spindles outside Lancashire do not amount to any
formidable figure, Lancashire can rely on obtaining a fair proportion of this
coming year's additional business, in spite of her costs being above those of
her competitors. Thus a fortunate accident has given her a breathing-space in
which to reorganize her affairs.

But it will only be a breathing-space, which it would be imprudent to treat otherwise. The danger is lest Lancashire may consider the revival of trade, when it comes, to be a justification of her past policy, and as a return of the "normal" times for which she has been waiting so long. But in truth the times will not be normal. There will be a temporary recovery based on raw cotton well below the cost of production, and on the time-lag, before cheaper producers can increase their spindleage. Present prices for raw cotton will not last for long; nor will the present limitations on spindleage elsewhere.

The mishandling of currency and credit by the bank of England since the war, the stiff-neckedness of the coal owners, the apparently suicidal behaviour of the leaders of Lancashire raise a question of the suitability and adaptability of our Business Men to the modern age of mingled progress and retrogression. What has happened to them—the class in which a generation or two generations ago we could take a just and worthy pride? Are they too old or too obstinate? Or what? Is it that too many of them have risen not on their own legs, but on the shoulders of their fathers and grandfathers? Of the coal owners all these suggestions may be true. But what of our Lancashire lads, England's pride for shrewdness? What have they to say for themselves?

9

The Smart Set and an Outsider, 1928

Aldous Huxley was himself a member of the highly-cultured Huxley family and very familiar with the smart upper-class life which he satirised in his novels of the 1920s. The aristocratic eccentric dabbling in science had a respectable ancestry; the position of the lower-class laboratory assistant, Illidge, is sketched here.

SOURCE: From pp. 30-34, *Point Counter Point* (hardbound edition) by Aldous Huxley. Copyright, 1928, 1956 by Aldous Huxley. By permission of Harper & Row, Publishers, Inc. (pp. 43-47 in the 1928 London edition. By permission of Chatto & Windus, Ltd. and Mrs. Laura Huxley.)

"There" said Lord Edward at last and straightened himself up as far as his rheumatically bent back would allow him. "I think that's all right, don't you?"

Illidge nodded. "Perfectly all right," he said in an accent that had certainly not been formed in any of the ancient and expensive seats of learning. It hinted of Lancashire origins. He was a small man, with a boyish-looking freckled face and red hair. . . .

Lord Edward filled his pipe. "Tail becomes leg," he said meditatively. "What's the mechanism? Chemical peculiarities in the neighbouring. . .? It can't obviously be the blood. Or do you suppose it has something to do with the electric tension? It does vary, of course, in different parts of the body. Though why we don't all just vaguely proliferate like cancers . . . Growing in a definite shape is very unlikely when you come to think of it. Very mysterious and. . ." His voice trailed off into a deep and husky murmur.

Illidge listened disapprovingly. When the Old Man started off like this about the major and fundamental problems of biology, you never knew where he'd be getting to. Why, as likely as not he'd begin talking about God. It really made one blush. He was determined to prevent anything so discreditable happening this time. "The next step with these newts," he said in his most briskly practical tone, "is to tinker with the nervous system and see whether that has any influence on the grafts. Suppose, for example, we excised a piece of the spine . . ."

But Lord Edward was not listening to his assistant. He had taken his pipe out of his mouth, he had lifted his head and at the same time slightly cocked it on one side. He was frowning, as though making an effort to seize and remember something. He raised his hand in a gesture that commanded silence; Illidge interrupted himself in the middle of his sentence and also listened. A pattern of melody faintly traced itself upon the silence.

"Bach?" said Lord Edward in a whisper.

Pongileoni's blowing and the scraping of the anonymous fiddlers had shaken the air in the great hall, had set the glass of the windows looking on to it vibrating; and this in turn had shaken the air in Lord Edward's apartment on the further side. The shaking air rattled Lord Edward's *membrana tympani;* the interlocked *malleus, incus,* and stirrup bones were set in motion so as to agitate the membrane of the oral window and raise an infinitesimal storm in the fluid of the labyrinth. The hairy endings of the auditory nerve shuddered like weeds in a rough sea; a vast number of obscure miracles were performed in the brain, and Lord Edward ecstatically whispered "Bach!" He smiled with pleasure, his eyes lit up. The young girl was singing to herself in solitude under the floating clouds. And then the cloud-solitary philosopher begain poetically to meditate. "We must really go downstairs and listen," said Lord Edward. He got up. "Come," he said. "Work can wait. One doesn't hear this sort of thing every night."

"But what about clothes," said Illidge doubtfully. "I can't come down like this." He looked down at himself. It had been a cheap suit at the best of times. Age had not improved it.

"Oh, that doesn't matter." A dog with the smell of rabbits in his nostrils could hardly have shown a more indecent eagerness than Lord Edward at the sound of Pongileoni's flute. He took his assistant's arm and hurried him out of the door, and along the corridor towards the stairs. "It's just a little party," he went on. "I seem to remember my wife having said... Quite informal. And besides," he added, inventing new excuses to justify the violence of his musical appetite, "we can just slip in without ... Nobody will notice."

Illidge had his doubts. "I'm afraid it's not a very small party," he began; he had seen the motors arriving.

"Never mind, never mind," interrupted Lord Edward, lusting irrepressibly for Bach.

Illidge abandoned himself. He would look like a horrible fool, he reflected, in his shining blue serge suit. But perhaps, on second thoughts, it was better to appear in shiny blue—straight from the laboratory, after all, and under the protection of the master of the house (himself in a tweed jacket), than in that old and, as he had perceived during previous excursions into Lady Edward's luscious world, deplorably shoddy and ill-made evening suit of his. It was better to be totally different from the rich and smart—a visitor from another intellectual planet—than a fourth rate and snobbish imitator. Dressed in blue, one might be stared at as an oddity; in badly cut black (like a waiter) one was contemptuously ignored, one was despised for trying without success to be what one obviously wasn't.

Illidge braced himself to play the part of the Martian visitor with firmness, even assertively.

Their entrance was even more embarrassingly conspicuous than Illidge had anticipated. The great staircase at Tantamount House comes down from the first floor in two branches which join, like a pair of equal rivers to precipitate themselves in a single architectural cataract of Verona marble into the hall. It debouches under the arcades, in the centre of one of the sides of the covered quadrangle, opposite the vestibule and the front door. Coming in from the street, one looks across the hall and sees through the central arch of the opposite arcade the wide stairs and shining balustrades climbing up to a landing on which a Venus by Canova, the pride of the third marquess's collection, stands pedestalled in an alcove, screening with a modest but coquettish gesture of her two hands, or rather failing to screen, her marble charms. It was at the foot of this triumphal slope of marble that Lady Edward had posted the orchestra; her guests were seated in serried rows confronting it. When Illidge and Lord Edward turned the corner in front of Canova's Venus, tiptoeing, as they approached the music and the listening crowd, with steps ever more laboriously conspiratorial, they found themselves suddenly at the focus of a hundred pairs of eyes. A gust of curiosity stirred the assembled guests. The apparition from a world so different from theirs of this huge bent old man, pipe-smoking and tweed-jacketed, seemed strangely portentous. He had a certain air of the skeleton in the cupboard—broken loose; or one of those monsters which haunt the palaces of only the best and most aristocratic families. The Beastie of Glamis, the Minotaur itself could hardly have aroused more interest than did Lord Edward. Lorgnons were raised, there was a general cramming to left and right, as people tried to look round the well-fed obstacles in front of them. Becoming suddenly aware of so many inquisitive glances, Lord Edward took fright. A consciousness of social sin possessed him; he took his pipe out of his mouth and put it away, still smoking into the pocket of his jacket. He halted irresolutely. Flight or advance? He turned this way and that, pivoting his whole bent body from the hips with a curious swinging motion, like the slow ponderous balancing of a camel's neck. For a moment he wanted to retreat. But love of Bach was stronger than his terrors. He was the bear whom the smell of molasses constrains in spite of all his fear to visit the hunters' camp; the lover who is ready to face an armed and outraged husband and the divorce court for the sake of an hour of his mistress's arms. He went forward, tiptoeing down the stairs more conspiratorially than ever—Guy Fawkes discovered, but yet irrationally hoping that he might escape notice by acting as though the Gunpowder Plot were still unrolling itself according to plan. Illidge followed him. His face had gone very red with the embarrassment of the first moment; but in spite of this embarrassment, or rather because of it, he came downstairs after Lord Edward with a kind of swagger, one hand in his pocket, a smile on his lips. He turned his eyes coolly this way and that over the crowd. The expression on his face was one of contemptuous amusement. Too busy being the Martian to look where he was going, Illidge suddenly missed his footing on this unfamiliar regal staircase with its inordinate treads and dwarfishly low risers. His foot slipped, he staggered wildly on the brink of a fall, waving his arms, to come to rest, however, still miraculously on his feet, some two or three steps lower down. He resumed his descent with such dignity as he could muster up. He felt exceedingly angry, he hated Lady Edward's guests one and all, without exception.

10

The Treasury View
of Economic Policy, 1929

Guided by Keynes, the Liberals produced a manifesto for the 1929 general election, entitled *We Can Conquer Unemployment*. The government took the unusual step of issuing a White Paper rebutting the arguments of the Liberals. This is an excellent brief statement of the narrow orthodoxy of treasury officials at that time.

SOURCE: *Parliamentary Papers 1928-29* (XVI Cmd. 3331). By permission of the Controller of H.M. Stationery Office.

MEMORANDA ON CERTAIN PROSPECTS
RELATING TO UNEMPLOYMENT:
MEMORANDUM PREPARED BY THE TREASURY, 1929

To sum up, we have always pursued the policy of providing the finance required for the economic development of the public services, and there is no justification for the charge that these services have been stinted. The proposals in the pamphlet that this programme should be greatly extended are open to very serious objection on financial grounds. The large loans involved, if they are not to involve inflation, must draw on existing capital resources. These resources are on the whole utilised at present in varying degrees of active employment, and the great bulk is utilised for home industrial and commercial purposes. The extent to which any additional employment could be given by altering the direction of investment is therefore at the best strictly limited. But the direction of investment can only be altered if we are prepared to offer sufficiently high money rates to counteract the attractions offered, e.g., in America. If, however, we do so, the damage done to home trade and employment by the imposition of such high rates would undoubtedly be much greater than any benefit they could obtain from the funds that could thereby be diverted from foreign investment. Moreover, this procedure would, of course, mean the restriction which might be serious of the development loans for the Dominions, as well as for foreign countries, on which our heavy industries have in the past largely depended for custom. Meanwhile, the issue of large additional Government loans, at an attractive rate of interest, would undoubtedly add to the costs of all

Government borrowings and impose therefore an extra charge (or prevent economies being realised) on the Budget. Although the maintenance of Government credit and the cheapening of Government borrowings may not be of paramount importance as against the social advantages of reducing unemployment (if it could be reduced by such means) there is no justification for depressing Government credit if (as seems to be the case) no great addition to employment could thereby be procured. It must be remembered that an increase in the cost of Government borrowings automatically increases the costs of borrowing for all public authorities, and eventually for private enterprise, too. Finally, on the long view, the undertaking of a large programme of Government expenditure, if it were successful in increasing employment temporarily, would tend to prejudice our export trades by encouraging our industries to struggle along on an uneconomic basis instead of reorganising themselves to meet present-day conditions.

11

The Interview Method of Recruitment to the Civil Service, 1931

The Royal Commission on the Civil Service which reported in 1931 rebutted criticisms that the interview method of recruitment was strongly biased in favour of those with the right educational and social background.

SOURCE: *Parliamentary Papers 1930-31* (X Cmd 3909). By permission of the Controller of H.M. Stationery Office.

REPORT OF THE ROYAL COMMISSION
ON THE CIVIL SERVICE 1929-31

Interview Test.

250. Four main types of interview are used in connection with recruitment to the Service:—

(i) The first type of interview, which is known as selection board procedure, is commonly used to fill specialist posts. Candidates are called upon to produce evidence showing that they possess certain necessary qualifications, but there is normally no written examination in specialist subjects. Appointments are made by the board after interviewing the candidates and a scrutiny of their written records.

(ii) In the second type a written examination in some subject is supplemented by a *viva voce* test. This, we understand, is common practice when modern languages are offered at examinations taken by candidates coming direct from school or University. This test, we think, is correctly described as a *viva voce*.

(iii) In the third type candidates at an open competition which includes written papers appear before a board whose object is to assess personal qualities which cannot be tested by a written examination. A varying proportion of the total marks in the examination as a whole are assigned to the interview test, and the marks obtained in that test are added to those obtained in the written papers. Normally, there is no qualifying mark in the interview test.

(iv) The fourth type, which has been called the "weeding-out interview" is held in connection with the Foreign Office and Diplomatic and Consular Services. No candidate can compete in the examination for posts in these Services unless he has first appeared before a board and been approved by them. The functions of this board are those of rejection rather than of selection. Appearance before this board is a preliminary to and does not form part of the competition for these Services.

251. We deal in paragraphs 257 and 258 with appointments to specialist posts where the selection board method of appointment is employed. We have no observations on the second type of interview, namely the *viva voce* proper. The "weeding-out interview", which is used in connection with the Foreign Office and Diplomatic and Consular Services, we regard as reasonable and proper arrangement, to which no objection can rightly be taken.

252. Our main concern is with the third type, namely, the interview which is used to assess personal qualities. The following table shows the main competitions which include this form of interview.

253. We received a considerable amount of evidence in regard to this form of interview test. In the first place it was suggested that it offered scope for the display of class prejudice. No evidence was adduced in support of this criticism, and the competition results support the view that no such prejudice exists. We are satisfied that there are no grounds for any suspicion of this kind.

254. In the second place evidence was submitted to the effect that on occasions there had been surprising variations between the marks awarded at the interview test to candidates who competed more than once for the same class. We do not propose to enter into the debatable question of the relative reliability of marks awarded at interviews and written examinations. Every method of testing candidates is, no doubt, exposed to its own particular hazards, and the method of interview is no exception to this rule. In this

Competition.	Maximum number of marks obtainable in the interview test.	Maximum number of marks obtainable in the whole examination.
Administrative class.	300	1,800 or 1,900
Foreign Office and Diplomatic Service.*	300	1,900 or 2,000
Consular Services.*	300	1,850 or 1,950
Tax Inspectorate group (i.e., Inspector of Taxes, and Third Class Officer, Ministry of Labour).	300	1,300
Officer of Customs and Excise	200	1,400
Probationary Assistant Engineer† and Probationary Inspector† in the Engineering department of the Post Office.	200	700
Assistant Preventive Officer,† Customs and Excise Department.	200	800

*The interview test which forms part of these competitions is distinct from the "weeding-out interview" referred to in paragraph 250.

†There is a qualifying mark in the interview test for these classes.

connection we attach some importance to Sir Stanley Leathes' statement that in his view the qualities which are judged at an interview are to some extent a corrective of those which are tested by a written paper. [Question 22,311.]

255. We recommend that the interview test (a method which is far from being confined to entry into Government Service) should continue to form part of the competitions of which the more important instances are given in paragraph 252. We regard as generally satisfactory the proportion of the total marks assigned to the interview. We do not recommend that the interview test should be made a qualifying test in regard to those competitions where such an arrangement does not already obtain.

256. We regard it as a matter of highest importance that the greatest care should be taken in choosing the personnel of interview boards. We feel sure that this is a matter to which the Civil Service Commissioners devote particular attention, with a view to securing the services of persons who possess the special qualifications and width of experience required for this duty.

12

The Labour Government, the Unions, and the Bank of England, 1931

The minority Labour Government of 1929-1931 collapsed in face of the financial crisis which became acute in the summer of 1931. On the one side the Bank of England pressed for drastic economies, while on the other the Trades Union Congress insisted that there should be no cuts in unemployment benefits.

SOURCE: Public Record Office: Cabinet Minutes (CAB 43 [31] and 44 [31], August 21st and 22nd 1931). Transcripts of Crown-copyright records in the Public Record Office appear by permission of the Controller of H.M. Stationery Office.

FRIDAY AUGUST 21ST, 1931, AT 10 A.M.

... the Cabinet received from the Chancellor of the Exchequer an account of the meeting which had taken place on the previous evening between the Cabinet Committee on the Report of the Committee on National Expenditure and a Committee of the General Council of the Trades Union congress. The meeting had been a friendly one, and Mr. Citrine, who acted as spokesman for the Committee, pointed out that in the view of the General Council, the Government had been mistaken in their method of approaching the problem. All through his statement, and in the subsequent discussion, it appeared that members of the General Council had no real appreciation of the seriousness of the situation; the statements made appeared to be based on a pre-crisis mentality, and the objections raised to the proposals were those which members of the Cabinet themselves would have taken had the circumstances been quite normal. With regard to the suggested economies, Mr. Citrine had stated that the General Council were opposed to any interference with the existing terms and conditions of the Unemployment Insurance Scheme ....

The Chancellor of the Exchequer added that he had replied to the points raised at some length, but that it must be realised that the Trades Union General Council were not prepared to accept the scheme of economies which had been prepared by the Government.

The Prime Minister informed the Cabinet that in view of the attitude adopted by the General Council, he had thought it necessary to see the Deputy Governor of the Bank of England. The Deputy Governor had expressed the opinion that arrangements for balancing the budget without recourse to very substantial economies would have a most detrimental effect on the situation . . . .

SATURDAY AUGUST 22ND, 1931, AT 9:30 A.M.

The Prime Minister reported that the financial situation had further deteriorated. The Chancellor of the Exchequer and himself had met the representatives of the Bank of England and the Leaders of the Opposition Parties on the previous afternoon, and had found that it was absolutely impossible to reach any agreement on the proposals which the Cabinet had authorised him to lay before those persons.

With regard to the Representatives of the Bank of England, the position was that it was essential that assistance of a substantial character must be obtained from both New York and Paris. In connection with the former, the Federal Reserve Bank had, on their own initiative, issued a very reassuring statement as to the Government's intentions, while the Bank of France had also been responsible for a very favourable notice in the Paris Press. He assured the Cabinet in the most emphatic terms that there was no ground whatever for the suggestion that the present crisis was in any respect due to a conspiracy on the part of the Banks, all of which were most anxious to render assistance to the government.

JOHN A. ARMSTRONG

The Communist Party as Ruler of Russia: Khrushchev's Rise Re-examined (1953-55)

THE PROBLEMS INVOLVED in investigating recent Soviet political history are so formidable that one is justified in treating the study as a special branch of historiography. For the early years of the Soviet regime—up to about 1930—political developments, while tortuous and occasionally obscure, in principle are no more difficult to study than the politics of many Western nations. Official accounts are reasonably accurate, and private documentation (for example, in the Trotsky archives) is abundant. For more recent periods, certain aspects of social, economic, and cultural history can be treated in the manner customary in modern Western historiography. But the embracing ("totalitarian") claims of the political system make it difficult to analyze even these aspects of contemporary history without attempting to determine the nature of official policy. Consequently, in spite of the great difficulties involved, anyone endeavoring to understand any major phase of recent Soviet development must come to grips with the problem of the relative significance of actors in the political system, their interaction in decision-making, and their influence on policy formation and implementation. For those who would go beyond the specific examination of historical events to elaboration of theories about the "nature" of Soviet social evolution, or who wish to compare its processes to those of other social systems, painstaking examination of the actual conditions of political life is even more essential. Consequently, despite his limitations, the work of the political historian is a prerequisite for all other approaches to understanding the U.S.S.R.

In the brief scope of this essay, I shall try to show how far political historiography can go in explaining a significant segment of Soviet development, as well as the refractory limits set to the historian's work. The period 1953-55 is useful for several reasons. It is close enough (as compared, for example, to the purges of the 1930s) to constitute an unquestionable element of contemporary history, yet sufficiently remote to permit resort to a variety of types of evidence. The evidence is much stronger and more abundant than what is available for the 1960s or even the 1940s.

The 1953-55 period also undoubtedly marked a turning point both in Soviet internal history and the relations of the U.S.S.R. to the rest of the world. At the beginning of 1953, Joseph Stalin had been the dictator of the U.S.S.R. for a quarter of a century. During his last years, Stalin became very rigid in his policies. In foreign policy, his support of the North Korean position in the Korean war led to a Western reaction which confronted the U.S.S.R. with a solid, heavily armed alliance led by the United States. Stalin's suspicion of "national liberation" forces also tended to isolate the U.S.S.R. from the increasingly important developments in the "third world." Within the Communist bloc, Stalin's insistence on conformity to Soviet policies led to drastic purges of most Eastern European Communist regimes, to a complete break with Yugo-slavia, and to strained relations with China. Within the U.S.S.R. itself Stalin apparently was plotting another "great purge" which would have produced a drastic upheaval in all spheres of life.

Stalin's death (March 5, 1953) reversed many of these extreme trends. Instead, many of the more flexible policies which have marked Soviet activity abroad during the past twenty years were begun. The Korean war was ended, and the "two camp" theory replaced by Soviet aid and diplomatic overtures to third-world countries. Within the Communist bloc and particularly within the Soviet leadership itself, however, changes were more complicated. Complications arose because all alterations in internal policies depended on the balance of political forces which emerged after Stalin's personal dictatorship ended. In many respects this balance has not been fully established, even after twenty years. But the new forces which would dominate Soviet policy-making began, at least, to emerge in the crucial years 1953-55 immediately following Stalin's passing. Essentially, this period is characterized by a struggle for succession in which one of Stalin's lieutenants, Nikita Khrushchev, established a commanding lead over his rivals. While the basic account of this struggle has been told many times, the passage of two decades has provided enough new evidence to warrant a brief reconsideration of those years.[1]

In my opinion the two years (or, to be more specific, the period from the September 1953 plenum of the Communist Party Central Committee to its July 1955 meeting) were the really decisive years of the post-Stalin political history of the U.S.S.R. In less than twenty-one months, the effort to establish a "collective leadership" of Stalin's principal lieutenants collapsed. The immediate result—which received, naturally, the most attention at the time—was the primacy of a new leader, Khrushchev. During the summer of 1953 Khrushchev appeared to be, at best, number three, inferior to Georgi M. Malenkov (the chairman of the council of ministers) and Old Bolshevik Vyacheslav M. Molotov, the foreign minister. By the end of the July 1955 plenum these men were humiliated and demoted, while Khrushchev had no evident rival for preeminence. A more far-reaching consequence of these events was the reestablishment of unquestioned primacy for the Party as a formal organization. Since Khrushchev (at least after September 1953) was the formal head of the Party, many observers interpreted Party ascendancy as an aspect of his effort to assume Stalin's dictatorial powers.[2] In retrospect, at least, the reassertion of Party supremacy represented a more fundamental institutional and ideological trend. It also constituted a significant part of the establishment of dominance not by a personal dictator, or even a small committee such as Stalin's lieutenants had constituted, but by an oligarchy formally defined by the Central Committee, although actually consisting of a bureaucratic interest group composed of the upper-stratum of Party officials. Ultimately—as the

---

[1] My own treatment appears in *The Politics of Totalitarianism* (New York: Random House, 1961), pp. 255-71. It contains many details relevant to the general framework of Soviet politics which the reader may wish to consult.

[2] The most elaborate and skillful interpretation of this nature was Myron Rush, *The Rise of Khrushchev* (Washington: Public Affairs Press, 1958). The appendix on "The Role of Esoteric Communication in Soviet Politics" is still a very valuable methodological treatment.

events of 1964 demonstrated—Khrushchev was more the instrument of this interest group than its manipulator. In making this observation, one need not assert that the 1964 outcome was inevitable; quite possibly Khrushchev could have replicated Stalin's reduction of the Central Committee to impotence. But if one searches for the origins of the way in which Soviet history has actually developed—as well as for unrealized possibilities of development—the period 1953-55 is crucial.

This essay is too brief to permit a thorough exploration of the social and economic factors affecting the evolution of political events. Instead, as indicated above, the purpose is to establish the facts of political history as a prerequisite for interpreting the broader aspects of societal development. But one must always be aware that even in a totalitarian system policy-makers do not act in a vacuum; the currents of societal development set material limits and may give rise to popular presssures which cannot be ignored. One must, therefore, at least allude to the factors which condition the policy-makers' choice, even though these factors may not determine specific policies. The account presented here assumes that policy-making is, in fact, an interaction between these social factors and the volition of policy-makers. The interpretation also rests on a conflict model; i.e., it assumes that the attitudes and interests of elites are so divergent that the policy-making process cannot satisfy all participants. Thus actual policy formation will reflect both an "instrumental " effort to solve societal problems and an antagonistic effort to secure advantage for individuals and groups.

II

The initial interpretation of contemporary Soviet politics is rarely the work of historians. Instead, diplomats, intelligence specialists, and journalists scrutinize the daily flow of material from the U.S.S.R. for clues as to what is happening in the closed political system. A principal motivation is the desire to predict the short-range political evolution, and thus to enable foreign governments to adjust their own policies. Journalistic "Kremlinology" is more colorful, but tne best Moscow correspondents are no less painstaking and cautious than their official counterparts. Such prediction is not the business of the historian; consequently he can avoid the excitement and hazards of day-to-day analysis of Soviet events. As will appear later, the historian's ability to review events from the perspective of even a decade or two provides him with an immense advantage. Nevertheless, a large part of the historian's documentation will consist of the same kind of current Soviet publications which constitute the Kremlinologist's fare.

The official announcement of the September 1953 plenum left no doubt that it was an important event: Khrushchev delivered a lengthy report stressing the serious deficiencies of agriculture, and outlining ways to overcome them. The plenum formally appointed him first secretary of the Party.[3] Clearly, his prestige was mounting. Yet, on the basis of the official announcements alone, observers could interpret his position as being in accord with Malenkov's, or even subordinate.

As Source 14 indicates, Malenkov had been the senior Party secretary (below Stalin) for a number of years; indeed, Khrushchev had less seniority in the central Party secretariat than Mikhail A. Suslov. Shortly after Stalin's death, however, Malenkov resigned (March 1953) from the secretariat, while retaining the premiership. While it is highly probable that he was obliged to give up one or the other post, it still seems likely that he regarded being head of the government as more important. In this capacity, during the summer of 1953 Malenkov vigorously promoted measures for improving the miserable standard of living which the Soviet population continued to endure at a time when prosperity had returned to most industrial nations. Here was a case where changing material limits combined with increasing popular pressures to make policy change almost unavoidable. Stalin's concentration on heavy industrial production for investment and armament meant that the plant capacity existed—as it had not in the early postwar years—for substantial consumers goods production. Relaxation of draconic labor control measures (begun under Stalin) and the rising educational levels of the population meant that the regime faced erosion of popular support if it did not take some steps to satisfy pent-up desires for material goods. Any leader who seemed to be satisfying these demands would be popular.

In early August 1953 Malenkov told the Supreme Soviet (to

[3] *Pravda*, September 13, 1953, as translated in *Current Digest of the Soviet Press V*, No. 37, p. 3. The *Current Digest* (hereafter *CDSP*) (Columbus, Ohio), is a weekly scholarly compilation of carefully selected items from the Soviet press, published since 1949. Where its meticulous translations are available, I have used them (with permission) in the hope that the reader will be encouraged to conduct further explorations in Soviet material available in English.

which, as premier, he was nominally responsible), that "hitherto we have not had the opportunity to develop light and food industry at the same rate as heavy industry. Now we can and consequently we must accelerate development of light industry in every way in the interests of securing a faster rise in the living standards and cultural level of the people."[4] Khrushchev's speech to the plenum seemed to echo this theme: "We were not able to ensure rapid development of heavy industry, agriculture, and light industry simultaneously. To do this, the necessary premises had to be created. These premises have now been established."[5] Even at the time, careful observers noted a nuance of difference between the speeches: Malenkov had called for the *same* rate of heavy and light industrial growth; Khrushchev avoided this explicit equation. In retrospect, it appears highly probable that the omission was not accidental, but in 1953 it was reasonable to assume that Khrushchev was merely carrying out the collective leadership's policy in the special area of agriculture. Further, it seemed plausible that Khrushchev—while clearly recognized as one of the "big three" in his top Party post—was a loyal second to Malenkov in broad policy matters.

III

During the autumn of 1953 and most of the following winter, the major public emphases on policy remained the same. Some observers thought they perceived increasing differences in Khrushchev's and Malenkov's pronouncements, but even today there is no certainty that such an "esoteric" conflict over policy was proceeding. What is clearer, in retrospect, is that fundamental personnel changes were shifting the balance between the government apparatus headed by Malenkov and the Party apparatus under Khrushchev.[6] Although tracing personnel alignments is as difficult and uncertain as the scrutiny of published materials to detect esoteric communication, both have become indispensable tools of Kremlinology. For the historian, use of personnel changes as evidence is often less risky, because they can be linked to known elements in the organizational structures of the U.S.S.R. and because the existence of *some* important alterations can be determined statistically.

[4] *Pravda*, August 9, 1953, trans. in *CDSP* V, No. 30, pp. 3 ff.
[5] *Pravda*, September 13, 1953, trans. in *CDSP* V, No. 37, pp. 3 ff.
[6] See *The Politics of Totalitarianism*, pp. 259 ff.

On the organizational side, the September plenum eliminated the political officers of the machine tractor stations (MTS). At various times under Stalin, these officers had been the key organizational bases for political control and indoctrination in rural areas. Since the MTS political officers were centrally directed, they constituted a kind of substitute for local Communist Party control. A considerable amount of evidence suggests that the police agencies actually directed the MTS political officers. If that is true, their elimination in the autumn of 1953 was part of vast organizational changes related to the dismantling of police agencies after the other members of the collective leadership eliminated Lavrenti Beria, the sinister police chief, in June 1953. Indeed, one way (although doubtless an oversimplified one) to look at the relations among Khrushchev, Malenkov, and Molotov during late 1953 is to regard the period as a fight for redivision of Beria's "empire." Clearly the Party apparatus under Khrushchev was most successful in taking over the rural aspects of this "empire," for the duties of the MTS political officers were transferred to newly designated district Party secretaries ("*raikom* secretaries for the MTS zones"). Many of the MTS political officers were reassigned to local Party work. Though it was not clear at the time, the historian can see retrospectively that the transfer of political functions was only the beginning of a process by which the MTS system itself was ultimately dismantled (1958). In place of the dominant economic position of the Ministry of Agriculture (a government agency) operating in rural areas through the MTS, the local Party organizations became relatively more powerful.

Individual changes are harder to assess unambiguously, but observers at the time regarded the removal of V. M. Andrianov as first secretary of the Leningrad *obkom* as a highly significant event. While it is possible that Andrianov was closer to Beria, there is no doubt that he had ties to Malenkov—and was linked to the latter in the repugnant "Leningrad affair" discussed below. The fact that the official announcement indicated explicitly that Khrushchev participated in the meeting which removed Andrianov strengthens the inference that Malenkov had suffered a setback. In retrospect, the fact that Andrianov's replacement was F. R. Kozlov appears equally significant. Later, Kozlov was to side with Khrushchev against the "anti-Party" group, including Molotov as well as Malenkov. For a time preceding his incapacitating illness (1963), Kozlov appeared to be the number two man, just behind

Khrushchev, in the Soviet leadership. On the other hand, Kozlov's promotion also appears, in retrospect, to indicate that more was at issue than a simple struggle between Khrushchev and his rivals. Later developments—too complex to discuss here—strongly suggest that Kozlov was far from a simple lieutenant of Khrushchev; instead, the Leningrad Party apparatus he led appears to have been a significant interest group in the bureaucratic elite, which may still be represented in the leadership (particularly by the present premier, A. N. Kosygin).[7]

As the preceding paragraph suggests, explanation of the significance of an individual personnel change is complicated and lengthy. Consequently, few can be treated in this essay. The third way in which personnel changes can be used to illuminate power rivalries is by aggregating a considerable amount of data concerning changes which cannot be treated individually. There are three basic difficulties in this method. A great deal of labor is required to compile lists of personnel changes, since they are rarely announced simultaneously. Fortunately, in the last twenty years this work has been done by an increasing number of agencies in Western countries, most of which are carrying out their task with great care. The basic information in Source 8 was compiled by Boris Meissner, an outstanding German scholar who later was a member of the first German Federal Republic diplomatic mission to Moscow. The data for April 1954-February 1956 was compiled by comparing several personnel directories published in the United States.[8]

A second difficulty is determination of the group of offices for which personnel changes should be studied. In Source 8, I have limited the examination to the major territorial Party officials in the RSFSR (Russian Soviet Federated Socialist Republic—which includes over half of the people and three-fourths of the area of the Soviet Union) although Meissner presents some

[7] See especially Myron Rush, *Political Succession in the USSR* (New York: Columbia University Press, 1965), p. 136; and Robert Conquest, *Russia after Khrushchev* (New York: Praeger, 1965), pp. 156-57. For a detailed, although somewhat speculative discussion of later relations between Khrushchev and Kozlov, see Robert M. Slusser, *The Berlin Crisis of 1961: Soviet-American Relations and the Struggle for Power in the Kremlin* (Baltimore: Johns Hopkins University Press, 1973).

[8] The principal directories available for this study are: lists in Leo Gruliow, ed., *Current Soviet Policies* (New York: Praeger, 1953) and *Current Soviet Policies II* (New York: Praeger, 1957) (Gruliow is editor of the CDSP); *Biographic Directory of the U.S.S.R.* (New York: Scarecrow Press, 1958), compiled by the Institute for the Study of the U.S.S.R. (Munich); and *Biographic Directory of Soviet Political Leaders* (Department of State, 1957, mimeographed).

additional data, and still more could be compiled. My reasons for doing this are partly to simplify the presentation. In addition, appointments to RSFSR Party offices, not being associated with one of the major Soviet rivals to the degree that, say, Ukrainian party offices or industrial ministerial offices were in 1953-54, are more apt to reflect subtle alterations in power relationships.

The fact that Meissner presents data on incumbents for three dates (to which I have added a fourth list) enables one to overcome, to a considerable extent, the third difficulty in utilizing aggregated personnel change data. It is meaningless to establish a rate of personnel change unless the rate can be compared to other periods. Unfortunately, much superficially impressive analysis of Soviet politics has overlooked this restriction, referring to "great" or even "sweeping" turnover in personnel without demonstrating that the rate, however large, was *abnormal*. Using the lists presented in Source 8, one can calculate turnover rates for two periods adjacent to the one which is our special concern. Thirty-two of the sixty-four incumbents of RSFSR territorial Party posts in April 1953 differed from the April 1950 incumbents. In April 1954 nineteen of sixty-five posts were filled with new appointees; and in February 1956 sixteen of sixty-eight.[9] At first glance, it might appear that the highest turnover rate was for the first period, with changes progressively decreasing thereafter. It seems most appropriate, however, to assume that turnover would normally be related to the length of the period involved. Since the first period is three years long, one may calculate that approximately 17 percent of the posts were filled with new men each year. A similar rate (13 percent per year) applies to the third period, which is twenty-two months long. For the period April 1953-April 1954, comprising a single year, the rate is 30 percent. A simple test of statistical significance indicates that the differences (17:13 percent) between periods one and three are not significant for the small numbers of appointments involved; i.e., that the differences in turnover may well have occurred by chance.

---

[9] Newly created positions are not counted, unless they are filled by transferring persons already holding RSFSR posts at the same level; persons transferred among previously existing positions are treated as old appointees. It might be slightly preferable to calculate attrition of old appointees than ratios of new appointees. In order to make the former calculation meaningful, however, one would have to determine what happened to the secretaries who were removed, which is not feasible (except, as noted below, in the calculation of Central Committee membership) within the limited scope of this study.

Conversely, the difference between either of these periods and period two (1953-54) is significant at the 5 percent level, i.e., there is only one chance in twenty that the marked increase in personnel turnover for that period was due to mere chance.[10]

Establishment of *statistical significance* is only a first step in utilizing quantitative evidence. The significance of the evidence *for the problem investigated* can only be inferred. Though precise quantitative information is not at hand, it is certain that nearly all of the 1953-54 RSFSR Party post changes occurred during the period which interests us, namely summer 1953-April 1954. Consequently, there is no doubt that the period of public harmony in the collective leadership coincided with peak turnover. It seems highly probable, however, that many of the territorial first secretaries replaced lost their posts because of some earlier association with Beria. Since assignments are made by the Party secretariat, the least that one can conclude is that Khrushchev and his associates were in an unusually good position to profit from these replacements. The historical precedent (Stalin's manipulation of territorial assignments when first he headed the Party secretariat in the early 1920s) strengthens this inference. There are many bits of direct evidence (too complicated to describe here) that the new appointees in late 1953 and early 1954 were in fact more sympathetic to Khrushchev, or at least more hostile to the central governmental apparatus headed by Malenkov, than the men they replaced.[11]

The matter is important, because precisely at the close of the period we have just been considering the Central Committee became the forum for policy disputes among the top leaders. According to formal announcements, the few changes in the composition of the Central Committee between 1952 and 1956 were largely limited to removal of members (like Beria's hench-

---

[10] A quick way to calculate significance level for this type of N (number) and percentage difference is to use a chart similar to a slide rule (see, for example, S. Rosenbaum, "A Significance Chart for Percentages," *Applied Statistics* VIII (1959), No. 1. This approach assumes that the "populations" (in our case, the personnel changes for each period) constitute "samples" of a larger chronological series. For a defense of this assumption (which many statisticians do not accept) see Karl Deutsch et al., "The Organizing Efficiency of Theories," *American Behavioral Scientist* VIII (1965): 30-33.

[11] For more details see particularly Robert Conquest, *Power and Policy in the U.S.S.R.* (New York: St. Martin's Press, 1961), pp. 232-33, 243, 247, 248, 256, 258, and Appendix II B; G. D. Embree, *The Soviet Union between the 19th and 20th Party Congresses, 1952-1956* (The Hague: Martinus Nijhoff, 1959), pp. 107 ff. and Appendix I; Wolfgang Leonhard, *The Kremlin since Stalin*, trans. Elizabeth Wickemann and Marian Jackson (New York: Praeger, 1962), pp. 83-87.

men) arrested or executed. Presumably these men were replaced by promotion of alternate members, but we do not know how the promotees were selected from the large number of candidates available. It seems likely, however, that the seven dismissed RSFSR territorial secretaries who were Central Committee members also ceased to function as active participants. Conversely, those newly appointed territorial secretaries who later (1956) were made Central Committee members (eight of the 19) may have participated in its deliberations informally.

IV

It is unlikely that these shifts (affecting only six percent of the Central Committee membership) decisively shifted the balance of power in the body, but the psychological effect on wavering members may have been considerable. In any event, in February 1954 Khrushchev used the Central Committee as a forum for a major new policy move, the effort to solve the agricultural shortages by opening (or reopening) cultivation of the "virgin lands" of southern Siberia, northern Kazakhstan, and certain other areas.[12] In contrast to his earlier agricultural measures, this move was not preceded by a governmental policy announcement; the new policy therefore appeared to be an initiative of the Party headed by Khrushchev. Consequently, even the official announcement implied a substantial shift in the government-Party balance, with governmental authority in the agricultural field virtually reduced to a formality. But this is an instance in which subsequent revelations go far beyond what could have been inferred from the information published at the time. If N. A. Bulganin's 1958 speech (Source 9) is accurate—it is corroborated by Madame E. A. Furtseva's speech (Source 11), although to be sure both were trying to curry favor with Khrushchev—all of Khrushchev's principal rivals opposed the virgin lands scheme as foolhardy. It is reasonable to suppose that both Molotov and Malenkov were sincere in their opposition to the new policy, for it was in fact a gamble. After several years of excellent harvests in the 1950s, drought almost eliminated grain production in virgin lands during

---

[12] See *Pravda* March 6, 1954, trans. *CDSP* VI, No. 9, p. 3, for the first report on the "recent" plenum; but *Pravda*, March 21, 1954, trans. *CDSP* VI, No. 12, pp. 3 ff., presented Khrushchev's speech to the plenum with the indication it had been given on February 23. The delay in publication suggested in itself that a covert dispute was taking place.

the early 1960s—a failure which discredited Khrushchev and probably played some part in his downfall. Quite probably Molotov and Malenkov expected this fiasco earlier, and hoped to avoid implication in it. But Molotov was a convinced adherent of the policies followed under Stalin, while Malenkov was in his way as much an innovator as Khrushchev. Consequently, it appears that Malenkov objected to the virgin lands scheme because even if it were successful in the short run, it could only strengthen Krushchev and the Party apparatus.

If this analysis is accurate, it shows that the latter group's interests were dominant on an issue like agriculture. But there is considerable evidence that the balance shifted several times between Khrushchev and Malenkov during the remaining months of 1954. Most of the indications are too complex (and still too undemonstrable) to warrant attention here.[13] One basic issue needs to be mentioned, however, because it points up a fundamental weakness of Khrushchev's rivals—their basic divergence on the wisdom of continuing Stalin's policies. This divergence was most apparent in foreign policy. As head of government, Malenkov was in a position to acquire the immense prestige which accrues to a statesman who initiates successful negotiations with other powers, whereas Khrushchev, as Communist Party chief, was limited in this area. In fact, in October 1954 Khrushchev made the most of his opportunities by becoming the first Soviet leader to visit Peking, as a "fraternal" Party emissary to Mao Tse-Tung. Malenkov, on the other hand, apparently envisaged a major opening in relations with the non-Communist great powers. In January 1954 he took the initiative, unprecedented for a Soviet leader, of recognizing that a nuclear war could mean the "destruction of civilization." After a few weeks, this declaration was implicitly rejected by military spokesmen, and later by Khrushchev, who reiterated the old position that, nuclear weapons or not, war would destroy capitalism rather than Soviet-type socialism. Possibly the military spokesmen played an independent part in this indirect argument, but it seems clear that Khrushchev was clever in rallying a wide range of "conservative" elements (including Molotov, who had direct responsibility for foreign

---

[13]The best treatments are in Leonhard, *op. cit.* pp. 83-107; Embree, *op cit.*; Conquest, *Power and Policy*; and Rush, *The Rise of Khrushchev*. Carl A. Linden, *Khrushchev and the Soviet Leadership, 1957-1964* (Baltimore: Johns Hopkins Press, 1966), pp. 27 ff. provides a more recent survey of this period.

affairs) to thwart Malenkov's effort to use his governmental post to take the initiative in foreign policy.[14]

Malenkov was also severely restricted in his role as rejuvenator of outworn policies by his fateful participation in Stalin's most abhorrent purges. The depth of revulsion against Malenkov among knowledgeable Soviet citizens has recently been confirmed by Roy Medvedev's semiclandestine history of the Stalinist period. Although Medvedev's book goes far beyond Soviet publications in condemning the atrocities of the Stalin period, he half excuses Khrushchev: "As a comparatively young politician, easily impressed (and not very bright), Khrushchev in the thirties was strongly influenced by Stalin, had faith in him, and feared him." Malenkov, on the other hand, Medvedev reports, personally interrogated and tortured prisoners.[15] For the decisive group, the Party elite, however, it was not Malenkov's activities in the 1930s which were unacceptable as much as his participation (with Beria) in the "Leningrad affair." This 1949 purge of major Party figures was still so fresh in the memories of the elite that—implicated as nearly all were to some extent in other purges—they could not feel safe with Malenkov in a commanding position.*

The "Leningrad affair" played a crucial part in Malenkov's demotion and humiliation. For those familiar with recent Soviet history, the announcement of December 24, 1954, that the former State Security chief, V. S. Abakumov, had been condemned for helping Beria in the Leningrad purge implied more than a continuing attack on Beria's henchmen.[16] Beria and most of his adherents had been executed without reference to this particular atrocity; why had the police director of the "Leningrad affair" alone been spared until this moment? The apparent answer was

---

*In 1949 A. A. Kuznetsov, several other high Party officials, and N. A. Voznesensky, chairman of the State Planning Commission, were arrested. After a carefully staged trial closed to the general public, they were executed. While the precise charges have never been revealed, the victims' main "crime" was opposition to the Politburo clique then in Stalin's favor. Most of the executed men had been followers of A. A. Zhdanov, who had died (apparently of natural causes) in 1948. In contrast to Malenkov and Beria, Zhdanov and his Leningrad associates had been involved in field supervision, especially during the crisis of World War II; consequently, they had remained relatively aloof from Kremlin intrigues. *See also Boffa's comments in* Source 14.

[14] Herbert S. Dinerstein, *War and the Soviet Union* (New York: Praeger, 1959), pp. 78 ff.; Raymond L. Garthoff, *Soviet Strategy in the Nuclear Age* (New York: Praeger 1958), pp. 22 ff.

[15] Roy A. Medvedev, *Let History Judge: The Origins and Consequences of Stalinism,* trans. Colleen Taylor, ed. David Joravsky and Georges Haupt (New York: Knopf, 1971), pp. 348, 350.

[16] *Pravda*, December 24, 1954, trans. *CDSP* VI, No. 49, p. 12.

that Malenkov's rivals were now strong enough to raise an issue which implicated him.

Subsequent information has confirmed this inference. Immediately after the overthrow of the "anti-Party" group (1957), Malenkov was denounced for his part in the "Leningrad affair," and further details appeared in Soviet speeches and publications throughout most of the Khrushchev period (see for example I. V. Spirodonov's 1961 speech, Source 10). But we know that the denunciations began long before this, at the January 1955 Central Committee plenum which was the real scene of Malenkov's defeat.

The official notice of this plenum (Source 3) was blandly misleading. Fortunately, less than two years later a Polish Communist party official, Seweryn Bialer, defected to the United States. Along with much other valuable information, he provided a summary of the secret proceedings of the January plenum. Since he could not bring a copy of the Party circular letter describing the proceedings, one must rely on his memory, always a somewhat unsatisfactory type of evidence. In Source 13 Bialer (now a member of the Columbia University faculty) has interspersed his recollections of the letter with his own analysis of its significance. It should be obvious that the student of Soviet affairs must make a careful distinction between these two elements of the Bialer article. Bialer's personal comments are helpful in assessing his recollection of the actual content of the confidential letter, however, for they suggest biases which might affect his memory. For example, Bialer's conviction (at that time) that Malenkov was no worse than Khrushchev apparently leads Bialer to depreciate the significance of the "Leningrad affair" charges made during the plenum, leading him to assert (inaccurately) that Malenkov had been "Khrushchev's aide" during the fight with Beria.

It is unusual for such a complete and accurate account of a confidential Central Committee circular to reach the West. What makes the January plenum account almost unique is that we have extended collaboration of the contents of this letter from a source with an entirely different point of view from Bialer's. Giuseppe Boffa was a loyal member of the Italian Communist Party. As such he had, while reporting on Soviet affairs, unusual access to confidential information. Like most Italian Communists, he was enthusiastic about Khrushchev. Hence his account of the January plenum circular letter stresses elements (like the Leningrad affair) which had been publicly revealed in the U.S.S.R. before his book appeared (in early 1959) and which fitted Khrushchev's anti-Stalinist tactics of the late 1950s. Nevertheless, Boffa recognizes implicitly (as noted, the English translation is faulty) that Malenkov was also attacked for emphasizing consumers goods, although (because Khrushchev had virtually adopted Malenkov's policy by 1958) Boffa avoids discussing the point.

The official announcement of Malenkov's demotion came more than a week after it had been decided at the Central Committee session, in a letter of resignation which he addressed to the Supreme Soviet. Formally, this was the correct procedure, for the head of government is supposed to be responsible to the legislative branch; but in fact Malenkov, as a Party member, was obliged to comply with the Central Committee directive to resign. The letter (Source 4) stresses his failures in agriculture and acknowledges the need for heavy-industry priority. Both Bialer and Boffa indicate that agriculture was also a major theme of the January plenum criticism. In a sense Bialer is correct in asserting that blaming Malenkov for agricultural failure was unwarranted. However, during Stalin's last years, Malenkov had publicly asserted that the current agricultural policies were successful. Khrushchev and his adherents obviously wanted to stress Malenkov's errors to show that the Party assumption of responsibility in the agricultural field represented a sharp break with the Stalinist past.

V

What is most striking is that both the rejection of Stalin's agricultural policy and the condemnation of his terrorization of the Party elite (the "Leningrad affair") occurred without overt rejection of the dead dictator. Indeed, the attack on Malenkov's consumers goods emphasis leaned heavily on Stalinist authority, as Dmitri Shepilov's article (Source 2) indicates. Published on the eve of the January plenum, this article was recognized even at that time to be an indirect attack on Malenkov. Its appearance evidently signalled a complete triumph for the heavy-industry emphasis, with a veiled threat (publicly repeated by Khrushchev shortly afterwards) to treat opponents of this emphasis as Stalin had treated the "right restorationists" (Nikolai Bukharin and his associates, denounced in the late 1920s and executed in 1938).

On this issue at least, Khrushchev and his associates were adhering to Stalinism in name, in style, and in substantive policy. There is no real evidence that this adherence was insincere, although, as indicated above, Khrushchev ultimately adopted most of Malenkov's policy on consumers goods. Very probably, however, Khrushchev's simultaneous acceptance of Stalinist tactics in foreign policy was an opportunistic concession to Molotov. Malenkov had been needed (as Bialer points out) to defeat Beria in 1953; Molotov was required to defeat Malenkov at the start of 1955. For Khrushchev and his adherents, divide and conquer was a clever tactic. Why Molotov went along with this is not so clear. Perhaps he feared Malenkov's ruthlessness, though Molotov had been ruthless enough under Stalin. The element of Malenkov's policy which Molotov most clearly resented—apart from concessions to Western powers—was relaxation of satellite controls in Eastern Europe. It is unquestionably significant that a "New Course" emphasizing consumers goods production in Hungary began slightly before Malenkov's stress on consumers goods. Just as Malenkov, heading the government, took the lead in the U.S.S.R., the Hungarian spokesman was the government head, Imre Nagy, as contrasted to the Stalinist party chief, Matyas Rakosi. Within a few days of Malenkov's "resignation" Rakosi deposed Nagy and placed him under house arrest. While Nagy's clandestine memoir does not (for obvious reasons) indicate hostility to the Khrushchev-Molotov coalition, the book does make it clear that Rakosi seized the opportunity to go beyond his Soviet Communist Party counterparts in eliminating a rival who had favored more concern for public welfare.[17]

At the same Supreme Soviet session where Malenkov was publicly demoted, Molotov gave a major address on foreign policy.[18] Generally, it adhered to the Stalinist "hard line" both toward non-Communist states and satellites. In a curious passage near the start of the message, Molotov appeared even to revise Stalin's doctrine in a pessimistic direction, by stressing the short distance the U.S.S.R. and some satellites ("people's democracies") had progressed on the road to socialism. At the time, Molotov's policy pronouncement was fulsomely praised by Khrushchev supporters like A. M. Puzanov, who had formally moved acceptance of Malenkov's resignation (Source 5). Many months later, in an extraordinary performance for a high-ranking Soviet official,

---

[17]Imre Nagy, *Imre Nagy on Communism* (London: Thames and Hudson, 1957), pp. 153, 252, 270, 276 ff.
[18]An English translation of the complete speech appears in *New Times* (Moscow), No. 7, February 12, 1955, pp. 12 ff.

Molotov publicly recanted his "erroneous formulation" (Source 7). The implications of both the original formulation and its recantation were confusing for contemporary observers. Much later, after Molotov was condemned for his part in the "anti-Party" affair, the significance of this episode was clarified in published speeches by victors like Anastas I. Mikoyan (Source 12). There seems little reason to question Mikoyan's assertion that Molotov's "formulation" was no slip of the tongue. By minimizing progress in the Communist bloc, Molotov was laying the ideological groundwork for continuing the rigid tutelage which had characterized Stalin's rule in Eastern Europe as well as the U.S.S.R. By minimizing the strength of the "socialist bloc," Molotov implied a continued need for strict exclusion of outside or heterodox influences.

As Bialer's and Boffa's accounts had made clear years before Mikoyan spoke, the real occasion for the break between Molotov and the Khrushchev group was rather different. Conceivably the latter might have tolerated opposition to their innovations in foreign policy couched in obscure ideological formulas, just as Molotov had apparently acquiesced in an innovation as significant as Nagy's new course. The sticking point was rapprochement with Yugoslavia. Both Beria and Malenkov apparently intended to end the bitterness caused by Stalin's high-handed condemnation of Tito—the first overt cleavage in the Communist bloc. For Molotov, however, admission of errors in dealing with Tito was hardly acceptable, for Molotov had acted as Stalin's mouthpiece in a series of increasingly vituperative exchanges with Tito.[19] To Khrushchev, on the other hand, reconciliation was not only expedient as a general foreign policy innovation, but offered the prospect of enhanced personal prestige, since he (as Party chief) could carry out the negotiations. As Bialer and Boffa relate (on the basis of the confidential circular letter on the July 1955 Central Committee plenum), Molotov opposed this move as soon as Khrushchev, having demoted Malenkov, felt able to risk it. Ultimately, the issue was joined at the July plenum, although once again the innocuous public announcement (Source 6) contains no hint of the violent debate which Bialer describes. What the contemporary public record does make clear is that Khrushchev and his followers regarded the Yugoslav rapprochement as a

---

[19] *The Soviet-Yugoslav Dispute: Text of the Published Correspondence* (London: Royal Institute of International Affairs, 1948), pp. 23, 33.

momentous step. Apart from the extended Central Committee consideration, the policy was discussed in at least four central committee meetings in the constituent union republics during the following weeks—the first foreign policy step to be considered at that level of CPSU organization since World War II.[20] The importance ascribed to the Yugoslav policy may have reflected a genuine conviction that it ensured a harmonious Communist bloc. In fact, however, only a year passed before more serious disturbances (first in Poland, then in Hungary) disrupted the bloc—and by 1958 relations with Yugoslavia were near-frigid. Perhaps Khrushchev was simply overoptimistic; but in retrospect the enormous attention devoted to the Yugoslav reconciliation seems to have been most significant in sealing the defeat of Molotov and his sanctification of Stalin's foreign policy.[21]

VI

In this brief analysis I have tried to show how policy and politics are intertwined in the U.S.S.R. More particularly, I have endeavored to provide some acquaintance with the kinds of evidence which enable us to examine this interrelation. The period September 1953-July 1955 is not typical even of recent Soviet history. Conflicts in the leadership were sharper, and evidence concerning them is much more detailed and reliable than is usually the case. Both factors make a reexamination of the period particularly useful, but the availability of a wide range of evidence is especially instructive.

As indicated above, official announcements and speeches published at the time the events occurred provide hardly a skeleton of the body of Soviet politics. If one took these announcements literally, policy disputes could scarcely be recognized; instead, various figures, obscure as the economists or as mighty as Molotov and Malenkov, would suddenly appear as inept, unsophisticated bunglers. Since our knowledge of human nature as well as earlier Soviet political history disinclines us to believe that participants in high politics are likely to be either as incompetent or as penitent as these announcements imply, one is led to seek hidden meanings

---

[20] See my analysis of union-republic central committee themes in *The Politics of Totalitarianism*, pp. 289, 395.

[21] If Khrushchev's alleged memoir is accurate, Molotov had been joined in opposition to the Yugoslav rapprochement by Suslov, an experienced and prestigious member of the secretariat. *Khrushchev Remembers,* ed. Strobe Talbott (Boston: Little, Brown, 1970), p. 377.

in Soviet publications—i.e., one examines them for esoteric language. The skilled Kremlinologist can do much with this method; but it is extremely laborious and, without corroborating evidence from other sources or subsequent developments, remains unsatisfying. Examination of personnel changes is equally laborious. While this method can provide information on turnover in office and types of office-holders, the relation of this information to the more crucial aspects of the political conflict must also remain inferential, and therefore in need of corroboration.

Fortunately the historian—as contrasted to the intelligence specialist or the journalist—can usually find corroborating evidence before completing his analysis. As many writers, following George Orwell, have noted, the labyrinthine turns of Soviet political developments often consign yesterday's truth to today's memory hole. But it also happens—though not so often—that yesterday's Party secret becomes today's propaganda theme. As shown above, a considerable amount of our information about the conflicts of 1953-55 is derived from speeches, years later, in which Khrushchev and his supporters sought to complete the discrediting of their defeated opponents. What is rather less common is the issuance of confidential circulars describing in detail these internal Party conflicts shortly after they took place. Still more unusual—and fortunate from our standpoint—is the availability of two detailed, independent reports of these circular letters. Increasingly during the past two decades, however, the Soviet regime has found it impossible to conceal from the outside world any information which is even moderately widely circulated within the U.S.S.R. In recent years the flow of clandestine manuscripts to the West has become a flood. They include such disparate items as the two cited in this essay—*Khrushchev Remembers*, a book which reveals a few important secrets of the regime, but which scholars have not yet fully authenticated by checking Khrushchev's tape recordings which are now available; and Medvedev's *Let History Judge*, unquestionably authentic but lacking much "inside" information.

For all the exceptional evidence available on 1953-55, one should not overlook the profound gaps in our information. Here I can only suggest a few unanswered questions. To begin with, there are the "deep" questions of causation which continue to puzzle students even where documentation is abundant and indisputable. To what extent were public pressures really responsible for policy innovations, as compared to the use of these innovations as ploys in the political conflict? It would seem that successive leaders felt obliged to seek ways to provide more consumers goods (including agricultural supplies). On the other hand, down to 1955 Khrushchev and his supporters apparently experienced no pressing need to renounce Stalinism in general. To what degree was a new policy of détente with the West and rapprochement in the Communist bloc really perceived as essential for "Soviet interests," as compared to the policy's utility as a means of enhancing the prestige of particular leaders? Other questions are more specific. How strong was Khrushchev relative to the Party apparatus, and to what degree did his ostensible initiatives merely reflect its interests? Was Malenkov's reliance on his government post simply a poor calculation, or at some point (perhaps during the struggle with Beria, prior to the period we consider) did he inadvertently surrender some key position? Was Molotov really so naive as to believe he could reformulate an ideological position to support his stand-pat policy, or did he think he had some firm commitment from the Khrushchev group? The questions are numerous, and it is unlikely that most will ever be answered conclusively. Many of the participants are dead, and it is unlikely—even if the Soviet regime should drastically change—that completely candid accounts of the conflicts exist. Indeed, we may even question, seriously, whether the tenets of Marxism-Leninism combined with the inarticulate pragmatism of the Soviet politician provide an adequate intellectual framework for explicating the conflict in which he is enmeshed. In other words, even candid accounts by Soviet political figures, if and when they become available, may fail to explain the obscure factors which motivated participants in the power struggles in the Kremlin.

FOR FURTHER READING

Periodicals:

Current Digest of the Soviet Press (now published in Columbus, Ohio) weekly, 1953-55. The most reliable selection and translation of major articles appearing in the U.S.S.R.

News from Behind the Iron Curtain (published in New York, now defunct) 1953-55. Valuable for its monthly treatment of Eastern European relations to the U.S.S.R.

Osteuropa (now published in Aachen, German Federal Republic) bimonthly, 1953-55. For those who read German, this is by far the best current discussion of Soviet politics.

Problems of Communism (Washington, United States Information Agency) bimonthly, 1953-55. The best current discussion of Soviet-bloc affairs in English.

Books:

Alliluyeva, Svetlana. *Twenty Letters to a Friend.* New York: Harper & Row, 1967. Memoir by Stalin's daughter, not highly sophisticated politically, but containing numerous interesting sidelights on events surrounding his death.

———. *Only One Year.* New York: Harper & Row, 1968. An expansion of the preceding work, containing more information on Khrushchev and other members of the post-Stalin leadership.

Armstrong, John A. *The Politics of Totalitarianism.* New York: Random House, 1961. My account, prepared a few years after the events discussed in this essay, of Stalin's last decades and Khrushchev's succession.

Biographic Directory of the U.S.S.R. New York: Scarecrow Press, 1958. The only relevant biographical work generally available to those reading only English.

Conquest, Robert. *Power and Policy in the U.S.S.R.* New York: St. Martin's Press, 1961, and Harper Torchbook paperback, 1967. A detailed and methodologically valuable discussion of the last years of Stalin's rule and the succession struggle.

Dinerstein, Herbert S. *War and the Soviet Union.* New York: Praeger, 1959. Useful for the relation of Soviet domestic pressures to major aspects of foreign policy.

Embree, George D. *The Soviet Union between the 19th and the 20th Party Congresses, 1952-1956.* The Hague: Martinus Nijhoff, 1959. The most detailed account of our period, but somewhat limited in sources and pedestrian in analysis.

Fainsod, Merle. *How Russia Is Ruled.* 2nd ed. Cambridge, Mass.: Harvard University Press, 1963. The most authoritative analysis of the Soviet Union under Stalin; treatment of the following decade is somewhat sketchy.

Gruliow, Leo (ed.). *Current Soviet Policies.* New York: Praeger, 1953. Expertly annotated from the *Current Digest of the Soviet Press*, for the period immediately preceding and following Stalin's death.

———. *Current Soviet Policies II.* New York: Praeger, 1957. Contains some material (similar to preceding item) on 1953-55 events.

Garthoff, Raymond L. *Soviet Strategy in the Nuclear Age.* New York: Praeger, 1958. A discussion of the interconnection of Soviet internal and foreign policies in the 1950s.

Khruschev Remembers. Ed. Strobe Talbott. Boston: Little, Brown, 1970. This alleged memoir is interesting, but should be used with caution until all portions have been authenticated by scholars.

Leonhard, Wolfgang. *The Kremlin since Stalin.* Trans. Elizabeth Wickemann and Marian Jackson. New York: Praeger, 1962. A very good analysis by a former German Communist who spent many years in the U.S.S.R.

Medvedev, Roy A. *Let History Judge: The Origins and Consequences of Stalinism.* Trans. Colleen Taylor, ed. David Joravsky and Georges Haupt. New York: Knopf, 1971. The most detailed effort by Soviet opposition writers to reconstruct the history of the Stalin period; rather disappointing for the events discussed in this essay.

Rush, Myron. *The Rise of Khrushchev.* Washington: Public Affairs Press,

1958. Valuable both as a detailed contemporary analysis and as a treatment of methodology.

———. *Political Succession in the USSR.* New York: Columbia University Press, 1964. A reexamination of Khrushchev's rise, with analytic comparison to other episodes of Soviet power conflict.

Salisbury, Harrison E. *American in Russia.* New York: Harper, 1954. A first-hand account by one of the few American journalists in the U.S.S.R. during 1949-54.

Schapiro, Leonard. *The Communist Party of the Soviet Union.* 2nd ed. New York: Vintage paperback, 1971. The most comprehensive treatment of the evolution of the principal element of the Soviet political system; excellent for background, though contains little on the 1953-55 period.

Shulman, Marshall D. *Stalin's Foreign Policy Reappraised.* New York: Atheneum paperback, 1965. An analysis of the continuities and discontinuities of Soviet foreign policy.

Slusser, Robert M. *The Berlin Crisis of 1961: Soviet-American Relations and the Struggle for Power in the Kremlin.* Baltimore: Johns Hopkins University Press, 1973.

SOURCES

I. Official Contemporary Publications

1

Official Statement on Plenary Session
of Communist Central Committee

SOURCE: *Pravda*, March 6, 1954, as translated in *Current Digest of the Soviet Press* VI, No. 9, p. 3. Translation copyright 1954 by *The Current Digest of the Soviet Press*. Published weekly at The Ohio State University by The American Association for the Advancement of Slavic Studies; reprinted by permission of the Digest.

The Central Committee of the Soviet Union held a plenary session recently.

The session heard and discussed a report by Comrade N. S. Khrushchev on further increasing the country's production of grain and putting virgin and idle lands into cultivation, and adopted a decree [text of decree follows in *Pravda*] on this matter.

Personnel of local Party, Soviet, agricultural and procurement agencies, chairmen of collective farms and officials of state farms took part in discussion of this question.

2

Dmitri Shepilov, "The Party General Line and Vulgarizers of Marxism"

SOURCE: *Pravda*, January 24, 1955, excerpt, as translated in *Current Digest of the Soviet Press* VI, No. 52, pp. 4-5. Translation copyright 1955 by *The Current Digest of the Soviet Press*. Published weekly at The Ohio State University by The American Association for the Advancement of Slavic Studies; reprinted by permission of the Digest.

Views utterly alien to Marxist-Leninist political economy and to the general line of the Communist Party on some fundamental questions of development of the socialist economy have begun to take shape of late among some economists and teachers in our higher educational institutions.

●　　●　　●　　●　　●

Grossly distorting the essence of Party and government decisions to increase production of consumers' goods, the authors of this conception assert that since 1953 the Soviet land has entered a new stage of economic development, the essence of which is allegedly a radical change in the Party's economic policy. While the Party used to put the emphasis on developing *heavy* industry, now, if you please, the center of gravity has shifted to developing *light* industry, to production of consumers' goods. Trying to present their imaginary formulae as requirements of the basic economic law of socialism, these economists propose setting an identical rate of development for heavy and light industry or even providing for preponderant development of light industry as compared with heavy industry throughout the entire period of completion of the building of socialism and gradual transition from socialism to communism.

If views of this kind were to become widespread, it would cause great harm to the entire cause of communist construction. It would lead to complete disorientation of our cadres on basic questions of the Party's economic policy. In practice it would mean that development of our heavy industry, which is the backbone of the socialist economy, would take a descending line, leading to decline in all branches of the national economy, not to a rise but a drop in the working people's living standards, to undermining the economic power of the Soviet land and its defense capacity.

The rightist restorationists, in their day, pressed the Party along this path, as we know. But the Party rejected these formulae of surrender.

●   ●   ●   ●   ●

Basing himself on the tremendous experience of socialist construction in our country, J. V. Stalin emphasized that such fundamental theses of the Marxist theory of reproduction as the thesis of division of social production into production of means of production and production of consumers' goods and the thesis of preponderant growth of production of means of production, that is, of heavy industry, under expanded reproduction, etc., are valid not only for capitalist economics but are of no less importance for socialist society under planning of the national economy.

3

Official Report on Plenary Session of Central Committee, Communist Party of Soviet Union

SOURCE: *Pravda*, February 2, 1955, translated in *Current Digest of the Soviet Press* VII, No. 4, p. 17. Translation copyright 1955 by *The Current Digest of the Soviet Press*. Published weekly at The Ohio State University by The American Association for the

Advancement of Slavic Studies; reprinted by permission of the Digest.

A plenary session of the Party Central Committee was held January 25 to 31. The session heard and discussed a report by Comrade N. S. Khrushchev on increasing the output of livestock products and adopted an appropriate decree.

4

Malenkov's Resignation

SOURCE: Moscow Radio, February 8, 1955, as reported in *New York Times*, February 9, 1955.

To the Chairman of the joint meeting of the Soviet of the Union and the Soviet of Nationalities:

I ask you to bring to the notice of the Supreme Soviet of the U.S.S.R. my request to be relieved from the post of Chairman of the Council of Ministers of the U.S.S.R. My request is due to practical considerations on the necessity of strengthening the leadership of the Council of Ministers and of the need to have at the post of Chairman of the Council of Ministers another comrade with greater experience in state work.

I clearly see that the carrying out of the complicated and responsible duties of Chairman of the Council of Ministers is being negatively affected by my insufficient experience in local work, and the fact that I did not have occasion, in a ministry or some economic organ, to effect direct guidance of individual branches of the national economy.

I also consider myself bound to say in the present statement that now, when the Communist Party of the Soviet Union and the workers of our country are concentrating special efforts for the most rapid development of agriculture, I see particularly clearly my guilt and responsibility for the unsatisfactory state of affairs that has arisen in agriculture, because for several years past I have been entrusted with the duty of controlling and guiding the work of central agricultural organs and the work of local party and administrative organs in the sphere of agriculture.

The Communist party, on the initiative and under the guidance of the Central Committee of the Communist Party of the Soviet Union, has already worked out and is implementing a series of large-scale measures for overcoming the lagging behind in agriculture.

Among such important measures is, undoubtedly, the reform of agricultural taxation, regarding which I think it is opportune to say that it was carried out on the initiative of and in accordance wtih the proposals of the Central Committee of the Communist Party of the Soviet Union. It is now evident what important role this reform played in the task of developing agriculture.

Now, as is known, on the initiative and under the guidance of the Central Committee of the Communist Party of the Soviet Union, a general program has been worked out to overcome the lagging behind in agriculture and for its most rapid development.

This program is based on the only correct foundation: The further development by every means of heavy industry, and only its implementation will create the necessary conditions for a real upsurge in the production of all essential commodities for popular consumption.

It is to be expected that various bourgeois hysterical viragos will busy themselves with slanderous inventions in connection with my present statement and the fact itself of my release from the post of Chairman of the U.S.S.R. Council of Ministers, but we, Communists and Soviet people, will ignore this lying and slander.

The interests of the motherland, the people and the Communist party stand above everything for everyone of us.

Expressing the request for my release from the post of Chairman of the U.S.S.R. Council of Ministers, I wish to assure the U.S.S.R. Supreme Soviet that, in the new sphere entrusted to me, I will, under the guidance of the Central Committee of the Communist Party of the Soviet Union, monolithic in its unity and solidarity, and the Soviet Government, perform in the most conscientious manner my duty and the functions which will be entrusted to me.

Chairman of the U.S.S.R. Council of Ministers
MALENKOV

5

Speech by Supreme Soviet Deputy
A. M. Puzanov

Puzanov held very important posts in subsequent years under both Khrushchev and his successors.

SOURCE: *Izvestia*, February 10, 1955, excerpt translated in *Current Digest of the Soviet Press* VII, No. 6, p. 22. Translation copyright 1955 by *The Current Digest of the Soviet Press*. Published weekly at The Ohio State University by The American Association for the Advancement of Slavic Studies; reprinted by permission of the Digest.

Comrade Deputies! We listened with great attention to the report made by Comrade Vyacheslav Mikhailovich Molotov, which explained the international situation with exhaustive clarity and set forth the foreign policy of the government of the U.S.S.R.

The Russian people and all other peoples of the Russian Republic, together with all peoples of the Soviet Union, consider this policy to be correct and to serve the cause of peace, and they support it completely and unreservedly. (*Applause*)

6

Communiqué on Plenary Session of Central Committee of Communist Party of the Soviet Union

SOURCE: *Pravda*, July 13, 1955, translated in *Current Digest of the Soviet Press* VII, No. 26, p. 6. Translation copyright 1955 by *The Current Digest of the Soviet Press*. Published weekly at The Ohio State University by The American Association for the Advancement of Slavic Studies; reprinted by permission of the Digest.

A plenary session of the Central Committee of the Communist Party of the Soviet Union was held July 4-12, 1955.

The plenary session discussed the following questions:

1.—Comrade N. A. Bulganin's report on tasks for the further development of industry, on technical progress and on improving the organization of production.

2.—The results of spring sowing, the tending of crops and the carrying out of the harvest, and the ensuring of the fulfillment of the agricultural produce procurement plan in 1955. The plenary session heard reports on this question by U.S.S.R. Deputy Minister of Agriculture Comrade V. V. Matskevich, U.S.S.R. Minister of State Farms Comrade I. A. Benediktov, U.S.S.R. Minister of Procurements Comrade L. R. Korniyets, Russian Republic Minister of Agriculture Comrade P. I. Morozov, Russian Republic Minister of State Farms Comrade T. A. Yurkin, and Comrade V. D. Kalashnikov, authorized representative of the Russian Republic Ministry of Procurements.

3.—Comrade N. S. Khrushchev's report on the results of the Soviet-Yugoslav talks.

4.—The convocation of the 20th Congress of the Communist Party of the Soviet Union.

The plenary session adopted appropriate resolutions on all the questions that were discussed.

The plenary session of the Central Committee of the Communist Party of the Soviet Union also elected Comrades A. I. Kirichenko and M. A. Suslov members of the Presidium of the Party Central Committee.

The Plenary session of the Party Central Committee also elected Comrades A. B. Aristov, N. I. Belyayev and D. T. Shepilov secretaries of the Party Central Committee.

•   •   •   •   •

Resolution of Plenary Session of Central Committee of Communist Party of the Soviet Union on Soviet Government Delegation's Report on Results of Soviet-Yugoslav Talks.

The plenary session of the Central Committee of the Communist Party of the Soviet Union, having heard Comrade N. S. Khrushchev's report on the results of the Soviet-Yugoslav talks, resolved:

To approve the results of the talks between the government delegations of the Union of Soviet Socialist Republics and the Federal People's Republic of Yugoslavia.

7

Letter from V. M. Molotov to Editors of the Magazine *Kommunist*

SOURCE: *Kommunist*, No. 14, 1955 (published in October 1955), pp. 127-28, Excerpt from translation in *Current Digest of the Soviet Press* VII, No. 38, p. 3. Translation copyright 1955 by *The Current Digest of the Soviet Press*. Published weekly at The Ohio State University by The American Association for the Advancement of Slavic Studies; reprinted by permission of the Digest.

I request that the following letter be published in the pages of the magazine Kommunist.

In my report to the Feb. 8, 1955, session of the U.S.S.R. Supreme Soviet I permitted an erroneous formulation concerning the question of the building of a socialist society in the U.S.S.R. The report stated, "Along with the Soviet Union, where the foundations of a socialist society have already been built, there are also people's democracies that have made only the first, though highly important, steps in the direction of socialism."

This erroneous formulation leads to the incorrect conclusion that a
socialist society has not yet been built in the U.S.S.R., that only the
foundations—that is, the basis—of a socialist society have been built; this is
not in accord with the facts, and conflicts with the frequent evaluations of
the results of the building of socialism in the U.S.S.R. that appear in Party
documents.

II. Personnel Changes

8

Secretaries of the CPSU Committees
Between April 1950 and February 1956

SOURCE: Boris Meissner, "Neuwahl des obersten 'Sowjet-
parlaments' und Parteisäuberungen," *Osteuropa* IV (June 1954),
220-25. Reprinted by permission.

THE REGIONAL PARTY CONGRESSES OF THE CPSU

The Moscow center of the Party used the election campaign for the
supreme Soviet of the USSR to hold Party meetings at the regional level
which led, in part, to significant personnel and organizational alterations in
the local Party leadership. In especially important regional Party administra-
tions, like the Moscow Party organization and the Communist Parties of the
Ukraine and Kazakhstan, the central committee secretariats were increased
above the norm of three secretaries.

● ● ● ● ●

PARTY PURGES IN THE RSFSR

The purges since the fall of Beria are not confined to a large portion of the
non-Great Russian Republics. As the following review of the party "generals"

of the Russian Republic (composed of the Party first secretaries) reveals, very fundamental changes have also taken place in the Great Russian regional Party organizations; in 6 territories and 47 old provinces almost two-thirds of the secretaries were changed. Secretaries of the six newly-established provinces are also new men. Leadership changes in the autonomous republics and the autonomous provinces were of lesser extent; only one-third of the Party secretaries were removed.

Of the Party first secretaries of the RSFSR, 13 members of the CPSU Central Committee seem to have been victims of the purges, including 9 full members (V. M. Andrianov, A. P. Yefimov, V. V. Lukyanov, A. I. Marfin, V. I. Nedosekin, B. T. Nikolayev, F. M. Prass, S. A. Vagopov, I. A. Volkov) and 4 candidate members (A. D. Bondarenko, K. D. Kulov, L. P. Lykova, F. A. Mamonov).

In addition to S. D. Ignatov, A. B. Aristov, T. F. Shtykov, A. S. Trofimov, F. Y. Titov, N. I. Gusarov, V. I. Zakurdayev, and N. G. Ignatov deserve special mention among the newly named RSFSR first secretaries. Aristov, the former first secretary of Cheliabinsk Province rose to be Central Committee Secretary and Central Committee Presidium member at the 19th Party Congress; after Stalin's death he was at first chairman of the Kharbarovsk territorial executive committee, and after the fall of Beria's plenipotentiary Goglidze Aristov took over the direction of the Kharbarovsk Party organization, the key position in the Far East. T. F. Shtykov, who has assumed direction of Novgorod Province, was the first postwar Soviet ambassador in North Korea; in 1939 he had been named a CPSU Central Committee candidate. Trofimov and Titov, the new first secretaries of Balashov and Ivanovo provinces, won their spurs as second secretaries of the Lithuanian and Latvian Republic Central Committees, where they played major roles in the Russification which accompanied Sovietization of the Baltic republics. Gusarov, who has replaced Nedosekin (a man of NKVD-MVD origins) as first secretary of the Tula Party committee, was Ponomarenko's successor and Patolichev's predecessor as first secretary of the Belorussian Party central committee. Zakurdayev, the new director of the Mordvin Party organization, was second secretary under Gusarov, and the first secretary of the Kaliningrad (Königsberg) province committee also comes from the Belorussian Party organization, where he was Minsk Province first secretary in the immediate postwar period.

N. G. Ignatov, the former director of the Krasnodar party organization, has constantly received new assignments during the past two years. At the 19th Party Congress he (like Aristov) became a Central Committee Secretary and a member of the CPSU Central Committee Presidium. After Stalin's death he was at first destined for a special assignment in the state apparatus but instead became second secretary (V. M. Andrianov's deputy) of the Leningrad Province committee and first secretary of the Leningrad city committee. In connection with Andrianov's removal, Ignatov was released from these posts and is supposed to have obtained a special assignment in the Party central office. But for some reason or other that did not take place, and Ignatov now reappears as first secretary of the Voronezh Province committee.

The alteration in the direction of the important Moscow Party organization is also worth noting. From January 27 to 29 the 11th Moscow city conference took place (*Pravda*, January 30, 1954). It installed a new city committee, which on January 30 elected the following bureau (*Pravda*, February 1, 1954): N. N. Andreyeva, P. I. Dimitriyev, I. F. Ignatov (not to be confused with N. G. Ignatov), I. V. Kapitonov, V. I. Krestyanov, V. I. Prokhorov, A. M. Pegov, Y. A. Furtseva, M. A. Yasnov. The following were designated secretaries of the Moscow city committee: first secretary I. V. Kapitonov, second secretary Y. A. Furtseva, secretary V. I. Prokhorov. P. I. Leonov was elected chairman of the auditing commission. On March 25-27 the 11th Moscow Province conference followed (*Pravda*, March 29, 1954), where I. V. Kapitonov rose, as first secretary of the Moscow Province Party committee, to direction of the Moscow Party organization in place of N. A. Mikhailov, who was sent as Soviet ambassador to Poland. The second secretary remained V. V. Grishin, while three new secretaries (including Moscow city bureau member I. F. Ignatov) were named to replace Y. I. Tretyakov. On March 29, 1954, the Moscow city committee met in a plenary session (*Pravda*, March 31, 1954), where Y. A. Furtseva rose to be first secretary of the city committee, and a completely new secretariat was named: I. T. Marchenko as second secretary, with V. F. Promyslov and D. A. Polikarpov named as additional secretaries. V. I. Prokharov, who had just been named secretary, was left out without any reason being given.

SECRETARIES OF THE TERRITORIAL AND THE PROVINCIAL COMMITTEES OF THE CPSU IN THE RSFSR

(Newly Formed Provinces in Italics:
Asterisks beside Secretaries Who Belong
to the CPSU Central Committee.)

[February 1956 column added by Armstrong; blanks indicate that the names of the incumbents are unknown. Meissner's section on secretaries of nationality districts—units of relatively small significance—has been omitted.]

I. Secretaries of the CPSU Territorial Committees in the RSFSR

	April 1950	April 1953	April 1954	February 1956
1. Altai	N. I. Belyayev	N. I. Belyayev	N. I. Belyayev*	K. G. Pysin
2. Krasnodar	N. G. Ignatov	V. M. Suslov	V. M. Suslov	V. M. Suslov
3. Krasnoyarsk	A. B. Aristov	S. M. Butuzov	N. N. Organov*	N. N. Organov
4. Maritime	N. N. Organov	D. N. Melnik	D. N. Melnik*	T. F. Shtykov
5. Stavropol	I. P. Boitsov	I. P. Boitsov	I. P. Boitsov*	I. P. Boitsov
6. Kharbarovsk	A. P. Yefimov	A. P. Yefimov	A. B. Aristov*	M. M. Stakhursky

II. Secretaries of the CPSU Provincial Committees of the RSFSR**

	April 1950	April 1953	April 1954	February 1956
1. Amur	F. R. Vasilyev	A. I. Sobenin	A. I. Sobenin	A. I. Loginov
2. Archangel	I. S. Latunov	I. S. Latunov	I. S. Latunov*	V. I. Ososkov
3. *Arsamas*	—	—	V. I. Ososkov	I. P. Ganenko
4. Astrakhan	F. N. Muratov	F. A. Mamonov	I. P. Ganenko	A. S. Trofimov
5. *Balashov*	—	—	A. S. Trofimov	M. K. Krakhmalov
6. *Belgorod*	—	—	M. K. Krakhmalov	A. U. Petukhov
7. Bryansk	A. N. Yegorov	A. D. Bondarenko	A. U. Petukhov	N. G. Ignatov
8. Gorky	D. G. Smirnov	D. G. Smirnov	D. G. Smirnov*	—
9. Grosny	I. K. Zhelagin	I. K. Zhelagin	I. K. Zhelagin*	
10. Ivanovo	V. V. Lukyanov	L. P. Lykova	F. E. Titov*	F. E. Titov
11. Irkutsk	A. I. Khvorostukhin	A. I. Khvorostukhin	A. I. Khvorostukhin*	B. N. Kobelov
12. Yaroslavl	G. S. Sitnikov	V. Nechiporenko	P. N. Alferov	P. N. Alferov
13. Kalinin	N. S. Konovalov	V. I. Kiselev	V. I. Kiselev*	F. S. Goryachev

*There is a misprint in the source which has been corrected by deleting the words "in the Autonomous Republics" from the text at this point.

**There is a misprint in the source which has been corrected by deleting the words "in the Autonomous Republics" from the text at this point.

II. Secretaries of the CPSU Provincial Committees of the RSFSR**

	April 1950	April 1953	April 1954	February 1956
14. Kaliningrad (Königsberg)	V. V. Shcherbakov	V. E. Chernyshev	V. E. Chernyshev*	V. E. Chernyshev
15. Kaluga	B. I. Panov	B. I. Panov	S. O. Postovalov	S. O. Postovalov
16. *Kamensk*	—	—	G. V. Yenyutin	G. V. Yenyutin
17. Kemerovo	E. F. Kolyshev	M. I. Gusev	M. I. Gusev*	S. M. Pilipets
18. Kirov	I. T. Bykov	A. P. Pchelyakov	A. P. Pchelyakov*	A. P. Pchelyakov
19. Kostroma	I. S. Kuznetsov	I. S. Kuznetsov	D. L. Zumtsov	L. Y. Florentyev
20. Kuibyshev	A. M. Puzanov	M. T. Yefremov	M. T. Yefremov	M. T. Yefremov
21. Kurgan		G. A. Denisov	G. A. Denisov*	G. F. Sizov
22. Kursk	V. Tishchenko	N. Goroshnikov	L. N. Yefremov	L. N. Yefremov
23. Leningrad	V. M. Andryanov	V. M. Andryanov	F. R. Kozlov*	F. R. Kozlov
24. *Lipetsk*			K. P. Zhukov*	K. P. Zhukov
25. *Magadan*			T. I. Ababkov	T. I. Ababkov
26. Molotov	F. M. Prass	F. M. Prass	A. I. Struyev	A. I. Struyev
27. Moscow	N. S. Khrushchev	A. N. Mikhailov	I. V. Kapitonov*	I. V. Kapitonov
28. Murmansk	A. M. Kutyrev	V. A. Prokofyev	V. A. Prokofyev*	V. A. Prokofyev
29. Novgorod	M. N. Tupitsyn	M. N. Tupitsyn	T. F. Shtykov	I. P. Tur
30. Novosibirsk	I. D. Yakovlev	I. D. Yakovlev	I. D. Yakovlev*	B. I. Deryugin
31. Omsk	N. V. Kiselev	I. K. Lebedev	I. K. Lebedev*	E. P. Kolushchinsky
32. Orel	L. I. Krylov	I. A. Volkov	F. R. Vasilyev	V. S. Markov
33. Pensa	I. K. Lebedev	Zvetkov	S. M. Butuzov*	S. M. Butuzov
34. Pskov	G. N. Shubin	M. Y. Kanunnikov	M. Y. Kanunnikov*	M. Y. Kanunnikov
35. Ryazan	A. N. Larionov	A. N. Larionov	A. N. Larionov*	A. N. Larionov

	1950	1953	1954	1956
36. Rostov-on-Don	N. S. Patolichev	N. V. Kiselev	N. V. Kiselev*	N. V. Kiselev
37. Sakhalin	D. M. Melnik	P. F. Cheplakov	P. F. Cheplakov	P. F. Cheplakov
38. Saratov	G. A. Borkov	G. A. Borkov	G. A. Borkov*	G. A. Denisov
39. Smolensk	V. P. Frontasyev	B. F. Nikolayev	P. I. Doronin	P. I. Doronin
40. Stalingrad	I. T. Grishin	I. T. Grishin	I. T. Grishin*	I. K. Zhelagin
41. Sverdlovsk	V. I. Nedosekin	A. M. Kutyrev	A. M. Kutyrev*	A. P. Kirilenko
42. Tambov	I. A. Volkov	A. M. Shkolnikov	A. M. Shkolnikov*	G. S. Zolotukhin
43. Tyumen	I. I. Afonov	F. S. Goryachev	F. S. Goryachev*	V. V. Kosov
44. Tomsk	A. V. Semin	V. A. Moskvin	V. A. Moskvin*	V. A. Moskvin
45. Chelyabinsk	A. V. Aristov	N. V. Laptev	N. V. Laptev	N. V. Laptev
46. Chita	G. I. Voronov	G. I. Voronov	G. I. Voronov*	G. I. Voronov
47. Chkalov	P. N. Korchagin	P. N. Korchagin	P. N. Korchagin*	D. S. Polyansky
48. Tula	I. A. Shalkov	V. I. Nedosekin	N. I. Gusarov	A. I. Khvorostukhin
49. Ulyanovsk	A. P. Bochkarev	I. P. Skulkov	I. P. Skulkov*	I. P. Skulkov
50. Veliki Luki	G. M. Boikachev	S. S. Rumyantsev	S. S. Rumyantsev*	—
51. Vladimir	P. A. Alferov	A. N. Kidin	A. N. Kidin*	K. N. Grishin
52. Volgoda	V. N. Derbinov	A. Baranov	A. V. Semin*	I. S. Latunov
53. Voronezh	K. P. Zhukov	K. P. Zhukov	N. G. Ignatov*	A. M. Shkolnikov

III. Secretaries of the CPSU Provincial Committees
in the Autonomous Republics of the RSFSR

	1950	1953	1954	1956
1. Tatar ASSR	Z. I. Muratov	Z. I. Muratov	Z. I. Muratov*	Z. I. Muratov
2. Bashkir ASSR	S. A. Vagapov	S. A. Vagapov	S. D. Ignatyev*	S. D. Ignatyev
3. Daghestan ASSR	A. D. Daniyalov	A. D. Daniyalov	A. D. Daniyalov*	A. D. Daniyalov

III. Secretaries of the CPSU Provincial Committees
in the Autonomous Republics of the RSFSR

	1950	1953	1954	1956
4. Buryat-Mongol ASSR	A. V. Kudryavtsev	A. U. Khakhalov	A. U. Khakhalov*	A. U. Khakhalov
5. Kabardin ASSR	T. K. Malbakhov	V. I. Babich	V. I. Babich	V. I. Babich
6. Komi ASSR	G. I. Osipov	G. I. Osipov	G. I. Osipov	G. I. Osipov
7. Mari ASSR	G. I. Kondratev	G. I. Kondratev	A. M. Spiridonov	A. M. Spiridonov
8. Mordvin ASSR	I. A. Piksin	V. I. Zakurdayev	V. I. Zakurdayev	V. I. Zakurdayev
9. North-Ossetin ASSR	K. D. Kulov	K. D. Kulov	V. M. Agkatsev	V. M. Agkatsev
10. Udmurt ASSR	P. N. Lysov	M. S. Suyetin	M. S. Suyetin	M. S. Suyetin
11. Chuvash ASSR	T. A. Akhasov	T. A. Akhasov	T. A. Akhasov*	T. A. Akhasov
12. Iakut ASSR	Y. Y. Vinokurov	S. Z. Borisov	S. Z. Borisov*	S. Z. Borisov

III. Official Retrospective Publications

9

Speech by N. A. Bulganin to the Plenum of the Central Committee of the CPSU

SOURCE: *Plenum Tsentralnogo Komiteta Kommunisticheskoy Partii Sovetskogo Soyuza 15-19 Dekabriya 1958 Goda: Stenograficheskii Otchet* (Plenum of the Central Committee of the CPSU, December 15-19, 1958: Stenographic Report), excerpt. Bulganin's speech is reported on page 340.

I well remember the situation in the Presidium of the Central Committee when Comrade Khrushchev raised the question of the virgin lands and their exploitation and when almost simultaneously the proposal for a new type of planning in agriculture was introduced. "This is an adventure," Molotov said. "We'll end up without grain," Molotov, Malenkov, and Kaganovich said. "It is necessary to wipe the slogan 'overtake the USA in production of animal products,' from the people's consciousness, we haven't got the fodder," they said.

10

Speech by I. V. Spiridonov to 22nd Party Congress

SOURCE: *Pravda*, October 20, 1961, excerpt as translated in *Current Digest of the Soviet Press* XIII, No. 48, p. 17. Translation copyright 1961 by *The Current Digest of the Soviet Press.* Pub-

lished weekly at The Ohio State University by The American
Association for the Advancement of Slavic Studies; reprinted by
permission of the Digest.

Along with the adventurist Beria, Malenkov took a hand in the so-called
"Leningrad case," which was fabricated and slanderous from beginning to
end. On Malenkov's conscience lie the deaths of totally innocent people and
numerous repressions. On his conscience lie the belittling of the dignity and
the compromising of the Leningrad Party organization. Could such a man as
Malenkov accept the denunciation of the cult of the individual with an open
heart? Of course not. He himself was not only a participant in but an
organizer of the distortions and lawlessness of that period. A similar burden
also weighed on Molotov, Kaganovich, and Voroshilov and united their efforts to seize leadership of the Party and the country for a struggle to retain
the ways that existed in the period of the cult of the individual.

11

Speech by E. A. Furtseva to
22nd Party Congress

SOURCE: *Pravda*, October 22, 1961, excerpt as translated in
Current Digest of the Soviet Press XIII, No. 50, p. 17. Translation
copyright 1961 by *The Current Digest of the Soviet Press*. Published weekly at The Ohio State University by The American
Association for the Advancement of Slavic Studies; reprinted by
permission of the Digest.

To get a clearer picture of the danger that this anti-Party group represented, we must again trace the positions they took on some of the basic
questions of domestic and foreign policy of recent years. The comrades will
recall the augmented session of the Central Committee Presidium in 1954,
which was attended by all the Ministers of the Soviet Union and by repre-

sentatives of public organizations. At that time, on Comrade Khrushchev's initiative, the Presidium was discussing the question of amalgamating Moscow's construction organizations into a single system under the Chief Moscow Construction Administration; heretofore these organizations had been scattered among 60 departments. This amalgamation was essential if we were to get moving on housing construction and establish an industrial base for construction work. Furthermore the dispersal of construction work affected the distribution of housing accommodations, because in many instances the departments had neglected to supervise this matter and permitted violations of the prescribed procedure. You should have seen the fury with which Molotov opposed this proposal. What arguments did he give? Only one, that the administration of construction must not be concentrated in a single chief administration under the Moscow Soviet, but that all the departments should concern themselves with this matter. Is any comment needed?

At that time the amount of housing being built yearly in Moscow was 500,000 square meters, while today the figure is 3,700,000 square meters, i.e., more than seven times as much. And this reorganization in the construction field after all affected not only Moscow but Leningrad and Kiev, too, and for that matter the whole country. This was a big issue of fundamental importance. It was a question of major reforms, of new features that had come into their own in the life of our state.

To continue, I would remind you that Molotov voiced his disagreement with the Party's new policy, with the measures the Party had mapped for the development of agriculture, starting with the overhauling of its planning and ending with the development of virgin and unused lands. And this was at a moment when our party's forces had to be brought into action swiftly and we had to gain time, so that the grain problem could be solved as quickly as possible. Steadily hewing to the policy that had been laid down, the Party successfully accomplished the task. As early as 1956 the state's purchases of grain came to 3,500,000,000 poods, or nearly double what they had been before. This was achieved through the development of the virgin lands. How, may I ask, could there have been any objection to these measures? But Molotov stubbornly opposed them.

12

Speech by A. I. Mikoyan to 22nd Party Congress

SOURCE: *Pravda*, October 22, 1961, as translated in *Current Digest of the Soviet Press* XIII, No. 51, p. 9. Copyright 1961 by *The Current Digest of the Soviet Press.* Published weekly at The Ohio State University by The American Association for the Advancement of Slavic Studies; reprinted by permission of the Digest.

How can the opposition of the conservative-dogmatic group be explained? Above all by the organic attachment of its members to the cult of the individual, which is alien to Marxism-Leninism, by their failure to understand that the country was entering a new stage of its development—the period of full-scale building of communism, that the world socialist system was turning into the dominant factor in the evolution of mankind while the imperialist camp had lost its determining role in international relations. Indeed, just before the 20th Congress of the C.P.S.U. Molotov, in a report at a session of the U.S.S.R. Supreme Soviet, openly questioned whether a socialist society had been built in the U.S.S.R. His statement was: "Along with the Soviet Union, in which the foundations of socialist society have already been built, there are those people's democracies that have taken only the first, but extremely important, steps in the direction of socialism." According to Molotov, it appeared that, first, socialism had not yet been built in the U.S.S.R.; second, the first steps toward socialism were being taken by only some of the people's democracies; and, third, there were people's democracies in which even these steps had not been taken.

You yourselves appreciate that with premises like these there could be no thought of a plan for building communism.

Influenced by criticism in the Central Committee, Molotov was forced to excuse himself in the pages of the magazine Kommunist; he tried to reduce the issue to one of erroneous formulation. But it was not an erroneous formulation that was involved. If only the foundations of socialism had been built, it was clearly impossible to pose the question of transition to the full-scale building of communism. If only some of the people's democracies had taken the first steps in the direction of socialism, it meant that the world socialist system had not formed and there could be no talk, therefore, of its

growing influence on the course of social development. This was a funda-
mentally wrong, non-Leninist assessment of the lineup of class and political
forces in the world of today.

The result of his underestimating the forces of socialism and, consequently, overestimating the forces of imperialism was that Molotov made
serious mistakes on questions of international development—on peaceful co-
existence and the possibility of preventing a world war, and on the multi-
plicity of the forms of transition to socialism in various countries.

IV. Unauthorized Revelations

13

The Truth About Malenkov's Resignation

Bialer was a Polish Communist official who defected to the
United States in 1956.

SOURCE: Seweryn Bialer, "I Chose Truth," *News from Behind
the Iron Curtain* V, No. 10 (October 1956), excerpts, pp. 8-14.
Reprinted by permission of Free Europe, Inc.

When I was given a Soviet Communist Party Presidium letter to the Soviet
Party *aktiv* at the Politburo office shortly thereafter, concerning Malenkov
this time, I wondered whether I would find an answer there to the questions
that haunted me—and I found it.

Because the reasons for Malenkov's removal have not yet been given to the
Russian people, or to the Party, or to the Polish people, I would like to tell
about the contents of that letter. These are the reasons mentioned in the
confidential letter, not those given in the press, which were so absurd that no
one could believe them. I shall enumerate them one by one.

The first charge concerned Malenkov's responsibility for serious errors in
the farm policy. This accusation was already known to me from Malenkov's
statement explaining his resignation. In the Soviet Politburo letter the charge

was amplified. It was said that Malenkov was in charge of farm policy. The state of farming in the Soviet Union was alarming, and Malenkov was chiefly responsible for this state of affairs.

When I read those charges, the following questions came to my mind. First, if Malenkov was responsible for the farm crisis, what could we say about Khrushchev, who had for many years been Party Secretary in the Ukraine, the granary of the Soviet Union? Secondly, if Malenkov knew so little about agriculture, what could be said about Bulganin, his successor, who, as I learned from his biography, had never had anything to do with farming? Thirdly, if Malenkov were little acquainted with agriculture, he knew even less about electric power stations, yet in spite of this he had been appointed Minister in charge of electric power stations. Finally, the first steps, which in the opinion of Khrushchev and the entire Politburo were to change the farm situation completely, had already been taken under Malenkov. Therefore, it was not Malenkov who was preventing implementation of agrarian reforms. Consequently, the question of farming was not involved. My suspicion was subsequently confirmed when, in spite of Malenkov's resignation, no really new resolutions on farm questions were announced.

What also struck me was that Beria too had been accused of being responsible for the farm crisis. This coincidence of charges brought against both Beria and Malenkov became even more striking when I read the rest of the letter. I shall write of this later, in connection with responsibility for the "Leningrad" affair.

Before taking up that matter, I should like to mention other charges brought against Malenkov in the Soviet Politburo's confidential letter. Attention was drawn to the danger of Malenkov's policy to the regular development of the People's Democracies. This charge was formulated cautiously and, like the whole letter, briefly: the policy followed by Malenkov could bring about a decrease of economic effort in the People's Democracies. I immediately understood what it was all about. At that time there was in the Polish Party great interest in the developments in Hungary after Imre Nagy had come to power. During that period, Hungary abandoned the principle of stressing heavy industry at any cost and by any means. Not only I but many other people also saw in it a great relief for the Hungarian people. During this period pressure was brought to bear on Party leadership in Poland by the *aktiv* to follow the Hungarian example more resolutely in establishing a proper relation between heavy industry and consumer goods production, so that the standard of living could be raised.

This pressure was firmly resisted by the Party leadership. They were at that time greatly displeased with the Hungarian comrades, who were making the situation in Poland more difficult. I remember especially clearly that Szyr* was furious when some of the activists maintained that Hungarian economic policy was more sensible than Polish.

Shortly after Malenkov's removal, even before I had the opportunity of

---

*Eugeniusz Szyr, head of the Polish State Planning Commission.

reading the Soviet Politburo's letter, I learned of Imre Nagy's dismissal, and that is why, when I read in the letter that Malenkov had been accused of endangering the orderly development of the People's democracies, I understood how this charge was justified from the viewpoint of the Soviet Politburo. Malenkov had, in fact, conducted a policy which might have brought some measure of relief in the economic situations of the captive countries. In the long run, however, this would mean an increase in the independence of those countries, and with such a policy Khrushchev and the rest of the Politburo could not agree. Besides, during Khrushchev's stay in Poland in the spring of 1955, I had been personally able to ascertain this, from listening to his very aggressive unpublished speeches.

The next charge in the letter concerned Malenkov's incorrect attitude toward the development of heavy industry. I was struck by the fact that Malenkov was actually accused of deviation from Stalinism, for one of Stalin's fundamental economic principles was the priority of heavy industry and the maintenance of a steady difference of tempo between heavy industrial and consumer goods industrial development. The simple conclusion occurred to me that whatever in Stalinism is convenient to the present Party leadership will without fail be maintained. I also remember that whereas formerly there were numerous discussions in the Party on the proper ratio between heavy industry and consumer goods industry, after Malenkov's dismissal these discussions were strictly forbidden.

Finally, there was yet another charge in the letter which gave me much to think about. The Soviet Politburo accused Malenkov of co-responsibility for the "Leningrad affair". The charge was formulated as follows: during the period of struggle against Beria, Malenkov adopted a conciliatory attitude toward him, and was, moreover, co-responsible for the "Leningrad affair." How can that be, I said to myself, since Malenkov had been Khrushchev's aide when Beria was purged? Still another question occurred to me: why wasn't Malenkov accused of this when Beria was accused? The answer was clear enough—Malenkov was indispensable in the fight against Beria, and his turn had not yet come.

The third step in Khrushchev's showdown with his Politburo rivals was to remove Molotov from all influence on political affairs in the Party leadership. This took place at the Plenum last July. How did it come about?

•   •   •   •   •

A few days after the meeting with Bierut* in the [Polish] Politburo office, *I was given a full stenographic record of the July* [1955] *Plenum to read. It was the only copy sent to Poland, for the use of the Polish Politburo. Only a very small number of members of the Party* aktiv *were permitted to read it.* The record was very long. The Plenum had lasted eight days, and some of the

*Boleslaw Bierut, head of the Polish Communist Party.

speeches had taken several hours, so I shall deal with only some of the problems discussed at the Plenum.

What was the chief subject discussed at the secret part of the July Plenum? After reading the record carefully, I saw that it concerned itself chiefly with the showdown between Khrushchev and the rest of the Soviet Politburo on the one hand, and Molotov on the other. The secret part of the July plenum was, therefore, the third step in clearing the way for the so-called collective leadership, i.e., for Khrushchev.

What was the platform of this showdown? The Yugoslav issue. The problem of the attitude of the Soviet Communist Party toward Marshal Tito and the Yugoslav Party. But it would not be fair to restrict the discussion to Tito's case alone. The fact is that the question of Yugoslav relations was only a point of departure for a long discussion of political and economic problems.

A good deal of space was given to discussion of a co-existence with the capitalist countries, to the problem of political relations between the Soviet Party and the Parties of the People's Democracies, to the problem of diplomatic relations with the People's Democracies. The question of the under-developed countries was also discussed, and the attitude toward Socialist Parties in the West, and the attitude toward Stalinism. However, the most important subject, and the basis for the showdown with Molotov, was the Yugoslav problem. What follows is based on the shorthand minutes of the secret part of the Plenum, about the showdown itself.

In February, at the Supreme Soviet meeting, Molotov's attitude had already appeared as differing from the line taken toward the Yugoslav problem by Khrushchev and most of the other Politburo members. In February, however, Khrushchev did not attack Molotov, because he needed him in the showdown with Malenkov. This is proved by the fact that the Soviet Politburo permitted his official address to the Supreme Soviet to express views which opposed those of the majority of the Politburo. Yet there is no doubt that the texts of such speeches are scrupulously approved by the Politburo, and primarily by the Party First Secretary, before they are delivered.

From the stenographic record of the secret part of the Plenum, it appeared that preparations for Molotov's removal began immediately after Malenkov's resignation. In the spring of last year, the Politburo held a meeting at which Molotov was criticized as Minister of Foreign Affairs for his attitude toward the Yugoslav problem and several other international problems. Molotov was accused of having hampered the re-establishment of Soviet-Yugoslav relations by every possible means.

Before Khrushchev and Bulganin left for Belgrade, the Politburo held another meeting, at which Molotov opposed the visit. Molotov was for re-establishment of international relations with Yugoslavia, but, for ideological reasons, resisted re-establishment of Party relations with the Yugoslav Communist Party. What he had in mind was not only the visit of Khrushchev and Bulganin to Belgrade, but also the character of their visit.

These facts were given by Khrushchev in his opening speech at the secret part of the July Plenum. Even after the Politburo discussions, Khrushchev continued, Molotov had still not changed his attitude. The disagreement found expression in the adoption of two Politburo resolutions. In one, the majority of the Politburo recognized the necessity of the Belgrade visit and the necessity of attempting to reconstitute inter-Party relations with Yugoslavia. In the second resolution, Molotov's attitude was described, appraised by Khrushchev and the rest of the Politburo, and a decision was taken to put the matter up for discussion at the forthcoming Plenum of the CC [Central Committee] of the CPSU.

At the July Plenum, Khrushchev once again charged Molotov with having prevented the re-establishment of international relations with Yugoslavia, and denounced his attitude on this issue as both erroneous and against the Party line.

The stenographic record showed that Molotov addressed the meeting, and that after several days of discussion the Plenum of the CC declared itself against Molotov. In addition to Khrushchev, Bulganin, Mikoyan, Kaganovich, Suslov, and Shepilov criticized Molotov severely. The discussion was accompanied by a series of personal skirmishes, abusive remarks flowed freely, and time and again the speeches were interrupted. This was particularly true during Molotov's speech.

I shall give an example: When Molotov was explaining his opinion that Party problems should not be discussed with Tito, because Tito was anti-Soviet and his views were far removed from Communism and rather close to those of the anti-Communists, Khrushchev interrupted him, shouting: "But in 1939 you could talk to Ribbentrop!" Incidentally, it occurred to me while I was reading the minutes that the comparison to Ribbentrop was not very flattering to Tito.

As a result of this violent discussion, Molotov made a short declaration toward the end of the secret meeting, a declaration which occupies not more than one page of the shorthand minutes, in which, in an extremely formal manner, he listed Khrushchev's charges and admitted that they were well founded. He also said that he yielded to the Central Committee's view of the Yugoslav problem. His declaration was so formal that I had no doubt when I read it that it was only an attempt to save what could still be saved. It was an attempt to take away from Khrushchev all the arguments that could be used as a basis for Molotov's dismissal.

The shorthand minutes showed that the discussion was full of Khrushchev's personal remarks about Molotov. Khrushchev therefore devoted a good deal of time in his closing speech to assurances that there was no question of a personal misunderstanding between himself and Molotov. Personally, he said, he had nothing against Molotov: his sole concern was the Party. These assurances were so numerous that I understood them to mean the opposite. Besides, even in his closing comments Khrushchev could not resist making a personal remark leveled at Molotov. He said, and I remember that passage extremely well, "Vyacheslav Mikhailovitch, all this is your wife's fault. It would be much better for you not to listen to her. She pushes you and makes you ambitious. She is your evil genius."

Such was the general outline of the showdown with Molotov at the secret session of the Plenum last July.

14

Malenkov's Resignation

SOURCE: Giuseppe Boffa, *Inside the Khrushchev Era*, translated by Carl Marzani (London: George Allen & Unwin Ltd., 1959, pp. 28-31 [Italian original edition, *La Grande Svolta*, Editori Riuniti, 1959, pp. 29-32]). Reprinted by permission of George Allen & Unwin Ltd.

Malenkov resigned as Premier on February 9, 1955, at one o'clock in the afternoon. The deputies, who had already been informed, received and accepted the resignation in complete silence. The procedure was rigorously constitutional but it was still a very unusual occurrence in Moscow, where such shifts at the head of the government had not taken place for a long, long time. Before the parliamentary sanction, the retirement of the Premier had been decided at a meeting of the Central Committee of the Communist Party, which had taken place at the end of January. Why the resignation? The letter of resignation gave two self-critical motives: inexperience in the direction of the total economy and past responsibilities for the present situation in the countryside. Most observers, however, sought the causes in a disagreement over the supremacy of heavy industry over light industry, for there had been a polemic in which Malenkov had been blamed for the confusion created by his speeches on this subject. Actually, however, quite different* criticisms had been directed by the Central Committee against the Premier who had taken over the direction of the government after Stalin's death.

The session of the highest Party organ had been concerned, once more, with the problems in agriculture, particularly with stock breeding. But given that development of thinking and reflections about all phases of Soviet life which had gone on during the preceding year, the discussion could not be restricted to the kolkhozes. The discussion moved toward past errors and paused there insistently. Not only the errors which had damaged the countryside, but also those errors, even more serious, which had negatively influenced all of Soviet life. For many years Malenkov had been secretary of the Party. In practice he was the first secretary, although that post did not exist officially at the time, and in that position had either countersigned or controlled all important decisions. For a long time, moreover, he had been directly respon-

---

*Italian version: "But that was not the essential; the substance of the criticism was different. . ." (*Ma l'essenziale non era qui; altra era la sostanca delle critiche . . .*)

sible for agricultural affairs. He could not, therefore, be ignorant of the real conditions in the countryside, particularly because many alarms had reached the Central Committee. Why then hadn't Malenkov ever talked about this? Why had he falsified the figures of the harvests? Worse, why had he done nothing to improve the situation? Nor was this all. The tragic and arbitrary character of the "Leningrad affair" was just being uncovered. Two major Party leaders had been arrested and sentenced with Malenkov's complaisant knowledge (two years later it was revealed that the arrest of Kusniezov [Kuznetsov] took place in Malenkov's office.). Even Malenkov admitted that he did have a "moral co-responsibility". One day Khrushchev was to say that Malenkov, under the influence of Beria, had become an instrument in the latter's hands. Finally, it was a fact, and this too was revealed and discussed at the January session although not known until his resignation, that at Stalin's death Malenkov and Beria had jointly shuffled the main organs of control, even before the Presidium was called together. The Central Committee was faced with a *fait accompli*, and because of the gravity of the moment no one raised objections. But so singular a procedure had not been forgotten.

The stenographic minutes of the January session of the Central Committee were communicated to all Party members and Malenkov's popularity was badly shaken. He had built for himself a small capital of personal prestige when he had announced to the Supreme Soviet, in August of 1953, the reduction of taxes on farmers. Also, it was under his direction that the slogan of an abundance of consumer goods within two or three years was launched. But this couldn't possibly become anything more than a slogan; superficial and hence actually demagogic. In view of the problems that later emerged, the slogan didn't even touch the economic realities of the situation; to give it content it would have had to be corrected, or more probably abandoned, and this independently of any decision as between the primacy of heavy or light industry. (From what I gathered, Malenkov himself had planned to keep temporary faith by buying consumer goods abroad with payments in gold. This would have been a most dangerous palliative, for once the gold was used up, the country would have been in a state similar to the one it had been in at the beginning, only worse for not having gold reserves. In other words, the country would neither have had the consumer goods, which would have been used up, nor the factories to produce them by themselves, nor the means to buy anything abroad.) At the time of Malenkov's resignation, all this was not clear, but his position was already heavily compromised. After the Twentieth Congress many organizations demanded his separation from the government. After his decisive defeat in 1957, only the least-informed observers could have been surprised that so few bemoaned his going.

A few months later a conflict with Molotov opened up in the directing circles of the Party. The substance of this conflict was of a different order. A self-critical letter appearing in the *Kommunist* led many to think that the differences were due, above all, to the theoretical question of whether socialism had been created in the Soviet Union or whether only the basis for socialism had been created. In reality this point was of secondary importance.

The centre of discussion was foreign affairs, for which Molotov had been responsible over many years.

•   •   •   •   •

After the disagreements within the Party leadership, Molotov openly opposed the new accord with Yugoslavia in the July meeting of the Central Committee. But he found himself isolated. He wouldn't admit any past errors or injustices in dealing with the Belgrade Communists. The Yugoslav regime was not for him an experiment based on ideological premises open to argument, but rather a profoundly reactionary government in its very essence and hence totally irreconcilable with Soviet positions. The Yugoslav question was not the only area of disagreement. He had braked the negotiations with Vienna, because in his opinion Austria would never be really neutral. And, of course, to some degree, his foreign policy of the preceding few years was being criticized. This was implicit in the new diplomatic initiatives of the USSR. There were other criticisms, explicit ones. Khrushchev criticized the haughty and tactless behaviour of Soviet functionaries in friendly countries, and Mikoyan criticized the methods of work of the Foreign Ministry, which were by no means clean of bureaucratic attitudes.

The July 1955 session of the Central Committee had a decisive role in the Soviet history of the next few years, a role perhaps not fully appreciated even today. Beside the isolation of Molotov, there was a first attempt to examine Stalin's activity and there was the decision to convene the Twentieth Congress of the Party.

A. JAMES GREGOR

The Ideology of Fascism

FROM THE VANTAGE POINT of the last half century, contemporary political historians and analysts have begun to perceive the outlines of a new system of political and social organization that began to take shape out of the massive dislocations that followed in the train of the First World War. That war destabilized a political and social system that the nineteenth century had every reason to believe was to be long-lived. In the last half of the nineteenth century, every index that measured stability and "progress" provided evidence to support the conviction that Europe, if not the world, had found a system that ensured tranquility and promised abundance. With retrospective insight we can say that beneath the relatively stable crust of nineteenth-century Europe social and political forces were in action that were to transform not only Europe, but the twentieth-century world as well. We live in a world that is, by and large, the product of the intersection of forces already operative prior to World War I itself. The war, apparently, did little more than accelerate a process that had already been initiated. With hindsight we can speak knowingly about those forces. At the time, and for an unreasonably protracted period thereafter, knowledgeable men were singularly incapable of assessing what was, in fact, transpiring. Even in the immediate past, many of the most competent European and

American scholars have been disposed to identify some of the most compelling products of the period immediately following the War as "episodic," as local and ephemeral "parentheses" in the history of Europe and the world.

Just such a collection of judgments has collected around what is identified as the "fascist phenomenon." Depending on the time period under scrutiny and the sensitivity of one's conceptual apparatus, the "phenomenon" is taken to include some or all of the actual or aspirant regimes that made their appearance in Italy, Germany, Spain, Portugal, Austria, Greece, Rumania, Hungary, Croatia, Norway, France, and Poland in the period between 1919 and 1945.[1] Through a kind of tacit consensus, most analysts agree that only movements that manifested themselves during that period can qualify as exemplars of generic fascism. As a consequence, the analysis is restricted, by definition, to that period and to those political movements. The spate of books devoted to the fascist phenomenon that have been produced over the last decade, therefore, frequently speak of a "fascist epoch" (now happily behind us) and "fascist movements" (now fortunately safely interred).[2] Occasionally disclaimers are bruited, and political journalists and sensationalists will conjure up images of a present "neo-fascist" specter—usually identified with some stodgy "Colonels' regime" or a political obscenity like the primitive tyranny that survives in Haiti.[3] Less silly, if not more intellectually satisfying, are the sometimes tortured analyses of "fascism" that make it little more than a political movement mobilized as a final desperate defense of "monopoly capitalism in its death throes."[4] In the context of such an account "fascism" remains a *current* problem—and it makes its appearance in the guise of ". . . the NDP in West Germany [and] the ultras in the United

---

[1] Cf. "International Fascism, 1920-1945," *Journal of Contemporary History* 1: 1 (1966); Stuart J. Woolf (ed.), *European Fascism* (New York: Random House, 1968) and *The Nature of Fascism* (New York: Vintage, 1969); Ernst Nolte, *Die faschistischen Bewegungen* (Munich: DTV, 1966); Nicholas M. Nagy-Talavera, *The Green Shirts and the Others: A History of Fascism in Hungary and Rumania* (Stanford: Stanford University, 1970).

[2] Cf. Ernst Nolte, *The Three Faces of Fascism* (New York: Holt, Rinehart and Winston, 1966).

[3] Cf. Angelo Del Boca and Mario Giovana, *Fascism Today: A World Survey* (New York: Pantheon, 1969).

[4] Mike Newberry, *The Fascist Revival: The Inside Story of the John Birch Society* (New York: New Century, 1961); Eric Hass, *The Reactionary Right: Incipient Fascism* (New York: New York Labor News, 1966); Editorial, "The New Fascist Danger," *World Marxist Review*, April 1962.

States. . . ."[5] Which "ultras" constitute a "fascist" peril and which do not is never very specific—but the advantage of this latter analysis is that "fascism" remains a current concern and is not simply relegated to a parenthesis in history.[6]

A METHODOLOGICAL PREAMBLE

We are concerned, in effect, with "interpretations" of "fascism," either a generic or a specific fascism—and contemporary historiography and political analysis seem to provide us with a variety of seemingly equally plausible, if mutually incompatible, accounts. Unhappily, what is to count as a satisfying interpretation of any simple or complex historical event remains, for most of us, little more than an account that manages, in some fashion, to abate somewhat, and in some obscure fashion, our puzzlement. After reading one or another version—and sometimes mutually exclusive accounts in serial order—we doff our hats one or more times, and identify what we have just read as "a compelling interpretation." It, or they, constitute "meaningful" or "insightful" accounts. "Meaningful" seems to signify that the account strikes some resonance in us—and "insightful" seems to mean that the account is suggestive of some kind of connections, linking historical events, that we might otherwise have missed.

Now that the passions generated by World War II have somewhat abated, what will count as "meaningful" is clearly different than it once was. Most scholars and students are no longer so concerned, for instance, with evoking or enjoying the sense of moral outrage that at one time attended their discussions of the fascist phenomenon. On the other hand, and furthermore, because of the sequence of events that followed the termination of World War II, there are a multitude of conceivable new connections between events, hitherto unimagined, that can be traced to produce novel "insights." We dignify cognitive efforts undertaken to point out such connections by characterizing them as "heuristic"—a somewhat pretentious way of saying that although the "interpretation" (or "reinterpretation" as the case might be) will be essentially nonrigorous, nonexperimental, and all but exclusively discursive, it *will* be "suggestive."

---

[5] Paul M. Sweezy, "Goldwaterism," *Monthly Review* 16: 5 (September 1964).
[6] Cf. Alexander Galkin, "Capitalist Society and Fascism," *Social Sciences: USSR Academy of Sciences* 2 (1970).

Heuristic accounts can, of course, be "meaningful" and "insightful" in a variety of fashions. Thus, each successive period of history pursues the assessment of fascism in a fashion calculated to produce an account that is "meaningful" and "insightful" in different ways. A more contemporary account might be "meaningful" insofar as it is more "detached," less characterized, for instance, by omnibus disapprobation—and "insightful" in that it might relate fascism (or more specifically, Mussolini's Fascism) to more general and more immediate European and world problems. While the contemporary historian might very well (and legitimately) restrict his account to no more than an exhaustive description of what transpired in Fascist Italy between 1922 and 1945,[7] a political analyst might just as well (and with equal legitimacy) attempt to identify some critical features of Mussolini's Fascism that relate it to broad currents in the modern world.[8] In effect, the latter strategy would attempt to suggest the rudiments of a more inclusive typology or a classificatory schema—and speak of Fascism as an instantial (and perhaps paradigmatic) member of an open class of mass mobilizing, developmental dictatorships with totalitarian aspirations. In so doing the account might (hopefully) prompt the hat-doffing response that we generally count as *prima facie* evidence of "meaningfulness" and "insightfulness."

Such a result might be achieved, it would seem, by providing a reasonably objective account of the ideology that animated the Fascist movement, conjoined with a number of comparative allusions to analogous movements. The rendering should be as accurate as possible—that is to say, the account of the ideology should rest on primary sources: it should be a stenographic summary of responsible Fascist argument. The allusions to analogous movements should, in their turn, be as specific as possible, given the limitations of time and space. Discharging such obligations is by no means easy. But it is the challenge that makes historical and political analysis so rewarding and so intrinsically interesting.

Within this context the discussion of the ideology of Fascism takes on certain properties. In the first place, any brief account cannot pretend to be exhaustive. Fascism was animated by a

---

[7] Renzo De Felice, *Le interpretazioni del fascismo* (Bari: Laterza, 1969).
[8] I have attempted something of that order in the final chapter of A. James Gregor, *The Ideology of Fascism* (New York: Free Press, 1969).

complex belief system whose spokesmen came from a variety of intellectual persuasions and who, as a consequence, articulated Fascist commitments in a variety of styles and frequently in such vague and ambiguous fashion that their individual postures often seemed, at least in part, mutually exclusive and contradictory. What one can attempt is a responsible restatement of Fascist ideology, based on the arguments of its principal and most authoritative spokesmen, calculated not only to reveal the stages through which it progressed, but to exhibit the central themes that characterize its substance. The selective reporting of Fascist ideology in the following discussion will be governed by just such considerations.

In the second place, given the intentions and restrictions of the account, no attempt will be made to review all the political, social, economic, and personality factors that influenced the activities of the actual historic Regime. The assumption subtending the essay will be, however, that the ideology of Fascism was not *simply* the reactive product of political, pragmatic, or personal concerns. A further assumption is that belief systems tend to be informed by a certain "logic" (using the word in its extended meaning) that shapes thought, to a considerable extent, independent of immediately "practical" concerns. Fascist ideology is conceived to have been just such a belief system, and tracing its "logic" involves the sorting out of the elements that came to constitute "the Fascist persuasion," the union of cognitive content and political style that we now identify with Fascism.

Finally, the following discussion will be governed by the plausible judgment that a political phenomenon as complex and as ramified as generic fascism was not the consequence of exclusively local and transient conditions. While the ideology of each movement might well be traced to intellectual currents prevalent in each historic and national environment, the shared similarities enjoyed by fascist movements (and non-fascist movements) in Europe suggest that generic fascism, and Mussolini's Fascism, might well have been, in substantial part, a response to general social and political problems that afflict the twentieth century.

THE ANTICIPATIONS OF FASCIST IDEOLOGICAL CONTENT

Fascism, as a system of thought—as a reasonably coherent collection of convictions about men in association—grew out of the intellectual subsoil of the first world conflict. While Fascist commentators never tired of alluding to a general catalog of "protofascist" ideas available as early as the first years of the nineteenth century, it has become increasingly obvious that the *substance* of Fascist thought derives from relatively specific sociological and philosophical traditions that manifested themselves during the last quarter of the nineteenth century and the first decade of the twentieth. The sociological tradition that provided Fascist ideologues with certain critical conceptual categories, analytic strategies, theoretical and descriptive claims, is that now identified principally with the names of Vilfredo Pareto (cf. Source 1), Gaetano Mosca (cf. Source 2), and Roberto Michels. More specifically, the substance of that tradition surfaced in the thought of Georges Sorel whose writings worked a major influence on the principal ideologues of Fascism. The philosophical tradition, which, in turn, afforded the normative supports for standard Fascist arguments, originated in the neo-Hegelianism and neo-idealism whose most notable advocates were Benedetto Croce and Giovanni Gentile. Gentile, of course, became the principal philosophical spokesman of Fascism and some of his students and followers (men of the caliber of Ugo Spirito and Balbino Giuliano) provided the most compelling justificatory arguments in support of the historic Regime.

We have only begun to sort out the complex interrelationship between men, ideas, and a specific political persuasion, but it is transparently clear that neither substantive sociological ideas nor normative philosophical convictions translate themselves directly into a *specific* political belief system. Mosca, for example, irrespective of the fact that a significant number of his ideas passed directly into Fascist apologetics, was politically an anti-Fascist. Croce, as everyone who is at all familiar with the period knows, was an equally determined anti-Fascist. All of which means that commitment to some one or another restricted collection of fundamental ideas does not necessarily make one a Fascist—or a Marxist—or a democrat. Political persuasions are the complex by-products of any number of intersecting intellectual, psychological, political, socioeconomic, familial, and historic variables. Our obligation here is not to identify the process that makes Fascists, but simply to reveal something of the "logic" of their persuasion. It is obvious that "commitment" to the *thought* of Karl Marx has produced men of *applied* Leninist, Stalinist, Maoist, and Castroite persuasion—men often at violent odds with each other. The distance between Leon Trotsky and Josef Stalin was easily as great as that between Gentile and Croce—and yet the two former were both as decidedly "Marxist" and "Leninist" as both Gentile and Croce were "neo-idealists" and "neo-Hegelians."

Almost every Fascist account, even the most incompetent, identified Fascist political and social ideas with the sociological tradition which included Pareto, Mosca, and Sorel.[9] Enzio Maria Olivetti, in one of the first mature statements of Fascist ideology, traced the substantive elements of Fascist doctrine to the "anti-individualist sociological tradition" popular in Antebellum Italy—a clear allusion to the tradition with which we are concerned.[10] Perhaps the most convincing way of documenting the impact of the ideas given currency by Pareto, Mosca, and Sorel is to trace something of their influence on the thought of Benito Mussolini who left, for all intents and purposes, a public record of that impact in a series of articles, pamphlets and reviews written in the period between 1903 and 1914 while he still identified himself as a revolutionary Marxist.

As early as 1903 (when he was but twenty) Mussolini expressed the conviction that "sentiments are the dynamic motives of human actions"—and that one of the cardinal sentiments moving men to act was a "sentiment of solidarity"[11] (cf. Source 6). Mussolini realized that such a conviction was a "scandal" among some of his "positivistic confreres"—for "materialists" seemed ill-disposed to recognize the historic role of "sentiment" in the processes that produce social change. During this period "orthodox Marxism" was, in fact, in the throes of a crisis characterized as a contest between a "positivistic" and a "non-positivistic" interpretation of Marxism. Revolutionary Marxism was to emerge from the crisis only in the guise of Leninism on the one hand, and Fascism on the other.

It is impossible, given the surviving information, to document the specific source of Mussolini's conviction concerning the influence of the "sentiment of solidarity." We know that Gustave Le Bon, in his *Psychology of Crowds,* employed such a sentiment as

---

[9]This is as true for the closing years of the Regime as it was at the commencement. Cf. for instance, Sergio Panunzio, *Che cos'é il fascismo* (Milan: Alpes, 1924), p. 77; Antonio C. Puchetti, *Il fascismo scientifico* (Turin: Bocca, 1926); Carlo Costamagna, *Dottrina del fascismo* (2d ed. Turin: Utet, 1940); Sergio Panunzio, *Teoria generale dello stato fascista* (2d ed. Padua: CEDAM, 1939), p. 13, n. 1; Aldo Bertelè, *Aspetti ideologici del fascismo* (Turin: Druetto, 1930), chaps. 2 and 3.

[10]Enzio M. Olivetti, *Sindacalismo nazionale* (Milan: Monanni, 1927), p. 95.

[11]Benito Mussolini, "Ne l'attesa," in *Opera Omnia* (hereafter referred to as *Opera*) (Florence: La fenice, 1951), I, p. 41.

an explanatory variable in accounting for mass behavior. We also know that Mussolini had, by 1902, already read Le Bon's book and had been enormously impressed.[12] But we also know that Pareto had explicitly employed Le Bon's concepts of psychosocial group building factors in his own exposition. Whether Mussolini gleaned his insight into the sentiments that foster group building or explain mass behaviors from Le Bon's volume written in 1895 or from similar ideas to be found in the work of Pareto as early as 1901 is impossible to say. We do know that both Le Bon and Pareto shared the same convictions about the "sentiment of solidarity" and its influence. In his essay, "An Application of Sociological Theories," written in 1901, Pareto refers to the functional role of sentiments in human behavior—and the notion that men possessed a prepotent dispositional "residue" of association or solidarity remained central to his explanation of collective responses throughout his subsequent works. Thus, whatever the explicit source of the notion, the idea that human beings are animated by a sentiment of solidarity or association came to Mussolini out of the sociological tradition with which we are concerned.

Furthermore, we know that as early as 1904 Mussolini was addressing himself to a "proletarian elite," a conscious and aggressive minority that was to serve as a "vanguard" of the revolution, a theme prominent in Pareto's account (Sources 1 and 6). Mussolini was clearly convinced, as was Pareto, that revolutions are "initiated" by such vanguard "elites"—elites that serve to mobilize masses to their "true interests."[13] Elites, Mussolini insisted—by exploiting sentiments of solidarity—marshalled individuals into "communities of consanguinity, of territory, of economic interest and intellectual affinity," to become the motive force of social change.[14] Revolutions become a social reality when individual men can be so mobilized (Source 6). The young Mussolini did not hesitate to identify such convictions as a "new conception of socialism, one profoundly 'aristocratic.' "[15]

These ideas were shared by any number of radical syndicalists

---

[12] "I have read all the works of Gustave Le Bon and I don't know how many times I have reread the *Psychology of Crowds*. It is a major work to which, even today, I frequently return." Mussolini, "Il progresso e la scienza," *Opera* XXII, p. 156; cf. Mussolini, *My Autobiography* (London: Paternoster, 1936), pp. 25, 36.

[13] Cf. Mussolini, " 'Le parole d'un rivoltoso,' " and "Intorno alla notte del 4 Agosto," in *Opera*, I, pp. 51f., 62.

[14] Mussolini, "Per Ferdinando Lassalle," *Opera*, I, pp. 65f.

[15] Mussolini, "La crisi risolutiva," *Opera*, I, p. 70.

then resident in Switzerland and with whom Mussolini interacted. The ideas can all be traced to the sociological tradition that included Pareto as one of its principal spokesmen. In October, 1904, Mussolini specifically referred to Pareto's *Socialist Systems* as a book that was the source of his convictions.[16] In April, 1908, he specifically identified Pareto's "theory of elites" as the "most ingenious sociological conception of modern times."[17]

In effect, and by the time he was twenty-five, Mussolini had committed himself to a number of substantive propositions about the nature of man and of men in association. He explicitly rejected the "contractual theory" of society which conceived men as individuals coming together to create rationally a rule-governed association. He insisted that men were social by intrinsic disposition (Source 6) and that they interacted in association because that association was sustained by a subtending "moral order," articulated by directive elites, and accepted by passive majorities. A minority of men, an elite, was gifted with the capacity of mobilizing the "torpid consciousness" of the majority to respond to their "true" interests.[18] Socialists were enjoined to constitute themselves "a vigilant and combative vanguard, in order to compel the masses never to lose sight of their ideal goals."[19]

In 1909 Mussolini delivered himself of a number of reviews of books and pamphlets written by men in the sociological tradition with which we are concerned. One of those books was entitled *Cooperazione* and was written by Roberto Michels who, at that time, still identified himself as a "revolutionary socialist" (Source 6). Michels, a student of Pareto, Mosca, and Sorel, gave expression to a conviction with which Mussolini had already identified: "Modern economic man exists only in so far as he is a member of an aggregate"—a conviction which, Mussolini insisted, "demolished that individualism which has been now reduced to a theory entertained only by litterateurs on holiday." Man, Mussolini held (taking his point of departure from Michels's tract), was a natural denizen of a collective—a collective animated by a sentiment of in-group solidarity and out-group enmity.[20] These were, again, convictions articulated in the sociological tradition of Pareto and Mosca (cf. Sources 1 and 2).

[16]Mussolini, " 'L'individuel et le social,' " *Opera*, I, pp. 73-75.
[17]Mussolini, "Intermezzo polemico," *Opera*, I, p. 128.
[18]Cf. Mussolini, "L'attuale momento politico," *Opera*, I, p. 120.
[19]Mussolini, "Al lavoro!" *Opera*, III, p. 6.
[20]Mussolini, "Fra libri e riviste," *Opera*, II, pp. 248f.

What becomes clear is that such ideas have significant implications for political conduct. In their simplest form these propositions maintain: (1) that individuals are creatures of both reason and sentiment and that for purposes of organization both aspects must be accorded their due significance; (2) that to satisfy material and/or sentimental concerns individuals must function as constituent parts of a rule-governed association; (3) that such associations are moved to action by minorities capable of setting into motion "torpid" or "indifferent" masses (cf. Sources 1 and 2).

Some of the further, if informal, implications of such notions include a disposition to conceive parliamentary maneuvering or the pursuit of exclusive economic interests as neither the sole nor most important strategies for a revolutionary movement (cf. Source 6). Both such strategies appeal to pervasive material interests and restricted rational concerns, but fail to tap reservoirs of psychic energy generally characterized as "ideal" or "sentimental." What is absent from such political strategies is a technique for creating a "psychological unity that reinforces the will and directs energies"—a sensitive and broad pedagogical and mobilizing task involving not only intellectual cultivation, but "paralogical" invocations—what Mussolini was, thereafter, forever to refer to as "myths."[21] What Mussolini clearly sought were techniques that would "create new personalities, new values, *homines novi*"—results that could not be realized through parliamentary tactics and appeals to exclusively material interests.[22] A truly competent revolutionary persuasion must be composed of ideal, as well as practical and doctrinal, constituents.[23] To mobilize masses in the service of ideal ends, the appeal to episodic, albeit real, interests can never be sufficient. What is required is a sustained recognition that one moral order must intransigently oppose itself to another. Parliamentarianism and economism are tactics suitable to an *intra*systemic struggle—the preparation for revolution requires the girding for *inter*system conflict—a conflict between integral communities, total systems in competition (cf. Source 6). It was within this context that Mussolini republished Sorel's small piece on "The Apology for Violence" in *La Lima* of June, 1908.[24]

[21] Cf. Mussolini, " '*La Voce*,' " *Opera*, II, p. 55.
[22] Mussolini, "La teoria sindacalista," *Opera*, II, p. 125.
[23] Mussolini, "Socialismo e socialisti," *Opera*, I, p. 142.
[24] Mussolini, "Per finire," *Opera*, I, pp. 147-49.

Mussolini's early objections to parliamentarianism in general and socialism's seeming fascination with electioneering[25] were rooted in an intellectual tradition that conceived men moved, in substantial part, by paralogical or nonrational sentiments—that conceived viable associations animated, in significant measure, by quasi-religious dispositions of discipline and sacrifice. Only if masses were organized by "resolute and audacious nuclei," capable of inspiring reason with faith, could the revolution, calculated to produce a new breed of man, make its appearance.[26] Mussolini's evident approval of Sorel's work turned on the preoccupation with individual and collective motivation shared by both men. Sorel, Mussolini maintained, was concerned with making political actors out of what would otherwise be historical "onlookers." What Sorel provided, again according to Mussolini's account, was a theory of individual and collective motivation. Sorel made plain that what we speak of today as "grand alternatives" succeed only insofar as they become "animating myths" for the masses. Historic myths are those symbolic and linguistic artifacts that elites, leading responsive masses, employ to reshape political and social commitments. As effective instruments, myths serve to define the moral universe in which men, individually and collectively, must operate. Men, as active moral agents, are necessarily members of an association which shares a sustaining sense of solidarity. Outside that association are out-groups against which in-group solidarity defines and articulates itself. The ultimate test and the ultimate measure of group cohesion and survival potential is the readiness to suffer and employ violence. Violence is a moral therapeutic insofar as it compels the agent prepared to suffer and employ it to make clear his commitments. It defines with precision the character and scope of his obligations. Violence not only "generates new energies," but "new moral values, new men who approximate in character the heroes of antiquity."[27] Violence becomes an agency of moral perfection for creatures for whom social and political activity is a result of the intersection of material, intellectual, moral, and sentimental concerns.

All these convictions, bruited by Mussolini before he was thirty years of age, and while he still identified himself as a Marxist, are clearly anticipations of some of the critical substantive constitu-

[25] Cf. for example, Mussolini, "Il socialismo degli avvocati," *Opera*, III, pp. 122-24, "Vecchiaia," *Opera*, III, pp. 130f.

[26] Mussolini, "La nostra propaganda," *Opera*, III, p. 26.

[27] Mussolini, "Lo sciopero generale e la violenza," *Opera*, II, p. 168.

ents of the belief system that was to become Fascism. They are documentary evidence of the persistent *anti-individualism* that came to characterize the standard justificatory rationale for the Fascist Regime. When, for example, the *Doctrine of Fascism* appeared in 1932, it insisted that Fascism was "opposed to all individualistic abstractions based on eighteenth century materialism"[28] —a clear allusion to the anti-contractualist and organicistic notions Mussolini early entertained concerning the associations to which individuals were naturally disposed. Mussolini was prepared to conceive each such association supported by an ensemble of obligations which shape and define the individual's relations to others within the community. Such "principles of solidarity," Mussolini maintained, "confine the will of individuals." They are overt manifestations of what he called "the fatal laws of solidarity" to which man "instinctively" responds. These "laws of solidarity" find expression in the patterned expectations which sustain associations of men in the struggle for existence, a struggle which, among men, is conducted on the organic, material, and superorganic level. Violence is the ultimate recourse in the contest, and is the ultimate test of obligation. Violence and the threat of violence provide the ultimate sanction governing the patterned responsibilities that shape interpersonal relations within and outside the association.[29]

What is important to note for our analysis is the fact that these basic anti-individualist and organicistic convictions were for Mussolini, during this early period, *association specific.* The specific associations to which individuals owed this ultimate allegiance were *classes.* Mussolini was, during this entire period, a convinced Marxist. He was recognized by his peers in the Socialist Party as a competent and reasonably orthodox Marxist theoretician. After 1912 he functioned as a national leader of the Party and ultimately assumed the editorship of the Party daily, *Avanti!* There was no suggestion during this period that Mussolini was anything other than an aggressive (and tendentious as well as radical) Marxist. The common claim that the young Mussolini was ignorant of Marxist theory is belied by the overwhelming weight of contemporary evidence available.[30] Mussolini was, in fact, a

[28]"The Doctrine of Fascism," in Charles F. Delzell (ed.), *Mediterranean Fascism, 1919-1945* (New York: Harper, 1970), p. 93, and Guido Bertolotto, *Die Revolution der jungen Voelker* (Berlin: Kittlers, 1934), pp. 20f.

[29]Mussolini, "La filosofia della forza," *Opera*, I, pp. 175f.

[30]I have reviewed some of the evidence in Gregor, *The Ideology of Fascism*, pp. 95-105.

Marxist, as orthodox as any during the period. "Orthodoxy," of course, is a term having variable meaning, but it generally refers to a disposition to adhere to a body of doctrine. The less well-defined that doctrine, of course, the wider the range of permissible behavior that can count as "orthodox." "Orthodoxy" was, as a consequence and during the period under consideration, broadly construed. A large number of social theorists during the period who identified themselves as Sorelian "syndicalists" were considered and considered themselves nonetheless "Marxist." In general, they shared the same collection of weighted judgments we have identified in the thought of the young Mussolini. They were just as disposed as he to appeal to Pareto, Mosca, and Michels to support their anti-individualist and elitist convictions. They, like Mussolini, larded over these convictions with invocations to the "proletariat." They, like he, were anti-clerical, anti-Christian, anti-militaristic, anti-bourgeois, anti-capitalist, anti-statist and anti-nationalist. They, like he, had identified the principal object of allegiance in the contemporary world as class membership—all their Marxist postures followed this identification by necessary implication.

For Mussolini, throughout this period and until the traumatic crisis of World War I, the only conceivable association that could claim ultimate allegiance for politically conscious men was *class* membership. Mussolini conceived, during this period, the associations in intersystemic competition to be *classes.* He spoke, for example, of socialists recognizing "only two nations in the world: that of the exploited and that of the exploiters."[31] His political strategy and tactics, his assumption of moral and social obligations, were a consequence of that supplementary and ancillary identification. He identified the object of his loyalty as an economic association, a class. The Church, the State, the Monarchy, and the organized military were all institutions organized in support of his class enemies. The irrepressible conflict he anticipated was explicitly a conflict between classes—the moral violence he advocated was directed against the bourgeoisie organized as a class. Mussolini construed any appeal to interests more general than those of class to be strategems designed to gull the working class into serving the economic, social, and political interests of the exploiting class.[32] When the syndicalists, Sorel among them,

---

[31] Mussolini, "Il contradittorio di Voltre," *Opera*, III, p. 137.
[32] Mussolini, "Nazionalismo," *Opera*, III, pp. 280f., "L'attuale momento politico e partiti politici in Italia," *Opera*, III, pp. 287f.

began to identify the nation as a conceivable object of loyalty, Mussolini was quick to condemn them as having betrayed their responsibilities to the proletariat as a class.

In retrospect it is clear that, theoretically speaking, the selection of one rather than another primary association was a *contingent*, rather than a necessary, choice. The organicistic analysis we have outlined committed one only to the recognition that men were, by nature, members of well articulated associations struggling for existence and welfare in a highly competitive world. Marxists (of whatever special persuasion) as well as nationalists, were all equally well aware of that. Marxists and nationalists distinguished themselves, not in terms of the analysis of the nature of men in association, but in terms of the associations they selected as worthy of men's primary loyalty. There was nothing in the analysis of man as a group animal, sustained by the influence of group building elites, that required the selection of *class* as the association of primary allegiance. Marxists, at that time, had opted for class identification because they were convinced that all available evidence indicated that economic associations, identified as "proletarian" and "bourgeois" classes, made up the roster of the principal historic actors in the world.

It is clear that others, reviewing available evidence, had come to different conclusions. During this period in Italy nationalists had begun to organize themselves politically. The arguments they mounted revealed the same collection of basic substantive commitments entertained by the young Mussolini. The relationship was so clear that as early as 1909 Georges Sorel—so important in the genesis of those social and political beliefs we have associated with the young Mussolini—identified Enrico Corradini, one of the principal founders and theoreticians of Italian Nationalism, as a "remarkably intelligent" man who realized "very well the value" of his own, Sorel's ideas.[33] Corradini did, in fact, speak (as did Sorel and Pareto) of man as an essentially social animal, a member of an organized and disciplined aggregate of "similars" (cf. Source 3). He spoke of that disposition to associate as the consequence of an "instinct of association," that revealed itself in sustained in-group amity and out-group enmity—with groups competing for both material and nonmaterial welfare[34] (cf. Sources 3 and 4).

---

[33] As cited, James Meisel, *The Genesis of Georges Sorel* (Ann Arbor: Wahr, 1951), p. 219.

[34] Enrico Corradini, *L'ombra della vita* (Naples: Ricciardi, 1908), p. 287.

Corradini spoke of group-sustaining interests in terms of economic benefits, ethnic provenience, geographic origins, and cultural affinities.[35] The competition that ensued between groups provided occasion for the ultimate test of group viability: intergroup violence. Corradini, like Sorel and Mussolini, understood the test of force as a moral challenge. The readiness to suffer and inflict suffering in the service of the community was the *prima facie* evidence of serious commitment—all other-regarding responsibilities held a place in a descending order of obligations. In war men reveal themselves as conscientious moral agents (cf. Source 3). Men, under such ultimate challenge, were no longer spectators in the moral universe but participants. Corradini, like Sorel and Mussolini, conceived of no more compelling test.[36]

Marxists and Nationalists alike shared a good deal of common intellectual baggage. The relationships between intellectual spokesmen for these ideas were complex but evident. Among Corradini's immediate associates, for example, was Scipio Sighele whose volume, *La folla delinquente,* anticipated the work of Le Bon by several years. Their ideas were so kindred that Sighele insisted that Le Bon had plagiarized. Pareto had, in the course of his *Sistemi,* cited both the work of Sighele and Le Bon, and it is clear that their ideas contributed to Pareto's own account.[37] Any reasonably careful analysis of the complex of ideas found in the works of Pareto, Sorel, Le Bon, Sighele, and Corradini reveals a relatively sustained similarity. By the time of the advent of World War I, representatives of the sociological tradition of Pareto, Mosca, and Michels, the syndicalist and Marxist persuasion of Sorel and the nationalist persuasion of Corradini, Sighele, and Alfredo Rocco were making effortless transit between each others' ideas.[38] They were all rooted in the same intellectual and theoretical subsoil—a subsoil they shared with the young Benito Mussolini.

THE ANTICIPATIONS OF FASCIST STYLE

While Fascist content was gradually articulating itself out of the

[35]Cf. Corradini, *Discorsi politici* (Florence: Vallecchi, 1923), pp. 36f., 61ff., 106f., 126.

[36]For a full statement of this collection of commitments, cf. "Il manifesto di 'Politica,' " in Franco Gaeta (ed.), *La stampa nazionalista* (Rocca San Casciano: Cappelli, 1965), pp. 9-22.

[37]Vilfredo Pareto, *I sistemi socialisti* (Turin: UTET, 1954), pp. 58, 83, 521, 523.

[38]I have provided a more extensive account of the cognitive affinities in Gregor, *Ideology of Fascism*, chapter 2.

body of thought available in antebellum Italy, the elements of what was to become the Fascist style were the possession of an improbable group of young intellectuals—artists and students—that collected themselves together as the Futurists of F. T. Marinetti.

When one speaks of political "style" one can be understood to refer to the *manner* in which one gives expression to one's convictions, rather than to the convictions themselves. Political styles distinguish themselves on the basis of manifestly different modes of expression. Political content can be expressed, for instance, in inflated and symbolic speech, exploiting imagery and invoking emotions—or it can find expression in measured prose and sophisticated locutions. The Futurists were to become masters of hyperbole, symbolic speech, and the exploitation of metaphor. They were prepared to advance broad and definitive evaluative judgments about the world and the men in it. They dichotomized their political universe, for example, into the "old moribund, useless, and irrelevant" and the "young, vital, functional and relevant" (cf. Sources 3 and 5). They were content to refer to themselves as "lunatics" who opposed the "funereal capitalist and bourgeois rationality" that debased the vitality of the Italian population.[39] They were advocates of "action" and "moral violence."

Futurist style was explicitly and/or implicitly predicated on several half-articulated convictions: (1) the behavior of men was governed, essentially, by both habits and learned, but essentially nonrational, attitudes; (2) in order to break through the inherited patterns of tradition and custom, truly innovative, aggressive, and youthful minorities are required—youths not burdened by the "pedantry, methodology, precision [and] accuracy" that supports the patterned behaviors that sustain the old order.[40] In effect Futurists were convinced that only a revolutionary minority (cf. Source 5) employing an evocative and histrionic style, could shake Italy out of its "bourgeois" lethargy. The Futurists were ready advocates of violence and confrontation. Nationalists like Giuseppe Prezzolini and Giovani Papini, who (for a time) made common cause with the Futurists, recognized that Futurist style

[39]Cf. Filippo T. Marinetti, "Uccidiamo il Chiaro di Luna!" and his Preface to G. P. Oucini's *Revolverate,* in Marinetti, *Teoria e invenzione futurista* (Verona: Mondadori, 1968), pp. 13-30.
[40]Cf., for example, B. Corra, "La scienza futurista," in Luigi Scrivo, *Sintesi del futurismo* (Rome: Bulzoni, 1968), pp. 152f.

could create the moral challenge that would "transform men" and once again make the "masses" "heroic." Armed with such convictions, the Futurists advertised themselves as a "vanguard" committed to "youth, force, and orginality at any cost," opposed to everything "professorial, old and slow." They were self-characterized as "purveyors of destruction in order to recreate," among the flaccid masses of Italy, as ready to take up sides in the revolutionary moral struggle that they anticipated would soon engulf the peninsula. They welcomed physical confrontation as a moral challenge that would "elevate the public to a higher comprehension of life."[41] Because they were convinced that most men were creatures of habit, the Futurists were unalterably opposed to the counting of noses in order to resolve social and political issues (Source 5). Their cry was "Down with sedentary majorities!"[42] The majority of men would have to be *driven* to assume moral postures—the most effective goad was exhortation, a carefully elaborated choreographic and histrionic program of invocation—the ultimate sanction was violence.

Futurists, in effect, had a strategy for mass mobilization. Conjoined with that strategy they had intuited convictions about what sentiments could most easily be invoked. Like the Nationalists, the Futurists conceived men disposed to identify most readily with those who shared with them economic, ethnic, geographic, historic, and sentimental affinities: co-nationals. The Futurists were nationalists. They sought an aggressive, dynamic, and productive Italy. They lamented the Italy of *dolce far niente,* the Italy that provided long-suffering workmen for the industrial complexes of England, France, and Germany. They deplored the Italy that played the role of a scavenger among nations—left to scramble for scraps at the feast of the dominant powers of Europe. They saw war not only as an occasion to redress the balance, but also as the occasion for the creation of the "new man" of the twentieth century (cf. Source 5). They shared, as a consequence, much of the political content of Nationalism as it found expression in the writings of Corradini. What they brought that was novel, was the political style in which that content was delivered. But for all that, Sorel and Corradini could hardly help but hear the echoes of their own substantive convictions in the inflated speech of Marinetti's Futurists.

[41] Marinetti, "In quest'anno futurista," *Teoria*, pp. 282-89.
[42] Marinetti, "Discorso ai Triestini," *Ibid.,* pp. 212f., 214.

THE ADVENT OF FASCISM

With the coming of World War I, Italian economic, social, and political life went into protracted crisis. Problems that had begun to collect throughout the first decade of the present century were exacerbated. Italy faced not only a political polarization defined in terms of aggressive class competition, but a population problem that saw about half a million Italians abandon their homeland each year in the effort to find circumstances where they might live above minimal survival levels. While it is true that by the beginning of the twentieth century Italy had begun to industrialize, it is equally true that it found itself afflicted with a singular lack of the most essential prerequisites for sustained industrial growth. The peninsula had literally no fossil fuels, no mineral resources, and precious little potential for hydroelectric power. Whatever industrial growth Italy enjoyed was accompanied by the massive translocation of manpower from the rural areas into the urban centers. More and more young men found themselves crowded into urban slums. Shorn of the traditional ties that had rendered them tractable, more and more of them gave themselves over to socialist and revolutionary blandishments. The coming of the war did nothing to solve any of these problems. What it did was to stimulate artificially certain kinds of industrial growth, accelerate the movement of masses of men from the rural areas to be mobilized into the military or to labor in the new urban industries, create an incredible national debt, and drain whatever resources the peninsula had.[43] But more than that, and more significant for our purposes, the war provoked a crisis among socialists from which the classical Marxism of the prewar years never successfully emerged.

In retrospect we can identify two problems which, of all the problems that afflicted classical Marxism, were never to be fully resolved within the theoretical confines of the available system of thought. One of those problems had to do with *the non-revolutionary disposition of the proletariat* as a politically organized class. The second turned on the difficulties which attended the whole issue of *the relationship of socialism and*

---

[43]There are a number of competent books devoted to this period. I have found Roberto Michels, *Sozialismus und Faschismus in Italien* (Munich: Meyer & Jensen, 1925) volume 2, particularly helpful. The first three chapters of Luigi Salvatorelli and Giovanni Mira, *Storia d'Italia nel periodo fascista* (Turin: Einaudo, 1964) provides a good survey.

nationalism. As early as 1895 Eduard Bernstein had provoked a searching reappraisal of classical Marxism on just these issues. Bernstein had argued that the proletariat, as a class, was reformist in fact, if not in theory. He argued that socialism's failure to come to grips with the reality of proletarian reformist aspirations had made socialism's political vocabulary visionary and its political strategies ineffectual. Moreover, he suggested that the laboring classes of each nation *did* have a significant investment in their politically defined national communities—and for socialists to fail to appreciate the extent of that investment was unrealistic. Berstein argued that men as a group, and the proletariat as a class, were motivated not only by immediate material interests, but by a collection of "ethical" or "ideal" sentiments. While the "orthodox" were content to mouth revolutionary slogans—to insist that the "workingmen have no fatherland," and that ethical or moral considerations were by-products rather than determinants of the historic process—Bernstein was prepared to take exception. The spokesmen for the Marxist "orthodoxy" of the time—including such notables as V. I. Lenin and Benito Mussolini—strenuously rejected his assessment. Nonetheless, men like Lenin and Mussolini were compelled to offer some account of the proletarian indisposition to undertake revolution. At about the same time that Mussolini began to insist that mass mobilization of the proletariat required the intercession of a self-conscious and aggressive elite (in the service of what he called an "aristocratic" socialism), Lenin was arguing that the proletariat would inevitably remain confined to struggles in the pursuit of its immediate economic interests unless an exiguous minority of declassed bourgeois revolutionaries mobilized their "spontaneous" energies to revolution.[44] Both Lenin and Mussolini responded to the criticisms to which Bernstein had given rise by contending that proletarians were passive because of the failure on the part of the leaders of socialism to mobilize and organize them effectively. Both explicitly committed themselves to the critical role of a select group of men, and the efficacy of their ideas, in mobilizing and organizing masses. Lenin drew on the ideas prevalent in his own intellectual environment—the ideas of Nicholas Chernyshevsky in particular—and Mussolini drew on those available in the sociological tradition of Pareto,

---

[44]I have attempted a more extensive discussion of Lenin's modifications of classical Marxism in A. James Gregor, *A Survey of Marxism* (New York: Random House, 1965), chapter 6, pp. 210-26.

Mosca, and Michels. Both Lenin and Mussolini were elitists, voluntarists, and activists.

During these prewar years Leninism began to take shape. At the same time, as we have suggested, the ideas that were to coalesce into Fascism made simultaneous appearance. Commentators speak of a "Mussolinian socialism" to begin to isolate those ideas, just as others speak of a "Leninist Marxism" to identify a "creative development" of Marxism that was contemporaneously taking place.

The issue of the relationship between socialism and nationalist sentiment, on the other hand, was not, for either Lenin or Mussolini, so easily resolved. Many socialists continued to maintain, irrespective of Bernstein's disclaimers, that national sentiment was nothing more than a bourgeois affliction. The Second International, for example, met with regularity to announce its internationalist orientation. The world, for socialist orthodoxy, remained divided between the oppressed and the oppressors, the international proletariat and the international bourgeoisie. The talk was of an "international brotherhood of workingmen," united against the depredations of an "international capitalist cabal." The conflict that was to herald the advent of the New World was to be a conflict of classes, not of nations. Men were to be mobilized by their class interests rather than any alternative collection of interests.

World War I revealed, to thinking socialists, how fragile such contentions actually were. Throughout Europe masses of men were caught up in a war fever that found expression in the cry for war uttered by mobs of working men in Berlin, Vienna, and Paris. Both Lenin and Mussolini were stupified by the display. Lenin refused to believe that the parliamentary contingent of the Social Democratic Party of Germany had voted, almost to the man, for the Kaiser's war credits or that the German proletariat was volunteering for war service. Mussolini found himself similarly incapable of understanding what was transpiring. As war broke out over Europe, the Socialist Party of Italy took an official stand on absolute neutrality. The war was a "brigand's war," a war between capitalists. The proletariat would not shed its blood for the capitalist class. Mussolini took part in the Party's deliberations— but we have compelling evidence that he was beset by almost intolerable personal doubts about the Party's stand. The socialists had long proclaimed that the proletariat could never be compelled to take up arms in the service of the bourgeois nation. Throughout

Europe, however, the proletariat was doing precisely what socialist theoreticians had insisted was impossible. The world, which orthodox socialism had insisted was historically stratified between the exploited and the exploiters, revealed itself to be vertically segmented into national communities composed of men of a variety of classes all mobilized to what they conceived to be a common defense.

From those fateful days in the late summer of 1914 until January 1915, Mussolini struggled to make sense of the events that had overtaken socialism. Under the impact of national loyalties, European socialism began to disintegrate rapidly. In France, Germany, and Russia socialists were volunteering for military service. In Italy, an entire wing of the radical syndicalists, typified by Filippo Corridoni, opted for war in the service of the nation. Mussolini, as an activist, felt increasingly confined and impotent by the Party commitment to "absolute neutrality" in the face of the catastrophic conflict that had enveloped the continent. On October 18, 1914, in the columns of *Avanti!*, Mussolini called for a review of the socialist commitment to "absolute neutrality." He reminded the Party that "national problems exist even for socialists"—and then proceeded to catalog some of the most impressive instances that involved them. He alluded to the Polish revolutionary socialist party that entertained a program of national liberation—to the Belgian and French socialists who had abandoned the doctrinaire notion that the proletariat has nothing national to defend and who had, as a consequence, volunteered to resist the German invaders—and finally, to the Italian socialists who responded to the voice of Italians within the borders of Austria-Hungary—and concluded that the socialists who refused to recognize the reality of the problem of national sentiment were "blind and dogmatic."[45]

Mussolini's call for reassessment of the Party's position on the war was the immediate cause of his resignation as editor of *Avanti!* and subsequent expulsion from the Party itself. Following his resignation and expulsion, Mussolini committed himself to Italy's intervention in the rapidly expanding conflict. The recriminations that followed were tortured. Party representatives raised strident objections to Mussolini's postures—and Mussolini responded in kind. In the course of the discussions it became quite evident that

---

[45] Mussolini, "Dalla neutralità assoluta alla neutralità attiva ed operante," *Opera*, VI, pp. 400f.

Mussolini had begun to maintain that there was a legitimate point of view concerning the war that was "national," and that the war issue could not be reduced to the interests of the "bourgeoisie" versus the interests of the "proletariat." Mussolini denied that there was a single and unambiguous "class" position *vis-à-vis* the war. He insisted that there were at least two manifestly distinct orientations among and within the bourgeois and proletarian elements in Italy. There were proletarians who had passed into the interventionist camp and there were capitalists opposed to the war. Class categories, in effect, were inadequate analytic concepts for sorting out what was transpiring in the course of the crisis.[46] The notion of the "nation" began to loom larger and larger in his deliberations. Finally, on November 10 and 11, 1914, Mussolini addressed an assembly of the Milanese section of the Socialist Party and affirmed that

the root of the psychological difficulty that afflicted socialists is to be found in their failure to examine national problems. The Socialist International never effectively occupied itself with such issues—and as a consequence the International is dead, overcome by events. . . . We must see whether there is any basis of conciliation between the nation, which remains an historic reality, and class, which is a living reality. It is certain that the nation represents a stage of human development that we have not, as yet, transcended. . . . The sentiment of nationality exists. It cannot be denied. The antipatriotism of old has dissipated itself. . . .[47]

While Mussolini went on to deny that he had marshalled himself into the ranks of the nationalists, it was evident that he was attempting to accommodate the concept "nation" into his system of beliefs. He continued to speak of the nation as a historic and psychological reality and asked whether "internationalism remains an absolutely necessary element of socialism, or whether the socialism of tomorrow might not occupy itself in finding conceptions that might integrate [the reality of] both nation and class."[48]

Events had seemed to provoke Mussolini to a re-examination of his own personal convictions. Until the crisis of 1914 he had been

---

[46]Cf. Mussolini, "Le ragioni del dissidio e le dimissioni," and "La neutralità socialista," in *Opera*, VI, pp. 409-12, 420f.

[47]Mussolini, "La situazione internationale e l'atteggiamento del partito," *Opera*, VI, pp. 427f.

[48]Mussolini, "Mussolini riconferma la sua avversione alla neutralità," *Opera, VI,* pp. 431.

content to identify *class* as the primary object of loyalty for all revolutionaries. The unanticipated and unprecedented events of 1914 seemed to disconfirm his conviction that the material and sentimental interests that invoked the allegiance of masses of men led to their organization into classes. The notion that men were committed to an international class rather than a national community seemed to be belied by the behavior of Germans, Frenchmen, Englishmen, Austrians, and Russians. The most active, resolute, and aggressive men seemed to have been animated by *national* rather than *class* sentiments. Belgians, Germans, and Frenchmen seemed to argue that the war involved their material, sentimental, and psychological interests with an intensity which had never attended the theoretical "class war." Invasion and military defeat, occupation and the excision of territory, would work against the concrete material interests of all men, whatever their class provenience. The cry of co-nationals, confined in territories occupied by powers alien in tradition and culture, found resonance in the emotions of men of all classes. Years later Mussolini was to maintain that the war had taught revolutionaries that an international class could hardly serve as the primary object of loyalty for men. The "international working class" was simply too large, shapeless, and meaningless a candidate community to serve as the association with which men could identify and in which men could define themselves.[49]

THE IDEOLOGY OF FASCISM

Interventionism provided the watershed for all the currents that were ultimately to reconstitute themselves as Fascism. As Mussolini abandoned a simple class analysis of historic and political events, and the concept "nation" began to figure more and more prominently in his analyses, the distance that separated him from the Nationalists began to diminish significantly. Both Mussolini and the Nationalists shared common convictions concerning the nature of man in association. Both conceived men moved by real and ideal motives, with masses responding mimetically to mobilization strategies employed by aggressive and intransigent elites (Source 3). Both conceived moral regeneration of individuals and masses to be a function of protracted and exacerbated conflict. Both dichotomized the world into in-groups and out-groups in real

---

[49] Mussolini, *My Autobiography*, p. 46.

and potential struggle. Both opposed the "sedentary and pusillanimous bourgeoisie." What had separated them in the past—their
respective primary objects of loyalty—no longer stood between
them. While Mussolini could vituperate against Corradini as late as
March of 1918, by 1919 Nationalists were joining Fascist squads
and Fascists had inscribed themselves members of Corradini's
Nationalist Party. By 1923 Corradini's Nationalists merged with
triumphant Fascism—and Corradini could dedicate the published
collection of his speeches to "Benito Mussolini, the Duce of
victorious Italy."

More interesting perhaps, for the purposes of exposition, is the
fact that during these same years Marinetti's Futurists became
more and more intimately involved in the development of Fascism. They brought to the collection of ideas that were to
constitute the substance of Fascism, an inimitable style. Since
Mussolini was convinced that history was made by resolute
minorities activating the elemental energies of the masses, Futurist
style, the histrionics and choreography of the streets, could readily
become a fundamental organizing and mobilizing instrument in
the Fascist armarium. By 1923, when Corradini could correctly
characterize Fascism as the first self-conscious revolutionary mass
mobilizing party,[50] the mobilizing was undertaken with the
strategies brought to Fascism by the Futurists.

The Futurists had been ardent interventionists and many had
passed into the ranks of the *Arditi,* the shock-troops of the Italian
army. Many of the Futurists had served on perilous missions with
the *Arditi* and had returned to civilian life possessed of their
country's highest decorations as well as an irrepressible conviction
that they had all the qualities to serve as a resolute revolutionary
elite in the new Italy that was to rise out of the ashes of the First
World War. When Mussolini organized the postwar Fascist movement, Marinetti and his Futurists were prominent among the
leadership as well as the rank and file. The Futurists and *Arditi*
brought to Fascism the principal trappings that were subsequently
to identify the movement. They brought to the movement the
Black Shirt and the battle cries. They brought the posturing and
the gestures, the slogans and the street locutions, that so endeared
Fascism to the crowds.

Years later Benedetto Croce was to insist that Fascism was, in
fact, a variant of Futurism—a clear exaggeration—but with equal

---

[50]Corradini, *Discorsi,* p. 13.

clarity a judgment that contained an element of truth which Fascist and non-Fascist commentators were quick to acknowledge. Recently Renzo De Felice maintained that the Futurists had infused a "new spirit" into the political activity of the Italian postwar period.[51] A perspicuous contemporary, Giuseppe Prezzolini, had earlier indicated as much.[52] Fascists themselves recognized that Futurism had provided the "sentimental and temperamental" adjuncts that gave Fascism its public character, but they correctly argued that Fascism's *content* found it origins in other sources.[53]

Futurism had materially assisted Fascism in resolving one of the principal problems that weighed upon prewar socialism—the problem of how one was to explain the non-revolutionary character of the proletariat. Orthodox socialism had never succeeded in energizing, mobilizing, and effectively organizing the masses that were beginning to collect in the standard metropolitan areas of Europe. Futurism, on the other hand, harbored an intuitive appreciation of the psychology of displaced and restive masses. The termination of World War I had created, in the urban centers of Northern Italy, a reservoir of mobilizable masses. The war had stopped the flow of outmigrants from Italy and had drawn inordinate numbers out of the countryside and thrown demobilized soldiers among them. All these combustible elements were to be found available in the urban centers of Northern Italy. All these groups found themselves trapped in an environment that began, immediately upon the end of hostilities, to suffer massive economic dislocation. The Italian *Lire,* measured in gold units, collapsed. Inflation swept away savings and security. Unemployment was pandemic. In 1919 there were almost nineteen hundred work stoppages that involved over a million and a half participants. The high hopes invoked by politicians during the war years were disappointed.

Many of the returning war veterans who collected in the cities were displaced and unemployable intellectuals. Italy suffered a supersaturation of dissident and classless intellectuals who had disproportionately borne the burden of war service. The socialists, in what was perhaps their most strategic failure of the immediate postwar years, rejected any rapprochement with the returning soldiers. Angelo Tasca, years later, was to denounce the intransi-

---

[51] Renzo De Felice, *Mussolini il rivoluzionario* (Turin: Einaudi, 1965), pp. 475-82; cf. James Joll, *Three Intellectuals in Politics* (New York: Harper, 1960), pp. 176-78.

[52] Giuseppe Prezzolini, *Fascism* (London: Methuen, 1926), pp. 84ff.

[53] Bertelè, *Aspetti ideologici*, pp. 45f., n. 10.

gent socialist position on the issue of attempting to accommodate returning war veterans.[54]

The survivors of the "generation of the front," those men whom Mussolini chose to call the "aristocracy of the trenches," the "warrior intellectuals," were to provide the critical and effective Fascist cadre so absent from the postwar socialist ranks.[55] Their effectiveness was not only a consequence of the endemic elitist disposition that seems to characterize intellectuals of any nationality, nor was it simply their facility with symbol manipulation. They adopted the political style developed by the Futurists. Masses could and were mobilized. The large membership collected by the Socialist and Popular parties after the war dissolved before the aggressive Fascist movement in the critical years 1921 and 1922. The Fascists were effective not least because they were infused with Futurist style and street tactics. The style and tactics were appropriate to a cadre composed largely of declassed intellectuals. The rank and file could be composed of disillusioned lumpenproletarian, proletarian, and petty bourgeois elements— the former alienated by the revolutionary talk of Socialism and its ineffective political action and the latter composed of a threatened petty bourgeoisie suffering downward mobility, diminishing resources, declining job opportunities, and the indifference of an unresponsive and insecure government.

The Fascists could mobilize these elements because they had an efficient cadre and a collection of slogans calculated to invoke common national sentiments. They promised aggressive action to dissident proletarians who had seen the Socialists bungle every opportunity afforded them for making revolution. They promised security and dignity to threatened artisans, shopkeepers, and civil servants. And they promised a general defense of *all* classes, the propertied and the propertyless, in an environment that gave every evidence of disintegrating into total disorder.

In June 1923, the Executive Committee of the Communist International, in attempting to analyze the events that had overtaken Italian socialism, recognized that Fascism had managed to mobilize the "small and middle bourgeoisie . . . the small landed peasantry . . . the intellectuals [as well as] many proletarian elements who, looking for and demanding action, [felt] dissatisfied

---

[54] Angelo Tasca, *Nascita e avento del fascismo* (Florence: La nuova Italia, 1950), pp. 518f.

[55] Cf. Michels's commentary on the role of returning war veterans and intellectuals, *Sozialismus und Faschismus in Italien,* II, pp. 253ff.

with the behavior of all political parties."[56] In fact, in their less tendentious moments Communists were prepared to admit that Fascism had in fact won a significant "political and ideological victory over the labor movement."[57] The political victory was at least in part the consequence of the adoption of the Futurist political style. But that adoption was, in itself, at least in part the consequence of Fascism's ideological convictions, convictions which Mussolini harbored as early as 1904. Fascism was prepared to invoke the mass mobilizing style of Futurism because Fascists entertained certain convictions about men in association, about the mimetism and suggestibility of crowds, about the energizing motives governing collective behavior. All of these convictions were drawn from the sociological tradition of which Pareto was perhaps the foremost spokesman—and these were convictions shared by syndicalists, nationalists and radical socialists of Mussolini's stamp. But Fascism's ideological victory was also a consequence of its synthesis of nationalist and syndicalist content—a special combination of elements that had, and has, a singular significance for Europe and, in our own time, the world. Once Mussolini had transferred his loyalty from the proletarian class to the Italian nation, his belief system underwent a transformation which ultimately revealed the shape of mature Fascist ideology. It was with the specific content that collected around Mussolini's core convictions that Fascism won its victory in 1922.

Having committed himself to intervention in 1914, Mussolini was prepared to grant that the Italian nation had legitimate interests independent of the interests of any constituent class or population category. There was a real general interest that found overt expression in the disposition of men of all walks of life, and all economic origins, to sacrifice in its defense. By the end of World War I Mussolini was prepared to articulate the conviction that Italy, as an integral unity including all classes and all categories of persons, was as disadvantaged as the proletarian class ever conceived itself to be. Italy was, in fact, a "proletarian nation." The entire nation, faced by the impostures and imperialisms of "bourgeois" or "plutocratic" nations, found itself denied sustenance and place.[58] Mussolini, in effect, was bruiting

---

[56] As cited in John Cammett, "Communist Theories of Fascism, 1920-1935," in *Science and Society* 21 No. 2 (Spring, 1967):151.

[57] Clara Zetkin, "Der Kampf gegen den Faschismus," in Ernst Nolte, *Theorien ueber den Faschismus* (Berlin: Kiepenheuer & Witsch, 1967), p. 99.

[58] Mussolini, "Atto di nascita del fascismo," *Opera*, XII, p. 323.

an idea that had been given common currency by Corradini as early as 1910[59] (Sources 3 and 6).

As a "proletarian" nation, every element of the Italian population became heir to all the sentiments that socialism had so long labored to inject into the intellectual climate of the peninsula. All Italians, irrespective of class or origin, could aspire to the future promised exclusively to the proletarian class by orthodox socialism. More than that, a "proletarian" Italy could make effective recourse to traditional loyalties and ingrained habits of its entire population. One could sacrifice himself for his country without suffering the conflict of loyalties that proved to be the nemesis of European socialists. The identification of the entire nation as "proletarian" forged the linch-pin of a system of beliefs that the Fascists baptized "national syndicalism"—a synthesis anticipated by Michels and Sorel . . . and Corradini as well (cf. Source 6).

Once the *entire* nation was characterized as disadvantaged, "proletarian," Fascists could treat the integral community as an effective productive unit. Italy as a whole was an exploited community—as socialists had insisted the workers had been exploited. Italy was exploited by "plutocratic" nations that used every "bourgeois" device to deny the nation its equitable share of the world's resources—"plutocratic" nations that had exploited every economic and diplomatic strategem to defend their advantage (cf. Source 6). Italy, like the proletarian class of yore, had been denied its "place in the sun." In giving credence to such convictions, *all* Italians could give themselves over to the defense of the fatherland in order to defeat oppression and exploitation—to their collective mutual advantage and in the pursuit of justice. These were to become the constant, and most successful, mobilizing themes of Fascist propaganda. As early as 1914 the young Dino Grandi, who was to serve among the highest echelons of Fascism's elite, insisted that the future of Europe would be dominated by "a class struggle between nations"—a conflict between "capitalist" and "proletarian nations."[60]

Both explicit and implicit in such an orientation were two programmatic themes that were equally recurrent and insistent in Fascist ideology: (1) the collaboration of all "productive classes" in the defense of the "proletarian" fatherland in the service of (2) the maximum development of the nation's productive capacities

---

[59] Corradini, "Principii di nazionalismo," *Discorsi*, pp. 92f.
[60] Dino Grandi, *Giovani* (Bologna: Zanichelli, 1941), pp. 39, 41f.

(cf. Source 6). Pareto, long prior to the advent of the First World War, had argued that the problems that faced most nations of the world were problems of *production* rather than socialist problems of *distribution.* As early as 1919 Mussolini insisted that the divisive class interests that divided Italians must be superseded by a more substantial and more pervasive interest: the need to increase the productive capacity of the "proletarian" fatherland.[61] In the documents that constitute the founding charter of the Fascist movement, Mussolini identified for Fascists but two unalterable programmatic commitments: one, the maintenance and expansion of the nation's productive capacity, and the other, the defense of the nation[62] (cf. Source 6). Sustained and incremental production required an intense collaboration of all productive elements in the national community. All the productive forces of the nation were to be marshalled in what Sergio Panunzio early called a "grand army" suffused with a "grand discipline" under the aegis of a youthful and dynamic elitist "hierarchy."[63] Maximization of production would provide the sinews for national defense (Source 6).

Within the context of these convictions all of Mussolini's ideas began to take on a special coherence. The surface features of Fascism began to take on substance. The *nation* was the association of primary loyalty to which men could give their allegiance. The out-groups against which the Italian in-group defined itself were advantaged nations, fat with "plutocratic" privilege. The constellation of obligations assumed by members of the association included disciplined and devoted labor in the service of increased national productivity. The ultimate test of loyalty was a readiness to serve the nation in times of international conflict. The national community was suffused by a sense of high moral tension out of which the "New Man" could be regenerated. That instrumental moral tension was to be sustained by what Fascists pleased to call "choreography, ceremony and ritual." Nationalist, syndicalist and Futurist elements were at once fused into the ideology of Fascism.

All that remained was to have the entire substance leavened with that final constituent: Fascism's conception of the state. Given the enterprisory, pedagogical, and tutelary functions of the revolutionary and national elite, the need for an organizing agency

---

[61] Mussolini, "Rettifiche di tiro," *Opera*, XII, p. 250.
[62] Mussolini, "Atto di nascita del fascismo," *Opera*, XII, p. 325.
[63] Sergio Panunzio, *Che cos'é il fascismo,* p. 16.

to superintend the entire process became obvious. By 1921 after considerable soul-searching and conflict (that revealed itself in the issuance of a number of mutually exclusive and contradictory postures), Mussolini explicitly adopted Giovanni Gentile's neo-idealist convictions concerning the state.[64] Roberto Farinacci, who was to serve as General Secretary of the Fascist Party, in his history of the period, refers explicitly to the decision to adopt Gentile's conception of the "ethical" and "totalitarian" state.[65]

Gentile had early identified himself with the interventionists, and his association with the Nationalists (irrespective of his considerable reservations) indicated a commonality of views. Ultimately, Gentile's convictions concerning the nature and function of the state became critical to the justificatory arguments of the Regime. His ideas were sufficiently acceptable to the Nationalists that the Fascist state, with its hierarchical and authoritarian features, could pass as the fulfillment of *either* Nationalist (cf. Source 4) or neo-idealist convictions. In any event, it was clear to Mussolini that once Fascism had assumed the collection of obligations entailed in the productionist and developmental intentions incorporated in the Fascist program, a strong and highly centralized state became a requirement. With that recognition, Fascist ideology was substantially complete. It was the consequence of the confluence of currents that, although sharing subtending similarities, developed separately in antebellum Italy. Their fusion took place in the charged atmosphere of postwar Europe.

Fascist ideology became the rationale for a mass-mobilizing, development dictatorship. It arose in a nation suffering retarded industrial development. Italy had only begun its industrial development when World War I threw the entire system into protracted crisis. Fascism undertook to resume that development in a drive toward industrial maturity. Given the circumstances in which it found itself, and the resources at its disposal, Fascism sought to accelerate the capital accumulation necessary for industrial expansion by suppressing labor unrest, controlling consumption, and intensively organizing industrial and managerial elements (a process that had already begun in prewar Italy). The major burden of the entire program fell, as it seems inevitably to fall in all developing nations, on the working classes. The state

[64] Cf. for example, Mussolini, "Il programma fascista," *Opera*, XVII, pp. 219, 221.
[65] Roberto Farinacci, *Storia della rivoluzione fascista* (Cremona: Cremona nuova, 1937), III, pp. 230-62, particularly p. 256.

administered a developmental program largely articulated by private industrial and managerial associations always under the threatening superintendence of the unitary (and increasingly dictatorial) Party. The Fascists made it clear that they had no intention of nationalizing private property as long as that property was effectively administered—and the Party and its leadership were to be the ultimate arbiters of what constituted effective administration. The profit rates of industry were to be maintained at as high a level as possible. Capitalists were not expected to squirrel away profits, but were given every incentive to reinvest in industrial expansion. To accelerate capital accumulation, wages and nonproductive consumption were to be held at the lowest tolerable levels. Economists will continue to argue how effective those policies were, and political analysts will continue to argue whether there were any alternatives open to the Fascists, but it is reasonably clear that Fascist ideology served this overall strategy. In the process Italy developed a modern infrastructure for modernization—expanding road and rail systems—increased agricultural yield—and developed a defensive and aggressive capability of sufficient magnitude to cause the more advanced nations of Europe to give it considerable berth.

Any number of commentators have highlighted these features of the regime. Peter Drucker, in the early thirties, alluded to what he termed the "noneconomic" policies of Fascism. Fascism's primary preoccupation, Drucker suggested, seemed to be "to keep the machinery of industrial production in good working order." The working classes were provided "noneconomic" benefits in order to permit increased investment in capital goods. Reduced consumption and high profit levels were strategies for creating capital for accelerated industrial investment. Drucker conceived "consumption management" to be the "secret" of totalitarian economic policy. If it was, it is clearly a perfectly rational economic strategy for a community undertaking a drive for industrial maturity.[66] The economy goes into phased develop-

[66] Peter Drucker, *The End of Economic Man* (New York: Harper, 1969), chapter 6, particularly pp. 156f. Cf. Paul Einzig's positive assessment of the Fascist developmental program, *The Economic Foundations of Fascism* (London: Macmillan, 1933), chapter 6 and passim. Compare in this context, S. Lombardini, "Italian Fascism and the Economy," in Stuart J. Woolf (ed.), *The Nature of Fascism*, pp. 152-64, particularly pp. 156f., and William G. Welk, *Fascist Economic Policy* (Cambridge: Harvard University, 1938). A Fascist account of the first eight years of Fascist rule is available in Antonio S. Benni, "Lo sviluppo industriale dell'Italia fascista," in *Lo stato Mussoliniano e le realizzazioni del fascismo nella nazione* (Rome: "La Rassegna Italiana," 1930); cf. also Delzell's editorial comments in *Mediterranean Fascism*, pp. 136-38.

ment without the dislocations that would attend a "revolution" that exterminates or alienates strategic managerial or enterprisory talents or "redistributes" scarce welfare benefits. The Fascist strategy was to make the propertied classes become the vehicle for the transmission of accumulated capital into developing industries. Heavy industry was favored at the expense of smaller, relatively noneconomic, units, and the process was conducted under the surveillance of the Party. Ideally, managerial and enterprisory elites were to be governed by the political hierarchy—but we know, as a matter of fact, that in many instances such strategic groups have enough autonomy and political leverage to defend themselves from any such developmental regime. Nonetheless, the specific aspirations of the Fascist state *were* totalitarian—and were calculated to control both labor and capital—and its overall policy was geared to the rapid industrialization of the peninsula.[67]

James Burnham has left us an account of Fascism that conceives it to have been a "managerial ideology,"[68] an ideology calculated to enhance the expansion and viability of industry as an integrated, disciplined, and rationalized national enterprise. In such an ideology there is emphasis on "saving," "work," and "discipline." Managerial ideologies are, in effect, animated by a work and sacrifice ethic—as one might well expect in a society going through the process of intensive and intensified capital production and accumulation. Labor organizations are domesticated and disciplined to state purpose—and noneconomic social benefits ("moral incentives") are substituted for "wasteful" consumption of capital in the form of commodities. We might add that the work ethic of Fascism not only served to restrict consumption in the service of capital accumulation, it provided the energy for labor intensive enterprises required in developing nations. The "voluntary" labor donated by domesticated labor organizations, for example, was a cost-free supplement to economic development. One works without material compensation for one's fatherland and the future of the nation in its entirety. One is subject to "moral incentives."

[67]This is the context in which books like Daniel Guerin, *Fascism and Big Business* (New York: Pioneer, 1939) and Ernesto Rossi, *Padroni del vapore e fascismo* (Bari: Laterza, 1966) might well be read. For a sober account of the relationship between the Fascist and the industrial hierarchies of Italy cf. Roland Sarti, *Fascism and the Industrial Leadership in Italy, 1919-1940* (Berkeley: University of California Press, 1971).

[68]James Burnham, *The Managerial Revolution* (New York: Day, 1941).

FASCIST IDEOLOGY AND HISTORY

If Fascist ideology was, in fact, essentially if not exclusively a rationale for a mass mobilizing, developmental dictatorship, its contemporary perceptions of the Soviet Union provide some interesting reflexive insights. Those perceptions tell us something about Fascists and their ideology—and perhaps offer some heuristic suggestions about a modern "neofascism."

While it is common knowledge that Fascism wore the mantle of an intransigent "anti-Bolshevism," it is less well known that serious Fascist ideologues entertained a rather subtle interpretation of the ideology that animated the Soviet experiment. By the mid-thirties serious Fascist literature was filled with articles devoted to the analysis of the Soviet experience. Characteristic of that literature was a distinction between various forms of "anti-Bolshevism." Fascists recognized the prevalence of a "reactionary anti-Bolshevism," an anti-Bolshevism of the threatened bourgeoisie who, after the deluge, sought a return to the *laissez faire* liberalism of the past. Fascists refused to identify with such "anti-Bolshevisms," and they lamented the disposition of some Europeans to identify Fascism with it.[69] Fascists argued that their "anti-Bolshevism" did not harken back to a restoration of prewar capitalism. They insisted that their "anti-Bolshevism" was a consequence of their recognition that the Soviets had misconstrued the challenge of the contemporary world. The Soviets continued to mouth internationalist, anti-statist, and "proletarian" slogans when the self-evident features of their regime attested to their abandonment of the entire substance of Marxism. Fascists indicated, with considerable satisfaction, that the internal policies of the Stalinist Regime had "involuted" the classical Marxism of Marx and Engels and had "dialectically" transformed the anarcho-syndicalist and anti-statist ideas of Lenin to produce a "political formula that galvanizes the Russian people in the service of industrial development—to nationalist purpose."[70] Stalinist formulae further provided for a restabilization of the family as the primary nucleus of a strong and centralized state; it made the state the central enterprisory and tutelary agency of the nation, and the nation was defended by military forces for whom the "defense of

---

[69]Francesco M. Pacces, "Antibolscevismo e antibolscevismi vari," *Critica fascista* 15, No. 17 (July 1, 1937): 289.
[70]Agostino Nasti, "L'Italia, il bolcevismo, la Russia," *Critica fascista* 15, No. 10 (March 15, 1937): 162.

the socialist motherland" was a primary obligation. Gone was the frenetic anti-religious, anti-militarist, anti-nationalist bias of the "revolutionary socialism" that had been the mortal enemy of Fascism.[71] Even in the discussions generated by this analysis, the disclaimers by Fascist discussants turned solely on what such internal developments meant for *international* relations. The most critical counterarguments contained clear recognition that Fascists generally agreed that Stalin's reforms of 1935 and 1936 had "dialectically thrown overboard the principles in whose name" the Russian Revolution had been conducted—and that "Marxist-Leninist principles" had been transformed into their " 'contraries,' that is to say, the ideas that provide body and substance to the Fascism of Mussolini."[72]

This kind of analysis had been countenanced by Mussolini himself. As early as 1933 Mussolini favorably reviewed Renzo Bertoni's *Il trionfo del fascismo nell'U.R.S.S.,* and suggested that the only viable course Russia could, in fact, follow was "an abandonment of Marx and an application of the principles of Fascism."[73] In 1934, in the principal journal of the Fascist Party, M. Ardemagni could correspondingly maintain that "in the course of its development the Russian revolution has gradually given evidence of fully abandoning Marxist postulates and of a gradual, if surreptitious, acceptance of certain fundamental political principles that characterize Fascism."[74] By 1938 Mussolini could, with considerable irony, identify Stalin as "a crypto-fascist."[75]

Sergio Panunzio, in a definitive study of Fascist ideology, published in a revised edition as late as 1939, indicated that while prewar socialism has been anti-state and anti-national, distributionistic and singularly "proletarian" in guise—and anarchic in disposition—the state system that had evolved in the Soviet Union under Stalin had begun to take on more and more of the features of paradigmatic Fascism.[76] As early as 1925 Panunzio had indicated that "Fascism and Bolshevism were phenomena that shared critical similarities."[77] He indicated that the Soviets had

[71] Berto Ricci, "Il 'fascismo' di Stalin," *Critica fascista* 15, No. 18 (July 15, 1937): 317-19.

[72] Tomaso Napolitano, "Il 'fascismo' di Stalin ovvero l'U.R.S.S. e noi," *Critica fascista* 15, No. 23 (October 1, 1937): 397.

[73] Mussolini, "Segnalazione," *Opera*, XXVI, p. 84.

[74] Mirko Ardemagni, "Deviazioni Russe verso il fascismo," *Gerarchia* 15 (July, 1934): 571.

[75] Mussolini, "Atto quinto finora," *Opera*, XXIX, p. 63.

[76] Panunzio, *Teoria generale*, pp. 5f., 8-10.

[77] Panunzio, *Lo stato fascista* (Bologna: Cappelli, 1925), pp. 145ff.

given every indication of having created an armed and authoritarian, anti-liberal state that had mobilized and disciplined masses to the service of intensive internal development. The state, possessed of hierarchical and juridical preeminence, generated, and allocated resources, articulated and administered interests, and assumed paramount pedagogical and tutelary functions.

This kind of analysis was not restricted to Fascists by any means. Trotsky spoke of the fateful similarities shared by Fascism and Stalinism—and both Prezzolini and Rudolfo Mondolfo, as early as 1925, remarked on the shared attributes that characterized the two revolutionary regimes.[78] The similarities include an intense nationalism, the instauration of an authoritarian and anti-liberal state under a "charismatic leader" activating "masses" that included all "sound" and "productive" population elements, a domestication of labor unions, and authoritarian control of the means of production by an enterprisory and managerial bureaucracy enjoying differential income and differential access to the levers of power. All of this took place within the confines of a political system dominated by a unitary party monopolizing the institutions of interest articulation and interest aggregation. Control over the means of communication and the prevalence of special means of social surveillance completed the picture of analogous political systems. The ultimate intentions of both were the creation of a modern and self-sufficient industrial system— economic autarchy that insured political and economic independence for what had been an underdeveloped national community. All that, coupled with instances of territorial aggression, provided a compelling picture of systemic symmetry. Drucker simply characterized the process by saying that "Russia has . . . been forced to adopt one purely totalitarian and fascist principle after the other," and Burnham could identify Bolshevism as one of the generic class of "managerial ideologies."[79] In 1936 Elie Halevy simply proceeded to "define" Bolshevism as one form of "fascism."[80] In our own time Bruno Rizzi, as a revolutionary socialist, could only lament that " . . . that which Fascism con-

---

[78] Leon Trotsky, *The Revolution Betrayed* (New York: Doubleday, 1937), p. 278; Giuseppe Prezzolini, "Ideologia e sentimento," and Rodolfo Mondolfo, "Il fascismo in Italia," in R. De Felice, *Il fascismo e i partiti politici Italiani* (Rocca San Casciano: Cappelli, 1966), pp. 522f., 549. Cf. also Bruno Rizzi. *Le lezioni dello Stalinismo* (Rome: Opere nuove, 1962).

[79] Drucker, *The End of Economic Man*, p. 246.

[80] Elie Halevy, *The Era of Tyrannies* (New York: Doubleday, 1965), p. 278.

sciously sought, [the Soviet Union] involuntarily constructed."[81]

Contemporary scholarship has produced an enormous literature around the concept "totalitarianism" and, whatever its cognitive merit, it does document the pervasive similarities between various forms of dictatorial and developmental dictatorships that took shape in the interwar years. This is not the place to review that literature.[82] What would seem more suggestive is to briefly consider its most recent development, that which conceives totalitarian systems to be a functional artifact of national communities in the process of rapid, if phased, development. The work of Ludovico Garruccio, for example, is devoted to an account of Fascism which characterizes it as an ideology of national development, variants of which can appear most readily in environments suffering delayed or thwarted development or protracted social, political, or economic deprivation.[83] In the same context George Lichtheim has recently suggested that the "Marxism-Leninism" of contemporary revolutionary movements is little more than a rationale for accelerated national development. That rationale, coined by declassed intellectuals, could equally well be couched in fascist, as well as socialist, locutions.[84] The political system that grows out of such developmental ideologies has a now familiar constellation of characteristics: it is an "anti-imperialist" nationalism—a struggle of "proletarian" nations against "plutocratic" nations. It advocates a national union of "all productive classes," including the "national bourgeoisie" and perhaps the "honest gentry" against all "anti-national, anti-popular and capitalist" foes in the pursuit of national sovereignty and independence. In order to attain those ends the masses and their hitherto autonomous organizations are mobilized into paramilitary and military hierarchies under the predominance of the unitary party dominated by the charismatic leader. At its best such a system produces a forced rate of industrialization, more often than not at

---

[81] Rizzi, *Le lezioni dello Stalinismo,* p. 38.

[82] Among the most important are Carl J. Friedrich and Zbigniew K. Brzezinski, *Totalitarian Dictatorship and Autocracy* (New York: Praeger, 1956); Hans Buchheim, *Totalitaere Herrschaft* (Munich: Koesel, 1962); William Kornhauser, *The Politics of Mass Society* (New York: Free Press, 1959); Emil Lederer, *State of the Masses* (New York: Fertig, 1967); Bruno Seidel and Siegfried Jenkner (eds.), *Wege der Totalitarismus-Forschung* (Darmstadt: Wissenschaftliche Buchgesellschaft, 1968).

[83] Ludovico Garruccio, *L'industralizzazione tra nazionalismo e rivoluzione* (Bologna: Mulino, 1969), "Le tre età dei fascismo,"*Il Mulino* 213 (January-February 1971): 53-73.

[84] George Lichtheim, *Imperialism* (New York: Praeger, 1971), pp. 158f.

the expense of the urban proletariat and the rural peasantry.[85] The strategic elements, the managerial and enterprisory elite, enjoy in varying measure and to varying degrees, social, economic, and political advantage. The sustaining morality of the system is a work and sacrifice ethic and the normative model of man is that of the "warrior-worker," the "warrior-peasant" or perhaps the "warrior-intellectual." In the process whole categories of citizens may be destroyed or exiled. The unitary party and authoritarian (and increasingly personalist) rule is sustained by regular "purges" which "purify" the revolutionary integrity of the movement. External intransigence and perhaps armed aggression seem to be a function of the success of the developmental drive and increased military capability. The "just and revolutionary war" can become the ultimate challenge for the "new man."

All of this leaves one with the sense of having been through this before—at some time between the wars. We are left with a feeling that perhaps Marx was not, after all, the prophet of our time. Perhaps in a curious, if not totally unanticipated, sense Mussolini was.

For Further Reading

Gregor, A. James. "Fascism and Modernization." *World Politics* 26: 3 (April, 1974).

———. *The Ideology of Fascism.* New York: Free Press, 1969.

———. *Interpretations of Fascism.* Morristown, N.J.: General Learning Press, 1974.

Hayes, Paul. *Fascism.* New York: Free Press, 1973.

Kedward, H. Roderick. *Fascism in Western Europe 1900-1945.* New York: New York University, 1971.

Nolte, Ernst. *The Three Faces of Fascism.* New York: Holt, Rinehart and Winston, 1966.

Schueddekopf, Otto-Ernst. *Revolutions of our Time: Fascism.* New York: Praeger, 1973.

Weber, Eugen. *Varieties of Fascism.* Princeton: Van Nostrand, 1964.

Woolf, Stuart J., (ed.). *The Nature of Fascism.* New York: Random House, 1969.

---

[85] Cf. for example, Walt W. Rostow, *The Stages of Economic Growth* (London: Cambridge University Press, 1969), pp. 47, 161 *passim.*

SOURCES

1

Vilfredo Pareto, *The Rise and Fall of Elites*

Pareto's *The Rise and Fall of Elites* was originally published in 1901 as *Un applicazione di teorie sociologiche.* We have no internal evidence that Mussolini, himself, was directly familiar with this piece of work, but all of Pareto's works were popular among the socialists and syndicalists with whom Mussolini interacted during this period. We do know that Mussolini read Pareto's *I sistemi socialisti* published in 1902 and was significantly influenced by the arguments it contained. The arguments that influenced him in the *Sistemi* are essentially those that appear in the *Applicazione.* All the revolutionary theoreticians with whom Mussolini was in contact during this period regularly referred to Pareto's work. Pareto's ideas were part of Mussolini's intellectual environment.

SOURCE: V. Pareto, "Un applicazione di teorie sociologiche," translated as *The Rise and Fall of Elites* (Introduction by Hans L. Zetterberg. Totowa, N.J.: Bedminster, 1968), pp. 27, 38, 59f., 62, 68f., 72, 74-78, 81, 83 and 85f.

First let us note that the greater part of human actions have their origin not in logical reasoning but in sentiment. This is principally true for actions that are not motivated economically. The opposite may be said of economic actions, especially those connected with commerce and industry. Man, although impelled to act by nonlogical motives, likes to tie his actions logically to certain principles; he therefore invents these *a posteriori* in order to justify his actions. So it happens that an action *A,* which in reality is the effect of a cause *B,* is presented by its author as the effect of a very often imaginary cause *C.* The man who thus deceives his fellowman begins by deceiving himself, and he firmly believes his own convictions . . . . Most human actions will continue to be determined, for many, many centuries to come, by sentiment. . . .

Except during short intervals of time, peoples are always governed by an elite. I use the word elite (*aristocrazia*) in its etymological sense, meaning the strongest, the most energetic, and the most capable—for good as well as evil. However, due to an important physiological law, elites do not last. Hence— the history of man is the history of the continuous replacement of certain elites: as one ascends, another declines. Such is the real phenomenon, though to us it may appear under another form.

The new elite which seeks to supersede the old one, or merely to share its power and honors, does not admit to such an intention frankly and openly. Instead it assumes leadership of all the oppressed, declares that it will pursue not its own good but the good of many; and it goes to battle, not for the rights of a restricted class, but for the rights of almost the entire citizenry. Of course, once victory is won, it subjugates the erstwhile allies, or, at best, offers them some formal concessions . . . .

When an elite declines, we can generally observe two signs which manifest themselves simultaneously:

1. The declining elite becomes softer, milder, more humane and less apt to defend its own power.

2. On the other hand, it does not lose its rapacity and greed for the goods of others, but rather tends as much as possible to increase its unlawful appropriations and to indulge in major usurpations of the national patrimony.

Thus, on one hand it makes the yoke heavier, and on the other it has less strength to maintain it. These two conditions cause the catastrophe in which the elite perishes, whereas it could prosper if one of them were absent. Thus, if its own strength does not weaken but grows, its appropriations too may increase, and if these decrease, its dominion may, though less frequently, be maintained with a lesser force. Thus the feudal nobility, at the time it arose, could increase its usurpations because its force was growing; thus the Romans and English elites could, while yielding where yielding was called for, maintain their own power. The French aristocracy on the other hand, eager to maintain its own privileges, and perhaps also to increase them, while its force to defend them was diminishing, provoked the violent revolution of the end of the eighteenth century. In short, there must be a certain equilibrium between the power a social class possesses and the force at its disposal to defend it. Domination without that force cannot last.

Elites often become effete. They preserve a certain passive courage, but lack active courage. It is amazing to see how in imperial Rome the members of the elite committed suicide or allowed themselves to be assassinated without the slightest defense, as long as it pleased Caesar. We are equally amazed when we see the nobles in France die on the guillotine, instead of going down fighting, weapon in hand. . . .

At present this phenomenon can be seen in almost all the civilized states, but is best observed in France and Belgium, which are more advanced in the radical-socialist evolution and show in some manner the goal toward which the evolution tends in general.

A superficial study is sufficient to show that the dominant class in these countries is weighed down by sentimental and humanitarian tendencies quite similar to those which existed toward the end of the eighteenth century. . . .

Elites in a stage of decline generally display humanitarian sentiments and great kindness; but this kindness, provided it is not simply weakness, is more seeming than real. Seneca was a perfect stoic, but he possessed great riches, splendid palaces, innumerable slaves. The French noblemen who applauded Rousseau knew how to make their "fermiers" pay; and the new love of virtue did not prevent them from dissipating in orgies with whores, the money extorted from the peasants, who were starving to death. Today in France a landowner collects, thanks to the duties on grain and cattle, thousands of lire from his fellow citizens; he donates a hundred lire or a little more to a "People's University," and with his purse thus fattened, appeases his conscience and hopes in addition, to be elected at the polls. To be moved with compassion for the poor and destitute in the midst of luxuries agreeably stimulates the senses. Many are landowners today and socialists in the future, and so they feed from two mangers at a time. That future is so far away, who knows when it will come! In the meantime it is sweet to enjoy one's wealth and to discuss equality, to pick up friendships, public offices, sometimes also to find good opportunities for making money, and to pay with words and future promises. There is always a profit to gain by bartering a sure asset for a promissory note signed for so long and uncertain a term. . . .

It is an illusion to believe that it is the people who stand at the head of the dominant class today. Those who stand there—and this is a very different matter—are part of a new and future elite which leans upon the people. . . . Where industry is highly developed, the working class is bound, sooner or later, to acquire great power. We need only watch what is happening in the countries where political elections take place: when a city becomes industrialized it is almost certain that it will send socialist or at least radical deputies to the parliament. In Italy, we see that Milan, where previously the "consorti" were in the majority, and Turin, which was monarchist, now vote socialist, republican, radical, because industry has grown exceedingly in these cities. Florence, where industrial growth is much slower, remains more faithful to the moderate party.

This general movement has been noted so many times that it is unnecessary to dwell upon it at any length; but, another movement, also of great importance is more recent and can be studied. I refer to the movement which enables part of the working class to earn high wages; which group therefore constitutes a first nucleus of the new elite.

The principal cause of this situation can be found in the enormous increase in savings and capital. After 1870 there were no great European wars which would have resulted in a grave diminution of savings, and if the growth of such savings was curbed by the waste due to state socialism or to graft and other malpractices of the dominant class, nevertheless all these causes combined could not prevent an overall increase in their total amount. As the proportion between capital and labor changes, the former becomes less precious while the latter grows in value. Wherever technically possible, the machine replaces man's physical energy. This can be done economically, among civilized nations precisely because there is no shortage of capital; among the other nations the conversion, though technically possible, is not often economical, and therefore man has a greater share in the physical work. Hence, where there is great abundance of capital, man turns necessarily to work in which the machine cannot compete with him, that is, work which requires judgment and intelligence. Moreover, there is also the added advantage of rigorous selection, since the incentive of high wages will secure the services of men with better than average intelligence to direct the machines. Two arms are sufficient for a digger, and if he is a Hercules with the strength of two ordinary men, he can be paid double, but not more, since his work could be done equally well by two other men. To drive a locomotive, on the other hand, one needs a man with judgment and intelligence. Should he be but a little deficient in these qualities, the situation could not be remedied by putting two engineers into the locomotive instead of one; two, three or even four mediocre engineers cannot achieve the output of one capable and intelligent engineer. Ten ignorant chemists in a chemical factory are not at all equivalent to one good chemist. And so we have here a very potent force incessantly at work, which divides labor into various strata, assigning great advantages to the superior ones. This is a principal factor in the formation of a new elite.

The great socialists, intent on squandering capital, pay no attention to all this. They do not understand the process by which they become unwittingly the helpmates of the old elite, obstructing the emergence of the new one, which can become strongly established only where capital is present in great abundance. The Marxists have a much clearer concept of this phenomenon, and they have understood, if not scientifically at least intuitively that their victory can only be realized if it is prepared by abundance of capital; or as they say: the socialist evolution must pass through a "capitalist phase."

Another rather rigorous selection, which is also instrumental in creating the new elite, is being accomplished by the workers' unions and syndicates. This in turn may be considered a consequence of the preceding facts, since these unions and syndicates can exist and thrive only where abundance of capital has permitted large-scale industry to develop and prosper, for at the source there must always be abundance of savings and capital. Let us not forget, however, that this very abundance appears to be, and in fact partly is, the cause of the phenomenon of which it is also a partial effect; for it is precisely the development of industry and the formation of the workers' new elite that contributes toward the growth of savings and capital.

Paul de Rousiers has very well observed the character of the evolution of labor in England, and in studying this evolution carefully, we will notice the same characteristics in the formation of the new elite. Speaking of trade union leaders, he says: "the quality that strikes you first about them is a practical mind, clear and precise, a realistic approach, a firm common sense resulting in a successful effort." These are exactly the qualities that are disappearing in the old elite which is about to die. "Precisely those who believe in the necessity of a profound overthrow of society, those who are seduced by the most advanced socialist theories, preserve within their minds the ideal of their dreams, while concentrating their efforts within the realm of facts so as to be successful in the details. . . . Moreover many among them are completely wrapped up on the pursuit of advantages which do not require in any way a revision of social institutions." They argue as strong men and do not indulge in the weak sentiments of humanitarianism that mark out bourgeoisie; they say "the condition of the weak cannot be bettered unless they struggle against their own weakness. . . . They need an energetic conscience, a virile sense of their moral responsibility. . . . A practical mind, high moral standards, and education, these are the three main qualities which assure the success of the trade union leaders." Are these not precisely the qualities which distinguish the elite (meaning 'the best') from the rest of mankind?

After the generals come the captains, the non-commissioned officers, the soldiers, and they are all selected men. There is never, to be exact, one elite stratum, there are only various strata which together constitute the elite. . . .

Only these unfortunate bourgeois humanitarians can dream of a government that is nothing but milk and honey, and demand that the carabinieri and soldiers should let themselves be stoned and wait till one of them drops dead before using arms. One can be sure that the police of the future elite will not be so patient, for the concepts of who shall be in command will be the concepts of vigorous youths and not of childish old men. . . .

Look at the vigorous discipline of the new elite. If it finds a culprit among its men, he is expelled immediately. The bourgeoisie, on the other hand, believes to act wisely if it closes its eyes on the most despicable offenses of its class. . . .

If somebody told you: "Here are two armies, A and B, confronting each other. In A there is no discipline whatever, little courage, no vigor, no faith in their own flag. These people do not even dare say clearly that they are fighting against B, but wish to pretend that they are at peace in the midst of war. They raise subscriptions to provide arms for B and are unwilling to spend a penny for their own. They prate and lose themselves in vain talk, they bring grist to their mills and seek to get something out. The best soldiers desert their own camp and go over to that of B. On the other hand, the men of B know what they want and they want it strongly, they maintain discipline, they have faith in their flag, they hold it high, they say very clearly that they want to defeat army A that they want to disperse and destroy it. They are tied together in a close group and each one of them is ready to make any sacrifice for his comrades and for the flag. They never dream of aiding the enemy, they procure arms for themselves and not for others. Their number grows constantly." Then you would be asked: "On whose side do you think will be the victory?" Would you be in doubt what to reply?

2

Gaetano Mosca, *The Ruling Class*

Mosca's *Elementi di scienza politica* was originally published in 1895. It was a book that was to have enormous impact on Italian political thought. The book was well known to all the socialists and syndicalists with whom Mussolini had contact and footnote references to it are easily found in the work of syndicalists like Sergio Panunzio and A. O. Olivetti who were later to become important ideologues of Fascism. Mussolini was probably familiar with Mosca's work, but because of Mosca's subsequent opposition to Fascism never formally alluded to it. There is little doubt that Mosca's thought influenced Fascist arguments.

SOURCE: From *The Ruling Class* by G. Mosca. Copyright © 1966 by McGraw-Hill, Inc. Used with permission of McGraw-Hill Book Company.

Among the constant facts and tendencies that are to be found in all political organisms, one is so obvious that it is apparent to the most casual eye. In all societies—from societies that are very meagerly developed and have barely attained the dawnings of civilization, down to the most advanced and powerful societies—two classes of people appear—a class that rules and a class that is ruled. The first class, always the less numerous, performs all political functions, monopolizes power and enjoys the advantages that power brings, whereas the second, the more numerous class, is directed and controlled by the first, in a manner that is now more or less legal, now more or less arbitrary and violent, and supplies the first, in appearance at least, with material means of subsistence and with the instrumentalities that are essential to the vitality of the political organism.

In practical life we all recognize the existence of this ruling class (or political class, as we have elsewhere chosen to define it). We all know that, in our own country, whichever it may be, the management of public affairs is in the hands of a minority of influential persons, to which management, willingly or unwillingly, the majority defer. We know that the same thing goes on in neighboring countries, and in fact we should be put to it to conceive of a real world otherwise organized—a world in which all men would be directly subject to a single person without relationships of superiority or subordination, or in which all men would share equally in the direction of political affairs. If we reason otherwise in theory, that is due partly to inveterate habits that we follow in our thinking and partly to the exaggerated importance that we attach to two political facts that loom far larger in appearance than they are in reality.

The first of these facts—and one has only to open one's eyes to see it—is that in every political organism there is one individual who is chief among the leaders of the ruling class as a whole and stands, as we say, at the helm of the state. That person is not always the person who holds supreme power according to law. At times, alongside of the hereditary king or emperor there is a prime minister or a major-domo who wields an actual power that is greater than the sovereign's. At other times, in place of the elected president the influential politician who has procured the president's election will govern. Under special circumstances there may be, instead of a single person, two or three who discharge the functions of supreme control.

The second fact, too, is readily discernible. Whatever the type of political organization, pressures arising from the discontent of the masses who are governed, from the passions by which they are swayed, exert a certain amount of influence on the policies of the ruling, the political, class.

But the man who is at the head of the state would certainly not be able to govern without the support of a numerous class to enforce respect for his orders and to have them carried out; and granting that he can make one individual, or indeed many individuals, in the ruling class feel the weight of his power, he certainly cannot be at odds with the class as a whole or do away with it. Even if that were possible, he would at once be forced to create another class, without the support of which action on his part would be completely paralyzed. On the other hand, granting that the discontent of the masses might succeed in deposing a ruling class, inevitably, as we shall later show, there would have to be another organized minority within the masses themselves to discharge the functions of a ruling class. Otherwise all organization, and the whole social structure, would be destroyed. . . .

We think it may be desirable . . . to reply at this point to an objection which might very readily be made to our point of view. If it is easy to understand that a single individual cannot command a group without finding within the group a minority to support him, it is rather difficult to grant, as a constant and natural fact, that minorities rule majorities, rather than majorities minorities. But that is one of the points—so numerous in all the other sciences—where the first impression one has of things is contrary to what they are in reality. In reality the dominion of an organized minority, obeying a single impulse, over the unorganized majority is inevitable. The power of any minority is irresistible as against each single individual in the majority, who stands alone before the totality of the organized minority. At the same time, the minority is organized for the very reason that it is a minority. A hundred men acting uniformly in concert, with a common understanding, will triumph over a thousand men who are not in accord and can therefore be dealt with one by one. Meanwhile it will be easier for the former to act in concert and have a mutual understanding simply because they are a hundred and not a thousand. It follows that the larger the political community, the smaller will the proportion of the governing minority to the governed majority be, and the more difficult will it be for the majority to organize for reaction against the minority. . . .

. . . As soon as there is a shift in the balance of political forces—when, that is, a need is felt that capacities different from the old should assert themselves in the management of the state, when the old capacities, therefore, lose some of their importance or changes in their distribution occur—then the manner in which the ruling class is constituted changes also. If a new source of wealth develops in a society, if the practical importance of knowledge grows, if an old religion declines or a new one is born, if a new current of ideas spreads, then, simultaneously, far-reaching dislocations occur in the ruling class. One might say, indeed, that the whole history of civilized mankind comes down to a conflict between the tendency of dominant elements to monopolize political power and transmit possession of it by inheritance, and the tendency toward a dislocation of old forces and an insurgence of new forces; and this conflict produces an unending ferment of endosmosis and exosmosis between the upper classes and certain portions of the lower. . . .

In fairly populous societies that have attained a certain level of civilization, ruling classes do not justify their power exclusively by de facto possession of it, but try to find a moral and legal basis for it, representing it as the logical and necessary consequence of doctrines and beliefs that are generally recognized and accepted. So if a society is deeply imbued with the Christian spirit the political class will govern by the will of the sovereign, who, in turn, will reign because he is God's anointed. So too in Mohammedan societies political authority is exercised directly in the name of caliph, or vicar, of the Prophet, or in the name of someone who has received investiture, tacit or explicit, from the caliph. The Chinese mandarins ruled the state because they were supposed to be interpreters of the will of the Son of Heaven, who had received from heaven the mandate to govern paternally, and in accordance with the rules of the Confucian ethic, "the people of the hundred families." The complicated hierarchy of civil and military functionaries in the Roman Empire rested upon the will of the emperor, who, at least down to Diocletian's time, was assumed by a legal fiction to have received from the people a mandate to rule the commonwealth. The powers of all lawmakers, magistrates and government officials in the United States emanate directly or indirectly from the vote of the voters, which is held to be the expression of the sovereign will of the whole American people.

This legal and moral basis, or principle, on which the power of the political class rests, is what we have elsewhere called, and shall continue here to call, the "political formula." (Writers on the philosophy of law generally call it the "principle of sovereignty.") The political formula can hardly be the same in two or more different societies; and fundamental or even notable similarities between two or more political formulas appear only where the peoples professing them have the same type of civilization (or—to use an expression which we shall shortly define—belong to the same social type). According to the level of civilization in the peoples among whom they are current, the various political formulas may be based either upon supernatural beliefs or upon concepts which, if they do not correspond to positive realities, at least appear to be rational. We shall not say that they correspond in either case to scientific truths. A conscientious observer would be oliged to confess that, if no one has ever seen the authentic document by which the Lord empowered certain privileged persons or families to rule his people on his behalf, neither can it be maintained that a popular election, however liberal the suffrage may be, is ordinarily the expression of the will of a people, or even of the will of the majority of a people.

And yet that does not mean that political formulas are mere quackeries aptly invented to trick the masses into obedience. Anyone who viewed them in that light would fall into grave error. The truth is that they answer a real need in man's social nature; and this need, so universally felt, of governing and knowing that one is governed not on the basis of mere material or intellectual force, but on the basis of a moral principle, has beyond any doubt a practical and a real importance.

Spencer wrote that the divine right of kings was the great superstition of past ages, and that the divine right of elected assemblies is the great superstition of our present age. The idea cannot be called wholly mistaken, but certainly it does not consider or exhaust all aspects of the question. It is further necessary to see whether a society can hold together without one of these "great superstitions"—whether a universal illusion is not a social force that contributes powerfully to consolidating political organization and unifying peoples or even whole civilizations.

Mankind is divided into social groups each of which is set apart from other groups by beliefs, sentiments, habits and interests that are peculiar to it. The individuals who belong to one such group are held together by a consciousness of common brotherhood and held apart from other groups by passions and tendencies that are more or less antagonistic and mutually repellent. As we have already indicated, the political formula must be based upon the special beliefs and the strongest sentiments of the social group in which it is current, or at least upon the beliefs and sentiments of the particular portion of that group which holds political preeminence.

This phenomenon—the existence of social groups each of which has characteristics peculiar to itself and often presumes absolute superiority over other groups (the *boria nazionale,* the national conceit, that Vico talks about!)—has been recognized and studied by many writers, and particularly by modern scholars, in dealing with the principle of nationality. Gumplowicz, for instance, pointed to its importance in political science, or in sociology if you will. . . .

In the formation of the group, or social type, many other elements besides more or less certain racial affinity figure—for example, community of language, of religion, of interests, and the recurring relationships that result from geographical situation. It is not necessary that all these factors be present at one and the same time, for community of history—a life that is lived for centuries in common, with identical or similar experiences, engendering similar moral and intellectual habits, similar passions and memories—often becomes the chief element in the development of a conscious social type.

Once such a type is formed, we get, to return to a metaphor which we have earlier used, a sort of crucible that fuses all individuals who enter it into a single alloy. Call it suggestion, call it imitation or mimetism, call it education pure and simple, it nevertheless comes about that a man feels, believes, loves, hates, according to the environment in which he lives. With exceedingly rare exceptions, we are Christians or Jews, Mohammedans or Buddhists, Frenchmen or Italians, for the simple reason that such were the people among whom we were born and bred.

3

Speeches of Enrico Corradini

"La vita nazionale" was delivered on January 26, 1905, before the Society for the Education of Women in Rome. "Sindacalismo, nazionalismo, imperialismo" was a speech delivered at the Accademia Olimpica in Vicenza in December 1909. "Principii di nazionalismo" was a communication delivered by Corradini at the founding congress of the Nationalist Party held in Florence on December 3, 1910. "Nazionalismo e socialismo" was a speech delivered before an audience at the Università Popolare on January 14, 1914. "Diritii e doveri nazionali dei produttori" was a speech given before an assembly of businessmen, the Camera del Commercio, on July 28, 1916, while Italy was involved in World War I. All these speeches were subsequently published in *Discorsi politici.*

SOURCE: *Discorsi politici* (Florence: Vallecchi, 1924), pp. 37f., 44; 57-61; 100f.; 214f., 220, 227-29; 345. Translation by A. James Gregor.

"NATIONAL LIFE"
("La vita nazionale")
(January 26, 1905)

Nations are the principal forces, they are the major organic forms [that make up] the world. The individual cannot be the measure of life, nor the possibility of life, nor [satisfy] the aspirations of man toward life. There is [of course] a life that is in us—and in me—in so far as we breath with the fulness of the heart and think with the most sublime intelligence. But that life is all inert and dreamlike. For life to be real, and for life to become a conscious activity, it is necessary to feel ourselves united with a certain number of our own kind. The family, the home, [for example] transcends the individual; that is to say, the family and the home constitute, in themselves, a transcendence of the individual.

Consider this transcendence a gradual expansion of life. . . . The home is a link in the chain of generations. By virtue of family life the father makes a gift of a name, of wealth, of abundance, of labor, of communication, of vital energy, of virtue, of a will and a mission to his son, through and in which to grow and to fulfill himself. The individual would be small if he were not enlarged in the spirit of the family. His tasks would be meager, if he did not have the patrimony of his forebears to make his own. The rules governing the family constitute the means to a fuller life. The family [quenches the] thirst for immortality, and everyone who enjoys an ancient lineage enjoys, if he is worthy, the privilege of feeling himself extended through time—just as every man enjoys the sense of prolonging himself, through his family, into the future. It is truly an appetite for existence that drives man to expand beyond himself, to escape from his one moment in time and from his atomic self, and to feel himself exist and work in a larger space and in a more inclusive time. [Such impulses] create admirable virtues and work admirable achievements. The family is the strength of generations for man and with that force he achieves that of which the individual alone is incapable.

The nation [like the family] is a multitude that contains in itself the force of many generations. With that force man creates the history of the world. . . . The nation is the maximum unity of the maximum number of kindred souls. . . .

This is the nation—it is a living thing grown large through centuries. . . . The world is sustained by both solidarity and antagonism. The conflicts [that result] are the entirety of its history. Nations are the principal organs of that conflict. Having suppressed [nations] one would suppress the protagonists of the world drama, that is to say they would suppress the drama itself. It is conceivable that one imagine antagonism of a still vaster kind, between federations of nations against each other, and something of that kind happened with the city-states when they expanded into nations. But if one expands [solidarity] to the limits of humanity where would one find humanity's [opposing] other? One would have to seek it in another planet. It is a problem better left to astronomers. . . .

The national virtue of which I have spoken without having identified it . . . , mother of all other virtues, . . . is solidarity. Thus I concerned myself with solidarity when I spoke of the conscience, the will and the courage that are necessary in popular leaders if they are to open a way for the people and indicate to them the means to their prosperity and power, their grandeur and their glory. . . .

Among citizens a sentiment must be cultivated as a consequence of which, when it is necessary, they will be prepared to sacrifice themselves unto death, not only for themselves and their children, but also for the children of their children and their most remote kindred. When we make the transit from the condition of [atomic] individuals to that of the nation, each of us becomes a component part of the nation. When the Fatherland suddenly manifests itself in us, we sense an impulse that arises from a seemingly unknown source—an enthusiasm that we have not hitherto known. Poetry, music and the Fatherland provide that impulse and that enthusiasm. They constitute the sign that we have lost ourselves in a larger being, as does the river in the sea.

"SYNDICALISM, NATIONALISM, IMPERIALISM"
("Sindacalismo, nazionalismo, imperialismo")
(December, 1909)

Syndicalists conceived the general strike in a grand and religious manner, infused with a moral substance all its own. The general strike requires that the workers be disciplined, patient, given to sacrifice, possessed of a solidarity with the future. . . . I am in sympathy with syndicalism in so far as it is critical of sentiments that today possess the force of instincts, and opinions that today have the force of dogma. You all know [the instincts and opinions to which I refer] : democracy, parliamentarianism, pacifism, humanitarianism and such. . . .

Let us see if there is a common substance shared by syndicalism and nationalism. Bear in mind that a doctrine, whatever doctrine, finds expression more in the action which the program evokes than in the program itself. Rather than in its programmatic fulfillment, each doctrine has influence in the world until it exhausts its potential for action. The Gospels were the program of Christianity. Can we really say that the program of the Gospels were carried out? Nonetheless, Christianity invoked that force necessary to transform the world. Similarly we can imagine a syndicalism that confines itself to the nation and does not go beyond it. A syndicalism that would cease to be international in character. Workers would unite, but no longer with the entire world, but would rather confine their union to the limits of the nation. They unite, but not to obtain dominion of the world, but of the nation. Should this occur the conflict between nationalism and syndicalism would be overcome. . . . Between syndicalism and nationalism there is this in common: both doctrines constitute a school of solidarity. You must . . . return to a conception of the world divided into continents and nations with the two antagonistic classes, labor and capital, reduced to components [of those continents and nations]. What then does the nation become? That which it is in substance: a corporation of classes, a large union. . . . Presuppose the class struggle to be a union of all classes in the interests of the nation—and the nation a harvest of common wealth. Just as a tree is rooted in the earth, the class struggle has its roots in the wealth of the nation. And nationalism is above all a doctrine of national economic solidarity, just as socialism and its new school . . . syndicalism, constitutes the doctrine of the economic solidarity of classes.

"PRINCIPLES OF NATIONALISM"
("Principii di nazionalismo")
(December 3, 1910)

We must begin with a recognition of this principle: there are proletarian nations, just as there are proletarian classes—nations, that is to say, whose conditions of life are disadvantaged when compared to other nations, just as is the case with classes. Given this premise, nationalism must first of all bruit about this truth: Italy is a nation that is materially and morally proletarian. . . . Italy finds itself circumstanced just as the proletariat did before the advent of socialism. The muscles of the workers were as strong in that early period as they are now, but the workers lacked the will to uplift themselves. They were blind to their condition. What occurred when socialism first spoke to the proletariat? The proletariat awakened, it saw for the first time its existential circumstances and anticipated the possibility of change. . . . Socialism united the workers and awakened them to struggle, creating in that struggle, the solidarity, the consciousness, the force, the arms, the new laws, the will to victory, and the pride . . . of the working class.

Similarly, . . . nationalism must do the same thing for the Italian nation. We must have . . . our own national socialism.

"NATIONALISM AND SOCIALISM"
("Nazionalismo e socialismo")
(January 14, 1914)

In reality workers and employers are united in the productive enterprise before they compete with respect to distribution. In different respects, but jointly, their wellbeing is tied to the fortunes of production, of commerce and the market. . . . Nationalism will continue to develop its program which is to carry the Italian nation from its present period of international inferiority to a level of superiority. The ascent has only begun. It is necessary to continue. . . . The definition, therefore, of nationalism is this: it is the socialism of the Italian nation in the world. Italy remains a proletarian nation in Europe and has need of its socialism. . . . All of the internal life of Italy, the economic and political life of the people and the state—and of its constitutive elements, individuals and classes—are subject to the actions and the power of foreign nations. . . . As it is with respect to the soil so is it with industry—the development of the means of production [is] retarded and impeded. In fact many Italian industries complain that they are weighted down with fiscal obligations and cannot develop. One cannot imagine that this is anything other than consequence of our dependency—the consequence of oppressive plutocratic nations taking advantage of a poor one.

Italy has a voice that makes these facts common knowledge. That voice is, in fact, the voice of nationalism.

Nationalism rests on an infrangible base . . . and on eternal principles: the principle of ethnicity, inescapable and eternal as the principle of individuality, . . . moreover, nationalism rests on the principle of production, which precedes and transcends that of distribution. . . .

The [orthodox] socialists destroy international and national production. . . . Against this we oppose our law, the law of production. . . .

"THE NATIONAL RIGHTS AND DUTIES OF PRODUCERS"
("Diritti e doveri nazionali dei produttori")
(July 28, 1916)

Just as in the political realm so is it in the economic: democracy tends to transform itself into oligarchy. This is because democracy, whether it is political or economic or of whatever sort, democracy, in the real and true sense, can consist in nothing other than a system of institutions from which power emanates, and power, by its very nature, manifests itself in a minority, precisely because it is the consequence of organization and organization culminates in a minority.

4

Corradini's "Manifesto"

The "Manifesto" was published in the first issue of the Nationalist theoretical journal, *Politica* 1 (1918) as the Nationalists prepared for the postwar political struggle. The "Manifesto" was probably written by Corradini and republished in *La Stampa nazionalista*.

SOURCE: *La stampa nazionalista* (edited by F. Gaeta. Rocca San Casciano: Cappelli, 1965), pp. 15-17. Translation by A. James Gregor.

In our work of spiritual reconstruction . . . our first obligation is to [reconsider] the idea of the relationship between society and the individual. Society is not, as demoliberal political philosophy insists, a simple *sum of individuals* which can be [entirely] reduced to its component elements, but rather, a real *organism* that has an existence and ends completely distinct from those of individuals. Out of the succession of generations of individuals society creates a continuous historic life. And its purpose is to contribute, in accordance with its special genius and intrinsic forces, to the development of world civilization. As opposed to the archaic idea of a universal human society entertained by medievalists and articulated and promulgated by the philosophy of the [French] Revolution [we contend that] human kind does not constitute a unified and immense society, composed of all humanity, but rather men live in numerous societies each of which is a distinct organism with its own life and its own goals, a fact established not only by history but by the biological and moral law governing social life.

This law is explicitly opposed to that bandied by liberal-democratic ideology. [The demoliberals], in the name of equality between all men, wished to abolish not only social hierarchies, but to establish a reign of perpetual peace in a united states of the world. [Demoliberalism] tends, in other words to disorganization, that is to say the dissolution of historic societies, [the dissolution] of the sole existing social reality in order to substitute a hypothetical society which today is outside the range of realization and which, tomorrow, will be outside the range of possibility. It is outside the range of possibility precisely because the suppression of the distinctions, the competition, the struggle between the various human societies, signifies the suppression not only of the life of single societies, but also the very life of mankind itself which is sustained in dynamic equilibrium. Struggle is, in fact, the fundamental law of the life of social organisms just as it is of biological organisms. Thanks to struggle [social and biological organisms] achieve form, consolidate and perfect themselves. As a consequence of struggle the healthiest, the most vital prevail over the weaker and those less adapted. In competition the struggle between peoples and races contributes to natural evolution. Therefore as opposed to the formula of democratic ideology—equality between individuals, and the consequent abolition of social hierarchies and internal disaggregation—equality between peoples and perpetual peace and immobility with respect to that which is external—we propose: discipline of the inequalities and a hierarchical organization within, and free competition and struggle between peoples without— because between unequals those better prepared and more adapted prevail, and perform those universal functions assigned to strong and capable peoples in the evolution of civilization.

In such a fashion, all the forms of struggle: from that bloodless economic and political competition to that of armed conflict (which constitute, in extreme cases, the ultimate recourse to which each people have the right and the duty) are directed [outside the community]. Within [the community], on the other hand, there is discipline, order and hierarchy which insures peace. One thus serves, in a manner compatible with life and social development, the cause of peace. Gradually as a society, consolidating itself internally, expands and enlarges its dominion, carrying its competition further afield over a wider range, the scope of peace is extended. The best way of providing a guarantee of peace is that which enlarges the range over which a single social organization, a single discipline and a single authority rules.

The state is born out of the ineluctable laws of life as struggle. The state cannot—as liberal democratic ideology would have it—separate itself from society, identifying itself with the organs of sovereignty, or with a political class . . . , or with individuals. . . . The state is a society organized under a supreme power and is therefore the necessary and historic form of social life—a form having continuity as against the transcient value of the individual. Thus our conception of the state is organic, dynamic and historic, while the liberal democratic conception is mechanical, static and anti-historic. Only in the [nationalist conception] do the institutions and phenomena in which the individual manifests himself in his function as an instrument or an organ of the ends of the state—particularly when the individual is called upon to make the supreme sacrifice in war—make any sense. For example the idea of liberty, conceived by the liberal theory as a natural or unlimited right of the individual with respect to the state, makes little sense. Individual liberties are concessions made by the state itself—the state which is primarily, and in the first instance, concerned with guaranteeing to individuals the conditions necessary for their organic development as personalities. Similarly, against the democratic and individualist principle of the sovereignty of the multitude, popular sovereignty, is opposed the concept of government by the most capable—that is to say, government by those capable of lifting themselves above the contingent interests of their time and to discern and effectuate the greater historical interests of the state.

All, governors and citizens, those in the more demanding directive roles and those who are subordinated—but no less important—are active agents of the life of the state. To serve the state is a duty of all of us, but it is also in the interests of all. The stronger, the more powerful, the richer the state, the more elevated, the more prosperous is the life of its citizens: *"civis romanus sum."*

5

Speeches of Filippo T. Marinetti

In the years prior to World War I, Marinetti regularly addressed large, often hostile, public assemblies. The following selections are from these public speeches. In some cases Marinetti added his impressions to the speeches as they were subsequently published. At the end of his "Discorso ai Tristini," a speech delivered to public meetings in Trieste, he adds not only his own impressions of the audience, but a brief account of the state of mind and the aggressive and volatile dispositions of his Futurists as well. The speeches, and his comments, were subsequently published in *Teoria e invenzione futurista.*

SOURCE: Filippo T. Marinetti, *Teoria e invenzione futurista* (Verona: Mondadori, 1968), pp. 211-16, 252-54, 282-89. Translation by A. James Gregor. Used with permission of the publishers.

DISCOURSE TO THE CITIZENS OF TRIESTE
("Discorse ai Triestini")
(April-June, 1910)

... In our struggle, we systematically deplore every form of obedience, docility, imitation; we deplore sedentary taste and all prudent hesitations; we struggle against majorities corrupted by power, and we spit on prevailing and traditional opinions, as well as on all those commonplaces of morality and philosophy.

In literature we propound the ideal of a great and potent scientific literature which, free from whatever artificial classicism and pedantic purism, enlarges upon the most recent discoveries, the new inebriation of speed and the heavenly life of aviators. . . .

Politically we are as far removed from international and antipatriotic socialism—ignoble exultation of the rights of the belly—as we are from that timorous and clerical conservatism that is symbolized by slippers and bed-warmers.

Every liberty and every progress within the grand circle of the nation!

We exalt patriotism, militarism. We sing of war, that cleansing of the world (*sola igiene del mondo*), that superb fire of enthusiasm and generosity, that noble bath of heroism, without which whole races succumb to the torpor of egoism, business interests, to narrowness of mind and of will. . . .

All these ardent and dynamic ideas exasperate and provoke opposition on the part of the public; but we futurists rejoice in the fact, because we fear only facile approval and the insipid praise of the mediocre. . . .

Down with museums! Rebury the dead! We glory in violence! Long live war! Death to pacifists! Down with sedentary majorities! Glory to the cruel!

The audience is scandalized; some of the shipwrecked spectators cling to their chairs [as though to save themselves]; others desperately cling to their own great round bald pates as though they sought to embrace the world in order to save it. Dying eyes search anxiously for lost crucifixes. The tumult of the crowd grows: it is the great insurrection of the mummies. Not a single Italian among them: they are all Austrians or lick-spittles. But vigorous youth triumphs. All the men are on their feet, and with blows and with shouts they force the cadavers to return to their tombs.

The burst of enthusiasm forces us out and carries us along the streets of Trieste.

We enter the Caffè Milano, a furnace from which the burning coals of excited hurrahs burst forth, erupt, and overwhelm us. At that grand fraternal table, the flushed cheeks, the inflamed voices, the brilliant ferment of poetry and patriotism . . . Armando Mazza is compelled to repeat for the third time the famous Manifesto [of Futurism]. All are set ablaze by the flow of alcohol. A youth, eyes burning with genius, rises to his feet and proclaims his futurist faith, his ardent commitment to our movement and the rebellion against the past . . . All listen to him intently, and he, possessed by an inspired madness, discharges a thousand paradoxical ideas in a loud voice.

"AGAINST LOVE AND PARLIAMENTARISM" (1911)
("Contro l'amore e il parlamentarismo")

. . . We defend, with the utmost enthusiasm the rights of suffragettes, including their infantile enthusiasm for the miserable and ridiculous right to vote.

In fact, we are convinced that if they come to possess that right with the requisite enthusiasm they will, involuntarily, help us to destroy that elaborate folly, that corrupt and banal thing, to which parliamentarianism has been now reduced.

Parliamentarianism is almost everywhere an empty form. It did have some good effect: it created the illusion of participation in the government on the part of the majority. I said "illusion," because it has been well established that the people cannot, and never can, be represented by representatives that it does not know how to select.

The people are always outside the government. But, on the other hand, parliament has produced the people.

The pride of the crowd (*folle*) has been enhanced by elective government.

The stature of the individual has been enhanced by the idea of representation. This idea, in turn, has hopelessly impaired our ability to judge intelligence, exaggerating inordinately the value of eloquence. This disability is increasing day by day.

For this reason I anticipate with pleasure the aggressive penetration of women into parliamentary life. Where could we find a more volatile and effective explosive?

Almost all the parliaments in Europe are nothing other than noisy chicken runs, troughs, or sewers.

"1915: IN THIS FUTURIST YEAR" (1915)
("1915: In quest'anno futurista")

STUDENTS OF ITALY!

Because an illustrious past weighed too heavily upon Italy, and an infinitely more glorious future was dawning under our too sensual sky, futurist energy was compelled to appear, six years ago, to organize itself, channelize itself, and find in us its engines, its means of illumination and propagation. Italy, more than any other country, had an urgent need of Futurism, because it was afflicted by [an inextricable involvement with] the past (*passatismo*). The afflicted hit upon their own cure. We are their doctors. And the remedy serves all the sick of every nation.

Our immediate program is to struggle indefatigably against Italian involvement with the past under all its repugnant forms: archeology, academic life, senile pursuits, quietism, cowardice, pacifism, pessimism, nostalgia, sentimentalism, eroticism, tourism, and so forth. Our ultraviolent, anticlerical, antisocialist and antitraditional nationalism arises out of the inexhaustible vigor of Italian blood and a battle against ancestor worship that, rather than unifying the race, renders it anemic and putrescent. We will succeed in the immediate program already (in part) realized by six years of incessant struggle.

Futurism, in so far as its total program is concerned is a . . . vanguard. It is the order of the day for all innovators . . . ; it is a love of that which is new; it is the impassioned art of speed; it emphatically rejects the antique and old, the slow, the erudite and the professorial; it is a new way of perceiving the world; a new reason to love life, an enthusiastic glorification of scientific discoveries and of modern technology; a banner of youth, of force, of originality at any cost; it is a collar of steel that undoes the habits of the nostalgics; it is an inexhaustible machine gun pointed against the army of the dead, the gout-ridden and the opportunists—those that we wish to divest of authority in order to place them under the control of audacious and creative youth. Futurism is a stick of dynamite under all the venerated ruins [of Italy].

The word "Futurism" implies a vast formula of rebirth—one that, being at one and the same cleansing (*igienica*) and exciting, reduces doubts, destroys scepticism and units all efforts in an imposing exultation. All innovators find themselves under the banner of Futurism, because Futurism proclaims the necessity of continual advance, and because it advocates the suppression of all cowardly strategems. Futurism is the contrived optimism (*ottimismo artificiale*) opposed to all chronic pessimisms; it is the continuous dynamism, the perpetual becoming and the untiring will. Futurism, is not confined by the laws of fashion nor affected by the erosion of time. It is neither a parsonage nor a school, but rather a great movement of solidarity of intellectual heroisms in which the pride of the individual is nothing, while the will to renew is everything. . . .

We are agents of destruction, but only to recreate. We clear away the debris in order to advance. We consider it futuristic to display absolute sincerity in thought and expression. . . .

Futurism is: the reinforcing and defense of Italian genius (creation and improvisation) against cultural obsessions (museums, libraries); solidarity of Italian innovators against the academic cabals, the opportunists, the plagiarists, the talkers, the professors and hotel keepers; a preparation of an atmosphere conducive to innovators; a conviction in the infinite progress of Italy; a heroic detachment in order to give to Italy and the world more force, more courage, more light, more liberty, more novelty, more elasticity; an order of the day and of battle with guns at our back in order never to retreat.

Futurism wishes to brutally introduce life into art; combat the old ideas of the aesthetes, static, decorative, effeminate, precious, fastidious—[ideas inimical to] action. In the last thirty years Europe has become morbid with a filthy socialistoid, antipatriotic, and internationalistic intellectualism that sunders body from spirit, produces a hypertrophied cerebral stupidity, that teaches pardon for trespasses, that pronounces universal peace and the disappearance of war whose horrors are to be replaced by the battle of ideas. Against this intellectualism that originates in Germany, Futurism exalts instinct, force, courage, sport and war.

Artists, finally alive, no longer poised on the pinnacles of aestheticism, wished to collaborate, as workers and soldiers, in world progress. Continual progress; the suppression of the dead, the old, the slow, the indecisive, the vile, the melifluous, the delicate, the effeminate, the nostalgic. Daily heroism. All the dangers and all the battles. . . .

We ferociously oppose the critics, useless or dangerous exploiters, and not the public which we want to elevate to a higher comprehension of life. We have frequently been misunderstood by the public. That was natural, given the idiotic superficiality of the few professorial imbeciles that act as its brain. The public will, however, understand us; it is a question of energy and that we have.

The crowds that have derided us have involuntarily admired in us the disinterested artists who heroically struggle to reinvigorate, rejuvenate and stimulate the genius of Italy. The great block of new ideas fashioned by us knocks about in the mud and on the stones, pushed and dirtied by the hands of happy urchins. They, mocking the strange external colors of that enormous plaything, are [nonetheless] affected by its incandescent and magnetic substance. This is not mere rhetoric: the very word Futurism has by itself done enormous good in Italy and in the world. Everywhere and with regard to every question, in parliaments, in communal councils, and in the streets, men divide themselves in terms of those committed to the past (*pasatisti*) and futurists.

6

Articles and Speeches of Benito Mussolini

"Nel'attesa" was an article by Mussolini published in the socialist paper *Il Proletario* 41, October 11, 1903. "L'uomo e la divinità" was a polemical monograph written by Mussolini when he was twenty-one years of age and was directed against the "Christian Socialism" of Alfredo Taglialatela. The monograph was published in 1904 by The International Library of Rationalist Propaganda, an organization of socialist intellectuals. "Per Ferdinando Lassalle" was an article written to commemorate the fortieth anniversary of the death of Ferdinand Lassalle, the founder of Germany's Social Democratic Party. The article was originally published in the Socialist journal *Avanguardia Socialista* 90, August 20, 1904. "La filosofia della forza" was an interpretive review of an exposition of the philosophy of Friedrich Nietzsche given by Claudio Treves at the communal theater of Forlì on November 22, 1908. Mussolini's review was published in three parts in the Socialist publication *Il Pensiero Romagnolo* 48, 49, 50 on November 29, December 6 and 13, 1908. "Lo sciopero generale e la violenza" was a review of Georges Sorel's book *Reflections on Violence* written for the Socialist publication *Il Popolo* and originally published on June 25, 1909. "Fra libri e riviste" was a review of Roberto Michels's book *Cooperazione* written for, and published by, the Socialist publication *Il Popolo*

on November 4, 1909. "Le ragioni del considetto 'pacifismo' "
was an article written for the principal socialist publication in
Italy of the period and of which Mussolini was Editor, *Avanti!* It
appeared in the issue of March 29, 1913. "Il valore storico del
socialismo" was a published summary of Mussolini's communication delivered before a Socialist conference in Florence on
February 8, 1914. The summary was published in *Avanti!* on
February 15, 1914. "Un altro passo" was an article written by
Mussolini for his own daily publication, *Il popolo d'Italia*, and
published on February 16, 1919. Mussolini had not yet officially
founded the "Fascist Movement." He had long since been
expelled from the official Social Party of Italy, but still considered himself a "productive socialist." "Atto di nascita del
fascismo" is a published account of Mussolini's speech before the
assembly that was to be the founding congress of the "Fascist
Movement." The speech was delivered on March 23, 1919, the
date celebrated in Fascist Italy as the "birthday" of Fascism. The
stenographic account of the speech was published the next day in
Mussolini's own daily, *Il Popolo d'Italia*. "Chi possiede, paghi!"
was an article Mussolini telephoned to *Il Popolo d'Italia*, which
published it on July 6, 1919. All of the speeches, articles, and
reviews mentioned above were republished in the *Opera omnia*.

SOURCE: Benito Mussolini, *Opera omnia* (Florence: la fenice,
1951-1963) I, p. 41; XXXIII, p. 23; I, pp. 66-67; 175f.; II, pp.
164-68; 249f.; V, p. 134; VI, 79-81; XII, p. 229; 325, 327; XIII,
p. 224. Translation by A. James Gregor.

"AT ATTENTION"
("Nel'attesa")
(October 11, 1903)

Psychology has demonstrated that sentiments are the dynamic motives of
human actions. For us [in this instance] it is the sentiment of solidarity that
compells us to action. . . .

"MAN AND THE DIVINITY"
("L'uomo e la divinità")
(March 26, 1904)

Man has been defined as a social animal. For man, as a consequence, life in
society has been natural to him since the earliest times.

"FOR FERDINANDO LASSALLE"
("Per Ferdinando Lassalle")
(August 20, 1904)

The moral idea is this: "The unlimited freedom of action by the individual himself is not sufficient. The solidarity of interests—communion and reciprocity of development—must culminate in a community that is morally integrated.". . .

Lassalle desired the voluntary association of workers "accomplished by universal suffrage and placed under the civilizing aegis of the state." Lassalle was a rabid *etatist*, but a state which, for him, was identified with the concept of community. Against the "modern barbarians," the manchestrians, he defended the ancient vestal fires of every civilization, the state. In the Lassallian conception, the state is the moral unity and union of individuals. It is the last integral phase of the evolutionary process in the life of communities—of the community of blood, of place, of economic interests, and of intellectual interests.

Its function is to conduct a struggle against nature, against misery, ignorance, powerlessness, and the slavery of every sort in which we, at the beginning of the struggle, find ourselves. Such a union, under the form of the state, must create the conditions in which individuals achieve a meaning and a level of life which isolated individuals could never have achieved. "The final and substantial end of the state is to bring human life to fulfillment and progressive development; it is the education of mankind to liberty". . . .

A form of psychological revolution must transform the mentality of the workers in order to have them acquire the technical and intellectual aptitudes indispensable to the management of communal production. It is in the syndicates that this "philosophy with a conscience," which Lassalle inherits from Fichte, must actuate itself. [It is this philosophy] to which the working classes must adapt themselves—which fosters in them a new morality of solidarity—while they accumulate the energies that will serve to accomplish the abolition of private property and the social and political organization requisite [to the future]. This Lassallian ideological conception has been transmitted to those workers, who having accepted it, entered into the ranks of Marxism.

"THE PHILOSOPHY OF FORCE"
("La filosofia della forza")
(November 29, December 6 and 13, 1908)

For Stirner and for Nietzsche and for all those whom Tuerck, in his *Der geniale Mensch* calls the "antisophists of egoism," the state is the organized oppression of the individual. But how has the state arisen? Was it a consequence of a social contract as Rousseau and his deluded followers pretended? No. Nietzsche, in his *Zur Genealogie der Moral* describes the genesis of the state in the following way:

It is a herd of blond animals of prey—it is a race of masters and conquerors who throw themselves upon a neighboring population that is disorganized, weak, and nomadic. It is an act of violence carried out by men who—in and because of their organization as warriors do not entertain the concept of regard for their neighbors, a concept of responsibility and of guilt. Their egoism of strength does not admit limitations. They feel the fullness of their life and the tensions of their energy only when they can crush another human being. Rather than suppress their primordial instinct of cruelty they afford it free expression. Their motto is the cry of the oriental sect of assassins: Nothing exists, all is permitted. And they add: to witness suffering is good, to effect suffering, better.

For all that, a principle of solidarity governs the relations of these blond beasts of prey. Even the conquerors obey the rules that the collectivity imposes to protect the cardinal interests of the caste and this can be construed as the first limitations on their autonomous will. Not only the warriors "constrain" themselves to a rigid discipline—a manifestation of, and the evidence for, a pre-existing solidarity of interests—but they are further compelled to preserve and protect the slaves that produce the material means of existence. It is not enough to create new tables of moral values, it is necessary to humbly produce bread. The individual can, therefore, never be "unique" in the Stirnerian sense of the word, since the fatal law of solidarity compels his submission. The social instinct is, according to Darwin, inherent in the very nature of man. The individual is inconceivable outside of an infinite chain of beings. Nietzsche sensed the "fatality" of what could be called the law of universal solidarity, and in order to escape contradiction [between the warrior's will to power and the necessity for social order] the Nietzschean superman—the Nietzschean hero, the sage and implacable warrior—unleashes his will to power against those outside his community.... But with war and external conquest, the circle of positive solidarity increases....

"THE GENERAL STRIKE AND VIOLENCE"
("Lo sciopero generale e la violenza")
(June 25, 1909)

In his introduction, Sorel develops his theory of "myths," as "myth" relates to the proletarian general strike. According to Sorel, if ideas have triumphed in the world, it is because they have, as myths, animated crowds—that is to say, [myths] characterize the actions which, undertaken in conflict, assist in the triumph of one's cause. The Christians had their myth in an apocalyptic vision of the definitive defeat of Satan, just as reformists, revolutionaries and Mazzinians have their myths. *Giovane Italia*, founded by the exile from Genoa, animated Italians as a mythic representation that moved them to conspiracy and battle. Similarly the myth of the general strike—considered as a final battle—provides, for the worker, the energy to realize the revolution. Those who oppose themselves to the myth because they conceive it utopian, forget that in all myths there [are utopian elements], and further that "in the contemporary revolutionary myths utopianism is almost absent. The contemporary myth motivates men to prepare themselves for the destruction of that which exists; utopianism serves to turn spirits to solely realizable reforms . . .".

. . . We do not desire to reap the patrimony of a decadent bourgeoisie. In the universal interests of man we prefer to face a bourgeois class that is militant, audacious, and conscious of its proper mission, a bourgeoisie that attains the fulness of its power and falls under the decisive stroke of the general strike. Proletarian violence, which compels capitalism to [assume manly character] in the industrial struggle and to devote itself to its productive functions, is perhaps the only means available to the nations of Europe, debased by humanitarianism, to rediscover their ancient vigor.

If a united and revolutionary proletariat faces a bourgeoisie that is wealthy and attracted by conquest, capitalist society will attain its historic perfection.

The peril that threatens the future of the world is to be found in the historic desire for peace at any price—in the universal embrace that attempts to suppress, under a torrent of humanitarian rhetoric, the harsh, irreducible antitheses of economic reality—and in a bourgeoisie that has lost its former faith in itself and in a socialism that had suffocated itself in the parliamentary bog.

. . . . All those who fear violence recall to mind the days of the Inquisition, the period of the Terror, the Jacobin tribunals and the ubiquitous guillotine. It is probable that a revolution conducted by ideologists, by people who make it their profession to think for others, in our case the proletariat, would reinvoke such punitive procedures; but proletarian violence has nothing to do with such eventualities. Proletarian violence is a simple act of war, and everything that pertains to war is carried out without hatred and without the spirit of revenge . . . ; social conflicts take on the character of simple battle, similar to those conducted by regular armed forces. . . . We have the right to expect that a socialist revolution conducted by syndicalists will not be tarnished by the abominations that characterize bourgeois revolutions.

Sorel draws a distinction between force and violence, a distinction necessary to dissipate many equivocations:

Force is employed to impose organization upon a social order governed by a minority; violence, on the other hand, serves to destroy that order.

Force is the expression of authority and violence is the expression of revolt. The former is the product of the bourgeois world, the latter the product of proletarian organization. Violence culminates in the general strike which, like a war of liberty, is "the sharpest manifestation . . . of rebellious masses." From the exercise of proletarian violence arises that which Sorel calls the morality of producers, the new morality which gives exuberant and epic life to the spirit and draws taut the psychic energies, to realize those conditions upon which the enterprise of free and humane men can be based. . . . Socialist violence provides the high moral values upon which rest the salvation of the modern world.

. . . Contemporary socialism in the Latin nations owes a great deal to Georges Sorel. Thanks to his work we have attained a more secure comprehension of Marxism which we would have otherwise received in an almost unrecognizable form from Germany. Stripped of all that ideological tinsel inherited from the democratic and Jacobin, not to say positivist, traditions, socialism "identifies itself with the general strike." Socialism is no longer a system of thought living in a future more or less remote, but a daily apprenticeship in revolutionary preparation, the continuous and violent application of the class struggle. The bourgeoisie and the proletariat are worlds apart. The first enhances itself with technical progress and colonial expansion while the latter prepares to expropriate that abundance. Expropriation will be the result of a general strike which constitutes a supreme catalyst, a Napoleonic battle, and, as Marx wished, it will be the occasion of a definitive break between two historic epochs.

Such an interpretation of the social future has nothing in common with the ideologies of official socialists who believe in the magic virtue of a single strategy. It is certain that a parliamentary vote of an assembly of lawyers, will not provide a society "in which production will be organized on the basis of an association of free and equal producers, relegating the machinery of the state to a museum of antiquities alongside the wheel and the stone axe."

[Such a society] will be the consequence, rather, of an immense collision in which the two opposing classes measure their strength in a decisive battle . . . . Sorel reinvokes in all its lucidity and historic significance, that notion of imminent catastrophe that reformists have been quick to reject as mistaken. . . .

This state of permanent warfare between the bourgeoisie and the proletariat will generate new energies, new moral values, new men who will approximate the heroes of antiquity.

The words of Georges Sorel with which I close these notes I commend to the meditation of my companions: it is necessary that socialists persuade themselves that the work to which they have committed themselves be recognized as grave, terrible and sublime.

"AMONG BOOKS AND MAGAZINES"
("Fra libri e riviste")
(September 4, 1909)

Dr. Roberto Michels—the noted German revolutionary socialist and a friend of Italy and Italians—has recently published, through the offices of Bocca in Turin, a book on *Cooperation*.

Michels begins his account of the phenomenon with the affirmation that "economic cooperation is the consequence of the law that [men] attempt to obtain maximal results with the least expenditure of effort."

Medieval cooperation based on the guild and the corporation, or that primitive cooperation such as one finds in the Russian *mir*, were struck down by the triumphant democracy of the French Revolution. . . .

All men that share an identity of interests, tend to defend themselves collectively in order to enhance their probability of success. This principle demolishes that individualism that now has been reduced to a theory entertained only by *litterateurs* on holiday.

Michels insists that "the modern economic man exists only in so far as he is part of an aggregate."

The truth of this is evident and hardly requires demonstration.

Michels has distinguished two elements of "cooperation"—each opposed to the other. One is positive and the other negative. The former manifests itself in the solidarity which characterizes the members of the group and the second in the struggle against antagonistic groups.

Michels attempts to provide a schematic account of this phenomenon so diffused in modern society, and his book will be welcomed among students of the social sciences.

"THE REASONS FOR SO-CALLED 'PACIFISM' "
("Le ragioni del cosidetto 'Pacifismo' ")
(March 29, 1913)

Struggle in society has been and always will be a struggle between minorities. To attempt to win over an absolute majority—quantitatively speaking—is an absurdity. It would be impossible to regiment the majority of the proletariat in economic and political organization . . . The class struggle is, essentially, a contest between minorities. The majority follows and submits. Is governance not a function of minorities, which in all nations imposes its will on the mass?

"THE HISTORIC VALUE OF SOCIALISM"
("Il valore storico del socialismo")
(February 8, 1914)

The mechanical or material possibility, or to use the expression, the empirical possibility, of revolution obtains. Of this the reformists themselves do not doubt—the difference is that they relegate the revolution to the very distant future. But is there the psychological possibility? One hears that modern man enjoys life and doesn't intend to risk it on a barricade. It could be. It is certain that today life is more precious, even for the lowliest peasant, than it was a century or two ago. But this is only the case under normal circumstances and cannot be said to be true for times of social crisis.

[Under crisis conditions] the masses lose that conservative equilibrium that keeps them tied to custom. Naturally [such a loss of equilibrium] requires an imposing cause—[it requires] that the agitation be profound, that the entire social atmosphere be charged.... There are those who wish to wait until an absolute majority supports them before making revolution. That is an absurdity. First of all the mass is a quantity; it is inert. The mass is static; only minorities are dynamic. Furthermore, labor organizations cannot hope to collect all recruitable workers into their unions.... The problem as I see it is to oppose the bourgeois minority with a socialist and revolutionary minority. In essence we are governed by a minority. Political life in Italy is governed, as it is in all civilized nations, by a minority to which the great mass submits. If this enormous mass is apathetic, and passively submits to an iniquitous regime that is unjust, why would it not accept a better governance?

We must create out of the bosom of the proletariat, a minority sufficiently numerous, sufficiently conscious, sufficiently audacious, that, at the opportune moment, it can substitute itself for the bourgeois minority. The masses will follow and submit.

"ANOTHER STEP"
("Un altro passo")
(February 16, 1919)

We must not permit the League of Nations to become a form of insurance for opulent, developed and rich nations that have nothing more to conquer in the world and only wish to conserve that which they have. In the League the members must be equal both juridically and economically. But in the League there are "bourgeois" and "proletarian" nations and the community and solidarity among them cannot endure forever.

"THE BIRTH OF FASCISM"
("Atto di nascita del fascismo")
(March 23, 1919)

We declare war against socialism, not because it is socialist, but because it is opposed to the nation. Everyone can involve themselves in the discussion concerning the program and tactics of socialism and what socialism might, in fact, be. But the official Socialist Party of Italy has been reactionary, absolutely conservative, and if it had its way, we would have no possibility of life in the world. The Socialist Party cannot take the lead in innovative action designed to reconstruct.... It is inevitably the case that the majority is static, while minorities are dynamic. We desire to be an active minority. We wish to draw the proletariat away from the Socialist Party. But if the bourgeoisie thinks that it will find in us a lightning rod, it deludes itself.... If the doctrine of syndicalism maintains that the masses can produce the necessary and capable enterprisory talent to assume the direction of labor, we will not oppose them—if that movement remains firm with respect to these two realities: the reality of production and that of the nation. . . . We have made the cornerstone of our political program the maximization of production.

"HE PAYS WHO POSSESSES"
("Chi possiede, paghi!")
(July 6, 1919)

Produce! That is the supreme imperative of the hour. Produce! insists the Honorable Nitti in his first circular to prefects. Industrialists, organizers, those in cooperatives, scholars, journalists—all those who perceive in unemployment and declining productivity the collapse of our fragile civilization—all cry in agreement, "Produce!"

I am modestly proud of having anticipated this necessity a year ago. I am proud to have emphasized the [role of] the forces of production when I changed the subtitle of this paper [from a "Socialist Daily" to a "Daily of Producers"]. Fools, the malevolent, the idiotic, conceived this to have been a form of "betrayal" of the immortal principles of democracy. Now everyone is prepared to admit that "production" is the first and principal problem. . . . which any social system—capitalist, socialist or communist—must resolve if it is not to perish in universal misery.

HAROLD C. DEUTSCH

The Genesis of the Military Conspiracy
Against Hitler

D OMESTIC OPPOSITION to the Hitler regime took every conceivable form and manifested itself in many quarters. It reflected all shadings of the political spectrum and drew support from every sector of society. An integral analysis of what can qualify as "German resistance" has not yet been attempted and indeed may have to await the perspective of another generation. The aspect on which attention has been mainly centered and which investigators have pursued most tirelessly certainly is that which led through a long chain of developments to their climax in the attempted coup on July 20, 1944.

PLACE OF THE MILITARY OPPOSITION

The grouping involved could boast a record of years of intensive conspiratorial activity, a wide-flung network of support, concrete plans for takeover, and some hope of success. Of necessity it clustered about military antagonists of the regime. Conspirators who could not claim some command over soldiers and police had scant chance of unseating Hitler. Only when a group civilian in

319

origin succeeded in coalescing with men of this stamp did its designs and resolution gain real significance.

Aside from having some access to instruments of power, those who formed this company had a number of other qualities which explain their place in history. Among them was a solidarity seldom achieved by clandestine movements within authoritarian societies. The roll of the leading figures as it read in 1938 differed little from what it was to be at such later high points as late 1939, 1943, and finally the summer of 1944. There was discernible an in again-out again movement by more opportunistic individuals that accorded roughly with the ebb and flow of Hitler's fortunes. But the solid core of steadfast adherents could be relied upon year after year. Such consistency betokened more than a mere community of material interests. It was based on a cement of moral and ethical principles that appealed not only to men of exceptional ideals but also to many ordinary persons.

A second feature that characterized what, for want of a better designation, we here call the Military Opposition is that it was largely civilian in composition as well as in origin. Such major military figures as General Ludwig Beck, the chief of the General Staff of the Army, were supporters of civilian supremacy and looked forward to no more than a brief period of transitional military rule. This accords with the fact that the resistance grouping with which we are concerned was the only one which could make any claim, or even a pretense, to reflect an across-the-board coalition of anti-Nazi elements. With the sole exception of the Communists,[1] there was some type of link with persons hostile to the regime from the far political right to the left wing of the Social Democrats. Such representation was perforce uneven in character and stood for different degrees of commitment and participation. Nevertheless, it must be judged genuine. In the end not only hundreds but thousands of Germans were affected in some fashion.

SOURCES OF INFORMATION

Tracing the course of deliberations and activities that are clandestine always bedevils the historical investigator with unusual complexities and difficulties. The secrecy that must be observed

---

[1] It was, in fact, a belated effort to bring in Communists which, in July 1944, helped to hurry matters and to lead to the tragic outcome on July 20. See also Source 1 on efforts to broaden the base of the Opposition.

puts a severe limit on what may be confided to paper. What is recorded is often phrased in language deliberately veiled or is concealed in coded messages and notations, including personal ones between individuals, to which it is sometimes impossible to find a key.

When the state and its leaders are the targets of conspiratorial activities, attackers and defenders tend to operate according to similar rules. Concealment is often a matter of life and death. Even after the contest has been resolved and victors and vanquished determined, there is much that compels or at least recommends continued reticence. It may still be necessary to guard methods of operation, avoid controversy in a period of partially restored national unity, and hush up mistakes or the more questionable means that may have been employed. Sometimes the problem is merely the reluctance of habitually close-mouthed people to conduct themselves in a fashion contrary to what has become instinctive with them.[2]

The historian is also hampered by restraint on the part of governments about making available to public scrutiny documentary records of clandestine operations. Traditionally police and intelligence files are the last to be opened to historians.[3]

What has been said here about the uphill task of tracing clandestine activities in general counts double in dealing with the history of the German Military Opposition. Not that it failed to produce an astonishing quantity of compromising paper. In part this was the result of pure carelessness, for most of the conspirators were rank amateurs at this hazardous game. The man scheduled to be Chancellor (prime minister) of a post-Hitler provisional government, Carl Goerdeler, systematically kept notes on conversations with persons he was trying to recruit and wrote voluminous memoranda that analyzed the problems that were likely to be faced by a liberated Germany. A major Military

---

[2] The writer vividly recalls his experience with Colonel Nicolai, the celebrated German Chief of Military Intelligence of World War I, who at first refused to comment about anything associated with his own role. Only repeated interviews and judicious needling on sensitive issues finally broke down his reserve.

[3] When, a few years ago, the British government reduced the waiting period for releasing documents on foreign relations from fifty to thirty years, this did not include the relevant Secret Service files. Foreign service documents that deal specifically with clandestine contacts are also at times excluded from early access. In looking for a report on a meeting between a British Foreign Office representative and Carl Goerdeler, leader of the group that is the subject of this essay, the writer found in the files of the London Public Record Office only a notation that the document in question would be made available in the year 2015!

Opposition leader, Colonel Hans Oster, left drafts of proposed radio proclamations in an officers' club. Only the amazing luck of the conspirators and the ineptitude of the *Gestapo* (Secret State Police) can explain that the oppositionists were not discovered years before they finally struck.[4]

It must not be assumed that the great mass of Opposition papers owed their existence largely to bungling. There was method and grim purpose in assembling the most formidable collection of documentary material—in effect, the archives of the Opposition. This began with a compilation of documents gathered by Hans von Dohnanyi, a brilliant young jurist, within the confines of Hitler's own Ministry of Justice. In this relatively secure haven, Dohnanyi, as the Minister's principal aide, was ideally placed to secure and store for eventual use whatever flowed into the Ministry by way of evidence on crimes committed by the regime or by those of its adherents who felt safe from prosecution as long as the Nazi state existed to shield them.[5]

During the Blomberg-Fritsch affair of 1938, which will be analyzed later, Minister of Justice Franz Gürtner entrusted Dohnanyi with the Ministry's part in investigating charges against General von Fritsch. In contending with this Nazi plot against the Army leadership, he became closely associated with top figures of the *Abwehr* (Armed Forces Military Intelligence) in their common effort to clear the general. In consequence, at the beginning of the war, Dohnanyi was enrolled in the *Abwehr*, whose resources were as made-to-order for ferreting out crimes in occupied Europe as those of the Ministry of Justice had been in getting wind of them in the domestic scene. The atrocities in Poland and later those in the Soviet Union, for example, were heavily documented by from-the-field reports, pictures, and films. The plans and activities of the Military Opposition itself, including the detailed story of such highlights as dealings with the British government through Pope Pius XII, were also carefully recorded. That part of the

---

[4] By no means all of these conspiratorial amateurs were so imprudent as those just mentioned. Thus a Benedictine monk, now administrator of the great monastery of Ettal in Bavaria, would carry no telephone numbers on his person when visiting Berlin, always looking up such numbers as he had not memorized. Interview with the Reverend Johannes Albrecht, June 28, 1970.

[5] The file that contained this material was marked "Chronicle of Nazi Crimes and Sharp Practice." Dohnanyi's activity was carried on with the full knowledge of Minister of Justice Gürtner, who knew volumes about the corruption and criminality of the regime but lacked the courage for a really serious confrontation with Hitler. See Harold C. Deutsch, *The Conspiracy Against Hitler in the Twilight War* (Minneapolis: University of Minnesota Press, 1968), p. 89. See also Source 1.

archives which was later captured by the Gestapo alone measured some eight feet of solid material.[6]

Dohnanyi himself was arrested in the spring of 1943 and from his prison cell sent frantic entreaties to his friends to destroy the vast hoard of incriminating material which by then had accumulated. This was interdicted by General Beck, who had both "a decent respect for the opinions of mankind" and a true historical viewpoint on the affairs of the Opposition. In particular, he felt that the preservation of these records was imperative to prove later to the German people and to the world generally that the conspiracy against Hitler had not been an improvised adventure cooked up when the war began to go badly in order to enable Germany to gain a better peace. The thought of facing such charges was bound to be unbearable for men who for six long years had persevered in their purpose in the face of innumerable frustrations and disappointments.

After Dohnanyi and several of his *Abwehr* associates had gotten themselves into deep trouble early in 1943, elementary caution demanded at least the removal of this compromising data from *Abwehr* headquarters. The entire mass was first transferred to the vaults of the Prussian State Bank. It was then determined to bury everything in the Schorf Heath where a member of the *Abwehr* group, Colonel Werner Schrader, had a hunting retreat. After a single automobile load had been dispatched, it proved impossible to get enough gasoline for further trips. The remainder was therefore carried to Army headquarters at Zossen near Berlin and deposited in a large safe in an underground chamber. There it was discovered and carted away by the Gestapo about two months after the disaster of July 20 and helped to fasten the noose around the necks of many of the conspirators. What had been taken to the Schorf Heath was burned in blind panic by Mrs. Schrader after her husband's suicide.

Chimneys were indeed smoking in many parts of Germany in the late summer and autumn of 1944. Wherever the Gestapo appeared to be closing in on its victims, they, or those to whom

[6] This appears to have been about two-thirds of what Dohnanyi and his friends had collected. The estimate of the captured part was given the writer by the official who transported it to Gestapo headquarters and confirmed by his superior who, together with him, took some four weeks to survey its contents. (Interviews with Franz Sonderegger, August 23, 1958, and Walter Huppenkothen, September 11, 1960.) Lieutenant Colonel Friedrich Wilhelm Heinz, who made the first big shift of the material from *Abwehr* headquarters after Dohnanyi's arrest, speaks of "two large passenger car loads." (Interview, August 24, 1958.)

they had entrusted their records, frantically did away with them. Diaries, letters, memoranda—papers of every imaginable description—were fed to the flames. And much that appears to have been hidden away by men who failed to survive has never been located.[7]

Little over half a year later, in a second holocaust of Opposition documents, agents of the collapsing regime swept away virtually all that had been seized by them. Into the same fires went the bulk of police records recounting what had been learned from observation, stalking, pursuit, and the interrogation of sometimes tormented prisoners.[8] Equally tragic for the historian as the demolition of the contents of the Zossen safe and the burning of what had been hidden in the Schorf Heath is the loss of the incredibly voluminous diary of Admiral Wilhelm Canaris, Chief of the *Abwehr*, who had resolved to document meticulously "how criminally the war had been begun and how dilettante had been Hitler's leadership."[9] Day after day over the years he had dictated to his faithful secretary his more significant conversations and whatever evidence had come his way.

Canaris's diary came into Gestapo hands a few weeks before the end of the war and what Hitler was told about its contents so infuriated him that he straightway ordered the execution of its author and of the entire *Abwehr*-associated group insofar as it was in his power. The chance that one of the microfilm copies then made still exists cannot be completely ruled out but must be reckoned as minimal. Only a few months before these lines were

---

[7] Thus detailed plans for takeover prepared in connection with the attempt of July 20 remain buried in the forest where Hitler's East Prussian military headquarters, known as Wolf's Lair, were established. (Interview with Ambassador Hans Herwarth von Bittenfeld, April 20, 1967.) The writer has had some contact with representatives of the Polish government with respect to permission to make a search if a more exact location can be established. He has also talked with the man who actually buried the papers but has not as yet been successful in securing his cooperation.

[8] There are many indications that Himmler had learned a good deal about the developing conspiracy before July 20, 1944. An analysis of this problem has been published by Hedwig Maier, "Die SS und der 20. Juli 1944," *Vierteljahrshefte für Zeitgeschichte* XIV, No. 3 (July, 1966), pp. 299-316.

One fortunate survival of material on the conspiracy consists of the reports addressed to Hitler on what the investigators learned through interrogations and documentary finds after July 20. These are published as: *Spiegelbild einer Verschwörung. Die Kaltenbrunner Berichte an Bormann und Hitler über das Attentat vom 20. Juli 1944. Geheime Dokumente aus dem ehemaligen Reichssicherheitshauptamt* (The pictorial mirror of a conspiracy. The Kaltenbrunner Reports to Bormann and Hitler about the assassination attempt of July 20, 1944. Secret documents from the former Reich Main Security Office), ed. by Karl Heinz Peter (Stuttgart: Seewald Verlag, 1961).

[9] See Deutsch, *Conspiracy*, p. 182.

written there was talk of some part of the diary having been found but this had been quickly discounted. For historians as well as for the lucky finder it would certainly prove a discovery of incalculable value.[10]

What does at this time exist in the way of primary source material on the history of the Military Opposition? Here and there have been found real nuggets in the way of documentary material. Prime examples are two diaries dug up in backyards in 1945 by relatives of deceased Opposition figures.[11] The two principal survivors of the group, Hans Bernd Gisevius and Erich Kordt, actually wrote memoirs in Switzerland and China while the war was still going on.[12] Another vital source is provided by the minutes of one of the three trials of Walter Huppenkothen, the principal Gestapo official directing the investigation of "the July criminals."[13]

In tracing the story of German resistance activities, the most important source in many cases is the memories of surviving resisters or of the friends and relations of those executed or murdered on or after July 20. To identify them, communicate with them, and persuade them to bear witness is often no easy or simple task and demands an extraordinary expenditure of time and resources. Historians dealing with aspects of the Military Opposition have not always been prepared to make the necessary sacrifices and sometimes have convinced themselves that it is not

[10] Over the years the present writer has spent many weeks in systematic search for possibly existing portions of Dohnanyi's "archives" and of the Canaris diary, interviewing at least a score of persons who might know something about their disposition. He is satisfied that the chances of sensational discoveries are virtually nonexistent. Some of the information the Zossen safe contained has come to light in duplicate copies that were preserved elsewhere. There are also a few specific entries of the Canaris diary, a copy of which he gave at times to one or another of his associates.

[11] In question are (1) Ulrich von Hassell, *The Hassell Diaries, 1938-1944: The Story of the Fight Against Hitler Inside Germany* (New York: Doubleday, 1947); and (2) Helmuth Groscurth, *Tagebücher eines Abwehroffiziers: Mit weiteren Dokumenten zur Militäropposition gegen Hitler* (Diary of an Abwehr officer: With additional documents on the Military Opposition against Hitler.) ed. by Helmuth Krausnick and Harold C. Deutsch in association with Hildegard von Kotze (Stuttgart: Deutsche Verlags-Anstalt, 1970).

[12] Hans Bernd Gisevius, *To the Bitter End* (Boston: Houghton Mifflin, 1947), and Erich Kordt, *Wahn und Wirklichkeit. Aussenpolitik des Dritten Reiches* (Delusion and reality. The foreign policy of the Third Reich) (Stuttgart: Union Deutsche Verlagsgesellschaft, 1947). Kordt later wrote more personal memoirs under the title, *Nicht aus den Akten* (Not from the records) (Stuttgart: Union Deutsche Verlagsgesellschaft, 1950).

[13] Transcript of testimony at the trial of Walter Huppenkothen, February 4-14, 1951, and Verdict, February 22. Three manuscript volumes in the writer's possession. Apparently these are the only complete minutes of one of the three Huppenkothen trials.

truly imperative to do so. To illustrate what may be involved, to
cover just the period 1938 through the spring of 1940, the author
of this essay has been obliged to interrogate (as prisoners in 1945)
or interview some two hundred persons at least six hundred times.
It is a constant race with the relentless march of death and all too
often the latter wins out.

In view of the emotional involvement of many who do consent
to testify, the customary handicaps of oral history are often
compounded. But it should be noted that the hazards and
impediments are no worse than those encountered in dealing with
memoirs and can in this instance be minimized by taking advantage of the opportunity for cross-examination. Another advantage
is that this type of research affords access to secondary figures
who are usually more objective and who seldom are moved to
write memoirs or set down anything whatsoever of their experience. Further, there is a frequent bonus in the willingness to loan
documentary material which might otherwise remain unknown or
at least not be forthcoming in reply to an appeal by letter.
Altogether, full exploitation of this resource constitutes one of the
most exciting and rewarding adventures in research of which the
historian of the recent period and his readers alone can hope to be
the beneficiaries.

HITLER'S RELATIONS WITH THE MILITARY BEFORE 1938

As with many complicated historical problems that have some
chronological framework, the Military Opposition against Hitler
can be dealt with most conveniently by considering the phases
or stages into which it most logically falls. A natural beginning
calls for a preliminary glance at the developing relationship
between Hitler and the military leadership and some consideration
of the military and civilian resistance elements which by the end
of 1937 had progressed sufficiently to provide some basis for a
process of coalescence. Next, attention is claimed by the catalyst
which provided the impulse to fusion—the Blomberg-Fritsch affair
in the first half of 1938. Thereafter the story centers in the various
phases or rounds of conspiratorial activity that culminated in the
attempt at takeover on July 20, 1944. It concludes with the grim
epilogue of the extermination of Germany's elite in the dying days
of the Third Reich.

This essay is concerned only with the first part of this

story—the background and crystallization of a recognizable and broad-based ingathering of oppositional forces of various types and diverse origin. From the moment when Hitler shouldered the government of the German Republic in 1933, it was evident to observers who knew something of history and German affairs that the relations between his regime and its armed forces (*Wehrmacht*) would be decisive in matters of vital national and international character. Without a doubt the outlook was full of uncertainties. Some of the Army leaders, such as the commander in chief, Colonel General Baron von Hammerstein, had seriously thought of using force to prevent the Nazi takeover. Virtually the entire general officer corps was beset by some doubts about the new order. It certainly had a distaste for the Nazi vulgarians who were thrusting themselves forward everywhere and it feared that Hitler would be too recklessly aggressive in foreign relations. But it could only welcome his evident intention to push rearmament and to follow a more vigorous national policy in pursuit of revising the peace settlement of 1919-1920.

A new team of military leaders who took over in 1933-1934 also made a favorable impression. Minister of War Werner von Blomberg was a seasoned commander and personally attractive. Hammerstein's successor, Werner von Fritsch, had a reputation for soldierly bearing, solid competence, and sterling integrity. And a new chief of the General Staff, Ludwig Beck, was widely regarded as intellectually the most distinguished soldier the Army had produced in a generation.

Hitler also began his rule with relative moderation. He curbed certain party extremists, avoided (except for a misstep with regard to Austria) serious adventures in foreign affairs, and kept within some bounds such disturbing aspects of Nazism as hostility to the churches, indeed to Christianity. On the whole the generals were inclined to give him the benefit of the doubt while throwing themselves into the congenial task of rebuilding the Army from the token status to which it had been condemned under the Weimar Republic.

The turning point year is usually agreed to be 1936. By then the economic and military comeback of Germany was taking on proportions and implying a future potential which inclined Hitler to begin taking chances in foreign relations. In his more intimate circle he began to talk about a major conflict which would be timed to the peaking of his arms program in the early or mid-forties.

This was mostly taken to be loose and fanciful verbiage. More seriously regarded was his increasingly reckless stance in critical international situations, such as when he remilitarized the German west bank of the Rhine in defiance of the Treaty of Versailles (spring 1936), began to intervene in the Spanish Civil war (summer 1936), and embarked on flirtations with increasingly aggressive Japan and Italy.

To men positioned to observe developments closely it was becoming clear that, however much he might cast dust in German and foreign eyes by stressing self-limiting policies like treaty revision, with which one could go only so far, he was actually preparing to commit Germany to unlimited expansionism based on fancies of race and "living space." Fritsch and Beck, in particular, found little to attract them in foreign and rearmament policies built on such principles. Such a program promised nothing but a succession of wars that ultimately would end in disaster for Germany.

Hitler, in turn, felt that he needed a new type of General Staff to accomplish his designs. He had said so as early as 1931 in conversations with an influential newspaper editor whose support he was wooing.[14] He saw future trouble in the way the generals dragged their feet every time he leaned toward international risk-taking, their total lack of response to the appeals of Nazism (Fritsch even returned the golden party badge Hitler had conferred on him), and their finickiness about everything that violated their professional or class taboos. He could hardly fail to foresee that they would resist and perhaps sabotage the extreme courses on which he was determined. Increasingly arrogant in his overestimate of his own talents and as an amateur in every area in which he exercised power, he resented also the claim of the military professionals to superiority in their field of competence. Perhaps most of all, he was incensed with the argument that the General Staff, as Beck often put it, was "the conscience of the Army" and must be heard whenever it seemed likely that the *Wehrmacht* might be employed as an instrument of national policy. Small wonder that Hitler became ever more receptive to the malicious insinuations of Nazi intriguers, such as Heinrich Himmler and Hermann Göring, who were jealous of the Army's semi-independ-

---

[14] See Harold C. Deutsch, *Hitler and His Generals, The Hidden Crisis of January-June 1938* (Minneapolis: University of Minnesota Press, 1974), p. 6.

ence and cherished private ambitions to gain control of this vital instrument of power.

Hitler was under greater obligation to Blomberg than to any other individual. The War Minister had fallen under his personal spell and had largely managed the *Wehrmacht* accordingly. One of his greatest services had been to curb the occasional impulse of Army leaders to intervene in areas where Nazi encroachments were becoming increasingly intolerable. On the debit side, as Hitler saw it, were Blomberg's efforts to preserve *Wehrmacht* autonomy, his hesitations about forcing the strong-willed Fritsch into line in various areas, and his tendency to recoil when matters became tense in international relations. If we are to believe Hitler's own description, the War Minister would then react like an "hysterical old maid." These failings were magnified in the dictator's eyes when his patience began to wear thin with everyone who threatened to be a brake on his aggressive designs.

Toward the end of 1937, Hitler determined to make what turned out to be his final effort to convert Fritsch to his policies. On November 5 he convened in his Chancellery what is known to history as the "Hossbach conference" because his Wehrmacht adjutant, Colonel Friedrich Hossbach, took rough notes and later wrote them up in what was to be the only record made of the meeting. (See Sources 3 and 4.)

Those invited were Blomberg, the Foreign Minister, Baron Konstantin von Neurath, and the three service chiefs, Fritsch, Göring, and Admiral Erich Raeder. Hitler led off by informing them that he was about to reveal his basic conceptions on foreign policy and that, in the event of his death, his words were to be regarded as his political testament. He dwelt in candid terms on the need for more German living space and announced that he was determined to change the map of Europe accordingly by force. The quickest gains at lowest cost could be expected in Austria and Czechoslovakia and the deadline for action concerning them would be the period 1943-1945. But a favorable international climate, such as a war of France and Britain with Italy, would provide an opportunity for moving as early as 1938.

The statement had considerable shock effect and three of the conferees—Blomberg, Fritsch, and Neurath—dared to take issue with it. Hitler's vexation later showed itself in such ways as rudeness to Neurath, whom he refused to receive for over two months. There is some argument among historians on just how much his frustration led directly to the fact that three months later all three of the men who had opposed him were out of office. Standing by itself, this circumstance is no proof that the two facts are inextricably connected. Indeed, the more evidence comes to light, the more manifest it is that in Hitler's calculations the days of all three were numbered even before November 5.[15] As he saw them, Neurath was soft and pusillanimous, Blomberg a weak reed to lean upon when it came to forcing the Army leaders into line, Fritsch a rigid, unimaginative traditionalist, Beck hesitant and indecisive. Each of these men still had something to offer him and their dismissal would have to be handled carefully. But they had become encumbrances and anything which arose to facilitate their exit would be welcome. In this sense, at least, the way from November 5 did lead directly to the formal dismissal of Blomberg, Fritsch, and Neurath on the following February 4.

IMMEDIATE BACKGROUND AND INITIATION OF THE 1938 WEHRMACHT CRISIS

The most persistent debate about the *Wehrmacht* crisis of the first half of 1938 concerns the degree to which opportunity was simply seized, as it were, on the wing, or made to order by the machinations of one or more of the Nazi hierarchs. It is widely assumed that, although chance undoubtedly played a role, those to whom it beckoned were not merely receptive but already had done much to pave the way for it. The argument revolves mainly about the relative involvement of Hitler, Göring, Himmler, and the latter's sinister henchman, Reinhard Heydrich. Historical analysis for the resolution of this dispute is badly hampered by the paucity of documentary evidence. And logical deduction from what we do know about the interests and motivations of the parties concerned cannot take us far enough nor nail down conclusions. Barring significant new documentary discoveries,[16] we are thus, as so often in affairs of the German Opposition, obliged to extend the

---

[15] Both the diary and oral testimony of General Gerhard Engel, Hitler's Army adjutant from 1938 to 1942, stress that in the months after their dismissal, Hitler almost obsessively repeated that he had to get rid of these men in any event. Interviews of May 4 and 11, 1970; diary entry of April 20, 1938, etc.

[16] Aside from what material may be in Soviet or East German hands, the most likely promise of turning up previously unknown documents lies in captured papers that are still in United States custody. In the early postwar years much was shipped in bulk to Washington without clear identification and simply stored away. Some of this material is now being examined for the first time in line with a broad program of "declassification."

boundaries of knowledge by relying on the still surviving witnesses, notably the oft-neglected secondary figures.

Let us begin with a summary of the stark and undisputed facts of the background and first stirrings of the crisis. The Hossbach conference had not only frustrated Hitler's aim to bring Blomberg and, especially, Fritsch into line with his policies, but had thrown sparks in a duel between Göring and the two generals over raw materials allocations. A spate of acid exchanges had left the *Luftwaffe* (Air Force) commander furious and somewhat out of countenance. Malice now gave an extra spur to his ambition to step into Blomberg's shoes, which of necessity also meant shouldering aside the man who had the inside track if he wanted the position—the head of the senior service, Fritsch.[17] Though the SS (Elite Guard) leaders, Himmler and Heydrich, had their own rivalries with Göring, they were always on hand for a common intrigue against the hated Army command. Since 1936 the two men, with at least the cognizance of Göring, had cherished a cunningly contrived file of misapplied data designed to give color to a charge of homosexuality against Fritsch. Hitler had not considered the time suitable for a showdown with the Army leadership and supposedly had directed the destruction of the incriminating dossier.

The next development spelled opportunity writ large—the injudicious marriage of Field Marshal von Blomberg to Eva Gruhn, a woman not only too humble in station for so exalted a bridegroom, but one with a police record for moral offenses including modeling for pornographic tableaux. Blomberg supposedly knew only that she had "something of a past." Military regulations obliged officers who wished to marry to secure approval of their superiors—in this case Hitler. For support to gain this and to be assured of backing against anticipated murmurs among the generals, Blomberg was so naive as to appeal to Göring, who readily agreed to help him along this road to ruin.

The simple marriage ceremony took place on January 12, Hitler and Göring acting as witnesses. Twelve days later Göring carried to the Fuehrer the file on the new Madame Field Marshal which had been assembled over the years by the morals police. Blomberg's fate was thereby sealed and the spotlight next shifts to Fritsch.

---

[17] General Bodenschatz, Göring's adjutant and intimate, unreservedly affirms that Göring's central ambition at this time was to take over command of the *Wehrmacht*. (Letter to Walter Baum, September 2, 1956, Institut für Zeitgeschichte, Munich, ZS 10.)

For Göring had also brought with him, or saw to it that Hitler received within a few hours, the dossier on the Army commander that had supposedly been burned in 1936 but was now "reconstituted" in an actually beefed-up condition. At least the previous nine days, and perhaps many more, had been devoted to this fattening process.

The dossier rested essentially on the testimony of Otto Schmidt, a professional blackmailer who in 1933 had "laid on the cross" an elderly cavalry captain named Achim von Frisch. The similarity of names had given the Gestapo ideas and led to a simple substitution by which the humble captain was promoted to colonel general and identified with the commander in chief of the Army. Confronted by Hitler and Göring with this file and the blackmailer in person, Fritsch was distraught and defended himself feebly. (See Source 6.) Under the illusion that his problem was to convince Hitler of his innocence, he condescended to submit to two Gestapo interrogations to which, as a military man, he was not subject. Meanwhile Hitler suspended him from duty and demanded his resignation, which he finally sent in on February 3.

So much, then, for a skeletal outline of the story as it is generally known. It confronts the historian with a particular challenge in his attempt to clarify the many uncertainties and points of controversy. Commonly agreed assumptions and actual proof are seldom farther apart than here in dealing with major problems of Third Reich history. Questions at issue in the main boil down into two categories:

(1) How much was there of an element of "plot" in the exploitation of Blomberg's folly and the wholly fortuitous circumstance of finding evidence on a military man with a name nearly identical with that of Fritsch? Assuming that the theory of a plot is substantiated, who were the plotters and by what courses did they prepare the ruin of the two generals?

(2) Was Hitler an accessory either before or after the fact? Did he actually believe in the guilt of Fritsch or even seriously doubt his innocence?

As indicated earlier, documentary sources are as inconclusive as they are fragmentary and new insight was likely to be gained only by searching out previously unheard witnesses. Though their ranks are steadily thinned by death,[18] a surprising number of them were

---

[18] Of over eighty who were questioned in 1969-1971 in connection with a study on the Blomberg-Fritsch affair, more than twenty had died by early 1974.

still available a few years ago. They fall basically into the following categories:

(1) Persons in the immediate entourage of Hitler or Göring, such as military adjutants who did duty at the Reich Chancellery.

(2) Fritsch's and Blomberg's friends, associates, and supporting staff such as adjutants and secretaries.

(3) SS and Gestapo members who had something to do with the affair or were in a position to observe some aspect of it.

(4) Judges and court officials involved in the investigation of the charges against Fritsch or in his court martial.

(5) "Volunteer helpers" of Fritsch—a miscellaneous group of persons who learned of his misfortune and hurried to his aid, often without his having the slightest awareness of this. On the whole these tended to have the best appreciation of what was at stake. This group looked for direction mainly to the *Abwehr* leadership, especially Admiral Canaris and Colonel Oster.

Only a small number of those whose testimony bears most significantly on the questions raised above can be brought into our story. Of special interest is the case of Dr. Erich Schultze, a close boyhood friend of Heydrich, who continued to be intimate with him despite his own career as a Social Democratic official who had had a serious run-in with the SS in East Prussia a few years before. About a month before Blomberg's marriage, Schultze first learned that a close Gestapo watch was underway on the goings and comings of Fräulein Gruhn. Further, Heydrich confided that the plot was also directed against Fritsch and Raeder, the latter being in the SS leader's black books for being largely responsible for his ouster from the Navy. The general and the admiral had agreed to act as witnesses at Blomberg's wedding and Heydrich gleefully anticipated that all three would be brought down in the ensuing scandal. As Schultze knew Fritsch from mutual participation in a small religious circle, he warned him, with the result that the Army commander and Raeder withdrew in favor of Hitler and Göring.[19]

This version of affairs differs so dramatically from all that had been previously assumed, that it was clearly incumbent to make the most intensive search conceivable to secure corroborative testimony. It was possible to locate six witnesses, including relatives of Fritsch and Blomberg, who were able to confirm the

---

[19] A similar attempt to warn Blomberg through a common friend, Reichsbishop Ludwig Müller, failed to reach the War Minister. Dr. Schultze was interviewed by the writer on at least nine occasions in the period 1969-1974.

fact of the withdrawal of Fritsch and Raeder at a late hour after having previously agreed to act for Blomberg at the wedding.[20]

That some members of the Gestapo were aware no later than January 15 of the existence of Captain von Frisch, and thus of Fritsch's own innocence, has been known from various sources since soon after the war. However, this did not constitute final proof that Himmler and Heydrich, not to speak of Göring or Hitler, had been definitely apprised of this. That Himmler and Heydrich knew no later than January 28 is now clear from the story told by Franz Josef Huber, a relatively high Gestapo official, who, in the absence from Berlin of the man whose job it would have been to conduct the interrogation, was called in cold to do so. Though an 82-page protocol of the interrogation of January 27 has lain in the Munich Institute for Contemporary History for many years, none of the German or foreign scholars who examined it there looked up Huber, who lived only about a mile away. Yet the man was able to give testimony of sensational import.

The interrogation disturbed Huber not only because of the rather spineless way in which Fritsch conducted himself, but because of an impression that the blackmailer Schmidt, with whom the general was again being confronted, was lying. That evening, when Gestapo department II-H which was charged with the pursuit of homosexuals was silent and empty, Huber decided to take a quick look around. What was his shock and amazement when he perceived on a desk a bank account book under the name of Achim von Frisch in which the withdrawals tallied exactly with the sums alleged by Schmidt to have been paid him by Fritsch. On the instant Huber, who felt as if he had been "stung by a tarantula," knew that there was no case against Fritsch at all but only against poor Captain von Frisch.[21]

On the following morning, Huber apprehensively carried his story to Himmler and Heydrich, putting the latter entirely out of countenance but drawing from the more phlegmatic Himmler only a dry commendation, "You have done well." But from that moment on he was given no further assignment in connection with the Fritsch case, though, needless to say, it continued to be pressed vigorously; and the SS chiefs in no way allowed it to be seen that they had lost any confidence in the guilt of the general.

[20]For the complete story see Deutsch, *Hitler and His Generals,* pp. 93-96.
[21] The information derived from Huber was conveyed in interviews of November 20, 1969, and June 1 and July 3, 1970.

With respect to the role of Göring, our interest is not titillated by melodramatic revelations, but from many directions the pieces fall into place to point to him as the moving spirit against both Blomberg and Fritsch. The legal defender of the latter, Count von der Goltz, was assured by no less a person than Werner Best, the specialist in matters of law of the *Gestapo*, that it had been Göring who set the dogs on Fritsch again by ordering the reactivation and expansion of the fatal dossier when it became evident that Blomberg's folly would soon create a vacancy into which Fritsch must not be allowed to slip.[22] There is also new confirmation for such of Göring's maneuvers as shipping off to Argentina a second lover of Eva Gruhn in order to leave the field clear for the infatuated Blomberg.[23]

As for Hitler's part, we must fall back largely on educated surmise in seeking to define it. Those who were closest to him during these days or in the months immediately following differ profoundly in their estimate of whether and to what degree he is believed to have been shocked, furious, bowled over, or just putting on a display of theatrics. These were tense, highly exciting days in which it was hardly necessary to feign agitation which many around him took for sincere and deep feeling. The keenest observer among his four military adjutants, the later General Engel, who after four years of closest contact judged him to be one of the great actors of world history, is sure that he did not for a single moment consider Fritsch guilty. That, also, is the conviction of the present writer.

The main though circumstantial evidence indicates that he was aware at all times after January 24 of the game being played. He had too intimate a knowledge of the character and ambitions of such henchmen as Göring, Himmler, and Heydrich and knew too well of what they were capable to be in any doubt as to who was behind what was happening to Fritsch. He was also tolerant, to say the least, about having his hand forced or wishes anticipated by those who sensed his deeper purposes. The best guess is that he had been told nothing about the plots of the Himmler-Göring combine while they were in process of formation and adjusting to developments before January 24. Thereafter, whether overtly or tacitly, he fell in with their aims and ruthlessly employed every

---

[22] Interviews with Goltz of November 1 and December 9, 1969. Best did not name Göring specifically but left no doubt about whom he meant.
[23] Complete story in Deutsch, *Hitler and His Generals*, p. 87.

expedient that promised to assist their implementation. Regarding Blomberg he appears to have been of two minds, for he was not immune to a sense of obligation. In all that had to do with eliminating Fritsch he showed a rare singleness of purpose.

THE COUNTERATTACK

Attention up to this point has of necessity concentrated on the activity of those whose intrigues and machinations provided the groundwork for the *Wehrmacht* crisis of 1938. Concern now shifts to the reactions of men who, though unable as yet to combine defense of Fritsch with a coup against the regime itself, achieved sufficient fusion of diverse hostile elements to come to the verge of one only a few months later.

What has just been said should not convey the impression that the Military Opposition sprang fully panoplied from the *Wehrmacht* crisis like Athena from the brow of Zeus. Segments which began to mesh during this period had been forming themselves, especially since 1936, around a number of nuclei. Two of those that can be identified were basically military in composition.[24] The more important of these from a longer range standpoint was growing in the *Abwehr* leadership. There Admiral Canaris had from the first favored the appointment to key positions of officers who were as antagonistic to the regime as they were professionally capable. This disposition was much accentuated by his experience during the Fritsch affair. Thus, in the aftermath of the annexation of Austria, he stipulated that only such Austrian intelligence officers should be transferred to his agency as were not Nazis.[25]

Canaris's readiness to embark on treasonable courses dates essentially from this period, whereas his chief of staff, Colonel Hans Oster, had reached that stage years earlier. Vigorously seconded by Hans Bernd Gisevius,[26] an official of the Ministry of the Interior who disposed over important contacts with disaffected police figures, Oster already had begun a recruitment

---

[24] For another previously unknown military group see Source 2.

[25] Karl Heinz Abshagen, *Canaris, Patriot und Weltbürger* (Stuttgart: Union Deutsche Verlagsanstalt, 1949), p. 182. The head of Austrian military intelligence, Major Erwin von Lahousen, was to all intents and purposes inducted into the *Abwehr* conspiratorial circle by Canaris's emissary, Major Groscurth, before he even left Vienna for Berlin.

[26] Gisevius died in February 1974 at the age of 67. Albeit something of a controversial figure and a man whose judgments were at times colored by personal feelings, his service to historians as the sole survivor of the inner "Oster circle" has been indispensable. He was gifted with an incisive mind and a phenomenal memory.

program calculated to draw together diverse elements from civilian agencies and the business world who were similarly contemplating the plunge into illegality.

A second military group, previously assumed to be only an offshoot of the above with whom it coalesced during the Blomberg-Fritsch affair, now appears already to have had some existence of its own. This centered about the later Field Marshal Erwin von Witzleben, commander of the Berlin military district, a distinguished soldier of simple, direct ways, who over the years was to prove one of the most steadfast Military Opposition personalities. No later than the summer of 1937, he and a number of his subcommanders in Berlin and in nearby garrisons had decided that things must not be allowed to continue in what seemed a steady drift toward international adventure. In September of that year they were busily reviewing the roll of prominent military personages to search out likely associates.[27] A number of other intriguing items of information fall into place in relation to what Witzleben was trying to do at this period.

Some would argue that for the time before 1938 it is scarcely possible to speak of either of the above Military Opposition segments as approaching a cohesive conspiratorial grouping. It is even more questionable to apply this term to a still amorphous confluence of civilians scattered throughout the Reich and in various quarters in Berlin. In fact, had it not been for a single man, it would not be possible to speak of it even in this fashion. This was Carl Goerdeler, who in March 1937 resigned as Lord Mayor of Leipzig in public protest against the destruction of the monument to the great Jewish composer Mendelssohn while he was out of the city.[28] Thereafter he was mostly underway in travels within and outside of Germany, everywhere denouncing, explaining, tying together, and pleading for "action," until he became known affectionately (and at times somewhat derisively) in Opposition circles as "the circuit rider." Abroad he carried, to strategically

---

[27] Oral history once more contributes an important item from a peripheral personage. In this case it is Ursula von Witzleben, wife of a relative of the future Field Marshal. At a family reunion on September 11, 1937, Witzleben confided to her his view of affairs and asked her about two generals whom she knew intimately and whom he and his "friends" hoped to win over (Interview of February 10, 1970). A previously known fragment about coincident activities in Potsdam involving the elite Infantry Regiment No. 9 assumes new meaning in this light. See Deutsch, *Hitler and His Generals,* pp. 45-47.

[28] The writer's own fascinating encounter with Goerdeler in June 1936, when he said exactly what he would do in such an event, is recounted in Deutsch, *Conspiracy,* pp. 11-12.

placed individuals, the message that there *was* resistance in Germany, that it was in process of organizing itself, and that in due time it would achieve the strength and summon the resolution to act.[29]

Until the beginning of the war, Goerdeler's recruits, and those of the already-converted whom he helped to bring together, were mostly, like himself, men of conservative leanings. As a leading light in political economy, his arguments appealed strongly to more perceptive leaders in the business world and to men in government who appreciated the fatal implications of Hitler's forced-draft economy. For the more sophisticated, there could hardly be much doubt any longer that Germany's limited resources were being mobilized for a single swift outpouring of power. The continued strain would before too long leave a choice only between national bankruptcy or a series of wars which in the end would lead to disaster. Goerdeler also maintained, especially in his arguments to soldiers, that the international climate, as he had observed it in his journeys, was now conducive to bringing Germany by diplomatic means most of what it felt itself entitled to by way of treaty revision. In this he was seconded by key individuals in the Foreign Office who had independently arrived at the same conclusion.

On February 4, 1938, Hitler announced to an amazed world a far-going *revirement* or turnover in government posts which he made to look as much as possible like one of Mussolini's "changing of the guard." Generals were transferred or retired, ministers changed, and ambassadors recalled—all to obscure the central fact that the targets were Blomberg, Fritsch, and Neurath. The Fuehrer himself assumed the powers of War Minister and the direct command of the *Wehrmacht*. In Fritsch's place he appointed Walther von Brauchitsch, a choice whose cynicism almost surpasses belief.

Ostensibly Blomberg was being sacked for having made a foolish and, by prevailing standards, a shameful marriage. The wholly innocent Fritsch had been hounded out of office with false charges and was being pushed as hard as the Nazi leaders dared toward total ruin. In his place Hitler now appointed a general who

---

[29] Unquestionably Goerdeler was almost naively optimistic, rigid in some of his thought, inclined to talk much too freely, and tended to sponsor unrealistic courses. Yet, as one leading oppositionist survivor has put it to the writer, "Where would we have been if there had not been Goerdeler to hold the torch, propagate the cause everywhere, and keep driving ahead?" (Gisevius interview, July 11, 1971).

was about to marry a woman whose background, though perhaps a shade less sordid, did not differ much in essentials from that of Fräulein Gruhn. And of this Hitler was fully aware through a previous *Gestapo* (or other) watch on Brauchitsch! Yet he financed the general's divorce, clearing the way for the fateful espousal and putting his new Army commander under heavy obligation. Most significant, Brauchitsch was condemned to guess how much the Fuehrer already knew, or might yet find out, about his affairs. It is hard to escape the conclusion that Hitler, at least in part, decided on Brauchitsch for the very reason that the man was so vulnerable as to be utterly in his power.[30] No wonder Brauchitsch proved so inhibited in his dealings with Hitler that his own chief of staff, General Halder, described him as standing before the Fuehrer "like a little cadet before his commandant."[31]

During the week previous to February 4 a fierce struggle, almost completely hidden from public view, had been going on. Its principal aspects were:

(1) Efforts by some of Fritsch's friends to induce him to withhold his resignation and instead make a ringing appeal for the support of the top commanders. There is much to indicate that this would have succeeded. Fritsch shrank from this because he did not yet sufficiently grasp the situation, such as Hitler's complicity in the plot against him, at least after the fact. He also felt inhibited about making what some might regard as a call for help in a largely personal quarrel and dreaded the responsibility for a possible civil war.

(2) Efforts by his volunteer supporters to alert commanding generals in the provinces to persuade them to intervene. At least three such attempts were made (by Goerdeler, Oster, and Gisevius). They failed because the generals in question, though deeply disturbed, were too stunned and felt too isolated.

(3) A struggle to force Hitler to abandon his evident intention to condemn Fritsch out of hand and to compel him to order an investigation by military judicial authorities and a court-martial. In this Fritsch's friends were successful, largely because it was

---

[30] Except for Hitler assisting with Brauchitsch's divorce by providing an 800 mark per month settlement for his first wife, the facts as they are here adduced were not known before the publication of the writer's *Hitler and His Generals*. The information about the background of the second wife came to him from a private source that cannot as yet be identified. Hitler's awareness of her past and Brauchitsch's previous relations with her rests on the testimony of General Engel (Interview, May 11, 1970).

[31] Deutsch, *Conspiracy*, p. 250.

brought home to Hitler that the generals simply would not settle for less. To the disgust of Göring and Himmler, who bent every effort to dissuade him, the Fuehrer grudgingly yielded. But he also concerted with them to set up an investigation and trial procedure that promised to make it next to impossible to clear Fritsch fully.

The investigation, which occupied nearly five weeks, was marked by constant pulling and pushing among the contending factions, whose moves involved an astonishing amount of clandestine activity on both sides. To handicap the defense as much as possible, Hitler decreed that a Gestapo investigation should continue parallel to the military one. (See Source 6.) A judge of Göring's own *Luftwaffe*, who might be assumed to cater to him, was charged with the direction of the latter, and the Fuehrer appointed himself as the ultimate judicial authority who would determine disputes as the case advanced and confirm the verdict.

Tracing all the twists and turns of the investigation makes exciting detective work and inevitably leaves some questions unanswered. Of those intimately concerned with the affair on either side, only Gisevius, a military judge of the investigative panel, Ernst Kanter, and Fritsch's defender, Count Rüdiger von der Goltz, survived into the sixties and the latter two are still with us today. Luckily all three of these men were tied in with one or another set of developments that helped decide the course of affairs. It is also fortunate that, though the minutes of the trial appear to be lost, the verdict, which includes a summary and analysis of the evidence, later turned up and was published in 1965. (See Source 7.)

INVESTIGATION AND TRIAL

It was difficult enough for Fritsch's defense to prove that on a certain, not fully determined, day in November 1933 he could not have been in a railway station complex where the act with which he was charged took place. To make its mission almost insurmountably tough, Hitler declared that he would not be content nor consider Fritsch cleared unless the blackmailer could be brought to repudiate his story. As Schmidt was a scoundrel of exceptional self-assurance, had been put through his paces until he was letter perfect in his recital, and had been told by both Göring and the *Gestapo* that he was not long for this world if he did not "stick to the truth," a euphemism for his tale as it then was, this was a formidable assignment.

Everything imaginable was done to Fritsch by his persecutors during the investigation to humiliate and demoralize him. Thus, a fishing expedition was instituted among nearly a score of his former grooms and orderlies in the hope that one or another of them would attribute to him some remark or gesture that could be made to give color to the charge of homosexuality. It was fortunate that all of them proved devoted to the kindly man they had served and could think of nothing to support such suspicions. However, the blow to Fritsch's dignity in having such a matter discussed in military stables throughout Germany may be imagined.

Schmidt was tripped up repeatedly on details of his story and on accusations he had made against others. Hitler, however, refused to declare himself satisfied when the military investigative panel appealed to him to suspend the case. Yet, as no shred of evidence supported Schmidt's story, the likelihood of acquittal in the court-martial in the form of "proven innocence" was becoming overwhelming. This gives color to the conviction of many that, in its desperation, the *Gestapo* contemplated the assassination of Fritsch in the form of a staged "suicide" when it insisted on a third interrogation of the general. If so, the plan was thwarted by ostentatious precautionary measures taken under the direction of Colonel Oster.

The sensational high point of the investigation was the discovery of the existence of Captain von Frisch. This was the fruit of the absurdly simple device of looking in the telephone address book for a name similar to that of Fritsch where the blackmailed party supposedly lived.[32] Indignant at what was being done to his former commander in chief, the good captain immediately admitted to his court-martial interrogators that Schmidt's story applied in all details to himself. Goltz was so triumphantly sure that this had decided matters that, carrying a large bouquet of roses, he reported the assumed happy outcome to Fritsch. But the brazen impudence of the Fuehrer of the German Reich was in no way inferior to that of the professional criminal Schmidt. The latter now insisted that there were two exactly similar cases and was backed in this incredible claim by Himmler. There was nothing for it but to make final preparations for the trial. A pathetic sidelight is that meanwhile Captain von Frisch was snatched up by the Gestapo as a "self-confessed homosexual." Though considerably

[32] Goltz interview, November 1, 1969.

knocked about before Hitler could be pressured into releasing him to the custody of the Ministry of Justice, the intrepid invalid refused to change an iota of the story he had told the court-martial investigators.

The trial of Colonel General von Fritsch began on March 10 but was interrupted a few hours later when the three service chiefs, Göring, Brauchitsch, and Raeder, who functioned among the judges, were called away to deal with preparations for the invasion of Austria. It is unlikely that we shall ever determine with any certainty just how much moves against that country were engineered to divert the attention of Army leaders and to give Hitler the international success he so badly needed. Suffice it to say that when the court-martial resumed on March 17, the political climate in Germany had swung much in the dictator's favor and, for the time being, precluded action against him.

Though we know very little about it, there is no doubt that both the *Abwehr*-associated circle of anti-Nazis and Witzleben's "friends," now working in increasingly close conjunction, were contemplating something of this nature, at least against the SS. They were mainly restrained by the difficulty of persuading the generals, notably Brauchitsch, to undertake anything while the court-martial was pending. It might look too much, they feared, as if they were trying to forestall a negative verdict.

In the upshot, the campaign to exonerate Fritsch proved a total success. At the critical moment in the proceedings, Goltz managed to lead Schmidt into committing so fatal an error that the astute Göring, who had arbitrarily seized the presiding function, realized that wisdom recommended his taking the lead in the direction in which things were now inevitably headed. A master in the art of bullying, he soon forced the befuddled miscreant to confess that his testimony really applied only to Frisch and that everything he had said about Fritsch was a lie.

AFTERMATH

From a short-range standpoint, the outcome of the Blomberg-Fritsch affair was a mixed one for all concerned. Hitler was, no doubt, infuriated by the exoneration of Fritsch, which placed him in no good light. He had also developed that animosity against the general which petty personalities at times experience against men whom they have wronged deeply. Despite this frustration, the Fuehrer had succeeded in ridding himself of the impediments which stood in the way of his more aggressive designs, had established direct control over the *Wehrmacht*, and had gained as successor to Fritsch a commander whom it would be no problem to intimidate whenever needful.

Hitler also displayed surprising finesse in avoiding a showdown with the generals over their demand for the "rehabilitation" of Fritsch in the form of appointing him to a new office or promoting him to the rank of Field Marshal. It was the struggle over this which prolonged the *Wehrmacht* crisis of 1938 into early June, when the pressures on the dictator mounted to the point where a wholesale resignation of top commanders threatened over this issue. (See Source 8.) At this delicate juncture rising tensions in relations with Czechoslovakia came pat to hand to again divert attention. In a speech Hitler made to the military leaders at the exercise ground at Barth on June 13, he dumfounded them by claiming that a war with Czechoslovakia was in prospect and had Brauchitsch appeal to their loyalties at "a time of national crisis." He presented alibis for not having done anything thus far to compensate Fritsch for the great injury he had suffered, proffered as a kind of payment on account his appointment to the honorary colonelcy of his old regiment, and promised more substantial honors later.

Basically Hitler thus seemed to have triumphed all along the line. As a matter of fact, however, by ridding himself of the exasperating brakes on his more extreme policies he left those who would oppose them no choice but the resort to illegality. Totalitarian tyranny has ever driven those who would not submit to it in this direction. Those military leaders who, like Witzleben, Canaris, and the comparative late-comer, Beck, were no longer in doubt about what was at stake for their country, now led the way to fusion with those civilian opposition elements which had revealed themselves during these trying months and shouldered many of the burdens in Fritsch's defense. The outcome was a conspiratorial combination which came close to striking during the Munich crisis of September and maintained essential cohesion for the six tragic years which separated the hidden *Wehrmacht* crisis of 1938 from the fatal July 20, 1944.

FURTHER READING

Brissaud, Andre. *Canaris.* New York: Grosset & Dunlap, 1974.
Bullock, Alan. *Hitler. A Study in Tyranny.* Rev. ed. New York: Harper & Row, 1962.

Craig, Gordon. *The Politics of the Prussian Army, 1640-1945.* Oxford: Clarendon Press, 1955.

Demeter, Karl. *The German Officer-Corps in Society and State, 1640-1945.* New York: Praeger, 1965.

Deutsch, Harold C. *The Conspiracy Against Hitler in the Twilight War.* Minneapolis: University of Minnesota Press, 1968.

———. *Hitler and His Generals: The Hidden Crisis of January-June 1938.* Minneapolis: University of Minnesota Press, 1974.

Fest, Joachim C. *Hitler.* New York: Harcourt Brace Jovanovich, 1974.

Foerster, Hermann. *Schuld und Verhängnis: Die Fritsch-Krise im Frühjahr 1938 als Wendepunkt in der Geschichte der nationalsozialistischen Zeit.* Stuttgart: Deutsche Verlags-Anstalt, 1951.

Gisevius, Hans Bernd. *To the Bitter End.* Boston: Houghton Mifflin, 1947.

Hassell, Ulrich von. *The Hassell Diaries, 1938-1944. The Story of the Fight Against Hitler Inside Germany.* New York: Doubleday, 1947.

Kielmansegg, Count Johann Adolf. *Der Fritsch-Prozess 1938: Ablauf und Hintergründe.* Stuttgart: Deutsche Verlags-Anstalt, 1949.

Müller, Klaus-Jürgen. *Das Heer und Hitler: Armee und nationalsozialistisches Regime 1933-1940.* Stuttgart: Deutsche Verlags-Anstalt, 1969.

O'Neil, Robert. *The German Army and the Nazi Party.* London: Cassell, 1966.

Rothfels, Hans. *The German Opposition to Hitler: An Assessment.* London: Oswald Wolff, 1961.

Schlabrendorff, Fabian von. *The Secret War Against Hitler.* London: Hodder & Stoughton, 1966.

Taylor, Telford. *Sword and Swastika. The Wehrmacht in the Third Reich.* New York: Simon & Schuster, 1953.

Weinberg, Gerhard. *The Foreign Policy of Hitler's Germany: Diplomatic Revolution in Europe, 1933-1936.* Chicago: University of Chicago Press, 1970.

Wheeler-Bennett, John W. *The Nemesis of Power. The German Army in Politics, 1918-1945.* 2nd ed. London: Macmillan; New York: St. Martin's Press, 1964.

SOURCES

1

From Christine von Dohnanyi's "Notations"

The following extract from the "Notations" of Christine von Dohnanyi throws light upon the recording by her husband, Military Judge Hans von Dohnanyi, of evidence on criminal activities of Nazi leaders and organizations, on aspects of the Fritsch affair, and on efforts to broaden the popular base of the military opposition.

SOURCE: Original document in the writer's possession. Translated by Harold C. Deutsch.

My husband did not gain serious contact with oppositionist officers until 1938. In January or February of that year, Gürtner (the Minister of Justice) was suddenly and urgently called to Hitler. With the strictest injunction to secrecy, extending even to the undersecretaries of the Ministry, he was handed the documents on the "Fritsch case" with the official request for an opinion. Actually Hitler said to Gürtner in handing him the file: "You will know at which end of the rope you are to pull." I remember this expression so well because my husband told me that Gürtner had passed him the documents with "the smile of an augur" and said thereto that he could only repeat the Fuehrer's words to him, which ought to suffice between them. He did not mean Hitler's end of the rope.

My husband was relieved of almost all his duties in order to work night and day on the clarification of the situation and on the refutation of the vile calumnies directed against the inconvenient general. For all those in the know this case was—after the murder of Schleicher—the second and conclusive effort to smash the oppositional elements in the Wehrmacht and to make the latter serviceable to the party. This contest with its nightly rendezvous, disguised telephone calls, anonymous letters, and attempts at assassination, during which an active Minister, the chief of the General Staff, and highest officials of the Military Court and other authorities of the Reich fought in continual danger to their lives with the Gestapo and the party, while externally all seemed quiet and order, was a situation typical of the Third Reich and possible only in it. . . .

My husband believed that after a brief period of a strong military dictatorship it would be possible to enlighten the people [on the true character of Nazism] by an appropriate counterpropaganda. With this in mind he, during the time of his service in the Ministry of Justice, undertook a project. At that period—usually with an order from Hitler prohibiting any judicial proceedings—almost all scandals within the party or its organizations were made known to the Minister of Justice. Without exception he would hand the information to my husband, who, under the title of "Chronicle," prepared a complete register of all these cases and thereby of the criminal acts of the party hierarchs with every detail. From murder and attempted murder in the concentration camps, from the horrors of these camps of which we have since learned so much, to the foreign exchange swindles of the Gauleiters [Nazi district leaders] and the dirt in the HJ [Hitler Youth] and SA [Brown Shirts] leadership, there was probably no delict which was not recorded in this Chronicle. It was maintained in association with a card file which made possible the location of the misdeeds of individual party personalities with the proper documentation. These notations were camouflaged by filing them with a few particularly prominent "criminal" cases on the monasteries, etc., so that the appearance of unintentional association was preserved. Over the years he extended and rounded out this material. There were speeches by Hitler, reports on the treatment of prisoners of war, films on atrocities in Poland, reports on the reason for "bloody Sunday" at Bromberg, directions of Goebbels on the Jewish pogroms, and more of this kind of material. My husband was convinced that these reports could be supplemented from the experience of other [government] departments and often said to me that these proofs must be sufficient to open the eyes of everyone who was willing to see on Hitler and his regime.

To make sure of public support of a coup, he regarded it as urgently necessary, to win not only the tolerance of the workers but their active cooperation with a military revolt. To his distress he here encountered with many officers a lack of understanding. Even fairly reasonable people, as he related it to me, would assure him that there was no longer a labor question. The unions had been smashed and to get any kind of effective resistance from this quarter was not to be anticipated. [In contrast] General Beck showed real understanding for my husband's efforts in this direction.

Through Ernst von Harnack, whom he had known for years, through his brother-in-law, Klaus Bonhoeffer, and through the latter's closest co-worker, Dr. Otto John, my husband established contact with Leuschner, Leber, and other union leaders. These were prepared for every type of cooperation and I recall how my husband one day said to me with relief: "Now we've done it; today Leuschner will call on Beck."

In those days, in the winter of 1939-40, the union leaders declared themselves ready, in the case of a military coup, to support it if necessary with a call to the workers for a general strike. Messengers were sent to all important centers to prepare for this. The money needed for these preparations was placed at our disposal by the industrialist Walter Bauer. Thus at that time went the cooperation of the various classes, and in this sense the civilians smoothed the road for the military.

2

Anti-Nazi Elements in the German Navy

The following item is included to illustrate how information concerning a previously unknown oppositional group comes to light from time to time. It is the more interesting and significant in that it pertains to anti-Nazi elements in the German Navy, which is usually contrasted with the Army with respect to a lack of vulnerability to hostile agitation against the regime. The information comes to us from a totally unexpected source, the memoirs of the late Governor Philip LaFollette of Wisconsin.

SOURCE: From *Adventure in Politics: The Memoirs of Philip LaFollette* edited by Donald Young. Copyright © 1970 by Donald Young. Copyright © 1970 by Isabel LaFollette. Reprinted by permission of Holt, Rinehart and Winston, Publishers.

On our return from Europe in 1936 we had met on the ship a man who was to become an intimate friend—Michael Obladen. He was the head of a large chemical firm in Hamburg and was one of the half dozen or so leading citizens of that city. He had asked us to visit him during our 1939 trip, and so we left Brussels for another look into Germany. He met us at the station and put us up as his guests at the leading hotel, because his young wife had just presented him with a son. The Obladens entertained us at an epicurean dinner in their exquisitely appointed home, and their friends did likewise.

Michael had intimated when I talked to him over the phone from Brussels that he wanted me to come to Hamburg for a mysterious and important reason. People who have never lived under a dictatorship have no appreciation of the hazards one takes in opposing the regime. I found out why Michael wanted me to come to Hamburg.

A men's luncheon was given me on board one of the Hamburg-American ships in the Hamburg harbor. The food and wine were of the best, but the point of the luncheon was not to entertain me. It was to give a high-ranking admiral in the German navy the opportunity at the close of the luncheon to say, "My aide whom you have met here today is a man of the highest integrity and trustworthiness. He would like to call on you tomorrow. I hope you will see him, listen to what he has to say, and know that you can have implicit confidence in what he tells you."

Before leaving the ship, the admiral's aide asked me for an appointment for the next morning. We set the hour, and he came to the hotel. He came up to our rooms and very seriously said, "Would you mind if we took a walk in the park?" When we entered the park, he said, "The only place one can be sure of in present-day Germany that the Gestapo can't tap one's conversations is when you're in the park."

He began our conversation by saying:

"Obladen has expressed explicit confidence in you, and he told me that he had explained to you that the least infected part of our service is the navy. We have a hundred men of rank and character who are prepared to act. We all know that we are risking not only our own lives but the lives of our families and maybe of our friends as well. We know far better than people outside of Germany what Hitler is leading to—unlimited disaster. We are ready to take the risk.

"Our group is ready, if we have certain assurances, to seize Hitler, Göring, Goebbels, and Himmler. The only thing we are apprehensive about is that if we act, there may be an internal upheaval which France might utilize as an opportunity to invade Germany and do us great harm. Few Americans realize how bitter we Germans are over what we feel was President Wilson's betrayal of us in 1918. Germany surrendered in the last war on what we believed was the solemn assurance that the peace would be written in terms of the Fourteen Points. None of us have the slightest faith in the assurance of any politician.

"What we want is to have an outstanding naval and military officer from your country and from Great Britain to give simultaneously a radio broadcast to the armed services. I suggest that an alert be given calling all of the British and American forces to hear a 'confidential' broadcast. It has occurred to us that the speakers could be someone from Britain like Field Marshall Lord Gort, chief of the Imperial General Staff, and perhaps your Admiral Leahy. It doesn't have to be either one of these two, but it must be of their stature. What they should say, in effect, is that speaking 'on my honor as an officer and a gentleman, I am thoroughly familiar with the plans and intentions of my government. I assure you we have no intention of attacking Germany. More than that, if Germany does not act aggressively, neither Britain nor the United States will permit any other power to attack Germany.'

"We are not trying to indicate the exact form of language. What we are asking for is the solemn pledge delivered, shall I put it obliquely, to these officers in the German navy who are ready to risk their necks to save Germany and the world from the holocaust for which we are headed unless something is done. We ask you to carry this word to responsible officers in the British government and to your president. You can assure them that the moment two such responsible military officers make the broadcast, we will act."

This was certainly the hottest potato I think I ever had dumped in my lap. Frankly, I didn't know what to do with it. Because we had our plans made to go on to Copenhagen and Stockholm, I decided to do nothing until I could think it over more carefully and perhaps get some advice. On our return from Scandinavia, we started homeward via Hamburg. I wanted another talk with Obladen to reconfirm the information I had been given a week before. He reiterated emphatically that what the naval commander had told me was completely reliable. He emphasized the point about the navy in Germany being the most independent and least Nazified service in Germany. He also pointed out that Hamburg and its vicinity had never completely lost the long tradition of the free cities of the Hanseatic League. In that section of Germany there was still a degree of independence. He told me that in the nationwide attacks on Jewish stores and synagogues during the previous November, the city least affected had been Hamburg. . . .

I telephoned Colonel Barnes in Brussels and asked him to meet me in the railroad station there. He met us, and I told him about the experience in Hamburg. I wanted his advice. Barnes, recognizing that I had no official position, advised me that it might be dangerous for me to pass this kind of suggestion to anyone in a foreign government—specifically the British government. He suggested that I should pass what I had learned to President Roosevelt but to no one else.

We arrived in London on March 1. On this visit I was astounded to find that aside from a few people like Vansittart, the English official world seemed unaware of what Hitler was up to on the continent. When I predicted that Hitler was headed for Czechoslovakia, most of the people I talked with were incredulous.

On March 17 Obladen came to breakfast with us during a brief visit to London. The news of Hitler's march into Czechoslovakia had come. Obladen paced the floor as he contemplated what lay ahead. He said, "I went through World War I. Twenty cousins of mine were killed. And now we are going through something even worse." His forebodings proved only too correct. Obladen survived most of the war, but near the end he lost his life.

A few days later we started for America. On arrival home I went to Washington to see Bob.* He felt it vital that I tell the President about the Hamburg incident. An appointment was arranged, and Bob and I had an hour with FDR.

After the usual amenities, I reported first on my impressions of France and predicted that if all-out war came, France would collapse in six months. The President reached over and patted my knee in an avuncular fashion and said, "Bob, Phil is a nice fellow but he just doesn't know what he's talking about when he makes that kind of a prediction."

*Senator LaFollette

I then gave him a detailed report of my experience in Hamburg. I told him that some German naval officers were ready to strike at Hitler and his inner circle if they could have assurances from appropriate American and British service officers that those countries had no intention of attacking Germany. I emphasized that no pledge by either American or British political leaders would have the slightest effect. The president at once said, "By Jove, that's a good idea. I can speak German and could make that radio broadcast myself." Nothing ever came of it. Perhaps Roosevelt thought the idea impractical or too dangerous. In any event, it has always seemed tragic to me that no attempt was made during the late thirties to support anti-Nazi elements in Germany.

3

Minutes of the "Hossbach Conference"

SOURCE: The following "Hossbach memorandum," actually a statement prepared from notes several days later, is printed in *Documents on German Foreign Policy, 1918-1945* (Washington: Goverment Printing Office, 1949-1966), Series D, I, 29-39.

Memorandum

BERLIN, November 10, 1937

MINUTES OF THE CONFERENCE IN THE REICH CHANCELLERY, BERLIN, NOVEMBER 5, 1937, FROM 4:15 to 8:30 P.M.

Present: The Führer and Chancellor,
          Field Marshal von Blomberg, War Minister,
          Colonel General Baron von Fritsch, Commander in Chief, Army,
          Admiral Dr. h. c. Raeder, Commander in Chief, Navy,
          Colonel General Göring, Commander in Chief, *Luftwaffe,*
          Baron von Neurath, Foreign Minister,
          Colonel Hossbach.
The Führer began by stating that the subject of the present conference was

of such importance that its discussion would, in other countries, certainly be a matter for a full Cabinet meeting, but he—the Führer—had rejected the idea of making it a subject of discussion before the wider circle of the Reich Cabinet just because of the importance of the matter. His exposition to follow was the fruit of thorough deliberation and the experiences of his 4½ years of power. He wished to explain to the gentlemen present his basic ideas concerning the opportunities for the development of our position in the field of foreign affairs and its requirements, and he asked, in the interests of a long-term German policy, that his exposition be regarded, in the event of his death, as his last will and testament.

The Führer then continued:

The aim of German policy was to make secure and to preserve the racial community [*Volksmasse*] and to enlarge it. It was therefore a question of space.

The German racial community comprised over 85 million people and, because of their number and the narrow limits of habitable space in Europe, constituted a tightly packed racial core such as was not to be met in any other country and such as implied the right to a greater living space than in the case of other peoples. If, territorially speaking, there existed no political result corresponding to this German racial core, that was a consequence of centuries of historical development, and in the continuance of these political conditions lay the greatest danger to the preservation of the German race at its present peak. To arrest the decline of Germanism [*Deutschtum*] in Austria and Czechoslovakia was as little possible as to maintain the present level in Germany itself. Instead of increase, sterility was setting in, and in its train disorders of a social character must arise in course of time, since political and ideological ideas remain effective only so long as they furnish the basis for the realization of the essential vital demands of a people. Germany's future was therefore wholly conditional upon the solving of the need for space, and such a solution could be sought, of course, only for a foreseeable period of about one to three generations.

Before turning to the question of solving the need for space, it had to be considered whether a solution holding promise for the future was to be reached by means of autarchy or by means of increased participation in world economy.

Autarchy:

Achievement only possible under strict National Socialist leadership of the State, which is assumed; accepting its achievement as possible, the following could be stated as results:—

A. In the field of raw materials only limited, not total, autarchy.

1) In regard to coal, so far as it could be considered as a source of raw materials, autarchy was possible.

2) But even as regards ores, the position was much more difficult. Iron requirements can be met from home resources and similarly with light metals, but with other raw materials—copper, tin—this was not the case.

3) Synthetic textile requirements can be met from home resources to the limit of timber supplies. A permanent solution impossible.

4) Edible fats—possible.

B. In the field of food the question of autarchy was to be answered by a flat "No."

With the general rise in the standard of living compared with that of 30 to 40 years ago, there has gone hand in hand an increased demand and an increased home consumption even on the part of the producers, the farmers. The fruits of the increased agricultural production had all gone to meet the increased demand, and so did not represent an absolute production increase. A further increase in production by making greater demands on the soil, which already, in consequence of the use of artificial fertilizers, was showing signs of exhaustion, was hardly possible, and it was therefore certain that even with the maximum increase in production, participation in world trade was unavoidable. The not inconsiderable expenditure of foreign exchange to insure food supplies by imports, even when harvests were good, grew to catastrophic proportions with bad harvests. The possibility of a disaster grew in proportion to the increase in population, in which, too, the excess of births of 560,000 annually produced, as a consequence, an even further increase in bread consumption, since a child was a greater bread consumer than an adult.

It was not possible over the long run, in a continent enjoying a practically common standard of living, to meet the food supply difficulties by lowering that standard and by rationalization. Since, with the solving of the unemployment problem, the maximum consumption level had been reached, some minor modifications in our home agricultural production might still, no doubt, be possible, but no fundamental alteration was possible in our basic food position. Thus autarchy was untenable in regard both to food and to the economy as a whole.

Participation in world economy:

To this there were limitations which we were unable to remove. The establishment of Germany's position on a secure and sound foundation was obstructed by market fluctuations, and commercial treaties afforded no guarantee for actual execution. In particular it had to be remembered that since the World War, those very countries which had formerly been food exporters had become industrialized. We were living in an age of economic empires in which the primitive urge to colonization was again manifesting itself; in the cases of Japan and Italy economic motives underlay the urge for expansion, and with Germany, too, economic empires, opportunities for economic expansion were severely impeded.

The boom in world economy caused by the economic effects of rearmament could never form the basis of a sound economy over a long period, and the latter was obstructed above all also by the economic disturbances resulting from Bolshevism. There was a pronounced military weakness in those states which depended for their existence on foreign trade. As our foreign trade was carried on over the sea routes dominated by Britain, it was more a question of security of transport than one of foreign exchange, which revealed, in time of war, the full weakness of our food situation. The only remedy, and one which might appear to us as visionary, lay in the acquisition of greater living space—a quest which has at all times been the origin of the formation of states and of the migration of peoples. That this quest met with no interest at Geneva or among the satiated nations was understandable. If, then, we accept the security of our food situation as the principal question, the space necessary to insure it can only be sought in Europe, not, as in the liberal-capitalist view, in the exploitation of colonies. It is not a matter of acquiring population but of gaining space for agricultural use. Moreover, areas producing raw materials can be more usefully sought in Europe in immediate proximity to the Reich, than overseas; the solution thus obtained must suffice for one or two generations. Whatever else might prove necessary later must be left to succeeding generations to deal with. The development of great world political constellations progressed but slowly after all, and the German people with its strong racial core would find the most favorable prerequisites for such achievement in the heart of the continent of Europe. The history of all ages—the Roman Empire and the British Empire—had proved that expansion could only be carried out by breaking down resistance and taking risks; setbacks were inevitable. There had never in former times been spaces without a master, and there were none today; the attacker always comes up against a possessor.

The question for Germany ran: where could she achieve the greatest gain at the lowest cost.

German policy had to reckon with two hate-inspired antagonists, Britain and France, to whom a German colossus in the center of Europe was a thorn in the flesh, and both countries were opposed to any further strengthening of Germany's position either in Europe or overseas; in support of this opposition they were able to count on the agreement of all their political parties. Both countries saw in the establishment of German military bases overseas a threat to their own communications, a safeguarding of German commerce, and, as a consequence, a strengthening of Germany's position in Europe.

Because of opposition of the Dominions, Britain could not cede any of her colonial possessions to us. After England's loss of prestige through the passing of Abyssinia into Italian possession, the return of East Africa was not to be expected. British concessions could at best be expressed in an offer to satisfy our colonial demands by the appropriation of colonies which were not British possessions—e.g., Angola. French concessions would probably take a similar line.

Serious discussion of the question of the return of colonies to us could only be considered at a moment when Britain was in difficulties and the German Reich armed and strong. The Führer did not share the view that the Empire was unshakable. Opposition to the Empire was to be found less in the countries conquered than among her competitors. The British Empire and the

Roman Empire could not be compared in respect of permanence; the latter was not confronted by any powerful political rival of a serious order after the Punic Wars. It was only the disintegrating effect of Christianity, and the symptoms of age which appear in every country, which caused ancient Rome to succumb to the onslaught of the Germans.

Beside the British Empire there existed today a number of states stronger than she. The British motherland was able to protect her colonial possessions not by her own power, but only in alliance with other states. How, for instance, could Britain alone defend Canada against attack by America, or her Far Eastern interests against attack by Japan!

The emphasis on the British Crown as the symbol of the unity of the Empire was already an admission that, in the long run, the Empire could not maintain its position by power politics. Significant indications of this were:

(a) The struggle of Ireland for independence.

(b) The constitutional struggles in India, where Britain's half measures had given to the Indians the opportunity of using later on as a weapon against Britain, the nonfulfillment of her promises regarding a constitution.

(c) The weakening by Japan of Britain's position in the Far East.

(d) The rivalry in the Mediterranean with Italy who—under the spell of her history, driven by necessity and led by a genius—was expanding her power position, and thus was inevitably coming more and more into conflict with British interests. The outcome of the Abyssinian War was a loss of prestige for Britain which Italy was striving to increase by stirring up trouble in the Mohammedan world.

To sum up, it could be stated that, with 45 million Britons, in spite of its theoretical soundness, the position of the Empire could not in the long run be maintained by power politics. The ratio of the population of the Empire to that of the motherland of 9:1, was a warning to us not, in our territorial expansion, to allow the foundation constituted by the numerical strength of our own people to become too weak.

France's position was more favorable than that of Britain. The French Empire was better placed territorially; the inhabitants of her colonial possessions represented a supplement to her military strength. But France was going to be confronted with internal political difficulties. In a nation's life about 10 percent of its span is taken up by parliamentary forms of government and about 90 percent by authoritarian forms. Today, nonetheless, Britain, France, Russia, and the smaller states adjoining them, must be included as factors [*Machtfaktoren*] in our political calculations.

Germany's problem could only be solved by means of force and this was never without attendant risk. The campaigns of Frederick the Great for Silesia and Bismarck's wars against Austria and France had involved unheard-of risk, and the swiftness of the Prussian action in 1870 had kept Austria from entering the war. If one accepts as the basis of the following exposition the resort to force with its attendant risks, then there remain still to be answered the questions "when" and "how." In this matter there were three cases [*Fälle*] to be dealt with:

Case 1: Period 1943-1945.

After this date only a change for the worse, from our point of view, could be expected.

The equipment of the army, navy, and *Luftwaffe*, as well as the formation of the officer corps, was nearly completed. Equipment and armament were modern; in further delay there lay the danger of their obsolescence. In particular, the secrecy of "special weapons" could not be preserved forever. The recruiting of reserves was limited to current age groups; further drafts from older untrained age groups were no longer available.

Our relative strength would decrease in relation to the rearmament which would by then have been carried out by the rest of the world. If we did not act by 1943-45, any year could, in consequence of a lack of reserves, produce the food crisis, to cope with which the necessary foreign exchange was not available, and this must be regarded as a "waning point of the regime." Besides, the world was expecting our attack and was increasing its counter-measures from year to year. It was while the rest of the world was still preparing its defenses [*sich abriegele*] that we were obliged to take the offensive.

Nobody knew today what the situation would be in the years 1943-45. One thing only was certain, that we could not wait longer.

On the one hand there was the great *Wehrmacht*, and the necessity of maintaining it at its present level, the aging of the movement and of its leaders; and on the other, the prospect of a lowering of the standard of living and of a limitation of the birth rate, which left no choice but to act. If the Führer was still living, it was his unalterable resolve to solve Germany's problem of space at the latest by 1943-45. The necessity for action before 1943-45 would arise in cases 2 and 3.

Case 2:

If internal strife in France should develop into such a domestic crisis as to absorb the French Army completely and render it incapable of use for war against Germany, then the time for action against the Czechs had come.

Case 3:

If France is so embroiled by a war with another state that she cannot "proceed" against Germany.

For the improvement of our politico-military position our first objective, in the event of our being embroiled in war, must be to overthrow Czecho-slovakia and Austria simultaneously in order to remove the threat to our flank in any possible operation against the West. In a conflict with France it was hardly to be regarded as likely that the Czechs would declare war on us the very same day as France. The desire to join in the war would, however, increase among the Czechs in proportion to any weakening on our part and then her participation could clearly take the form of an attack toward Silesia, toward the north or toward the west.

If the Czechs were overthrown and a common German-Hungarian frontier achieved, a neutral attitude on the part of Poland could be the more certainly counted on in the event of a Franco-German conflict. Our agreements with Poland only retained their force as long as Germany's strength remained unshaken. In the event of German setbacks a Polish action against East Prussia, and possibly against Pomerania and Silesia as well, had to be reckoned with.

On the assumption of a development of the situation leading to action on our part as planned, in the years 1943-45, the attitude of France, Britain, Italy, Poland, and Russia could probably be estimated as follows:

Actually, the Führer believed that almost certainly Britain, and probably France as well, had already tacitly written off the Czechs and were reconciled to the fact that this question would be cleared up in due course by Germany. Difficulties connected with the Empire, and the prospect of being once more entangled in a protracted European war, were decisive considerations for Britain against participation in a war against Germany. Britain's attitude would certainly not be without influence on that of France. An attack by France without British support, and with the prospect of the offensive being brought to a standstill on our western fortifications, was hardly probable. Nor was a French march through Belgium and Holland without British support to be expected; this also was a course not to be contemplated by us in the event of a conflict with France, because it would certainly entail the hostility of Britain. It would of course be necessary to maintain a strong defense [eine Abriegelung] on our western frontier during the prosecution of our attack on the Czechs and Austria. And in this connection it had to be remembered that the defense measures of the Czechs were growing in strength from year to year, and that the actual worth of the Austrian Army also was increasing in the course of time. Even though the populations concerned, especially of Czechoslovakia, were not sparse, the annexation of Czechoslovakia and Austria would mean an acquisition of foodstuffs for 5 to 6 million people, on the assumption that the compulsory emigration of 2 million people from Czechoslovakia and 1 million people from Austria was practicable. The incorporation of these two States with Germany meant, from the politico-military point of view, a substantial advantage because it would mean shorter and better frontiers, the freeing of forces for other purposes, and the possibility of creating new units up to a level of about 12 divisions, that is, 1 new division per million inhabitants.

Italy was not expected to object to the elimination of the Czechs, but it was impossible at the moment to estimate what her attitude on the Austrian question would be; that depended essentially upon whether the Duce were still alive.

The degree of surprise and the swiftness of our action were decisive factors for Poland's attitude. Poland—with Russia at her rear—will have little inclination to engage in war against a victorious Germany.

Military intervention by Russia must be countered by the swiftness of our operations; however, whether such an intervention was a practical contingency at all was, in view of Japan's attitude, more than doubtful.

Should case 2 arise—the crippling of France by civil war—the situation thus created by the elimination of the most dangerous opponent must be seized upon *whenever it occurs* for the blow against the Czechs.

The Führer saw case 3 coming definitely nearer; it might emerge from the present tensions in the Mediterranean, and he was resolved to take advantage of it whenever it happened, even as early as 1938.

In the light of past experiences, the Führer did not see any early end to the hostilities in Spain. If one considered the length of time which Franco's offensives had taken up till now, it was fully possible that the war would continue another 3 years. On the other hand, a 100 percent victory for Franco was not desirable either, from the German point of view; rather were we interested in a continuance of the war and in the keeping up of the tension in the Mediterranean. Franco in undisputed possession of the Spanish Peninsula precluded the possiblity of any further intervention on the part of the Italians or of their continued occupation of the Balearic Islands. As our interest lay more in the prolongation of the war in Spain, it must be the immediate aim of our policy to strengthen Italy's rear with a view to her remaining in the Balearics. But the permanent establishment of the Italians on the Balearics would be intolerable both to France and Britain, and might lead to a war of France and England against Italy—a war in which Spain, should she be entirely in the hands of the Whites, might make her appearance on the side of Italy's enemies. The probability of Italy's defeat in such a war was slight, for the road from Germany was open for the supplementing of her raw materials. The Führer pictured the military strategy for Italy thus: on her western frontier with France she would remain on the defensive, and carry on the war against France from Libya against the French North African colonial possessions.

As a landing by Franco-British troops on the coast of Italy could be discounted, and a French offensive over the Alps against northern Italy would be very difficult and would probably come to a halt before the strong Italian fortifications, the crucial point [*Schwerpunkt*] of the operations lay in North Africa. The threat to French lines of communication by the Italian Fleet would to a great extent cripple the transportation of forces from North Africa to France, so that France would have only home forces at her disposal on the frontiers with Italy and Germany.

If Germany made use of this war to settle the Czech and Austrian questions, it was to be assumed that Britain—herself at war with Italy—would decide not to act against Germany. Without British support, a warlike action by France against Germany was not to be expected.

The time for our attack on the Czechs and Austria must be made dependent on the course of the Anglo-French-Italian war and would not necessarily coincide with the commencement of military operations by these three States. Nor had the Führer in mind military agreements with Italy, but wanted, while retaining his own independence of action, to exploit this favorable situation, which would not occur again, to begin and carry through the campaign against the Czechs. This descent upon the Czechs would have to be carried out with "lightning speed."

In appraising the situation Field Marshal von Blomberg and Colonel General von Fritsch repeatedly emphasized the necessity that Britain and France must not appear in the role of our enemies, and stated that the French Army would not be so committed by the war with Italy that France could not at the same time enter the field with forces superior to ours on our western frontier. General von Fritsch estimated the probable French forces available for use on the Alpine frontier at approximately twenty divisions, so that a strong French superiority would still remain on the western frontier, with the role, according to the German view, of invading the Rhineland. In this matter, moreover, the advanced state of French defense preparations [*Mobilmachung*] must be taken into particular account, and it must be remembered apart from the insignificant value of our present fortifications—on which Field Marshal von Blomberg laid special empahsis—that the four motorized divisions intended for the West were still more or less incapable of movement. In regard to our offensive toward the southeast, Field Marshal von Blomberg drew particular attention to the strength of the Czech fortifications, which had acquired by now a structure like a Maginot Line and which would gravely hamper our attack.

General von Fritsch mentioned that this was the very purpose of a study which he had ordered made this winter, namely, to examine the possibility of conducting operations against the Czechs with special reference to overcoming the Czech fortification system; the General further expressed his opinion that under existing circumstances he must give up his plan to go abroad on his leave, which was due to begin on November 10. The Führer dismissed this idea on the ground that the possibility of a conflict need not yet be regarded as so imminent. To the Foreign Minister's objection that an Anglo-French-Italian conflict was not yet within such a measurable distance as the Führer seemed to assume, the Führer put the summer of 1938 as the date which seemed to him possible for this. In reply to considerations offered by Field Marshal von Blomberg and General von Fritsch regarding the attitude of Britain and France, the Führer repeated his previous statements that he was convinced of Britain's nonparticipation, and therefore he did not believe in the probability of belligerent action by France against Germany. Should the Mediterranean conflict under discussion lead to a general mobilization in Europe, then we must immediately begin action against the Czechs. On the other hand, should the powers not engaged in the war declare themselves disinterested, then Germany would have to adopt a similar attitude to this for the time being.

Colonel General Göring thought that, in view of the Führer's statement, we should consider liquidating our military undertakings in Spain. The Führer agrees to this with the limitation that he thinks he should reserve a decision for a proper moment.

The second part of the conference was concerned with concrete questions of armament.

                                                            HOSSBACH

CERTIFIED CORRECT:
Colonel (General Staff)

4

Göring's Testimony

SOURCE: Göring's testimony at his Nuremberg trial on the import of the "Hossbach conference" is printed in *International Military Tribunal: Trial of the Major War Criminals before the International Military Tribunal, 14 November 1945-1 October 1946.* 42 vols. (Nuremberg, 1947-49), IX, pp. 306-7.

DR. STAHMER: On 5 November 1937 a discussion with the Führer took place at the Reich Chancellery, a record of which was prepared by a certain Colonel Hossbach, and that has been referred to as Hitler's last will. It has repeatedly been the subject of the proceedings here. May I ask you for a short explanation as to what significance this conference had. I am going to have that document shown to you. It is Document Number 386-PS.

GÖRING: This document has already been shown to me here, and I am fairly familiar with the contents. This document played an important role in the Indictment, since it appears under the heading "Testament of the Führer." This word "testament" is, in fact, used in one place by Hossbach.

As far as the technical aspect of this record is concerned, I want to say the following: Hossbach was the adjutant of the Führer, the chief adjutant. As such, he was present at the meeting and took notes. Five days later, as I have ascertained, he prepared this record on the basis of his notes. This is, therefore, a record which contains all the mistakes which easily occur in a record, which is not taken down on the spot by alternating stenographers, and which under certain circumstances contains the subjective opinions of the recorder or his own interpretations.

It contains a number of points, as I said at the time, which correspond exactly to what the Führer had repeatedly said; but there are other points and expressions which I may say do not seem like the Führer's words.

During the last months I have seen too many records and interrogations which in part had nothing to do with it nor with the interpretation which had been given to it; for that reason I must here too point out the sources of mistakes.

As far as the word "testament" is concerned, the use of this word contradicts the Führer's views completely. If anybody at all knows anything about these views, it is I.

The decision that I was to be the successor was not made first on 1 September 1939, but as early as the late autumn of 1934. I have often had the opportunity of discussing the question of a so-called political testament with the Führer. He turned it down, giving as his reason the fact that one could never appoint a successor by means of a political testament, for developments and political events must allow him complete freedom of action at all times. Quite possibly one could set down political wishes or views, but never binding statements in the shape of a will. That was his view then and as long as I stood in his confidence.

Now what did he aim at in this discussion? The Minister of War, the Commander-in-Chief of the Army, the Commander-in-Chief of the Navy and the Luftwaffe and the then Reich Foreign Minister were called together. Shortly before the Führer had informed me, as I was there earlier, that he was going to call this meeting mainly in order, as he called it, to put pressure on General Von Fritsch, since he was dissatisfied with the rearmament of the Army. He said it would not do any harm if Herr Von Blomberg would also exercise a certain amount of pressure on Von Fritsch.

I asked why Von Neurath was to be present. He said he did not want the thing to look too military, that as far as the commanders-in-chief were concerned it was not so important, but that he wanted to make it very clear to Commander-in-Chief Fritsch that the foreign political situation required a forced speed in armament and that for that reason he had asked the Foreign Minister, who knew nothing about the details, to come along.

The statements were then made in the way the Führer preferred on such occasions. He went to great lengths to picture things within a large political framework and he talked about the whole world situation from all angles; and for anybody who knew him as well as I did the purpose which he pursued was obvious. He was quite clearly aiming at saying that he had great plans, that the political situation was such and such, and the whole thing ended in the direction of a stronger armament program. I should like to say that, if the Führer, a couple of hours later, had talked to another group, for instance, diplomats of the Foreign Office, of Party functionaries, then he probably would have represented matters quite differently.

Nevertheless, some of these statements naturally do reflect the basic attitude of the Führer, but with the best intentions I cannot attach the same measure of significance to the document as is being attached to it here.

5

A Friend's Attempt to Help Fritsch Fails

SOURCE: Item from Joachim von Stülpnagel, "75 Jahre Meines Lebens" (75 years of my life), unpublished manuscript in the Military Archives, Freiburg, Germany, p. 356. Translation by Harold C. Deutsch.

Two or three days before the fateful event an unknown masculine voice called me at my office and said: "You are a friend of General von Fritsch. He is in greatest danger." I answered: "Who is speaking to me?" I received no reply as the caller had hung up. Of course I immediately drove to Fritsch. He did not know of anything and we thought of the possibility of some assassination attempt from the side of the party, which did not trouble Fritsch further. He correctly surmised that a man in his position in such times was always in some danger.

After what happened next I can only assume that the caller was some decent man in the Gestapo who wanted to warn Fritsch. The cause for his action was soon to become clear. Shortly thereafter I received a call from an adjutant of Fritsch, requesting that I come immediately. When I arrived, I found him sitting in complete despair at his desk. He described the monstrous scene that had taken place in Hitler's room from which he had returned shortly before. The accusation of homosexuality by Hitler, the confrontation with the crimnal, his own speechlessness, his word of honor that he was not guilty, and, finally, his plea for a court-martial investigation are known. After he had replied affirmatively to my question, can you as a friend assure me of your innocence, I said to him: "You have acted wrongly with Hitler, for if he brought you into this grotesque situation and failed to throw out the calumniator when you gave your word of honor, you should have, in default of a weapon, assailed the criminal with a chair." (I know, of course, that it is much easier for a non-involved person to determine the right course than it is for one who is caught off guard, especially a man of such high mind as Fritsch, who was disconcerted by so mean a trick.) I reflected on what after such a calamity I could advise Fritsch to do and proposed to him:

(1) An immediate summons to the top generals, declare on his word of honor that everything was a pack of lies, and appeal to them to declare their solidarity with him for the protection of the concept of honor.

(2) A request to attorney Dr. Count Goltz to represent him in the judicial

clarification. He was a man of high mind, even though a National Socialist, and for this very reason would be able to deal more effectively with his party associates.

Fritsch accepted the second proposition but had doubts about the first. He thought that he was now sidelined and would have to await whatever would be done by the leading generals, whose senior representative was Rundstedt.

Thus affairs took their fatal course!

6

The Court-Martial Panel
Refutes the Gestapo's Arguments

The two investigative groups, the *Gestapo* and the court-martial panel, were charged by Hitler with keeping each other informed of their activities and of what they learned. They were to have observers at each other's interrogations. The *Gestapo* frequently violated these rules, but they were scrupulously observed by the court-martial panel as it was evident that its rival would make a great to-do about any slip. The following document provides an example where such an accusation was actually made by Himmler but energetically refuted. The three signatures are those of the judges of the court-martial panel.

SOURCE: Original manuscript in the possession of Mrs. Helle Sack, who provided a copy. Translated by Harold C. Deutsch.

Berlin-Charlottenburg
21 March 1938

NOTATION FOR THE RECORD

The Reichsführer SS and Chief of the German Police has maintained that, in the judicial proceedings against Colonel General (ret.) Baron von Fritsch the Secret State Police, contrary to the order of the Fuehrer, was not informed of the time of the first interrogation of Captain (ret.) von Frisch. Against this claim it is established that:

(1) The encounter took place on 2 March between 18 and 20 o'clock in Lichterfelde-East in the residence of Captain (ret.) von Frisch.

(2) As early as that morning the Secret State Police was notified by telephone that it should summon the witness von Frisch for immediate interrogation. About 12 o'clock an official of the Gestapo appeared to state that the witness was too ill for interrogation.

(3) Thereupon the Gestapo was requested to furnish the address of the attending physician. This was done.

(4) The attending physician, on being called by the Chief Investigator, declared that the witness von Frisch was indeed unable to go to the court house but that there were no serious objections to his being interrogated in his residence.

(5) Thereupon at about 17 o'clock Criminal Inspector Fehling, on the particular order of the Chief Investigator, was informed by Military Judge Dr. Sack of the declaration of the physician and that the Chief Investigator would immediately proceed to the residence of von Frisch in Lichterfelde-East in order to interrogate him as a witness. Criminal Inspector Fehling remarked thereto that Captain (ret.) von Frisch was in no sense of interest in the case of Colonel General (ret.) Baron von Fritsch. Von Frisch, he said, was a seriously ill man near 70. Also, the withdrawals from his bank account in the period in question were insignificant.

(6) No official of the Gestapo appeared at the interrogation which began only after about 20 minutes in the residence and, with brief intermissions, lasted until about 20 o'clock. Also, in a meeting that morning in which nine witnesses provided by the Gestapo to the Chief Investigator were interrogated, no official of the Gestapo took part.

(7) On the next morning Criminal Inspector Fehling was present in the Reich Military Court. In the presence of Military Judge Biron he was asked by Military Judge Sack about the bank withdrawals of von Frisch in November/December 1933. Criminal Inspector Fehling again gave the assurance that the withdrawals had been minimal. He said that he would comply with a request to send the court a bank statement, though another official was now charged with the investigation. The bank statement has not been received to date.

(8) After the charge had been made [by Himmler] that the Gestapo had not been informed of the time of the interrogation of Captain (ret.) von Frisch, Military Judge Sack on 5 March 1938, in the presence of Military Judges Biron and Dr. Kanter, reproached Criminal Inspector Fehling that *he* (Fehling) had received the appropriate notice. Criminal Inspector Fehling declared roughly as follows:

"Yes, that is true. You did tell me the time. It was my fault that this information was not passed on. We were so busy that day that in the morning also we were unable to send any officials."

Reich Military Judge	Reich Military Judge	Reich Military Judge
Biron	*Dr. Kanter*	*Dr. Sack*
(for #3 & 5 on information provided by Military Judge Dr. Sack)	(for #8)	(for #4 on information from Military Judge Biron)

7

Evaluation of the Evidence

This is the second part of the verdict in the court-martial of General von Fritsch. It was formulated by one of the civilian judges along lines indicated by Göring, who had usurped the function of presiding office of the court. Göring was especially eager that the verdict should imply that, though Fritsch in the end had been proved not guilty, appearances against him had been sufficient to justify Hitler's pursuing the case. The verdict was first published in 1965 by the German periodical *Der Spiegel.*

SOURCE: From the book, *The Secret War Against Hitler* by Fabian von Schlabrendorff. Copyright, © 1965, by Pitman Publishing Corporation. Reprinted by permission of Pitman Publishing Corp.

SECOND PART.

THE EVALUATION OF THE RESULT OF COLLECTED EVIDENCE.

A

The picture which evolved at the end of the main trial is completely different from that which led to the ordering of the investigation. It is also quite different in many points from the picture that was disclosed at the end of the preliminary investigation proceeding and at the time the main trial was ordered.

I.

Schmidt's accusations against Colonel-General von Fritsch in 1936 were put forward in a way that, taken by themselves, offered grounds for serious suspicion. They did, however, show some gaps. This was outbalanced by the fact that Schmidt, in an unusually large number of cases, had accused of homosexual acts people who later had been brought to trial and sentenced on the basis of his accusations, or where at least his statements had proved correct.

The fact that the man who made the accusations had a long criminal record and was an extremely dangerous and morally worthless blackmailer was under the circumstances not sufficient *in itself* to let the accusation appear baseless from the start. The fact that the accusation was directed against a blameless man of great merit also *in itself* could not justify the assumption that the accusations made under such circumstances had been invented. There have been too many sad examples of homosexual tendencies and acts among all groups and classes of people, and by persons who are mentally and culturally outstanding and irreproachable in other respects. It is also evident that such people cannot be considered reliable in their statements about their tendencies.

Added to that was the following in this special case:

Schmidt's accusations appeared so incredible to all concerned that he was put under the greatest pressure to tell the truth. The president of the court himself, who was present during part of the preliminary inquiries, did that, and Schmidt was given every opportunity by both the president and officials of the Secret State Police to retract his accusations against the Colonel-General. He did not do so, but persisted in his statements. Finally—long before the main trial—he told the president that if it were the express wish that he should retract his statements because of political reasons, he would do so. He insisted, though, that his statements were true.

The following, also has to be pointed out: the Fuehrer directed the Reichminister of Justice, on January 27, 1938, to give his opinion on the case. After examining the files which at that time were unavailable to the Minister, he sent the following communication to the Fuehrer:

My Fuehrer!

On the 27th of this month, you directed me to express my opinion on the case v. F., and you later explained this directive through separate questions. The documents available to me were: 22 court files, 7 Secret State Police files, 2 protocols on the interrogations of v. F. on the 27th and 28th of this month.

I also had the opportunity to get a personal impression of the witnesses. Otto Schmidt and Martin Weingaertner.

After careful examination of these documents I have come to the following conclusions:

1.

The serious accusation of having committed homosexual acts with a homosexual prostitute has been made against v. F.

2.

V. F. denies any and all homosexual activity or inclination.

He has so far not disproved the accusation. He has up to now not submitted the announced alibi proof.

3.

The other charges (in the cases of Wermelskirchen and Zeidler) would be considered an aggravating circumstance by the prosecution in connection with the accusation under 1.

4.

The decision of guilty or not guilty cannot be made by me; that remains—without regard to the person, his rank or position—the task of the court.

II.

The circumstances and considerations mentioned in connection with what was said earlier about the case history were the reasons the trial became necessary.

These proceedings had the goal of clearing up the case in a *main trial*, and of doing this before a court whose members were the Commanders-in-Chief of the three branches of the Armed Forces and the two highest military judges of the Reich.

The directive of the Fuehrer to this court had a purpose which differed from the ordinary rules covering criminal charges. The court received the assignment to examine the accusations against the Colonel-General. It was to give its opinion in what was something like a trial of establishment of facts—that the accusations were true or not proven or that the Colonel-General was not guilty.

B.

I.

The main trial has not uncovered the slightest proof of any homosexual inclination on the part of Colonel-General (Ret.) Baron Werner von Fritsch.

The witnesses who have known the Colonel-General so well over such a long period of time as have Major-General Count von Sponek, Major Siewert, and Captain von Both never even harbored the slightest suspicion that the Colonel-General could possibly be homosexually inclined. The witness

Kunau, who has held the position of housekeeper to the Colonel-General since 1926, has made the same statement.

The declarations of fifteen of the Colonel-General's orderlies, who were all interrogated, show that the Colonel-General never made advances to any one of them. He never even talked about sexual matters with any of these orderlies.

The fact that the Colonel-General occasionally pinched the ear of one or another of these orderlies when they were unable to answer a question is completely harmless.

This picture is not changed by the so-called Wermelskirchen and Zeidler cases. The Colonel-General occasionally pinched the ears of those boys. They were his guests for lunch. Wermelskirchen came for two years almost without interruption, Zeidler for one month. The Colonel-General ate with them, and after the meals sometimes worked with them on topography, or questioned them on other matters designed to improve their knowledge. If during such occasions the boys were inattentive, he pinched their ears. Once—according to earlier statements, several times—he slapped Wermelskirchen across the buttocks. The boys did not see anything wrong in that at the time, nor do they today. The anxiety of the mothers can be explained by the thoughts by which all parents of adolescent boys were beset at the time.

The *personal impression* the main trial has conveyed to the court was that these slight physical contacts were in no way offensive.

In this connection it must be pointed out that these cases were examined only because Colonel-General Baron von Fritsch, during a meeting with the Fuehrer on January 26, 1938, had himself mentioned Wermelskirchen.

II.

The fact that the main trial has failed to show any proof whatsoever of homosexual inclinations by the Colonel-General is still important for the examination of the accusations made by Schmidt. These accusations have to be examined and evaluated without regard to the fact that Schmidt finally retracted them.

For such an evaluation of Schmidt's statements, one should not be influenced solely by the fact that there are contradictions in them. Schmidt had been interrogated many times in the course of years, and especially during the preceding months. Experience shows that during such frequent interrogations even truthful witnesses cannot avoid contradicting themselves. Schmidt's contradictions, however, assume a special importance when viewed in connection with the "von Frisch" case. More will be said about the latter.

III.

1. Schmidt from the start declared that the gentleman who committed a homosexual act with Weingaertner at the Wannsee station wore a fur coat

with a fur collar. This description of the man is found in all statements to the Secret State Police during 1936. The fur coat had aroused Schmidt's interest to such a degree that even during his first interrogation by the witness Haeusserer (protocol copy of July 8 or 9, 1936) he described the fur coat in detail. "Each time we met . . . he wore a fur coat which had black cloth on the outside. The collar was made of valuable brown fur." In the interrogation of August 26, Schmidt says: "The man wore a dark fur coat with a dark brown collar, also of fur." The same day, he said in another interrogation: "I want to remark that v. F. did not take off his fur coat." In the interrogation of September 3, 1936, Schmidt described the man as the "gentleman in the fur coat."

The officials of the Secret State Police who carried out these interrogations, Police Captain (now retired) Haeusserer and Criminal Secretary Loeffner, declared under oath that Schmidt made his statements voluntarily, independently, and without pressure. Haeusserer also said, upon being interrogated by the chief of investigation, that he had attached special importance to setting down carefully and in exact detail all the statements Schmidt had made on small items, so that other later statements and explanations could be based upon that protocol.

Accordingly there cannot be any doubt that in 1936 Schmidt considered the fur coat an especially outstanding mark of identification and description. Because the man supposedly wore the fur coat during each of their meetings, Schmidt must have seen the coat on three occasions, each time for a lengthy period. During later interrogations, Schmidt played down this statement.

Colonel-General (Ret.) Baron Werner von Fritsch never had a fur coat of this kind, or indeed any civilian fur coat at all. This is evident from the testimony of the Colonel-General himself and from its confirmation by Miss Kunau, who has been his housekeeper since 1926 and therefore knows all his clothes.

Mr. von Frisch, however, does possess a fur coat.

2. According to statements to the Secret State Police in 1936, the man Schmidt blackmailed was a *heavy smoker.* In his testimony on August 26, 1936, to Criminal Secretary Loeffner, Schmidt says of the man who watched the young men in the railroad-station lobby: "The gentleman in the meantime also had lighted a cigar." Then later: "Shortly after leaving the railroad-station exit, the two (Bavarian Joe and the gentleman) stopped on the street and each lighted a cigar or cigarette, then they went farther into the street. Before the gentleman and Bavarian Joe lighted their smokes, they spoke to each other." During the same interrogation, it says in the description of their parting: "Then the two persons each lighted a cigar and parted right after." In the same interrogation, it says about the incident in the second-class waiting room, which Schmidt later denied completely in connection with the Colonel-General: "First I received a cigar from his cigar case." In the interrogation of August 26, the testimony says about the incident in the

second-class waiting room in Lichterfelde in January 1934: "*We* (Schmidt and the man) each had Asbach-Uralt and smoked cigars. Whether Buckner (Heiter) also smoked a cigar, I cannot say."

During the interrogation of the Colonel-General by the Secret State Police on January 27, 1938, it was established that the Colonel-General has not smoked for many years.

Schmidt's later statements about the smoking were more and more subdued. In the first interrogation before the chief of investigations, on February 22, 1938, Schmidt did not mention anything at all on his own initiative about the gentleman's smoking in the station lobby. His description of the two men's visit to the Privatstrasse was as follows: "From there, I saw the flame of a match. Obviously they, or one of them, had lighted a cigar or cigarette." With regard to the incident in the waiting room in January 1934, Schmidt said of the gentleman: "He said to me during the conversation: 'Oh, I shall smoke a cigar too.' Thereupon I offered him the box, and he lighted a cigar. He smoked that to the end. He smoked only that one cigar." During the same interrogation Schmidt said, in reply to a question, that he could not remember whether the gentleman had also smoked a cigar in the station lobby.

Schmidt answered these questions in a similar manner during the main trial.

The main trial established through statements of the Colonel-General and Major-General Count von Sponeck, and through Miss Kunau that the *Colonel-General was a non-smoker.* The Colonel-General declares that he has not smoked since 1926. The witnesses confirm that they never saw him smoke.

Mr. von Frisch is a heavy smoker.

3. Schmidt said during his first interrogation (July 8 or 9, 1936) that, when they returned from the Ferdinandstrasse to the Lichterfelde-Ost station on that first evening, the gentleman showed him a bank on the other side of the station—"I believe it was the Dresdener Bank"—where Schmidt was to wait for him the following day. In the second interrogation (August 26, 1936), Schmidt added: "When we came through the station to the other side, he showed me that bank which is located on the left side of the station, and from which he was going to get the money." Then, later, of the next morning: "I stood in the Bahnhofstrasse at the corner of the Jungfernsteg at the telephone booth and watched the entrance of the bank at No. 3, Jungfernsteg. . . . Shortly afterward, v. F. came out of the bank." These statements clearly apply to the Depositenkasse of the Dresdener Bank in Lichterfelde-Ost.

During both the preliminary investigation and the main trial, Schmidt spoke no more of the Dresdener Bank. Also, he no longer stated that he was shown the bank from which the money was to be picked up. There is no word about coming out of the bank on the morning after the first blackmail. During the incident of January 1934, he (Schmidt) maintained that the

Colonel-General was standing in front of the Commerz-und-Privatbank (located diagonally across the street from the Dresdener Bank.)

The Colonel-General did not have an account either with the Dresdener Bank or the Commerz-und Privatbank. Mr. von Frisch had an account with the Depositenkasse of the Dresdener Bank in Lichterfelde. There he and Schmidt picked up the money.

4. From the very beginning of the court-martial proceedings, the question of a possible relationship between the Colonel-General and the house at No. 21 Ferdinandstrasse was given special attention. *Not the slightest evidence was found that there existed any connection whatsoever between the Colonel-General and the house at No. 21. Mr. von Frisch lives at No. 20 Ferdinandstrasse.*

5. It has already been pointed out that several items on which Schmidt later changed or modified his initial testimony of 1936 do not apply to the Colonel-General. They do, however, apply to Mr. von Frisch. The von Frisch case, with the exception of one point, is clear.

Schmidt himself admits the von Frisch case almost in the way it is described by von Frisch.

Von Frisch, on his part, admits all the details Schmidt attributes to the Colonel-General:

Homosexual act—November 1933—Privatstrasse at the Wannsee station—blackmail attempt by Schmidt—picking up part of the initial sum of 500 marks at a house in the Ferdinandstrasse—meeting on the following morning—coming out of the Dresdener Bank—transfer of the rest of the 500 marks in the waiting room—payment of 1000 marks with participation of another blackmailer, again in the waiting room—Asbach-Uralt cognac—cigars—fur coat—later payment of another 1000 marks—receipt for the total blackmail sum of 2500 marks—signature Kroeger.

All this conforms almost perfectly to the statements Schmidt made about the von Fritsch case to the Secret State Police in 1936, when he was much closer to the affair.

The importance of the von Frisch case, first uncovered during the preliminary court-martial investigations, for evaluating the von Fritsch case is evident. There may be cases in which blackmail attempts against two different persons are similar in appearance and sequence of events. However, it seems most improbable that there could be two cases where the similarity is so great as in this case.

The similarity begins with the name and the clothing. It continues over the approximate time of the commission, the manner, and the locale of the act. In both cases, the blackmailed persons go to Lichterfelde-Ost. They go to the same street, into houses located next to one another. The money is withdrawn from the same bank. The sums paid are both the same amount. In both cases, a second blackmailer participates, both times in the waiting room of the Lichterfelde-Ost station. Both times during these meetings Asbach-Uralt is imbibed and cigars are smoked. After the last payment, a receipt is given for a total sum of 2500 marks.

Considering these similarities in name, locale, time, and course of events of the blackmail, the differences in the descriptions of the two cases play only a small part. They refer to the fact that in one case Schmidt claims to have spoken to the man he blackmailed in the tunnel of the Wannsee station, in the other in Lichterfelde-Ost. There are differences concerning the name, the presentation of the identification card, and the trip to Lichterfelde, which in the von Fritsch case was supposedly made by both men together; concerning the numbers of the houses (20 and 21); the manner of payment of the first 500 marks (in the von Fritsch case in one lump sum, in the von Frisch case in two payments); and concerning the walk from the house to the station, which in the von Fritsch case supposedly was made by both men together. In the time element there is a difference insofar as the von Frisch case supposedly occurred prior to the von Fritsch case.

These slight variations are unimportant seen against the similarities of the main points and the important secondary details.

6. Any remaining doubt was dispelled in the main trial by the witness Ganzer.

It is unthinkable that Schmidt—if indeed he had at the time known the Colonel-General and had been looking for him—would have looked for him in the vicinity of the Lichterfelde-Ost station. Schmidt is a very experienced blackmailer. The stupidity of such unplanned behavior is not to be expected of him.

Instead, on his trips to Lichterfelde with Ganzer as well as during his own visits there, Schmidt was thinking only of the von Frisch case. He spoke to Ganzer of a Captain or Rittmeister he had already blackmailed with Siefert. He spoke of a sickly old man whose house he knew, in whose home he had been, who offered cognac and who had a nurse. This was the man he wanted to blackmail anew with Weingaertner's discharge papers, because of the incident at the Wannsee station. At another time Ganzer was supposed to imitate Weingaertner. All that can apply only to the von Frisch case.

In addition Siefert, who at that time saw a good deal of Schmidt and whom Schmidt told a lot about his blackmailing, is of the opinion that Schmidt most certainly would have told him if at that time he had known something about a Colonel-General.

7. Just for the sake of completeness, it is pointed out that several contradictions have not been cleared up. The following are to be mentioned.

The von Frisch case had its beginning at the Wannsee station after intercourse with a man whose (prison) discharge papers Schmidt wanted to use for blackmailing von Frisch. The man whose discharge papers were involved was Weingaertner. Weingaertner admits the act at the Wannsee station but denies having committed the act with *von Frisch*, just as von Frisch admits the act but denies having committed it with Weingaertner.

This contradiction is of no importance in this case. It can possibly be explained by the fact that the few moments during which the two men saw each other by light were too short to enable sure recognition of each other after more than four years. In addition, the appearance of von Frisch must have changed considerably during the intervening years as a result of his illness.

On the other hand, the possibility cannot be ruled out that Weingaertner may have committed some other act of the same kind at the Wannsee station and that a second line of connections leads to Lichterfelde through Otto Schmidt.

Also not clarified is the following contradiction, which could possibly play a part in this connection:

Schmidt always stated that the act he claims to have observed, in which Weingaertner was involved, took place in the depths of the Privatstrasse, behind the fence. Weingaertner stubbornly persisted in saying that it happened near the entrance. From the statements of the railroad workers Just and Koehler, it seems highly likely that the fence was closed regularly at dusk, even when the scaffolding had been erected. It therefore would seem possible that Schmidt, shortly before the closing of the fence, did observe something at the spot he states he did. That would be especially so if Weingaertner, contrary to what he says, should have had dealings there with other people.

There was no reason further to examine these questions in the trial against the Colonel-General. There was also no reason to examine a number of other questions which came up through Schmidt's statements.

IV.

From the facts as they have been related so far, it becomes evident that Schmidt has falsely accused the Colonel-General.

Both Schmidt and Heiter finally admitted this during the main trial. How and under what circumstances this confession was made has already been described in detail above.

This confession rounds out the case and closes it once and for all.

Therefore, this is established:

The main trial proceedings have shown the innocence of Colonel-General (Ret.) Baron Werner von Fritsch in all points.

The accuracy of the transcript is attested to
Berlin-Charlottenburg, March 30, 1938.

(signed) Dr. Sack

Reichs War Tribunal Judge
as documentation official of
the main office.

8

Efforts in Behalf of Fritsch

The following memorandum was prepared immediately after the trial of General von Fritsch by Admiral Canaris and Colonel Hossbach. It was inspired by General Beck and was meant to be used with General von Brauchitsch to persuade him to put pressure on Hitler to "rehabilitate" Fritsch and remove the SS leaders.

SOURCE: Original document in the writer's possession. Translated by Harold C. Deutsch.

(probably March 19 or 20, 1938)

POSITION WITH RESPECT TO THE CASE OF
COLONEL GENERAL BARON VON FRITSCH

The outcome of the trial is unsatisfactory for the restoration of the honor of Colonel General Baron von Fritsch and thereby for the reputation of the Army and the entire Wehrmacht, as well as for freeing them from the nightmare of a Cheka [Bolshevik-type political police].

Proposals for further measures.

Should the Fuehrer as commander in chief of the Wehrmacht not undertake satisfactory measures on his *own* initiative, it will be necessary to consider whether the Army as the service most immediately attacked and defamed should undertake steps *under the leadership of its commander in chief* with the commander in chief of the Wehrmacht.

It will be necessary to consider whether the leading military personalities should be included in this step. In question would be:

Colonel General von Rundstedt,

Colonel General von Bock as commander in chief of the 8th Army in
    Austria (very imperative!),

General of Infantry List,

General of Artillery Beck, chief of the General Staff of the Army.

Should one wish to go beyond the framework of the Army, there would come into question:

General Field Marshal Goering

General Admiral Dr. h.c. Raeder, Commander in chief of the Navy
General of Artillery Keitel, Chief of the High Command of the Wehrmacht
There is need for dispatch so that the commander in chief of the Wehrmacht is not diverted in wrong directions by the innuendos of other forces.

Proposals for demands:

As demands that are to be made to the commander in chief of the Wehrmacht are proposed:

a. The rehabilitation of Colonel General Baron von Fritsch in an impressive fashion before the public, as not only the Wehrmacht, but also a wider public have learned something of the true reason for the departure of Colonel General Baron von Fritsch.

   One of the most effective means and also one that would serve the interests of the Fuehrer would be a personal visit of the Fuehrer to Colonel General Baron von Fritsch.

b. Important changes in the leadership of the Gestapo.

   Here in first line would be Himmler, Heydrich, Joost (SD), Best, Meisinger, Fehling, among others.

Considerations for the Justification of this Step and Its Demands.

a. The action of 4 Feb. was undertaken on the basis of the incorrect assumption of the guilt of Colonel General von Fritsch without awaiting the outcome of the court-martial.

b. The purpose of this step is the unequivocal restoration of the honor of the former commander in chief of the German Army and of that of the entire Wehrmacht, as well as to liberate the Wehrmacht from the nightmare of a Cheka.

c. Continued healthy cooperation between the Wehrmacht and those responsible for defaming Colonel General Baron von Fritsch, and thus also of the insulting and vile attack on the Army by the participating figures of the Gestapo, is under the prevailing circumstances intolerable.

   Moreover, the attention of the Fuehrer must be called in an insistent and determined manner to the evil game that has been played with his name and reputation. It must also forcefully be emphasized that the measures demanded are in the Fuehrer's own interests. Among other things, it should be mentioned that it was the clear duty to inform the Fuehrer about the indications that there was a double.

d. Finally, in order to make an impression on the Fuehrer, one must avoid attacking the institution of the Gestapo as such. It must be said to him that there are enough decent and honest National Socialists to occupy these positions of trust.

e. In view of the possibility of some kind of objection of the Fuehrer, it should be considered that the Fuehrer knows exactly and controls the psyche of the people but is not alive to the need of keeping clean the escutcheon of a Wehrmacht and its leaders.

f. Sharpest rejection of interpreting the steps undertaken as mutiny, a military coup, or some other action against the party.

g. The veterans of the great war and the soldiers of the Wehrmacht of the National Socialist state are among the best, most unselfish, and disinterested National Socialists.

GODFREY N. UZOIGWE

From the Gold Coast to Ghana:
The Politics of Decolonization

O N MARCH 6, 1957, the one hundred and thirteenth anniversary of the Bond of 1844 when certain Fante chiefs formally alienated part of their sovereignty to Britain, the British territory of the Gold Coast became the sovereign and independent nation-state of Ghana. And neither Africa nor Britain was to be the same again. On the one hand, the independence of Ghana accelerated "the wind of change" which had been blowing acro'ss Africa since the end of World War II; and on the other, it changed Britain's feeling of uncertainty toward its African colonies, noticeable since the interwar years, to one of utter despondency. In these senses, at any rate, the history of the decolonization process is part and parcel of European history. And even on the general philosophical level, it is at least arguable that since by the twentieth century Europe, as a result of imperialism and colonialism, had become bigger than itself, European history of this century would be meaningless if shorn of its extra-European dimensions. These explanations justify, in our view, the validity of this chapter in a book on twentieth-century Europe. Ghana provides the classic case study on which we hope to construct a hypothesis for the

377

decolonization process in twentieth-century Africa, a hypothesis, if you will, to end all hypotheses!

I. THEORETICAL FRAMEWORK:
TOWARD A FORMULA FOR DECOLONIZATION

The decolonization process in Africa has naturally attracted a lot of journalistic and scholarly attention in recent years. The speed with which Europe made its political exit from Africa baffled even the most inveterate African nationalist. The attempt to explain this major revolution in the twentieth century has been confounded by myths as well as realities. Communist scholars, for example, emphasize the primacy of African resistance movements but are silent on the interesting question of African collaboration with the colonizers. Western scholars, on the contrary, while studiously weak on resistance movements, have not really studied the character of African collaboration. They have, however, propagated many myths about African reaction to colonialism. African societies, they argue, generally welcomed the establishment of the European *pax*; only the few anti-modernizers were against it. The majority of the Africans realized that it was useless to resist the superior might of the Europeans who, armed with their strong military and economic power, were generally master of the situation and could therefore contain any resistance. Faced with such a situation, Africans were docile and helpless. But they were smart enough to realize that nothing could be gained from resistance while there was a lot to gain from collaboration. Resistance movements brought with them social and political disintegration.

How, then, can one explain the various resistance movements recorded in African history? They were, according to Jack Gallagher and Ronald Robinson, mere "romantic, reactionary struggles against the facts, the passionate protest of societies which were shocked by a new age of change and would not be comforted."[1] They noted, however, with more validity, that the earlier resistances differed from the later and "defter nationalisms" which "planned to reform their personalities and regain their powers by operating in the idiom of the westernizers."[2]

---

[1] Ronald E. Robinson and John Gallagher, "The Partition of Africa," in F. H. Hinsley (ed.), *The New Cambridge Modern History, Vol. XI: Material Progress and World-wide Problems, 1870-1898* (Cambridge: Cambridge University Press, 1962), p. 640.
[2] *Idem.*

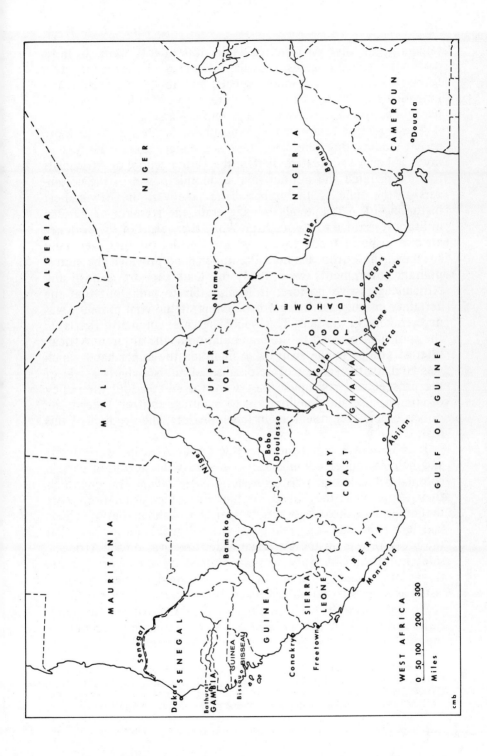

Others argue that African resistance movements were, in most cases, directed not against colonial rule *per se* but against its cruel forms or against its seamier aspects; and that some groups and individuals resisted colonialism purely for selfish motives and hardly because of nationalist aspirations so-called.[3]

These interpretations have come under severe attack in more recent studies. But here, too, there is a danger that a new type of myth is being formulated. Just as the earlier school of Africanists had exaggerated the military and economic power of the colonizers at the time of the imperialistic takeover, the new radical historians of Africa tend to exaggerate the strength of African military resistance to colonialism. While the weight of the evidence at our disposal tends to tilt to the conclusion that, generally speaking, the Europeans held the upper hand provided the metropolitan governments were ready to lend support against any African aggressive posture, it is also fair to point out that the certainty of this aid being forthcoming at the vital moment was never taken for granted. This being the case, colonial officials on the spot had to resort to the manipulation of the different African interest groups in the struggle to maintain the upper hand which was vital for the success of colonialism. Understandably afraid of the prospects of resistance, they were forced to adopt the policy of compromise and amelioration to maintain control. Indeed, the policy of indirect rule was, in large measure, the product of this fear.

It is therefore nonsensical to assert that Africans were docile and helpless under colonial rule. So also is the notion of certain colonial officials that African societies were *tabula rasa* on which they wrote what they liked; or that Euro-African relations were tantamount to those between Prospero and Caliban, between gods and lesser mortals. The reality of the colonial situation was that the pressure was on the European side; time was on the Africans' side. European authority was maintained by the sword—or the threat of it—and by bribing Africans into loyalty. Such a policy lasted as long as it maintained its credibility but no longer.

We will attempt to formulate a hypothesis for the decolonization process in Africa with the aim of reflecting more accurately the relationship between Africans and Europeans and how changes

---

[3] These views are summarized by T. O. Ranger, "African Reactions to the Imposition of Colonial Rule in East and Central Africa," in L. H. Gann and Peter Duignan (eds.), *Colonialism in Africa, 1870-1960: Volume One: The History and Politics of Colonialism, 1870-1914* (Cambridge: Cambridge University Press, 1969), pp. 293-304.

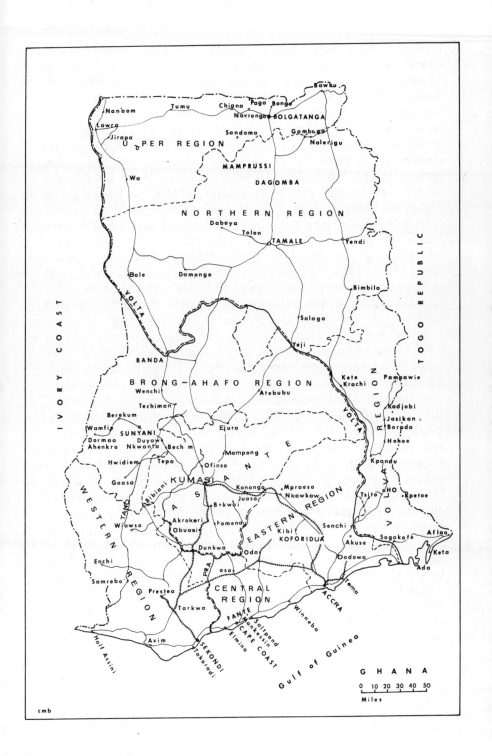

in these relationships led to the collapse of colonialism. The Gold Coast (Ghana) therefore is the peg on which we will hang our hypothesis. Briefly, the hypothesis asserts that collaboration between conqueror and conquered is as old as history; that when a technologically superior society conquers an agrarian or less technologically advanced society, and the conquest is accepted as a *fait accompli*, there is an inevitable tendency for the weightier class of the agrarian society and the officials of the technological society to collaborate the one with the other. Why? Because the superior power has certain advantages to offer to the weightier group of elites in the occupied society who hope to benefit tremendously by such a connection. These include prospects for patronage, honors, titles, official appointments, capital, wealth, education, etc., as rewards for collaboration. The colonizing power needs this collaboration badly because it is hopelessly deficient in manpower resources which happen to be the major strength of the agrarian society. If this hypothesis is accepted, it then follows that colonial rule inevitably involves an unwritten bargain—or sometimes a written bargain such as the Buganda Agreement of 1900—with terms understood, if not necessarily spelled out. The role of the agrarian collaborators is clear: to keep the masses quiet. To make the bargain worthwhile for the foreign collaborators, they invest the local collaborators with sufficient authority—where this is felt necessary—to make it possible for them to deliver the goods because if the colonial power has to intervene physically and directly to promote its interests, the rationale for the bargain falls to the ground. As Lord Frederick D. Lugard, the advocate of indirect rule, put it: ". . . if a native chief has lost prestige and influence to such a degree that he has to appeal to government to enforce his orders he becomes not merely useless but a source of weakness to the administration."[4] To which his disciple, Sir Donald Cameron, added: "[If the masses] are not prepared to accept the orders of the so-called authority unless we compel them to do so, then of course the administration we set up is not indirect and the native authority set up on such a basis is a sham and a snare."[5] Some local collaborators, aware of these difficulties, bargained strenuously for better terms before they would collaborate.

The novelty of this theory is that the bargain is not one-sided.

[4] Cited in D. A. Low and R. C. Pratt, *Buganda and British Overrule, 1900-1955: Two Studies* (London and New York: Oxford University Press, 1960), pp. 204-5.
[5] *Idem.*

Colonialism operated on the basis of "you scratch my back and I scratch yours." In other words, there is a considerable degree of interdependence inherent in a colonial situation. Colonial rule was not as easy as it appeared. Collaboration whether of the African or European variety was basically dishonest. It was a dangerous game in which the ruler as well as the ruled had to be sharp in order to survive. European proconsuls, as they pranced from place to place oozing an appearance of calm, control, and dignity, were, in fact, as Ronald Robinson put it, "up to their eyes in the politics of their so-called subjects, operating a system of checks and sticks for enemies and of baits and carrots for friends. . . . They were in the business of traditional faction and client-making."[6] The genius of colonialism is that they succeeded for over half a century in maintaining this precarious balance. Its weakness was that European policy makers were overtaken by the logic of events which they were not farsighted enough to foresee. As the colonial era was drawing to a cataclysmic conclusion, they found themselves being directed, rather than directing, the march of inevitable historical forces. They also discovered, rather belatedly, that they had carefully nurtured a ground which proved very fertile for their overthrow. And their despondency was complete.

The genius of African nationalism, on the other hand, is its superb pragmatism which enabled it to beat the Europeans in their own game and allowed them to depart with honour. African nationalism triumphed over colonialism because it won the game of collaboration. For, once the African nationalists learned to ride most of the political horses in the country, and succeeded in persuading the grassroots peasantry to change from passivism to activism by joining forces with the elitist and other resisting groups, the European rider was bound to fall off. And the nationalists were left to carry on the act. The quality of their performance, however, is not here our concern. Nowhere is this hypothesis more relevant than in the study of the politics of decolonization in the Gold Coast.

II. PRE-TWENTIETH-CENTURY BACKGROUND:
THE GOLD COAST AND EUROPE TO 1900

The term "Gold Coast" was a name applied to a stretch of coast

---

[6] R. E. Robinson, "The Extra-European Dimensions of Imperialism," Seminar paper read at Makerere University, 1969 (unpublished).

in West Africa running from the vicinity of the Tano river
eastward to the Volta river. Strictly speaking, therefore, the Gold
Coast was precisely a coast along which Europeans had constructed forts for the purposes of trade. But it was also a region famous
for its gold deposits—hence the name "Gold Coast." The name was
never seriously meant to apply to the several hinterland states—
Fante, Asante, Dagomba, Banda, Mamprussi—which were annexed
piecemeal by Britain to form the colony and protectorate of the
Gold Coast. Like most contemporary European colonies in Africa,
the boundaries of the Gold Coast were artificial in the sense that
they were contemptuous of geographical and ethnic divisions. The
successor nation-state of Ghana inherited these colonial boundaries. Added to the new Ghana was also that portion of Togoland
which had been under British mandate since the defeat of
Germany in World War I.

Ghana is a small country. About the size of the British Isles or
one-fourth that of Nigeria, its population at the time of independence in 1957 numbered no more than five million. The
non-African population was a mere thirteen thousand, of whom
nine thousand were British. About 55 percent of the population
were Christian, 5 percent were Muslim, and the remaining 40
percent practiced various African religions. There were no European settlers in the Gold Coast because, unlike in Kenya, European ownership of land was forbidden. The European population
comprised mainly government officials and representatives of the
various European firms. This absence of European settlement
made the decolonization process much easier and much faster. For
in countries settled heavily by Europeans, there is the tendency of
these settlers to complicate our decolonization equation by
forming a prefabricated collaborating group which actively works
against African interests. The African nationalist in such a region,
confronted with two enemies all at once, has been forced to
employ other tactics in the politics of decolonization.

The Gold Coast came into contact with Europe in the fifteenth
century. Europeans, however, were not the first foreigners to visit
the country. The Carthaginian Admiral Hanno, for example, had
visited West Africa as early as 500 B.C. and had established trade
on a regular basis between West Africa and Carthage. The Gold
Coast came within the orbit of this trade. The Carthaginians
exchanged their cloth and beads for gold through the process of
what Herodotus called "dumb barter" or silent trade. Egyptian
traders were later involved in the gold trade and established small

commercial posts along the coast for this purpose. With the Roman conquest of Carthage and Egypt, their sea trade with West Africa came to an end; but the trans-Saharan caravan trade routes remained open.

The opening of the Euro-West African trade toward the close of the fifteenth century led to the decline in importance of the trans-Saharan trade. West Africa turned toward the sea. Europeans built a chain of forts along the Gold Coast for the purpose of conducting their trade in ivory, gold dust, spices, and slaves. Between the seventeenth and eighteenth centuries slaves had become the main focus of this trade. This was also the period of great prosperity. Between 1642 and 1803 the two dominant European powers in the Gold Coast were the Dutch and the English. Portugal, the first European power to establish a strong presence in this region, had been superseded by the Dutch after 100 years of settlement. The Dutch, indeed, had held a hegemony over the West African trade until the intervention of other European countries. England, particularly, employing the expedient of chartered companies, broke this hegemony by the close of the eighteenth century. Earlier the Danes (1642), Swedes (1647), and Brandenburgers (1682) had joined the competition. The Swedes, however, wound up their operations in 1661, the Brandenburgers in 1732, the Danes in 1850, and the Dutch in 1872. By the nineteenth century, then, Britain and France were the only major European powers in serious competition in West Africa. Within the Gold Coast itself, the British were, after 1872, without any foreign competitor.[7]

Britain achieved its dominant position through gradual and

---

[7] For general history of Gold Coast-European relations to the nineteenth century, the following works are recommended: Walter W. Claridge, *A History of the Gold Coast and Ashanti*, 2 vols. (London: John Murray, 1915); W. E. Ward, *A Short History of the Gold Coast* (London: Allen & Unwin, 1953); J. W. Blake, *Europeans in West Africa, 1450-1560*, 2 vols. (London: Hakluyt Society, 1942); Richard F. Burton and Verney L. Cameron, *To the Gold Coast for Gold* (London: Chatto & Windus, 1883); John D. Fage, *Ghana: A Historical Interpretation* (Wisconsin: University of Wisconsin Press, 1966, ed.), Chapters II and III, John D. Fage, "The Administration of George Maclean on the Gold Coast, 1830-44," *Trans. Gold Coast and Togoland Historical Society*, 1, 4 (1955): 104-20; George E. Metcalfe, "After Maclean: Some Aspects of British Gold Coast Policy in Mid-nineteenth Century," *Ibid.* 5(1955): 178-92; A. Adu Boahen, "Asante, Fante and the British, 1800-1880," in Jacob F. Ade Ajayi and Ian Espie (eds.), *A Thousand Years of West African History* (Ibadan and London: Ibadan University Press and Nelson, 1966), pp. 346-63. Historical documents covering a good deal of this period are printed in G. E. Metcalfe, (ed.), *Great Britain and Ghana: Documents of Ghana History, 1807-1957* (Accra and London: Nelson & Sons, Ltd., 1964).

consistent growth. This growth started with British involvement in the internal affairs of the Asante empire which led to the annexation of Southern Ghana in 1874, immediately following the ousting of the Dutch two years earlier. Up till 1821 British administration of the Gold Coast trading posts was the responsibility of chartered companies. The relationship between the merchants and the coastal states was a sort of equal partnership marked by rough friendship—a partnership which gradually cracked at the expense of the Africans. In 1821, therefore, the colonial office took direct control over the administration of the forts; but decline in trade, lack of progress in propagating Christianity and Western education, and mounting administrative expenses caused the British government to decide to withdraw altogether from Southern Ghana. This decision was strongly opposed by British merchants who feared that a British withdrawal would leave them as the easy prey of the mighty power of Asante which had already fought two engagements with British forces, winning the first and losing the second. A compromise was reached whereby the colonial office consented to hand over the administration of the forts to a Committee of British Merchants to whom it granted an annual subsidy of £4,000. Their jurisdiction, however, was strictly confined to the inhabitants of the forts. They were forbidden to interfere in the politics of the hinterland.[8]

The second chartered company administration lasted from 1828 to 1843 when the British government once more assumed direct responsibility of the forts. The relevant achievement of this administration from our point of view was the supplanting of Asante power and jurisdiction in the south by that of the British. There was by 1843, in effect, the existence of an undeclared British protectorate. Clearly, the Committee of Merchants had gone beyond their mandate. The success of this administration is largely credited to the policy of a young and dashing Scotsman called George Maclean who was chosen by the merchants to be their proconsul in the Gold Coast. Maclean's rule lasted from 1830 to 1844. During this period he extended British authority along all the coastal states and for some forty miles into the interior. The territories thus added to the Crown had, of course, no legal basis. What drove the government to intervene, however, were the series of charges of maladministration brought against Maclean's company, especially the charge of conniving at the slave trade. The

[8]Metcalfe, *Documents*, Chapters 4, 5, and 6.

Parliamentary Select Committee appointed to investigate these charges recommended the resumption of direct responsibility by the Crown, and the retention, under British suzerainty, of the territories illegally seized by Maclean.[9] Edward George Stanley (1799-1869), 14th Earl of Derby and British Colonial Secretary, did not accept the Committee's recommendation as a whole. But he did follow up the recommendation that Fante chiefs should be persuaded to accept British jurisdiction. Surprisingly—but understandably given the standing menace of Asante—a group of nineteen Fante chiefs signed the famous document known as the "Bond" of 1844 (Source 1) which alienated part of their sovereignty to the British Crown.

The importance of this document has been exaggerated by historians, nationalists, and politicians. It has come to be regarded as either the *Magna Carta* or the *Munich* of Ghana history depending, of course, on who was assessing it. In reality, the document was neither. It was not even a treaty but, as the name suggests, a "bond" executed by the chiefs "before his Excellency the Lieutenant-Governor." In short, the British were not a contracting party; it was a unilateral declaration by the chiefs concerned to accept British jurisdiction. In effect, they "were renouncing part of their sovereignty," writes J. D. Fage, "and, though this was but vaguely perceived at the time, converting their states into the semblance of a British protectorate, though one in which British authority was limited to judicial and police matters and did not legally extend into the sphere of administration."[10] It should be borne in mind that this curious document was signed primarily as a counterweight to Asante aggression; and that whatever its strengths and weaknesses, it represents formal British relationship with the Gold Coast and assured British authority on the coast. Maclean, demoted to the position of Judicial Assessor, worked hard on this job to extend British administration of Justice. He died in 1847 of malaria, but by the 1860s the English legal system had replaced African customary law in the coastal states. Administratively, too, progress was being made. The Gold Coast, hitherto administered together with Sierra Leone, became a separate dependency of the Crown in 1850.

The new administration built roads, hospitals, and schools as part of the policy of promoting Western civilization. But these were expensive undertakings which necessitated the policy of

[9] Metcalfe, *Documents*, Chapters 7, 8, and 9, especially nos. 116, 117, and 135.
[10] Fage, *Ghana: A Historical Interpretation*, pp. 74-75.

direct taxation as a means of raising revenue. This measure was especially necessary because the economy was growing sluggishly and trade had suffered a slump. But Africans, always viewing taxation as synonymous with loss of independence, vigorously opposed the government's Poll Tax Ordinance. A lot of unrest developed between the coastal states and British administrators. The most serious of these was the Christiansborg Revolt of 1854 when some coastal chiefs and elders "made a solemn compact never to pay tax again" and insulted the "honour of the British flag."[11] The revolt was vigorously suppressed in order "to make them feel the moral and physical superiority of the British Government."[12] Although the government suppressed the revolt, it found it difficult to collect the tax. Attempts to increase customs duties as a way of offsetting the financial losses arising from the failure of the Poll Tax Ordinance enraged British merchants who joined the Africans in their protests against government policy.

The major threats to British authority, however, came from the Asante. In March 1863 an Asante army invaded the Gold Coast, defeated the British in several engagements, and then withdrew triumphantly. If the British could not protect the Fante, what use was the "Bond" to them? It was, in part, as a move to demonstrate British capability of defending the Fante, that Governor Richard Pine in 1864 launched an offensive against Asante. The heavy rains took such a terrible toll of the soldiers that the expedition was called off. British prestige suffered a severe setback. The economic crisis, the Poll Tax imbroglio, and the mismanagement of the Asante Wars of 1863-4, drove the government to set up, in 1865, yet another Parliamentary Select Committee with instructions to look into the affairs of all the West African settlements and make recommendations. The Committee recommended, *inter alia*, the discouragement of further expansion of British authority in the Gold Coast; the pursuit of a policy which would lead to the "ultimate withdrawal from all [the West African territories] except probably Sierra Leone," and retrenchment in government expenditure.[13]

These recommendations were not heeded. Fante leaders became

---

[11] Quoted in David Kimble, *A Political History of Ghana: The Rise of Gold Coast Nationalism, 1850-1928* (London: Oxford University Press, 1963), p. 179.

[12] *Idem.*

[13] Parliamentary Papers, 1865, V(412), *Report of Select Committee on State of British Settlements on the West Coast of Africa*. Cf. also J. J. Crooks, *Records of the Gold Coast Settlements, 1750-1874* (Dublin: Browne & Nolan, 1923).

suspicious of the steady growth and entrenchment of British influence and jurisdiction. John Aggery, elected King of Cape Coast in January 1865, emerged as the leader of his people in protest against increasing British interference in their affairs. Determined to defy the British, he became particularly vocal after the Cape Coast riot of September 1865 involving drunken West Indian soldiers and the townspeople had resulted in the death of about three persons. King Aggery was accused of aiming "to set aside the sovereignty and the power of the Queen at Cape Coast Castle."[14] He was consequently deposed and deported to Sierra Leone in 1867. The interesting thing about this charge was that King Aggery could have brought it with more propriety against the British. The extent to which British jurisdiction had been extended since 1844 went beyond the limits set by the Bond.

In 1868 the Fante, partly in response to the spirit of coastal nationalism which had accelerated since King Aggery's accession to power, partly worried by Asante invasions southward, and partly as a consequence of the Anglo-Dutch exchange of forts in 1867, met at Mankessim to reflect on the future of their country. The result of their deliberations was the formation of the Fante Confederation which is generally accepted as marking the beginning of modern Ghana nationalism (Source 2). In 1869 the Confederation proclaimed its independence of Britain. It set up a Supreme Court and introduced a Poll Tax to defray administrative costs. In October 1871 the Mankessim Constitution containing forty-seven articles was published (Source 3). British authorities reacted swiftly to this challenge. The leaders were arrested, accused of treason, and imprisoned. They were released a month later on the order of the colonial secretary; but the confederacy disintegrated within the next two years. And in July 1874 the British government formally annexed the Gold Coast and turned it into a Crown colony.

Between 1874 and 1886 the Gold Coast was governed in union with the colony of Lagos. After 1886 it was once more separately administered until the union with Asante in 1901. Politically, the administration of the new colony progressed more or less smoothly until the end of the century. Here, the classic collaboration game was in operation. With the conquest of Southern Ghana, both the chiefs and the Western educated elite (henceforth

---

[14]C. O. 96/74, Carnarvon to Blackall, 23 February, 1867 quoted in Metcalfe, *Documents*, no. 258, p. 318. For details of King Aggery's revolt see *Ibid*, Chapter 18.

to be known as the "intelligentsia") struggled to make the best of the colonial situation. The spirit of Mankessim did not, however, die out completely, for the Fante Confederacy surfaced again, in the 1890s, as the Aborigines Rights Protection Society (henceforth ARPS) via the *Mfantsi Amanbuw Fekuw* (founded in 1889), a sort of cultural organization which had a lot of reverence for land as the cornerstone of communal existence.

The ARPS apparently drew some inspiration from the well-known humanitarian organization in London, the Aborigines Protection Society. It was the ARPS which successfully opposed the Public Lands Bill (1897) and which was largely responsible for the passage of the Concessions Ordinance (1900) which safeguarded African land tenure, thereby making it possible for Africans of the Gold Coast to escape the fate of the Kikuyu of Kenya. The membership of the ARPS included chiefs, businessmen, lawyers, doctors, and journalists. By 1912 it had a membership of 100 persons and until 1925 it was recognized by the British governor as the proper channel of African opinion. Clearly, the new organization was a much milder form of Fante nationalism than the Confederacy idea. Nevertheless, it was one of the earliest forms of political organization in black Africa.[15] Besides the ARPS, there mushroomed among the African intelligentsia who had flocked to the urban centers in this period several clubs and societies which served the purposes of expanding social contacts and fostering common interests. These associations helped to break down ethnic barriers and paved the way for the nationalism of later years.

To the north of the Gold Coast colony lived the Asante who, together with the Fante, form the Akan or Twi speaking people. These two groups make up more than 40 percent of the population of modern Ghana. By 1750 the Asante and the Fante had emerged as the two leading states in the Gold Coast. Asante had established a vast and fairly well-organized empire with its capital at Kumasi. Its king was called the Asantehene. The Fante, on the other hand, were made up of small states organized rather loosely. They had neither a king nor an acceptable overlord. By 1824 the Asante had achieved the complete conquest of the southern states, including Fanteland, and were, indeed, presiding over an empire larger than modern Ghana of which Asante now forms only a part.

---

[15] David E. Apter, *The Gold Coast in Transition* (Princeton, N.J.: Princeton University Press, 1955), p. 35.

It was the desire to recover their lost independence that forced the Fante to ally themselves with the British. Thus, the British were drawn into the Asante-Fante wars. Between 1823 and 1900 the Asante fought eight wars against the British and their Fante allies. It was these wars which were largely responsible for the disintegration of the Asante empire. The major blow, however, was delivered by the war of 1873-4. By the Fomena Treaty of 1874 the Asante were forced to renounce what remained of their sovereignty in the southern states which the Maclean Treaty of 1831, following the Asante defeat of 1826, had already greatly reduced. And after 1874, Britain adopted the deliberate policy of encouraging loyal components of the Asante empire to declare their independence of Kumasi. British policy toward the Asante, as the governor of the Gold Coast put it in October 1875, was the breaking "up of Ashanti into two or more tribes who would be independent of each other."[16] During the reign of Kwaku Dua III, popularly known as King Prempeh I, the Asante strove to counteract the effects of this policy with some measure of success. In reality, then, the period between 1883 and 1895 in Asante history was one of revival rather than of decline. In 1896 Britain invaded Kumasi and occupied it without serious opposition. King Prempeh was captured and exiled to the Seychelles Island in the Indian Ocean; in 1900 Britain achieved the complete conquest of Asante. By an imperial Order-in-Council of September 26, 1901, Asante was annexed to the British Crown as a state "conquered by Her Majesty's forces."[17] It was proclaimed a protectorate and not a colony. Another Order-in-Council of the same date annexed the Northern Territories of the Gold Coast.[18] These three regions made up the British colony and protectorate of the Gold Coast. Thus, the simple relationship, based on trade, between Britain and the coastal states since the fifteenth century, had ended in British conquest and domination.

III. THE AGE OF CRITICISM AND REASON, 1901-1945

By 1901 the "new imperialism" had triumphed in the Gold

---

[16] Quoted in Boahen, "Asante, Fante and the British," *loc. cit.*, p. 358.

[17] *Parliamentary Papers*, 1901 (Cd. 501) xlviii, Hodgson to C. O. 29 January, 1901. no. 79.

[18] See Metcalfe, *Documents*, no. 437, pp. 523-4; c.f. G. N. Uzoigwe, *Britain and the Conquest of Africa: The Age of Salisbury* (Ann Arbor: University of Michigan Press, 1974), pp. 90-92.

Coast as elsewhere in Africa. The triumph, however, was still superficial and precarious and time was needed for its consolidation. The African intelligentsia, discontented and frustrated, yet had sufficient confidence in themselves and in the vitality of their institutions under the impact of the European presence to believe that the conquest was bound to be a temporary affair. "The foreigner comes and goes," the *Lagos Standard* of July 11, 1906, comforted its readers; "that he must do if he means to abide here long; but the native has it all to himself. He stays on forever . . . ." During the interwar years this confidence was largely eroded. The rump of what may be called nationalist organizations had become conservative, having fallen prey to a British policy of faction and client making. Attracted by the lure of office and other ophelimities accruing from loyalty to the imperial superstructure, they did not demand independence for the Gold Coast but indulged in mild and reasoned criticism of British overrule.

The genius of colonialism is its ability to manufacture collaborators and use them for its own purposes. Since the Bond of 1844, British officials had indulged in this game of collaboration and client making. They had built schools and churches not only with the aim of propagating European civilization and demonstrating its superiority to African civilization, but also as part of this process. They built roads, increased trade, erected magnificent houses, founded exclusive clubs, and led a sophisticated way of life which was the envy of the few African intelligentsia who were the products of European institutions. Even before the beginning of the twentieth century, British officials had made it possible for bright young men from the colony to study in Britain. The Africans of the colony displayed amazing receptivity to the opportunity offered them; to be educated in England became the ambition of many prominent families. This process had its roots, not in the nineteenth century, but in the early years of the European contact. The Africans had not demanded this type of education. It was the missionaries who rammed it down their throats. After initial opposition to missionary programs, the Africans came to realize that the ability to read and write largely accounted for the Europeans' domination over them, and were anxious to acquire as much of this knowledge as possible.

Unfortunately, colonial education owed nothing to African antecedents, for it would have defeated its purpose had that been the case. Its aim had been, in part, to destroy the foundations of African systems of thought believed to be "barbarous." It was also a literary sort of education which, as an educated Ghanaian chief put it, filled boys' heads "with stuff which they did not understand, much less apply. . . . As we were taught, so did we teach."[19] Education, nevertheless, offered Africans better jobs, released them from manual labour, gave them the opportunity to visit Europe, and increased their prestige and authority among their less fortunate comrades. It did not therefore matter to them what they studied provided they studied something which would elevate their status in society. The result of these developments was that by the turn of the century, the Gold Coast boasted of a sizeable Western-educated elite, urbane in outlook, sophisticated in politics, and reasoned in their arguments for the nationalist cause. They became preposterously arrogant and consequently alienated themselves not only from the chiefs but from the masses as well. They had proved to be extraordinarily teachable in European ways, much to the chagrin of those Britons who seriously believed that Africans were an unteachable lot. The arrogance of the African intelligentsia made matters worse. Thus, throughout the second half of the nineteenth century, European officials and traders heaped abuses on them. "The educated natives," they claimed, were "the curse of the West Coast." They were utterly distrusted and made the scapegoat for colonial difficulties.

And yet since the 1850s the government had adopted the development of African education as official policy. Between 1850 and 1919 elementary education expanded significantly. By 1919 the total enrollment in elementary schools was 27,318 including 4,600 girls; the average attendance was 21,928; and the Grants-in-Aid from the government totalled £6,599.[20] Before 1876 post elementary education was available, for those who could afford it, primarily in England and to a lesser extent in Sierra Leone. Study abroad broadened their horizons and sharpened their criticisms of the government. But it also brought the criticism that foreign education alienated Africans from their own people. Between 1876 and 1919, therefore, a conscious effort was made, largely through African and missionary initiative, to expand secondary education in the Gold Coast. Only the few privileged African families could afford university education. These were not wanting in the Gold Coast, and by the dawn of the

[19] Nana Annor Adjaye, *Nzima Land* (London, 1931), cited in Kimble, *Political History of Ghana* p. 61.
[20] Kimble, *Political History of Ghana*, p. 78.

twentieth century, the Gold Coast had produced more of this class than either Sierra Leone or Nigeria, their nearest rivals.

The government and commercial firms had good reasons for not obstructing African education. For them it was a necessary evil. They needed Africans in the government service, in schools, in churches, and in the commercial firms. The alternative would have been a massive importation of Britons to perform these functions. But the British empire was worldwide and there were not enough Britons to go round. Even if there were, West Africa had a low priority in terms of European settlement largely because of its notoriety in European literature as the "white man's grave." Moreover, the colonial government was still militarily weak and badly needed African collaboration. When, therefore, from the 1870s the African intelligentsia began to be more vocal in their demands for advancement, the government had reluctantly to meet their demands. It was at this stage that color discrimination began to play a serious part in Euro-African relations. Africans were becoming competitors rather than inferiors. Colonial educational aims appeared to have been misconceived. Terms such as "discontented and unprincipled natives, principally mulattoes and semi-educated blacks (who appear to be an evil inseparable from all negro communities)",[21] scribbled in official documents as early as the 1850s and 1860s began to be more openly heard. The term "educated native" increasingly became a joke in British circles; their claim to African leadership was equally ridiculed. Thus in 1909 Sir John Rodger noted, with great insight, that Britain, having through the process of its educational system turned out "black and brown Englishmen" in large numbers, turned round to curse "the finished article when the operation is complete."[22]

This was perhaps inevitable, for, as the government had suspected, the Western-educated African, far from being an obedient "Uncle Tom," was arrogantly becoming an ambitious one. He saw himself as the natural ruler of his people in the new age. The government reacted to this challenge by playing another card in the collaboration game, namely, the demotion or deposition of collaborators who became too big for their boots in such a way as to avoid a mass revolt and their replacement by other interest groups who could be more easily managed. Thus it was that

[21] Quoted in *Ibid*, p. 39, f.n.1.
[22] *The African Mail*, July 9, 1909.

between 1897 and 1920 the government carefully excluded most of the African intelligentsia from public office, cut off patronage entirely except for the very few, and effectively frustrated their aspirations. And although elementary and secondary education continued to expand, opportunities for study abroad for higher degrees were correspondingly being closed. At the same time, the government deliberately raised standards for official appointments. Europeanization of the public service progressed apace; de-Africanization was carried out with a vengeance. This was made possible because by the beginning of the twentieth century the balance of military power in the Gold Coast was decisively in Britain's favour. It was also becoming easier for Britons to accept appointments in the tropics since medical research had improved health conditions in such climates. Of 274 senior civil service officers listed in 1908 only five were Africans. It also soon became clear that many of the newly recruited Britons were of doubtful quality. This led the great Casely-Hayford to complain that "Patronage" and not ability or qualification "rules the day at Downing Street."[23]   Indeed, when Sir Hugh Clifford became governor of the Gold Coast in 1912, he was bluntly told by the African intelligentsia that prior to his arrival "the educated natives, especially the lawyers, were beginning to entertain the fear ... that they were not wanted in the country."[24] During the war years little was done to redress their grievances.

It would be wrong to assume that during this period the rump of the old Gold Coast elite—products of the nineteenth century— had been completely eclipsed. Far from it. But they no longer were an important political power group. Concentrated mainly in the colony, they still managed to perpetuate their class. Protected by the legal classification of British subjects, and shielded by the umbrella of English law, they could form political associations, practice law, run newspapers, and mildly criticize the government in the same way that His Majesty's loyal opposition did in Britain. Such luxuries were not permitted to those who resided in the protectorates. Led by Casely-Hayford, they formed a class by themselves and made no serious efforts to enlarge their number. For the most part they ignored the masses and were ignored by them. Indeed, by the end of World War I, they had decided to

[23] Joseph E. Casely-Hayford, *Gold Coast Native Institutions* (London: Sweet & Maxwell, 1903), p. 218.

[24] Quoted in Kimble, *Political History of Ghana*, p. 100.

come to terms with colonialism but reserved for themselves the function of being its watchdog. They pleaded for colonial amelioration and protested against colonial excesses in urbane and polished phrases. The African press, which only a handful of Africans could read, was their greatest instrument. They also still dominated the ARPS, but by 1918 that organization had lost touch with public opinion, had become close to the administration, and thus was politically dead as a nationalist weapon. The government rewarded them for their loyalty by allowing them to monopolize the few nominated seats allocated to Africans in the Legislative Council (henceforth Legco).

And yet many of these early nationalists were great men any society in the world would have been proud to have raised. Among them was John Mensah Sarbah (1864-1910), C.M.G., barrister-at-law, great statesman, scholar and jurist who led the Gold Coast elite until his death in 1910. His *Fanti Customary Laws,* first published in 1897, is a brilliant attempt to use a sociological and legal work to serve nationalist ends without offending the imperial overlord. In his *Fanti National Constitution* (1906), he defends African backwardness in relation to Europe, stresses once more the importance of traditional African institutions, and urges more African participation in government.

There was the inimitable Joseph Ephraim Casely-Hayford (1866-1930). Teacher, journalist, lawyer, statesman, disciple of Edward Blyden, he was an intellectual and philosopher *par excellence.* He succeeded Sarbah in 1910 to the elite leadership of the Gold Coast. In three important works he attempted to find a solution to the dilemmas of the African elite brought about by the new imperialism. His *Gold Coast Native Institutions* (1903), while emphasizing the importance of these institutions, called for "a healthy imperial policy for the Gold Coast and Ashanti." His *Ethiopia Unbound* (1911) has been described as "an intellectual autobiography in the form of a novel that sought to rally negroes throughout the world in defence of their culture, institutions and racial integrity." In 1915 he wrote his *William Waddy Harris, the West African Reformer, the Man and his Message.* This is a religious work, being the life of the itinerant Grebo prophet and preacher, whose mass oratory and charismatic leadership fascinated Casely-Hayford. We watch him, after this book, moving cautiously away from defensive middle-class nationalism to West African populism. In 1919, he founded the National Congress of British West Africa. Its first conference was held in Accra in 1920.

The Congress became the organ of English speaking West Africa, demanding colonial amelioration rather than self-government. Its delegation to England to press this demand was frustrated by the embittered West African colonial governors who persuaded their government that the chiefs, not the intelligentsia, spoke for the people. Nothing was achieved in London then or even thereafter. In the 1920s the Congress became very snobbish, ridiculously elitist, and conservative. In the Gold Coast, its members went so far as to entertain the governor, and as a result its credibility as an instrument of effective decolonization was lost. It was Casely-Hayford himself who emphasized the elitist character of the movement, thereby destroying the traditional alliance of the intelligentsia and chiefs characterized by the old ARPS. Some chiefs rallied round the very influential chief Nana Ofori Atta and attacked the Congress. The British deliberately encouraged these divisions in the hope that the Congress would die as a result. When Casely-Hayford died in 1930 the Congress died with him.

Besides Sarbah and Casely-Hayford, there were several important publicists and patriots engaged in this sort of middle-class nationalism. A good representative of this group was the Reverend Samuel Richard Brew Attoh Ahuma (1863-1921). Rhetoric was his forte. His *Gold Coast Nation and National Consciousness* (1911) was an exuberant call for the recognition of a Gold Coast nation along the line demarcated by the imperialist powers. Less restrained and dignified than either Sarbah or Casely-Hayford, he was nevertheless full of praises for that "highest organized form of government in creation" (the British empire) under whose "one umbrageous flag—a flag that is the symbol of justice, freedom, and fair play" the Gold Coast was being welded together.[25]

Clearly, one characteristic of the nationalism of this period was its lack of militancy, its lack of appeal to the masses, its middle-class and conservative orientation, and its profession of loyalty to the British crown. Given this sort of situation, the colonial administration had little to worry about. The individuals British officials were dealing with were "gentlemen," forming a class by themselves and apart from the common folk for whom their language had no meaning. They were no cynics, no embittered and hardened nationalists, but individuals who stoutly believed in the efficacy of British justice and fair play which they

---

[25] See pp. 1-11; cf. Henry S. Wilson (ed.), *Origins of West African Nationalism* (London: Macmillan; New York: St. Martins Press, 1969), p. 267.

naively hoped would, in the distant future, surrender the mantle of authority to themselves as the legitimate heirs to the colonial administration. Another factor in the government's favor was the economic expansion which characterized the period between 1902 and 1913 which, with its increased prosperity, did not create a conducive climate for militant colonial agitation. The outbreak of World War I afforded the intelligentsia and the chiefs the opportunity to demonstrate their loyalty to the crown.

In 1916, the government, feeling quite secure, increased African representation in the Legco to six. They were all unofficial members nominated by the governor from among those loyal to the administration. The rest of the Council included eleven officials and the governor (all British). The Legco had been established in the Gold Coast in 1850. Its duty was to advise the governor with respect to local opinion for legislative and budgetary decisions. The governor was its president and all his advisers were "gentlemen." The first African representative to the Council was James Bannerman, a mulatto and wealthy merchant, who was one of its foundation members. In 1850-51, Bannerman was the acting governor of the colony and consequently the first president of the Council. The first African member of unmixed blood was appointed in 1861. He was G. K. Blankson, another wealthy merchant. But as a result of the exclusion policy adopted toward the African intelligentsia, African representation in the Council grew very slowly. By 1901 it included only two Africans, one of whom was J. M. Sarbah. Governor Clifford's action in 1916 was therefore hailed as a great constitutional advance. Indeed, the political aim of the ARPS since the 1890s had been the democratization of the Legco, the influence of which as a colonial legislature was overvalued. It must be pointed out that before 1946 the Legco had no competence beyond the colony. In other words, it had no representations from Asante and the Northern Territories, for whom the governor legislated directly.

Guggisberg and the Politics of Indirect Rule, 1919-1927

So far the colonial government was firmly seated in the saddle. No serious attempts had been made to rock the boat. The masses were ignored but had remained remarkably quiet. No serious attention had been paid to the chiefs and they had created no trouble for the government. The arrogant intelligentsia had been quietly tamed. But the government was aware that the intelligentsia were still capable of some mischief. A new policy had therefore to be adopted. In 1919 Sir Gordon Guggisberg, former army engineer and an unemployed brigadier-general since the close of World War I, succeeded Sir Hugh to the governorship of the Gold Coast. Sir Gordon devised several ambitious programs for the country's development and appeared to be revising the anti-elitist policy of his predecessors. But he soon ran into difficulties with the elite because of his arrogant conviction that he knew more than anyone else what was best for the country. As he discovered to his chagrin, his priorities were precisely the reverse of the Gold Coast intelligentsia's.

Consequently, the new governor turned to the chiefs for support. It was Guggisberg who, by working in partnership with the chiefly classes, first introduced the principle of indirect rule in the Gold Coast. This policy, by implication, meant that the chiefs were the legitimate leaders of the masses—the role which the intelligentsia had carved out for themselves. Indeed, if the progressive leadership of the African masses was not their role, what then was the use of them! Thus was created a rivalry between the chiefs and the intelligentsia for leadership in the Gold Coast. The new chiefly collaborators soon came to be dismissed by the intelligentsia as lackeys of colonialism who should be destroyed. A situation like this always worked in favor of the colonizer. Here was a classic example of divide and rule. It was clear to the government that the intelligentsia were politically impotent because the masses found their language incomprehensible. The chiefs, on the contrary, still wielded considerable influence. It was also clear that colonialism would succeed so long as the masses were kept in control. The chiefs, not the intelligentsia, were better equipped to perform this function. The intelligentsia therefore were expendable; the chiefs were not—at least, not yet.

In the strict sense, Guggisberg's system of government was an amalgam of indirect rule through the chiefs and direct authority exercised by the governor although he showed preference toward the former system.[26] This is not surprising because colonial proconsuls ideally aimed to concern themselves with high affairs of state, thereby avoiding any headlong collision with their various puppets and traditional structures. Chiefs, under indirect rule, were left to do the dirty work for the colonial administration. Sooner or later, they incurred the opprobrium of the various interest groups among their so-called subjects. The masses, while

---

[26] *Annual Report on the Gold Coast* (1931-1932), p. 4.

indifferent to the intelligentsia during this period, steadily became more distrustful of the chiefs as agents of colonial rule. The colonial administrators, by not getting directly involved with local issues, seemed to stand above these local squabbles. They were seen—and wished to be seen—as arbitrators and peacemakers. And yet, most of the so-called chiefs were mere executors of central government policies. The problem then arises whether, in fact, it is really correct to speak of indirect rule when, in the final analysis, no local policy seriously opposed by the colonial government had any chance of success.[27]

At the apex of the colonial administration in the Gold Coast was the governor. Below him, in descending order of hierarchy, were the Executive and Legislative Councils. Both were advisory bodies to the governor in the direct government of the colony. There was also the colonial senior civil service made up of a class of technical experts and political officers who wielded a lot of influence, and without whom colonial administration would have been inoperative.[28] It was they who supervised the chiefs and recommended their promotion or demotion either for alleged incompetence or overt disloyalty. These developments were not lost sight of by the masses. Before the imposition of European rule, the king or the chief was the highest authority in the land. Now, under colonial rule, it was obvious that real power lay elsewhere.

In 1920 Guggisberg expanded the new-style Legco to include eleven official and nine unofficial members. The unofficial members included three chiefs, three members of the intelligentsia from the colony, and three European merchants. They were all directly appointed by the governor. No militant nationalist had any chance of serving in such a body. The government preserved its majority in the Council, which therefore did not really have any power. It was, however, allowed to discuss government

---

[27]For discussions of indirect rule in the Gold Coast see, for example, Gordon Guggisberg, "The Goal of the Gold Coast," *Journal of the African Society* XXI, LXXXII (January 1922): 81-91; W. Ormsby-Gore, "The Meaning of 'Indirect Rule' ", *Journal Royal African Society* 34 (July 1935): 283-86; Ransford Slater, "The Gold Coast of Today," *Ibid* 27, 108 (July 1928): 321-28; R. S. Rattray, "Present Trendencies of African Colonial Government," *Journal Royal African Society* 33, 130 (January 1934): 22-36; A. Victor Murray, "Education Under Indirect Rule," *Ibid.* 27, 36 (July 1935): 227-68; C. Thurston Shaw, "Further Difficulties of Indirect Rule in the Gold Coast," *Man* 45, 20 (March-April 1945): 27-30; F. Agbodeka, "Nationalism in the Gold Coast, 1900-1954," *Tarikh* 3, 4(1971): 22-32.

[28]This was Lord Lugard's view—see Frederick D. Lugard, *The Dual Mandate in British Tropical Africa* (Edinburgh: Wm Blackwood & Sons, 1926), p. 128.

legislation publicly. The intelligentsia, naturally, were not enthusiastic about these changes.

When their disquietude became obvious, the governor, observing that the "time had come for giving Africans greater and better representation," initiated certain measures which he hoped would make all concerned happy.[29] The first was the Municipal Corporations Bill (1924) which provided for an elected majority in the newly created Municipal Councils. The Council was empowered to govern the municipality and pursue policies approved by the government. The franchise was given only to those who owned a house or rented one at the value of £5. This was a kind of indirect rule without the chiefs. It was supported by the intelligentsia but was reluctantly shelved when the poorer masses ferociously attacked it. Thus, Guggisberg's attempt to placate the intelligentsia by giving them something to do had failed. On April 8, 1925, therefore, he introduced a new constitution which is known as the *Guggisberg Constitution* in which he established, for the first time, the principle of direct elections in the provinces. The constitution created provincial councils of chiefs which not only served as electoral colleges electing six unofficial African members to the newly reconstructed Legco but were also intended to serve as forums where African opinion could be given expression. To avoid the total alienation of the intelligentsia who lived primarily in the municipalities of Accra, Cape Coast, and Sekondi—where incipient nationalism was gradually developing—the new constitution provided for the election of three African unofficial members to the Legco by the ratepayers of these municipalities. It also provided for the election of five unofficial European members, thus bringing the total of unofficials to fourteen. The government's official representation was accordingly increased to fifteen, excluding the governor.[30] The unofficials were regarded by the governor as partners in government rather than as providing a loyal opposition. The government never seriously hid its conviction that the idea of a Legco was undemocratic and benevolently paternalistic. In reality, the Legco exercised little authority and the government usually got its way. "The theory of a Legislative Council with an official majority," writes Martin Wight, "is that of a morally homogeneous advisory body. Its subordination to the

[29] Quoted in F. M. Bourret, *Ghana: The Road to Independence* (Stanford, Calif.: Stanford University Press and London: Oxford University Press, 1960), p. 41.

[30] See Gordon Guggisberg, *The Gold Coast: A Review of Events of 1920-1926 and the Prospects of 1927-1928* (Accra: Govt. Printer, 1927).

executive government is its primary feature, its composition only secondary; and the organization of the party system would be as improper as it is unnecessary."[31] The intelligentsia, convinced that it was government policy to work in partnership with the chiefs and to leave them out in the cold, opposed the constitution but lacked sufficient influence to ensure its demise. Guggisberg's public defence of his constitution amply justified their fears. He bluntly rejected the intelligentsia's desire for a parliamentary system of government which would have given them more influence at the expense of the chiefs. As the *Gold Coast Leader* of May 22, 1926 put it: "The issue is one of life and death with us, for if you perpetuate the possibility of the return of dummies [chiefs] to the Legislature, our national independence is gone forever. Probably that is what has been aimed at all the time, to so gag the people that while they have a machinery obstensibly of an advanced type, yet to be truly and really voiceless in the affairs of their country." The newspaper was perfectly correct but the majority of the chiefs, including some western-educated elite from chiefly families such as Dr. J. B. Danquah and Nana Sir Afori Atta, favored the constitution. The government had, in David Apter's words, moved "to bolster the waning support of the chiefs and to avoid incipient nationalism by building a more representative system based partly on the traditional democracy of the Gold Coast tribal system." [32] It must, however, be stressed that the constitution applied only to the colony.

Guggisberg's system of indirect rule was a temporary victory for the government in the politics of decolonization. While the masses, and, to a lesser extent, the chiefs had been able to kill the Municipal Corporations Bill, the intelligentsia were powerless to kill the 1925 Constitution which ostensibly favoured the chiefs. More importantly, Guggisberg managed to end the alliance between the chiefs and the intelligentsia formed in the 1890s but which, since the formation of Casely-Hayford's National Congress of West Africa (opposed by the chiefs), had been experiencing severe strains. The chiefs were now listened to with more respect and courtesy by the government, which regarded them "as the repositories of Gold Coast wisdom." Honors usually reserved for His Majesty's loyal and faithful subjects were showered on them; their advice on local

---

[31] Martin Wight, *The Gold Coast Legislative Council* (London: Faber & Faber, 1947), quoted in Apter, *Gold Coast in Transition*, p. 137.
[32] Apter, *Gold Coast in Transition*, p. 133.

affairs came to be usually accepted; their claim (in many cases justified) as the legitimate ruling African aristocracy was enhanced; and for the colonial authorities, they were the undisputed spokesmen for the African masses. And because the traditional African system of government was supposed to be democratic, it was sincerely believed by the government that indirect rule was the best means of keeping in touch with African public opinion. The intelligentsia furiously denied these assumptions but they were benignly ignored. The government made it perfectly clear that it preferred what it called the "orderly progress" of chiefly rule to the lugubrious vaticinations of a few ambitious intelligentsia.

And yet, it was obvious that indirect rule was a good example of "government by seduction." It would be wrong, however, to regard the chiefly collaborators as being necessarily on the side of the colonizers during the independence struggle. There was, on the contrary, a struggle between the chiefs and the intelligentsia for leadership in the Gold Coast when, and if, independence came. The chiefs, indeed, were fighting for survival as a class and naturally allied themselves to the power (in this case, the colonial government) which appeared to them to be well disposed toward their interests. By appearing deferential to the authorities as well as enthusiastic in their new roles, they hoped to manipulate the colonizers into granting them more authority and influence over their African subjects as a whole. Far from being traitors to their people, they were playing for high stakes and the government knew it. But as long as they could prevent a mass revolt against colonialism, the government played along with them. Moreover, should they prove too big for their new boots, the government could easily change the rules of the game and restore the discontented intelligentsia to favor. In the meantime, it was good colonial politics to discredit the intelligentsia in the eyes of the masses, turn chiefs against intelligentsia, and watch the drama in amused satisfaction.

The intelligentsia, frustrated and powerless, did not preach the overthrow of colonialism but resorted to reasoned criticism of colonial rule which they usually "rounded off . . .by a declaration of loyalty to Empire."[33] The intelligentsia, however, were right on one point: indirect rule, whatever its strengths and weaknesses,

---

[33] Martin Wight, *Legislative Council*, quoted in T. Peter Omari, *Kwame Nkrumah: The Anatomy of an African Dictatorship* (London: C. Hurst & Company, 1970), p. 21.

did not operate in the idiom of nationalism and was, in the final analysis, prejudicial to nationalist aspirations. By relying on indirect rule in sustaining the politics of collaboration, both the British and the chiefs proved, in the end, to be too clever by half, a point noted by R.S. Rattray with much propriety. "In introducing indirect rule in this country," he warned fellow officials, "we would therefore appear to be encouraging on the one hand an institution which draws its inspiration and validity from the indigenous religious beliefs, while on the other we are systematically destroying the very foundation upon which the structure that we are striving to perpetuate stands. Its shell and outward form might remain, but it would seem too much to expect that its vital energy could survive such a process."[34] It did not survive for long. British officials' desire to devise a new structural synthesis—indirect rule—from the clash of European and African norms served only to confuse role differentiation, created tension, and gradually led to the weakening of authority and influence on the part of the chiefs. Indeed, by the end of World War II, many of the chiefs had used up most of their credits with their subjects. They were increasingly portrayed as imperialist lackeys although, unlike their contemporaries in Buganda, they still retained sufficient influence to keep their part of the bargain. In other words, mass revolt against the Gold Coast chiefs was slow in coming. But come it did. By the 1950s the revolt of the masses under the leadership of Kwame Nkrumah had driven them into oblivion.

Period of Transition, 1928-1945

The period between 1928 and 1945 saw the groundwork for the revolt against colonialism. It is characterized by the rise of Youth Associations, literary and discussion groups, and local coalitions which carried on political agitation primarily through the African press and in spite of the chiefs. Their membership was drawn from the products of the various mission and government schools, particularly from Achimota College set up by Guggisberg in the 1920s. The young intelligentsia of the 1930s belonged to a different generation from that of Sarbah and Casely-Hayford. They appeared, on the average, less well educated, less sophisticated, and less urbane in their prose than their seniors. Given to rhetoric and rabble-rousing, they significantly failed to form large

---

[34] Quoted in Apter, *Gold Coast in Transition*, pp. 140-41.

political organizations capable of attracting the illiterate masses to their ranks. They, too, did not preach the overthrow of colonialism and may be described as moderate nationalists. They, however, rejected the conservatism of the older intelligentsia and appeared more willing to interest the rank and file in their type of politics. Indeed, they had a broader conception with respect to the solution of Gold Coast problems than the earlier organizations.

The most influential group of these new types of coalitions was the *Youth Movement* which had a wider appeal than such earlier organizations as the ARPS and the National Congress. This movement probably drew its inspiration from the Nigerian Youth League organized by Professor Eyo Ita in 1932. The Gold Coast variety was formed by Dr. J.B. Danquah in 1938. It was called the Gold Coast Youth Conference and published a pamphlet entitled *First Steps toward a National Fund* (Accra,1938) which recognized the Asante Confederacy Council, the ARPS, and the Joint Provincial Council of chiefs as the legitimate agents of authority in the country. This was an important step toward mending the breach between the intelligentsia and the chiefs. This is not surprising because Danquah was both from a chiefly family and a member of the intelligentsia. Its main thrust, however, was the issue of race. The pamphlet admonished the youth of the country to stop their habit of aping the Europeans and disdaining African standards and life styles. "Neither the integrity nor ability nor the spirit of cooperation," it wrote, "is wanting in the African. The youth of the country does not believe that these calumnies are true of the Africans as such, or of the Europeans as such, for that matter. Individuals may prove themselves dishonest, incompetent, self-centred and vain not because they are Africans but because they have been so brought up. Heredity alone is not responsible for what an individual turns out to be in society; environment counts for much, and the social milieu, and it is the duty of the country's leaders to improve the environment and the conditions of the social balance in which the growing child must weigh his future possibilities." This is the language of national awakening but hardly one of revolution. Nothing was said of decolonization or indeed of colonialism.

In 1941 the movement published its Youth Manifesto which had political, economic and social objectives.[35] Politically it

---

[35] Rita Hinden, "Africans in Conclave," *New Statesman and Nation* (September 6, 1941), pp. 226-27.

sought a clear African majority in Legco; an elected majority in the Executive Council; a majority of African mayors in the municipal councils; increased opportunities for Africans in the civil service, the appointments of whom should be made by a Selection Board with African majority membership. Economically, it desired the expansion of the economy to reduce reliance on one export crop—cocoa; industrialization to minimize heavy dependence on European imported food and household goods; the heavy taxation of European-owned mines in order to increase local revenues; reduction in the high interest payments on foreign loans and pensions paid to retired European officials; the fostering of the cooperative movement; a government subsidy to local producers; protected tariffs and capital advances for the purchase of machinery and equipment. Socially it demanded free primary education, the schools to be controlled by the government; 60 percent government support for running all approved high schools; pensions for all teachers to be the government's responsibility; state control of all hospitals, which would treat all serious tropical diseases entirely free; and payment of medical officers manning these hospitals to be sufficiently high so that they did not have to charge private fees to make ends meet. This enlightened and expensive manifesto with its socialist orientation was, in effect, demanding self-government for the Gold Coast and what it called the creation of "a new and better social order for the Gold Coast people." Such proposals had, of course, no hope of success. That its authors believed that such concessions were possible without organized political action showed their ignorance of colonial politics. One thing the movement achieved, however, was the temporary bridging of the gulf between the chiefs and the non-chiefly intelligentsia. Indeed, the attendance at its conference held in April 1941 included paramount chiefs from the provinces of whom some were illiterate and many more barely literate. In attendance also were those Africans educated in Europe and America who practiced their various professions in the Gold Coast.

The literary and other groups which mushroomed in this period had a narrower appeal than the youth movements, for they were mainly concerned with the betterment of their particular interest groups. The Achimota Discussion Group formed in the 1930s, for example, pressed for the admission of capable Africans into the senior civil service. Other coalitions with narrow interests, but still politically significant, included the various literary clubs, the

Ratepayers Association, the Gold Coast Farmers Association, the Agricultural and Commercial Society, the Trade Unions, the Boy Scout organizations, and other solidarity groups.

The characteristic of these groupings was that they operated not in the idiom of the Africans but in that of the westernizers. As David Apter put it: "Wooed and accepted by liberal British educators, they discussed Gold Coast problems long and earnestly. An intellectual elite emerged, often divorced, as far as social habits were concerned, from the less well-educated youth and the larger social organizations of the tribe."[36] But no leader emerged with both the foresight and charisma to consolidate them into a political party, broaden their appeal to the masses, and turn them into a revolutionary force for the decolonization process. The revolutionary elements were present. The various cocoa hold-ups[37] (strikes organized for better pay and better working conditions by holding up cocoa production) during the hard years of the 1930s, the riots, strikes, faction fights, disputes which usually erupted into violence, and the various acts of disobedience against the paramount chiefs show conclusively that the Gold Coast was in ferment. But there was no revolutionary leadership available to exploit the situation. The attempt of these moderate nationalists to press for the unity of the colony, Asante, and the Northern Territories which led to the formation in 1933 of the Central National Committee of the Gold Coast failed because of lack of organized and sustained pressure. They were deftly bribed into silence and the committee which would have formed the basis of a political party collapsed.

The government also acted swiftly in an attempt to nip this rising nationalism in the bud. In 1939, the 1925 Constitution was amended to enable individuals other than chiefs to be eligible for election to the Legco by the Provincial Councils. This amendment would appear to be a sop to the sensibilities of the intelligentsia since it removed the legal disability which precluded them from larger representation in the Legco. In practice, however, only sympathetic (to the chiefs) professional men had any chance of election by these Provincial Councils. In 1942 the colonial office took the further step of appointing two loyal Africans to the Executive Council, thus allowing Africans to participate, for the

---

[36] Apter, *Gold Coast in Transition*, p. 130.
[37] For a study of some of these cocoa problems see Sam Rhodie, "The Gold Coast Cocoa Hold-up of 1930-1931," in *Transactions Hist. Soc. of Ghana* IX (1968): 105-18.

first time, in the highest policy-making body of the Gold Coast. And in 1944 approval was given to Asante representation in the Legco. These constitutional developments were, however, not enthusiastically greeted by the intelligentsia, who felt that African representatives in these councils were either chiefs or those generally known to be loyal to the colonial administration.

IV. THE AGE OF REVOLUTION:
NKRUMAH AND POPULAR PARTICIPATION IN POLITICS, 1946-1951

By 1945 the British were still riding most of the political horses in the Gold Coast. Only the most progressive of the colonial officials entertained thoughts of granting independence to the country after a political apprenticeship of some further fifty years or even more. Events in the next few years gave them a bad jolt. As the war was drawing to an end, Sir Alan Burns, the governor (1941-47), perhaps sensing that some trouble lay ahead, decided to introduce a new constitution which he hoped would stem the tide of revolution. This new constitution, known as the *Alan Burns Constitution* of 1946, was the major constitutional advance in the Gold Coast since 1925. It was worked out after consultations with the Joint Provincial Council, the Asante Confederacy Council, and the Municipalities. Its main importance is that it made the Gold Coast the first colony in sub-Saharan Africa to be granted an elected official majority in the Legco. Its composition, however, was not democratic and the African unofficial majority turned out to be mere window dressing since they had no power to change government policy. More importantly, the constitution did not disturb the comfortable official majority enjoyed by the more influential Executive Council which was not responsible to the Legco.[38]

The constitution was indeed "outmoded at birth." It spoke the language of the Gold Coast nationalists of the 1920s. But many changes, internal and external, had taken place since the 1920s that had rendered Burns's ideas anachronistic. It was no wonder then that the nationalists of 1946 opposed it and agitated for its overthrow. And yet, for Britons interested in colonial affairs it was a very bold step toward self-government. The gulf between the ruling and the ruled was such that the strong opposition this

[38] See Martin Wight, *Legislative Council*, Appendix 2, pp. 239-67, for a reproduction by this constitution. Cf. Alan Burns, in *Gold Coast Legislative Council Debates*, II (Accra, 1946), 5.

constitution aroused could not be comprehended among informed opinion in Britain. Such was the vehemence of the opposition of the intelligentsia that they were driven, rather belatedly, to form the first political party in the Gold Coast at a meeting held at Saltpond on December 27, 1947. The party that emerged was called the United Gold Coast Convention (henceforth UGCC). One of its major aims was "to ensure that by all legitimate and constitutional means the control and direction of the Government shall within the shortest possible time pass into the hands of the people and the chiefs."[39] Its major weakness was that it made no plans to attract—and did not in fact attract—mass support; and it was even opposed by some chiefs. The government was not threatened by such a tame body. But it mildly rebuked its leaders, the lawyers of the coastal municipalities, for having "not so far contributed to the solution of the practical and urgent problems facing the country but [having] confined [themselves] to an appeal to nationalist feelings."[40]

In an effort to revitalize the party and make it into a popular movement Kwame Nkrumah was invited by Danquah, the leading spirit of the new party, to become its general secretary. Nkrumah had in 1935 gone to the United States where he studied at Lincoln University and the University of Pennsylvania. It was in America that he learned the ground rules of political organization, for he was actively involved in student politics as well as in the Movement for Colonial Freedom. He also "made time," as he put it, "to acquaint myself with as many political organizations in the United States as I could. These included the Republicans, the Democrats, the Communists and the Trotskyites. It was in connection with the last movement that I met one of its leading members, Mr. C. R. L. James, and through him I learned how an underground movement worked. I was also brought into contact with organizations such as the Council on African affairs, the Committee on Africa, the Committee on War and Peace Aims, the Committee on African Students, the Special Research Council of the National Association for the Advancement of Coloured People and the Urban League. My aim was to learn the technique of

---

[39] Quote in Kwame Nkrumah, *Ghana: The Autobiography of Kwame Nkrumah* (London: Nelson & Sons, Ltd., 1959, ed.), p. 57. This is one of the better autobiographies in twentieth-century African history. It contains a lot of primary materials and is substantially reliable.
[40] *Annual Report on the Gold Coast* (1947); cf. Dennis Austin, *Politics in Ghana, 1946-1960* (London: Oxford University Press, 1970 ed.), p. 7.

organization. I knew that when I eventually returned to the Gold
Coast I was going to be faced with this problem . . . I concentrated
on finding a formula by which the whole colonial question and the
problem of imperialism could be solved. I read Hegel, Karl Marx,
Engels, Lenin and Mazzini. The writings of these men did much to
influence me in my revolutionary ideas and activities, and Karl
Marx and Lenin particularly interested me as I felt sure that their
philosophy was capable of solving these problems. But I think that
of all the literature that I studied, the book that did more than
any other to fire my enthusiasm was *Philosophy and Opinions of
Marcus Garvey* published in 1923. Garvey, with his philosophy of
Africa for the Africans and his Back to Africa movement, did
much to inspire the Negroes of America in the 1920's . . ."
Nkrumah's experiences and ideas about decolonization were
published in a pamphlet entitled *Towards Colonial Freedom.*[41]

Nkrumah's political apprenticeship was completed in London
where he had gone in 1945 to study law and complete his Ph.D.
thesis in philosophy. But involvement in the numerous
anti-colonial politics in London forced him to give up further
academic studies. He was one of the stars of the Pan-African
Congress held at Manchester in 1945 which demanded freedom for
the colonies. It was in London, too, that he struck up a life-long
friendship with George Padmore, the radical West Indian political
activist and an ex-Communist who was to serve as his political
mentor for the struggle ahead.

When Nkrumah eventually returned to the Gold Coast in 1947
to serve as the Secretary General of the UGCC, he discovered that
the new party had established only a few branches. Within six
months, he built up a respectable party organization. The draft
constitution of the party had concerned itself primarily with the
colony proper and only to a small degree with the rest of the
country. He saw to it that the party was organized throughout the
country. To help him in this organizational work, he drew up a
program of action which was revolutionary in terms of the Gold
Coast of 1948 (Source 4).

Events in February 1948 played into Nkrumah's hands and
greatly helped his movement in the long run. In that month, a
sub-chief called Nii Kwabena Bonne had organized a countrywide
boycott of European and Syrian goods to force them to lower the
exorbitant prices they charged for these goods. He was supported

[41] Nkrumah, *Autobiography*, pp. 36-39.

enthusiastically by many chiefs and commoners in the Gold Coast. The boycott, which lasted for a month, was effective. It was, however, anti-inflationary rather than nationalistic in its aims. Nii Boone and his followers did not belong to any political party. And although Nkrumah was later accused of being the instigator of the boycott, he claimed that he had nothing to do with it because he was still new in the country and was preoccupied with party organization, but that he was naturally sympathetic to it.

On February 29, however, Nkrumah delivered his maiden speech entitled "The Ideological Battles of our Time" at a large gathering in Accra. At the end of the speech, he "realized," as he put it, "more fully than ever before, from the reaction of the crowd, that the political consciousness of the people of the Gold Coast had awakened to a point where the time had come for them to unite and strike out for their freedom and independence."[42] Earlier, on February 28, the boycott had been called off, but on that same day the Ex-Servicemen's Union had undertaken a peaceful demonstration. It is generally agreed that the boycott and the demonstration were unconnected. The demonstrators soon came into conflict with the police. The clash resulted in the shooting of two ex-servicemen and the wounding of five Africans. The news of this incident sparked off the 1948 riots which led to the death of twenty persons and the wounding of 237. Nkrumah and the UGCC exploited these riots for nationalist purposes; and the government reacted as expected, even if unwisely, by detaining Nkrumah, Danquah, and two other leading members of the party in a Kumasi prison in the interest of "public safety and the maintenance of public order."[43] They were later removed to the Northern Provinces when the plan of some Asante youths to shoot their way into the prisons and release the detainees was discovered. Students from all over the country went on strike to protest their detention. Clearly, the events of 1948 had turned Nkrumah and his fellow nationalists into martyrs of the decolonization process. And the Gold Coast was not to be the same again.

The violence of 1948 caused a lot of dismay in British circles. Hitherto the various annual reports had expressed lusty confidence in the future of the Gold Coast. It was a well-endowed country. It

[42]*Ibid.*, pp. 62-63.
[43]This document entitled "The Removal Order, 1948" dated 12th March, 1948 is reproduced in Nkrumah, *Autobiography*, pp. 65-66.

belonged to a class by itself among British possessions in Africa. Its intelligentsia were "men of sobriety and practical wisdom." Politically sophisticated and superbly reasoned in their arguments for the nationalist cause, they had become, as Martin Wight put it, "the pioneers of political advance and the touchstone of political competence in Africa."[44] In the Asante Kingdom, the institutions of government before the imperialistic takeover compared favourably with any of their kind in sub-Saharan Africa. And the non-Kingdom states of the north had created no particular obstacle to colonial rule. In terms of *per capita* income and in terms of Western education in relation to population, the Gold Coast was second to none in sub-Saharan Africa. It was understandable, therefore, why the country was praised as "a model colony," "a peace loving country" whose people would move toward self-rule in an "orderly and constitutional progress." Indeed, Governor Burns had declared in October 1946 that he had "great confidence in these extremely sensible people. They know their limitations and they are very keen to take advice provided they know the man giving them advice is really sincere."[45]

Why, then, did these "moderate" and "extremely sensible people" reject the 1946 Constitution? Supposing one agrees with the government and admits that the rejection was the work of a few disgruntled and ambitious intelligentsia, while the silent majority who knew what was good for them favored it, how then can one explain the 1948 riots? The colonial authorities, dismayed and confused, could offer no explanation which would not destroy their earlier confidence. The truth of the matter was the politics of collaboration had worked so smoothly in the Gold Coast that the government had failed to grasp the depth of nationalist aspirations among the intelligentsia and disquietude among the masses who only needed a strong leader to rouse them out of their complacency. The emotion which the 1948 riots engendered would hardly had been called for had the disturbances occurred, for example, in India, or, for that matter, in Nigeria. And yet the rioters had no proclaimed objective of ending British overrule. The success of the boycott and the arrogant defiance displayed by the rioters proved to Gold Coast nationalists how woefully they had failed, all these years, to exploit the most revolutionary instrument at their disposal. To the government it

---

[44] Wight, *Legislative Council*, p. 207.
[45] Quoted in Austin, *Politics in Ghana*, p. 3.

showed that the chiefs, whose authority and influence had been badly disrupted by the celebrated policy of indirect rule, were, when the chips were down, in no position to keep the masses quiet. Now, if they proved unable to do this, what then was the point of the bargain we have talked about so often in these pages? In short, what was the use of indirect rule? I should not be understood to be arguing that the Gold Coast masses were imbued with a sense of nationalism. My point is that their importance as the major revolutionary material for nationalist ends was not grasped by the Western-educated leaders of the Gold Coast before the rise of Nkrumah. From their experiences in other parts of the Commonwealth the British authorities might have been expected to realize the power of the revolutionary masses. Yet they appeared to labor under the strange belief that the same colonial chiefs who, as more and more people came to know where the real power lay in a colonial situation, were becoming a laughing stock could hold the masses in check indefinitely. The way in which the nationalist movement spread like wildfire after 1948 is sufficient proof that nationalistic feelings were easily exploitable among the masses.

The exciting thing about the study of the politics of decolonization is how the colonizer is driven by internal contradictions and external imponderables to move from one expedient to the other to ensure the survival of colonialism. Sensing danger in 1946, Sir Alan Burns had introduced the 1946 Constitution as an antidote to nationalism. Events in the next two years proved that his measures were more than a generation too late. Moreover, it never occurred to him that a minor and inconsequential chief could call a boycott and sustain it for a whole month. Nor did he reckon with the genius of a charismatic young man called Francis Kwame Nkrumah, educated in America of all places. Recalled in 1947, Sir Alan was succeeded as Governor by Sir Gerald Creasy who, faced with the violence of 1948, confessed that he had been "overtaken by events."[46] The British government, which had a penchant for commissions of inquiry, promptly ordered one. In April 1948 the commission, headed by Mr. Aiken Watson, arrived in Accra. They were instructed "to enquire into and report on the recent disturbances in the Gold Coast and the underlying causes, and to make

---

[46] Quoted in *Ibid.*, p. 11.

recommendations on any matter arising from their enquiries." By June the Watson Commission had completed its work and issued its startling report.[47] Having discussed the causes of the disturbances—which were seen in local, political, economic, and social terms—it recommended the introduction of responsible government in the Gold Coast, that is, that Africans should have control of their internal affairs. In other words, the country was to have a legislative assembly on parliamentary lines. The Executive Council was to be replaced by a Board of nine ministers, five being African members of the assembly and four *ex officio*. These ministers were to be nominated by the governor, the nomination to be approved by the resolution of the assembly. The African ministers could only be removed on a 3/4 vote of censure. Now, at last, the stark truth has appeared. Indirect rule was to die. The chiefs no longer had any significant part to play in a self-governing Gold Coast. The report had thus struck down with one deadly blow the cornerstone propping up the edifice of colonial administration as set up by Clifford, Guggisberg, and Burns.

What, then, should be done? Faced with a major condemnation of its colonial policy, the British government reserved strong objections to the report but was not prepared to reject it outright. Instead, it appointed an all-African representative committee under the Chairmanship of Mr. Justice (later Sir Henley) Coussey to consider the report's recommendations and submit its own proposals for a new constitution.[48] This, indeed, was a beautiful move in the short run but short-sighted in the long run. If an all-African committee, headed by a respectable African judge, were, hopefully, to reject the institution of self-rule, the government would then be in a better position to boast about how little Mr. Watson and his colleagues knew of African conditions! On the other hand, should their proposals appear more radical than those of the Watson committee, the government was not bound to accept them. Once more, the government had proved itself out of touch with Gold Coast opinion. It could—and did—fill the Coussey Committee with moderates, but it was becoming evident that these moderates no longer carried much weight with

[47] See *Report of the Commission of Enquiry into Disturbances in the Gold Coast, 1948* [Watson Report] (London: H.M.S.O., 1948), Colonial no. 231.

[48] See *Statement by His Majesty's Government on the Report of the Commission of Enquiry into the Disturbances in the Gold Coast*, 1948, *Ibid.*, Colonial no. 232.

the masses. Indeed, Nkrumah's first criticism of the commission was devoted to the manner of the nomination of its members by government. The report, published in 1949 and accepted by the government with some reservations, was a compromise between the Watson report and the UGCC demand for self-government.[49] It unanimously recommended, for example, an executive composed mainly of Africans, responsible, not to the governor, but to an indirectly elected legislature. The governor would retain his veto power as well as certain reserved rights. The chiefs, too, were to be represented in the new legislature. A new constitution based on these proposals would come into effect in 1951. The Coussey report was accepted by the Legco as an important step toward responsible government.

Two significant events took place during this period. Dr. Danquah, as well as some leading members of the UGCC, agreed to participate in the Coussey Committee. On this point they, for all intents and purposes, parted company with Nkrumah and the more radical elements of the party. Equally importantly, regional jealousies among the leaders of the Gold Coast themselves began to appear as independence was in the offing. The riots therefore had not only thrown the British into confusion but were also, as Dennis Austin put it, "the violent herald of a struggle for power soon to be conducted by new leaders who drew their support from a much broader, more popular level than had hitherto been active in national politics, and the demands shortly to be revised by Nkrumah and the Convention People's Party implied a far greater upheaval in local society than the earlier struggle between the chiefs and the intelligentsia."[50]

The CPP and the Nkrumah Phenomenon

In criticizing the Coussey Committee Nkrumah had noted that "A most important section of the community . . . had been entirely excluded from the Committee. These were the workers—the farmers, the miners, the petty traders—and the trade union movement. It was little wonder that dissatisfaction set in among a large section of the community who felt that as the

---

[49] See *Gold Coast: Report to His Excellency the Governor by the Committee on Constitutional Reform*, 1949 [Coussey Report], *Ibid.*, Colonial no. 248 and *Gold Coast: Statement by His Majesty's Government on the Report of the Committee on Constitutional Reform, 1949, Ibid.*, Colonial no. 250.
[50] Austin, *Politics in Ghana*, p. 12.

radical elements had been left out, the true political aspirations of the people could never be satisfied. This dissatisfaction became so acute that . . . I felt obliged to take action."[51] It was, then, to these radical elements and the masses that he turned for support. The UGCC had been a middle class and an upper middle class party led mainly by coastal lawyers, merchants, and educated individuals from chiefly families. In reality, they could not be described as true radicals. They believed in moderation, ordered progress, and rule by an African aristocracy of intellect and of birth. But they were African nationalists all the same and had no illusion that with the chiefs they were the legitimate successors to the colonial administration.

Nkrumah and his "parlour boys"—as his supporters were contemptuously called—had other ideas. While Danquah and some leading members of the UGCC participated in the Coussey Committee, Nkrumah went about organizing a new party dedicated to no compromise with colonialism. Such a party, he reckoned, was what the country needed. He had already used his position as the Secretary General of the UGCC to popularize himself with the masses. In 1948, shortly after his release, he had founded the Ghana National College which pledged to "combine the best in Western culture with the best in African Culture."[52] Its major aim, however, was to train "an awakened intelligentsia" from "among so-called subject people" who would become "the vanguard of the struggle against alien rule."[53] In the same year he launched a newspaper called the *Accra Evening News*. The first edition of this paper appeared on September 3, 1948. That was also the day the Working Committee of the UGCC relieved him of his post as Secretary General. The gap between Nkrumah and his colleagues therefore widened; the *Accra Evening News* became the vanguard of Nkrumah's radical movement. As Nkrumah put it: the paper became the movement's "chief propagandist, agitator, mobiliser and political educationist. Day by day in its pages the people were reminded of their struggle for freedom, of the decaying colonial system and of the grim horrors of imperialism."[54] The paper's mottos: "We prefer self-government with danger to servitude in tran-

---

[51]Nkrumah, *Autobiography*, p. 71. For the next few papers, I will rely on Nkrumah's *Autobiography* since it is the best available account of developments in this period.
[52]*Ibid.*, p. 74.
[53]*Idem.*
[54]*Ibid.*, p. 76.

quility."–"We have the right to live as men."–"We have the right to govern ourselves"–became household words. At last, a Gold Coast politician was speaking in a language comprehensible to the masses. The literate and barely literate Gold Coasters alike waited daily to purchase the paper. Within a short time, demand had outstripped supply because of limited resources. The success of the *News* drove Nkrumah to launch the *Morning Telegraph* in Sekondi and the *Daily Mail* in Cape Coast during the same year. Threatened by this phenomenon, the government and the UGCC leadership resorted to the well-worn practice of libel suits to drive Nkrumah into bankruptcy. They failed. Clearly, the colonial government had lost the initiative in the politics of decolonization. It now responded to moves made by the radical nationalists. The *Accra Evening News*, for example, quickly became the *Ghana Evening News* when the former was threatened with extinction.

Another major step taken by Nkrumah to radicalize the masses was the formation of the Youth Study Group. This group was later merged with the Asante Youth Association and the Ghana Youth Association and became the nationalist movement known as the Committee on Youth Organization (CYO) which demanded "Self-Government Now." In 1948 it published the *Ghana Youth Manifesto* which likened its war against colonialism to the war against fascism in Europe. Identifying the youth of the Gold Coast with youth all over the world, it stated: "To British Youths we send special greetings. You are lovers and exponents of freedom and democracy. Thousands of you fought in this last war against fascism to maintain your well-earned freedom. . . . We trust that you, Youth of Britain, would co-operate with us in our struggle for freedom and self-government so that we could both freely work together to build the Brave New World which is the dream of us youth." Addressing itself to its supporters, it said: "Youth of the Gold Coast, the new Ghana, the struggle for self-government gains unrelenting momentum, that brings us daily near our goal. However hard the struggle, whatever the stratagems of the imperialists, or whatever the opportunism of traducers, stooges, and quislings to lead us astray, we shall not deviate an inch from our avowed goal" which was "a constitution that would give this country nothing less than FULL SELF-GOVERNMENT."A comparison of the demands contained in this pamphlet with those contained in Danquah's *First Steps Towards a National Fund* ten years earlier shows that a major political revolution had occurred in the Gold Coast. The supposedly sensible London *Times* of May

24, 1949, reacted to this development by blaming it on the activities of "a single-minded and hard-working fanatic" (Nkrumah). It was the CYO and the radical press which agitated furiously against the Coussey Committee. The CYO drew up its own version of a constitution which would be acceptable to the people of the Gold Coast and sent it to the Commission.

When the breach between Nkrumah and the UGCC became unbridgeable, the CYO decided to form The Convention Peoples' Party (CPP)—the party that was to lead the Gold Coast to independence within eight years. The main thrusts of its six point program were "Self-Government Now" and the unity of the country in freedom (Source 5). The formation of the party was announced on June 12, 1949 before an Accra audience estimated by Nkrumah to have numbered sixty thousand. At this meeting Nkrumah's mass oratory was at its best. Having related the history of the decolonization struggle in the Gold Coast since 1946 (as he understood it), he went on to explain why he demanded immediate self-government, why he broke with the UGCC, and requested their endorsement (which was given unanimously) of his course of action. Various attempts by moderate elements to unite the two Gold Coast parties having failed, Nkrumah formally resigned from the UGCC (to avoid being dismissed) and vowed before his supporters: "This very day I will lead you." And the meeting ended with one of the excited female supporters singing "Lead Kindly Light," a hymn which henceforth became a feature of CPP rallies. The messianic strain in Nkrumah has a long history!

Nkrumah's pledge to die in the cause of Ghana, if need be, he later asserted, "marked the final parting of the ways to right and left of Gold Coast nationalism; from the system of indirect rule promulgated by British imperialism to the new political awareness of the people. From now on the struggle was to be three-sided, made up by the reactionary intellectuals and chiefs, the British Government and the politically awakened masses with their slogan of 'Self-Government Now'."[55] And the die was cast. Nkrumah and his supporters traversed the length and breadth of the Gold Coast organizing his party and recruiting the grass roots peasantry, youths, and women into its ranks. The great success he attained demonstrated that the British government's silent majority, contented and happy with the existing political order, never really

[55]*Ibid.*, p. 89.

existed. Even in the remotest villages, the CPP's color of "red, white and green, could be seen flying on rough wooden poles."[56] This was political organization at its best. Much of this success was attributed "to the efforts of women members" who, from "the very beginning ... have been the chief field organizers." They "travelled through innumerable towns and villages in the role of propaganda secretaries" and were "responsible for the most part in bringing about the solidarity and cohension of the Party."[57] There is the story of one of these women who slashed her face with a razor blade in public after a fiery speech protesting Nkrumah's imprisonment in 1950. The youth of the country, too, worked tirelessly for the party, and the three radical newspapers crashed in their accompaniments to round off each incomparable solo performance by their leader. The Gold Coast was in great ferment. The slur of "verandah boys, hooligans and Communists" cast on these revolutionary elements in Gold Coast politics did nothing to stem the tide of the revolution of the masses. "For, if a national movement is to succeed," as Nkrumah notes, "every man and woman of goodwill must be allowed to play a part."[58] The CPP gave the masses of the country the opportunity to free their country and they performed their parts with great exuberance and gusto.

In 1946, the British rider was seated firmly on the political horse in the Gold Coast; by 1949, he was in serious danger of falling off the horse. George Padmore, Nkrumah's political mentor since their London days, urged his disciple to push the Briton off. But the disciple demurred. The rider must be allowed to fall off the horse out of exhaustion. To expedite this process, however, Nkrumah developed the concept of "nonviolent positive action" which he described "as the adoption of all legitimate and constitutional means by which we could attack the forces of imperialism in the country. The weapons were legitimate political agitation, newspaper and educational campaigns and, as a last resort, the constitutional application of strikes, boycotts, and noncooperation based on the principle of absolute nonviolence as used by Gandhi in India" (Source 6). It was clear, nevertheless, that the Gold Coast was not India and that the concept of *satyagraha* ("soul force") embedded in Hindu religious culture was alien to

[56]*Idem.*
[57]*Idem.*
[58]*Ibid.*, p. 90.

African patterns of behavior. In the meantime, it was politically expedient to employ such tactics in the hope that the government would not provoke the employment of physical force to test its validity.

When the Coussey Report was published in October 1949, the CPP summoned what it called the "Ghana People's Representative Assembly" on November 20, and secured its denunciation as "unacceptable to the country as a whole." The assembly also reaffirmed "that the people of the Gold Coast be granted immediate self-government, that is, full Dominion status within the Commonwealth of Nations based on the Statute of Westminster."[59] Some of the leading chiefs dissociated themselves from these views and a major split occurred between the CPP and the chiefly class. Ignoring the chiefs for the moment, Nkrumah sent an ultimatum to the government to accept the legitimate demands of the people or risk the application of his "Positive Action." And to show that he was serious, he caused "a stirring article" to be published in the *Evening News* headed: "The Era of Positive Action Draws Nigh." The masses were also warned to be prepared for the inevitable showdown. Government attempts to shut up the newspapers by crippling libel suits failed to succeed, and the Governor, determined to do something before things got out of hand, persuaded Nkrumah to abandon the campaign on the promise that he would consider his demands sympathetically. Such was the influence that Nkrumah had over the masses that they promptly obeyed his orders to draw in their horns for the moment. But when nothing was forthcoming from the government, the Trade Union Congress (TUC) called a strike (January 1950). Fearing the loss of control over the movement, Nkrumah was forced to declare "Positive Action" on January 8. This involved a general strike from which only hospital workers were exempted. "The response of the people," claimed Nkrumah, "was instantaneous. The political and social revolution of Ghana had started."[60] But a counter-campaign by the government through the use of the radio nearly ruined the strategy as people started going back to work after a few days. It was at this point that Nkrumah demonstrated once more his genius as a political agitator. He spoke at a men's rally "where the whole of Accra appeared to be assembled." Employing all the tactics in the mass oratory business

[59]*Ibid.*, p. 93.
[60]*Ibid.*, p. 97.

at which he excelled, and making use of his tremendous charismatic personality, he re-established his leadership of the movement and fired the "blood" of his audience to such an extent that "no Government propaganda machine could have succeeded in pacifying them or controlling them. . . . The tension was soon sensed throughout the whole town and it was hardly surprising to any of us when at seven o'clock that evening an emergency was declared for the whole country and a curfew imposed."[61] The general strike, however, was a complete success. The government reacted by imposing a strict censorship of the press, closed the offices of the radical press, and forbade all public meetings. Nkrumah and the leaders of his party were arrested, tried for sedition, and imprisoned. In this move, the government was supported by the Joint Provincial Council of chiefs and the leaders of the UGCC. It was at this point that Nkrumah declared "that if the chiefs would not co-operate with the people in their struggle for freedom then a day might come when they 'will run away and leave their sandals behind them' ."[62] The situation in the Gold Coast was so serious that British, Lebanese, and Syrian nationals were used as special constables and they treated the Africans with overzealous brutality. The ex-servicemen appeared once more on the scene, and in a clash with government forces two African policemen were killed.

In an attempt to diffuse the explosive situation, Sir Charles Noble Arden-Clarke, the governor of the Gold Coast since 1949, decided to embody the Coussey Committee's recommendations into a constitution. The proposals were accepted by the Legco and promulgated as the Gold Coast (Constitution) Order in Council, 1950. Popularly known as the *Arden-Clarke Constitution,*[63] it granted the Gold Coast a greater form of internal autonomy than hitherto, the first African colonial government, indeed, to be granted such a constitutional advance. The constitution also extended the franchise for direct and indirect elections to all British subjects and protected persons—male or female—over twenty-one years of age and who were not disqualified by virtue of criminal offences or mental disability. The CPP was sorely unimpressed. The next step taken by the government was the

---

[61] *Ibid.,* pp. 97-98.
[62] *Ibid.,* p. 99.
[63] See *The Gold Coast (Constitution) Order in Council 1950* (London: H.M.S.O., 1950), no. 2094.

announcement of the first Gold Coast General Election to be held
in February 1951, the old Legco having been dissolved for the last
time at the close of 1950. As a result of this election the CPP
emerged as the majority party in the country (Source 7). It won
thirty-four of the thirty-eight seats in the new Assembly while the
UGCC won only three. The National Democratic Party (NDP),
made up of the remnants of the defunct Mambii Party and
members of the Ratepayers' Association of Accra, and led by Nii
Amaa Ollenu, as well as the Peoples Democratic Party (PDP),
backed only by the *Asante Kotoko*, an ethnic solidarity group,
was not represented. The remaining seat was won by an independent. Nkrumah himself was elected while still in prison by a
stunning 22,780 votes out of a possible 23,122. Sir Charles was
forced to release him from prison and invited him to become the
first Leader of Government Business in the Gold Coast.[64] This
post was equivalent to that of Prime Minister, the latter title being
formally conferred on Nkrumah in 1952.

V. TRIUMPH OF REVOLUTION:
THE BRITISH RIDER FALLS OFF THE HORSE, 1952-1957

The landslide victory of the CPP in the 1951 elections, wrote
George Padmore, a close observer of contemporary Gold Coast
politics, "caused consternation in British official circles and spread
despondency and alarm among the African chiefs and right-wing
parties."[65] Before the elections, informed British observers had
not expected a landslide. The *Economist* of February 3, 1951, for
example, noting with dry humour that there was "no Gallup poll
in the Gold Coast to guide election prophets," did, however,
forecast that the CPP "will command about a third of the
Assembly and that about three of the Ministers will come from
their ranks." The success of the CPP confounded those who had
confidently believed that the silent majority of Gold Coast
Africans—99 percent to be sure—supported the government.
Equally seriously, many of the chiefly representatives in the new
Assembly decided to join the winning team and threw in their lot
with the CPP. And by the time the Assembly met for the first
time, the CPP majority was so overwhelming that the presence of

---

[64] For a study of this election see J. H. Price, "The Gold Coast General Election,
1951," *Journal African Administration* 3, 2 (April 1951): 65-77.
[65] George Padmore, *The Gold Coast Revolution: The Struggle of an African People
from Slavery to Freedom* (London: Dennis Dobson, 1953), p. 118.

the opposition, now dispirited and confused, was a mere formality. Clearly, the long struggle to win the covert or overt loyalty of the grass roots peasantry which was at the heart of the colonial government's game of collaboration had been lost. The masses, who never really understood what the right-wing intellectuals were talking about, had now deserted their chiefs to whom they had looked for leadership for most of the colonial period. They had been won over by a new radical element of the Gold Coast composed of individuals not supposed to have the natural right to rule. This was a development of revolutionary proportions. To those of the elite who considered themselves as forming the black aristocracy of the Gold Coast, namely, the UGCC leaders, the rule of the plebeians was an unmitigated tragedy. Their feeling was put across forcibly by an upper-class African conservative, barrister Francis Awoonor-Williams (the hyphen in his name apparently inserted in imitation of the British aristocracy). Urging the return of the old aristocractic order, he stunned progressive elements all over the world by asserting that "true aristocracy, after true religion, is the greatest blessing a nation can enjoy." Individuals "of the old school of politics," he went on, "were men of education and substance, and merchant princes working in the interests of the country. . . . Apart from one or two members of the Convention People's Party, their leaders and supporters are the flotsam and jetsam and the popinjays of the country, men who had suddenly loomed large into men of substance. . . . It is, therefore, the bounden duty of every well informed citizen to unite to save the social and political order." He blamed the rise of the masses on "the unfortunate adoption by the Coussey Committee of universal manhood suffrage at the threshold of parliamentary self-government in the country."[66] In the Gold Coast of the 1950s reactionaries such as Awoonor-Williams were becoming an embarrassment, rather than an asset, to the colonial government.

Times had changed. The gusty wind of revolution had suddenly burst upon the Gold Coast. The government had tried, unsuccessfully, to keep its potent force in control. And since the chiefs, not for want of trying, had also failed to keep their part of the collaboration bargain, the government was forced to realign the political horses in the country. In the process it spelled its own doom. And yet there was the consolation that it was better to

[66] Quoted in *Ibid.*, p. 126.

retreat with dignity than to be forced out with ignominy. The conciliatory speech of the British colonial secretary, Mr. James Griffiths, published in *The Times* of February 21, 1951 in reaction to the results of the election, may be termed a concession speech. And Nkrumah's studied response to the British Minister after his release from prison did help to allay the fears of some conservative British parliamentarians who prematurely saw a "Red Shadow Over the Gold Coast." Nkrumah had stated: "I came out of goal and into the Assembly without the slightest feeling of bitterness to Britain." And later on he had clarified his position: "I stand for no racialism, no discrimination against any race or individual, but I am unalterably opposed to imperialism in any form."[67] The air was cleared, at any rate for the present, and there began a new type of collaboration which led the Gold Coast to full independence within a few years. The remarkable thing about this period of Gold Coast's colonial history is not only how the governor and Nkrumah worked closely as a team and how the British government accepted their apparent defeat graciously but also Nkrumah's amazing pragmatism in consenting to work within the framework of the 1950 Constitution which he had dismissed as "bogus and fraudulent."

Nkrumah knew the dangers of collaboration. The CPP could easily be manipulated by the colonial authorities into complacency and conservatism. If that happened, the opposition would be given a ready-made campaign issue. Although independence was around the corner, it had not yet been achieved. Nkrumah therefore decided to mix radical utterances with calculated moderation in collaboration. "The die is cast," he reminded his supporters. "The exploited and oppressed people of colonial Africa and elsewhere are looking up to us for hope and inspiration. Progressive people in Britain and elsewhere are also solidly behind us. The torch of the Liberation Movement has been lifted up in Ghana for the whole of West Africa and it will blaze a trail of freedom for other oppressed territories. Long Live the Convention People's Party! Long Live the Liberation Movement throughout the World!"[68] Already he had grasped the dimensions of his revolution and was determined not to let his admirers down.

His first major action was to invite all the opposition parties,

---

[67]Nkrumah, *Autobiography*, p. 113.

[68]*Ibid.*, pp. 117-18; for an opposition party member's view of events in this period see K. A. Busia "The Prospects of Parliamentary Democracy in the Gold Coast," *Parliamentary Affairs* V, 2(1952).

including the chiefs, to join with him to begin another campaign of "Positive Action" if the British government rejected a motion of "Self-Government Now" which he intended to introduce as soon as possible. This move, calculated more to embarrass the opposition than to form a united party made up of strange bedfellows, had the desired effect. The opposition refused to respond to his challenge and their claim to political integrity and sincerity became more questionable than ever. Nkrumah's next move, also calculated to keep the flame of revolution alight, was to launch what he termed the phase of "Tactical Action" in the politics of decolonization. This move was adopted to placate those who wished to quicken the pace of revolution and, at the same time, not to alarm British officials. Part of Nkrumah's "tactical action" was the Africanization of the civil service which was predominantly manned by British officials. It will be remembered that in British territories with internal self-government, control of the civil service, the police, the judiciary, defense, external trade, and foreign affairs resided in the hands of the colonial governor. Nkrumah had therefore to seek the approval of Whitehall for his proposal and had to show good faith if that approval was to be granted. The government, anxious to avoid any showdown, did not stand in his way and the program was guardedly enforced in order to avoid a total breakdown of the government machinery. This period also saw the pursuit of various internal policies intended to placate the party's rank and file and avoid a palace revolt, and the adoption of measures to strengthen the party's hold on the country.

The British government was also strongly pressed to change Nkrumah's official title to that of Prime Minister. This request was granted and on March 21, 1952 Nkrumah was officially elevated to the rank. In the meantime, the CPP, uncomfortable under the 1950 Constitution, pressed for a further constitutional advance. The British government consented to consider any constitutional changes submitted in consultation with the chiefs and the people. Having made the necessary consultation, the Nkrumah government issued in June 1953 a white paper in which it set out its proposals for "the limited transitional period which is necessary in order that the requisite constitutional and administrative arrangement for independence can be made."[69] These proposals were unani-

---

[69] *The Gold Coast Government's Proposals for Constitutional Reform* (Accra, 1953). Cf. also *Dispatches on the Gold Coast Government's Proposals for Constitutional*

mously approved by the Legislative Assembly. With his hand strengthened, Nkrumah moved, on June 10,1953, the independence motion popularly called the "Motion of Destiny" which demanded immediate full independence for the Gold Coast (Source 8). The acclamation that this motion brought about was so loud that the Legislature was forced to adjourn "for fifteen minutes." Outside the Assembly, the shouting and rejoicing was taken over by the waiting crowd who spread the news downtown. There never was any fear that the British government was going to oppose this motion. On the contrary, it passed into law the necessary statutory instrument which amended the 1950 Constitution to meet the demands of the CPP government.[70] The general election of June 1954 confirmed these proposals as well as Nkrumah's leadership. The CPP won 72 seats out of 104 seats in the new Assembly and formed a government which, for the first time in British colonial Africa, had an all-black cabinet.[71]

As full independence drew nearer, the various factions in Gold Coast politics outplayed by the CPP in the politics of decolonization joined together to form an opposition party called The National Liberation Movement. Drawing its support mainly from Asante, and led by Dr. K.A. Busia, it demanded a federal constitution, regional autonomy, and the creation of a House of Chiefs (equivalent to the House of Lords in Britain) before full sovereignty would be granted to the country. And to demonstrate that they meant business, periodic acts of violence were committed in Asante. Nkrumah thus found himself in the embarrassing situation of either employing the repressive forces of colonialism against his own people or risking the breakdown of law and order. It was at this juncture that the British government decided to invite Sir Frederick Bourne, a retired old colonial hand in the Indian Civil Service, to visit the Gold Coast as Constitutional Adviser and to make the necessary recommendations.[72] His report,

---

Reform Exchanged Between the Secretary of State for the Colonies and H. E. the Governor, 24 August 1953 to 15 April 1954 (London: H.M.S.O., 1954), Colonial no. 302. See also Anon., "Self-government in the Gold Coast, Progress of a Constitutional Experiment," *Round Table* (September 1952): 326-32; Asa Briggs, "Nationalism in the Gold Coast," Parts 1 & 2, *Fortnightly* (January-June 1952): 152-57, 231-36; Anon., "The Gold Coast: Constitutional Reform,*"Information Digest* (August 1953): 11-12.
[70]*Gold Coast Colony and Ashanti (Legislative Council) Order in Council 1954* (London: H.M.S.O., 1954), Colonial no. 353.
[71]For a study of this election see George Bennett, "Gold Coast General Election of 1954," *Parliamentary Affairs* 7, 4(1955): 430-30. See also C.P.P., *Forward to Freedom with the Common People: Manifesto for the General Election* 1954 (Accra, 1954).
[72]Anon., "The Gold Coast: Further Developments in the National Liberation

issued on December 23, 1955, rejected federalism because it would "slow down development and introduce an intolerable handicap to the administration of the country." He, however, recommended "a very substantial transfer of power from the central government to the regions."[73] These recommendations were embodied in the Gold Coast Government White Paper of April 20, 1956, which outlined the constitutional proposals for Gold Coast independence as a full member of the British Commonwealth of Nations. The salient points of these proposals included a unitary constitution, the devolution of power from the center to the six regions, the establishment of a House of Chiefs with only consultative and advisory powers in each of the regions, and the change of the name of the Gold Coast to Ghana.[74]

The choice of the name, Ghana, is significant insofar as it can be seen as a weapon in the politics of decolonization. The empire of Ghana was the first of the major empires of the Western Sudan. Before its destruction in the eleventh century by the Almoravids of Morocco, it had developed a high degree of civilization and tremendous military power comparable to that of the most developed European empire of the period. The capital of the Ghana empire was situated some 1000 miles from modern Ghana. There is no strong historical evidence to suggest that modern Ghana ever came within the sphere of influence of the medieval empire. It was Dr. J.B. Danquah who claimed to have created the "Ghana myth." He claimed that after the fall of Ghana its descendants moved southeastward to become the forebears of the Akan peoples of modern Ghana.[75] The same claim was made by Dr. Kwame Nkrumah. In making this claim these nationalists were reminding the British that the founding of empires and the development of civilizations were not unknown to African peoples. As Nkrumah put it, the name was chosen to kindle "in

---

Movement," *African Digest* 11, 7 (February 1955): 8-11; Anon., "A Nascent Dominion: African Self-Government in the Gold Coast," *Round Table* (March 1955): 149-55; Barbara Ward (Jackson), "The Gold Coast: an Experiment in Partnership," *Foreign Affairs* 32, 4(1954): 608-16; Kwame Nkrumah, "Movement for Colonial Freedom," *Phylon*, Fourth Quarter (1955): 397-409.

[73] *Report of the Constitutional Adviser* [Bourne Report], (Accra, 19550.

[74] *The Gold Coast Government's Revised Constitutional Proposals for Gold Coast Independence* (Accra, 1956).

[75] Joseph B. Danquah, "The Culture of the Akan," *Africa* 22, 4(October 1952) and "The Akan Claim to Origin from Ghana," *West African Review* XXVI (November-December 1955): 963-70 and 1107-11; see also Raymond A. Mauny, "The Question of Ghana, an Historical Approach," *African Affairs* XXIV (1954): 200-212; J. S. Hutton, "Medieval Ghana and Modern Ghana," *Party* 6 (June 1957): 35-46.

the imagination of modern West African youth ... the grandeur and the achievements of a great medieval civilization which our ancestors had developed many centuries before the European penetration and subsequent domination of Africa began."[76] The people of the Gold Coast "took pride in the name, not out of romanticism, but as an inspiration for the future." The choice was a popular one, and with independence in the air the historical validity of the name was of no consequence whatever.

In May 1956, the Colonial Secretary announced in the House of Commons that "if a general election is held Her Majesty's Government will be ready to accept a motion calling for independence within the Commonwealth passed by a reasonable majority in a newly elected legislature and then to declare a firm date for this purpose."[77] Consequently, a general election was held in July 1956, the main issue being the proposals contained in the White Paper. The CPP won the election with a large majority and on August 3, Nkrumah moved the final independence motion in the Legislative Assembly. It was passed unanimously. On February 7, 1957, the British government passed the *Ghana Independence Act* which provided "for and in connection with, the attainment by the Gold Coast of fully responsible status within the British Commonwealth of Nations."[78] A firm date for independence was set for March 6, 1957 to coincide with the anniversary of the "Bond." This act was quickly followed on February 22 by the *Ghana (Constitution) Order-in-Council, 1957* which established the first constitution of Ghana. The Gold Coast Legislative Assembly was prorogued but immediately replaced by the first National Assembly of Ghana (Source 9).

On the morning of March 6, 1957 the British rider formally and ceremoniously got off the political horse in the Gold Coast. And Dr. Francis Kwame Nkrumah and his CPP were left to carry on the act. Ghana, however, retained the British queen as the Head of State in the same way as Canada, Australia, and New Zealand still do.[79] But on July 1, 1960 Ghana decided formally to become a

---

[76]Nkrumah, *Autobiography*, p. 221.
[77]Quoted in *Ibid.*, pp. 208, 229.
[78]*The Proposed Constitution of Ghana, 1957* (London: H.M.S.O., 1957), Cmd, 71.
[79]For a discussion of events in this period see Anon., "The Birth of Ghana: Independence for the Gold Coast," *Round Table* (December 1956): 48-56; John Hatch, "Policies and Politics in the Gold Coast," *Africa South* 1, 1 (October-December, 1957): 107-15; H. Wiseman, "The Gold Coast, from Executive Council to Responsible Cabinet," *Parliamentary Affairs* 10, 1 (1956-1957): 27-35; R. B. Davidson, "The Challenge of Ghana," *Political Quarterly* (July-September, 1957): 271-84; Charles Arden-Clarke,

Republic within the Commonwealth with Nkrumah as its first President and Head of State. Summing up his victory, Nkrumah had stated with much propriety: "We had succeeded because we had talked with the people and by so doing knew their feelings and grievances. And we had excluded no one. For, if a nationalist movement is to succeed, every man and woman of goodwill must be allowed to play a part."[80] The chiefs and the so-called intellectuals of the Gold Coast did not understand the rules of the game. The colonial officials did. But by supporting the chiefs whose influence they had inadvertently disrupted by the application of *Indirect Rule*, they discovered when it was too late that they had backed the wrong horse. And yet one must wonder whether in a colonial situation there will ever be the right horse to back!

FOR FURTHER READING

A. *Primary Sources*

George E. Metcalfe (ed.). *Great Britain and Ghana: Documents of Ghana History, 1807-1957*. Accra and London: Nelson & Sons, Ltd., 1964. Very useful source material, competently selected and edited.

J. J. Crooks. *Records Relating to the Gold Coast Settlements*. Dublin: Browne & Nolan, 1923. Useful supplement to Metcalfe's *Documents*.

Henry S. Wilson (ed.). *Origins of West African Nationalism*. London: MacMillan, St. Martin's Press, 1969. Another useful collection of documents, from which pre-twentieth century Ghanaian nationalism can be seen within the context of West African nationalism.

Kwame Nkrumah. *Ghana: The Autobiography of Kwame Nkrumah*. London: Nelson & Sons, Ltd., 1959. One of the better autobiographies of African nationalists. Contains very valuable source material.

B. *Secondary Sources*

David Apter. *Ghana in Transition*. New York: Antheneum Publishing Company, 1963. An updated version of the same author's *The Gold Coast in Transition*. Princeton, N.J.: Princeton University Press, 1955.

F. M. Bourret, *Ghana: The Road to Independence*. Stanford, Calif.: Stanford University Press and London: Oxford University Press, 1960.

Martin Wight. *The Gold Coast Legislative Council*. London: Faber & Faber, 1947.

David Kimble. *A Political History of Ghana: The Rise of Gold Coast Nationalism 1850-1928*. London: Oxford University Press, 1963.

"Gold Coast into Ghana: Some Problems of Transition," *International Affairs*, XXXIV (1958): 49-56.
    [80] Nkrumah, *Autobiography*, p. 90.

John D. Fage. *Ghana: A Historical Interpretation*. Wisconsin: University of Wisconsin Press, 1966 ed.

Dennis Austin. *Politics in Ghana*. New York: Oxford University Press, 1970 ed.

L. Rubin and P. Murray. *The Constitution and Government of Ghana*. London: Sweet & Maxwell Ltd., 1961.

Thomas Hodgkin. *Nationalism in Colonial Africa*. New York: New York University Press, 1969, ed. A general study of African nationalism.

Immanuel Wallerstein. *Africa: The Politics of Independence*. New York: Vintage Books, Alfred A. Knopf, 1961. Another general study of African nationalism.

SOURCES

1

The Fante Bond, 1844

SOURCE: G. E. Metcalfe (ed.), *Great Britain and Ghana: Documents of Ghana History 1807-1957* (London: The University of Ghana and Thomas Nelson, 1964), pp. 195-96.

HILL TO STANLEY
CAPE COAST CASTLE, 6 MARCH, 1844.

Private and confidential.

My Lord,

An opportunity offering for England tonight, I am induced thus hurriedly to acquaint your Lordship, that several of the chiefs from different parts of the country adjacent to Cape Coast, have visited me today in great state to pay their respects on the transfer of the Government.

I have for some days been aware that an idea was believed by the natives of its being the intention of Her Majesty's Government to pronounce freedom to all slaves within the limits over which jurisdiction has been exercised. I need not tell your Lordship that an attempt to carry any such measure would cause a revolution.

The chiefs were delighted on my informing them that it was quite an idle report, and that the export slave trade was all that we prohibited. They expressed satisfaction on my telling them they were not at liberty to ill-use their domestic slaves, and if a person inherited a slave, that person was not at liberty to sell the slave again, but such slave was to be considered a member of the family.

I considered it a good opportunity of establishing an agreement to their being under our jurisdiction, and drew up the document of which the enclosed is a copy, and which the chiefs readily signed. This will, I hope, my Lord, meet with your approbation, and I think it quite sufficient to establish the powers of the Foreign Jurisdiction Act. I beg to mention the chiefs expressed great satisfaction at the appointment of Captain Maclean to preside over the trial of offenders.

I shall take the earliest opportunity of visiting Accra and the other forts, and I have already applied to the senior naval officer for a vessel of war to convey me to the different stations, when I shall endeavour to get the chiefs of those districts to sign a similar agreement. . . .

DECLARATION OF THE FANTE CHIEFS (THE "BOND") 6 MARCH, 1844.

1. Whereas power and jurisdiction have been exercised for and on behalf of Her Majesty the Queen of Great Britain and Ireland, within divers countries and places adjacent to Her Majesty's forts and settlements on the Gold Coast, we, the chiefs of countries and places so referred to, adjacent to the said forts and settlements, do hereby acknowledge that power and jurisdiction, and declare that the first objects of law are the protection of individuals and property.

2. Human sacrifices and other barbarous customs, such an panyarring, are abominations and contrary to law.

3. Murders, robberies and other crimes and offences will be tried and inquired of before the Queen's judicial officers and the chiefs of the district, moulding the customs of the country to the general principles of British law.

Done at Cape Coast Castle, before his Excellency the Lieutenant Governor on this 6th day of March, in the year of our Lord, 1844.

[The marks of:]

    Cudjoe Chibboe, king of Denkera
    Quashie Ottoo, chief of Abrah
    Chibboe Coomah, chief of Assin
    Gebra, second chief of Assin
    Quashie Anka, chief of Donadie
    Awoosie, chief of Domonassie
    Amonee, chief of Annamaboe
    Joe Aggrey, chief of Cape Coast. . . .

[C.O. 96/4]

2

Casely-Hayford on the Fante Confederacy

SOURCE: J. E. Casely-Hayford, *Gold Coast Native Institutions*
(London: Phillips, 1903), pp. 182-189.

The Constitution of the Fanti Confederation, otherwise known as the "Mankessim Constitution," deserves more than a passing notice in the political annals of the Gold Coast. A careful study of the provisions thereof leaves the impression upon the mind how harmful, and yet how useless, it is at any time for a Government to attempt to set back the onward tide in the progress of a nation under its protection. It is harmful, because it entails waste of national energy; it is useless, because you may as well expect the spider not to weave anew its web after a wanton child has destroyed it once, twice, and yet again. . . .

When . . . we come to examine the attitude of the local administration upon the presentation of the Constitution, it will be quite obvious that section I of Article 8 thereof could form no ground of objection.

Second Object.—"To direct the labours of the Confederation towards the improvement of the country at large."

This section requires no comment.

Third Object.—"To make good and substantial roads throughout all the interior districts included in the Confederation."

Article 26, which, really, should be construed with section 3 of Article 8, directs that the said roads should be made "fifteen feet broad, with good deep gutters on either side, and that the attention of the Confederation be first directed to the main road connecting Edgimacoe, Ayan, Ayanmain, and Mankessim, with the coast."

Fancy the Aborigines of the Gold Coast, thirty-two years ago, thinking of the necessity of good roads, fifteen feet wide, connecting the principal producing district with the sea coast! But they were not suffered by the local Administration to try to open up their own country, and it so happens that it is only now that, under an energetic Administration, there is anything like a serious attempt to grapple with the question of good roads. Thus, waste, absolute waste, of golden opportunity is the record of a whole thirty-two years in the country's history. One is inclined, therefore, to agree with Mr. Salmon, speaking as a private British citizen, and not as the Administrator of the Gold Coast, that progress is not the keynote of the Crown Colony system.

Fourth Object.—"To erect school-houses and establish schools for the education of all children within the Confederation, and to obtain the services of efficient schoolmasters."

Articles 21 to 25 must be read with section 4 of Article 8, which directs the establishment of national schools in Brofoo country, Abrah, Ayan, Goomowah, Eckumfi, Edgimacoe, Denkira, and Assin; the attachment of normal schools to each national school for technical instruction in carpentry, masonry, agriculture, architecture, etc.; special provision for female education, and provision for meeting the expense of school building, and ensuring the attendance at school of all children between the ages of eight and fourteen.

What a far-reaching policy is foreshadowed in the 'object' under discussion! Why, it meant the emergence of the country in two or three generations from a lower to a higher order of civilisation. It meant providing the country with that incalculable boon, good, intelligent mothers, to guide the growing minds of their offspring. It meant well laid out towns and sanitary arrangements, commensurate with an advanced stage of society. It meant lastly, and most important of all, the flooding of the country with contented men, each sitting under his own vine and fig-tree, close to Mother Earth, instead of a certain class of concession mongers and breathless speculators on the Exchange. What a dream to be frustrated by stupid officialism and red tape!

Surely, whatever may be said against the Constitution now before us, it will be admitted by all fair-minded men that its policy was an enlightened one, and that it sought to do for the country what His Majesty's Government have not yet showed any visible signs of accomplishing.

Why, it looks like beginning afresh, does it not, for the Aborigines of the Gold Coast, thirty-two years after the Constitution, to inaugurate a scheme of national education, somewhat after the model foreshadowed in the said Constitution, which has received the hearty support of the present enlightened Administration? Yes, we have to weave it all over again, you see. What a waste of time, and the energy of a past generation!

Fifth Object.—"To promote agricultural and industrial pursuits, and to endeavour to introduce such new plants as may hereafter become sources of profitable commerce to the country."

It is conceivable that the Gold Coast might be a cotton-producing country to-day if the Confederation had been allowed to work out its constitution.

Sixth Object.—"To develop and facilitate the working of the mineral and other resources of the country."

The above are the modest objects of the Confederation. . . .

Throughout the Articles you trace in vain what could have been the cause of offence to the local Administration until you come to Article 44, where provision is made for the purpose of carrying on the administration of the Federal Government, to pass laws, etc., for the levying of such taxes as may be necessary. In other words, the question as to whether any native authority should be suffered to levy taxes in the country was the crux of the contention between the Local Administration and the Confederators. Innocently asked the leaders of the movement, "How possibly are we to go to work at all without money?" They did not know then, as events proved subsequently, that, notwithstanding all protestations to the contrary, the intention of the British Government was not to allow the people self-government at all, but to govern the country as a Crown Colony. And, of course, the Constitution went diametrically against that policy.

3

The Mankessim Constitution or Constitution of the New Fante Confederacy, 1871

SOURCE: G. E. Metcalfe (ed.), *Great Britain and Ghana: Documents of Ghana History 1807-1957* (London: The University of Ghana and Thomas Nelson, 1964), pp. 335-39.

QUASSIE [KWASI] EDOO AND OTHERS TO SIR A. E. KENNEDY

Mankessim, 24 November, 1871.

Sir,

We, the kings and chiefs and others assembled at Mankessim, beg most respectfully to forward you the enclosed copy of a Constitution framed and passed by us after mature deliberation.

We have united together for the express purpose of furthering the interests of our country.

In the Constitution it will be observed that we contemplate means for the social improvement of our subjects and people, the growth of education and industrial pursuits, and, in short, every good which British philanthropy may have designed for the good of the Gold Coast, but which we think it impossible for it at present to do for the country at large.

Our sole object is to improve the condition of our peoples, not to interfere with, but to aid our benefactors on the sea coast, and we count upon your Excellency giving us at times that assistance which may be necessary to carry out our humble efforts.

We beg to forward a copy of the Constitution . . . for the information of the Right Honourable the Secretary of State for the Colonies.

(Signed)	Quassie Edoo	(his X mark)
	Anfoo Otoo	(his X mark)
	Kings President . . .	
	Qow Yanfoo	(his X mark)
	king of Ayan.	
	Thomas Solomon	(his X mark)
	chief of Dominassie.	
	W. E. Davidson, Vice-President.	
	J. F. Amissah, Secretary.	

For the kings and chiefs assembled at Mankessim and all the members of the Confederation.

CONSTITUTION OF THE NEW FANTE CONFEDERACY.

To all whom it may concern.

Whereas we, the undersigned kings and chiefs of Fanti, have taken into consideration the deplorable state of our peoples and subjects in the interior of the Gold Coast, and whereas we are of opinion that unity and concord among ourselves would conduce to our mutual well-being, and promote and advance the social and political condition of our peoples and subjects, who are in a state of degredation, without the means of education and of carrying on proper industry; we, the said kings and chiefs, after having fully discussed and considered the subject of meetings held at Mankessim on the 16th day of October last and following days, have unanimously resolved and agreed upon the articles hereinafter named.

Article 1. That we, the kings and chiefs of Fanti here present, form ourselves into a committee with the view of effecting unity of purpose and of action between the kings and chiefs of the Fanti territory.

2. That we, the kings and chiefs here assembled, now form ourselves into a compact body for the purpose of more effectually bringing about certain improvements (hereinafter to be considered) in the country.

3. That this compact body shall be recognised under the title and designation of the 'Fanti Confederation'.

4. That there shall be elected a president, vice-president, secretary, under-secretary, treasurer and assistant-treasurer.

5. That the president be elected from the body of kings, and be proclaimed king-president of the Fanti Confederation.

6. That the vice-president, secretary and under-secretary, treasurer and assistant-treasurer, who shall constitute the ministry, be men of education and position.

7. That it be competent to the Fanti Confederation thus constituted to

receive into its body politic any other king or kings, chief or chiefs, who may not now be present.

8. That it be the object of the Confederation:

i. To promote friendly intercourse between all the kings and chiefs of Fanti, and to unite them for offensive and defensive purposes against their common enemy.

ii. To direct the labours of the Confederation towards the improvement of the country at large.

iii. To make good and substantial roads throughout all the interior districts included in the Confederation.

iv. To erect school-houses and establish schools for the education of all children within the Confederation, and to obtain the service of efficient schoolmasters.

v. To promote agricultural and industrial pursuits, and to endeavour to introduce such new plants as may hereafter become sources of profitable commerce to the country.

vi. To develop and facilitate the working of the mineral and other resources of the country.

9. That an executive council be formed, composed of [the ministry]... who shall be ex-officio members thereof, together with such others as may be hereafter from time to time appointed.

10. That in order that the business of the Confederation be properly carried on during the course of the year, each king and principal chief shall appoint two representatives, one educated, the other a chief or headman of the district of such king and principal chief, who shall attend the meetings which the secretary may deem necessary to convene for the deliberation of state matters.

11. That the representatives of the kings and chiefs assembled in council shall be known under the designation of the 'Representative Assembly of the Fanti Confederation' and that this assembly be called together by the secretary as state exigency may require.

12. That this representative assembly shall have the power ... of exercising all the functions of a legislative body.

13. That the representatives of each king and chief be responsible to the nation for the effectual carrying out of the bills, resolutions &c passed at such meetings and approved of by the king-president. ...

15. That the National Assembly shall appoint an educated man to represent the king-president, and act as vice-president of the Confederation; and that the vice-president shall preside over all meetings convened by the secretary.

16. That there shall be in the month of October of each year, a gathering of the kings, principal chiefs, and others within the Confederation, when a recapitulation of the business done by the Representative Assembly shall be read, and the programme of the ensuing year discussed.

17. That at such meetings the king-president shall preside, and that it be the duty of the king-president to sanction all laws &c passed by the Representative Assembly, so far as they are compatible with the interests of the country.

18. That the king-president shall not have the power to pass any, or originate any laws . . . &c nor create any office or appointment, excepting by and under the advice of the ministry.

19. That the representatives of the kings and principal chiefs hold office as members of the Representative Assembly for three years, at the expiration of which it shall be competent for the kings and chiefs to reelect the same or appoint other representatives.

20. That the members of the Ministry and Executive Council hold office for three years, and that it be competent to the National Assembly to re-elect all or any of them and appoint others. . . .

[Articles 21-27. Details of school and road-building programme.]

28. That a site or town, unanimously agreed upon, be chosen as the nominal capital of the Confederation, where the principal business of the State should be conducted.

29. That provincial assessors be appointed in each province or district, who shall perform certain judicial functions and attend to the internal management thereof. . . .

[Articles 30-33. Duties of Secretary and Treasurer.]

34. That it be the duty of the under-secretary. . .

To hear and determine, with an assistant appointed by the Secretary, cases which may be brought from the provincial courts.

To arrange important appeal cases for the hearing of the Executive Council, which shall constitute the final court of appeal of the Confederation. . . .

[Articles 35-6. Duties of assistant-treasurer and provincial assessors.]

37. That in each province or district, provincial courts be established to be presided over by the provincial assessors.

38. That it be the duty of the Ministry and Executive Council:

To advise the King-President in all state matters. . . .

To hear, try and determine all important appeal cases brought before it by the under-secretary, option being allowed to any party or parties dissatisfied with the decision thereof to appeal to the British Courts. . . .

39. That three of the "ex-officio" members of the Executive Council, or two ex-officio and two non-official members of the Executive Council shall form a quorum of said Council. . . .

40. That one-third of the members composing the Representative Assembly shall form a quorum.

41. That all laws. . . &c be carried by the majority of votes in the Representative Assembly or Executive Council, in the latter the Vice-President possessing a casting vote.

42. That it be the duty of the National Assembly, held in October of each year . . .

To elect from the body of kings the President for the ensuing year. . . .

To consider all programmes laid before it by the Executive Council. . . .

To place on the "stool" in cases of disputed succession thereto, the person elected by the Executive Council, with the concurrence of the principal inhabitants of the town, croom or district.

43. That the officers of the Confederation shall render assistance as directed by the executive in carrying out the wishes of the British Government. . . .[1]

[H.C.171 of 1873]

C. S. SALMON[2] TO SIR A. E. KENNEDY

Cape Coast Castle, 4 December, 1871.

. . . The Constitution was handed to me in Government House by Mr. Davison the Vice-President and Mr. Brew Assistant-Secretary. I refused to forward it officially to your Excellency on their part. The parties have never applied for any sanction to their proceedings. I officially proclaimed them to be illegal some time since. . .

The people of the country, the merchants and traders, and all the kings and chiefs, except those immediately interested, are one and all utterly opposed to this new Confederacy. Kings Edoo of Mankessim and Otoo of Abrah are the only two cognisant of the actual proceedings, and even they have been partially imposed on. . . . Four of these mentioned as kings are very small chiefs. The majority of the names appended to the Constitution have been put down without the knowledge or consent of the parties themselves.

I have arrested all the Ministry except Grant. Warrants are out against the other members of the Executive Council. I have sent for the judge. The parties will be tried in the Judicial Assessor's Court. . . . If the kings come down I shall send a magistrate to Mankessim . . . to make enquiries and to obtain the seal.

This dangerous conspiracy must be destroyed for good, or the country will become altogether unmanageable. The people could not stand a double taxation. The Government have for a long time been attempting to do what this Confederation states to be its object; but they, the originators of it have,

---

[1]The list of adherents is given as consisting of the chiefs of Mankessim, Abrah [Abura], Ayan [Anyan], Coomendah [Komenda], Edjumacoo [Ajumako], Incoosoocoom [Nkusukum], Assin, Dominassie [Dominasi], Donnassie [Odonasi?], Saltpond, Tuarcoh [Tuakwa?], Abrarsempah [Abakrampa], Batdazah [?], Quarman [Kwamang], Aduddzi [?], Trupessedardir [Mpesedadi?], Bookah [?], Adoomanoo [?], Ampinafoo [Apimanim?], Abbankrome [Obakrom?], Acrofome [Akrofuom?], Arnum [?], Abiror [?], Ichafu [Eduafu?]. But cf. Nos. 280 and 282 below.

[2]Colonial Secretary and Acting Administrator of the Gold Coast.

more than all else, hindered us, by keeping up a state of feuds and destroying unity and confidence. . . .

[H.C. 171 of 1873]

KIMBERLEY TO KENNEDY

London, 16 January, 1872.

Sir,

I have received your despatch of the 16th ult. transmitting despatches from the Administrator of the Gold Coast, reporting the proceedings of the so-called Fantee Confederation, and the steps which he had taken to check what he regarded as a dangerous conspiracy.

As the information before me does not lead me to attach so much importance to this movement, I cannot but regret that persons claiming to hold office under the Confederation should have been arrested, although they were subsequently, and apparently after a short interval, released on bail; and if on the receipt of this despatch, the proceedings which the Administrator contemplated in the Judicial Assessor's Court should not have taken place, you will instruct him to stay all proceedings and to free the parties from bail.

But whilst I feel it necessary to give these directions, I fully recognise that the Administrator acted under a strong conviction that it was incumbent upon him to take the promptest and most effective measures for putting down a movement which, in his judgement, infringed the conditions of the British Protectorate, and was likely to prove delusive and injurious to the natives who would be affected by it.

There is hardly room for question that some of the articles in the constitution of the Confederation were practically inconsistent with the jurisdiction of the British Government in the protected territory. I think that the Administrator might have confined himself to issuing a proclamation warning British subjects from taking office under the Confederation and stating that those who did so would be held responsible for their acts. He would have been quite right also in declining to recognize in any way the 'Constitution' until the articles had been approved by Her Majesty's Government, and in publishing Mr. Grant's disavowal of participation in the proceedings of the Confederation.

Her Majesty's Government have no wish to discourage any legitimate efforts on the part of the Fantee kings and chiefs to establish for themselves an improved form of government, which, indeed, it is much to be desired that they should succeed in doing; but it is necessary that all parties concerned should understand, that so long as they live under the protection of Great Britain, the protecting Government must be consulted as to any new institutions which may be proposed.

The manner in which the new 'Constitution' was brought into operation and certain acts performed under it, without any previous communication with the British authorities, would be more likely to tend to discord and disorder than to further the ends which the promoters of the Constitution profess to have in view.

[H. C.171 of 1873. The minutes on which the despatch was based are in C.O.96/89]

·4

Kwame Nkrumah: Program for the Revitalization of the United Gold Coast Convention, January 20, 1948

SOURCE: From *The Autobiography of Kwame Nkrumah*, first published in 1957. Copyright Panaf Books Ltd., 243 Regent Street, London W1R 8PN (pp. 58-60 in the Thomas Nelson 1959 edition).

. . . Once more I set out on a room hunt and eventually managed to hire an old office of the United Africa Company, the biggest British firm in West Africa. I managed to secure the services of a typist and in a few days got the office fairly well set up. The first thing I did was to call a meeting of the Working Committee of the Convention on 20th January 1948. At this meeting I laid before the members for their consideration the programme which I had drawn up for the organisation of the Movement. This included the following points:

SHADOW CABINET

The formation of a Shadow Cabinet should engage the serious attention of the Working Committee as early as possible. Membership is to be composed of individuals selected *ad hoc* to study the jobs of the various ministries that would be decided upon in advance for the country when we achieve our independence. This Cabinet will forestall any unpreparedness on our part in the exigency of Self-Government being thrust upon us before the expected time.

ORGANISATIONAL WORK

The organisational work of implementing the platform of the Convention will fall into three periods:

First Period:

(*a*) Co-ordination of all the various organisations under the United Gold Coast Convention: *i.e.* apart from individual Membership, the various Political, Social, Educational, Farmers' and Women's Organisations as well as Native Societies, Trade Unions, Co-operative Societies, etc., should be asked to affiliate to the Convention.

(*b*) The consolidation of branches already formed and the establishment of branches in every town and village of the country will form another major field of action during the first period.

(*c*) Convention Branches should be set up in each town and village throughout the Colony, Ashanti, the Northern Territories and Togoland. The chief or Odikro of each town or village should be persuaded to become the Patron of the Branch.

(*d*) Vigorous Convention weekend schools should be opened wherever there is a branch of the Convention. The political mass education of the country for Self-Government should begin at these weekend schools.

Second Period:

To be marked by constant demonstrations throughout the country to test our organisational strength, making use of political crises.

Third Period:

(*a*) The convening of a Constitutional Assembly of the Gold Coast people to draw up the Constitution for Self-Government or National Independence.

(*b*) Organised demonstration, boycott and strike—our only weapons to support our pressure for Self-Government.

5

Convention People's Party:
Six Point Program, January 12, 1949

SOURCE: From *The Autobiography of Kwame Nkrumah*, first published in 1957. Copyright Panaf Books Ltd., 243 Regent Street, London WlR 8PN (pp. 82-83 in the Thomas Nelson 1959 edition).

Much discussion took place on the name to be given to this party. The most popular suggestion that was made was "The Ghana People's Party." This would have been adopted but for one vital reason. Owing to the fact that the rank and file of the people had learnt to associate my name with that of the United Gold Coast Convention, I felt that the omission of the word "Convention" from the name of this new party, would arouse doubt and suspicion in the minds of the people who would regard it as a completely new party with new ideas and new promoters. And so, in order to carry the masses with us, we all agreed that at all costs "Convention" must appear as a part of the name. The name we eventually agreed upon was the Convention People's Party.

We then drew up a six-point programme for the C.P.P. which was as follows:

(1)   To fight relentlessly by all constitutional means for the achievement of full "Self-Government NOW" for the chiefs and people of the Gold Coast.

(2)   To serve as the vigorous conscious political vanguard for removing all forms of oppression and for the establishment of a democratic government.

(3)   To secure and maintain the complete unity of the chiefs and people of the Colony, Ashanti, Northern Territories and Trans-Volta.

(4)   To work in the interest of the trade union movement in the country for better conditions of employment.

(5)   To work for a proper reconstruction of a better Gold Coast in which the people shall have the right to live and govern themselves as free people.

(6)   To assist and facilitate in any way possible the realisation of a united and self-governing West Africa.

It was with this programme that we launched the Convention People's Party and started organising for the struggle that lay ahead.

6

Kwame Nkrumah:
"What I Mean by Positive Action"

SOURCE: G. E. Metcalfe (ed.), *Great Britain and Ghana: Documents of Ghana History 1807-1957* (London: The University of Ghana and Thomas Nelson, 1964), pp. 688-89.

Party Members, Friends and Supporters,

In our present vigorous struggle for Self-Government, nothing strikes so much terror into the hearts of the imperialists and their agents than the term Positive Action. This is especially so because of their fear of the masses responding to the call to apply this final form of resistance in case the British Government failed to grant us our freedom consequent on the publication of the Coussey Committee Report.

The term Positive Action has been erroneously and maliciously publicised no doubt by the imperialists, their concealed agent-provocateurs and stooges. These political renegades, enemies of the Convention People's Party and for that matter of Ghana's freedom, have diabolically publicised that the C.P.P.'s programme of action means riot, looting and disturbances, in a word violence. . . This is the way our struggle is being misrepresented to the outside world; but the truth shall ultimately prevail.

It is a comforting fact to observe that we have cleared the major obstacle to the realisation of our national goal in that ideologically the people of this country and their Chiefs have accepted the idea of Self-Government even now. . . . What is left now is chiefly a question of strategy and the intensity and earnestness of our demand. The British Government and the people of Britain, with the exception of die-hard imperialists, acknowledge the legitimacy of our demand for Self-government. However, it is and must be by our own exertion and pressure that the British Government can [alone be made

to] relinquish its authority and hand over the control of affairs, that is, the
Government, to the people of this country and their Chiefs. . . .

From our knowledge of colonial liberation movements, Freedom or
Self-Government has never been handed over to any colonial country on a
silver platter. The United States, India, Burma, Ceylon and other erstwhile
Colonial territories have had to wage a bitter and vigorous struggle to attain
their freedom. Hence the decision by the Convention People's Party to adopt
a programme of non-violent Positive Action to attain Self-Government for the
people of this country and their Chiefs.

We have talked too much and pined too long over our disabilities—
political, social and economic; and it is now time that we embarked on
constitutional positive steps to achieve positive results. We must remember
that because of the educational backwardness of the Colonial countries, the
majority of the people of this country cannot read. There is only one thing
they can understand and that is Action.

By Positive Action we mean the adoption of all legitimate and constitutional means by which we can cripple the forces of imperialism in this
country. The weapons of Positive Action are:

1. Legitimate political action.
2. Newspapers and educational campaigns, and
3. as a last resort, the constitutional application of strikes, boycotts, and
   non-co-operation based on the principle of absolute non-violence. . . .

Mr. C. V. H. Rao in his book entitled *Civil Disobedience Movement in
India* has this to say:

"Constitutional agitation without effective action behind it of organised
national determination to win freedom is generally lost on a country like
Britain, which can appreciate only force or its moral equivalent. . . . An
important contributory factor to the satisfactory settlement of a disputed
issue, is the extent and the nature of the moral force and public sympathy
generated by the righteousness of the cause for which suffering is undergone
and the extent of the moral reaction it has produced on the party against
which it is directed."

The passive sympathy of the masses must be converted into active
participation in the struggle for freedom: there must also be created a
widespread political consciousness and a sense of national self-respect. These
can only be achieved when the mass of the people understand the issue. These
are not the days when people follow leaders blindly. . . .

Positive Action has already begun by our political education, by our
newspapers, agitation and platform speeches and also by the establishment of
the Ghana Schools and Colleges as well as the fearless and legitimate activities
of the C.P.P.

But as regards the final stage of Positive Action, namely, National
Non-violent Sit-down-at-home Strikes, Boycotts and Non-co-operation, we
shall not call them into play until all the avenues of our political endeavours

of attaining Self-government have been closed. Accordingly we shall first carefully study the Report of the Coussey Committee. If we find it favourable, we shall accept it and sing alleluya. But if we find it otherwise, we shall first put forward our own suggestions and proposals and upon refusal to comply with them we shall invoke Positive Action straight away. . . .

What we all want is Self-government so that we can govern ourselves in our own country. We have the natural, legitimate and unalienable right to decide for ourselves the sort of government we want and we cannot be forced against our will into accepting anything that will be detrimental to the true interests of the people of this country and their Chiefs. . . .

Therefore, whilst we are anxiously awaiting the Report . . . I implore you all in the name of the Party to be calm but resolute. Let us advance fearlessly and courageously armed with the Party's programme of Positive Action based on the principle of absolute non-violence.

Long live the Convention People's Party
Long Live the forward march of the people of this country.
Long live the new Ghana that is to be.

7

Convention People's Party: General Election Manifesto, 1951

SOURCE: G. E. Metcalfe (ed.), *Great Britain and Ghana: Documents of Ghana History 1807-1957* (London: The University of Ghana and Thomas Nelson, 1964), pp. 704-7.

Our Appeal to the People of Ghana to Vote C.P.P. Ghanaians!

1. If you believe in the justice of our cause.
2. If you believe that we too must be free to manage our own affairs in our own country as the British do in theirs.
3. If you believe that imperialism is a hindrance to our national progress.
4. If you believe that we too, given the opportunity, can achieve greatness for our country and leave noble heritage to our country.

5. If you believe that no foreigner, no matter how sincere he is, under an imperialist Colonial Government can make greater sacrifices than we can to improve her.
6. If you believe that our natural resources must no longer be exploited mainly for the benefit of Aliens, but for our benefit too.
7. Above all, if you believe that Self-Government is the only solution to the evils that plague us, and therefore must be fought for and won now, then your duty is clear—VOTE C.P.P. AT THE GENERAL ELECTIONS.

WHY THE C.P.P. IS CONTESTING THE 1951 ELECTION.

... We were not surprised when the nominated members of the Coussey Committee, in spite of hundreds of telegrams, memoranda and newspaper articles sent to them by the general public demanding immediate self-government, produced half-baked proposals which they considered acceptable as the basis for the improvement on of colonial rule. True to type, the nominated men turned deaf ear to the whole country's demand for S.G. NOW, and the people were justified for believing that "Nominations by Colonial Governments in any shape or form are an abomination. . . ."

HOW DID THE COUSSEY COMMITTEE
LET THE COUNTRY DOWN?

Among other objectionable proposals, the Coussey Committee recommended that Ghana should remain under colonial servitude and degradation for many more years.

1. That the British Governor should retain as much power as he had under the old Colonial system, by wielding the powers of *VETO* and *CERTIFICATION*; thus, bills passed by all the 75 representatives of the people could only have the force of law if the Governor agreed.
2. That the most important ministries of *DEFENCE, FINANCE* (the country's life blood) *EXTERNAL AFFAIRS* and *JUSTICE* should *NOT* be held by the people's representatives but by "civil service ministers" who will be appointed by and be ultimately responsible to the Secretary of State for the Colonies in far-away London.
3. That the election of the representatives in all but the 4 municipalities of Accra, Cape Coast, Sekondi-Takoradi and Kumasi should be indirect, which process can easily lend itself to corrupt practices and abuse in a country where bribery and corruptions are rife.

The task of fighting to remove these objectionable proposals cannot be entrusted to the same men who framed them. . . .

WHAT DOES THE PARTY STAND FOR?

You know, we all know, the whole world knows that C.P.P. stands for full SELF-GOVERNMENT NOW and the end of foreign control of our affairs. . . . This is our native land, and we can no longer tolerate a foreign imperialist government; we are of age. . . .

OUR MESSAGE TO GHANA. . . .

Ghanaians, yours is the task of deciding whether you will be free NOW or subject yourselves to years of meddlesome, oppressive foreign colonial rule. . . . Once get the right men in, Victory will be ours at no distant date and NOT in 15 or 20 years as imperialists have been promising us.

THEREFORE

Vote wisely and God will save Ghana from the imperialist.
Long live the Convention People's Party.
Long live Kwame Nkrumah.
Long live the forward march of the common people of Ghana to their
  rightful and just inheritance.
SEEK YOU FIRST THE POLITICAL KINDGOM AND ALL THINGS WILL BE ADDED INTO IT.

OUR PROGRAMME

. . . Our entry into the Assembly in full strength will open up better opportunities to struggle for immediate self-Government. Whilst that struggle is proceeding, the C.P.P. will do all in its power to better the condition of the people of this country; it must be pointed out however that the implementation of this development programme can only be possible when S.G. has been attained, and we are in full control of our own affairs.

(A) POLITICAL. . . .

The aim of the Convention People's Party is full SELF-GOVERNMENT NOW.
It will fight for and get. . . .
   (1) A free and democratic National Assembly elected on the basis of Universal Adult Suffrage at 21 years;
   (2) Direct elections with no property or residential qualifications for candidates seeking election;

(3) Not less than 100 Constituencies of about 50,000 people each to elect representatives to the National Assembly.

(4) A Senate for Chiefs. . . .

(B) ECONOMIC.

The Convention People's Party aims at launching a Five-year Economic Plan for both social and economic development of this country in order to afford the people an increasingly higher standrad of living which has long been denied to them under the Crown Colony system of government. What follows is a brief account of what the Party intends to do when the country gets FULL Dominion Status and the Party is entrusted with the running of the government. . . .

The immediate materialisation of the Volta Hydro-Electric Scheme and the electrification of the whole country is one of the prime objectives of the Party. . . .

The immediate development of facilities for a modern communication and transport system . . . is another major objective. . . . The Railway system will be modernized (e.g. double track railway) and extended to the Northern Territories and Trans-Volta. Various branch lines and a coastal line extending from Half-Assini to Aflao will also be built. . . . Roads also will be modernised and extended. . . . Water transport . . . will be encouraged by the building of canals to join rivers. . . .

The party aims at a progressive mechanisation of agriculture. . . . It also aims at raising the standard of living among the peasants by bringing pipe-borne water, electric lights, good housing, education and other social and cultural amenities to the towns and villages. Special attention will be given to the Swollen Shoot Disease. . . . Farmers will be given control of the vast funds with the Cocoa Marketing Board to use for the benefit of the farmers primarily and the country in general. One of the important objectives . . . is to redeem for the farmers the numerous farms that have been mortgaged. . . .

The timber industry will be controlled and expanded for the benefit of the people. . . . A large programme of afforestation will be undertaken and measures will be taken to check and remedy soil erosion. . . . The fishing industry will be helped with the provision of canning factories . . . and modern facilities for catching fish and marketing same. . . .

The industrialisation of the country is one of the principal objectives of the Party, and under Dominion Status it will carry it out with all energy. Imperialism is incompatible with industrialisation of a colonial country. It is only under self-government that this country can be industrialised in the way it should. Under the industrialisation programme the Party envisages numerous manufacturing factories (e.g. canning, meat, electrical goods, building materials, machinery, cutlery, crockery, provision, hardwares and textile plants) springing up in all parts of the country. . . .

The retail trade in the country needs great improvement by the allowance of fair discount on wholesale prices, so that the Market women and the smaller African retailers can have a fair margin of profit. . . .

To control the economy of the country it is imperative that a National Bank be established. . . .

(C) SOCIAL. . . .

One of the first objectives of the Party is to create avenues of employment for all with good pay and better conditions of work. Jobs for all will be achieved [by the economic programme]. . . . An important innovation which the Party intends to introduce . . . is the system of weekly wages. . . . The Party will help promote Hire Purchase Systems. . . .*

The country needs a unified system of education with free and compulsory elementary, secondary and technical education up to the age of 16 years. . . . The Party will bring the University College to a full university status at once. . . . The Party lays special importance on Adult Education and will see to it that a planned campaign to liquidate illiteracy from this country in the shortest possible time is vigorously undertaken. . . .

The scandalous insanitary conditions in towns and villages are some of the gravest indictments of the imperialist regime in this country and constitute one of the fundamental reasons for our demand for full self-government NOW. Imperialism . . . cannot help us. For one of the unwritten laws of imperialism is to keep colonial people poor in mind and body so as to exploit them the better. The aim of the Convention People's Party is to remove this stain; it intends to establish hospitals . . . clinics and sanatoriums all over the country and to inaugurate a Free Medical Service. . . . The C.P.P. intends as one of its principal aims to establish a country-wide network of pipe-borne water supply for use in homes and factories. At no very distant date it should be possible to see water on the tap in most homes in the country. . . .

Hard Work.

Self Government or Dominion Status by itself does not produce bread or kenkey; it only releases a colonial people from imperialist bondage and exploitation, and enables them to get work, decent wages and to attain a higher standard of living. . . .

Taxation.

Under the present colonial rule, taxation has been most unpopular because people do not get returns commensurate with taxes they pay. Under self-government taxes would still be levied on all who should pay taxes, but the C.P.P. would see that taxation brings with it, social education, cultural and economic rewards for the whole community. . . .

Exploited and oppressed Ghanaians, this is your chance to save your country!

VOTE C.P.P.!!!

*Installment buying (Ed.).

8

The Motion of Destiny, 1953

SOURCE: From *The Autobiography of Kwame Nkrumah*, first published in 1957. Copyright Panaf Books Ltd., 243 Regent Street, London WlR 8PN (pp. 156-70 in the Thomas Nelson 1959 edition).

From April to June of 1953 I met many groups and organisations throughout the country collating views on constitutional reform. The following month the government White Paper was published and on 10th July, 1953, I moved a motion on constitutional reform, my independence motion which has become popularly known as "The Motion of Destiny."

On this day, every seat in the Assembly was filled and crowds were standing outside anxious to take part in what was going on in the House. The atmosphere was one of rejoicing, almost as if independence had already been won. A cheer went up as I entered and took my place and again as I stood to deliver my motion. This was followed by deep silence.

"Mr. Speaker," I began, "I beg to move that this Assembly in adopting the Government's White Paper on constitutional reform do authorise the Government to request that Her Majesty's Government as soon as the necessary constitutional and administrative arrangements for independence are made, should introduce an Act of Independence into the United Kingdom Parliament declaring the Gold Coast a sovereign and independent State within the Commonwealth; and further, that this Assembly do authorise the Government to ask Her Majesty's Government, without prejudice to the above request, to amend as a matter of urgency the Gold Coast (Constitution) Order in Council 1950, in such a way as to provide *inter alia* that the Legislative Assembly shall be composed of members directly elected by secret ballot, and that all Members of the Cabinet shall be Members of the Assembly and directly responsible to it.

"Mr. Speaker, it is with great humility that I stand before my countrymen and before the representatives of Britain, to ask this House to give assent to this Motion. In this solemn hour, I am deeply conscious of the grave implications of what we are about to consider and, as the great honour of proposing this Motion has fallen to my lot, I pray God to grant me the wisdom, strength and endurance to do my duty as it should be done.

"We are called upon to exercise statesmanship of a high order, and I would repeat, if I may, my warning of October, that 'every idle or ill-considered word—will militate against the cause which we all have at heart.'. . . .

"In seeking your mandate, I am asking you to give my Government the power to bring to fruition the longing hopes, the ardent dreams, the fervent aspirations of the chiefs and people of our country. Throughout a century of alien rule our people have, with ever increasing tendency, looked forward to that bright and glorious day when they shall regain their ancient heritage, and once more take their place rightly as free men in the world.

"Mr. Speaker, we have frequent examples to show that there comes a time in the history of all colonial peoples when they must, because of their will to throw off the hampering shackles of colonialism, boldly assert their God-given right to be free of a foreign ruler. To-day we are here to claim this right to our independence. . . ."

"The freedom we demand is for our children, for the generations yet unborn, that they may see the light of day and live as men and women with the right to work out the destiny of their own country.

"Mr. Speaker, our demand for self-government is a just demand. It is a demand admitting of no compromise. The right of a people to govern themselves is a fundamental principle, and to compromise on this principle is to betray it. . . .

"The right of a people to decide their own destiny, to make their way in freedom, is not to be measured by the yardstick of colour or degree of social development. It is an inalienable right of peoples which they are powerless to exercise when forces, stronger than they themselves, by whatever means, for whatever reasons, take this right away from them. If there is to be a criterion of a people's preparedness for self-government, then I say it is their readiness to assume the responsibilities of ruling themselves. For who but a people themselves can say when they are prepared? How can others judge when that moment has arrived in the destiny of a subject people? What other gauge can there be?

"Mr. Speaker, never in the history of the world has an alien ruler granted self-rule to a people on a silver platter. Therefore, Mr. Speaker, I say that a people's readiness and willingness to assume the responsibilities of self-rule is the single criterion of their preparedness to undertake those responsibilities.

"I have described on a previous occasion in this House what were the considerations which led me to agree to the participation of my party in the General Election of 1951, and hence in the Government of the Gold Coast under the terms of the 1950 Constitution Order in Council. In making that decision, I took on the task of proving to the world that we were prepared to perform our duties with responsibility, to set in motion the many reforms which our people needed, and to work from within the Government and within the Assembly, that is, by constitutional means, for the immediate aim of self-government. We have only been in office, Mr. Speaker, for two and a half years, and we have kept these objectives constantly in mind. Let there be no doubt that we are equally determined not to rest until we have gained them. We are encouraged in our efforts by the thought that in so acting we are showing that we are able to govern ourselves and thereby we are putting an end to the myth that Africans are unable to manage their own affairs, even when given the opportunity. We can never rest satisfied with what we have so far achieved. The Government certainly is not of that mind. Our country has proved that it is more than ready. For despite the legacies of a century of colonial rule, in the short space of time since your Representative Ministers assumed the responsibilities of office, we have addressed ourselves boldly to the task of laying sound economic and social foundations on which this beloved country of ours can raise a solid democratic society. The spirit of responsibility and enterprise which has animated our actions in the past two years will continue to guide us in the future, for we shall always act in the spirit of our Party's motto: *'Forward ever, backward never.'* For we know notwithstanding that the essence of politics is the realisation of what is possible.

"Mr. Speaker, we have now come to the most important stage of our constitutional development; we can look back on these stages through which we have passed during these last few years: first, our discussions with the Secretary of State leading to the changes of last year; then the questions posed in the October statement, which were to be answered by all parties, groups and councils interested in this great issue; the consultations with the Territorial Councils, with the political parties, with the Trades Union Congress. We have proceeded logically and carefully, and as I view it, the country has responded fully to my call. Every representation which we received—and there were many—has received my careful consideration. The talks which I had with the political parties and the Trades Union Congress, and the committees of the Asanteman and Joint Provincial Councils, were frank and cordial.

"I had also received a special invitation to attend a meeting in Tamale with the Territorial Council, the Traditional Rulers and the Members of the Legislative Assembly. Naturally I accepted the invitation, because it was clear that if I had not held discussions with the Northern Territories, the unity of the Gold Coast might have been endangered and our progress towards self-government might have been delayed. The reverse has been the case. We have adapted some of our proposals to meet Northern Territories wishes, and have been able to set their minds at rest on several issues of the greatest importance to them and to the Gold Coast as a whole. Mr. Speaker, sir, the days of forgetting about our brothers in the North, and in the Trust Territory, are over. . . .

"Mr. Speaker, knowing full well, therefore, the will of the chiefs and people whom we represent, I am confident that with the support of this House, Her Majesty's Government will freely accede to our legitimate and righteous demand to become a self-governing unit within the Commonwealth.

"I put my confidence in the willing acceptance of this demand by Her Majesty's Government, because it is consistent with the declared policy of successive United Kingdom Governments. Indeed, the final transition from the stage of responsible government as a colony to the independence of a sovereign state guiding its own policies, is the apotheosis of this same British policy in relation to its dependencies.

"Mr. Speaker, pray allow me to quote from Britain's own Ministers. Mr. Creech Jones, as Colonial Secretary in the first post-war Labour Government, stated that 'The central purpose of British Colonial policy is simple. It is to guide the Colonial Territories to responsible self-government within the Commonwealth in conditions that ensure to the people concerned both a fair standard of living and freedom from oppression from any quarter.'

"Again, on 12 July, 1950, in the House of Commons, Mr. James Griffiths, Mr. Creech Jones' successor, reiterated this principle: 'The aim and purpose,' he said, ' is to guide the Colonial Territories to responsible self-government within the Commonwealth and, to that end, to assist them to the utmost of our capacity and resources to establish those economic and social conditions upon which alone self-government can be soundly based.'

"Last, I give you the words of Mr. Oliver Lyttelton, Colonial Secretary in Her Majesty's Conservative Government of to-day: 'We all aim at helping the Colonial Territories to attain self-government within the Commonwealth.'

"Nor is this policy anything new in British Colonial history. The right to self-government of Colonial Dependencies has its origin in the British North American Act of 1867, which conceded to the provinces of Canada, complete self-rule. The independence of the other white Dominions of Australia and New Zealand was followed by freedom for South Africa. And since the end of the Second World War, our coloured brothers in Asia have achieved independence, and we are now proud to be able to acknowledge the sovereign States of India, Pakistan, Ceylon and Burma.

"There is no conflict that I can see between our claim and the professed policy of all parties and governments of the United Kingdom. We have here in our country a stable society. Our economy is healthy, as good as any for a country our size. In many respects, we are very much better off than many sovereign states. And our potentialities are large. Our people are fundamentally homogeneous, nor are we plagued with religious and tribal problems. And, above all, we have hardly any colour bar. In fact, the whole democratic tradition of our society precludes the *herrenvolk* doctrine. The remnants of this doctrine are now an anachronism in our midst, and their days are numbered.

"Mr. Speaker, we have travelled long distances from the days when our fathers came under alien subjugation to the present time. We stand now at the threshold of self-government and do not waver. The paths have been tortuous, and fraught with peril, but the positive and tactical action we have adopted is leading us to the *New Jerusalem*, the golden city of our hearts' desire! I am confident, therefore, that I express the wishes and feelings of the chiefs and people of this country in hoping that the final transfer of power to your Representative Ministers may be done in a spirit of amity and friendship, so that, having peacefully achieved our freedom, the peoples of both countries—Britain and the Gold Coast—may form a new relationship based on mutual respect, trust and friendship. Thus may the new partnership implicit in the Statue of Westminister be clothed in a new meaning. For then shall we be one of the 'autonomous communities within the British Empire, equal in status, in no way subordinate one to another in any aspect of their domestic or external affairs, though united by a common allegiance to the Crown, freely associated as members of the British Commonwealth of Nations,' in accordance with the Balfour Declaration of 1926, which was embodied in the Statue of Westminister in 1931.

"To-day, more than ever before, Britain needs more 'autonomous communities freely associated.' For freely associated communities make better friends than those associated by subjection. We see to-day, Mr. Speaker, how much easier and friendlier are the bonds between Great Britain and her former dependencies of India, Pakistan and Ceylon. So much of the bitterness that poisoned the relations between these former colonies and the United Kingdom has been absolved by the healing power of a better feeling that a new friendship has been cemented in the free association of autonomous communities.

"These, and other weighty reasons, allied with the avowed aim of British colonial policy, will, I am confident, inspire Britain to make manifest once more to a sick and weary world her duty to stand by her professed aim. A free and independent Gold Coast, taking its rightful place in peace and amity by the side of the other Dominions, will provide a valid and effective sign that freedom can be achieved in a climate of good will and thereby accrue to the intrinsic strength of the Commonwealth. The old concepts of Empire, of conquest, domination and exploitation are fast dying in an awakening world. Among the colonial peoples, there is a vast, untapped reservoir of peace and goodwill towards Britain, would she but divest herself of the outmoded, moth-eaten trappings of two centuries ago, and present herself to her colonial peoples in a new and shining vestment and hand us the olive branch of peace and love, and give us a guiding hand in working out our own destinies.

"In the very early days of the Christian era, long before England had assumed any importance, long even before her people had united into a nation, our ancestors had attained a great empire, which lasted until the eleventh century, when it fell before the attacks of the Moors of the North. At its height that empire stretched from Timbuktu to Bamako, and even as far as to the Atlantic. It is said that lawyers and scholars were much respected in that empire and that the inhabitants of Ghana wore garments of wool, cotton, silk and velvet. There was trade in copper, gold and textile fabrics, and jewels and weapons of gold and silver were carried.

"Thus may we take pride in the name of Ghana, not out of romanticism, but as an inspiration for the future. It is right and proper that we should know about our past. For just as the future moves from the present so the present has emerged from the past. Nor need we be ashamed of our past. There was much in it of glory. What our ancestors achieved in the context of their contemporary society gives us confidence that we can create, out of that past, a glorious future, not in terms of war and military pomp, but in terms of social progress and of peace. For we repudiate war and violence. Our battles shall be against the old ideas that keep men trammelled in their own greed; against the crass stupidities that breed hatred, fear and inhumanity. The heroes of our future will be those who can lead our people out of the stifling fog of disintegration through serfdom, into the valley of light where purpose, endeavour and determination will create that brotherhood which Christ proclaimed two thousand years ago, and about which so much is said, but so little done.

"Mr. Speaker, in calling up our past, it is meet, on an historic occasion such as this, to pay tribute to those ancestors of ours who laid our national traditions, and those others who opened the path which made it possible to reach to-day the great moment at which we stand. As with our enslaved brothers dragged from these shores to the United States and to the West Indies, throughout our tortuous history, we have not been docile under the heel of the conqueror. Having known by our own traditions and experience the essentiality of unity and of government, we constantly formed ourselves into cohesive blocs as a means of resistance against the alien force within our borders. And so to-day we recall the birth of the Ashanti nation through Okomfo Anokye and Osei Tutu and the symbolism entrenched in the Golden Stool; the valiant wars against the British, the banishment of Nana Prempeh the First to the Seychelle Islands; the temporary disintegration of the nation and its subsequent reunification. And so we come to the Bond of 1844. Following trade with the early merchant adventurers who came to the Gold Coast, the first formal association of Britain with our country was effected by the famous Bond of 1844, which accorded Britain trading rights in the country. But from these humble beginnings of trade and friendship, Britain assumed political control of this country. But our inalienable right still remains, as my friend George Padmore, puts it in his recent book, *The Gold Coast Revolution*, and I quote—'When the Gold Coast Africans demand self-government to-day they are, in consequence, merely asserting their birthright which they never really surrendered to the British who, disregarding their treaty obligations of 1844, gradually usurped full sovereignty over the country.'

"Then the Fanti Confederation—the earliest manifestation of Gold Coast nationalism occurred in 1868 when Fanti Chiefs attempted to form the Fanti Confederation in order to defend themselves against the might of Ashanti and the incipient political encroachments of British merchants. It was also a union of the coastal states for mutual economic and social development. This was declared a dangerous conspiracy with the consequent arrest of its leaders.

"Then the Aborigines Rights Protection Society was the next nationalist movement to be formed with its excellent aims and objects, and by putting up their titanic fight for which we cannot be sufficiently grateful, they formed an unforgettable bastion for defence of our God-given land and thus preserved our inherent right to freedom. Such men as Mensah-Sarbah, Atta Ahuma, Sey and Wood have played their role in this great fight.

"Next came the National Congress of British West Africa. The end of the first Great War brought its strains and stresses and the echoes of the allied slogan, 'We fight for freedom' did not pass unheeded in the ears of Casely-Hayford, Hutton-Mills and other national stalwarts who were some of the moving spirits of the National Congress of British West Africa. The machinations of imperialism did not take long to smother the dreams of the people concerned, but to-day their aims and objects are being more than gratified with the appointment of African judges and other improvements in our national life.

"As with the case of the National Congress of British West Africa, the United Gold Coast Convention was organised at the end of the Second World War to give expression to the people's desire for better conditions. The British Government, seeing the threat to its security here, arrested six members of the Convention and detained them for several weeks until the Watson Commission came. The stand taken by the Trades Union Congress, the farmers, students and women of the country, provides one of the most epic stories in our national struggle.

"In June, 1949, the Convention People's Party with its uncompromising principles led the awakened masses to effectively demand their long lost heritage. And to-day, the country moves steadily forward to its proud goal.

"Going back over the years to the establishment of constitutional development, we find that the first Legislative Council to govern the country was established in 1850; thirty-eight years later the first African, in the person of John Sarbah, was admitted to that council. It was not until 1916 that the Clifford Constitution increased the number of Africans, which was four in 1910, to six. But these were mainly councils of officials.

"The Guggisberg Constitution of 1925 increased the unofficial representation in the council almost to par with the officials. This position was reversed by the Burns Constitution of 1946 which created an unofficial majority. The abortive Colony-Ashanti Collaboration of 1944 was the prelude to this change.

"The Coussey Constitution of 1951 further democratised the basis of representation; and now, for the first time in our history, this Government is proposing the establishment of a fully elected Assembly with Ministers directly responsible to it.

"We have experienced Indirect Rule, we have had to labour under the yoke of our own disunity, caused by the puffed-up pride of those who were lucky to enjoy better opportunities in life than their less fortunate brothers; we have experienced the slow and painful progress of constitutional changes by which, from councils on which Africans were either absent or merely nominated, this august House has evolved through the exercise by the enfranchised people of their democratic right to a voice in their own affairs and in so doing they have shown their confidence in their own countrymen by placing on us the responsibility for our country's affairs.

"And so through the years, many have been laid to final rest from the stresses and dangers of the national struggle and many, like our illustrious friends of the Opposition, notwithstanding the fact that we may differ on many points, have also contributed a share to the totality of our struggle. And we hope that whatever our differences, we shall to-day become united in the demand for our country's freedom.

"As I said earlier, what we ask is not for ourselves on this side of the House, but for all the chiefs and people of this country—the right to live as free men in the comity of nations. Were not our ancestors ruling themselves before the white man came to these our shores? I have earlier made reference to the ancient history of our more distant forebears in Ghana. To assert that certain people are capable of ruling themselves while others are not 'ready,' as the saying goes, smacks to me more of imperialism than of reason. Biologists of repute maintain that there is no such thing as a 'superior' race. Men and women are as much products of their environment—geographic, climatic, ethnic, cultural, social—as of instincts and physical heredity. We are determined to change our environment, and we shall advance in like manner.

"According to the motto of the valiant *Accra Evening News*—'We prefer self-government with danger to servitude in tranquillity.' Doubtless we shall make mistakes as have all other nations. We are human beings and hence fallible. But we can try also to learn from the mistakes of others so that we may avoid the deepest pitfalls into which they have fallen. Moreover, the mistakes we may make will be our own mistakes, and it will be our responsibility to put them right. As long as we are ruled by others we shall lay our mistakes at their door, and our sense of responsibility will remain dulled. Freedom brings responsibilities and our experience can be enriched only by the acceptance of these responsibilities.

"In the two years of our representative Government, we have become most deeply conscious of the tasks which will devolve upon us with self-rule. But we do not shrink from them; rather are we more than ever anxious to take on the reins of full self-government. And this, Mr. Speaker, is the mood of the fundamental choice between colonial status and self-government, we are unanimous. And the vote that will be taken on the motion before this Assembly will proclaim this to the world.

"Honourable Members, you are called, here and now, as a result of the relentless tide of history, by Nemesis as it were, to a sacred charge, for you hold the destiny of our country in your hands. The eyes and ears of the world are upon you; yea, our oppressed brothers throughout this vast continent of Africa and the New World are looking to you with desperate hope, as an inspiration to continue their grim fight against cruelties which we in this corner of Africa have never known—cruelties which are a disgrace to humanity, and to the civilisation which the white man has set himself to teach us. At this time, history is being made; a colonial people in Africa has put forward the first definite claim for independence. An African colonial people proclaim that they are ready to assume the stature of free men and to prove to the world that they are worthy of the trust.

"I know that you will not fail those who are listening for the mandate that you will give to your Representative Ministers. For we are ripe for freedom, and our people will not be denied. They are conscious that the right is theirs, and they know that freedom is not something that one people can bestow on another as a gift. They claim it as their own and none can keep it from them.

"And while yet we are making our claim for self-government I want to emphasise, Mr. Speaker, that self-government is not an end in itself. It is a means to an end, to the building of the good life to the benefit of all, regardless of tribe, creed, colour or station in life. Our aim is to make this country a worthy place for all its citizens, a country that will be a shining light throughout the whole continent of Africa, giving inspiration far beyond its frontiers. And this we can do by dedicating ourselves to unselfish service to humanity. We must learn from the mistakes of others so that we may, in so far as we can, avoid a repetition of those tragedies which have overtaken other human societies.

"We must not follow blindly, but must endeavour to create. We must aspire to lead in the arts of peace. The foreign policy of our country must be dedicated to the service of peace and fellowship. We repudiate the evil doctrines of tribal chauvinism, racial prejudice and national hatred. We repudiate these evil ideas because in creating that brotherhood to which we aspire, we hope to make a reality, within the bonds of our small country, of all the grandiose ideologies which are supposed to form the intangible bonds holding together the British Commonwealth of Nations in which we hope to remain. We repudiate racial prejudice and national hatred, because we do not wish to be a disgrace to these high ideals.

"To Britain this is the supreme testing moment in her African relations. When we turn our eyes to the sorry events in South, Central and East Africa, when we hear the dismal news about Kenya and Central African Federation, we are cheered by the more cordial relationship that exists between us and Britain. We are now asking her to allow that relationship to ripen into golden bonds of freedom, equality and fraternity, by complying without delay to our request for self-government. We are sure that the British Government will demonstrate its goodwill towards the people of the Gold Coast by granting us the self-government which we now so earnestly desire. We enjoin the people of Britain and all political parties to give our request their ardent support.

"The self-government which we demand, therefore, is the means by which we shall create the climate in which our people can develop their attributes and express their potentialities to the full. As long as we remain subject to an alien power, too much of our energy is diverted from constructive enterprise. Oppressive forces breed frustration. Imperialism and colonialism are a two-fold evil. This theme is expressed in the truism that 'no nation which oppresses another can itself be free.' Thus we see that this evil not only wounds the people which is subject, but the dominant nation pays the price in a warping of their finer sensibilities through arrogance and greed. Imperialism and colonialism are a barrier to true friendship. For the short time since we Africans have had a bigger say in our affairs, the improved relations between us and the British have been most remarkable. To-day there exists the basis of real friendship between us and His Excellency the Governor, Sir Charles Arden-Clarke, and the *ex-officio* Ministers of Defence and External Affairs, of Finance and of Justice. I want to pay tribute to these men for their valuable co-operation in helping us to make a success of our political advance. . . .

"Unless, therefore, our claim to independence is met now, the amicable relations which at present exist between us and the British may become strained. Our chiefs and people will brook no delay. But I feel confident that our claim, because of the reasons I have already given, will be accepted and our amity towards Britain will be deepened by our new association.

"The strands of history have brought our two countries together. We have provided much material benefit to the British people, and they in turn have taught us many good things. We want to continue to learn from them the best they can give us and we hope that they will find in us qualities worthy of emulation. In our daily lives, we may lack those material comforts regarded as essential by the standards of the modern world, because so much of our wealth is still locked up in our land; but we have the gifts of laughter and joy, a love of music, a lack of malice, an absence of the desire for vengeance for our wrongs, all things of intrinsic worth in a world sick of injustice, revenge, fear and want.

"We feel that there is much the world can learn from those of us who belong to what we might term the pretechnological societies. These are values which we must not sacrifice unheedingly in pursuit of material progress. That is why we say that self-government is not an end in itself. . . .

"Mr. Speaker, we can only meet the challenge of our age as a free people. Hence our demand for our freedom, for only free men can shape the destinies of their future. . . .

"Mr. Speaker, 'Now God be thank'd, Who has match'd us with His hour!' I beg to move."

The acclamation that burst forth was such that one expected the roof and walls to collapse. As soon as the cheering was heard by those waiting outside, they took it up as well. Members from both sides of the House came to congratulate me and, in the words of the official Legislative Assembly debates—"The House was suspended for fifteen minutes."

J. A. Braimah, Minister of Communications and Works, then seconded the motion, and after it had been debated upon for a few days it was carried unanimously.

9

The Ghana (Constitution)
Order in Council, 1957

SOURCE: G. E. Metcalfe (ed.), *Great Britain and Ghana: Documents of Ghana History 1807-1957* (London: The University of Ghana and Thomas Nelson, 1964), pp. 729-53.

At the Court of Buckingham Palace,
the 22nd day of February, 1957.
Present,
The Queen's Most Excellent Majesty in Council.

Whereas by the Ghana Independence Act, 1957,[1] provision is made for and in connection with the attainment by the Gold Coast of fully responsible status within the British Commonwealth of Nations under the name of Ghana with effect from a day (hereinafter referred to as 'the appointed day') which, by virtue of section 5 of the said Act is the sixth day of March, nineteen hundred and fifty-seven, unless before that date Her Majesty has, by Order in Council, appointed some other day to be the appointed day for the purposes of that Act:

Now, therefore, Her Majesty, by virtue and in exercise of the powers conferred upon her by the British Settlements Acts, 1887 and 1945,[2] the Foreign Jurisdiction Act, 1890,[3] the Ghana Independence Act, 1957, and of all other powers enabling Her, in that behalf, is pleased, by and with the advice of Her Privy Council to Order, and it is hereby ordered, as follows:—

Part I. Preliminary.

1. [Definition.]
2. [Citation and commencement.]
3. [Revocation and amendment.]

Part II. The Governor-General.

4. [Appointment of Governor-General.]
5. [Salaries of Governor-General &c.]

---

[1] 5 & 6 Eliz. 2. cap. b.
[2] 50 & 51 Vict. cap. 54 and 9 & 10 Geo. 6. cap. 7.
[3] 53 & 54 Vict. cap. 37.

Part III. The Executive.

6. The executive power of Ghana is vested in the Queen and may be exercised by the Queen or by the Governor-General as Her representative.

7. There shall be a Cabinet of Ministers of not less than eight persons, being Members of Parliament, who shall be charged with the general direction and control of the Government of Ghana and who shall be collectively responsible to Parliament.

8. [Vacation of Office.]

9. [Official Oath.]

10. [Precedence of Ministers.]

11. [Summoning of Cabinet.]

12. [Presiding in the Cabinet.]

13. [Transaction of business in the Cabinet.]

14. [Assignment of responsibilities to Ministers.]

15. The Attorney-General shall be a person who is a public officer and he shall be vested with responsibility for the initiation, conduct and discontinuance of prosecutions for criminal offences triable in courts-constituted under the provisions of the Courts Ordinance[4] or any Act repealing and re-enacting with or without modification, or amending the provision of that Ordinance. . . .

16. [Parliamentary Secretaries.]

17. [Permanent Secretaries.]

18. [Secretary of the Cabinet.]

19. [Duties of Secretary of the Cabinet.]

Part IV. Parliament.

20. (1) There shall be a Parliament in and for Ghana which shall consist of Her Majesty the Queen and the National Assembly.

(2) The National Assembly shall consist of a Speaker and not less than one hundred and four Members to be known as Members of Parliament; but the number of Members may be increased from time to time by the creation of further electoral districts under the provisions of sections 33, 70 and 71, but in any event the total number of Members shall not exceed one hundred and thirty.

21. The Speaker shall be a person, not being either the holder of any public office, or a Minister or Parliamentary Secretary, elected by the Members of Parliament. . . .

22. [Deputy Speaker.]

23. [Voting at elections of Speaker and Deputy Speaker.]

24. Subject to the provisions of section 25 of this Order, any person who—

    (a)   is a citizen of Ghana: and

    (b)   is of the age of twenty-five years or upwards; and

    (c)   is able to speak and, unless incapacitated by blindness or other

---

[4] Laws of the Gold Coast, 1951, cap. 4.

physical cause, to read the English language with a degree of proficiency sufficient to enable him to take an active part in the proceedings of the Assembly;

shall be qualified to be elected as a Member of Parliament, and no other person shall be qualified to be so elected or, having been so elected, shall sit or vote in the Assembly.

25. [Disqualifications for Members.]
26. [Tenure of office of Members.]
27. [Decision of questions as to membership.]
28. [Reporting and filling of vacancies.]
29. [Penalty for unqualified person sitting or voting.]
30. [Staff of the National Assembly.]

Part V. Legislation and Procedure in the Assembly.

31. (1) Subject to the provisions of this Order, it shall be lawful for Parliament, to make laws for the peace, order and good government of Ghana.

(2) No law shall make persons of any racial community liable to disabilities to which persons of other such communities are not made liable.

(3) Subject to such restrictions as may be imposed for the purposes of preserving public order, morality or health, no law shall deprive any person of his freedom of conscience, or the right freely to profess, practise or propagate any religion.

(4) Any laws in contravention of subsection (2) or (3) of this section or section (34) of this Order shall to the extent of such contravention, but not otherwise, be void.

(5) The Supreme Court shall have original jurisdiction in all proceedings in which the validity of any law is called in question and if any such question arises in any lower court, the proceedings in that court shall be stayed and the issue transferred to the Supreme Court for decision.

32. (1) No Bill for the amendment, modification, repeal or re-enactment of the constitutional provisions of Ghana (other than a Bill to which section 33 of this Order applies) and no Bill to which paragraph (b) of subsection (2) of this section applies shall be presented for the Royal Assent unless it has endorsed on it a certificate under the hand of the Speaker that the number of votes cast in favour thereof at the third reading in the Assembly amounted to not less than two-thirds of the whole number of Members of Parliament. For the purposes of this subsection, the expression 'constitutional provisions' means this Order, the existing Orders and any Act (or instrument made under an Act) that amends, modifies, reenacts (with or without any amendment or modification) or makes different provision in lieu of any provision of this Order, the existing Orders or any such Act (or instrument) previously made.

(2) Without prejudice to the provisions of subsection (1) of this section, no Bill for—

(a)   The enactment, modification, repeal or re-enactment (with or

ithout any amendment or modification) of any of the pro-
isions of this Order specified in the Third Schedule to this Order;

or

abolishing or suspending any Regional Assembly or diminishing
the functions or powers of any Regional Assembly,

shall be presented for the Royal Assent unless it has endorsed on it a
certificate (in addition to the certificate required under subsection (1) of this
section) under the hand of the Speaker that the Bill has been referred to all
the Regional Assemblies, and, in the case of a Bill to which paragraph (a) of
this section applies, to all Houses of Chiefs, in accordance with subsection (3)
of this section and has been approved by not less than two-thirds of the total
number of the Regional Assemblies (including, in the case of a Bill to which
paragraph (b) of this subsection applies, any Regional Assembly affected by
the Bill) and, if amendments have been made to the Bill by the National
Assembly since it was so approved by the Regional Assemblies, that such
amendments have been made and are not, in the Speaker's opinion, amendments of substance.

(3) [Details procedure for reference to Regional Assemblies.] . . .

33. (1) No Bill for effecting any alteration in the boundaries of a Region
which seeks to transfer an area or areas containing less than ten thousand
registered electors, other than a Bill which creates a new Region, shall be
introduced in the Assembly unless the alteration to which the Bill seeks to
give effect has been approved by a majority of members present and voting at
a meeting of the Regional Assembly of every Region whose boundaries will
be affected.

(2) No Bill for effecting any alteration in the boundaries of a Region
which seeks to transfer an area or areas containing not less than ten thousand
registered electors shall be introduced in the Assembly unless the alteration to
which the Bill seeks to give effect has been approved by referendum in every
Region from which it is proposed to transfer any area and by a majority of
members present and voting at a meeting of the Regional Assembly of any
Region in which it is proposed to incorporate any part of the area
transferred. . . .

[(4)-(7) give further details of procedure.]

34. [Compulsory acquisition of property.] . . .

35. When any Bill affecting the traditional functions or privileges of a Chief is
introduced into the Assembly and is read a first time, the Speaker shall
forthwith refer such Bill to the House of Chiefs of the Region in which the
Chief exercises his functions as such and no motion shall be moved for the
second reading of the Bill in the Assembly until three months after the day
on which the Bill was introduced into the Assembly.

36. [Standing Orders.] . . .

37. [Presiding in the Assembly.] . . .

38. [The Assembly may transact business notwithstanding vacancies.] . . .

39. No business except that of adjournment shall be transacted in the

Assembly if objection is taken by any Member present that there twenty-five Members present besides the Speaker or Member pres

40. (1) Save as otherwise provided in this Order, all questions p decision in the Assembly shall be determined by a majority of the the Members present and voting; and if upon any question befo Assembly, the votes of the Members shall be equally divided the motion shall be lost.

(2) (a) The Speaker shall have neither an original nor a casting vote: and (b) any other person, including the Deputy Speaker, shall when presiding in the Assembly, have an original vote but no casting vote.

41. (1) Save as is provided in subsection (2) of this section, and subject to the provisions of this Order and of the Standing Orders of the Assembly, any Member may introduce any Bill, or propose any motion for debate in, or may present any petition to, the Assembly, and the same shall be debated and disposed of according to the Standing Orders of the Assembly.

(2) Except with the recommendation or consent of the Governor-General signified thereto, the Assembly shall not proceed upon any Bill, motion or petition which, in the opinion of the Speaker or Member presiding, would dispose of or charge the Consolidated Fund or other public funds of Ghana, or revoke or alter any disposition thereof or charge thereon, or impose, alter or repeal any rate, tax or duty.

42. (1) No Bill shall become a law until Her Majesty has given her assent thereto.

43. [Words of enactment.] ...

44. [Oath of Allegiance.] ...

45. [Privileges of the Assembly and Members.] ...

46. (1) There shall be a session of the Assembly once at least in every year, so that a period of twelve months shall not intervene between the last sitting of the Assembly in one session and the first sitting thereof in the next session. ...

47. [Prorogation and dissolution.] ...

(3) The Governor-General shall dissolve the Assembly at the expiration of five years from the date of the first sitting of the Assembly after the last preceding general election, if it shall not have been sooner dissolved. ...

48. There shall be a general election at such time within two months after every dissolution of the Assembly as the Governor-General shall by Proclamation published in the Gazette appoint.

63. The whole of Ghana shall be divided into the following Regions:—

(a)   The Eastern Region, which shall comprise those parts of Ghana which on the first day of January, 1957, were comprised in the Eastern and Accra Regions of the Gold Coast;

(b)   the Western Region, which shall comprise that part of Ghana which on the first day of January, 1957, were comprised in the Western Region of the Gold Coast

(c)   the Ashanti Region which shall comprise the whole of Ashanti;

(d)   the Northern Region which shall comprise the whole of the Northern Territories and Northern Togoland;

(e)   the Trans-Volta/Togoland Region which shall comprise that part of Ghana which on the first day of January, 1957 was comprised in the Trans-Volta/Togoland Region of the Gold Coast.

(2) In each Region there shall be a Head of the Region, who, except in the case of the Ashanti Region, shall be chosen by the House of Chiefs of the Region and shall hold office for such period as may be prescribed by Act of Parliament. The Asantehene shall be the Head of the Ashanti Region.

64. (1) For the purpose of fulfilling the need for a body at regional level with effective powers in specified fields, a Regional Assembly shall be established by Act of Parliament in and for each Region.

(2) A Regional Assembly shall have and exercise authority, functions and powers to such extent as may be prescribed by Act of Parliament relating to

(a)   Local Government;

(b)   Agriculture, Animal Health and Forestry;

(c)   Education;

(d)   Communications;

(e)   Medical and Health services;

(f)   Public Works;

(g)   Town and Country Planning;

(h)   Housing;

(i)   Police; and

(j)   such other matters as Parliament may from time to time determine. . . .

65. [Membership of local government councils.] . . .

66. The Office of Chiefs in Ghana as existing by customary law and usage, is hereby guaranteed.

67. (1) Within twelve months of the appointed day or as soon thereafter as may be practicable, a House of Chiefs shall be established by Act of Parliament in and for each Region. . . .

68. [Determination of matters of a constitutional nature involving chiefs.] . . .

Part X. Elections and the Delimitation of Electoral Districts.

69. (1) Voting for the election of Members of Parliament shall be by secret ballot on the basis of adult suffrage.

(2) Every citizen of Ghana, without distinction of religion, race or sex, who—

(a)   is not less than twenty-one years of age; and

(b)   is subject to no legal incapacity as defined by Act of Parliament on the grounds of non-residence, unsoundness of mind, crime, or corrupt or illegal practices or non-payment of rates or taxes; and

(c)   either owns immovable property within, or has, for a period of not less than six months out of the twelve months preceding the date of an application to be registered, resided within the electoral district in respect of which application is made,

shall be entitled to be registered as an elector for the election of Members of Parliament.

70. (1) For the purposes of the election of Members of Parliament, each Region of Ghana shall be divided into areas, which shall be known as electoral districts. The total number of electoral districts shall not be less than one hundred and four or more than one hundred and thirty. Electoral districts shall be so delimited that the number of persons resident in each such district at the time of delimitation is, as nearly as practical considerations admit, the same, but, in dividing any Region into electoral districts, regard shall be had to the physical features of the Region and its transport facilities and no electoral district shall be partly in one Region and partly in another Region. Each electoral district shall return one Member to Parliament.

(2) Until other provision is made in pursuance of section 33 or 71 of this Order, the number of electoral districts in the whole of Ghana shall be one hundred and four and the allocation of electoral districts between the various parts of Ghana shall remain as it was immediately before the appointed day.

71. (1) Within two years of the taking of each general census in Ghana, the Governor-General shall, in the manner prescribed in subsection (5) of this section, appoint a body to be known as the General Electoral Delimitation Commission . . . which shall review the delimitation of the electoral districts existing at the time of its appointment and shall submit a report to the Governor-General regarding the number of persons then residing in each electoral district together with such recommendations as the Commission deems necessary for a fresh delimitation of electoral districts in accordance with the provisions of section 70 of this Order. . . . [The Governor-General may also appoint interim Commissions.]

If such Interim Commission is satisfied that the number of persons resident in [an] electoral district is, on the basis of the best available information, in excess of one hundred and seventy per centum of the average number of persons resident in each of all other electoral districts, the Interim Commission shall submit a report to the Governor-General together with a recommendation for the division of the said electoral district into two electoral districts. . . .

(5) Each General Commission, Area Committee or Interim Commission

shall consist of three persons appointed by the Governor-General who shall select persons who he is satisfied are not actively engaged in politics. . . .

Part XI. Transitional Provisions. . . .

73. (1) The Legislative Assembly constituted under the existing Orders and in being immediately prior to the appointed day shall continue in being thereafter as the first National Assembly of Ghana within the meaning of subsection (2) of section 20 of this Order. . . .

85. (1) The Governor-General shall, within three months after the appointed day, or as soon thereafter as may be possible, appoint a Regional Constitutional Commission consisting of a Chairman who shall be the Chief Justice or a Judge nominated by him, two Commissioners representing each Region who shall be persons nominated by the Territorial Council of each Region and not more than six Commissioners appointed by the Governor-General.

(2) The Regional Constitutional Commission shall enquire into and report on the devolution to Regional Assemblies of authority, functions and powers relating to the matters specified in subsection (2) of section 64 of this Order and in particular, and without prejudice to the generality of the foregoing, shall make recommendations as to the composition of each Regional Assembly, the executive, legislative, financial and advisory powers to be exercised by it, the funds required to meet the capital and recurrent expenditure to be incurred by it, the provision of such funds and the legislation required to give effect to its recommendations. . . .

The Third Schedule.

The following definitions in subsection (1) of section 1:—

"Ashanti," "the Assembly," "the Consolidated Fund," "judicial officer," "the Northern Territories," "Northern Togoland," "public office," "public officer," "the public service," "Region."

Subsections (2), (3), (4), (5), and (6) of section 1.
Section 6
Section 20
Subsections (1), (2), (3), and (4) of section 31.
Sections 32 to 35.
Subsections (1) and (2) of section 42.
Subsection (1) of section 46.
Subsection (3) of section 47.
Sections 48 to 58.
Subsection (1) of section 61.[5]
Sections 62[6] to 64.
Sections 66 to 69.

[5] Deals with the post of Auditor-General
[6] Section 62 provides for an annual Audit of Accounts. The territorial definitions in the first subsection are those of 1950 and 1954.

This Schedule
[Statutory Instruments, No. 1. of 1957[7]]

10

The Gold Coast Press, 1822-1957

SOURCE: Dennis Austin, *Politics in Ghana, 1946-1960* (London: Oxford University Press under the auspices of The Royal Institute of International Affairs, 1970), p. 422. Reprinted by permission.

THE GOLD COAST/GHANA PRESS

The earliest newspaper in the country was the *Royal Gold Coast Gazette & Commercial Intelligence* which appeared handwritten in 1822; the first regular newspaper was James Brew's *The Gold Coast Times* in 1874. By the end of the nineteenth century some nineteen papers had existed at one time or other, limited in circulation to a few hundred but of a high standard of journalistic writing, a tradition continued by J. E. Casely Hayford's *The Gold Coast Leader* between 1902 and his death in 1929. A new development began in 1931, the year of Danquah's *West African Times* (later the *Times of West Africa*) when Danquah, Nnamdi Azikiwe, Wuta Ofei, and C. S. Adjei attacked different aspects of colonial policy in flamboyant language. When the restrictions imposed during the war on the import of newsprint were lifted, and nationalist demands gathered force, newspapers, newssheets, weekly journals, pamphlets appeared in great number—including Nkrumah's Accra *Evening News* (3 September 1948)—hard-hitting, raucous, simply-written, crudely-printed. A mass circulation was not achieved until the appearance at the end of 1950 of the *Daily Graphic*, a subsidiary of the London overseas *Daily Mirror* Group, which was at first boycotted, then copied and, after independence, largely ignored by nationalist opinion except on the rare occasion when it ventured to comment on local political issues.

At independence, the position had been reached when, compared with the

[7]47 pages in original.

twenty daily papers of 1950, there were only five of any political importance: the *Evening News* (CPP–1948), the *Liberator* (NLM–1954), the *Ashanti Pioneer* (Independent-opposition–1939), the *Daily Graphic* (neutral–1950), and the twice-weekly *Ashanti Times* (owned, written, and published since 1947 by the Ashanti Gold Fields Corporation). The rise and decline in the number of papers may be set down as:

	1870–1900	*1901–30*	*1937*	*1948*	*1950*	*1959*
Daily	2	–	1	6	20	5
Weekly*	5	7	4	8	7	5
	7	7	5	14	27	10

*including 1 vernacular weekly.

Source: *Report on the Press in West Africa* (Ibadan, 1960), p. 38.